"Ken Boa is one of the most gifted writers and scholars in the Christi... world. This is a brilliantly done apologetics reference. The title tel... ...faith is not an unreasonable faith."

Charles W. Col... DC

"I know of no better analysis of Christian ... ...uth Has Its Reasons. It is comprehensive and rigorous... ...udable. However, the book's greatest virtue is its ability to lo... ...importance of apologetics in the life of the church as well as in the personal faith of the individual believer."

Francis J. Beckwith, author of *David Hume's Arguments against Miracles*

"Applying the principle of 'unity in diversity' to apologetic systems, this book integrates the best insights of each approach. In challenging readers to maximize the stunning reasons for faith in concert with the magnetic power of transformed hearts, *Faith Has Its Reasons* charts the right course for the future of apologetics."

David K. Clark, author of *Dialogical Apologetics*

"An excellent, thorough survey of apologetic approaches."

John M. Frame, author of *Apologetics to the Glory of God*

"This volume is an excellent overview of the field of apologetics. It gives not only a superb historical survey but also a look at the different types and approaches to the subject. The book makes for a good starter into an understanding of a biblical defense of the faith. It could be used with high school and college Sunday school classes, and it has value as a perfect textbook for college or seminary use. . . . This reviewer is so inspired with this volume he plans to go back through and study the text in more detail. In some ways it may be said that the book has in it almost everything you want to know about this important field of study."

Mal Couch, Tyndale Seminary

"Exceedingly useful."

John Warwick Montgomery, author of *Faith Founded on Fact*

Faith
Has Its Reasons

*Integrative Approaches
to Defending the Christian Faith*

Contents

Part Three: *Evidentialist Apologetics: Just the Facts*

Christianity Vindicated by Science
History as the Medium of Revelation
Experience Founded on Evidence

Scripture as Source
The Uniqueness of Christianity
The Case for God
The Inductive Problem of Evil
Miracles as Evidence for God
Jesus: The Evidence

The Evidentialist Model
Evidentialism Illustrated
The Strengths of Evidentialist Apologetics
The Weaknesses of Evidentialist Apologetics

Part Four: *Reformed Apologetics: God Said It*

John Calvin
Modern Roots of the Reformed Approach
Herman Dooyeweerd
Cornelius Van Til
Gordon H. Clark
Alvin Plantinga

Biblical Standard for Defining Truth
The Vindication of Reformed Theology
Toward a Christian Philosophy
Christianity Against False Science
Revelation as Interpreting History
The Problem with Experience

Part Five: *Fideist Apologetics: By Faith Alone*

The Personal Problem of Evil
Miracles as God Revealing Himself
Jesus: The Christ of Faith

The Fideist Model
Fideism Illustrated
The Strengths of Fideism
The Weaknesses of Fideism

Part Six: *Integrative Approaches to Apologetics*

Precursors of Integrative Approaches
Edward John Carnell
Francis A. Schaeffer
David K. Clark
C. Stephen Evans
John M. Frame

Perspectival Approaches to Defending Truth
Apologetics and Theology
Apologetics and Philosophy
Christianity and Science
Revelation and History
Apologetics and Experience

Scripture as Truth
Myth, Truth, and Religion
God Who Makes Himself Known
Solutions to the Problems of Evil
Miracles as Signs
Jesus: The Answer

Preface

How to relate the Christian worldview to a non-Christian world has been the dilemma of Christian spokespersons since the apostle Paul addressed the Stoic and Epicurean philosophers in Athens. Twenty centuries of experience have not simplified this task, as new challenges have arisen in every century and new methods and approaches to defending the Christian faith have been formulated in response.

In this introductory textbook on Christian apologetics—the study of the defense of the faith—you will be inducted into this two-millennia-long discussion. You will overhear the greatest apologists of all time responding to the intellectual attacks on the Bible in their day. You will take a guided tour of the four major approaches to apologetics that have emerged in the past couple of centuries. Along the way you will pick up insightful answers to such questions as:

- Why is belief in God rational despite the prevalence of evil in the world?
- What facts support the church's testimony that Jesus rose from the dead?
- Can we be certain Christianity is true?
- How can our faith in Christ be based on something more secure than our own understanding without descending into an irrational emotionalism?

At least formal differences in theory and method have sharply distinguished leading Christian apologists. At the same time, many apologists draw on a variety of methods and do not fit neatly into a single "cookie-cutter" theory of how to defend the Christian faith. In this book, we will identify four "approaches" or idealized types of Christian apologetic methodologies. We will look at the actual apologetic arguments of leading apologists and see how their methods compare to those idealized approaches. We will then consider the work of apologists who have advocated directly integrating two or more of these four basic approaches. Our goal is to contribute toward an understanding of these different apologetic methods that will enrich all Christians in their defense of the faith and enable them to speak with clearer and more relevant voices to our present day and beyond.

SARAH AND MURALI

While apologetics as an intellectual discipline seeks to develop answers to questions that at times may seem abstract, ultimately its purpose is to facilitate bringing real people into a relationship with the living and true God. In this book we will illustrate how the various apologetic methods would be applied in conversations with two very different hypothetical individuals: Sarah and Murali.

Sarah is a college sophomore pursuing a degree in psychology at a state university. Raised in a conservative Protestant home, she began to question the faith of her childhood in high school, as Christianity increasingly seemed a harsh and uncaring religion to her. In her first year at the university she took introductory courses in philosophy, psychology, and English literature that cast doubt on Christian beliefs and values. Her philosophy professor especially had gone out of his way to ridicule "fundamentalism" and had attacked the Christian worldview at its root. Sarah found the "problem of evil"—the question of why a good, all-powerful God would allow so much evil in his world—to be an especially strong argument against Christianity. She was also exposed to theories of biblical criticism that denied the historical accuracy of the Bible and reinterpreted the biblical miracles as myths. When she went home for the summer after her first year at State, Sarah was a self-confessed skeptic.

Murali came to the United States from India to attend medical school and ended up staying and establishing a practice there. Although he was raised as a Hindu and still respects his family's religion, Murali is not particularly devout. Troubled by the centuries of conflict in the Indian subcontinent between Hindus and Muslims, he has concluded that all religions are basically good and none should be regarded as superior to another. Absolute claims in religion strike him as both unprovable and intolerant, and he resents efforts by both Muslims and Christians to convert him or his family to their beliefs. Although religions speak about God and adherents experience the transcendent in different ways, he believes it is all really the same thing. When Muslims or Christians attempt to convince him that their religion is the truth, Murali asks why God has allowed so many different religions to flourish if only one of them is acceptable to God.

Throughout this book we will periodically ask how a skilled and astute advocate of a particular approach to apologetics would respond to Sarah and Murali. In this way we will see how the various apologetic methods can be applied in concrete situations. We will see their weaknesses as well as their strengths. This will help us think through how the different apologetic methods may be integrated to greater effectiveness in defending the faith.

Fundamental to apologetics is answering questions commonly raised by non-Christians about the truth of Christianity. While many such questions are broached in this book, we will concentrate on those that are basic and crucial to the validity of the Christian faith. These questions are part of the unbelieving stance typified by our model non-Christians, Sarah and Murali. Those questions are the following:

1. Why should we believe in the Bible?
2. Don't all religions lead to God?
3. How do we know that God exists?
4. If God does exist, why does he permit evil?
5. Aren't the miracles of the Bible spiritual myths or legends and not literal fact?
6. Why should I believe what Christians claim about Jesus?

TOM, JOE, CAL, AND MARTINA

In this book we will be analyzing four basic approaches to apologetics. Again, these are idealized types; when we consider the apologetic work of actual Christian apologists we find that there are actually many more than four approaches. However, most of the methods that Christians use in apologetics are closely related to one of these four basic approaches. We might think of them as "families" of apologetic approaches, with those classified in the same type as sharing certain "family resemblances" with one another. Membership in one family does not preclude some resemblances to another family. Our analysis of apologetic approaches into these four types closely parallels that found in other surveys of major types of apologetics, though with some minor differences (see the Appendix.)

What distinguishes these four basic approaches to apologetics? To put the matter as simply as possible, each places a distinctive priority on reason, fact, revelation, and faith respectively. In our illustrations with Sarah and Murali, we will also present four Christians utilizing the four approaches in an astute, representative manner. For reasons that will become clear by the end of Part One, we call these four apologists Tom (after Thomas Aquinas, a thirteenth-century theologian), Joe (after Joseph Butler, an eighteenth-century Anglican bishop), Cal (after John Calvin, the sixteenth-century French Reformer), and Martina (after

Martin Luther, the sixteenth-century German Reformer). Tom's apologetic approach places a strong emphasis on logic, and is called *classical apologetics*. Joe's approach emphasizes facts or evidences, and is called *evidentialism*. Cal's approach emphasizes the authority of God's revelation in Scripture; because of its close identification with Calvinist or Reformed theology, this approach is here called *Reformed apologetics*. Finally, Martina's approach emphasizes the need for personal faith and is referred to here as *fideism* (from the Latin *fide*, "faith"). These are differences in emphasis or priority, since apologists favoring one approach over another generally allow some role for reason, facts, revelation, and faith. (Even fideism, which is typically suspicious of apologetic argument, offers a kind of apologetics that uses reason and fact.)

The four approaches diverge on apologetic method or theory regarding the following six questions, all of which will be discussed in this book in relation to each of the four views:

1. On what basis do we claim that Christianity is the truth?
2. What is the relationship between apologetics and theology?
3. Should apologetics engage in a philosophical defense of the Christian faith?
4. Can science be used to defend the Christian faith?
5. Can the Christian faith be supported by historical inquiry?
6. How is our knowledge of Christian truth related to our experience?

Although each approach answers these questions in different ways, those answers are not necessarily mutually exclusive. In practice, many apologists do not fit neatly into one of the four categories because they draw somewhat from two or even more approaches to answer these questions about apologetics. We see this as a healthy tendency. In fact, we will argue that all four approaches have value and should be integrated together as much as possible.

THE PLAN OF THE BOOK

This book is divided into six parts. Part One introduces the subject of apologetics, and includes a review of the thought of leading apologists in church history and an overview of the four basic approaches to apologetics.

Parts Two through Five present parallel treatments of each of the four approaches. Each part is divided into four chapters. The first chapter of each part traces the roots of the apologetic approach and introduces the thought of five major apologists (chapters 4, 8, 12, and 16). These five apologists are associated with that approach or idealized type in different ways: some are precursors to that approach as it has emerged in modern times, some are advocates of a "pure" form of that approach, and some represent significant variations in that approach. The second chapter analyzes the method and its view of the six questions mentioned above concerning knowledge, theology, philosophy, science, history, and experience (5, 9, 13, and 17). The third chapter examines the method's answers to the six questions about Scripture, other religions, God, evil, miracles, and Jesus (6, 10, 14, and 18). The fourth chapter of each part summarizes the method and illustrates it with a sample dialogue between our two fictional non-Christians and one of the four model Christian apologists (7, 11, 15, and 19). Each of these latter chapters also discusses the major strengths and weaknesses of the apologetic approach illustrated in the dialogue.

Finally, Part Six discusses ways to integrate the four basic approaches. Its structure closely parallels Parts Two through Five, and thus it begins with a chapter noting the precursors to an integrative strategy and introducing the thought of five modern apologists who have proposed or utilized such integrative systems (chapter 20). These five apologists integrate the four approaches in different ways, with one approach typically dominating to some extent. The next two chapters propose integrative strategies to understanding the relation of apologetics to theories of knowledge, theology, philosophy, science, history, and experience (21), and to answering the six questions concerning Scripture, other religions, God, evil, miracles, and Jesus (22). We are *not* here advocating a "fifth approach" or offering an integrative system of our own to replace or supplant other apologetic systems. Rather, we are encouraging Christians to use whatever method or methods they find useful while enriching their defense of the faith by learning from apologists who favor other approaches. The final chapter makes the case for a plurality of apologetic methods in view of the differences among apologists and non-Christians, the different needs people have, and the different questions people ask (23). The following table shows the overall plan of the book from Part Two through Part Six.

This second edition of *Faith Has Its Reasons* has been thoroughly updated and in other respects revised. Wherever possible we have drawn on more recent publications of living apologists and made note of recent studies pertaining to apologists and apologetic issues. A number of reviewers of the first edition made some insightful criticisms that we have taken into consideration in this revision. It may be impossible, even in a book of this length, to treat such a vast array of thinkers and diversity of issues without simplifying and even omitting some significant aspects of the subject matter. We encourage you to use this book as an *introduction* to the field of apologetics—a handbook to your reading of the groundbreaking apologists of the past and the present.

We pray that this book will be useful in helping you to "sanctify Christ as Lord in your hearts, always being ready to make a defense to everyone who asks you to give an account for the hope that is in you, yet with gentleness and reverence" (1 Peter 3:15).

PART TWO	PART THREE	PART FOUR	PART FIVE	PART SIX
4. APOLOGISTS/ REASON	8. APOLOGISTS/ FACT	12. APOLOGISTS/ REVELATION	16. APOLOGISTS/ FAITH	20. APOLOGISTS/ INTEGRATION
Roots	Roots	John Calvin	Roots	Precursors
B. B. Warfield	Joseph Butler	Modern Roots	Martin Luther	Edward J. Carnell
C. S. Lewis	James Orr	Herman Dooyeweerd	Blaise Pascal	Francis A. Schaeffer
Norman L. Geisler	Clark H. Pinnock	Cornelius Van Til	Søren Kierkegaard	David K. Clark
Peter Kreeft	John Warwick Montgomery	Gordon H. Clark	Karl Barth	C. Stephen Evans
William Lane Craig	Richard Swinburne	Alvin Plantinga	Donald G. Bloesch	John M. Frame
5. CLASSICAL APOLOGETICS: **Reasonable Faith**	9. EVIDENTIALIST APOLOGETICS: **Faith Founded on Fact**	13. REFORMED APOLOGETICS: **Christianity in Conflict**	17. FIDEIST APOLOGETICS: **Reasons of the Heart**	21. CONTENDING FOR THE FAITH
Rational Tests for Determining Truth	Methods for Discovering Truth	Biblical Standard for Defining Truth	Divine Call to Obey the Truth	Perspectival Approaches to Defending Truth
Foundation of Theology	Defense of Theology	Vindication of Theology	Making Theology Personal	Apologetics & Theology
Constructive Use of Philosophy	Critical Use of Philosophy	Toward a Christian Philosophy	Critiquing the God of the Philosophers	Apologetics & Philosophy
Christianity Consistent with Science	Christianity Vindicated by Science	Christianity Against False Science	Christianity & the Reality Beyond Science	Christianity & Science

PART TWO	PART THREE	PART FOUR	PART FIVE	PART SIX
Revelation Confirmed in History	History as the Medium of Revelation	Revelation Interpreting History	Revelation Transcending History	Revelation & History
Proof from Experience	Experience Founded on Evidence	Problem with Experience	Faith Is Experience	Apologetics & Experience
6. THE RATIONALITY OF THE CHRISTIAN WORLDVIEW	10. PRESENTING EVIDENCE THAT DEMANDS A VERDICT	14. TAKING EVERY THOUGHT CAPTIVE	18. CALLING PEOPLE TO ENCOUNTER GOD	22. REASONS FOR HOPE
Scripture as Conclusion	Scripture as Source	Scripture as Foundation	Scripture as Witness	Scripture as Truth
Disproving Other Worldviews	Uniqueness of Christianity	Antithesis between Christian & Non-Christian Religion	Christian Faith: Not Another Religion	Myth, Truth, & Religion
Proving God's Existence	The Case for God	Belief in God as Basic	To Know God Is to Know God Exists	God Who Makes Himself Known
Deductive Problem of Evil	Inductive Problem of Evil	Theological Problem of Evil	Personal Problem of Evil	Solutions to the Problems of Evil
Miracles as the Credentials of Revelation	Miracles as Evidence for God	Miracles as Revealed by God	Miracles as God Revealing Himself	Miracles as Signs
Jesus: Alternatives	Jesus: Evidence	Jesus: Self-Attesting	Jesus: Christ of Faith	Jesus: The Answer
7. APOLOGETICS/ LIMITS OF REASON	11. APOLOGETICS/ INTERPRETATION OF FACT	15. APOLOGETICS/ AUTHORITY OF REVELATION	19. APOLOGETICS/ SUBJECTIVITY OF FAITH	23. SPEAKING THE TRUTH IN LOVE
Classical Model	Evidential Model	Reformed Model	Fideist Model	One Body, Many Gifts: Apologists
Classical Apologetics Illustrated	Evidentialism Illustrated	Reformed Apologetics Illustrated	Fideist Apologetics Illustrated	One World, Many Individuals: People
Strengths	Strengths	Strengths	Strengths	One Process, Many Stages: Needs
Weaknesses	Weaknesses	Weaknesses	Weaknesses	One Faith, Many Questions: Problems

Part One

What Is Apologetics?

Chapter 1

Defining Apologetics

Apologetics may be simply defined as the defense of the Christian faith. The simplicity of this definition, however, masks the complexity of the problem of defining apologetics. It turns out that a diversity of approaches has been taken to defining the meaning, scope, and purpose of apologetics.

FROM *APOLOGIA* TO APOLOGETICS

The word "apologetics" derives from the Greek word *apologia*, which was originally used of a speech of defense or an answer given in reply. In ancient Athens it referred to a defense made in the courtroom as part of the normal judicial procedure. After the accusation, the defendant was allowed to refute the charges with a defense or reply (*apologia*). The accused would attempt to "speak away" (*apo*—away, *logia*—speech) the accusation.[1] The classic example of such an *apologia* was Socrates' defense against the charge of preaching strange gods, a defense retold by his most famous pupil, Plato, in a dialogue called *The Apology* (in Greek, *hē apologia*).

The word appears seventeen times in noun or verb form in the New Testament, and both the noun *(apologia)* and verb form *(apologeomai)* can be translated "defense" or "vindication" in every case.[2] Usually the word is used to refer to a speech made in one's own defense. For example, in one passage Luke says that a Jew named Alexander tried to "make a defense" before an angry crowd in Ephesus that was incited by idol-makers whose business was threatened by Paul's preaching (Acts 19:33). Elsewhere Luke always uses the word in reference to situations in which Christians, and in particular the apostle Paul, are put on trial for proclaiming their faith in Christ and have to defend their message against the charge of being unlawful (Luke 12:11; 21:14; Acts 22:1; 24:10; 25:8, 16; 26:2, 24).

Paul himself used the word in a variety of contexts in his epistles. To the Corinthians, he found it necessary to "defend" himself against criticisms of his claim to be an apostle (1 Corinthians 9:3; 2 Corinthians 12:19). At one point he describes the repentance exhibited by the Corinthians as a "vindication" (2 Corinthians 7:11 NASB), that is, as an "eagerness to clear yourselves" (NIV, NRSV). To the Romans, Paul described Gentiles who did not have the written Law as being aware enough of God's Law that, depending on their behavior, their own thoughts will either prosecute or "defend" them on Judgment Day (Romans 2:15). Toward the end of his life, Paul told Timothy, "At my first *defense* no one supported me" (2 Timothy 4:16), referring to the first time he stood trial. Paul's usage here is similar to what we find in Luke's writings. Earlier, he had expressed appreciation to the Philippians for supporting him "both in my imprisonment and in the *defense* and confirmation of the gospel" (Philippians 1:7). Here again the context is Paul's conflict with the government and his imprisonment. However, the focus of the "defense" is not Paul but "the gospel": Paul's ministry includes defending the gospel against its detractors, especially those who claim that it is subversive or in any way unlawful. So Paul says later in the same chapter, "I am appointed for the *defense* of the gospel" (Philippians 1:16).

Finally, in 1 Peter 3:15 believers are told always to be prepared "to make a *defense* to everyone who asks you to give an account for the hope that is in you." The context here is similar to Paul's later epistles and to Luke's writings: non-Christians are slandering the behavior of Christians and threatening them with persecution (1 Peter 3:13–17; 4:12–19). When challenged or even threatened, Christians are to behave lawfully, maintain a good conscience, and give a reasoned defense of what they believe to anyone who asks. (We will discuss this text further in chapter 2.)

The New Testament, then, does not use the words *apologia* and *apologeomai* in the technical sense of the modern word *apologetics*. The idea of offering a reasoned defense of the faith is evident in three of these texts (Philippians 1:7, 16; and especially 1 Peter 3:15), but even here no science or formal academic discipline of apologetics is contemplated. Indeed, no specific system or theory of apologetics is outlined in the New Testament.

In the second century this general word for "defense" began taking on a narrower sense to refer to a group of writers who defended the beliefs and practices of Christianity against various attacks. These men were known as the *apologists* because of the titles of some of their treatises, and included most notably Justin

Martyr *(First Apology, Dialogue with Trypho, Second Apology)* and Tertullian *(Apologeticum)*. The use of the title *Apology* by these authors harks back to Plato's *Apology* and to the word's usual sense in the New Testament, and is consistent with the fact that the emphasis of these second-century apologies was on defending Christians against charges of illegal activities.

It was apparently not until 1794 that *apologetics* was used to designate a specific theological discipline,[3] and there has been debate about the place of this discipline in Christian thought almost from that time forward. In 1908 B. B. Warfield cataloged some of these alternate perceptions before offering his own conclusion that apologetics should be given the broad task of authenticating the facts of God (philosophical apologetics), religious consciousness (psychological apologetics), revelation (revelational apologetics), Christianity (historical apologetics), and the Bible (bibliological apologetics, Warfield's specialty).[4] Greg L. Bahnsen summarizes Warfield's catalog:

> Some attempted to distinguish apologetics from apology, but they differed among themselves respecting the principle of distinction (Dusterdieck, Kubel). Apologetics was variously classified as an exegetical discipline (Planck), historical theology (Tzschirner), theory of religion (Rabiger), philosophical theology (Schleiermacher), something distinct from polemics (Kuyper), something belonging to several departments (Tholuck, Cave), or something which had no right to exist (Nosselt). H. B. Smith viewed apologetics as historico-philosophical dogmatics which deals with *detail* questions, but Kubel claimed that it properly deals only with the *essence* of Christianity. Schultz went further and said that apologetics is concerned simply to defend a generally *religious* view of the world, but others taught that apologetics should aim to establish *Christianity* as the final religion (Sack, Ebrard, Lechler, Lemme).[5]

This debate continued throughout the twentieth century. In this chapter we will offer definitions of the apologetics word group and consider just how best to conceive of the discipline of apologetics.

APOLOGETICS AND RELATED TERMS

It has become customary to use the term **apology** to refer to a specific effort or work in defense of the faith.[6] An apology might be a written document, a speech, or even a film; any medium of communication might conceivably be used.

An **apologist** is someone who presents an apology or makes a practice of defending the faith. Apologists might (and do) develop their apologies within various intellectual contexts. That is, they may offer defenses of the Christian faith in relation to scientific, historical, philosophical, ethical, religious, theological, or cultural issues.

The terms *apologetic* and *apologetics* are closely related, and can be used synonymously. Here, for clarity's sake, we will suggest one way of usefully distinguishing these terms that corresponds to the way they are often actually used. An **apologetic** (using the word as a noun) will be here defined as a particular approach to the defense of the faith. Thus, one may hear about Francis Schaeffer's apologetic or about the Thomistic apologetic. Of course, we often use *apologetic* as an adjective, as when we speak about apologetic issues or William Paley's apologetic thought.

Apologetics, on the other hand, has been used in at least three ways. Perhaps most commonly it refers to the discipline concerned with the defense of the faith. Second, it can refer to a general grouping of approaches or systems developed for defending the faith, as when we speak about evidentialist apologetics or Reformed apologetics. Third, it is sometimes used to refer to the practice of defending the faith—as the activity of presenting an apology or apologies in defense of the faith. These three usages are easily distinguished by context, so we will employ all three in this book.

Finally, **metapologetics** refers to the study of the nature and methods of apologetics. This term has come into usage only recently and is still rarely used.[7] Mark Hanna defined it as "the field of inquiry that examines the methods, concepts, and foundations of apologetic systems and perspectives."[8] While apologetics studies the defense of the faith, metapologetics studies the theoretical issues underlying the defense of the faith. It is evident, then, that metapologetics is a branch of apologetics; it focuses on the principial, fundamental questions that must be answered properly if the practice of apologetics is to be securely grounded in truth. A **metapologetic** may then be defined as a particular theory of metapologetics, such as Cornelius Van Til's Reformed metapologetic or Norman Geisler's neo-Thomistic metapologetic.

THE FUNCTIONS OF APOLOGETICS

Historically, apologetics has been understood to involve at least three functions or goals. Some apologists have emphasized only one function while others have denied that one or more of these are valid functions of apologetics, but in general they have been widely recognized as defining the task of apologetics. Francis Beattie, for example, delineated them as a *defense* of Christianity as a system, a *vindication* of the Christian worldview against its assailants, and a *refutation* of opposing systems and theories.[9]

Bernard Ramm also lists three functions of apologetics. The first is "to show how the Christian faith is related to truth claims." The truth claims of a religion must be examined so that its relation to reality can be discerned and tested. This function corresponds to what Beattie calls defense. The second function is "to show Christianity's power of interpretation" relative to a variety of subjects—which is essentially the same as what Beattie calls vindication. Ramm's third function, the refutation of false or spurious attacks, is identical to Beattie's.[10]

John Frame likewise has outlined "three aspects of apologetics," which he calls proof, defense, and offense. Proof involves "presenting a rational basis for faith"; defense involves "answering the objections of unbelief"; and offense means "attacking the foolishness (Psalm 14:1; 1 Corinthians 1:18–2:16) of unbelieving thought."[11] Frame's book then follows this outline: proof (chapters 3–5), defense (6–7), and offense (8).

The first three parts of Robert Reymond's fourfold analysis of the task of Christian apologetics follow the same pattern. (1) Apologetics answers particular objections—obstacles like alleged contradictions between scriptural statements and misconceptions about Christianity need to be removed (defense). (2) It gives an account of the foundations of the Christian faith by delving into philosophical theology, and especially epistemology (vindication). (3) It challenges non-Christian systems, particularly in the area of epistemological justification (refutation). To these Reymond adds a fourth point: (4) Apologetics seeks to persuade people of the truth of the Christian position.[12] In a sense, this last point could be viewed simply as indicating the overall purpose of apologetics, with the first three points addressing the specific functions by which that purpose is accomplished. On the other hand, treating persuasion as a separate function is helpful, since it involves elements that go beyond offering an intellectual response (the focus of the first three points). Persuasion must also consider the life experience of the unbeliever, the proper tone to take with a person, and other matters beyond simply imparting information.

We may distinguish, then, four functions, goals, modes, or aspects of apologetics. The first may be called *vindication* (Beattie) or *proof* (Frame) and involves marshaling philosophical arguments as well as scientific and historical evidences for the Christian faith. The goal of apologetics here is to develop a positive case for Christianity as a belief system that should be accepted. Philosophically, this means drawing out the logical implications of the Christian worldview so that they can be clearly seen and contrasted with alternate worldviews. Such a contrast necessarily raises the issue of criteria of verification if these competing truth claims are to be assessed. The question of the criteria by which Christianity is proved is a fundamental point of contention among proponents of the various kinds of Christian apologetic systems.

The second function is *defense*. This function is closest to the New Testament and early Christian use of the word *apologia*: defending Christianity against the plethora of attacks made against it in every generation by critics of varying belief systems. This function involves clarifying the Christian position in light of misunderstandings and misrepresentations; answering objections, criticisms, or questions from non-Christians; and in general clearing away any intellectual difficulties that nonbelievers claim stand in the way of their coming to faith. More generally, the purpose of apologetics as defense is not so much to show that Christianity is true as to show that it is *credible*.

The third function is *refutation* of opposing beliefs (what Frame calls "offense"). This function focuses on answering, not specific objections to Christianity, but the arguments non-Christians give in support of their own beliefs. Most apologists agree that refutation cannot stand alone, since proving a non-Christian religion or philosophy to be false does not prove that Christianity is true. Nevertheless, it is an essential function of apologetics.

The fourth function is *persuasion*. By this we do not mean merely convincing people that Christianity is true, but persuading them to apply its truth to their life. This function focuses on bringing non-Christians to the point of commitment. The apologist's intent is not merely to win an intellectual argument, but to persuade people to commit their lives and eternal futures into the trust of the Son of God who died for them. We might also speak of this function as evangelism or *witness*.

These four aspects or functions of apologetics have differing and complementary goals or intentions with respect to reason. Apologetics as proof shows that *Christianity is reasonable*; its purpose is to give the non-Christian good reasons to embrace the Christian faith. Apologetics as defense shows that *Christianity is not unreasonable*; its purpose is to show that the non-Christian will not be acting irrationally by trusting in Christ or by accepting the Bible as God's word. Third, apologetics as refutation shows that *non-Christian thought is unreasonable*. The purpose of refuting non-Christian belief systems is to confront non-Christians with the irrationality of their position. And fourth, apologetics as persuasion takes into consideration the fact that *Christianity is not known by reason alone*. The apologist seeks to persuade non-Christians to trust Christ, not merely to accept truth claims about Christ, and this purpose necessitates realizing the personal dimension in apologetic encounters and in every conversion to faith in Christ.

Not everyone agrees that apologetics involves all four of these functions. For example, some apologists and theologians have claimed that proof is not a valid function of apologetics—that we should be content to show that Christianity is not unreasonable. Or again, some Christian philosophers have urged against trying to argue that the non-Christian is being irrational to reject Christianity. Many apologists have even abandoned the idea that apologetics might be useful to persuade people to believe in Christ. Such opinions notwithstanding, all four functions have historically been important in apologetics, and each has been championed by great Christian apologists throughout church history.[13] It is to the efforts of those apologists, then, that we turn in the next chapter.

For Further Study

Howe, Frederic R. *Challenge and Response: A Handbook for Christian Apologetics*. Grand Rapids: Zondervan, 1982. The first two chapters discuss the definition of apologetics (13-24) and the relationship between evangelism and apologetics (25-33), with Howe arguing for a sharp distinction between the two.

Mayers, Ronald B. "What Is Apologetics?" Chapter 1 in *Balanced Apologetics: Using Evidences and Presuppositions in Defense of the Faith*, 1-14. Grand Rapids: Kregel, 1996. First published as *Both/And: A Balanced Apologetic*. Chicago: Moody, 1984. Helpful treatment of the meaning of *apologia* and of the relationship between apologetics and philosophy.

Warfield, Benjamin B. "Apologetics." In *The New Schaff-Hertzog Encyclopedia of Religious Knowledge*, ed. Samuel Macauley Jackson, 1:232-238. New York: Funk & Wagnalls, 1908. Reprinted in *Studies in Theology*, 3-21. The Works of Benjamin B. Warfield 9. New York: Oxford University Press, 1932; Grand Rapids: Baker, 1981. Still hard-to-match analysis of the nature of apologetics and its place in the academic disciplines.

Chapter 2
A Brief History of Apologetics

While apologies or defenses of the Christian faith go all the way back to the first century, the formal science of apologetics is a more recent development. In this chapter we will survey the history of apologetics in three stages. First, we will discuss in some detail apologetics in the New Testament itself. Second, we will give detailed attention to the thought of the leading apologists prior to the Reformation, notably Augustine, Anselm, and Thomas Aquinas. Third, we will present a more cursory overview of apologetics from the Reformation to the present.[1] In later chapters we will consider the apologetic thought of several modern Christian thinkers in more detail.

APOLOGETICS IN THE NEW TESTAMENT

Although perhaps none of the New Testament writings should be classified as a formal apologetic treatise, most of them exhibit apologetic concerns.[2] The New Testament writers anticipate and answer objections and seek to demonstrate the credibility of the claims and credentials of Christ, focusing especially on the resurrection of Jesus as the historical foundation upon which Christianity is built. Many New Testament writings are occupied with polemics against false teachings, in which the apologetic concern is to defend the gospel against perversion from within the church.[3]

Apologetics In Luke–Acts

Of all the New Testament writings, the two volumes by Luke (his Gospel and the Acts of the Apostles) are the most overtly apologetical in purpose.[4] In his prologue (Luke 1:1–4) Luke announces that his work is based on careful historical research and will present an accurate record of the origins of Christianity. The very structure and content of this two-part work suggests it was written at least in part as a political apology for Paul: Acts ends with Paul under house arrest yet preaching freely in Rome, and both books emphasize that Jesus and the apostles (especially Paul) were law-abiding persons. In Acts the motif of Jesus' resurrection as vindication, his fulfillment of Old Testament messianic prophecies, and the charismatic phenomena on and after the Day of Pentecost are used as cumulative evidences of the messianic lordship of Jesus (Acts 2:36) and of the authority of the apostolic truth claims. Along the way Luke uses the speeches of the apostles to present apologetic arguments to a wide variety of audiences, both Jewish and Gentile.

One of these speeches, Paul's address to the Athenians in Acts 17, has been extraordinarily important in Christian reflections about apologetics throughout church history; it is the only substantial example of an apology directed to a non-Jewish audience in the New Testament (though see Acts 14:15–17). Thus this one speech has traditionally been regarded as a paradigm or model of apologetics.[5]

According to Luke (Acts 17:18), Paul's message of Jesus and the Resurrection was misunderstood as teaching new deities. Luke reports this accusation in terms identical to those describing the Athenians' charge against Socrates in Plato's *Apology*, which strongly suggests that Luke sees Paul's speech here as a Christian counterpart to the Socratic apology. Challenged to explain his position by Stoic and Epicurean philosophers, Paul set his message in a rational context in which it would make sense to his philosophically minded audience. The speech was quite unlike those Paul delivered to Jewish audiences, which emphasized Jesus as the fulfillment of Old Testament messianic promises and quoted Old Testament proof texts liberally. In fact, Paul used a form of speech recognized by the Greeks as a philosophical address, such as was commonly used by the Stoics and Cynics of his day.

Throughout the speech Paul speaks biblical truth but uses Stoic terms and argues in Stoic fashion, even quoting a Stoic poet in support of his argument (verses 24–29). Essentially, the point of this first and longest part of the speech is that idolatry is foolish and that the Stoics themselves have admitted as much, though they had failed to abandon it completely. Paul uses this inconsistency in Stoic philosophy to illustrate the Athenians' ignorance of God (cf. verse 23). Having proved his major premise, Paul then announces that God has declared an end to ignorance of his nature and will by revealing himself. Paul concludes that the Resurrection is proof of God's intention to judge the world through Jesus Christ (verses 30–31). This scandalized the Athenians (verse 32), in part because Greek thought generally found the idea of physical resurrection foolish, and in part because the idea of a final judgment was offensive to them.

The result of Paul's apology was that some believed, some scoffed, and some expressed interest (verses 32–34). These reactions cover the three possible responses to the gospel, and the small number of those who believed should not be taken to mean that Paul's speech was a failure. Nor should 1 Corinthians 2:2 be taken to mean that Paul abandoned philosophical reasoning (as his use of Greek logic and rhetoric in 1 Corinthians 15 makes clear), but that he refused to avoid the central issue with the Corinthians even though it was scandalous to them. Thus Christian apologists are right to view Paul's speech to the Athenians as a model of Christian apology.

Apologetics in Paul's Writings

Closely related to Paul's thought in his Athenian address is his argument in Romans 1. Paul takes over Hellenistic Jewish apologetics here on the folly of Gentile culture (chapter 1, first half of chapter 2), then argues that the Jews are not above the same sins as the Gentiles (second half of chapter 2). Along the way he sets forth some notions about the knowledge of God that have been extremely important for apologetics.[6] According to Paul, God's existence and divinity are clearly revealed in nature. All human beings, he says, "knew God," but they suppressed the truth, refusing to acknowledge God and falling into idolatry instead (1:18–25).

The statement that people "knew God" (verse 21) has been understood in two ways. (1) It may mean that all people once knew God but don't any longer. The past tense of the verb certainly allows for this interpretation, and in support it may be noted that Paul elsewhere consistently says that the Gentiles do *not* know God (besides Acts 17:23, see 1 Corinthians 1:21; Galatians 4:8; 1 Thessalonians 4:5; 2 Thessalonians 1:8; Titus 1:16). (2) It may mean that all people in some limited sense know God but refuse to worship him properly. In support of this view, it has been pointed out that the godless must know something about God to be able to "suppress" the truth about him and refuse to "acknowledge" him (Romans 1:18, 28). In other words, since the suppression continues, so must the knowledge being suppressed.[7] These two views can be reconciled. The true knowledge of God—in which one *knows God*, not merely knows that there is a God of some kind—was once had by all people, but no longer. All human beings continue to know that there is a God and continue to be confronted with internal and external evidence for his deity, but generally speaking they suppress or subvert this knowledge into idolatrous religion of varying kinds.

Paul's letters elsewhere repeatedly deal with apologetic issues that arose as both Jews and pagans who had confessed Christ and become associated with the churches Paul had founded developed radically different interpretations of the meaning of Christ. In 1 Corinthians 1–2 Paul warned the Corinthian believers against trying to accommodate the gospel to the wisdom of the Greeks. Paul is not advocating a kind of anti-intellectualism. Christianity promotes a true wisdom that mature Christians find intellectually superior to anything the world can produce, one based on God's revelation rather than human speculation (1 Corinthians 1:18–21; 2:6–16).[8] In 1 Corinthians 15 Paul refuted errors about the resurrection of the dead by reminding the Corinthians that the resurrection of Christ was a historical fact (verses 3–11). Paul argues that the heretics—who deny our future resurrection—are inconsistent if they affirm Jesus' resurrection since, if he was raised, we can be too. They are also inconsistent if they do not affirm Jesus' resurrection since, if Jesus was not raised, there is no point to their affirming faith in Jesus at all (verses 12–19). This is a classic model of apologetic argument, locking opponents of gospel truths in a logical dilemma.[9]

In his epistle to the Colossians, Paul refuted errors about Christ's person that arose apparently from a religious context in which unbiblical Jewish and Greek ideas were mixed with an acknowledgment, however inadequate, of Jesus Christ. In this context Paul condemns not philosophy per se, but manmade philosophies that are not "according to Christ" (Colossians 2:8). Paul boldly co-opted Greek religious terms such as *plērōma*, a term used to denote the "fullness" of the divine beings that inhabited the cosmos, to convey Christian ideas—in this case, the idea that all deity dwelled in Christ (2:9).

Apologetics in John's Writings

The apostle John followed a strategy similar to Paul's adoption of Greek philosophical and religious terms in his Gospel, in which the preincarnate Christ is called the **Logos** ("Word," John 1:1, 14; cf. 1 John 1:1). The notion of a preexistent Word involved in God's creation of the universe had Old Testament associations (for example, Genesis 1:3; Psalm 33:6, 9). Still, to any Gentile or Hellenistic Jewish reader the term *Logos* would have immediately conjured up Platonic and Stoic notions of the universal Reason that was believed to govern the cosmos and was thought to be reflected in the rational mind of every human being (cf. John 1:9). Yet the announcement by John that this Logos was personal—that he was

God's Son (verses 1, 14, 18; cf. 20:31) and had become incarnate (1:14)—was shocking to both Jews and Greeks. It required a completely new way of looking at God and humanity to believe that Jesus was the divine Logos incarnate.[10]

The Apologetic Mandate in 1 Peter 3:15

Our survey of New Testament apologetics would not be complete without taking notice of 1 Peter 3:15, which has often been regarded as the classic biblical statement of the mandate for Christians to engage in apologetics.[11] Peter instructs believers to "sanctify Christ as Lord in your hearts, always being ready to make a defense [*apologia*] to everyone who asks you to give an account [*logos*] for the hope that is in you, yet with gentleness and reverence" (NASB). Three key observations should be made about this text.

First, Peter is definitely instructing believers to make a reasoned defense of their beliefs. *Logos* (the same word used in John 1:1 to refer to the preexistent Christ) is a very flexible word, but in this context it clearly refers to a rational explanation or account. The word *apologia*, while not meaning "apologetics" in the modern technical sense, does indicate that Christians are to make the best case they can for their confession of Jesus Christ as Lord.

Second, this apologetic mandate is given generally to all Christians, requiring them to give reasons for faith in Christ to anyone who asks for them. In the context Peter is specifically urging believers to be ready to do this when threatened with suffering for their faith (see 1 Peter 3:13–14, 16–17), but there is no basis for limiting the mandate to such situations. The language is quite general ("always . . . to everyone who asks you") and makes the apologetic mandate a standing order for the church.

Third, Peter instructs us to engage in apologetics with proper attitudes toward both the non-Christians with whom we are speaking and the Lord about whom we are speaking: "with gentleness and reverence." The term "gentleness" indicates the manner in which we are to answer those who challenge our faith (again, in context this includes both "seekers" and those who are antagonistic to the Christian message). The term "reverence" (*phobos*, almost always translated "fear") is translated "respect" in some versions, and this is often understood as referring to respect toward the people to whom we are speaking. However, Peter has just said we are not to show *phobos* toward people (3:14), and elsewhere says we are to show *phobos* toward God (1:17; 2:17). Almost certainly, then, Peter is telling us to conduct our defense of the faith with an attitude of holy fear or reverence toward Christ, whom we honor as Lord (3:15). We do so by striving to be faithful to Christ both in what we say and in how we live (verse 16).

THE EARLY CHURCH FATHERS

In the postapostolic era, the new challenges that confronted the burgeoning church as it spread throughout the Roman Empire required a new apologetic counterthrust. Rabbinic Judaism, fully developed Gnosticism, persecuting paganism, and Hellenistic culture and philosophy all opposed the fledgling church. The religious apologists defended Christianity against these attacks and sought to gain converts to the faith by arguing for the superiority of the Christian position. There were also political apologists who argued that the church should be tolerated by the state.

The apologists of the second century[12] modeled their arguments after contemporary philosophical refutations of polytheism and the critiques of pagan philosophy by Hellenistic Jews. Of the many apologists from this period, the most important by far was **Justin Martyr** (ca. 100–165),[13] a convert to Christianity from Platonism. In his *Dialogue with Trypho the Jew*, Justin used messianic prophecies from the Hebrew Scriptures to prove that Jesus is the Messiah. In his two *Apologies* he appealed for the civil toleration of Christianity and argued that it was in fact the true philosophy. To show that Christianity should be tolerated, he refuted common errors and rumors (for example, that Christians were atheists and that they ate flesh and drank blood) and presented Christianity as a morally superior religion. To support his claim that it was the true philosophy, Justin made the first attempt in postbiblical history to correlate John's doctrine of the Logos with Greek philosophy, arguing that Christianity was superior to Platonism and that any truth in Plato was actually plagiarized from Moses. Arguably, Justin's doctrine was less than consistently biblical, notably in his strongly subordinationist view of Christ. However, his efforts were commendable given his place in Christian history (even before the process of collecting the New Testament canon was completed) and in view of his role as a pioneer in Christian theologizing and apologetics.

The third-century Alexandrians "continued to assimilate arguments from Platonic and Stoic philosophers as well as Jewish controversialists."[14] Clement of Alexandria wrote a number of theological discourses and an apologetic work called *Protrepticus*, a more sophisticated and persuasive work than those of the second-century apologists. By far the most important Greek apologist of the third century was **Origen** (ca. 185–254),[15] whose lengthy *Contra Celsum* ("Against Celsus") was a reply to Celsus's philosophical, ethical, and historical criticisms of Christianity. In it, for example, Origen argued that Jesus did not do his miracles by sorcery, offered an impressive historical defense of Jesus' resurrection against an early hallucination theory and other objections, and showed that the miracle stories of paganism are far less credible than those of the Gospels.[16] It is with good reason that Origen's book has been ranked as one of the classics of apologetics.[17]

AUGUSTINE

In the fourth and fifth centuries, pagan religions were on the wane and Christianity was on the ascendancy throughout the empire, particularly after the edict of Constantine in 313. Christian apologists, both Latin and Greek, wrote with pride of the progress and life-changing effects of Christianity. They also became more systematic in their presentation of Christianity as a worldview in contrast to competing philosophies, notably Neoplatonism.

The greatest apologist and theologian of this period and indeed of the first millennium of Christian history was, by nearly everyone's reckoning, Aurelius **Augustine** (354–430), the bishop of Hippo, whose apologetic and theological writings ranged widely over the areas of human culture, philosophy, and history.[18] Augustine was won to the Christian faith after trying Manicheism, a dualistic philosophy that viewed both good and evil as ultimate realities, and Platonism, which convinced him that Manicheism was false and so, by his own testimony, helped him on the path to Christianity. His earlier apologetic works, not surprisingly, were in large part devoted to refuting Manichean philosophy (*On the Catholic and Manichean Ways of Life*, *Of True Religion*, *On the Usefulness of Belief*).

As Augustine became more involved in church life, his apologetic works became more diversified. Over the course of his life he wrote numerous works championing Christianity over paganism, refuting heresies plaguing the church, and expounding Christian truth in a positive manner in teaching manuals and in sermons for the edification of Christians. An original and multigifted writer, thinker, and scholar, Augustine was able to develop an apologetic that was built on a stronger metaphysical or worldview base. While his worldview was at first heavily Platonic, as he matured his theology and philosophy became significantly less Platonic and more and more biblical. Specifically, Augustine became the first Christian theologian and apologist to embrace a thoroughly Pauline view of faith and of God's sovereignty in salvation and in human history. This Pauline theology, in turn, enabled him to develop the first philosophically sophisticated, biblically sound, and comprehensive Christian view of the world and of history. Such a Christian philosophy was necessary to combat pagan philosophies, including Platonism, the philosophy he considered closest to Christianity. All such philosophies were corrupt and incapable of bringing people to God. Augustine's Christian philosophy was expounded most fully in one of his last works, *The City of God*, widely regarded as one of the five or ten most important books in the history of Western thought.[19]

Augustine's teaching on apologetical issues has inspired apologists and theologians from his day to the present. In his approach, faith and reason are interactive in coming to know the true God in Jesus Christ. Reason precedes faith in that a rational mind and recognition of the truth of what is to be believed must exist if we are to believe anything.[20] But faith precedes reason in that the truths of the Christian faith are in large part unseen—not only is God invisible, but the redemptive acts of God in Jesus Christ occurred in the past and cannot be directly witnessed. Because these truths cannot be seen, they must be accepted on the authority of God's revelation as given in Scripture and witnessed by the church.[21] These truths can then be understood as the believer comes to appreciate their significance from the inside. "For understanding is the reward of faith. Therefore do not seek to understand in order to believe, but believe that thou mayest understand."[22] Augustine, then, was the first apologist to enunciate the principle of believing in order to understand, or faith seeking understanding *(fides quaerens intellectum)*, but for him it was only one side of the coin. He frequently expressed this interactive or interdependent view of faith and reason in such statements as "For faith is understanding's step; and understanding faith's attainment."[23] Moreover, he emphasized (in his later writings) that both faith and reason are enabled by God's grace. He declared that "no one is sufficient for himself, either to begin or to perfect faith; but our sufficiency is of God."[24]

This does not mean that non-Christians know nothing about God. Augustine cited Romans 1:20 to show that some philosophers, especially Platonists, have been able from the creation to recognize the fact of a Creator God. The line of reasoning by which even pagans can be made to admit a Creator is essentially what philosophers would later call a **cosmological argument**, reasoning from the changeableness of all things in the world (Greek *cosmos*) to the existence of an unmade Maker of all things. This was one of a number of arguments by which Augustine reasoned that knowledge of God was available to pagans.[25] But this knowledge cannot prevent them from falling into idolatry and polytheism.[26] The true worship of God can be found only by placing faith in Jesus Christ.

Such faith is not a groundless faith: "they are much deceived, who think that we believe in Christ without any proofs concerning Christ."[27] Augustine wove the proofs he found compelling into an apologetic consisting of a number of strands. These proofs included fulfilled prophecy, the consistent monotheistic faith and worship of the church, the miracles of the Bible, and especially the "miracle" of the massive conversion of much of Roman society to faith in a crucified God even when such faith brought martyrdom.[28]

ANSELM

By the seventh century Christianity had absorbed Greco-Roman culture and triumphed in its struggle against paganism. The church was the central vehicle of Western culture, and its apologists during the Middle Ages directed their efforts in three directions—toward unconverted Judaism, the threat of Islam, and the rational ground for belief.[29] Two Christian philosophers of the Middle Ages who stand out for their contributions to apologetics, and whose works continue to be read and debated today, were Anselm and Thomas Aquinas.

Anselm (1033–1109), the bishop of Canterbury, was one of the most creative and original philosophers the Christian church has ever produced.[30] He emphasized the side of Augustine's view of faith and reason that viewed faith as prior to reason or understanding. "For I do not seek to understand in order to believe but I believe in order to understand [*credo ut intelligam*]."[31] Although his philosophical arguments are often treated simply as rationalistic proofs designed to convince atheists, for him they were expressions of the search for understanding of one who already believed. On the other hand, he did intend at least some of his arguments as proofs to answer unbelievers and to confront them with the truth, as we shall see.

The most famous by far of these philosophical arguments has come to be known as the **ontological argument**,[32] the development of which in Anselm's *Proslogion* was a groundbreaking effort in apologetics. The essence of the argument is that the notion of a being of unsurpassable greatness is logically inescapable. From the *idea* of "that than which nothing greater can be thought," Anselm inferred the existence or *being* (Greek *ontos*, hence "ontological" argument) of God.

The argument has been interpreted in several markedly divergent ways. Frequently it has been treated as a rational proof of the existence of God, and as such it has usually (but not always) been rejected by both Christian and non-Christian philosophers. Some philosophers have taken it to prove that *if* there is a

God, he must be a necessary being (that is, a being that *must* exist, that cannot *not* exist) rather than a contingent being (one that might or might not have existed). Others have argued that it proves that necessary existence must be acknowledged for some being, either for the cosmos itself or for a being transcendent to the cosmos. Still others have offered radical reinterpretations of the argument. For example, Karl Barth took it to mean that God must reveal himself in order to be known. Charles Hartshorne reworked it to prove his "process" view that God is not the greatest possible being but is forever *becoming* a greater being and, in comparison to all others, is unsurpassably great. This bewildering diversity of interpretations of Anselm testifies to the provocative genius of his argument.

Anselm's other major contribution to apologetics is found in his book *Cur Deus Homo* ("Why God became a man" or "Why the God-man"), in which he argued that God became a man because only God in his infinite being could provide an infinite satisfaction or atonement for man's sin.[33] Anselm prefaced the work with the observation that the church's teachers discussed "the rational basis of our faith . . . not only to confound the foolishness of unbelievers and to break through their hardheartedness, but also in order to nourish those who, having hearts already cleansed by faith, delight in the rational basis of our faith—a rational basis for which we ought to hunger once [we have] the certainty of faith."[34] The first part of the work "contains the answers of believers to the objections of unbelievers who repudiate the Christian faith because they regard it as incompatible with reason. And this book goes on to prove by rational necessity—Christ being removed from sight, as if there had never been anything known about Him—that no man can possibly be saved without Him."[35] At the beginning of the book Anselm explained that he wrote it at the request of other believers. They asked for the book "not in order to approach faith by way of reason but in order to delight in the comprehension and contemplation of the doctrines which they believe, as well as in order to be ready, as best they can, always to give a satisfactory answer to everyone who asks of them a reason for the hope which is in us."[36] Later Anselm pointed out that "although they [unbelievers] seek a rational basis because they do not believe whereas we seek it because we do believe, nevertheless it is one and the same thing that both we and they are seeking."[37]

These statements in *Cur Deus Homo* make it clear that Anselm did see his work as apologetic in purpose. While careful to disavow any intention of displacing faith as the basis of Christian certainty, Anselm did hope to offer reasoned arguments that would show unbelievers that Christian faith has a rational basis. Evidently he viewed these arguments as designed to render unbelievers without rational excuse and even to persuade them to accept the Christian faith. But while such arguments might help in bringing a person to faith, for Anselm such faith would have to be placed, not in his rational arguments, but in the God-man himself.

THOMAS AQUINAS

In the thirteenth century Christian Europe was shaken by the rediscovery and distribution of the philosophical works of Aristotle and the strong impetus given to the Aristotelian worldview by the very capable Spanish-Arab philosopher Averroes. The growing influence of Averroist thought in European universities led to a crisis for Christian thought. Some scholars at the universities were embracing an uncritical Aristotelianism, while others, especially high-ranking church officials, uncritically condemned anything Aristotelian. Albert the Great was one of the earliest philosophers to rise to this challenge, writing *On the Unity of the Intellect against Averroes*. But it was Albert's disciple, **Thomas Aquinas** (1225–1274), who would offer a response to this challenge that would change the course of Christian philosophy and apologetics.[38]

Aquinas sought to combat the challenge of the Greco-Arabic worldview by creating a Christian philosophy utilizing Aristotelian categories and logic. In the *Summa Contra Gentiles*, he presented an apologetic directed primarily against Averroism but also offering a sweeping, comprehensive Christian philosophy in Aristotelian terms.[39] His *Summa Theologiae* was a systematic theology intended to instruct Christian students in theology; it is important for its opening apologetic sections and its theology of faith.[40]

The view of faith and reason taken by Aquinas is often contrasted sharply with that of Augustine, but despite semantic and structural differences, their views are not very far apart. According to Aquinas, some truths about God are discoverable through reason or through faith, while others are discoverable only through faith. Yet even those truths discoverable through reason are commended to faith because our reason is finite, prone to error, clouded by sin, and always uncertain, while faith is absolutely reliable because it is founded on God's revelation.

Aquinas is perhaps best known for his **five ways**, five arguments for the existence of God. These theistic arguments have been the subject of enormous debate for over two centuries.[41] Aquinas himself did not put great emphasis on the five ways, which take up only a few pages in both *Summas*. According to Aquinas, that God (or, a God) exists is vaguely recognized by all; that it is *God*, however, is not universally recognized. God's existence may be inferred from the nature of the world as changing, causative, contingent, graduated, and ordered (the five ways). These proofs (according to Aquinas himself) show that a God exists, but do not prove God per se; for Thomas, faith in God ought to be based on his revelation in Scripture, not on the proofs. The proofs were apparently offered not as a refutation of atheism (which was not a serious option in Aquinas's day), but to show the coherence of Christianity with Aristotelianism.

Interestingly, Aquinas was himself a critic of some types of theistic proofs. For example, he rejected Anselm's ontological argument. Aquinas gave particular attention to arguments based on philosophical proofs against the eternity of the world. He concluded that philosophy could neither prove nor disprove the eternity of the world and therefore could not prove God's existence from the fact of the world's origination in time. Instead, he insisted, we believe that the world is not eternal because we know from God's revelation in Scripture that the world was created by God.

Aquinas used the traditional evidences for Christianity in much the same fashion as Augustine, including the conversion of the masses, fulfilled prophecy, and miracles.[42] He was careful to point out, though, that these arguments show that Christianity is plausible and can be used to refute objections, but cannot be used to prove Christianity to nonbelievers.

THE REFORMATION

The primary concern of the Protestant Reformers of the sixteenth century was the doctrine of salvation. In their view the Aristotelianism of the **Scholastics**—the medieval theologians on whose teachings the sixteenth-century Roman Catholic system was based—had led to a confusion and perversion of the gospel of salvation through faith in Jesus Christ. Moreover, the Renaissance was marked by an infatuation with pagan antiquity, especially Plato and Neoplatonism, and the result was a further corruption of the Christian message in what came to be known as humanism. Originally **humanism** was essentially an intellectual approach to literature and learning, emphasizing the study of the classics (and of the Bible) directly instead of through medieval commentaries. By the sixteenth century, though, Catholic humanism (as represented, for instance, by Erasmus) was characterized by a man-centered philosophy emphasizing human dignity and freedom at the expense of the biblical teachings on sin and grace.[43]

The doctrine of justification by faith in Jesus Christ alone was the heart and soul of the ministry of **Martin Luther** (1483–1546), the Augustinian monk who lit the torch of the Reformation with his Ninety-five Theses protesting legalistic abuses in the church.[44] In Luther's estimation reason, particularly as employed in medieval theology, had obscured the gospel of justification. He therefore emphasized the limitations of reason and rejected the traditional theological project of employing logic and philosophy to explicate and defend the Christian faith.

Luther admitted that non-Christians can gain a "general" knowledge about God through reason, discerning that a God exists, that he is good and powerful, and the like. However, reason is incapable of helping them know who the true God is or how to be justified in his sight. Such "particular" knowledge is available only in the gospel, and can be appropriated only by faith. Not only is reason unhelpful in gaining a saving knowledge of God, it is actually an enemy of faith.

If Luther was the father and chief polemicist of the Reformation, **John Calvin** (1509–1564)[45] was arguably its chief theologian. His *Institutes of the Christian Religion* and biblical commentaries are still read and discussed today, even by nontheologians. As with Luther, Calvin's principal apologetic labors were directed against Roman Catholic criticisms of the Reformation gospel.

Unlike Luther, Calvin held that faith is always reasonable. However, he also insisted that faith often *seems* unreasonable to us because our reason is blinded by sin and spiritual deception. Such blindness is evident in the philosophies of the pagans, which at times come close to recognizing the truth but in the end always distort the truth of God's revelation of himself in nature. To remedy our spiritual blindness, God has given us his Word in Scripture, which is so much clearer and fuller in its revelation, and, through the redeeming work of Jesus Christ, God has also given us his Spirit, who enables us to understand his Word. Because God's Word comes with his own divine, absolute authority, it cannot be subjected to our reasoning or tests. Faith needs no rational justification and is more certain than rationally justified knowledge, because it is based on God's revelation in Scripture.

APOLOGETICS FACES SKEPTICISM

Until the post-Reformation period most Europeans took Christianity for granted, and the major religious debates were primarily intra-Christian disputes about the *meaning* of specific key doctrines of the faith. But the seventeenth century saw the rise of religious skepticism that challenged the very *truth* of the Christian faith. This skepticism led to new developments in apologetics. Some apologists responded to the rationalistic critiques of Christian doctrine by expressing a skepticism of their own—regarding the reliability of human reason—and proposing an approach to religion that emphasizes faith as a response of the heart. Other apologists accepted the rationalistic challenge and sought to answer it by proving that Christianity was just as rational as the conclusions of modern science.[46] These two approaches were typified by Blaise Pascal in the seventeenth century and Joseph Butler in the eighteenth century.

In his classic work *Pensées* ("Thoughts"), the French Catholic mathematician and apologist **Blaise Pascal** (1623–1662) rejected the traditional rational arguments for God's existence and emphasized the personal, relational aspects involved in a non-Christian coming to faith in Jesus Christ. Pascal pointed out that some things that are clear to one group of people may be unclear or doubtful to another group. He was one of the first apologists to argue that apologetics should take into account the differences among people. Christians who would defend the faith must seek to show that it is not irrational, that it is great news if it is true, and that in fact it can be proved to be true.

Pascal sought to strike a balance between two extremes. He did not want to abandon reason altogether, but he also did not want its importance or value in knowing Christ to be exaggerated. God has given enough evidence of the truth of Christianity that those who want to know the truth will see it, but he has not shown himself in a way that would compel faith in those who don't care or don't want to believe. Pascal was especially concerned about those who don't give serious thought to the issue. He urged them to realize that if Christianity is true and they fail to believe, they are in most serious danger.

Despite the eloquence and depth of Pascal's "thoughts," his approach to the defense of the faith was to remain a minority report. Natural science, through such giants as Galileo and Newton, achieved major breakthroughs during the seventeenth century and revolutionized our view of the world. In the wake of these developments, most apologists for the next three centuries understood the apologetic task as primarily one of showing the scientific credibility of the Christian faith. More broadly, apologetics became focused on providing empirical evidence, whether scientific or historical, in support of Christianity. Laying the groundwork for this empirical approach was John Locke (1632–1704), a British philosopher who developed one of the earliest formulations of empiricism.

The classic work of apologetics in an empirical mode was **Joseph Butler**'s book *The Analogy of Religion, Natural and Revealed, to the Constitution and Course of Nature* (1736). Butler (1692–1752), an Anglican bishop, sought to defuse objections to the orthodox Christian faith posed by deists, who favored a purely natural religion that was in principle available to all people in all times and places and that could be proved by reason. On this basis they came to question and finally reject the notion of a revealed religion that could not be rationally proved and was known only to those who had heard the revelation.

Butler argued, in response, that the intellectual difficulties found by deists in believing the Christian revelation have analogies in our knowledge of the natural world. In making this case he could assume as a given that God exists, since the deists agreed with this assumption. His use of analogies was not intended to prove either that God exists or that Christianity is true, but merely that it is *not unreasonable* to believe in the Christian revelation. This was the burden of almost the entirety of Butler's book; only in a concluding chapter did he review the positive evidences for the truth of Christianity. Throughout his book Butler's approach was empirical, focusing on facts and evidences, and the conclusions were couched in terms of probability. In taking this approach he sought to meet the deists on their own grounds, and he denied that he thought Christian faith should be *based* on the sorts of probabilistic arguments he was presenting.

THE RISE OF MODERN APOLOGETICS

Butler's apologetic efforts in *The Analogy of Religion* were widely regarded as a worthy response to the natural religion of the deists. However, Christian apologetics was forced to reinvent itself with the advent of the **Enlightenment**.[47] The skepticism of the Scottish philosopher David Hume (1711–1776) prepared the way for this movement, which rejected all revelation claims and all natural religion or natural theology, and declared the autonomy of human reason. Hume convinced many that the teleological or design argument, the argument from miracles, and other standard Christian apologetic arguments were unsound. The German Enlightenment philosopher Immanuel Kant (1724–1804), who reported having been awakened from his "dogmatic slumbers" by Hume's writings, likewise critiqued the cosmological and ontological arguments for the existence of God.

These successive waves of attack on Christianity forced orthodox Christians to develop apologetic responses. Such responses varied depending on the theological convictions and philosophical temperament of the apologist as well as the content of the unbelieving attack.

One of the earliest apologists to respond to Hume was **William Paley** (1743–1805). Paley systematized the evidential arguments of this time in two works, *A*

View of the Evidences of Christianity and *Natural Theology*. The latter work was a classic presentation of the teleological argument. He skillfully multiplied illustrations (most famously his illustration of the watch found in the desert, for which an intelligent maker must be posited) and arguments for design and for the evidential value of miracles. The force of his apologetic was severely weakened, though, by the rise of evolutionary biology in the late nineteenth century. Charles Darwin's *Origin of Species* (1859) seemed to offer a naturalistic explanation for the order and diversity in life, encouraging many in the West to abandon belief in God as the Creator. Paley also defended the reliability of the New Testament writings. In the nineteenth century such historical apologetics, centering on the New Testament accounts of Jesus' life, death, and especially his resurrection, came to the fore with works by such apologists as Richard Whately and Simon Greenleaf.

An older contemporary of Paley was **Thomas Reid** (1710–1796), a Scottish Calvinist who developed a philosophy later known as Scottish Common-Sense Realism. Reid's philosophy, like Paley's, was in large part an answer to his fellow countryman Hume. Whereas Hume had been skeptical not only of miracles and the existence of God but also of cause-and-effect and of objective right and wrong, Reid held that our knowledge of all these things was simply a matter of common sense. Philosophers who question these things have let theory obscure the obvious. Our knowledge of cause and effect and right and wrong is self-evident and an incorrigible aspect of our constitution as created by God, whether we acknowledge God's existence or not.

Reid's epistemology (or theory of knowledge) was dominant at Princeton Theological Seminary in the nineteenth and early twentieth centuries. The "Old Princetonians" affirmed that one could argue for the truth of the Christian revelation on the basis of "common sense" presuppositions about the nature of truth, reason, morality, and the world. **Charles Hodge** (1797–1878), the most famous Calvinist theologian at Old Princeton, maintained that although reason must submit to God's revelation in Scripture, reason must first discern whether Scripture is indeed a revelation from God. The non-Christian must therefore be invited to use reason and "common sense" to evaluate the evidences (miracles, fulfilled prophecy, etc.) for Christianity. Hodge also maintained the validity of most of the traditional arguments for God's existence, even recommending the works of Butler and Paley. **B. B. Warfield** (1851–1921), one of the last professors at Princeton before its reorganization and shift to liberal theology, continued Hodge's apologetic approach. The thrust of Warfield's apologetic was to argue against liberalism that a Christianity devoid of supernaturalism is, first, a Christianity that denies God, and second, really no Christianity at all.

In nineteenth-century Europe the efforts of Christian thinkers to defend Christian faith were directed largely against the philosophies of Kant and another German philosopher, Hegel. In Denmark the "melancholy Dane," **Søren Kierkegaard** (1818–1855), strongly denounced both the cold confessional Lutheran orthodoxy and the abstract philosophical system of Hegel. Kierkegaard called on Christians to repent of their merely intellectual profession and to believe passionately and personally in Christ. His *Philosophical Fragments* and *Concluding Unscientific Postscript* rejected the traditional theistic proofs and arguments for the deity of Christ on the grounds that a rational approach to Christianity ran afoul of the central paradox of Jesus Christ as God incarnate.

Somewhat later the Scottish theologian **James Orr** (1844–1913) responded to the Enlightenment challenge. He was one of the first apologists to present Christianity as a worldview, arguing that the weight of the evidence from various quarters supported the Christian view of God and the world.

In the Netherlands one of Orr's contemporaries, the Calvinist theologian and politician **Abraham Kuyper** (1837–1920), developed the notion of the **antithesis**. There is, said Kuyper, an absolute antithesis between the two sets of principles to which Christians and non-Christians are fundamentally committed (for example, God as sovereign versus man as autonomous). In short, Christians and non-Christians cannot see eye to eye on matters of fundamental principle. The non-Christian is incapable of verifying or testing the revelation of God in Scripture because, since Scripture is the Word of God, its teachings must be accepted as first principles or not at all. Therefore Christianity cannot be proved to the non-Christian on the basis of philosophical arguments or historical evidences, because these presuppose Christian principles. There can be no common or neutral ground between Christian and non-Christian. Thus, traditional apologetics must be abandoned. Negatively, Christian apologists should seek to expose the anti-Christian religious root of all non-Christian thought. Positively, they should attempt to model the truth of Christianity to the world by reconstructing society according to biblical principles.

Kuyper's seminal ideas were developed into a full-fledged philosophy by others, among whom the best-known figure was **Herman Dooyeweerd** (1894–1977). According to Dooyeweerd, traditional apologetics, especially that of Thomas Aquinas, was based on an unbiblical dualism between nature and grace—between what can be known by the non-Christian by nature through reason alone and what can be known only by God's gracious revelation through faith. The task of Christian philosophy is to commend the Christian worldview while exposing the inadequacy of all other worldviews to provide a secure footing for knowledge and ethics.

Another Christian thinker influenced by Kuyper was **Cornelius Van Til** (1895–1987), professor of apologetics at Westminster Theological Seminary. Van Til's approach was essentially a creative synthesis of the Old Princetonian and Kuyperian philosophical-apologetical positions. He agreed with the Common-Sense Realist view taught at Old Princeton that sense perception, logic, moral values, and the like were guaranteed to us by God's creating us and the world. He also agreed with Old Princeton that apologetics should offer proof for the Christian position. But Van Til integrated this position with the Kuyperian doctrine of the antithesis. Common-Sense Realism had held that non-Christians live in a God-created universe and thus operate on the basis of Christian presuppositions, whether they acknowledge that fact or not. For the Old Princetonians this meant that Christians might appeal to these shared presuppositions in traditional apologetic arguments. In Van Til's thinking, however, the Kuyperian doctrine of the antithesis indicated that the non-Christian so suppresses these presuppositions when thinking about matters of principle that no argument appealing to them will connect.

For Van Til the great mistake of traditional apologetics was in using rationalistic arguments that concluded that the truths of Christianity are *probably* true. He thought such probabilistic arguments—which he claimed dominated apologetics since Butler's *Analogy*—detracted from the certainty of faith and the absolute authority of Scripture as the written word of God. In place of such arguments, he urged Christian apologists to argue by *presupposition*. Such a presuppositional apologetic has two steps. The first is to show that non-Christian systems of thought are incapable of accounting for rationality and morality—to show that ultimately all non-Christian systems of thought fall into irrationalism. The second step is to commend the Christian view as giving the only possible presuppositional foundation for thought and life. For Van Til, such a presuppositional argument is the *only* legitimate apologetic method.

While Van Til was teaching his presuppositional version of Reformed apologetics in Philadelphia, on the other side of the Atlantic the most popular Christian apologist of the twentieth century was giving radio addresses in Britain and writing books. **C. S. Lewis** (1898–1963) was a scholar of medieval literature who converted to Christianity in midlife. His apologetic works included *The Problem of Pain* (on the problem of reconciling human suffering with an all-good God), *The Screwtape Letters* (from a senior devil instructing a junior devil in the art of temptation), *Miracles* (defending belief in miracles), and *Mere Christianity* (defending belief in God and Christ). Lewis insisted that Christianity was based on reasonable evidence, and that once a person had embraced the faith, the true attitude of faith was to believe despite such seeming evidence against Christianity as one's personal suffering and losses. Among the most popular arguments he developed was the "trilemma" (as it was later called): since Jesus claimed to be God, one must either (1) reject him as a liar, (2) dismiss him as a lunatic, or (3) accept him as Lord. Since the first two alternatives contradict Christ's evident sincerity and sanity, Lewis argued, we must conclude that he really is Lord. Lewis's writings have had a tremendous influence on Christian apologetics. Among contemporary apologists most indebted to Lewis is the Roman Catholic philosopher **Peter Kreeft**, whose articulation of the gospel is surprisingly evangelical and whose philosophy is essentially Thomistic.

An older contemporary of C. S. Lewis who took a very different view of apologetics was the Swiss theologian **Karl Barth** (1886–1968). While Lewis had converted from skepticism to Anglican Christianity, Barth had converted from German theological liberalism to a radically Christ-centered faith. Unable to swallow liberalism any longer and unwilling to go back to a premodern, conservative Protestant orthodoxy, Barth found it necessary to reconstruct Christian theology according to a new paradigm. His central and constant claim was that God is known *only* in Jesus Christ. On the basis of this premise, Barth rejected both liberalism, which thought it could find God in man's own moral and spiritual sense, and fundamentalism, which, Barth argued (erroneously), treated the Bible as an end rather than as a means to knowing God in Christ. He also rejected natural theology, the project of trying to prove God from nature, for the same reason. According to Barth, apologetics as usually conceived is unfaithful to the principle that God can be known only through his self-revelation in Jesus Christ.

Conservative evangelicals generally have rejected Barth's approach to theology and disagreed with his negative assessment of apologetics. However, some evangelicals who dissent from the belief in biblical inerrancy while maintaining an evangelical view of Christ and salvation have expressed appreciation for Barth, even while critiquing some of his views. Notable in this regard are **Bernard Ramm** and **Donald Bloesch**. Ramm, whose textbooks on apologetics were widely used in conservative evangelical circles in the 1960s and 1970s, in the 1980s argued that Barth's theology, though needing some correction, provided a paradigm for avoiding the extremes of liberalism and fundamentalism. Bloesch, a systematic theologian, agrees with Barth's criticisms of traditional apologetics but is more critical of his theology.

More conservative evangelical apologetics was dominated in the second half of the twentieth century by the debates over Van Til's presuppositionalism. During the 1950s three American apologists offered three different answers to Van Til's challenge to traditional apologetics. One was **Gordon H. Clark** (1902–1985), a Reformed philosopher whose emphasis on deductive logic led to a fierce debate with Van Til that divided the presuppositionalist movement. Clark maintained that the laws of logic and the propositions of Scripture provide the only reliable basis for knowledge. Clark's most eminent disciple was **Carl F. H. Henry** (1913–2003), one of the leaders of the new evangelicalism represented by such institutions as Fuller Theological Seminary and the magazine *Christianity Today*.

The second major apologist of the 1950s was **Edward John Carnell** (1919–1967), another new evangelical, who was president of Fuller Seminary for much of the 1950s. Carnell's books set forth a semi-presuppositional apologetic that approached Christianity as a hypothesis to be verified by showing that it alone is systematically consistent and practically livable. Like the presuppositionalists, Carnell rejected the traditional proofs for the existence of God. However, against the presuppositionalists he insisted that in the nature of the case apologetic arguments for the historical truth claims of Christianity, most notably the resurrection of Jesus, could only be based on probabilities. Carnell taught a generation of students, many of whom went on to become accomplished apologists themselves. Among these was **Gordon Lewis**, who defended a Carnellian approach to apologetics in his textbook *Defending Christianity's Truth Claims*.

The third major apologist to emerge in the 1950s was **Stuart Hackett**. Unlike the apologists mentioned so far, Hackett was avowedly non-Calvinistic. He called for "the resurrection of theism" (in a book of that title) as a rational philosophical system, defended the traditional theistic proofs, and offered one of the first detailed critiques of Van Til. Whereas Dooyeweerd, Van Til, Clark, Carnell, and many other apologists agreed that Hume and Kant's criticisms of traditional theistic proofs and evidential apologetics were valid, Hackett strenuously disagreed and in particular offered a head-on critique of Kant's criticisms.

William Lane Craig, a student of Hackett, has published a number of major apologetic works in which he has moved from a position similar to Hackett's to a more eclectic one. Craig's writings are evenly divided between sophisticated defenses of the existence of God (based primarily on philosophical and scientific forms of the cosmological argument) and equally sophisticated historical and theological defenses of the resurrection of Jesus Christ. Although his approach has strong affinities with evidentialism, in general his apologetic approach is best classified in the classical tradition.

In 1971 *Jerusalem and Athens*, a volume of essays in honor of Van Til, was published. It included several critical essays to which Van Til responded. Beginning with the publication of this book, at least two different ways of understanding and developing Van Til's presuppositionalism have been defended. The first one (which actually predates *Jerusalem and Athens*) may be called the *transcendental* interpretation, and was articulated especially by **Robert D. Knudsen** (1924–2000), a former student of Van Til who became his colleague at Westminster, where he taught apologetics until 1995. According to Knudsen, Van Til's apologetic is best understood as transcendental, that is, as one that presents Christianity as the only position that can give an adequate account of the possibility of truth, reason, value, and our existence. For Knudsen, Van Til's apologetic was essentially Kuyperian, and Van Til should be regarded as a member of the school of the Calvinistic philosophy, along with Dooyeweerd and other Reformed thinkers.

The second interpretation of Van Til's thought originated from **John M. Frame**, a student of Van Til who became a professor of apologetics at Westminster's sister campus in California. Frame developed an epistemological theory he called *perspectivalism* that sought to integrate rational, empirical, and existential (or personal) aspects of human knowledge. In his 1987 book *The Doctrine of the Knowledge of God*, Frame presented perspectivalism as a systematic refinement of Van Til's position, giving more positive appreciation to logic and factual evidence while remaining true to Van Til's vision of a thoroughly Reformed, presuppositional apologetic. Frame has also applied his perspectivalism to ethics, while his colleague **Vern S. Poythress**, a professor of New Testament at Westminster in Philadelphia, has applied perspectivalism to systematic theology and hermeneutics.

In the 1970s Van Til's most notable critic was **John Warwick Montgomery**, a Lutheran apologist who contributed a satirical essay to *Jerusalem and Athens* entitled "Once upon an A Priori" that characterized Van Til's position as abandoning all reasoned argument for the Christian faith. Montgomery, inspired especially by the nineteenth-century legal scholar and apologist Simon Greenleaf, contended for an "evidentialist," empirically based apologetic that focused on the historical argument for the resurrection of Jesus based on principles of legal evidence. Evidentialists in Montgomery's school of thought also generally accord more weight to scientific evidences for creation than to philosophical arguments for God's existence. Numerous apologists today focus their efforts in an "evidential" direction, though without necessarily subscribing to a thoroughgoing evidentialist theory of apologetics. Such evidential apologists would include **J. P. Moreland**, who has made significant contributions to developing a Christian philosophy of science as well as defending the historical reliability of the Gospels. Another evangelical who favored an evidence-based apologetic and critiqued Van Til in *Jerusalem and Athens* was **Clark Pinnock**. In the 1980s and 1990s Pinnock, like Bernard Ramm, moved away from the conservative stance he had taken earlier, dissenting from biblical inerrancy and questioning other aspects of evangelical theology.

Also critical of Van Til was **Norman Geisler**, an evangelical scholar who argued for a classical apologetic based mainly on the thought of Thomas Aquinas. Although several Roman Catholic theologians, such as Étienne Gilson and Jacques Maritain, have defended a Thomistic approach to apologetics and theology, Geisler has been one of the few contemporary evangelical Protestants to advocate such an approach. His approach involves three main stages of argument. First, he examines various limited theories of knowledge that attempt to base all knowledge solely in reason, or in empirical fact, or in experience and shows them to be inadequate. In place of such epistemologies, he defends the twin principles of unaffirmability (anything that cannot consistently be affirmed is false) and undeniability (anything that cannot be consistently denied is true) as providing a reliable and adequate test for truth. Second, Geisler examines all the major worldviews (including atheism, pantheism, etc.) and attempts to show that only theism (the monotheistic worldview common to traditional forms of Judaism, Islam, and Christianity) passes the test of truth. A key aspect of this second stage is a reconstructed version of the Thomistic cosmological argument. Third, Geisler argues on probabilistic grounds that Christianity is the true form of theism. Here his argument focuses on the resurrection of Jesus Christ and the historical reliability of the biblical writings. His works have contributed greatly to evangelical apologetics and have been influential and appreciated even among those who do not accept his Thomistic method.

Another apologist who published apologetic works in the late 1960s and early 1970s was **Francis Schaeffer** (1912–1984). Like Van Til, Schaeffer emphasized the need to challenge non-Christian presuppositions, especially the relativism that became so prevalent in Western culture during the tumultuous 1960s. Also like Van Til, Schaeffer criticized apologetic arguments that were based on probabilities rather than certainties. Schaeffer, however, invited non-Christians to test the claims of Christianity to see if it is consistent and livable, making his apologetic in some respects more akin to Carnell's than to Van Til's.

During the same period Reformed philosopher **Alvin Plantinga** published his *God and Other Minds*. In this and other books Plantinga led the way in developing a school of thought known as the "new Reformed epistemology," which was not influenced positively or negatively by Van Til. Plantinga argued that belief in God is rationally justified even if the believer cannot offer any evidence for that belief, just as we are rational to believe other things (notably in the existence of other minds) even if we cannot prove they exist. The focus of the new Reformed epistemology is on justifying belief rather than challenging unbelief. Yet its approach has some affinities with presuppositionalism, perhaps most notably its rejection of evidentialism (the claim that beliefs are rational only as they are justified by appeals to evidence). The school came into prominence in 1983 with the publication of *Faith and Rationality*, co-edited by Plantinga and Wolterstorff. The new Reformed epistemology and presuppositionalism are the two major varieties of Reformed apologetics today.

During the last two decades of the twentieth century, a number of apologists attempted to integrate the subjective, existential perspective propounded by Kierkegaard into an essentially traditional apologetic; notable among these is the Christian philosopher **C. Stephen Evans**. Still other apologists argued explicitly for the usefulness of a variety of apologetic methods in encounters with persons of differing beliefs and temperaments. A recent example of the latter is **David K. Clark**, whose book *Dialogical Apologetics* defended a "person-centered approach" to apologetics as distinguished from what he views as competing "content-oriented" approaches.

While debate over diverse apologetic methods continues in the twenty-first century, an increasing number of thinkers are claiming that the age of apologetics is over. These thinkers argue that apologetics assumes the ideal of rational knowledge that is the basis of modern rationalistic objections to Christianity. With the supposed death of modern rationalism and the advent of postmodernism, both anti-Christian rationalism and Christian rationalistic apologetics are said to be outmoded. Other Christian thinkers, on the other hand, argue that the contemporary situation is more complex. Postmodernism, they suggest, has not so much abandoned the rationalist ideal as it has qualified it. A place remains for apologetics, they conclude, though it must take into account the recent developments of postmodern thought.

The growing diversity of approaches to the study and practice of apologetics has made it necessary to devise some way of classifying these approaches and sorting out the various issues over which they differ. In the next chapter we will present an overview of these issues and offer an analysis of the major apologetic approaches.

For Further Study

Brown, Colin. *Christianity and Western Thought: A History of Philosophers, Ideas, and Movements. Vol. 1, From the Ancient World to the Age of Enlightenment.* Downers Grove, Ill.: InterVarsity, 1990. Tends toward a fideist view of apologetics and Christian philosophy.

Bush, L. Russ, ed. *Classical Readings in Christian Apologetics, A.D. 100-1800.* Grand Rapids: Zondervan, Academie, 1983. See also the concluding chapter reviewing the history of apologetics since 1800. (Russ uses the term *classical* in its more customary sense, not in the technical sense used in this book.)

Craig, William Lane. *The Historical Argument for the Resurrection of Jesus During the Deist Controversy.* Texts and Studies in Religion 23. Lewiston, N.Y.: Edwin Mellen Press, 1985. Closest thing to an evidentialist review of the history of apologetics. In a lengthy first chapter, Craig covers the New Testament, the church fathers, and Thomas Aquinas (1-70).

Demarest, Bruce A. *General Revelation: Historical Views and Contemporary Issues.* Grand Rapids: Zondervan, 1982. Textbook survey written from a classical apologetics perspective.

Frame, John M. *Cornelius Van Til: An Analysis of His Thought.* Phillipsburg, N.J.: Presbyterian & Reformed, 1995. See especially Part IV, where Frame, a presuppositionalist, presents a more positive assessment of the thought of classical and evidentialist apologists than the assessment of his teacher Van Til (see below).

Mayers, Ronald B. *Balanced Apologetics: Using Evidences and Presuppositions in Defense of the Faith.* Grand Rapids: Kregel, 1996. Includes an in-depth study of the history of apologetics that seeks to balance the classical and evidentialist approaches with Reformed apologetics (87-195).

Miller, Ed. L., ed. *Believing in God: Readings on Faith and Reason.* Upper Saddle River, N.J.: Prentice Hall, 1996. Excellent collection of readings from Tertullian, Augustine, Anselm, Aquinas, Calvin, Pascal, Paley, Kierkegaard, Swinburne, Plantinga, and many others.

Van Til, Cornelius. *A Christian Theory of Knowledge.* Phillipsburg, N.J.: Presbyterian & Reformed, 1969. The standard presuppositionalist survey of the history of Christian philosophy and apologetics, giving special attention to the church fathers, Roman Catholic thought, the differences between Kuyper and Warfield, and Buswell's apologetic.

Chapter 3

Issues and Methods in Apologetics

The preceding survey of the history of apologetics illustrates the wide variety of approaches that have been developed to defend the Christian faith since the first century. Christian apologists have faced different challenges from different quarters and at different times, and they have sought to defend their faith in a variety of ways. This has led to considerable disagreement over such metapologetical issues as the following:

- the theory of knowledge one assumes in presenting Christianity as truth
- the value of theistic proofs
- the degree of certainty that Christianity provides
- the relationship between faith and reason and between philosophy and Christianity
- the role of evidences in apologetics
- the existence and nature of common ground between Christians and non-Christians

Coming to terms with these issues and approaches is the purpose of this book.

FOUR TYPES OF APOLOGETIC SYSTEMS

Until the twentieth century, only a few writers grappled seriously with the issue of apologetic method. As Avery Dulles noted, this is no longer the case: "The 20th century has seen more clearly than previous periods that apologetics stands or falls with the question of method. In the past few decades apologetical science has merged to an increasing degree with the epistemology of religious knowledge."[1] The reason for this close relationship between apologetic science and religious epistemology is that modern thought since Kant has been in epistemological crisis. How do we know what we think we know? This question has been viewed as especially troublesome for religious knowledge claims, and Christian apologetics has necessarily been forced to deal with it.

Because of the importance of epistemology for modern doubts and denials of the Christian revelation, the most fundamental assumptions that distinguish the apologetic systems that have developed in modern Christian thought are epistemological. Edwin A. Burtt, in his *Types of Religious Philosophy,* cataloged four principal methods of pursuing theological questions: the rationalistic, the empirical, the authoritarian, and the intuitive.[2] Applying Burtt's typology of religious philosophy to apologetics in particular, we may distinguish four basic approaches to apologetics, which we have called classical apologetics (corresponding to what Burtt calls the rationalistic method), evidentialism (empirical), Reformed apologetics (authoritarian), and fideism (intuitive).[3] Each of these four approaches to apologetics, though it had precursors in earlier periods of church history, emerged as a distinct approach to apologetics grounded in an explicit epistemology in the late nineteenth and the twentieth centuries. We will briefly describe each of these here.

Classical apologetics, as we are using the term in this book, refers to an apologetic approach that emphasizes the use of logical criteria (for example, the law of noncontradiction, self-consistency, comprehensiveness, coherence) in determining the validity of competing religious philosophies. These criteria are used to refute the truth claims of non-Christian worldviews and to establish the existence of God through theistic proofs. The approach in its modern form is characterized by a "two-step" method of apologetics in which one first makes a case for theism (the worldview that affirms the existence of one Creator God) and then presents evidence that this God has revealed himself in Christ and in the Bible. The most famous Christian thinker commonly regarded as paving the way for this approach was the thirteenth-century theologian Thomas Aquinas. In modern evangelical apologetics it is perhaps best represented by Norman L. Geisler. We discuss this approach in Part Two, "Classical Apologetics: It Stands to Reason."

Evidentialism seeks to ground the Christian faith primarily on empirically and historically verifiable facts. Evidentialists often draw a parallel between the scientific method of testing theories and theological verification. They argue that a high degree of probability can be established in favor of Christianity, and that this is the same kind of credibility as that associated with confirmed scientific laws. The evidence does not necessarily constitute proof, but it is sufficient to answer objections and to show that belief in Christianity is not unreasonable. Rather than a two-step method of first defending theism and then defending Christianity, as in the classical approach, evidentialists consider the evidence for creation, for the inspiration of the Bible, and for the divine identity of Christ (especially based on his resurrection from the dead) as part of an overall case for the reality of the Christian God. Joseph Butler is commonly regarded as the pioneer of this apologetic type, and in recent decades it has been especially associated with the Lutheran scholar John Warwick Montgomery. We discuss this approach in Part Three, "Evidentialist Apologetics: Just the Facts."

The term *classical apologetics* is sometimes used to refer to evidentialism as well as the more rationally-oriented form discussed above. We have chosen to use the term in its narrower sense for two reasons. First, evidentialism is a distinctly modern development that in some respects represents a repudiation of key aspects of the traditional, classical approach to apologetics. Second, what we are terming classical apologetics, though it emphasizes rationality in general and deductive reasoning in particular, should not be confused with the modern philosophical tradition known as *rationalism*, which regards the rational mind as the sole source of knowledge. The more "rational" approach to apologetics typically rejects rationalism in this sense. Other recent publications have also distinguished classical apologetics from evidentialism.[4]

Reformed apologetics argues that we ought to ground reason and fact on the truth of the Christian faith, rather than trying to prove or defend the faith on the basis of reason or fact.[5] Empirical and rational approaches to religious truth are doomed to failure by the moral impairment (though not the technical efficiency) of the human mind fallen in sin; worse, they assume the self-sufficiency of human beings to employ reason and interpret the facts independent of divine revelation. Therefore, apologetic systems based on such epistemologies are both inadequate and inappropriate to defend the faith. The only means of argumentation between the two groups must be indirect, that is, on the level of fundamental assumptions or presuppositions. Most Reformed apologists seek to show that while non-Christian belief systems cannot account for the validity of reason, fact, and truth, Christian theism can. This approach was inspired by the theology of John Calvin; its most influential modern advocate was Cornelius Van Til. We discuss this approach in Part Four, "Reformed Apologetics: God Said It."

Fideism may be (and has been) defined in a variety of ways. The term derives from the Latin *fide*, meaning "faith." It has commonly been used as a pejorative term for the position that one should "just believe" in God or Christ apart from any reasoning or evidence. (Some critics have alleged that Reformed apologetics is fideistic in this sense; as we shall see, this characterization is mistaken.) More broadly, fideism maintains that human knowledge of truth (including, and especially, religious truth) is at bottom a personal matter of the heart or the will rather than of the intellect. Personal, existential experience with God cannot be grounded in rational analysis or scientific and historical evidences, since it is a matter of the heart. Fideists often stress the paradoxical and personal-encounter dimension of Christian truth. They emphasize the transcendence and hiddenness of God and repudiate natural theology and theistic proofs. Fideism argues from humanity's basic existential needs to the fulfillment of those needs in Christianity. While in many respects fideism has tended to reject apologetics as an intellectual discipline, some Christian apologists have seen value in its emphasis on the personal, subjective dimension in faith and religious commitment. On the Roman Catholic side, Blaise Pascal is often regarded as having anticipated this approach. The Protestant fideist tradition, though, is based in Lutheran pietism and is rooted in significant ways in the thought of Martin Luther himself. (It should be emphasized that neither Pascal nor Luther can properly be described as fideists. Rather, certain elements of their thought anticipated or prepared the way for the eventual emergence of fideism.) The Christian thinker who represents fideism in its purest form is the nineteenth-century Danish philosopher Søren Kierkegaard. We discuss the fideist perspective in Part Five, "Apologetics as Persuasion."

Four Approaches to Apologetics			
Classical	Evidentialist	Reformed	Fideist
rational	empirical	authoritarian	intuitive
Thomas Aquinas	Joseph Butler	John Calvin	Martin Luther
Norman Geisler	John W. Montgomery	Cornelius Van Til	Søren Kierkegaard
"Tom"	"Joe"	"Cal"	"Martina"

How would astute advocates of these four approaches respond to the apologetic challenges posed by Sarah and Murali, our two hypothetical non-Christians? Recall that Sarah is a skeptic who has departed from the Christian faith because of its moral demands and who is troubled by the problem of evil, while Murali is a nominal Hindu living in America who believes all religions are basically the same. (See the preface for more detailed profiles of these two characters.) Our four astute apologists, each representing one the four approaches, we have named Tom, Joe, Cal, and Martina (see above chart for their respective approaches). Although we present specifics on how these approaches would be applied in conversations between these imaginary apologists and non-Christians in the remainder of this book, we offer a glimpse here.

Tom's approach to both Sarah and Murali would follow a two-step method common in classical apologetics. First, he would expose the logical incoherence of their positions. He might explain to Sarah that the concept of evil on which she bases her rejection of God's existence logically implies an absolute moral standard, which can only come from a transcendent Creator. Tom would probably tell Murali that it is logically impossible for religions that affirm such different worldviews as pantheism (Hinduism) and monotheism (Judaism, Islam, and Christianity) all to be true. Second, Tom would offer carefully constructed answers to the non-Christians' objections, proving that those objections have failed to prove any logical incoherence in the Christian position. He would likely respond to Sarah's problem of evil by explaining that God has a higher purpose for allowing evil and will eventually overcome evil with good. He would probably also insist that while God has allowed evil, he is not its cause; human beings have caused evil by the exercise of their free will. In response to Murali's argument that God must approve of different religions if he allowed so many to flourish, Tom would likewise attribute the different religions to the freedom of human beings to go their own way. He would then propose examining the worldview of each religion to determine which of them, if any, offered a coherent view of the world.

Joe's basic approach as an evidentialist would be to present facts that he believes support the Christian position and undermine the non-Christians' objections. He would probably point out to Sarah the abundant evidence for a good and powerful Creator and argue that this outweighs the evidence of evil against belief in God. The facts Joe adduces might be wide-ranging, but are likely to include scientific evidence for the universe's beginning and intelligent design as well as historical evidence for the miraculous acts of God in the Bible. Joe would present the same facts to Murali as evidence against nontheistic religions and in support of the claim that the God of the Bible is actually the real God.

Cal's Reformed approach would preclude making direct appeals to deductive reasoning or empirical facts in the manner of Tom or Joe. In Cal's estimation, Sarah and Murali are committed to a spiritually jaundiced way of using reason and looking at facts. He would therefore take what he calls an indirect approach, which, like Tom's, involves two basic steps. First, Cal would argue that both Sarah and Murali presuppose their own self-sufficiency or "autonomy" to judge for themselves what is true and right. Sarah's judgment that God must not be good if he allows evil presupposes that she is able to determine for herself, from within herself, the standard of goodness to which even God must conform. Murali's complaint that God should not have allowed so many different religions if he wanted us to believe in only one also presupposes his competency to judge what God should or should not do. Cal would then remind them of what they already know in their hearts: that they are not God and that their arrogant pretensions to autonomy are symptomatic of their fallenness with all mankind in sin. Second, Cal will argue that only on the presupposition that the God of Scripture is real can we even give a coherent account of the concepts of goodness and justice to which Sarah and Murali appeal in their arguments against Christianity. Sarah's argument from the problem of evil presupposes that there is a standard of goodness against which evil is judged; yet, in denying the existence of God she is left without any rational basis for judging anything to be evil. Murali's claim that God must accept many different religions since he has allowed them to flourish presupposes that God is just or fair, but this idea cannot be justified except on the basis that God is the personal Creator and Judge spoken of in Scripture.

Our fourth apologist, Martina, would take a very different approach from those of the other three. In her view the direct arguments of Tom and Joe and the indirect argument of Cal are all problematic because they treat God as an object of rational argument rather than as a Person with whom Sarah and Murali need to have a relationship. Martina would focus on relating to them as individuals rather than refuting their arguments. She would get to know them and try to help them see the personal issues underlying their questions and objections. For example, she might try to lead Sarah to realize that she was already questioning God before her philosophy professor gave her intellectual ammunition against Christianity. Was it God that seemed uncaring, or some Christians she knew? Martina would likely emphasize that God's compassion and love are far greater than any sentimentalism human beings may express. God really wants our good, even when that good can be achieved only through suffering. Martina might ask Murali why, if he thinks all religions are good ways to the same goal, he doesn't seem to be following any of them seriously. The one thing that nearly every religion insists is necessary is a deep personal commitment, and Murali doesn't have that. Martina might challenge him to examine the different religions with the question, to which one can he commit himself wholly? For herself, Martina would likely say, she refuses to make an absolute commitment to any philosophy or religion. God—not just the idea of God, but the personal God who speaks and acts and loves us in Jesus—is alone worthy of our absolute commitment and trust.

ISSUES IN APOLOGETICS

These four approaches to apologetics differ in many ways. In this book we will focus on a dozen critical issues that represent in a systematic way the full range of issues facing the apologist.[6] These issues are divided into two groups of six issues each. The first group deals with *metapologetic* issues—foundational questions about the stance apologetics should take toward human knowledge and experience. The second group deals with *apologetic* issues—the most common questions or objections that non-Christians (or Christians dealing with doubt or confusion) raise to the Christian truth claim.

Metapologetic Questions

Apologetics is a discipline that seeks to defend the Christian view of God, the world, and human life. As such, it relates comprehensively to every area of human knowledge and thought. Apologists understand these relations differently. These differences are typified in the stance taken by apologists toward the following six questions.

1. On what basis do we argue that Christianity is the truth?

On the basis of what understanding of knowledge and truth should the Christian apologist seek to lead non-Christians to the knowledge of Christianity as the truth? As we have seen, this question is at the core of what distinguishes the four approaches discussed in this book. The classical apologist sees reason as the ground of apologetic argument. The evidentialist seeks to build a case for Christianity from the facts. The Reformed apologist contends that God's revelation of himself in Jesus Christ and in Scripture is the proper ground for all thinking about reason, fact, and human experience. The fideist presents experience of God in Jesus Christ as self-justifying apart from argument. These varying approaches are based on different epistemologies, or theories of knowledge. (**Epistemology** is concerned with the nature and ground of knowledge—what knowledge is, and how we know what we know—and especially with the justification of knowledge claims.) Thus the classical apologist adheres to a broadly rationalist epistemology, the evidentialist to an empirical or fact-based epistemology, the Reformed apologist to an authoritarian epistemology (with Christ and Scripture the supreme authorities), and the fideist to a subjectivist, experience-based epistemology. Tied up with these epistemologies are varying beliefs about the kind of certainty that can be afforded through apologetic argumentation, the existence and identity of "common ground" or relevant shared truth between Christians and non-Christians, and the relation between faith and reason.

This metapologetic question also relates directly to an apologetic question. Non-Christians object to the absolute truth-claim made by Christians on behalf of the gospel. Most people in our society today do not believe in absolute truth and consider any absolute religious claims particularly onerous. The rise of postmodernism represents the newest wave of assaults on the belief in absolute truth. The responses to this question from the four apologetic approaches will naturally parallel their answers to the question in its metapologetic form. Thus the classical apologist will argue that denials of absolute truth are irrational. The evidentialist will typically argue that while absolute rational *certainty* for the claims of Christ is unavailable, those claims can be supported by the facts, perhaps beyond reasonable doubt. The Reformed apologist will commonly contend that all people at bottom do believe in absolute truth and even presuppose that belief at every turn. The fideist will generally respond that absolute truth is not a matter of propositional knowledge or factual information anyway, but is a Person who is known in relationship, not in mere words. Fideists are more likely than advocates of other apologetic approaches to find value or points of contact in postmodernism, since that movement eschews the modernist assumption of scientific and rational objectivity and views belief systems primarily as functions of the individual and the community.

2. What is the relationship between apologetics and theology?

This relationship is a primary issue in metapologetics, though its importance is often overlooked. This question is important in two ways.

First, there is significant debate concerning the theological foundation of apologetics. To some extent apologetical methods are related to the way one understands and interprets Christian theology. The close relationship between theology and apologetics is especially evident in Reformed apologetics, because it originated from and is almost completely tied into the Reformed tradition in systematic theology. On the other hand, some Reformed theologians engage in rational and evidential apologetics, although those we are calling Reformed apologists regard these thinkers as inconsistent Calvinists who have slipped into a Thomistic or Arminian apologetic methodology. Thus one cannot avoid theology when considering how to do apologetics. Apologists disagree, for example, about whether God's revelation in nature can be sufficiently understood by non-Christians to arrive at belief in God. This disagreement is closely tied to a debate over the effects of sin on human reasoning.

Second, apologists hold different views about the relationship of apologetics as a discipline to the discipline of theology (particularly systematic theology). Some apologists view apologetics as a branch of theology (whether major or minor), while others regard it as a preparation for theology. The debate is significant because it affects our understanding of the rules or methods followed in apologetics as well as the purpose and scope of apologetics.

3. Should apologetics engage in a philosophical defense of the Christian faith?

Apologetics is often viewed and practiced almost as if it were synonymous with philosophy of religion—as a discipline that seeks to apply the tools of philosophy to defining and proving key beliefs of Christianity. On the other hand, some apologists show great disdain for philosophy, regarding it as the enemy of Christian faith. Historically, some apologists have sought to defend Christianity in terms drawn from the non-Christian philosophies of such thinkers as Plato or Aristotle or Kant. Meanwhile other apologists have regarded such efforts as inevitably compromising the Christian message that is supposedly being defended. This issue must be considered in developing an approach to apologetics.

4. Can science be used to defend the Christian faith?

For many non-Christians today, science poses the most formidable intellectual objections to Christian faith. Yet Christian apologists differ markedly in their view of the proper stance to be taken toward science. Some embrace the findings of science enthusiastically, claiming to find in them direct confirmation of the Christian faith. Others take the opposite position, viewing science in general with suspicion and regarding certain prevailing theories of science as inimical to the Christian faith. Still other apologists view science as irrelevant, since to them the Christian faith deals with issues that transcend the physical world that is the field of scientific inquiry.

5. Can the Christian faith be supported by historical inquiry?

The diversity of views on science among apologists is paralleled by a similar diversity concerning history. Some apologists stake the truth of the Christian message on its historical verifiability. Others, while agreeing that the faith is based on historical events, place little emphasis on historical inquiry or warn against believing that the central events of redemption can be verified "objectively" according to the canons of historical study. Still others regard the faith as in principle not subject to historical inquiry because it deals with the eternal, not the temporal.

6. How is our knowledge of Christian truth related to our experience?

All human beings process new information and ideas by relating them in some fashion to their own experiences in life. This fact necessitates giving some consideration to how apologetics should relate to experience. Some apologists seek to analyze human experience in terms of universal truths in which the Christian message can be grounded. Others eschew argumentation about experience and instead call on non-Christians to experience God's love in Christ. Still others view all experience as untrustworthy and argue that it needs to be tested and interpreted in light of the authoritative teaching of Scripture. Some answer to the question of experience must be given, or at least assumed, by every apologist.

How each of the four apologetic approaches answers these six metapologetic questions, and how these answers may be integrated, will be considered in the second chapter of each of the remaining parts of this book (chapters 5, 9, 13, 17, and 21).

Apologetic Questions

In the preface we introduced six common questions or objections to the Christian faith that are commonly brought up by non-Christians. We will comment briefly on each.

1. Why should we believe in the Bible?

All Christian apologists have as part of their "job description" the task of persuading people to accept the Bible as God's word—as inspired Scripture. Apologists take different approaches to accomplishing this task. Some see the question of the Bible as the conclusion or end point of their apologetic. Typically they seek to demonstrate logically the truth of the biblical worldview, then to defend the truth of the central biblical claims on behalf of Jesus Christ, and only then to present the Bible as God's word. Other apologists defend the truth and inspiration of the Bible inductively, by treating the Bible as a source and defending the authenticity and accuracy of that source in every major aspect. In contrast to these approaches, some apologists insist that the divine authority of the Bible must be presented as the only viable foundation for all knowledge; for them the inspiration of Scripture is the beginning, not the end, of the argument. Still other apologists focus not on ·

defending the doctrine of biblical inspiration but on leading non-Christians to encounter Jesus Christ personally through the reading of Scripture.

2. Don't all religions lead to God?

On the assumption that (absolute) truth claims in religion are unjustifiable, many people today argue that all religions are adequate to meet the needs that Christianity does. Apologists employing different methods tend to respond to this belief in different ways. Some try to show that all non-Christian religions are illogical. Others present evidence to support Christianity's unique status among the religions of the world. Still others cut through the objection by responding that Christianity isn't a religion at all.

3. How do we know that God exists?

All Christian apologists, of course, are concerned to bring non-Christians to the knowledge of God. However, they differ markedly in what sorts of arguments they regard as viable means of convincing non-Christians that God even exists. Some apologists employ arguments designed to prove conclusively that God exists, while others use arguments claiming only to show that it is not unreasonable to believe that God exists. Still others are critical of traditional arguments for God's existence, preferring either an indirect argument or no argument at all. Some apologists, in fact, assert that arguments for God's existence can actually interfere with or impede genuine faith.

4. If God does exist, why does he permit evil?

Ask ten non-Christians at random to give two objections to the Christian faith, and very likely nine of them will mention what is known as the problem of evil: How is it that there is evil in the world created by an all-powerful and all-loving God? Christian apologists respond to this challenge with different argumentative strategies. Some argue for the coherence of the Christian worldview as inclusive of evil and suffering. Others contend that the question is impudent and cannot be rationally answered. As this is probably the number one objection to the Christian faith, apologists must wrestle seriously with this question.

5. Aren't the miracles of the Bible spiritual myths or legends and not literal fact?

Modern criticism of the Bible has resulted in the widespread belief that the books of the Bible were in general not written when or by whom they have traditionally been understood to have been written. Worse, it is commonly believed that the narratives of the Bible are not historical accounts but later myths or legends that have only tenuous roots in fact. In particular, many people today view the biblical accounts of such foundational miraculous events as the crossing of the Red Sea in the Exodus or the resurrection of Jesus from the dead as symbolic myths teaching perennial spiritual truths rather than as miraculous historical events. Christian apologists approach the biblical miracles in different ways. Some seek to make them credible by first proving the existence of God. Others appeal directly to the historical evidence to show that these events occurred, and actually cite the biblical miracles as evidence of God's existence. Others, though, view miracles as God's activity in the world in response to faith and criticize traditional apologetic arguments as seeking to base faith on miracles. Once again, apologists who agree that the biblical miracles occurred have markedly different approaches to defending belief in those miracles.

6. Why should I believe what Christians claim about Jesus?

Most non-Christians are willing to grant that belief in Jesus can be helpful or meaningful to Christians, but balk at the claim that belief in Jesus is necessary for all people because what Christians believe about Jesus is *the* truth. In addition, many non-Christians today believe that biblical scholarship has called into question the traditional Christian view of Jesus as the supernatural, risen Savior and Lord. Apologists employ a variety of arguments designed to lead non-Christians to see and accept the truth claims of Jesus. Some reason that Jesus must be what the Bible says he is because no other explanation makes sense. Others present factual evidence for the life, the death, and especially the resurrection of Jesus, maintaining that it is sufficient to refute modern antibiblical theories about Jesus and to establish the Christian truth claims about him. Still other apologists argue, in effect, that Jesus himself is his own best argument: that non-Christians need simply to be confronted with the person of Jesus in the Gospels. They recognize that biblical scholarship does not deliver to us the traditional, biblical Christ, but contend that it could not and indeed should not do so: the Christ of faith transcends the "Jesus of history" and must be found by faith, not by historical inquiry. Thus, on so basic a question as why non-Christians should believe in Jesus, Christian apologists have offered some strikingly different answers.

How each of the four apologetic approaches answers the six apologetic questions raised here, and how these answers may be integrated, will be considered in the third chapter of each of the remaining parts of this book (chapters 6, 10, 14, 18, and 22).

For Further Reading

Cowan, Steven B., ed. *Five Views on Apologetics*. Counterpoint series. Grand Rapids: Zondervan, 2000. This book contains contributions by William Lane Craig ("The Classical Model"), Gary R. Habermas ("The Evidential Model"), John M. Frame ("The Presuppositional Model"), Kelly James Clark ("The Reformed Epistemology Model"), and Paul D. Feinberg ("The Cumulative Case Model"). The models of Habermas and Feinberg are variations of what we are calling evidentialism, while the models of Frame and Clark are variations of what we are calling Reformed apologetics.

Geisler, Norman L. *Christian Apologetics*. Grand Rapids: Baker, 1976. See Part One, "Methodology" (13-147), for a classical apologist's survey of different theories of knowledge as they relate to apologetic method.

Lewis, Gordon R. *Testing Christianity's Truth Claims: Approaches to Christian Apologetics*. Chicago: Moody, 1976. Includes chapters on an evidentialist (Buswell), a classical apologist (Hackett), two Reformed apologists (Gordon Clark, Van Til), and a fideist (Barrett), followed by four chapters developing and defending Carnell's approach.

Ramm, Bernard. *Varieties of Christian Apologetics: An Introduction to the Christian Philosophy of Religion*. Grand Rapids: Baker, 1962. Profiles the life and thought of three thinkers each for three types of systems, stressing subjective immediacy (Pascal, Kierkegaard, Brunner), natural theology (Aquinas, Butler, Tennant), and revelation (Augustine, Calvin, Kuyper). (Ramm's second type includes what we are calling both classical and evidentialist apologetics.) The first edition, entitled *Types of Apologetic Systems* (Wheaton, Ill.: Van Kampen Press, 1953), included chapters on Van Til and Carnell instead of Calvin and Kuyper.

See Appendix for more detailed discussion of the books by Cowan, Lewis, and Ramm.

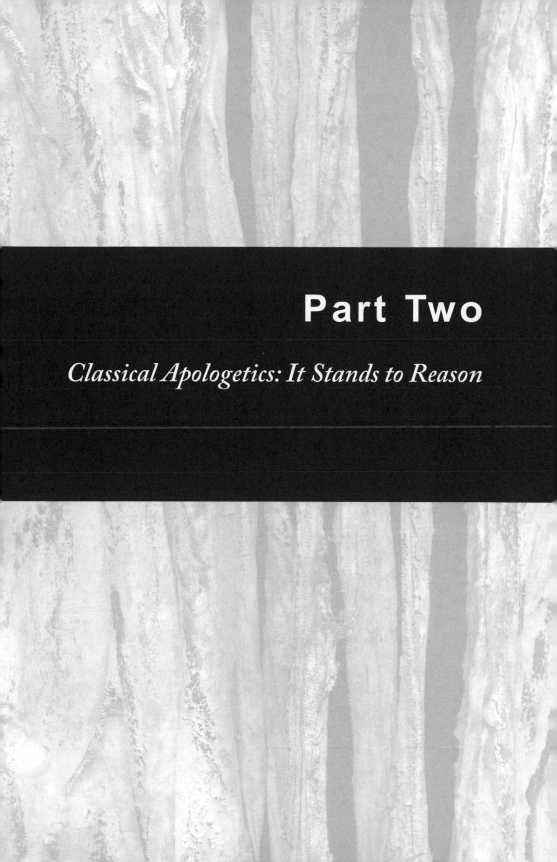

Part Two

Classical Apologetics: It Stands to Reason

Chapter 4

Apologists Who Emphasize Reason

The classical apologetical tradition, as the term *classical* suggests, is the dominant approach to apologetics in church history, especially prior to the modern period. It emphasizes the presentation of Christianity as *rational*—as logically coherent and supportable by sound arguments—and offers what its advocates consider *proofs* of various types (though especially philosophical proofs) for the existence of God as a first step in defending the truth claims of the Christian faith. As we are using the term in this book, "classical apologetics" also refers to an idealized type that is more or less fully exemplified in apologists in that tradition. Of necessity, then, we will be offering generalizations; that is, what we say about apologetics of this idealized type or approach is generally applicable to apologists in the classical tradition, but one must allow for considerable variations and exceptions. One other qualification needs to be made: as a distinct approach and explicit methodological stance, classical apologetics, like the other three basic approaches discussed in this book, is actually a modern development.

In this chapter we will examine the roots of classical apologetics and consider briefly the thought of five modern classical apologists, among whom is Norman L. Geisler, who represents perhaps the "purest" form of this approach.

HISTORICAL ROOTS OF CLASSICAL APOLOGETICS

Classical apologetics, more than the other three systems discussed in this book, draws on the apologetic thought of Christian theologians and philosophers throughout church history. Indeed, most advocates of the classical approach count it an important point in their favor that their approach is in line with the major apologists from the early and medieval church. The authors of the book *Classical*

Apologetics, for example, assert with regard to "the classic Christian view" that "theistic proofs" are a valid part of apologetics. "From the Apologists to the dawn of our own era, this has been the central teaching of the church, Eastern, Roman, Protestant, the teaching of the creeds and of the theologians."[1] Although this claim is arguably overstated, there is a significant tradition of Christian apologetics throughout church history in which theistic proofs played a major role. Since we have already given a fairly detailed survey of the history of apologetics in chapter 2, we will review that history only very briefly here.

The classical apologists lay great emphasis on the *examples* of apologetic argument found in the New Testament (especially Paul's apologetic speech in Athens in Acts 17). Elements of the classical method were developed by the Apologists of the second century, most notably **Justin Martyr**. Certain aspects of the apologetic thought of Augustine continued this classical tradition. He made use of philosophical proofs for God's existence, especially but not exclusively in his earlier writings. To prove that this God had revealed himself in Christ, Augustine cited miracles and fulfilled biblical prophecy and emphasized the dramatic growth and triumph of the church through centuries of persecution and suppression.

It is in the medieval period, though, that the classical approach began to receive systematic formulation. **Anselm** offered his ontological argument for the existence of God both to edify believers and to challenge and persuade unbelievers. He also presented an argument for the necessity of God becoming man in order to redeem us that proved the point, he claimed, without assuming any knowledge about Christ. Anselm was careful to add that in the end faith was to be placed in God and in his revelation in Scripture, not in Anselm's arguments. Still, his approach was quite rationally oriented.

Likewise, **Thomas Aquinas** developed a number of philosophical arguments for the existence of God and expounded Christian teaching on the nature of God in Aristotelian philosophical categories. Thomas rejected Anselm's ontological argument, preferring various forms of the cosmological argument, but both types of argument are philosophical arguments for theism. Again, Thomas was very careful to say that such philosophical proofs were not the basis of faith or a substitute for faith. According to Thomas, those who rely on philosophical argument alone will never have an adequate knowledge of God. Yet his theistic proofs have often been utilized as a line of defense against atheism, which was not even a serious problem in his day. Thomas's approach to philosophy (known as **Thomism**) has inspired many succeeding works of classical apologetics.

While many of the Reformers in the first generation of the Protestant Reformation rejected or denigrated classical apologetic arguments, not all of them did. Philip Melanchthon, in particular, was in his later years more appreciative of classical apologetics than Martin Luther had been, and presented arguments in the Thomistic fashion in the later editions of his *Loci communes*. Likewise, many Calvinist theologians in the seventeenth century found greater value in philosophical proofs of a classical type than had John Calvin himself. When deism and other forms of skepticism arose in the seventeenth century, Protestants typically answered with arguments rooted in the classical apologetics of Anselm and Aquinas. **Natural theology**, the construction of arguments defending or proving a theistic worldview on the basis of rational considerations apart from divine revelation, became a regular part of Christian apologetics.

In the nineteenth century the classical theistic proofs were endorsed and utilized by a wide variety of Christian theologians and apologists, including **Charles Hodge**, whose three-volume *Systematic Theology* was probably the most influential work of its kind published in nineteenth-century America. In the twentieth century Roman Catholic philosophers, most notably Étienne Gilson and Jacques Maritain, rekindled an interest in Thomistic philosophy, which is probably more popular and influential now than ever before among both Catholic and Protestant apologists.

In the rest of this chapter we will examine in some detail the apologetic contributions of four modern apologists in the classical tradition. Although they have their differences, they all endorse an approach that seeks to offer a rational method of proof (however variously the proofs may be derived) for the Christian position.

B. B. WARFIELD

Benjamin Breckinridge Warfield (1851–1921) was a professor of theology at Princeton Theological Seminary from 1871 until the end of his life.[2] During that half-century he wrote an impressive array of books and articles in the fields of New Testament criticism and theology, historical theology, and systematic theology.[3] Although few of his works would be classified as apologetics per se—in fact, Warfield wrote no book on the subject—virtually all his writings had a strong apologetic purpose and thrust to them. He was the last and arguably the most brilliant representative of the so-called Old Princeton school of theology and apologetics. A few years after he died, Princeton Seminary was reorganized under liberal theological leadership, and the mantle of Old Princeton was taken up by Westminster Theological Seminary in nearby Philadelphia. Westminster was founded by Warfield's former student and younger colleague at Princeton, J. Gresham Machen (1881–1937).[4]

What engulfed Princeton shortly after Warfield's death was in fact the main focus of his apologetic labors throughout his ministry: the rise of liberal theology grounded on an antisupernaturalist approach to the Bible and Christianity. Arguably the primary concern of Warfield's apologetics was to uphold the supernatural character of Christianity. This meant arguing, first of all, that unless Jesus Christ was a supernatural person, specifically truly God incarnate, and unless he rose supernaturally from the grave, Christianity is simply not true. It is one thing for avowed non-Christians to reject the supernatural; it is another thing entirely for professing Christians to do so. Warfield lamented the fact that many people were rejecting Christianity while clinging to it in name. That people do this is testimony to the significance of Christianity in the world, but it is still misleading.[5]

Thus, for Warfield a great deal of apologetics was simply explaining why Christianity could not be affirmed or accepted without the supernatural. A naturalistic Christianity is a mere moralism, a philosophy of human self-improvement inspired by the idea of the divine. True Christianity is a religion of redemption, a revelation of the real God's grace reconciling us and transforming us through faith in Jesus Christ. Although Warfield unabashedly defended Calvinism as the most consistent form of Christianity, in fact the general tenor and focus of his apologetics was supportive of the most basic elements of orthodox Christianity: the truth of the Bible, the deity of Christ, and the virgin birth, sinlessness, miracles, atoning death, and resurrection of Christ.

Part of Warfield's agenda for reclaiming supernatural Christianity as the only true Christian religion was to show that this is what the Christian church had always believed and its best theologians had always taught. He also wanted to show that the premodern Christian theologians' belief in the supernatural was not an irrational or blind faith, but one grounded in evidence. In making this case he expressed appreciation for the great apologists in the classical apologetic tradition such as Augustine, Anselm, and Aquinas (though above all Augustine). He also held in high regard Joseph Butler and William Paley, apologists who paved the way for the evidentialist approach, and Blaise Pascal, whose apologetic in significant ways moved in a fideist direction.[6] Although they took apologetics in new directions, these three men were to a great extent consistent with the classical tradition, and thus Warfield could see them as contributing to the development of apologetics as he understood it. He gave considerable attention to showing that the theology of the knowledge of God taught by Augustine and Calvin was consistent with a rational apologetic for the Christian faith.[7]

According to Warfield, the science of theology takes as its primary data the facts of Scripture. But for theology to be properly grounded, we must know that the Bible is indeed inspired Scripture from God. Ultimately this means that the first principles of theology must be to establish the fact of God's existence. Warfield distinguished five subdivisions of apologetics based on five subjects. The first three are God, religion, and revelation, by which he means that apologetics "must begin by establishing the existence of God, the capacity of the human mind to know Him, and the accessibility of knowledge concerning Him."[8] From there apologetics must go on "to establish the divine origin of Christianity as the religion of revelation in the special sense of the word," and finally "to establish the trustworthiness of the Christian Scriptures as the documentation of the revelation of God for the redemption of sinners."[9]

Warfield thus advocated a two-step method of defending the Christian faith. First, one establishes the truth of God's existence and the possibility of knowing God. Second, one shows from the evidence that God is known in his revelation in Christ and in Scripture. Sometimes Warfield subdivides these two steps, as when he writes (with A. A. Hodge), "In dealing with sceptics it is not proper to begin with the evidence which immediately establishes Inspiration, but we should first establish Theism, then the historical credibility of the Scriptures, and then the divine origin of Christianity."[10] The method of first establishing theism (belief in God) before one seeks to establish the truth of Christianity is at the heart of the classical approach to apologetics.

Not everyone agrees that Warfield was a classical apologist. Most notably, Kim Riddlebarger, in his excellent dissertation on Warfield, interprets Warfield as an evidentialist.[11] He specifically distinguishes Warfield's method from that of Norman Geisler (whom we discuss below) or R. C. Sproul and John Gerstner, the lead authors of the book *Classical Apologetics*.[12] His reason for categorizing Warfield as an evidentialist is that the classical theistic proofs play little role in Warfield's apologetic, although Warfield acknowledged their validity.[13] Riddlebarger also shows that Warfield's defense of the resurrection of Christ as an historical event focused on the evidences.[14] (Still, this would be the case with a classical apologist as well as an evidentialist.) His strongest point for classifying Warfield as an evidentialist is Warfield's contention that a "non-miraculous world-view" might be overturned by the factual evidence for miracles.[15] However, Warfield is here focusing on establishing a more robust Christian theism, including miracles, over against a "world-view" such as deism. His argument here is thus compatible with understanding his basic method as the "two-step" classical approach (first show that God exists, then show that God has miraculously revealed himself). In any case, Riddlebarger's excellent analysis shows that the line between classical and evidentialist apologetics was in practice a blurry one even in Warfield's day.

For Warfield, apologetics is essentially a theological discipline. Indeed, it occupies a primary place in the theological curriculum. It has the inestimably important task of establishing the fundamental truths and principles on which Christian theology rests. In this sense it might be described as a "pretheological" discipline, but in the broader sense Warfield regarded it as the first of the theological disciplines.

It should be noted, then, that strictly speaking Warfield distinguished apologetics as a formal, theoretical discipline at the head of theology, from what he called apology. *Apology* is a branch of practical theology and deals with the pragmatic question of how Christians should explain and defend their beliefs when speaking with non-Christians.[16]

C. S. LEWIS

Clive Staples Lewis (1898–1963), known to his friends as "Jack," was almost without doubt the most popular Christian apologist internationally in the twentieth century.[17] A British scholar of medieval literature who converted to Christianity in midlife, Lewis did not develop a specific apologetic system but approached the claims of Christianity from several directions.[18]

Having converted from atheism to Christianity, he gave much attention to refuting the philosophical objections to the Christian faith that had bothered him as an atheist.[19] Thus the focus of his apologetic writings is to defend the Christian claim that a real, personal, and moral Creator exists to whom we are all accountable and who has intervened in human affairs through miracles, especially the miraculous Person of Jesus Christ. Lewis never tired of emphasizing to skeptics that he was not recommending that they believe in Christ because it would make them happier, but because it was true: "As you perhaps know, I haven't always been a Christian. I didn't go to religion to make me happy. I always knew a bottle of Port would do that."[20]

Lewis's best-known apologetic work, *Mere Christianity*, was really a combination of three books *(The Case for Christianity, Christian Behaviour,* and *Beyond Personality)*. In it he refuted atheism, naturalism, and dualism, and presented a case for the unique claims of Christ. A 1993 *Christianity Today* poll found it far and away the most influential book in readers' Christian lives, apart from the Bible.[21] In its original form as BBC radio talks during World War II, *Mere Christianity* may actually have contributed in some measure to the Allied victory by encouraging faith and hope among the British people.

Lewis's apologetic efforts, unlike those of many in the classical tradition, were not limited to rational argument but adopted a variety of genres, reflecting his literary flair. *The Pilgrim's Regress* uses allegory to treat many issues in the philosophy of religion.[22] *Surprised by Joy* is a biographical apologetic that develops the experience of intense longing for the transcendent.[23] Lewis's three-volume space trilogy *(Out of the Silent Planet, Perelandra,* and *That Hideous Strength)* and seven-volume *Chronicles of Narnia* defend the Christian worldview through imagination instead of reason.[24] Lewis explained his apologetic purpose by noting that "any amount of theology can now be smuggled into people's minds under cover of romance without their knowing it."[25] By stripping Christian truths "of their stained-glass and Sunday school associations," one could sneak past the "watchful dragons" that keep unbelievers from seriously considering those truths.[26] Lewis's humor, wit, and style have thus attracted many non-Christian readers to his books. As Burson and Walls observe, "One should not underestimate the power of style in apologetics, especially in our day. Lewis is an excellent example of how style and substance can work hand in glove to achieve maximum impact."[27] In 1988 over 40 million copies of Lewis's books were in print.[28] No wonder, then, that *Time* magazine labeled him the twentieth century's "most-read apologist for God."[29]

> For the child at heart he created the land of Narnia and the untamed lion/savior, Aslan. For science fiction readers he traveled to Perelandra with Ransom. For the philosopher and theologian he reasoned about pain and miracles, as well as debating doctrines of Christianity and the philosophy of men. For the lover of myth, he wrote an adaptation of the myth of Cupid and Psyche. For the pain stricken he observed grief and spoke of prayer. For those enchanted with rhythm and rhyme he wrote poetry. For those concerned with the afterlife he wrote about Heaven and Hell and

exposed the mind of Satan. For the weak and questioning he wrote letters of personal encouragement and advice.[30]

Lewis's approach to apologetics defies simple categorization precisely because of the diverse ways in which he sought to display and defend the truth of "mere Christianity." However, we agree with Norman Geisler and David K. Clark, both of whom classify Lewis as a classical apologist.[31] (We will refer to various elements of Lewis's apologetic in the next two chapters, where we elaborate on the classical apologetic model.) When dealing with outright atheism, Lewis generally offered philosophical arguments for belief in God in preparation for presenting the case for Christianity—though not the specific arguments that most classical apologists prefer. Moreover, toward the end of his career, Lewis found that arguments for belief in God's existence were not as helpful as he once assumed:

> It is very difficult to produce arguments on the popular level for the existence of God. And many of the most popular arguments seem to me invalid. . . .

> Fortunately, though very oddly, I have found that people are usually disposed to hear the divinity of Our Lord discussed *before* going into the existence of God. When I began I used, if I were giving two lectures, to devote the first to mere Theism; but I soon gave up this method because it seemed to arouse little interest. The number of clear and determined atheists is apparently not very large.[32]

In the above comments, Lewis sounds closer in spirit to the evidentialist approach of launching directly into the factual evidence for Jesus' divine acts and identity without first trying to make a case for theism.[33] One should note, though, Lewis's explanation for this change in tactic: he did not find it necessary or helpful to argue separately for theism because apparently few of his listeners were dogmatic atheists. The implication is that Lewis would have continued to argue for theism before discussing the evidence for Christianity if the opposition to theism had been more forceful.

Lewis, then, may be broadly described as a classical apologist, with the qualification that (like most apologists) he did not espouse an explicit apologetic method derived from a formal theory of apologetics. Indeed, in his published writings he never discussed apologetic theory. Rather, he employed varying tactics and modes of argument and persuasion in order to address people's questions, doubts, and skepticism in interesting and effective ways.

NORMAN L. GEISLER

One Christian apologist who *has* advocated a formal theory of apologetic method is Norman L. Geisler, whose books on apologetics, philosophy of religion, ethics, and biblical studies have made him a key figure in Christian apologetics. He has authored, co-authored, and edited some sixty books.[34] A philosopher by training, Geisler has taught apologetics and theology at several major evangelical seminaries since the late 1950s, and is the president of Southern Evangelical Seminary in Matthews, North Carolina, which he co-founded in 1992. He was also a prominent member of the Evangelical Theological Society,[35] culminating in his serving as president in 1998.

Although Geisler is evangelical Protestant in his theology, he is a convinced Thomist in his philosophy and apologetics. His approach to apologetics proceeds in two steps.[36] First the apologist builds a case for theism by demonstrating how it conforms to rational criteria used to evaluate the truth claims of competing worldviews. Having shown that theism is true according to these criteria, the apologist may then present the evidence for the historical truth claims of Christianity.

Geisler elaborates this two-step method (characteristic of classical apologetics) in a series of "Twelve Points that Show Christianity is True":

1. Truth about reality is knowable.
2. The opposite of true is false.
3. It is true that the theistic God exists.
4. If God exists, then miracles are possible.
5. Miracles can be used to confirm a message from God (i.e., as an act of God to confirm a word from God).
6. The New Testament is historically reliable.
7. The New Testament says Jesus claimed to be God.
8. Jesus' claim to be God was miraculously confirmed by:
   a. His fulfillment of many prophecies about Himself;
   b. His sinless and miraculous life;
   c. His prediction and accomplishment of His resurrection.
9. Therefore, Jesus is God.
10. Whatever Jesus (who is God) teaches is true.
11. Jesus taught that the Bible is the Word of God.

12. Therefore, it is true that the Bible is the Word of God (and anything opposed to it is false).

Geisler says that this argument "builds the case for Christianity from the ground up"—that is, it begins with undeniable points and proceeds from those to show that Christianity is true.[37] The first five points correspond to the first step of the classical argument, while the last seven points correspond to the second step.

Geisler's two most important works, for our purposes, are his *Philosophy of Religion* (the second edition of which was co-authored with Winfried Corduan) and *Christian Apologetics*. In view of his influence in contemporary evangelical apologetics, we will review the argument of both of these books in some detail.

Geisler's Philosophy of Religion

Geisler divides philosophy of religion into four major divisions, dealing with (1) religious experience, (2) God and reason, (3) religious language, and (4) the problem of evil. We will consider each of these subjects in turn.

Religious experience. The issue dominating the first part of Geisler's *Philosophy of Religion* is whether experiences of God or the supernatural can be considered rational. Geisler argues that they can because "the history of mankind, sacred or secular, supports the thesis that by nature man has an irresistible urge to transcend himself" (63–64).[38] Nevertheless, he argues that verification is necessary to discern *that* there really is a God to fulfill the human need for transcendence

God and reason. Such verification can be found in a philosophical theistic proof. In the second section of the book, titled "God and Reason," Geisler examines the function of theistic proofs and defends a version of the cosmological argument. He maintains that "the theist need not be concerned about showing that God's nonexistence is *inconceivable* but only that it is *undeniable*. After all, what the theist seeks is not mere rational inconceivability but existential undeniability. That is, the theist seeks a necessary *Being*, not a necessary Thought at the end of his argument" (100–101). The theistic proof that Geisler regards as fundamental is the cosmological argument, which is based on the principle of causality. He examines three other standard philosophical arguments for God's existence—the argument from design in nature, the argument from morality, and the ontological argument—and argues that in each case the principle of causality is assumed. If this principle is accepted, Geisler maintains, each of these three arguments will depend on a causal form of the cosmological argument.

Religious language. The third part of Geisler's book focuses on the problem of religious language. Even if a sound argument for the existence of God can be made, how can we intelligently speak about that which transcends all our experience? Geisler maintains that every negation implies a prior affirmation, and that therefore purely negative God-talk is meaningless. The positive knowledge of God implied by negative God-talk requires that language about God be understood **univocally**—as having an identity of meaning when referring to both God and creatures—to avoid a descent into religious skepticism. Without such univocal understanding, Geisler (along with the late medieval philosopher Duns Scotus) maintains that we would be using words without really knowing what they meant. On the other hand, Geisler also agrees with Aquinas that God cannot possess perfections in the same way created things possess them.

The problem of evil. In the fourth and final part of *Philosophy of Religion*, Geisler considers three ways to relate God and evil. The first, atheism, affirms the existence of evil and denies the existence of God. Atheists reason that if God exists, he is not essentially good, since he should destroy all evil but does not. Moreover, God evidently cannot do the best, since this is not the best of all possible worlds. Geisler argues that although God has not yet destroyed evil, he will do so, and in a way that leads to the best possible world. The second alternative is illusionism, the denial of the reality of evil. Geisler points out that illusionism cannot account satisfactorily for the origin of the illusion of evil. The third alternative affirms both God (though not necessarily the biblical God) and evil. Some options in this category, such as dualism, finite godism, and sadism, are incompatible with theism. Geisler raises logical objections to each option and turns to solutions to the problem of evil that are open to theism. After examining the alternatives available to the theistic God, Geisler concludes that "the morally best world is better than a morally good world or than no moral world at all" (354). That this world, despite its temporary degradation due to sin, is the best way to the best world will eventually be confirmed at the end of history in the Final Judgment.

Geisler's Christian Apologetics

Geisler's textbook *Christian Apologetics* is divided into three parts. In the first part he considers how to test competing truth claims. Having chosen a test for truth, he applies it to the major worldviews in the second part and argues that theism—the view that the world was created by a God who is able to perform miracles—is the true worldview. Finally, in the third part he presents evidence in support of the Christian faith.

Apologetic method. Geisler critically evaluates seven methodological approaches to the question of God: agnosticism, rationalism, fideism, experientialism, evidentialism, pragmatism, and combinationalism. He concludes that each of these epistemological methods makes a contribution but is inadequate as a test for truth. In their place he proposes *unaffirmability* as the test for the falsehood of a worldview and *undeniability* as the test for the truth of a worldview. Unaffirmability occurs when a statement is directly self-defeating, such as "I cannot express myself in words," or indirectly self-defeating, such as "I know that one cannot know anything about reality" (142).[39] Undeniability applies to statements that are definitional or tautologous, such as "Triangles have three sides," as well as to statements which are existentially self-confirming, such as "I exist" (143–144). These tests for truth should be compared to the first two points of Geisler's 12-point argument (truth is knowable and the opposite of true is false).

Theistic apologetics. Using the two tests of unaffirmability and undeniability, Geisler seeks to demonstrate that all nontheistic worldviews are directly or indirectly unaffirmable, and only theism is affirmable and undeniable. He examines several competing worldviews (deism, pantheism, panentheism, atheism) and argues that all of them fail the test for truth. For example, deism is a self-defeating position because it acknowledges the miracle of an *ex nihilo* creation but denies that other miracles are possible. Pantheism is self-defeating because it involves a person (the pantheist) claiming that individual finite selves (such as the pantheist) are less than real. Dogmatic atheism, in its insistence that God must not exist because of the reality of evil, must assume God (as the ground of morality) in order to disprove God. By contrast, Geisler develops a revised cosmological argument with undeniable premises (something exists, nothing comes from nothing) "that leads inescapably to the existence of an infinitely perfect and powerful Being beyond this world who is the current sustaining cause of all finite, changing, and contingent beings" (258). This conclusion corresponds to the third point of Geisler's 12-point apologetic.

Christian apologetics. Having established the validity of the theistic worldview, Geisler then deals with miracles, the role of history and the establishment of the historical reliability of the New Testament, the deity and authority of Jesus Christ, and finally the inspiration and authority of the Bible. Since he is shifting from judging between worldviews to judging within the theistic worldview (that is, Islam, Christianity, and Judaism), he moves away from the criteria of unaffirmability and undeniability to the probabilistic criterion of systematic consistency (comprehensiveness, adequacy, consistency, coherence). Geisler argues that given the truth of theism, one must acknowledge the possibility of miracles (the fourth point of Geisler's 12-point apologetic). Furthermore, the existence of God guarantees that history has meaning and that it is possible for human beings to know historical events. This means that God could use miracles in history to confirm his message (the fifth point). From these premises Geisler proceeds to examine the case for Christianity. He argues that the New Testament writings may be regarded as authentic and reliable (point #6), and then applies the methods of historical investigation to those documents to show that Jesus Christ claimed to be God (point #7) and that he vindicated this claim by fulfilling Old Testament prophecies and rising from the dead (point #8). The most systematically consistent interpretation of these facts is that Christ was, in truth, the Son of God (point #9). On the basis of Christ's divine authority, then, Christians believe the Bible to be the word of God (264–265; compare points #10–12).

PETER KREEFT

Peter Kreeft is a Roman Catholic professor of philosophy at Boston College. He has written numerous books and has emerged as a Christian apologist whose works are popular among Protestants as well as Catholics.[40]

Even more so than Geisler, Kreeft models his approach on the work of Thomas Aquinas. Kreeft edited and annotated one of the best digests of Aquinas's major work, the *Summa Theologica*,[41] and in his *Handbook of Christian Apologetics*, co-authored with Ronald K. Tacelli, he self-consciously modeled his method on that of Aquinas. In fact, they "even thought of titling it *Summa Apologetica*" (12).[42] The book is divided into chapters dealing with broadly defined issues (e.g., God, evil, the Resurrection, the Bible), and each issue is subdivided into more specific questions or problems. In turn each question can, they say, be broken down into seven parts, though for the sake of readability they do not cover all seven for each question. The seven parts are as follows (20):

1. Definition of terms and the meaning of the question
2. The importance of the question, the difference it makes
3. Objections to the Christian answer to the question
4. Answers to each of these objections
5. Arguments for the Christian answer from premises accepted by the unbeliever as well as the believer
6. Objections to *these* arguments
7. Answers to each of these objections

The crux of this method is found in the fifth part, in which the apologist presents arguments for the Christian position "from premises accepted by the unbeliever as well as the believer." The arguments thus function as proofs that should be acceptable to unbelievers if they are constructed properly and if the unbelievers reason properly. "The arguments in this book demonstrate that the essential Christian doctrines are true, unless they are bad arguments; that is, ambiguous, false or fallacious." Not all the arguments have conclusive demonstrative force, though; some are "probable" and function more as "clues" that gain persuasive force when "considered cumulatively" (18).

Although for Kreeft apologetics at its core offers positive arguments as proofs (both demonstrable and probable) for the Christian position, most apologetic argumentation is taken up with answering objections to these proofs or other objections to the Christian faith (parts 3–4, 6–7 above). Following Aquinas, Kreeft is confident that "every possible argument against every Christian doctrine has a rational mistake in it somewhere, and therefore can be answered by reason alone" (39).

Kreeft's approach is well illustrated by his handling of arguments for the existence of God. He admits that some people do not personally need proofs of God's existence in order to believe in him, but he points out that the arguments can help others take belief in God seriously. Moreover, Kreeft and Tacelli acknowledge at the outset that their arguments for God's existence differ in demonstrative power. For example, arguments from miracles or religious experience "claim only strong probability, not demonstrative certainty," and were included "because they form part of a strong cumulative case." They believe the arguments with the most demonstrative certainty are the cosmological arguments based on Aquinas's "five ways," but these proofs "are not the simplest of the arguments, and therefore are not the most convincing to most people" (49). In the end they offer twenty distinct arguments for God's existence; while not depending too heavily on any one argument, the authors express confidence that "all twenty together, like twined rope, make a very strong case" (50). These references to a "cumulative case" in which multiple arguments work together "like twined rope" are actually more characteristic of the evidentialist approach to apologetics. This should not be surprising, since many apologists today freely utilize different sorts of arguments. Still, the overall approach that Kreeft and Tacelli take in their book follows the classical model: first argue for the theistic worldview, then argue more specifically for the truth of the Christian revelation.

While the rational structure of his apologetic is especially rooted in Thomistic philosophy, Kreeft is greatly indebted to C. S. Lewis for the practical expression of much of his approach.[43] Kreeft and Tacelli conclude their *Handbook* by reprinting the essay "Man or Rabbit?" which "we think is the most effective essay written by the most effective Christian apologist of our century, C. S. Lewis" (388).[44] Kreeft is perhaps best known for his books in which various characters, some fictional and some historical, engage in dialogue about ethical, philosophical, and religious questions. In one of these, *Between Heaven and Hell*, he imagines a discussion between C. S. Lewis, who represents Kreeft's Christian position, and two men who happened to die on the same day as Lewis (22 November 1963)—John F. Kennedy, representing the modernist or humanist tradition, and Aldous Huxley, representing the mystical or pantheist tradition. Early in the dialogue Lewis and Kennedy discuss the grounds of Lewis's faith in Christ:

Kennedy: If you want to be so logical, I challenge you: prove to me logically that Jesus is God and not just man.

Lewis: All right.

Kennedy: What?

Lewis: I just said, "All right." Why the surprise?

Kennedy: I thought you were going to say something about mysteries and faith and authority and the church. Do you mean you are going to try to *reason* yourself into the old faith?

Lewis: Not myself; I'm already there. But you, perhaps.

Kennedy: Did you reason yourself into it? Did you arrive at your belief by reason alone?

Lewis: Reason *alone?* Of course not. But I looked before I leaped. I reasoned before I believed. And after I believed too—I mean, once I believed, I was convinced by the way reason backed up faith. It couldn't prove *everything*, but it could give strong arguments for many things, and it could answer all objections.

Kennedy: All objections?

Lewis: Certainly.

Kennedy: That sounds pretty arrogant to me. Who are you to answer all objections?

Lewis: No, no, I don't claim that *I* can answer all objections but that *reason* can—that all objections are answerable.

Kennedy: Why do you believe that?

Lewis: If truth is one, if God is the author of all truth, both the truth of reason and the truth of faith (I mean divine revelation), then there can never be a rational argument against faith that's telling, that's unanswerable. Faith may go beyond reason but it can never simply contradict reason.[45]

WILLIAM LANE CRAIG

William Lane Craig's work has put him at the forefront of evangelical apologetics in the early twenty-first century. The scholarly depth and range of his work and his effectiveness as an apologist are very impressive. Most academics make their mark in only one field, and as specialization increases, that field tends to be ever narrower. Craig is one of the leading evangelical theorists in at least three areas of academic research. The first is the cosmological argument, an approach to proving God's existence that Craig has developed along both philosophical and scientific lines, both with great sophistication.[46] Craig is also widely viewed as one of the leading evangelical scholars in the historical argument for the resurrection of Jesus, an extremely well plowed field that has produced new fruit through Craig's efforts.[47] Yet a third area in which Craig is a leading evangelical researcher is the philosophical analysis of the attributes of God. Craig has given special attention to the doctrine of God's omniscience, defending an orthodox (though frankly Arminian[48]) theological understanding of this doctrine with a rigorous and fresh approach.[49] Craig has also published extensively on the question of God's relation to time.[50]

Besides writing both technical and popular books defending these three aspects of Christian faith, William Lane Craig has written one of the best recent textbook introductions to the subject of apologetics[51] and co-authored a major textbook on Christian philosophy.[52] In addition, he has publicly debated atheists and skeptics widely, with great success. Some of these debates have been published,[53] most notably his 1997 debate on the Resurrection with radical New Testament scholar John Dominic Crossan[54] and his 1998 debate with renowned atheist philosopher Antony Flew.[55] Craig's debate with Flew was held on the fiftieth anniversary of the famous 1948 BBC radio debate between Fredrick Copleston and Bertrand Russell. A few years later, in 2004, Flew abandoned atheism, announcing that he had concluded that some sort of God exists, although he still did not accept the Christian view of God.[56]

In most of his earlier works Craig did not identify himself as an advocate of any particular apologetic methodology. However, in 2000 Craig defended the classical model in a book on different apologetic methods.[57] That he is a classical apologist may also be seen in his apologetics textbook and in some of his more wide-ranging debates, where he follows a fairly traditional, classical pattern. He opens by presenting arguments for the existence of God and follows these with arguments for the truth of Christianity (based mainly on the evidence for Jesus' resurrection and deity). Still, some of Craig's arguments have been extremely influential in evidentialist apologetics. Here we will present an overview of his textbook on apologetics, *Reasonable Faith*.

Craig begins by exploring the question, "How do I know Christianity is true?" According to Craig, the key to answering this question is "to distinguish between *knowing* Christianity to be true and *showing* Christianity to be true" (31).[58] "We *know* Christianity is true primarily by the self-authenticating witness of the Holy Spirit. We *show* Christianity is true by demonstrating that it is systematically consistent" (48). In other words, Christian apologetics does not pretend to create the grounds for knowing that Christianity is true, but rather points to or presents Christianity as rational as a means of encouraging unbelievers to receive the witness of the Spirit.

Rather than launching immediately into arguments for God's existence, Craig begins his apologetic by showing "the absurdity of life without God" (chapter 2). This argument is not intended to prove that Christianity is true, but to show "the disastrous consequences for human existence, society, and culture if Christianity should be false" (51). "If God does not exist, then life is futile. If the God of the Bible does exist, then life is meaningful. Only the second of these two alternatives enables us to live happily and consistently. Therefore, it seems to me that even if the evidence for these two options were absolutely equal, a rational person ought to choose biblical Christianity" (72).

Given that God's existence would give meaning to life, we do not believe in God in an irrational attempt to convince ourselves that life has meaning. We believe in God because there is proof that he exists. "Thus, people are without excuse for not believing in God's existence, not only because of the internal testimony of the Holy Spirit, but also because of the external witness of nature" (77). Arguments in support of belief in God "provide an intellectual, cultural context in which the gospel cannot be dismissed simply as a logical absurdity and is therefore given an honest chance to be heard" (78). Craig surveys the traditional arguments for God's existence, including the ontological, cosmological, teleological, and moral arguments, and finds "quite a number of the proffered theistic arguments to be sound and persuasive and together to constitute a powerful cumulative case for the existence of God" (91–92). Craig's favorite theistic argument is the *kalām* cosmological argument, which was originally formulated by medieval Arabic Muslim philosophers. Craig concludes that, "amazing as it may seem, the most plausible answer to the question of why something exists rather than nothing is that God exists. This means, in turn, that the first and most fundamental condition for meaning to life and the universe is supplied" (121–122).

In chapter 4 Craig defends the possibility of miracles. He concludes that the philosophical objections from such thinkers as Spinoza and Hume are without merit. His final words on the subject indicate that for him the reasonableness of belief in miracles rests on the reasonableness of belief in God: "Once the non-Christian understands who God is, then the problem of miracles should cease to be a problem for him" (155). This line of reasoning is characteristic of the classical approach, which rests belief in the possibility of miracles on belief in God.

In chapter 5 he considers the question of the possibility of historical knowledge as a prelude to the examination of the historical claims of the New Testament concerning Jesus Christ. Here the major error to be combated is historical relativism, the belief that our distance from the past and our lack of neutrality or objectivity makes it impossible for us to know what actually occurred in the past (169–172). In answer to the objection that we lack direct access to the past, Craig argues that we may test theories about the past using the same criterion of systematic consistency that we use in other matters of truth. "The historian should accept the hypothesis that best explains all the evidence" (184). To the objection that objectivity in historical knowledge is impossible, Craig points out that our ability to distinguish history from propaganda and to criticize poor history reveals our ability to access genuine historical facts (185–187).

Craig L. Blomberg, an evangelical New Testament scholar, wrote chapter 6 on "the historical reliability of the New Testament" to document that it is "probable that a substantial *majority* of the details in the gospels and Acts do describe what Jesus and the apostles actually said and did" (226). In chapter 7 William Lane Craig turns the discussion directly to Jesus' claims about himself as reported in the Gospels. "At the center of any Christian apologetic must stand the person of

Christ; and very important for the doctrine of Christ's person are the personal claims of the historical Jesus" (233). Craig admits "that the majority of NT scholars today do not believe that the historical Jesus ever claimed to be the Son of God, Lord, and so forth" (243). But while Jesus' use of these titles for himself is widely questioned, the self-understanding they express can be clearly traced back to Jesus himself in the rest of what he said about himself (244). Suppose we take only the sayings of Jesus admitted by the extremely liberal "Jesus Seminar" to be authentic. Even these sayings show Jesus as someone who "thought of himself as being the Son of God in a unique sense," who "claimed to speak and act with divine authority" and to be "able to perform miracles," and who "claimed to determine people's eternal destiny before God" (244–252). Radical critics refuse to draw the obvious conclusion—that Jesus claimed to be God—not because of a lack of evidence but because of their prejudice against the Christian doctrine (253).

The importance of Jesus' claims to deity is that they "provide the religio-historical context in which the resurrection becomes significant, as it confirms those claims" (253). This leads Craig to the capstone of his apologetic, the historical argument for the resurrection of Jesus (chapter 8).

> The case for the historicity of the resurrection of Jesus seems to me to rest upon the evidence for three great, independently established facts: the empty tomb, the resurrection appearances, and the origin of the Christian faith. If these three facts can be established and no plausible natural explanation can account for them, then one is justified in inferring Jesus' resurrection as the most plausible explanation of the data. (272)

The structure of Craig's apologetic closely parallels that of Norman Geisler, with some minor differences. Both begin by considering matters of epistemology and then move to defend the existence of God, primarily on the basis of a form of the cosmological argument. (Craig uses a version of the *kalām* argument originated by medieval Muslim philosophers, while Geisler uses a form of the cosmological argument dependent on the medieval Christian philosopher Thomas Aquinas.) Having established the credibility of belief in God's existence, both apologists argue for the possibility of miracles and then for the possibility of historical knowledge of such miracles. They then move to specifically Christian claims, making the case for the reliability of the New Testament, from there to Jesus' claims to deity and the evidence for his resurrection, and conclude that

Jesus' resurrection confirms his claims to deity and therefore the truth of all that Jesus taught.

In the conclusion to his book, Craig presents "the ultimate apologetic," which he says "will help you to win more persons to Christ than all the other arguments in your apologetic arsenal put together" (299). This ultimate apologetic is to show people our love for God and our love for one another (299–301). "This, then, is the ultimate apologetic. For the ultimate apologetic is: your life" (302).

CONCLUSION

Although the five apologists profiled in this chapter are all identified with the classical apologetical tradition pioneered by Thomas Aquinas, some distinct differences among them should not be overlooked. Norman Geisler is perhaps the most unremittingly rationalist of the five, by which we mean that deductive logic plays the most comprehensive role in his apologetic. Even Geisler, however, is not a thoroughgoing rationalist.

Peter Kreeft's and William Lane Craig's methods differ somewhat from that of Geisler. While upholding the rational ideal of deductive proof for theism, Kreeft and Craig also draw on a wide variety of arguments that fall short of deductive proof and employ them in defense both of theism and of Christianity per se in cumulative-case arguments. Thus these two apologists show some affinities for the evidentialist approach that defends theism using inductive, empirical evidences. What makes their method classical is that they follow the pattern of defending theism as a worldview within which the historical evidences for Christianity (miracles, fulfilled prophecy) are to be considered. In this respect, as we have just seen, Craig's apologetic follows essentially the same structure as Geisler's.

B. B. Warfield, writing at the beginning of the rise of the Reformed apologetic tradition, articulated a fairly traditional, classical apologetic. Yet Warfield, who was himself a Calvinist, anticipated in certain respects the Reformed apologetic of Cornelius Van Til. He regarded theistic arguments as reminders of the immediate awareness of recognition of God that all human beings have because of their creation in the image of God. His affirmation that the facts of Christianity are also Christian doctrines anticipated Van Til's teaching that all facts are interpreted facts. Warfield's apologetic also has affinities with the evidentialist approach, notably in his view that evidence for miracles could be in some sense part of the case for God's existence.

Finally, C. S. Lewis's apologetic, while broadly fitting the classical approach, also had affinities with other approaches. Lewis's stock method was to argue first for God's existence and then for Christianity, but in later years he often found it prudent to start immediately with the evidence for Christ's deity. In this respect his later method was similar to that of evidentialism (although his reason for not arguing for theism first was that he found it largely unnecessary). Lewis also showed the sensitivity to personal, relational concerns that characterizes the fideist approach. For him apologetics was a function of the whole human person, dealing as much with the imagination as with the intellect, and ultimately was concerned with the personal reality of Christ himself.

In the following chapters, we will examine the classical approach in greater detail, drawing on the writings of these five classical apologists and other modern apologists who follow in that tradition.

For Further Study

Hackett, Stuart C. *The Reconstruction of the Christian Revelation Claim: A Philosophical and Critical Apologetic*. Grand Rapids: Baker, 1984. An apologetics textbook by William Lane Craig's philosophy professor at seminary, advocating a "rational empirical" theory of knowledge as the basis for a classical defense of Christianity.

Jones, Charles Andrews, III. "Charles Hodge, the Keeper of Orthodoxy: The Method, Purpose and Meaning of His Apologetic." Ph.D. diss., Drew University, 1989. A dissertation on the apologetic of the premier systematic theologian of Old Princeton.

Moreland, J. P. *Scaling the Secular City: A Defense of Christianity*. Grand Rapids: Baker, 1987. An apologetics textbook taking an approach very similar to that of William Lane Craig— generally classical in structure with some evidentialist leanings in content.

Noll, Mark A., ed. *The Princeton Theology, 1812-1921: Scripture, Science, and Theological Method from Archibald Alexander to Benjamin Breckinridge Warfield*. Grand Rapids: Baker, 1983. A helpful collection of essays and excerpted writings from Old Princeton.

Sproul, R. C. *Defending Your Faith: An Introduction to Apologetics*. Wheaton, Ill.: Good News Publishers—Crossway Books, 2003. Recent text by a popular Reformed theologian and classical apologist in the tradition of Warfield. Sproul discusses the task of apologetics, delineates "four essential principles of knowledge" from which he will make his case (the law of noncontradiction, the law of causality, the reliability of sense perception, and the validity of analogical language for God), presents his argument for God from the existence of the universe, and finishes with the case for the authority of the Bible, relating it to both Jesus' teaching and the testimony of the Holy Spirit.

Chapter 5

Classical Apologetics: A Reasonable Faith

In the previous chapter we surveyed a number of apologists working in the classical tradition. Although they vary among themselves especially on the extent to which they use deductive or inductive arguments to formulate their apologetic as a whole, all emphasize the importance of showing the theistic worldview to be reasonable in order to present the evidences for the facts of Christianity effectively to nontheists. It is this methodological principle, however differently understood and applied, that typifies the classical apologetic approach. In this chapter we consider how this principle is related to various crucial areas of human knowledge that have an important bearing on the truth claims of Christianity.

RATIONAL TESTS FOR DETERMINING TRUTH

In the classical approach, there is no substantive conflict between faith and reason. The Christian worldview is a reasonable faith, a step into the light of reason and truth rather than a leap into the darkness of irrationality and subjectivity. To show this reasonableness, classical apologists stress the need to compare and evaluate conflicting worldviews by means of certain epistemological criteria, chief among which is logical consistency or rationality. This does *not* mean that classical apologists are pure rationalists in their epistemology. All would be quick to acknowledge that **rationalism** per se (according to which, reason is the sole test of truth) is an inadequate approach to religious knowledge. Rationalism wrongly elevates human reason to the level of an ultimate arbiter of truth. Moreover, because God transcends the universe, the human mind cannot arrive on its own at substantive knowledge about God.

Geisler's treatment of rationalism is representative of the classical approach. The strength of rationalism, he argues, lies in its stress on the inescapability of the law of noncontradiction, its recognition of the *a priori* categories of knowledge, and its emphasis on the intelligibility of reality. In spite of these positive features, Geisler maintains that the standard forms of rationalism are deficient because they fail to demonstrate that their first principles are rationally necessary. Logic is an indispensable and excellent negative test for truth—it is very useful in disproving truth claims—but it is insufficient alone as a positive test for truth.[1] This does *not* mean that Geisler does not view logic as a test for truth, but only that logic cannot discover truth *alone*. He explains why he is not a rationalist as follows:

> A rationalist tries to *determine* all truth by human reason. A reasonable Christian merely uses reason to *discover* truth that God has revealed, either by general revelation or by special revelation in the Bible.[2]

Warfield argued that rationalism erred in insisting that every doctrine of Christianity had to be tested and proved before the bar of reason before any of it could be believed. Reason may examine the truth claims of the Christian religion as a whole, he agreed, but it would be unreasonable to deny that some truths about the transcendent God and his relationship to mankind might be beyond our capacity to prove rationally.

> It certainly is not the business of apologetics to take up each tenet of Christianity in turn and seek to establish its truth by a direct appeal to reason. Any attempt to do this, no matter on what philosophical basis the work of demonstration be begun or by what methods it be pursued, would transfer us at once into the atmosphere and betray us into the devious devices of the old vulgar rationalism, the primary fault of which was that it asked for a direct rational demonstration of the truth of each Christian teaching in turn.[3]

Such comments about the limits of rationality alone should not obscure the primary role that logic or reason plays in classical apologetics. According to Geisler, logic "is the basis of all thought about God."[4] In a statement he was to make repeatedly in his writings, Warfield asserted that "we believe in Christ because it is rational to believe in Him, not even though it be irrational."[5] Indeed, Warfield contends, there cannot be true faith that is not rationally grounded in evidence. The purpose of apologetics is to elucidate these rational grounds. This does not at all mean that people must be able to demonstrate the truth of Christianity in order to be Christians. In fact, people may have faith and be completely at a loss to analyze or explain the grounds of their faith. Yet such rationally explicable grounds must exist, according to classical apologists. Warfield explains:

> A man recognizes on sight the face of his friend, or his own handwriting. Ask him how he knows this face to be that of his friend, or this handwriting to be his own, and he is dumb, or, seeking to reply, babbles nonsense. Yet his recognition rests on solid grounds, though he lacks analytical skill to isolate and state these solid grounds. We believe in God and freedom and immortality on good grounds, though we may not be able satisfactorily to analyze these grounds. No true conviction exists without adequate rational grounding in evidence. . . . The Christian's conviction of the deity of his Lord does not depend for its soundness on the Christian's ability convincingly to state the grounds of his conviction.[6]

Although classical apologists do not think the truth of Christianity depends on the strength of their arguments, this does not mean they are dubious about the rational validity of those arguments. Geisler's own approach, though not a thoroughgoing rationalism, uses arguments based on a dual test for truth that is largely rationalist. Unaffirmability is used as the negative test, while undeniability is the positive test. A statement is unaffirmable if the act of affirming it actually contradicts it ("I cannot utter a single sentence in English"). A statement is undeniable if it is true by definition ("A triangle has three sides") or if the act of denying it actually affirms it ("It is not true that I exist").[7] According to Geisler, the main problem with a purely rationalistic argument like the ontological argument (which reasons from the idea of an unsurpassably great being to the existence of that being, i.e., God) is that it assumes that something exists:

> Of course, if something exists, then the ontological argument takes on new strength; for if something exists it is possible that something necessarily exists. But the point here is that there is no purely logical way to eliminate the "if." I know undeniably but not with logical necessity that I exist.[8]

In his main argument for God's existence—a form of the cosmological argument—Geisler's only empirically grounded premise is that some changing being or beings exist. The rest of the argument proceeds rationally to reach the conclusion that God exists.[9] An argument of this sort is highly rationalistic even though it is not an exercise in pure rationalism.

The rational test of unaffirmability is frequently used in classical apologetics, in particular to show that non-Christian philosophies are untenable. One such philosophy is the tradition of relativism and postmodernism that emerged as a potent cultural force in the last decade of the twentieth century. **Relativism** is the belief that statements of fact or value are true from some perspectives but not from others; in short, all truth is relative. This has been a dominant view of knowledge in much Eastern religion and philosophy, as well as in the New Age movement. Advocates of these belief systems find nothing troubling about affirming flatly contradictory claims. **Postmodernism** is a cultural movement that has applied relativistic thinking in various fields of thought, including architecture, law, ethics, literature, the arts, philosophy, and even theology. Classical apologists firmly resist relativism in all its forms as a logically incoherent view of knowledge. They point out that a statement of relativism such as "Every point of view is only partial" is self-defeating because, if expressing only a partial point of view, it is not true for all points of view—which means that some points of view are total, not partial. If the statement is said to express the total truth, of course, then the statement becomes an example of the kind of knowledge the statement itself asserts cannot be had.[10]

While classical apologists use arguments that, if sound, yield certain conclusions, they are often content to conclude simply that belief in God, as well as in Christ, is reasonable. For example, C. S. Lewis argues that at a minimum Christianity must have some rational plausibility; it is not a religion of indifference to reason or evidence. "We know, in fact, that believers are not cut off from unbelievers by any portentous inferiority of intelligence or any perverse refusal to think. Many of them have been people of powerful minds. Many of them have been scientists. We may suppose them to have been mistaken, but we must suppose that their error was at least plausible."[11]

Lewis thinks "there is evidence both for and against the Christian propositions which fully rational minds, working honestly, can assess differently. . . . There is no reason to suppose stark unreason on either side. We need only suppose error. One side has estimated the evidence wrongly. And even so, the mistake cannot be supposed to be of a flagrant nature; otherwise the debate would not continue."[12] Likewise, William Lane Craig has explained that he does not attempt to prove that it is necessarily *irrational* to disbelieve in the Resurrection, but that the Resurrection is the *best* explanation of the known facts.[13]

Craig's view of the relationship between faith and reason merits closer consideration. He has set forth that view most fully in the first chapter of his textbook on apologetics, *Reasonable Faith*. He begins by surveying the thought of such thinkers as Augustine, Aquinas, John Locke, Wolfhart Pannenberg, and Alvin Plantinga. He then develops his own answer to the question, "How do I know Christianity is true?" The key to answering this question, he says, is "to distinguish between *knowing* Christianity to be true and *showing* Christianity to be true" (31).[14] He discusses these two issues separately.

First, Craig suggests that "the way we know Christianity to be true is by the self-authenticating witness of God's Holy Spirit" (31). A person who has this witness from the Holy Spirit "does not need supplementary arguments or evidences" to know that he is having that experience, because it is a direct experience of God and not merely the basis of an argument about God (32). Craig finds this doctrine clearly taught in the New Testament (32–34). "For the believer, God is not the conclusion of a syllogism; he is the living God of Abraham, Isaac, and Jacob dwelling within us" (34). The unbeliever's problem is not a lack of arguments or evidence but resistance to this witness of the Spirit (35–36). Given this ultimate, grounding role of the witness of the Spirit in our knowledge of the truth of Christianity, "the only role left for argument and evidence to play is a subsidiary role. . . . A person who knows Christianity is true on the basis of the witness of the Spirit may also have a sound apologetic which reinforces or confirms for him the Spirit's witness, but it does not serve as the basis of his belief" (36). To make apologetic argument the basis of faith "would consign most believers to irrationality" and let people who had not been given good arguments for Christianity off the hook (37).

When it comes to *showing* that Christianity is true, the roles of the Holy Spirit's witness and of argument "are somewhat reversed." Showing that Christianity is true involves presenting "sound and persuasive arguments for Christian truth claims" (38). These arguments may be either deductive or inductive, but in both forms of reasoning "logic and fact are the keys to showing soundly that a conclusion is true" (40). A truth claim that "is logically consistent and fits all the facts known in our experience" passes the test for truth known as *systematic consistency*.[15] This test does not "guarantee the truth of a world view"; it merely shows that worldview to be probably true. This does not undermine the absolute commitment required in faith because while we can only *show* Christianity to be probably true by argument, we can *know* Christianity to be true with complete assurance by the Spirit's witness (40). Moreover, the Holy Spirit can and does use rational argumentation as a means through which he brings people to faith (46–47).

Craig recognizes that many people today who espouse some form of Eastern religion or New Age teaching will dismiss his appeal to logical consistency. These belief systems often *encourage* people to hold contradictory ideas together. Craig finds such ideas "frankly crazy and unintelligible" (41). The claim that logic and other self-evident principles are not universally true "seems to be both self-refuting and arbitrary." He asks us to consider the claim that "God cannot be described by propositions governed by the Law of Contradiction." If this statement is true, then it itself expresses a proposition that is not governed by the law of contradiction. But that means that its contrary is also true: God can be described by propositions governed by the law of contradiction (42). Craig then shows that the same problem applies to postmodernism. His own view that the truth about Christ is known ultimately by the witness of the Spirit and not by rationalism might be described as a kind of postmodern view of knowledge. But postmodernists per se claim "that there is no objective truth about reality" (43), and such a claim is again "self-refuting and arbitrary" (44).

Craig concludes by explaining that he finds his approach to faith and reason both liberating for Christians and effective in evangelism:

> It is tremendously liberating to be able to know that our faith is true and to commend it as such to an unbeliever without being dependent upon the vagaries of argument and evidence for the assurance that our faith is true; at the same time we know confidently and without embarrassment that our faith is true and that the unbeliever can know this, too, without our falling into relativistic subjectivism. . . . Success in witnessing is simply communicating Christ in the power of the Holy Spirit and leaving the results to God. Similarly, effectiveness in apologetics is presenting cogent and persuasive arguments for the Gospel in the power of the Holy Spirit, and leaving the results to God (49, 50).

Although Geisler believes that rational arguments for the truth of God's existence can be had, he agrees that such apologetic arguments cannot produce faith. "Rational arguments offer proof but do not necessarily persuade unbelievers of God's existence. They may be objectively correct but not always subjectively convincing. This is because they are directed at the mind but are not directive of the will. They can 'lead the horse to water,' but only the Holy Spirit can persuade a person to drink."[16]

THE FOUNDATION OF THEOLOGY

Generally speaking, classical apologists understand the purpose of apologetics to be showing the rationality of the foundational truths and principles on which Christian theology is based. As Ronald B. Mayers has explained, this meant that apologetics was often virtually equated with theological prolegomena, notably in Thomism. Mayers himself rejects this equation. He argues that **theological prolegomena** is a branch of theology that "assumes the truth of the Christian faith" and seeks to clarify its underlying assumptions, while apologetics seeks "to demonstrate the *truthfulness* of Christianity and the viability of the theologian's assumptions."[17] One can see, though, that even in Mayers's view there is a very close relationship between the two disciplines.

Warfield has articulated the classical understanding of the purpose of apologetics as justification of the grounds of theology perhaps more explicitly than anyone:

> It is, in other words, the function of apologetics to investigate, explicate, and establish the grounds on which a theology—a science, or systematized knowledge of God—is possible; and on the basis of which every science which has God for its object must rest, if it be a true science which claims to a place within the circle of the sciences. It necessarily takes its place, therefore, at the head of the departments of theological science and finds its task in the establishment of the validity of that knowledge of God which forms the subject-matter of these departments. . . .[18]

Warfield insists that apologetics must be distinguished from apologies and even from the science of apology. The place to study "the theory of apology" and "to teach men how to defend Christianity" is "in practical theology" alongside homiletics and similar disciplines. The science of apology "of course presupposes the complete development of Christianity through the exegetical, historical and systematic disciplines," and as such should be treated along with polemics and the like as a theological discipline, either systematic or practical.[19] But apologetics is a theoretical discipline that seeks to establish the reality of the subject matter with which all theology, including the study of apology, is concerned. "So soon as it is agreed that theology is a scientific discipline and has as its subject-matter the knowledge of God, we must recognize that it must begin by establishing the reality as objective facts of the data upon which it is based."[20]

Insofar as the unbeliever is invited to examine the apologetic argument for the truth of the fundamental claims and principles of Christian theology, this view of apologetics has generally been associated with a high view of human reason even after the Fall. Classical apologists do subscribe to the biblical doctrine of the Fall and the resulting effects of sin on human thinking, but they generally argue that human depravity cannot have completely debilitated the capacity of human reason to understand God's truth. Man is in need of the grace of God to respond to special revelation, but he is capable of understanding general revelation to a considerable extent and can formulate rational arguments to prove the existence of God. Moreover, the non-Christian is capable of understanding that such rational arguments cannot enable him to know God personally, much less savingly, and therefore to recognize that special, redeeming revelation from God is needed.

The crucial point here is that for the classical apologist, theology is a discipline to which people are invited *after* becoming Christians. Thus he seeks to keep theological questions of controversy among Christians on the back burner in apologetic arguments directed to non-Christians. C. S. Lewis was typical of many classical apologists in that he understood the task of apologetics to be defending the basic message of "mere Christianity" and not arguing for one theological or denominational tradition within Christianity. "Our divisions should never be discussed except in the presence of those who have already come to believe that there is one God and that Jesus Christ is His only Son."[21] Lewis acknowledged that the theological issues that divide Christians may be important, but the apologist as such should not be concerned to press one viewpoint on those issues: "Each of us has his individual emphasis: each holds, in addition to the Faith, many opinions which seem to him to be consistent with it and true and important. And so perhaps they are. But as apologists it is not our business to defend *them*. We are defending Christianity, not 'my religion.'"[22]

THE CONSTRUCTIVE USE OF PHILOSOPHY

Norman Geisler's thinking has been greatly influenced by the work of Aquinas, and his apologetic system reflects a modified version of Thomistic philosophy. Thus he believes that Christian theology is not inimical to philosophy but can be expressed within the context of a metaphysical system. In their textbook on philosophy Geisler and co-author Paul Feinberg assert that "philosophy serves in the construction of the Christian system and in the refutation of contrary views" (73).[23] They quote with approval C. S. Lewis's statement that "good philosophy must exist, if for no other reason, because bad philosophy needs to be answered" (74).[24] Philosophy is the necessary prerequisite to systematic theology and to apologetics, because both require "the philosophical tools of clear, consistent, and correct thinking" (76). Apologetics "involves the construction of good arguments or the supplying of good evidence in justification of the basic truth of Christianity. . . . This task falls squarely on the shoulders of philosophy." Philosophy is also necessary to the task of polemics and to the effort of communicating the Christian worldview. Geisler does not believe that the "glasses" of one's non-Christian worldview are cemented to one's face and can be removed only by a supernatural conversion, but he does acknowledge that people view things according to the models or paradigms they have embraced. "One task of Christian philosophy, then, is to work on a pre-evangelistic level to get the outsider to look around the edges or through the cracks of his glasses, or to take them off and try a set of 'theistic glasses' on for size. Philosophy performs the process indicated by these metaphors through philosophical argumentation" (78).

Stuart Hackett, an evangelical philosopher whose students included William Lane Craig, identified philosophy with apologetics perhaps as forcefully as anyone has. Hackett notes that philosophy deals with such questions as the possibility of knowledge (epistemology), the ultimate nature of reality (metaphysics), and our proper conduct in the light of reality (ethics). He then suggests that apologetics also seeks to defend a particular set of answers to these questions. "In this broad sense, apologetics is practically coextensive with the whole philosophical enterprise: it is not merely a defense—it is rather a defense of conclusions which the rational analysis of human experience fully justifies."[25]

The importance of philosophy to classical apologetics is emphatically affirmed in J. P. Moreland and William Lane Craig's textbook, *Philosophical Foundations for a Christian Worldview*.[26] "One of the awesome tasks of Christian philosophers is to help turn the contemporary intellectual tide in such a way as to foster a sociocultural milieu in which Christian faith can be regarded as an intellectually credible option for thinking men and women" (2). Of all the disciplines in the university curriculum, philosophy "is the most foundational of the disciplines, since it examines the presuppositions and ramifications of every discipline at the university—including itself!" (3). Philosophy is important for Christians, first of all, as "an aid in the task of apologetics" (14). "When an objection against

Christianity comes from some discipline of study, that objection almost always involves the use of philosophy" (15).

CHRISTIANITY CONSISTENT WITH SCIENCE

Classical apologists generally try to maintain a balanced view of science, neither uncritically endorsing it nor hypercritically rejecting it. They believe apologists should seek to show that Christianity is consistent with the scientific facts, and that this usually, though not always, includes comparing what Christianity says about the world and mankind with what current scientific theorists have concluded. But scientists can be wrong, and the way science is applied by both scientists and nonscientists often leads to error. This means that Christians should be cautious about endorsing current scientific theory too uncritically, as theories change. B. B. Warfield issued a warning to that effect: "Science, philosophy, scholarship, represent not stable but constantly changing entities. And nothing is more certain than that the theology which is in close harmony with the science, philosophy, and scholarship of today will be much out of harmony with the science, philosophy, and scholarship of tomorrow."[27]

Such caution is typical of classical apologetics. One must indeed use the most current findings by scholars and scientists, but at the same time their findings are not to be accepted uncritically. This point appears repeatedly in the writings of C. S. Lewis. For example, he observed:

> Science is in continual change and we must try to keep abreast of it. For the same reason, we must be very cautious of snatching at any scientific theory which, for the moment, seems to be in our favour. We may *mention* such things; but we must mention them lightly and without claiming that they are more than "interesting." Sentences beginning "Science has now proved" should be avoided. If we try to base our apologetic on some recent development in science, we shall usually find that just as we have put the finishing touches to our argument science has changed its mind and quietly withdrawn the theory we have been using as our foundation stone.[28]

This does not mean that we may not appeal to scientific evidence for Christian truth claims, merely that we must present this evidence with due caution. Lewis exemplifies the approach he here recommends in another place when he applies modern scientific theories about the beginning of the universe to the cosmological argument:

> If anything emerges clearly from modern physics, it is that nature is not everlasting. The universe had a beginning, and will have an end. But the great materialistic systems of the past all believed in the eternity, and thence in the self-existence of matter. . . . This fundamental ground for materialism has now been withdrawn. We should not lean too heavily on this, for scientific theories change. But at the moment it appears that the burden of proof rests, not on us, but on those who deny that nature has some cause beyond herself.[29]

The sum of the matter is that Lewis is confident scientific breakthroughs will not change the situation radically with respect to the scientific credibility of Christianity. They may lend some support to the Christian faith, but one must be careful not to exaggerate this support naively. In any case, science will not disprove Christian teachings.

> Each new discovery, even every new theory, is held at first to have the most wide-reaching theological and philosophical consequences. It is seized by unbelievers as the basis for a new attack on Christianity; it is often, and more embarrassingly, seized by injudicious believers as the basis for a new defence.

> But usually, when the popular hubbub has subsided and the novelty has been chewed over by real theologians, real scientists and real philosophers, both sides find themselves pretty much where they were before. So it was with Copernican astronomy, with Darwinism, with Biblical Criticism, with the new psychology.[30]

Norman Geisler, while finding much value in the scientific evidence for the creation and design of the universe and for the creation of life and of mankind, is likewise cautious about overstating the case. "Since science is limited and progressive, we should not expect complete agreement in every detail with the biblical presentation. However, the amount of present agreement is striking."[31] He warns that "scientific evidence by its nature does not yield full proof of things, except on a very limited, material level in some controlled situations." He concludes that "one must temper dogmatism about scientific arguments. Perhaps it is simply sufficient to say that the prevailing view in the scientific community presents evidence that strongly supports what Christians have always believed on biblical (and some even on philosophical) grounds. . . ."[32]

On the basis of this stance toward science, evangelical apologists during the hundred years following the publication of Charles Darwin's *Origin of Species* tended to give cautious, qualified acceptance of the theory of evolution while rejecting naturalistic evolutionism as a philosophical dogma rather than a scientific theory. So conservative a theologian and apologist as B. B. Warfield accepted the theory of evolution and argued that it could be reconciled with Scripture. Yet Warfield was critical of Darwinism as a philosophy, and wrote articles specifically on Darwin and the religious implications of his work.[33]

While C. S. Lewis was not opposed to the scientific theory of evolution, which deals with change within limits, he took issue with what he called the myth of popular evolutionism. "To the biologist Evolution is a hypothesis. It covers more of the facts than any other hypothesis at present on the market and is therefore to be accepted unless, or until, some new supposal can be shown to cover still more facts with even fewer assumptions. . . . In the Myth, however, there is nothing hypothetical about it: it is basic fact: or, to speak more strictly, such distinctions do not exist on the mythical level at all." Lewis puts his finger on the humanistic, philosophical belief of evolutionism when he concludes: "In the science, Evolution is a theory about *changes:* in the Myth it is a fact about *improvements.*"[34]

Although Lewis has been enormously popular among evangelicals, most evangelical apologists since his time have not followed him in accepting theistic evolution. Since about 1960, evangelical apologists have tended to reject theistic evolution as a serious option and have instead argued for some form of creationism. Classical apologists, though, have generally expressed a greater degree of openness to other modern scientific theories. These include the belief that the universe is billions of years old instead of the thousands of years posited by young-earth creationists. Both Geisler and Craig have endorsed the old-earth view, though Geisler more tentatively than Craig.[35]

J. P. Moreland has for many years engaged in the most sophisticated analysis by any classical apologist of the nature of science and of its relation to Christian theological truths. He has, in fact, written an entire book and numerous articles on the subject.[36] The burden of Moreland's extensive research and writing on science and Christianity may be summed up under four headings.

First, he argues against naturalism and especially scientism that science can legitimately be practiced within the framework of a theistic worldview. *Scientism*, or what philosopher of science John Kekes calls "scientific imperialism," is the belief that science alone yields genuine knowledge or truth. Moreland argues that scientism is self-refuting because the claim that science alone produces truth is not learned scientifically.[37] He documents extensively the various sorts of limits to science that preclude any sort of scientism.[38] The refutation of scientism and its presupposed worldview of naturalism opens the door to theism as a proper worldview context in which science may be practiced.

Second, Moreland urges caution in assuming a naively realist view of science. Although he thinks "a scientific theory should be understood along realist lines in the absence of sufficient evidence to the contrary," he cautions that in some instances we should be reticent to grant that a scientific theory describes reality as it actually is.[39] If the theory attempts to explain in totality phenomena that lie outside the proper domain of science, or if it conflicts with a rationally well established conclusion about reality, then the theory should be viewed as a construct that does not describe reality itself.[40] This "eclectic" approach to scientific theories gives methodological rigor to the classical apologists' characteristically cautious acceptance of scientific theories and developments.

Third, Moreland explores the various models for relating science and theology and explains why the two fields should be viewed as overlapping. Over against those who would "protect" religion or faith from science by relegating theology to the realm of values or spiritual matters, he insists that theology does deal with some aspects of the physical world (such as its creation by God). Thus "science and theology really do interact on common ground,"[41] and effort must be made to reconcile or integrate science and theology.[42]

Fourth, Moreland argues that creationism can be a legitimate idea within the discipline of science. His main contention here is that science should not be defined in such a way as to exclude creationism *a priori* from the discipline of science. For example, he argues that the definition of science affirmed in Judge William R. Overton's 1981 decision in the Little Rock creationism trial assumed both naturalism (the belief that nature is all that exists) and a naive view of the nature of science.[43] He concludes that other arguments designed to prove that creationism cannot be science (regardless of the evidence!) misunderstand the nature of creationism as well as assume an erroneous view of science.[44] He has also argued that a careful study of Genesis and of the biological facts shows that creationism, at least of a generic form, is reconcilable with the physical evidence as well as consistent with Scripture.[45] Although he shows an openness to young-earth creationist arguments, Moreland appears to lean toward an old-earth position, freely drawing on modern cosmology for evidence of the beginning and intelligent design of the universe.[46]

Moreland's approach to science well illustrates the central method of classical apologetics. His objections to scientism and naturalism, as well as to definitions of science that exclude creationism, focus on the question-begging and self-defeating nature of these positions.

REVELATION CONFIRMED IN HISTORY

According to classical apologists, history is important to apologetics because it is in history that God has revealed himself. As Warfield explained, Christianity is not a religion of "ideas," that is, of timeless, "eternal verities," but is rather "a religion of fact."

> A God who is only an idea, and who never intervenes in the world of fact, can never actually save a soul that is real from sin that is real. For the actual salvation of an actual sin-stricken soul we require an actual Redeemer who has actually intervened in the actual course of history. . . . Christianity is a historical religion, all of whose doctrines are facts. He who assaults the trustworthiness of the record of the intervention of God for the redemption of the world, is simply assaulting the heart of Christianity.[47]

To show that Christianity is rational, then, it is necessary to show that God has revealed himself in history—specifically as recorded in Scripture. But logically, before that can be shown, one must know that it is possible for God to have revealed himself to us in history. At this point the modern apologist confronts the question of whether historical knowledge is even possible. The notion of historical relativism has been around for a while, but it has gained fresh strength in the wake of postmodernism and its dictum that all knowledge, including historical knowledge, is relative and subjective. Moreover, even if the possibility of historical knowledge is admitted, many skeptics argue that we cannot have such knowledge of alleged miracles.

In his *Christian Apologetics*, Geisler addresses the supposed subjectivity of historical knowledge by arguing that scientific knowledge is conceded to be possible despite the subjective dimensions of the scientific enterprise. He admits that "no human historian can be objective" if this is defined to mean possessing absolute knowledge. But historians can have an objective view of the past if this is understood to mean "a *fair but revisable* presentation." In this sense, "it can be argued that history can be just as objective as some sciences" (290).[48] The very fact that we are able to distinguish "between propaganda and history" proves that history is not "entirely in the mind of the beholder" (291).

Geisler denies that "facts speak for themselves" if this is taken to mean "that facts bear only *one* meaning and that they bear it evidently." He agrees that "there are no so-called bare facts," but insists that the meaning that facts bear is assigned to them by minds and does not emanate from the facts themselves (291).

> Finite minds may give differing interpretations of them or an infinite Mind may give an absolute interpretation of them, but there is no one objective interpretation a finite mind can give them. Of course, if there is an absolute Mind from whose vantage point the facts are given absolute or ultimate meaning, then there is an objective interpretation of the facts which all finite minds should concur is the ultimate meaning. If theism is the correct world view . . . then there is an objective meaning to all facts in the world. All facts are theistic facts, and no nontheistic way of interpreting them is objective or true. (292)[49]

For Geisler, then, the objectivity of all knowledge of facts, including knowledge of history, rests on the truth of the theistic worldview. If God exists, then all facts are what they are because God says so, and we have true or objective knowledge insofar as we accept the meaning of the facts as given by God. Arguments for the theistic worldview, then, come logically prior to arguments about historical fact, since our objective knowledge of those facts depends on our considering them within the context of the correct worldview.

Likewise, Geisler argues that the fact that historians inevitably make selective use of materials to construct their interpretations of the past does not make objectivity impossible, but it does make it important that events be seen in the right context. Ultimately this means that the *meaning* of events cannot be interpreted "without assuming an overall hypothesis or world view by which the events are interpreted" (293). "Hence, the problem of objective meaning of history, like the problem of objective meaning in science, is dependent on one's Weltanschauung [worldview]" (294). For the classical apologist, the truth of the theistic worldview can and should be established prior to considering the historical facts pertaining to Christianity, making objective knowledge of those facts possible.

PROOF FROM EXPERIENCE

Classical apologists do not build their case for theism primarily on religious experience. However, they recognize that the Christian faith does not call people merely to believe that God exists, but rather to experience a personal relationship with God. The biblical concept of God is not only infinite and transcendent but also personal and immanent. The Christian faith is based on revelation from this infinite-personal God, and there can be no awareness of a revelation that is not experienced. Thus, if theism is to be defended as more than an academic theory, it is necessary to defend the validity and rationality of religious experience. For this reason classical apologists take pains to argue that it is rational to believe that people can have experiences of God and that these experiences can result in an immediate knowledge of God.

In Part One of *Philosophy of Religion*, Norman Geisler and Winfried Corduan offer three main arguments in defense of religious experience. First, *religious experience is unique*—it differs radically from moral or aesthetic types of experience. Moral experience, for example, unlike religious experience, cannot overcome failure and guilt. Aesthetic experience may produce wonder and admiration but not worship and adoration (18–24).[50]

Second, *the religious impulse, if not religious experience per se, is universal.* Classical apologists contend that the universality of religious experience across centuries and cultures points to a basic human drive toward self-transcendence. Even those who claim not to be religious betray their desire for the transcendent. Geisler and Corduan observe that "humans are incurably religious. When one way to transcend is cut off, people find another. . . . The sacred or secular history of humanity supports the thesis that by nature a person has an irresistible urge to transcend himself" (61).

Classical Christian apologists affirm that to be real, this transcendental urge must be more than a subjective projection or wish fulfillment; it must have an objective and independent basis in something real. The universality of this need, illustrated by such diverse thinkers as Freud, Schleiermacher, Heidegger, Tillich, Sartre, Beckett, Kafka, Nietzsche, Hume, and Kant, is itself proof for many classical apologists that the transcendent exists. They maintain that the premise that "what human beings really need really exists" is based on the experience of human expectations and the potentiality for all human needs to be met (74). "Some people may think that needs are real but cannot be fulfilled; few people (if any) will really believe it, and no person can consistently live with that belief" (75). Skeptics may deny that the human need for transcendence can be fulfilled, but no one can live consistently with the logical implications of a universe devoid of the divine (no ultimate meaning, purpose, value). Even atheists generally admit the human need to transcend, though they allow no object to fulfill this need.

Third, *religious experience is too ubiquitous to be explained away.* Geisler and Corduan reason that the evidential value of religious experience could only be discounted by making the radical claim that every person in the history of the world who claimed to have a religious experience has been totally deceived. Since this would be an onerous claim to prove, the conclusion that some reality exists that corresponds to the universal need for transcendence stands. Thus there must be a basis in reality for at least some religious experience. "For if even one religious person is right about the reality of the Transcendent, then there really is a Transcendent. It seems much more likely that such self-analyzing and self-critical men as Augustine, Blaise Pascal, and Kierkegaard were not totally deceived than that total skepticism is right" (76).

In his debates with atheists, William Lane Craig routinely ends his opening statements by affirming that human beings can not only know about God's existence but can also know God by experience. However, he cautions, "This isn't really an *argument* for God's existence. Rather, it's the claim that you can know that God exists wholly apart from arguments, simply by immediately experiencing Him. . . . For those who listen, God becomes an immediate reality in their lives."[51] His purpose in citing the experience of God, then, is not "to hold forth my experience as evidence to others of God's existence, but to invite others" to experience God.[52]

For Further Study

Geisler, Norman L., and J. Kerby Anderson. *Origin Science: A Proposal for the Creation-Evolution Controversy.* Grand Rapids: Baker, 1987. Geisler's major contribution to a Christian view of science.

Geisler, Norman L., and Ronald M. Brooks. *Come, Let Us Reason: An Introduction to Logical Thinking.* Grand Rapids: Baker, 1990. A textbook on logic, with numerous illustrations of the application of deductive reasoning in apologetics and theology.

Hoffecker, W. Andrew. *Piety and the Princeton Theologians: Archibald Alexander, Charles Hodge, and Benjamin Warfield*. Grand Rapids: Baker, 1981. Explores the view of spiritual experience taken by Old Princeton.

Moreland, J. P. *Christianity and the Nature of Science: A Philosophical Investigation*. Grand Rapids: Baker, 1989. In-depth discussion of a Christian view of science by a classical apologist with training in science (see also Moreland, *Scaling the Secular City*, 185-223).

_____. *Love Your God with All Your Mind: The Role of Reason in the Life of the Soul*. Colorado Springs: NavPress, 1997. On the importance of developing a Christian mind for personal growth, evangelism, apologetics, and worship.

_____, and William Lane Craig. *Philosophical Foundations for a Christian Worldview*. Downers Grove, Ill.: InterVarsity, 2003. Two leading classical apologists team together in a massive textbook treating the nature of philosophy, epistemology, philosophy of science, and other subjects relevant to apologetics.

Chapter 6

The Rationality of the Christian Worldview

Classical apologists seek to show that the Christian worldview is rational or reasonable and therefore worthy of belief. The characteristic approach they take to accomplish this task is a two-step or two-stage argument. First, classical apologists seek to demonstrate that theism—the general type of worldview that affirms the existence of one personal Creator God and that is associated historically with Judaism, Islam, and Christianity—is true. Arguments of a deductive logical structure—"proofs" in the usual strict sense—are typical of this stage, although many apologists in this tradition also use empirical arguments (especially for creation) and claim only to show that there are good reasons to think that God exists. In the second step or stage of the apologetic, the classical apologist argues that, given the existence of God, the evidence for Jesus Christ and the inspiration of the Bible are sufficient to show that Christianity is true. At this stage the arguments are usually more inductive, and in fact are typically identical to the sorts of arguments used by evidentialists in regards to such subjects as the resurrection of Christ.

William Lane Craig explains the method in just this way. He acknowledges that the main argument he favors in support of belief in God does not prove everything we might like about God, but is rather proof "simply of a Personal Creator of the universe, and then the argument can proceed from there."

> Has this Creator remained distant and aloof from the world that he has made, or has he revealed himself more fully to humankind that we might know him more completely? Here one moves to the claims of Jesus of Nazareth to be the unique personal revelation of such a Creator. It will

then be the Christian evidentialist's turn to take over the oars from the natural theologian.[1]

SCRIPTURE AS CONCLUSION

One of the most fundamental questions concerning apologetic method is the role that Scripture plays in apologetic argument. In general, classical apologists seek to make the existence of Scripture as a body of inspired and authoritative writings *the conclusion of the whole apologetic.*

For example, B. B. Warfield argued that the inspiration and inerrancy of Scripture were the conclusion toward which apologetics worked, not its presupposition or starting point. "In dealing with sceptics it is not proper to begin with the evidence which immediately establishes Inspiration, but we should first establish Theism, then the historical credibility of the Scriptures, and then the divine origin of Christianity." On the basis of the divine origin of Christianity, one may then go on to argue for the inspiration of Scripture.[2]

Warfield's placement of Scripture at the end of the apologetic argument is reflected explicitly in the structure of some textbooks on apologetics from a classical approach. Norman Geisler's *Christian Apologetics* is a perfect example.[3] Geisler discusses apologetic methodology in Part One and argues for the existence of God in Part Two. In Part Three he presents an apologetic for Christianity per se, beginning with a defense of the belief in the supernatural (chapter 14) and continuing with a defense of the possibility of knowing that God had intervened supernaturally in history (15). Next, Geisler defends the historical reliability of the New Testament (16) as a prelude to giving an argument for the deity and authority of Christ (17). Only after all this has been established does he conclude with a final chapter on the inspiration and authority of the Bible (18). "The evidence that the Bible is the written word of God is anchored in the authority of Jesus Christ."[4] As we saw in our overview of Geisler's apologetic in chapter 4, the inspiration of Scripture is the twelfth point in his 12-point argument for Christianity.

In treating the authority of Scripture as the conclusion toward which an apologetic is directed, classical apologists seek to avoid begging the question by assuming the authority of Scripture in apologetic arguments directed to unbelievers. These apologists argue that "reason must judge the credentials of any alleged revelation."[5] Doing so is not seen as arrogant or impious because, classical apologists explain, God gave us our faculty of reason and directed his revelation to it. Therefore God expects us to employ our reasoning abilities both to recognize his true revelation and to detect the fraudulent revelations of other religions. As Stephen Neill put it: "Reason is not the affirmation of the arrogant autonomy of man, fashioning a universe according to his own ideas. It is that faculty in man which makes it possible for him to receive the revelation of God, to receive revelation in the form of the Word of God. But, to receive it, he must be humble, and ready to listen to God, whenever and however He speaks."[6]

Classical apologists believe that human beings are responsible to use their reasoning faculties to "test the spirits to see whether they are from God" (1 John 4:1). They deny that testing revelations from God is a manifestation of human autonomy that elevates the mind as the final authority for truth. Rather, just as it is reasonable to look for credentials before submitting to a human authority in any given field, so it is reasonable to submit to the authority of revelation once it is shown to be well founded on the basis of God-given rationality. As Gordon R. Lewis argues, "To be responsible before the Bible, the unbeliever must have enough judgment to know why he should determine his lifestyle by Scripture rather than the Koran or the Book of Mormon. The use of systematic consistency to distinguish the Bible from the Koran in no way detracts from the Bible's authority. It verifies the Bible's claim above all competitors."[7]

Negatively, classical apologists seek to refute common objections to biblical inspiration. This refutation involves both direct answers to specific objections and observations about the assumptions or presuppositions of those who reject biblical inspiration or inerrancy. Geisler, for example, in *Inerrancy*, a book he edited for the International Council on Biblical Inerrancy, contributed a chapter entitled "Philosophical Presuppositions of Biblical Errancy." There he examines the modern neoevangelical drift from the historical biblical doctrine of inerrancy. He traces the current crisis in biblical authority to philosophical presuppositions derived from various unbiblical philosophies.[8] Geisler's thesis is that "contemporary neoevangelical denials of inerrancy borrow from one or more of these alien and unjustified philosophical presuppositions."[9] The solution to such antibiblical presuppositions, for classical apologists like Geisler, is to reexamine the worldviews of those who hold them and make the case for a theistic worldview in which the inspiration and inerrancy of Scripture will not be philosophically scandalous.

DISPROVING OTHER WORLDVIEWS

A **worldview** is the sum of a person's basic assumptions, held consciously or subconsciously, about life and the nature of reality. These assumptions or presuppositions are sometimes "only brought to mind when challenged by a foreigner from another ideological universe."[10] Classical apologists generally maintain that while there may be many internal variations, the actual number of basic worldviews is quite limited. James W. Sire catalogs and contrasts several of these in *The Universe Next Door*, and then comments:

> The fact is that while worldviews at first appear to proliferate, they are made up of answers to questions which have only a limited number of answers. For example, to the question of prime reality, only two basic answers can be given: Either it is the universe that is self-existent and has always existed, or it is a transcendent God who is self-existent and has always existed. Theism and deism claim the latter; naturalism, Eastern pantheistic monism, New Age thought and postmodernism claim the former.[11]

There are different ways of categorizing worldviews because of areas of overlap. Sire devotes separate chapters to eight basic worldviews: Christian theism, deism, naturalism, nihilism, existentialism, Eastern pantheistic monism, the New Age, and postmodernism.[12] Norman Geisler and William Watkins in *Worlds Apart*, another evangelical overview of worldviews, distinguish seven worldviews, and their list differs in some respects from Sire's (deism, pantheism, panentheism, finite godism, polytheism, atheism, and theism). There is more overlap here than may meet the eye: Sire's naturalism is the same worldview as atheism, and nihilism and existentialism are philosophies that seek to apply the atheistic worldview to human life. Moreover, pantheism includes both Eastern pantheistic monism and the New Age. Narrowing the options enables the apologist to show non-Christians the fundamental choices that need to be made. Once they realize there are only a few basic worldviews, the excuse that there are so many beliefs in the world drops away.

One way classical apologists demonstrate that the number of worldview choices is finite and manageable is by presenting the major worldviews as the conclusions to a series of choices between two opposing alternatives. Doing so also allows the apologist to identify the critical issues that need to be addressed in choosing a worldview. Here again the classical approach's characteristic emphasis on logic is evident. The following chart presents this schema.[13]

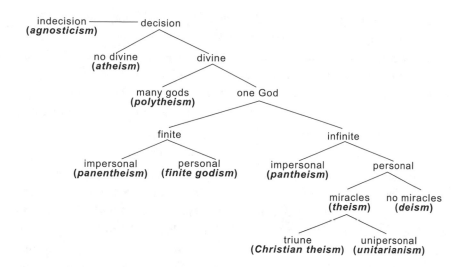

C. S. Lewis reduced the number of worldviews even further, to three. In broad terms, he held that most if not all people hold to some variation of three views of reality: materialism or atheism, Hinduism (of which Buddhism was a simplification), and Christianity (of which Islam was a simplification). For Lewis, the best options could be narrowed down to Hinduism and Christianity, and from there to Christianity alone because of the person and work of Christ.[14]

Having narrowed the worldview options to a manageable number, whether two, three, seven, or more, the classical apologist then examines the alternatives to theism in order to show that they are to be rejected. The basic strategy here is to show that these other worldviews are rationally incoherent. Other considerations may also be pressed (for example, that they are in conflict with specific facts, or that they are unlivable), but the characteristic emphasis of the classical approach to refuting non-Christian worldviews is to show that such worldviews are logically self-contradictory or self-refuting.

If nontheistic worldviews can be eliminated and theism established as the most credible one, this would reduce the number of viable world religions to three: Judaism, Christianity, and Islam. The classical apologist can then point to various evidences that Christianity is the true fulfillment of original (Old Testament) Judaism and that both Judaism and Islam fail to reckon adequately with the claims of Christ.

Although classical apologists argue that non-Christian religions as well as worldviews are false, they do not claim they are false in every respect. Rather, they typically argue that non-Christian belief systems incorporate significant truths, but also contain grave errors about God and his relation to the world, and so in the end must be deemed inadequate. Thus non-Christian belief systems do contain truth, but as a whole their final answers to life's most fundamental questions are false. Again, the reason for acknowledging truth in other belief systems can be seen graphically from the worldviews chart: most of the worldviews clearly do make one or more right choices.

For example, C. S. Lewis frequently asserted that other religions contained much truth. "And it should (at least in my judgment) be made clear that we are not pronouncing all other religions totally false, but rather saying that in Christ whatever is true in all religions is consummated and perfected."[15] Geisler is careful to note positive features of such worldviews as pantheism, deism, and even atheism before presenting his critical arguments against those beliefs.[16] The Calvinist theologian B. B. Warfield showed himself consistent with the classical tradition when he made much the same point as Lewis:

> Christianity does not stand in an exclusively antithetical relation to other religions. There is a high and true sense in which it is also their fulfilment. All that enters into the essence of religion is present in them no less than in it, although in a less pure form. They too possess the idea of God, the consciousness of guilt, the longing for redemption: they too possess offerings, priesthood, temples, worship, prayer. Israel's Promise, Christianity's Possession, is also the Desire of all nations.[17]

The classical approach to refuting these non-Christian worldviews may be illustrated with pantheism. Most nontheistic religions have affirmed one of the many forms of **pantheism**, all of which in some way identify or equate God with the All—so that God is in some sense the ultimate and only Reality. Pantheism is closely related to **monism**, according to which reality is ultimately one and not many, a unity rather than a plurality. The rediscovery of Eastern (particularly Indian) culture and the promulgation of Eastern thought in the West have stimulated pantheistic thinking in Western culture, notably in what has come to be known as the New Age movement.

Geisler notes that pantheism is a comprehensive philosophy that focuses on the unity of reality and seeks to acknowledge the immanence and absolute nature of God. In spite of these positive insights, pantheism is an inadequate worldview because "it is actually unaffirmable by man."[18] Specifically, it is self-defeating for a pantheist to claim that individual finite selves are less than real. To assert "*I* believe that *I* am not an individual" is to utter a self-refuting statement (because it assumes the existence of the individual who says "I" while at the same time denying it). Pantheism wrongly assumes "that whatever is not really ultimate is not ultimately or actually real."[19] Pantheism also cannot adequately account for evil (its assertion that evil is an illusion is meaningless, since pain that is felt is real), and it is unable even to distinguish good from evil (since in theory all is one, nothing can be evil as opposed to good). Geisler also argues that to say that God and the universe are one says nothing meaningful about God and is indistinguishable from atheism.[20]

PROVING GOD'S EXISTENCE

Disproving nontheistic worldviews and philosophies of life does not necessarily prove theism. Classical apologists, therefore, offer a variety of arguments in support of theism.

The complexity of religious knowledge, and the fact that it concerns a transcendent reality, makes proving God's existence quite complex. There is considerable disagreement among apologists over the value and relevance of the theistic proofs. Immanuel Kant's critique of the traditional theistic proofs continues to be influential, and most philosophers and theologians have moved away from the scholastic mentality of solid and unequivocal arguments for God's existence. Classical apologists, while upholding the validity of most or all of the traditional theistic proofs, are generally more cautious about how compelling they are. They believe that arguments for God's existence can show the reasonableness of belief in God even though they may be less than definitive or not persuasive to everyone.

In brief, four major arguments for God's existence have dominated classical apologetics. The first is the **ontological argument**. First formulated in explicit terms by the eleventh-century philosopher Anselm of Canterbury, this argument reasons from the idea of God as the greatest, most perfect, or necessary being to the existence of that God. The second and third theistic arguments have ancient roots but received their classical formulation from Thomas Aquinas in the thirteenth century, and are known as the cosmological and teleological arguments. The **cosmological argument** reasons from the existence of the world (Greek, *cosmos*) to the existence of God. The **teleological argument** (from the Greek *telos*, "goal") reasons from the evidence of design in the world to the existence of God as the one who created things with a specific purpose or goal. The fourth major theistic argument emerged in modern times and is the **moral argument**, which reasons from the objectivity and absolute character of moral judgments to the existence of a transcendent God as the ground of morality.

One of the most vigorous twentieth-century defenses of the theistic proofs is *The Resurrection of Theism*, by the evangelical classical apologist Stuart Hackett. In this book Hackett defends the cosmological and teleological arguments specifically against Kant's criticisms. He concludes that the traditional arguments for God lead "to the firm conclusion that theism alone actually poses a solution to the metaphysical problem."[21]

Respect among philosophers for the traditional theistic arguments was at an all-time low for much of the twentieth century. In the late 1960s the Calvinist philosopher Alvin Plantinga helped revive serious interest among professional philosophers in the ontological argument. And in the early 1980s a detailed defense of the cosmological argument by the evangelical classical apologist William Lane Craig (a student of Hackett) prompted philosophers to take it far more seriously as well. The seriousness with which these and other theistic proofs are now viewed can be seen by reviewing academic philosophy journals such as *Religious Studies* and the *International Journal of Philosophy and Religion*.

Classical apologists are careful to issue certain caveats about the use of theistic proofs. One such caveat is that the theistic arguments as they are popularly understood are often invalid; that is, they need to be formulated carefully and rigorously if they are to be valid. Second, most people actually do not need to hear theistic arguments, since they are not atheists. What they need is evidence that God is the kind of God found in Scripture. [22]

Another caveat, issued by classical apologetics in the Calvinist tradition, is that theistic arguments remind unbelievers of what they already know but have been trying to deny. Warfield, for example, argued that from one perspective everyone already has knowledge of God, though most do not own up to it. People cannot be completely ignorant of God, although they can completely ignore God.[23] We cannot escape all awareness of God. "God is part of our environment."[24] The arguments, though, are still useful and valid.

> This immediate perception of God is confirmed and the contents of the idea developed by a series of arguments known as the "theistic proofs." These are derived from the necessity we are under of believing in the

real existence of the infinitely perfect Being, of a sufficient cause for the contingent universe, of an intelligent author of the order and of the manifold contrivances observable in nature, and of a lawgiver and judge for dependent moral beings. . . . The cogency of these proofs is currently recognized in the Scriptures, while they add to them the supernatural manifestations of God in a redemptive process, accompanied at every stage by miraculous attestation. From the theistic proofs, however, we learn not only that a God exists, but also necessarily, on the principle of a sufficient cause, very much of the nature of the God which they prove to exist.[25]

We will now consider three of the four major theistic arguments, focusing on their classical formulation as philosophical proofs for God's existence. (The teleological argument will be discussed in chapter 10.) Because of its continuing importance in the classical apologetic tradition, the cosmological argument will receive special attention.

The Moral Argument

The moral argument can be viewed as one aspect of a larger argument for God's existence known as the anthropological argument. This broader argument reasons from specific aspects of human nature to the existence of God, and includes arguments from morality, aesthetics, human thought and reason,[26] and the need for meaning, purpose, and hope.

The **moral argument** relates to the universality of moral experience and holds that unless there is a God, there is no ultimate basis for moral law. Classical apologists answer the objection that ethical judgments vary from place to place by arguing that, regardless of time or culture, there is a built-in concept of normative conduct, a universal sense of "ought" and "should." It is true that people can acknowledge the moral law without seeing this as a theistic proof, but this does not mean that such a law could have real validity apart from God. The real thrust of this argument lies in the fact that when people express approval or criticism of the actions of others, they are behaving as if theism were true, that is, as if there are such things as absolute rights and absolute wrongs.[27] Classical apologists typically argue that one would have to assume this position in order to criticize it as wrong.

A good example of the moral argument in classical apologetics is the opening section of C. S. Lewis's *Mere Christianity*. Lewis begins that book by noting that human beings have the idea that they ought to behave in certain ways—what Lewis calls the Law of Human Nature—and yet they do not behave in those ways (26).[28] After arguing that this Law is real and does not derive from human beings themselves but is instead "something above and beyond the ordinary facts of men's behaviour" (30), he asks what lies behind the Law. "We want to know whether the universe simply happens to be what it is for no reason or whether there is a power behind it that makes it what it is" (33). The Law shows us that there is such "a Power behind the facts, a Director, a Guide" (34). Lewis hastens to caution, "We have not yet got as far as the God of any actual religion, still less the God of that particular religion called Christianity. We have only got as far as a Somebody or Something behind the Moral Law. We are not taking anything from the Bible or the Churches, we are trying to see what we can find out about this Somebody on our own steam" (37). Lewis goes on to argue that we can infer that this Somebody is rather like a mind, one unyielding in his moral expectations of us, and one whose expectations we have failed to meet (37–38). This strategy of formulating an argument for a general notion of God prior to introducing specific Christian claims is characteristic of the classical approach.

The Ontological Argument

The **ontological argument** is the only philosophical theistic proof that reasons in a purely *a priori* fashion (from certain assumptions or ideas as given). The first form of this argument as developed by Anselm was largely ignored until René Descartes revived it in the seventeenth century. The Cartesian formulation was later refuted by Kant, but it continues to resurface in contemporary philosophy of religion, along with Anselm's second form, which adds the concept of necessary existence. Influential advocates of some form of the ontological argument have included Charles Hartshorne (a process theologian who uses it to support a panentheist worldview) and Alvin Plantinga (a Reformed philosopher).[29]

There are many forms of the ontological argument, some too technical to discuss here. Perhaps one of the simplest forms (if any of them may be called simple) is based on Anselm's second version of the argument as restated by various modern philosophers.[30]

1. The existence of a necessary Being must be either (a) a necessary existence, (b) an impossible existence, or (c) a possible but not necessary existence.

2. But the existence of a necessary Being is not an impossible existence because (so far as we can see) there is nothing contradictory about this concept.
3. Nor is the existence of a necessary Being a possible but not necessary existence, since this would be a self-contradictory claim.
4. Therefore, the existence of a necessary Being is a necessary existence.
5. Therefore, a necessary Being necessarily exists.

Although classical apologists employ a wide variety of arguments for God's existence, most do not accept the ontological argument. Most apologists and philosophers continue to accept the rebuttal that the ontological argument commits the fallacy of deducing the existence of God from the concept of God. For example, the formulation given above can be criticized by alleging that all point 4 means is that *if* a necessary Being exists, his existence must be a necessary existence. This still leaves open whether a necessary Being exists in the first place. Most classical apologists concur with Geisler's conclusion: "No valid ontological proof has been given that makes it rationally inescapable to conclude that there is a necessary Being."[31]

The Cosmological Argument

The **cosmological argument** reasons from the nature of the world as temporal and contingent to the conclusion that an eternal, necessary being must exist. Proponents argue that if anything now exists, something must be eternal, or else something not eternal must have emerged from nothing. Since the notion of something emerging from an absolute nothing is generally considered absurd, the principal options are that either the universe is eternal or it is the product of an eternal and necessary being. Two main forms of the cosmological argument enjoy widespread support among contemporary classical apologists.

One form reasons from the fact of a beginning for the universe to the existence of a Beginner. This argument is known as the *kalām* cosmological argument, and was first developed by medieval Muslim philosophers. As articulated by William Lane Craig, the *kalām* argument is essentially a philosophical, deductive proof.[32] It may be formulated as a series of logical alternatives, as follows.[33]

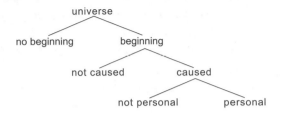

Craig himself offers the following simple form of the argument:

Whatever begins to exist has a cause.

The universe began to exist.

Therefore, the universe has a cause.

Craig argues that the first premise is "intuitively obvious" and should be accepted without trying to base it on something else.[34] He then defends the second premise on both philosophical and scientific grounds. His principal argument here is a philosophical argument based on the impossibility of a temporally infinite past. The idea of time extending backward infinitely (what is known as an **infinite regress**), through an actually infinite series of moments or events, is said to be inherently irrational. Therefore, on *a priori* philosophical grounds, this argument concludes that the universe must have had a beginning.[35] The third statement is a conclusion that follows necessarily from the foregoing two premises but leaves open the question of what this cause is. Craig offers additional philosophical and scientific arguments in support of the belief "that it is a personal being who caused the universe."[36]

Although the *kalām* argument as originally formulated is a deductive philosophical proof, Craig and other classical apologists supplement this rather abstract argument with the scientific evidence that the universe had a beginning. The argument here is based on the virtual consensus among cosmologists that this beginning occurred in what is called the big bang. It has been pointed out that even if a series of big bangs were postulated (for which there is no evidence), it is clear that the universe would not oscillate through such a series from eternity.[37]

The second major form of the cosmological argument originates from Thomas Aquinas; its most notable advocate among contemporary apologists is Norman Geisler.[38] Geisler developed a modified form of the Thomistic cosmological argument that begins with the premise, not that the universe must have had a beginning (as in the *kalām* argument), but that there are undeniably finite, contingent, and temporal things. According to Geisler, the *kalām* argument is suggestive but not demonstrative. In brief, his argument states that "if any finite being exists, then an infinite Being exists as an actual and necessary ground for finite being."[39] If the universe is contingent, it requires a cause—and its ultimate cause cannot be contingent because of the problem of infinite regress. (Note that both Craig's and Geisler's versions of the cosmological argument appeal at some point to the impossibility of an infinite regress.) There must be, then, an uncaused or necessary being. Geisler sets out the argument in several of his books; here is one of his earliest and simplest versions:

1. Some limited, changing being(s) exist(s).
2. The present existence of every limited, changing being is caused by another.
3. There cannot be an infinite regress of causes of being.
4. Therefore, there is a first Cause of the present existence of these beings.
5. The first Cause must be infinite, necessary, eternal, simple, unchangeable, and one.
6. This first uncaused Cause is identical with the God of the Judeo-Christian tradition.[40]

Geisler explicates and defends each premise in detail, and then systematically argues that none of the usual objections validly apply to his restated cosmological argument. According to him, this argument from "existential causality," while not rationally inescapable, passes the test of undeniability.

Opponents have raised a variety of objections to these arguments. For example, they claim that reasoning from the finite, temporal, or contingent nature of all things in the universe to the conclusion that the universe itself is finite, temporal, or contingent commits the *fallacy of composition*. This fallacy occurs when the attributes of the parts are attributed to the whole (for example, it would be a mistake to reason from the premise that all atoms are invisible to the conclusion that all physical objects, since they are composed of atoms, should also be invisible!). One answer to this objection is that arguments appealing to composition are often valid (for example, if all the pieces of a puzzle are red, the puzzle as a whole will also be red). Furthermore, at least some forms of the cosmological argument do not appeal to composition. For example, Geisler's argument appeals to the existence of *any* or *some* finite beings; it does not require the assumption that the universe as a whole is finite.

Another criticism of the cosmological argument is that it moves from finite effects to an infinite cause. A finite effect, it is argued, requires only a finite cause. Classical apologists maintain that this criticism misunderstands the argument. It is true that a finite effect implies *for itself* only a finite cause, but such a finite cause must itself have been caused, and so forth. That is, a finite effect can be directly produced by a finite cause, but ultimately the whole reality of finite causes requires an infinite cause—an "uncaused cause," as it is often called.

Yet another objection is that the argument begs the question by assuming what it sets out to prove. The *kalām* argument, in particular, is often criticized for reasoning from the inconceivability of an actual infinite series to its nonexistence. It is suggested that what seems inconceivable to the human mind is not necessarily nonexistent. Defenders of this form of the cosmological argument typically respond that the issue is not subjective inconceivability (what one person's mind can conceive) but objective irrationality (whether the concept is rationally coherent).

THE DEDUCTIVE PROBLEM OF EVIL

The problem of evil has been used by such thinkers as David Hume, H. G. Wells, and Bertrand Russell to challenge the rationality of belief in the existence of an omnipotent and benevolent God. Theists believe the problem is soluble, "since the events we condemn and the moral law by which we condemn them are both traceable to the same Source."[41] Historically, the problem has most commonly been set forth formally as an apparent contradiction among three propositions (often called the **inconsistent triad**):

1. God is all-loving (God *would* eliminate evil if he could).
2. God is all-powerful (God *could* eliminate evil if he wanted).
3. Evil exists (God *does not* eliminate evil).

This problem has elicited a number of **theodicies**,[42] or explanations for the occurrence of evil in a world made by God, but classical apologists agree that these three propositions are not incompatible or inconsistent with one another. In essence, there are five logically distinguishable responses to this problem. One may (1) deny that God exists (atheism), (2) deny that God is all-loving (dualism), (3) deny that God is all-powerful (finitism), (4) deny that evil exists (illusionism), or (5) affirm that all three of the propositions in the list above are true (theism). The strategy used by classical apologists is to criticize proposed theodicies that solve the problem by denying one of these propositions and then to show that affirming all the propositions is not irrational.

Atheism. The first alternative, atheism, argues that an all-good and all-powerful God must not exist, because he could destroy all evil and would want to destroy all evil, but does not. Moreover, God evidently cannot do the best, since this is not the best of all possible worlds. Most classical apologists relate these objections to the implications of a world where moral creatures have been given the freedom to make real choices, and to the concept that if an all-perfect, all-powerful God does exist, there must be a good purpose for evil. Moreover, although God has not *yet* destroyed evil, he will do so, and in a way that leads to the best possible world. That is, although "*this is not the best of all possible worlds, it is the best of all possible ways (i.e., a necessary way) to achieve the best of all possible worlds.*"[43]

Dualism. While the older forms of religious dualism are not influential today, various theories that question the absolute goodness of God continue to be defended. Classical apologists reject the view that God's goodness is different from what humanity calls good, because it renders the goodness of God nugatory and meaningless. In a similar way, they criticize the views that God is somehow "beyond" good and evil, or that all evils are punishments for sin, as inadequate and distorted solutions.

Finitism. The theodicy that God is unable to control or stop evil has been advocated by John Stuart Mill, William James, Edgar S. Brightman, and the Jewish rabbi Harold Kushner. Classical apologists criticize this view because a finite God cannot assure the final triumph of good, and being finite, would need a Creator to explain its existence.

Illusionism. The denial of the reality of evil is an approach to the problem that is standard in much of Eastern religion and philosophy, and has gained ground in Western culture. Geisler points out that illusionism cannot account satisfactorily for the origin of the illusion of evil. He also observes that there is no practical difference between viewing pain and evil as illusions or viewing them as actual realities.

Theism. In addition to offering logical objections to each of these options, classical theists develop a positive case for the theistic solution to the problem of evil. Geisler's argument is a good model of the classical approach. He considers five hypothetical alternatives for theism:

1. God could have created nothing at all.

2. God could have created only beings who were not free.
3. God could have created beings who were free to sin but did not sin.
4. God could have created beings who were free but must sin.
5. God could have created beings who were free to sin and did sin.

The first and second options appear least desirable, and the fourth appears incoherent (if beings *must* sin, they are not free). The third option would appear to be the most desirable, but Geisler argues that what is logically possible and even morally desirable may not be actually achievable. In short, according to Geisler, if God created beings who were free to sin, he could not at the same time guarantee that they did not sin. "The actual alternatives for theism are dictated by the kind of world we do have, not the kind of world there might have been."[44]

Geisler continues by distinguishing the metaphysical, moral, and physical aspects of the problem of evil, all of which must be resolved to have a complete theodicy. Concerning the metaphysical problem, Geisler follows the lead of Augustine and Aquinas: "Metaphysically speaking, evil has no essence or being of its own; it is a privation of the essence or being of another."[45] Evil is the lack of good resulting from the corruption actualized by human freedom. Thus the answer to the metaphysical problem of evil leads to the moral problem of evil, which Geisler traces to human freedom. Classical apologists usually make this **free-will defense** a centerpiece of their theodicy. They point out that the same conditions that are necessary for a volitional response to love also create the possibility of a rejection of that love. "Even God could not create free men without at the same time creating men who were free to rebel."[46]

The classical apologist, then, reasons that evil, or at least the possibility of evil, is a necessary condition and byproduct of a maximally perfect moral world. After examining the alternatives available to the theistic God, Geisler concludes that "a world with evil is a morally necessary prerequisite to the most perfect world possible. A less perfect moral world is possible, but then it would not be the most perfect moral world that an infinitely perfect God could achieve. In brief, permitting evil is the best way to produce the best world."[47] That this world is the best way to the best world will eventually receive **eschatological verification**—a confirmation at the end of history, in the Final Judgment, of the truth of this answer to the problem of evil.[48] This is an affirmation of the biblical promise that evil will disappear in the consummation of history. "Evil belongs to history; it is not in the eternal constitution of things."[49] Suspension of final judgment is necessary because of the historically bound and finite character of the human perspective. In the meantime, Geisler maintains, we have enough evidence to see that the present world fulfills the necessary conditions, in light of human freedom, that will lead to the best possible world:

> But an optimally perfect moral world should contain four components: the process leading to the final achievement of a world where humans are free but never will do any evil; a world wherein is permitted the full and final uncoerced exercise of moral freedom; a world in which there is permitted the presence of enough evil to provide both the condition for the achievement of higher moral virtues and a comprehensive lesson of the wrongness of evil for free creatures; a world where free creatures learn for themselves why evil is wrong.[50]

Finally, Geisler maintains that all physical evil is to be explained either as a consequence of God's granting free choice to creatures or as a contribution to God's purpose to produce the greatest good. Some physical evil results directly and indirectly from one's own free choices and directly and indirectly from the free choices of others. God may use some physical evil as a warning about moral evils or greater physical evils. Some physical evil occurs because higher forms of life live on lower forms.

Geisler responds to a number of objections to his theodicy with respect to physical evil, including the implication that the end justifies the means. He contends that God has utilitarian *goals* (the greatest good for the greatest number in the long run) but does not employ utilitarian *means* (doing evil that good may come). Geisler therefore rejects the idea that a good end justifies evil means.[51]

MIRACLES AS THE CREDENTIALS OF REVELATION

The miracles of the Bible are not incidental but integral to Christian theism. Before the modern era, they were generally viewed as contributing to the apologetic for Christianity. In the modern era, the philosophical and scientific objections raised against miracles have led to a reversal of their status in apologetics. Now, instead of citing the biblical miracles in defense of the Christian faith, apologists frequently find themselves having to defend the biblical miracles and even the very possibility of miracles. Thus miracles have seemingly been transformed from an apologetic asset to an apologetic liability.

Christian apologists have responded to these modern assaults in a variety of ways. The basic strategy taken by classical apologists has been threefold. First, they emphasize that miracles are rational concepts in the context of a theistic worldview. Second, they give special attention to answering *a priori* objections to miracles that are based on philosophical or scientific misconceptions. And third, they argue that given a theistic worldview, the miracles of the Bible do provide evidential support or confirmation for the Christian faith.

Consider first the matter of the worldview context of miracles. In an atheistic or naturalistic worldview, miracles are by definition impossible because there is no reality beyond the physical universe to effect the miraculous. Likewise in a pantheistic or panentheistic worldview, the divine is really a function or aspect of the universe, and again miracles are impossible. In a sense the pantheist might regard everything as a "miracle," that is, as a manifestation of the divine. But, as Warfield points out, a definition of miracle that broadens the concept to everything renders the concept meaningless. Warfield observes that whereas deism regards God as utterly transcendent and denies that God ever intervenes in the world, pantheism regards God as purely immanent and on that basis holds that God never needs to intervene because everything that occurs is an expression of the divine. Thus both deism and pantheism deny the supernatural, though pantheism does so by redefinition: "When the natural is defined as itself supernatural, there is no place left for a distinguishing supernatural."[52] Thus the key to defending belief in miracles according to classical apologists is to defend theism. Once it is understood that the universe was created by an infinite-personal God who is both transcendent and immanent, the possibility that this God could do miracles is a given. Note how Craig overcame his own intellectual prejudice against miracles: "In my own case, the virgin birth was a stumbling block to my coming to faith—I simply could not believe such a thing. But when I reflected on the fact that God had created the entire universe, it occurred to me that it wouldn't be too difficult for him to create the genetic material necessary for a virgin birth! Once the non-Christian understands who God is, then the problem of miracles should cease to be a problem for him."[53] In his debate with radical New Testament scholar John Dominic Crossan (who teaches that after the crucifixion Jesus' body was not given a proper burial and was eaten by dogs), Craig pressed this very point. During the dialogue Craig led Crossan, who professes to believe in God as a matter of faith but not fact, to reveal that in his opinion God's existence is not an objective reality:

Craig: During the Jurassic age, when there were no human beings, did God exist?

Crossan: Meaningless question.

Craig: But surely that's not a meaningless question. It's a factual question. Was there a Being who was the Creator and Sustainer of the universe during that period of time when no human beings existed? It seems to me that in your view you'd have to say no.

Crossan: Well, I would probably prefer to say no because what you're doing is trying to put yourself in the position of God and ask, "How is God apart from revelation? How is God apart from faith?" I don't know if you can do that.[54]

Craig comments on this exchange at the end of the book: "What this exchange revealed is that on a factual level Dr. Crossan's view is, as I suspected, atheism. 'God' is just an interpretive construct which human beings put on the universe in the same way that 'Christ' is an interpretive construct which Christian believers put on the purely human Jesus. In this light, it is no surprise at all that Dr. Crossan believes neither in miracles nor in the resurrection of Jesus as events of history."[55]

It is essential to the theistic worldview to believe not only in a God, but also that this God created the world as a place of order. Only in a world where natural law ordinarily operates could we even recognize an event as a miracle, as C. S. Lewis argues:

> First we must believe in a normal stability of nature, which means we must recognize that the data offered by our senses recur in regular patterns. Secondly, we must believe in some reality beyond Nature. When both beliefs are held, and not till then, we can approach with an open mind the various reports which claim that this super- or extra-natural reality has sometimes invaded and disturbed the sensuous content of space and time which makes our "natural" world. The belief in such a supernatural reality itself can neither be proved nor disproved by experience.[56]

For example, if babies were conceived in completely random and unpredictable ways, sometimes following sexual relations and sometimes not, no one would be surprised to learn that a young peasant girl had become pregnant before getting married. Only in a universe where babies normally came in the same way time after time would a virgin birth be recognizable as a special act of the Creator. The theistic worldview is not to be confused with the magical worldview in which "impossible things are happening every day."[57] In the theistic worldview God is providentially involved in everything that occurs, but he also intervenes and acts more directly or overtly in the world to accomplish special purposes. These overt interventions are called miracles. In a theistic universe the possibility of miracles cannot be fairly ruled out. This means, as Lewis points out, that the "various reports which claim that this super- or extra-natural reality has sometimes invaded and disturbed the sensuous content of space and time which makes our 'natural' world" should be approached with an open mind and evaluated on their own merits rather than rejected out of hand.[58]

The second aspect of the classical apologetic for miracles is the refutation of *a priori* objections to belief in miracles based on philosophical or scientific misconceptions. For example, it is often maintained that miracles are *scientifically impossible*—that they "transgress," "violate," or "contradict" the laws of nature. Apologists counter that this is based on a "misleading analogy between nature's laws and the laws of society."[59] The biblical miracles are not *anti*natural but *super*-natural; they are not caused *contrary to* nature *(contra naturam)*, but are rather caused by an agent who *transcends* nature *(extra naturam)*, God. The laws of science are descriptive of how nature normally operates, not prescriptive of what must always occur; they do not legislate what God, who transcends space and time and instituted those laws in the first place, can or cannot do. Classical apologists point out that it would require a metaphysical assumption that the universe is a system closed to any influences apart from the four-dimensional space-time continuum to maintain that the laws of nature could not be superseded by a higher principle on certain occasions. The idea of a deterministic or mechanistic universe is not scientific but metaphysical, as is theism. The underlying issue with respect to miracles, then, is whether God exists; if so, miracles are possible.

Third, classical apologists argue that, given a theistic worldview, the biblical miracles provide positive evidence for the truth claims of Christianity. This is because belief in God does not automatically imply an endorsement of any or all miracle claims. Although the reality of God's existence proves that miracles *may* have occurred, it does not prove that they *have* occurred. (If it did, theists would have to accept all miracle claims of all religions, or at least admit that any of them might be true.) Whether miracles have in fact occurred is a matter of history, and must be determined by historical investigation. Classical apologists do not ask that biblical miracle claims be accepted uncritically. They do, however, insist that once the existence of the type of God described in the Bible is conceded, the historical evidence for miracle claims must be taken seriously. They urge that the same canons of historical criticism that are applied to other historical records be applied as well to the biblical accounts without prejudging the case with metaphysical assumptions. Once this is done, classical apologists believe that the biblical miracles will be found to be in a class by themselves, and that the evidence for these miracles will be seen as compelling.

In one sense classical apologists argue that the question of miracles cannot be addressed until one has established agreement that God exists. However, Christianity entails certain unique claims about the nature and purposes of God, such as that he is triune or that he intends to save a segment of humanity on the basis of his gracious redemption rather than their works. The miracles of Jesus Christ in particular reveal *this* God to be the true God. In a sense, then, the biblical miracles do function as proofs, not of "a God" in a generic sense, but of *God*, the true, biblical God.

JESUS: THE ALTERNATIVES

Having demonstrated the possibility of the supernatural, the classical apologist is ready to defend the actuality of the biblical miracles and in particular the claims to deity made by and about Jesus Christ. Norman Geisler's argument for the deity of Christ is typical of the classical approach, and basically proceeds in two steps: (1) Christ claimed to be God; (2) Christ proved himself to be God.[60]

An alternate form of the argument lays out all the alternatives to the Christian view of Jesus as God and then shows that they must be rejected. The simplest form of this process-of-elimination argument is known as the Trilemma,[61] and presents three possibilities—Jesus really was God (or *Lord*), Jesus knew he wasn't God (a *liar*), or Jesus mistakenly thought he was God (a *lunatic*). Apologists need say almost nothing in refutation of the second and third views, since nearly everyone recognizes Jesus to have been at the very least a person of great wisdom and moral courage. This leaves as the only possibility, though, that Jesus really was God.

For the Trilemma argument to be complete, however, it must take into consideration that Jesus did not even claim to be God (step one of Geisler's argument). There are two lines of reasoning by which non-Christians have denied that Jesus claimed to be God. They have either denied that he made the claims to deity reported in the Gospels or argued that these should be interpreted to mean something other than a claim to deity. The one clear alternative way of interpreting Jesus' claims to deity is to interpret them in an Eastern religious sense as mystical affirmations of a unity with God that all people potentially may realize. We thus have a total of five possible views of Jesus—a set of alternatives that Peter Kreeft has called the Quintilemma.[62] We may represent the Quintilemma as a series of dilemmas, as follows:

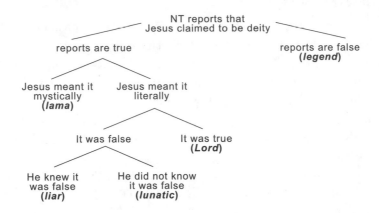

Again, classical apologists believe that a great deal has been gained if one can simply show that Jesus did in fact claim to be God. After all, most people will hesitate to assert that Jesus *falsely* made such a claim for himself. This is why most skeptics and unorthodox believers simply deny that Jesus ever made such lofty claims.

We will sketch here how classical apologists dispose of the four non-Christian alternatives and thus conclude in favor of the Christian view that Jesus was God.

Jesus' Claims: The Gospels' Reports

The primary premise of the Quintilemma is that the Gospels report Jesus claiming to be God. Perhaps the simplest way of undercutting the argument is to dismiss the Gospel reports as historically unreliable. Admittedly many New Testament scholars today contend that Jesus did not claim to be deity; the Gospel accounts of Jesus claiming divine titles or prerogatives, they contend, are later mythical or legendary accretions and do not represent the views of the historical Jesus.

Evangelical scholars and apologists have given enormous attention to rebutting modern skepticism about the historical reliability of the New Testament, especially of the Gospels. Classical apologists appeal to the same types of evidences in defense of the Gospels and the rest of the New Testament as do evidentialist apologists (whose treatment of these matters we will discuss in Part Three), with the aim of showing that the Gospel accounts of the life, teachings, death, and resurrection of Jesus Christ possess both authenticity and reliability. Their *authentic-*

ity has to do with determining that the New Testament as we now possess it is an accurate representation of what the writers originally wrote. Their *reliability* has to do with determining whether the writers had access to the facts of which they speak, and whether they are credible, faithful witnesses to those facts.

The issue of credibility, or believability, is of course at the heart of the matter. There are two aspects to this question, both of which classical apologists address. The first is whether the New Testament writers, particularly the Gospel writers, *want to be believed* as reporting historical fact. Against those who claim that the Gospels did not have an historical purpose, classical apologists such as Geisler argue that it is highly improbable that the early church had no biographical interests, and explain why the Gospels are vastly different from folklore and myth. The second issue is whether the Gospel writers *can be believed* as reporting historical fact. Here classical apologists employ a two-pronged defense. Positively they point to the archaeological and secular testimony to the events recorded in the Gospels. Negatively they emphasize that there is nothing incredible about the miracle accounts in the Gospels if the existence of God is admitted.

One aspect of the classical apologetic response to the claim that the Gospel accounts are legendary reflects the distinctive method of the classical approach. As we noted, the Gospels purport to be historical accounts about Jesus. Geisler observes that critics of the Gospels have often alleged either that the apostles and other eyewitnesses had experienced hallucinations of Jesus risen from the dead or that the apostles (or later Christians) had fabricated their accounts about Jesus performing miracles, rising from the dead, and claiming to be deity. Geisler argues that neither of these explanations work and that we should conclude that the Gospels tell us the truth about Jesus.[63] But this argument amounts to an application of the Trilemma to the apostles: either they were delusional (*lunatics*), or they (or the Gospel writers) were *liars*, or they were telling the truth and Jesus really presented himself to the apostles as the *Lord*.

Jesus' Claims: What They Meant

The second line of defense against the Christian view of Jesus as God is to argue that he really did not claim to be God in the Jewish sense. Although there are various heretical distortions of the biblical teaching that Jesus is God, we are here concerned with interpretations that take Jesus' claims completely outside of any professing Christian context. In practice there is only one such interpretation: that when Jesus spoke or acted as if he were God, this is to be understood in an Eastern, pantheistic, and mystical sense. That is, in this view God is all or in all, and Jesus was merely claiming to have realized what is potentially or ultimately true about all of us—that we are all God. But this means that Jesus was a kind of Eastern guru or lama, a religious holy man who had realized his oneness with the divine and had sought to transmit this understanding to others.

Classical apologists have responded to this theory with a battery of arguments. Peter Kreeft and Ronald Tacelli well represent the classical response when they assert that Jesus could not have been a mystical guru "for one very simple reason: because he was a Jew."[64] Kreeft and Tacelli point out a number of glaring contradictions between the teachings of Judaism in general and Jesus in particular and, on the other hand, those of mystics and gurus. The Jewish belief that Jesus taught was a public faith in a personal Creator who could be known because he had taken the initiative and revealed himself. Eastern gurus taught a secret, mystical experience of an impersonal divine reality in all things that is beyond knowledge but can be experienced by those who pursue it with religious fervor.[65] Kreeft and Tacelli present a number of other differences and conclude: "So we have eight flat-out contradictions, all of them crucially important, between the teaching of Jesus as we have it in the New Testament and the teaching of the Eastern mystics and gurus. To classify Jesus as a guru is as accurate as classifying Marx as a capitalist."[66]

Jesus' Claims: Were They True?

If Jesus really did claim to be God, and if he meant this in the Jewish sense of being the personal Creator of the universe, then the simpler Trilemma comes directly into play. Classical apologists know that if they can reduce the options to these three—liar, lunatic, or Lord—they will have a convincing case for all but the most jaundiced, hostile opponent of Christianity. The reason is simple: even the most avowed non-Christians are incapable of convincing themselves, let alone others, that Jesus was a deceiver or demented. And those really are the choices if Jesus claimed to be God and yet was merely a human being. C. S. Lewis made this point in what may be the most often quoted passage in twentieth-century apologetic literature:

> A man who was merely a man and said the sort of things Jesus said would not be a great moral teacher. He would either be a lunatic—on a level with the man who says he is a poached egg—or else he would be the Devil of Hell. You must make your choice. Either this man was, and is, the Son of God: or else a madman or something worse. You can shut

Him up for a fool, you can spit at Him and kill Him as a demon; or you can fall at His feet and call Him Lord and God. But let us not come with any patronising nonsense about His being a great human teacher. He has not left that open to us. He did not intend to.[67]

For Further Study

Craig, William Lane. *The Cosmological Argument from Plato to Leibniz*. New York: Macmillan, 1980. An historical study of the cosmological argument, reviewing the most influential versions of the argument in the history of philosophy.

_____. *The* Kalām *Cosmological Argument*. Library of Philosophy and Religion. New York: Macmillan, 1979. An exposition and defense of the *kalām* argument.

Geisler, Norman L. *Is Man the Measure? An Evaluation of Contemporary Humanism*. Grand Rapids: Baker, 1983. Good example of a classical apologetic critique of a non-Christian worldview.

_____. *Miracles and Modern Thought*. Grand Rapids: Zondervan, 1982. A defense of the possibility of miracles and answers to objections from modern skeptics.

_____. *The Roots of Evil*. Grand Rapids: Zondervan, 1978. More popular exposition of the approach to the problem of evil found in his *Philosophy of Religion*.

Geivett, R. Douglas, and Gary R. Habermas, eds. *In Defense of Miracles: A Comprehensive Case for God's Action in History*. Downers Grove, Ill.: InterVarsity, 1997. Several of the essays seek to defend miracles by placing them in the context of a theistic worldview.

Kreeft, Peter. *Making Sense Out of Suffering*. Ann Arbor: Servant, 1986. A classical apologist's sympathetic treatment of the problem of evil.

Lewis, C. S. *God in the Dock: Essays on Theology and Ethics*. Edited by Walter Hooper. Grand Rapids: Eerdmans, 1970. Important collection of essays that includes "Evil and God," "Miracles," "Myth Becomes Fact," "Horrid Red Things," "The Grand Miracle," "Christian Apologetics," and many more of relevance.

_____. *Miracles: A Preliminary Study*. 2nd ed. New York: Macmillan, 1960. Arguably Lewis's most ambitious, rigorous apologetic work, thoughtfully revised in light of criticisms he received of the first edition.

_____. *The Problem of Pain*. London: Centenary Press, 1940; New York: Macmillan, 1943; paperback ed., 1962. Lewis's insightful treatment of the problem of evil, still somewhat unusual in its approach.

Moreland, J. P., and Kai Nielsen. *Does God Exist? The Debate between Theists and Atheists*. Buffalo: Prometheus Books, 1993. Classical apologist philosopher with some evidentialist leanings debates an influential atheist philosopher; includes analyses by and discussions with other atheist and Christian philosophers.

Warfield, B. B. "The Question of Miracles." In *Selected Shorter Writings of Benjamin B. Warfield*, edited by John E. Meeter, 2:167-204. Nutley, N.J.: Presbyterian & Reformed, 1970.

_____. "The Resurrection of Christ a Historical Fact" and "The Resurrection of Christ a Fundamental Doctrine." In *Selected Shorter Writings of Benjamin B. Warfield*, edited by John E. Meeter, 1:178-192 and 1:193-202. Nutley, N.J.: Presbyterian & Reformed, 1970. These essays illustrate Warfield's classical apologetic approach to the defense of belief in the supernatural character of Christianity.

Chapter 7

Apologetics and the Limits of Reason

In this concluding chapter on classical apologetics, we will summarize this model or paradigm for apologetics, illustrate its use in practical apologetic encounters, and then consider its major strengths and weaknesses.

THE CLASSICAL APOLOGETICS MODEL

As explained in chapter 3, we are summarizing each model of apologetic system under two headings (metapologetics and apologetics) and six specific questions under each heading. Here we apply this analysis to the classical apologetics model.

Metapologetic Questions

Metapologetic questions deal with the assumptions or approaches taken by an apologetic method to the relationship between apologetics and various areas or kinds of knowledge. In chapter 5 we considered the approach taken in classical apologetics to epistemology (the theory of knowledge), theology, philosophy, science, history, and experience. Here we summarize our findings in that chapter.

1. On what basis do we claim that Christianity is the truth?

Classical apologetics emphasizes *logic* in its defense of the Christian faith as a form of knowledge. Apologists in this tradition may speak of logic, reason, rationality, coherence, or consistency; these are all different ways of referring to what we might call the "structural integrity" of a belief system. The form of argument given priority in classical apologetics is *deductive* in form. In theory deductive arguments yield certain conclusions, but this is so only if one knows with certainty that the premises are true. Thus, in practice classical apologists do not typically claim absolute certainty for their arguments. They also prefer to apply deductive reasoning in their critiques of non-Christian belief systems and in their rebuttals to objections to Christian beliefs. The most decisive form of criticism in classical apologetics is to show that a non-Christian belief or objection is logically *self-defeating* or self-referentially incoherent. This criticism is applied especially to relativism, both in Eastern religion and philosophy and in the New Age movement and postmodernism. All these movements are regarded as self-refuting and therefore incoherent on their face.

Logical argument in apologetics does not produce faith, nor is it the proper basis of Christian assurance or knowledge; these are the work of the Holy Spirit. Rather, the purpose of apologetic argument is to serve as means through which the Holy Spirit can lead nonbelievers to acknowledge the truth of Christianity.

2. What is the relationship between apologetics and theology?

Classical apologists typically regard the intellectual discipline of apologetics as in some sense preceding theology. That is, apologetics seeks to defend the basic principles and assumptions of Christian theology—to explain why we ought to believe in the Christian faith as revealed in Scripture and practiced in the Christian church. In this model, apologetic argument cannot assume or be based on theological positions, because the purpose of apologetics is to convince people to embrace the Christian revelation that is the basis of all theology. For this reason classical apologists see their mission as defending "mere Christianity" and not any specific theological camp within Christianity.

3. Should apologetics engage in a philosophical defense of the Christian faith?

Classical apologetics has the most positive view of philosophy in general, and even of non-Christian philosophy, of the four approaches to apologetics. The classical apologist views the apologetic task as articulating the Christian position in a way that communicates that position clearly and faithfully in terms that people of non-Christian worldviews and religions can understand. This does not mean that non-Christian philosophies are accepted without qualification, but that the Christian thinker uses the categories and insights of non-Christian systems of thought in order to make Christian thought intelligible to the non-Christian. Classical apologists tend to see a great deal of overlap in subject matter and method between apologetics and philosophy.

4. Can science be used to defend the Christian faith?

Classical apologists take a cautiously positive approach to the findings and theories of science. While not generally suspicious of science, they urge caution in jumping too quickly to endorse scientific theories in fields where theories have historically come and gone. Still, they regard modern developments in science, especially in cosmology, as encouraging confirmation of key aspects of the Christian theistic worldview. Classical apologists of the early twentieth century tended to accept tentatively the biological theory of evolution, though more recently evangelical classical apologists have tended to embrace some form of old-earth creationism.

5. Can the Christian faith be supported by historical inquiry?

The main concern that classical apologists have regarding history is to show that true knowledge of the past is possible. They admit that competing worldviews and other factors tend to skew our perceptions of the past. For this reason they typically conclude that an accurate view of history, especially with regard to the significance of past events, requires adherence to a true worldview. In other words, one must have a theistic view of the world and of history to understand the past correctly.

6. How is our knowledge of Christian truth related to our experience?

Classical apologists do not place heavy emphasis on arguments from experience. However, they do contend that the commonality of religious experience and the virtual universality of the religious impulse prove there is a transcendent reality toward which human beings incorrigibly yearn. What all or nearly all people need must exist in some form; so if people have a need for God, then there must be a God. To deny the existence of the transcendent, one would have to contend that everyone in history who has had a religious experience was totally deceived in thinking he had experienced transcendent reality.

Apologetic Questions

Apologetic questions deal with issues commonly raised by non-Christians themselves. In chapter 6 we considered the approach classical apologetics takes to answering questions about the Bible, Christianity and other belief systems, the existence of God, the problem of evil, the credibility of miracles, and the claims of Jesus Christ. Here we summarize our findings in that chapter.

1. Why should we believe in the Bible?

In one sense all Christian apologists urge that the Bible should be believed because it is *true*—indeed, because it is God's word of truth. But the four apologetic methods approach this question in different ways. Classical apologists commonly reserve it for the end of the apologetic task. Only after the existence of God, the credibility of his intervening in history, and the deity of Jesus Christ have been shown to be true do they seek to establish the inspiration and authority of Scripture. In their view we believe in the Bible because we believe in the God revealed in Christ—not the other way around. Moreover, they are generally frank about saying that reason may be validly used to test and verify the claim of the Bible to be a revelation from God. Doing so does not elevate reason above Scripture; rather, it takes account of the fact that God communicated his revelation to us in a rational form and expects us to recognize and receive it through our faculty of reason.

2. Don't all religions lead to God?

Classical apologists tend to approach the question of the revelatory character of non-Christian religions by analyzing those religions in terms of their worldviews. By reducing alternative belief systems to a manageable number, the apologist can analyze the basic worldview options and show that theism is the correct one. This reduces the number of viable world religions to three: Judaism, Christianity, and Islam. Classical apologists then point to various evidences that Christianity is the true fulfillment of original (Old Testament) Judaism and that both Judaism and Islam fail to reckon adequately with the claims of Christ. But they do not claim there is no truth in non-Christian religions. In fact, they argue that God reveals himself to all people and that all religions reflect that revelation, albeit in partial and corrupt form. In this sense non-Christian religions can be viewed as expressions of hope or longing for the full and redemptive revelation of God in Jesus Christ.

3. How do we know that God exists?

Although classical apologists are generally careful to point out that there is no substitute for a personal relationship with God through faith in Christ and the indwelling presence of God by his Holy Spirit, they do maintain that the existence of God can be demonstrated rationally. While most of them do not endorse all the traditional theistic proofs, they all endorse one or more of those arguments in some form. Further, while most are not averse to arguments that appeal to scientific facts or other inductive evidence, the primary form of theistic argument most classical apologists favor is deductive. The most commonly used theistic proofs in the classical tradition are the cosmological argument (which reasons from the world to God), the teleological argument (which reasons from order or design to God), the moral argument (which reasons from moral absolutes to God as the absolute source of morality), and the ontological argument (which reasons from the idea of God to the existence of God).

4. If God does exist, why does he permit evil?

Classical apologists usually address the problem of evil in its historically most influential form as a logical conundrum: How can God be all-powerful and all-loving, yet permit evil? This seeming contradiction is typically resolved by showing that it is logically necessary, or at least logically possible, for God to permit evil in order for God's loving purpose in creation to be realized. The most common answers focus on the beginning and the end. Evil originated because God created beings with a capacity for choice (the free-will defense). Evil will be overcome both because God will one day eliminate it and because God will bring about a greater good as a result of the evil he has temporarily permitted.

5. Aren't the miracles of the Bible spiritual myths or legends and not literal fact?

Classical apologists defend the coherence of belief in miracles. They attribute modern denials of the biblical miracles to an antisupernatural mind-set that at its root is a product of a nontheistic worldview. Thus miracles must be defended primarily by defending the theistic worldview and showing that they are neither impossible nor implausible given the existence of God.

6. Why should I believe in Jesus?

Classical apologists regard faith in Jesus as the core issue in apologetics. To press the claims of Christ, they urge nonbelievers to choose how they will view Jesus. Nonbelievers are told there are only so many alternatives in light of the Gospels' reports that Jesus claimed to be God. One might say that Jesus made no such claim—but then how did Jews come to believe this about a crucified man? Or one might suggest that he did claim to be God but meant it in the Eastern mystical sense that we are all one with God—but is this doctrine likely to have fallen from the lips of a Jewish rabbi? If one chooses neither of these options, one must believe that Jesus was either wrong about being God or right. If he was wrong, he was either a liar or a lunatic. If he was right, then he was indeed Lord. The one explanation that can't stand up to the evidence is that Jesus was merely a great teacher.

The following table presents an overview of the classical model of apologetics with these twelve questions in mind.

Issue		Position
Metapologetics	KNOWLEDGE	Logic is the primary test of worldviews Postmodernism is self-refuting Spirit's witness is the ground of knowledge
	THEOLOGY	Apologetics establishes foundation of theology Apologetics defends "mere Christianity"
	PHILOSOPHY	Apologetics overlaps philosophy's subject matter Substantive use of non-Christian philosophy
	SCIENCE	Cautiously accepts established theories Science and theology overlap, both rational Typically old-earth creationism
	HISTORY	Objective view of history difficult but possible Right view of history requires right worldview
	EXPERIENCE	Religious experience not irrational Argument from religious desire
Apologetics	SCRIPTURE	Reason used to test Scripture's credentials Begin with theism, conclude with inspiration Fulfilled prophecy proves inspiration if God exists
	RELIGIONS	Religious pluralism is illogical Nontheistic worldviews are incoherent
	GOD	Generally deductive proofs favored Cosmological, moral arguments most common
	EVIL	Deductive problem of evil: Is theism inconsistent? Beginning: evil result of free choice of creatures End: world with evil best way to best world
	MIRACLES	Miracles credible given a theistic worldview Miracles do not contradict natural law
	JESUS	Jesus' claim to deity excludes him as mere man Quintilemma: Legend, lama, liar, lunatic, Lord?

CLASSICAL APOLOGETICS ILLUSTRATED

In this first of four dialogues we will present in this book, a Christian named Tom becomes involved in a discussion with Sarah and Murali while waiting in line to see a movie. Tom is a computer programmer. He has read widely in philosophy and apologetics; his favorite author is C. S. Lewis. In fact, he has brought a copy of Lewis's *Problem of Pain* with him to read while waiting to see the movie. Sarah notices the book and asks him about it:

Sarah: That book sounds interesting. What's it about?

Tom: It's about the question of why there is pain and death in the world if the world was made by an all-powerful and all-loving God.

Sarah: That seems like an obvious contradiction to me.

Tom: Yes, I know it seems like one. But I think it's only an apparent contradiction, not a real one. I think a good answer can be given that will resolve the problem.

Murali: Excuse me, may I say something? This question is of interest to me as well.

Tom: Sure. By the way, my name's Tom. What's yours?

Murali: Murali. I am from India.

Sarah: My name's Sarah. Nice to meet you guys.

Tom: Likewise. Murali, you were going to say something?

Murali: Yes. You said you thought there was a good answer to the question about evil in the world if God is good. I have found that there are many religions and they all have answers that satisfy the people who believe them. I do not believe there is only one right answer to the question.

Tom: Let me ask you a question, then. Do you think all the answers given to this question by the different world religions are equally valid?

Murali: Yes, I think so. After all, as I said, they are helpful to the people who believe them. And none of us is really in a position to say that our answer to this great question is better than anyone else's.

Tom: Well, I don't claim to have a perfect understanding of the issue, but I do think some answers are better than others. And they can't all be right. For example, Taoism and other religions have taught that good and evil are co-eternal realities that balance each other out. If Taoism is right, evil is just part of the way things have always been and always will be. Christianity, on the other hand, teaches that evil has not always existed but began when creatures with free will chose to abuse their freedom by doing wrong. If Christianity is right, evil is not just part of the way things have always been, and some day evil will be completely gone. Now, these can't both be right, can they?

Murali: You are looking at these religions using Western logic. On that logical level the two religions seem to contradict each other. But at a higher level both are true.

Sarah: Wait a minute. I'm not convinced that either of these religions gives a good answer to the question. And I certainly don't see how they can both be true. Either evil has always been around, or it hasn't. Which do you think it is, Murali?

Murali: I think it depends on how you look at things.

Tom: Well, how do you look at things?

Murali: I don't have a very strong opinion on the question either way. I just think that whichever way you want to answer the question is fine for you, and that it's wrong to claim that *your* answer is the only right answer.

Tom: But Murali, I'm not interested in finding an answer that is "fine for me." I'm interested in finding an answer that is *true*. If one person's answer to the problem of evil is right, it must be true, and any answer that contradicts it must be false. For example, I believe that evil exists because creatures like us have chosen to abuse the free will that God gave us. That answer assumes that other answers that contradict it must be false. For example, saying that evil resulted from a conflict among the gods, as in ancient polytheism, or that evil is an illusion, as the New Age movement claims, simply cannot agree with the belief that evil is a choice made by creatures to rebel against their Creator. So if you say my answer is not the only right answer, you're saying it is the wrong answer.

Sarah: But you're assuming that God exists.

Tom: Not really. I'm saying that *if* God exists, then the problem of evil has to be solved by understanding who God is and what his purpose is in creating this world. But I don't simply assume God exists. I think there are good reasons for believing that God exists. I'd be happy to share those reasons with you if you're interested.

Sarah: I took a course in philosophy last year, and most philosophers today agree that there's no way to prove that God exists.

Tom: Well, that depends on what you mean by "prove." If you studied philosophy, then you probably know that there are lots of good arguments that show that it is more reasonable to believe that God exists than that he doesn't.

Sarah: But these arguments don't seem to me to outweigh the problem of evil. After all, it's a blatant contradiction. If God is all-powerful, he could stop evil anytime he wants to. If God is all-loving, then he'd want to stop it right away, maybe even before it got started. But evil has been around for a long time, and God hasn't done anything to stop it. So it seems that either God doesn't exist at all, or that if he does exist he either isn't all powerful or he isn't all loving. Which is it?

Tom: Your dilemma has another solution. God may allow evil because, as an all-loving God, he has a greater good in mind that necessitates allowing evil to exist, and as an all-powerful God, he has the ability to bring about that greater good despite all the evil that happens.

Sarah: What exactly is this greater good that requires God to allow evil in the world?

Tom: God has a plan to bring about the best of all possible worlds, a world with finite creatures with the capacity to love one another. For him to carry out that plan, he had to give us the freedom to do good or evil.

Sarah: Why? Why couldn't he just make everybody choose to do good?

Tom: I'm not sure I understand this perfectly myself, but it seems to me that if God *made* everybody do good all the time, then it wouldn't really be good. You see, God is a God of love, and he wants us to be creatures who love him and love each other. But even God can't *make* people love others. He can do a lot to make it possible for us to love, but in some sense that love has to be freely *given*. But evidently people who have the capacity to give freely must also have the capacity, at least at first, to withhold freely. And that's what's happened. Creatures that God created with the capacity to love or not to love have chosen not to love God, and the result has been that we have had a very hard time loving each other as well.

Murali: But insisting that one's religion is the only true religion has been one of the main reasons for people not getting along in this world. In the part of the world where I come from, Hindus and Muslims kill each other over religion. In the Middle East it's the Jews against the Muslims. In Northern Ireland it's been the Catholics against the Protestants. People need to stop being so intolerant of the religions of other people and try to get along. Any religion is good as long as it isn't made into a reason to hate and kill people of other religions.

Sarah: It sounds like most of the world's religions have made the problem of evil worse, not better. Maybe we'd be better off with less religion and more education.

Tom: I'm inclined to agree with both of you more than you might think. I agree that religion has often been made the basis for hating and killing other people. But religion has also been made the basis for loving and caring for other people. I think that any religion that teaches hatred and violence against other people because of their beliefs is wrong.

Sarah: But doesn't Christianity have a long history of teaching those things? Look at the Crusades, and the Inquisitions. Look at the long history of anti-Semitism in Christianity. I don't think Christianity is exempt from the charge of teaching hatred and violence against others because of their beliefs.

Tom: Again, I think you might be surprised to hear that I agree with you. But I'm not saying Christianity as a religion has always been right. Far from it. Christians, especially Christians in positions of political power, have done some terrible things. When they do evil, they disobey God himself. That's what evil is, whether it's Christians or non-Christians doing it.

Murali: But if you agree that Christians also do evil, why insist that Christianity is the only right religion? What is the advantage in believing in Christianity rather than any other religion, if its people do the same things as people in other religions?

Tom: There's no advantage in being a member of the Christian religion if a person does not take the central teaching of Christianity seriously.

Murali: And what is that central teaching?

Tom: I'm glad you asked! The central teaching of Christianity is that God sent his Son Jesus into the world to take our evil and turn it around to bring about our ultimate good.

Sarah: You're talking about Jesus dying on the cross, right?

Tom: Exactly.

Sarah: I used to believe all that stuff about Jesus. But now it just doesn't add up.

Tom: Who do you think Jesus was, then, if you don't think he was the Son of God?

Sarah: I'm not sure. I don't think anyone really knows much about the real Jesus. I mean, I'm sure he was a good teacher and all that. In his time I suppose he helped people, inspired them to live better lives. But all that stuff about him doing miracles and being God on earth seems to me to have been myths that people came up with long after Jesus was gone.

Tom: How long after, do you think?

Sarah: I don't know exactly. I've heard that the Gospels were written maybe a hundred years after Jesus. No one knows for sure.

Tom: Actually, the most extreme dates in modern scholarship for the Gospels place them about forty to seventy years after the death of Jesus. Jesus died in A.D. 33, and nonconservative scholars date the Gospels between about 70 and 100. So within forty years the first Gospel, Mark, presented Jesus as the miracle-working Son of God.

Sarah: Forty years is still a pretty long time.

Tom: Yes, but it's still within the lifetime of most of the people who knew Jesus personally. But besides the Gospels, we also have a number of epistles in the New Testament, especially ones written by the apostle Paul. Paul wrote his epistles between about 50 and 65, beginning less than twenty years after Jesus' death. And Paul says he saw Jesus risen from the dead, and that Jesus was the Son of God. So we can go back to the very first generation of Christians, and what we find is that they always believed that Jesus was the miracle-working Son of God who had died on the cross and risen from the dead. And they always believed that Jesus himself had claimed to be the Son of God in the flesh. If you take just the statements in the Gospels that even the most radical scholars agree Jesus said, you find a Jesus who thought of himself as speaking with divine authority and performing divine works. So the idea that Jesus claimed to be the Son of God very clearly goes back to Jesus himself; it can't be explained away as a later myth.

Murali: But, if I may, this claim to be the Son of God is hardly unique. All the great religions of the world have made similar claims about their great religious figures, have they not? In India, where I come from, we were taught that God manifests himself in many ways. Are we not all God's children?

Tom: There is a sense in which all people might be called God's children. But Jesus was clearly claiming something unique—something no other major religious leader has ever claimed. Remember, Jesus was a Jew. The Jews did not believe that God is manifest in many figures, as in Hinduism, or that we are all a part of the divine All. They believed that there was a basic distinction between the Creator and the creature. Their God was the transcendent yet personal Creator, Master, and Judge of the universe. And here's Jesus, who was obviously a man, claiming to be that kind of God. Jesus forgave the sins of others. He claimed to have been the one who had sent prophets to Israel warning them of God's judgment. He said, "No one comes to the Father except through me." No, Jesus wasn't claiming merely to be a human being who had realized our common divinity. He was claiming to be our Maker, Redeemer, and Judge.

Sarah: That's just your interpretation.

Tom: I invite you to read the Gospels for yourself and draw your own conclusion about who Jesus claimed to be. I think you'll find that he
did not leave open to us the option of thinking of him as merely a
great teacher. If he claimed to be God in the flesh but was really
only a mere man, then he was either one of the biggest liars the
world has ever known or he was crazy in the head. Which do you
think?

Murali: I certainly wouldn't say that Jesus was either a liar or a crazy man.
Everything I have heard or read about Jesus leads me to believe
that he was a wonderful person. But I have never thought about
Jesus in this way before.

Sarah: I wouldn't say anything bad about Jesus, either. But I'm still not sure
this idea that he was God couldn't have been a misunderstanding.

Tom: Fair enough. Why don't you read the New Testament for yourselves
and see what you think? If you're interested, I'd be happy to get
together with either or both of you later and discuss it further.

Murali: I'd like that very much.

Sarah: I'm not sure.

Tom: That's fine. Let me give you my phone number and e-mail address and
you can contact me at your convenience if you decide you'd like to
continue this discussion.

Murali and Sarah: Okay!

NOTABLE STRENGTHS OF CLASSICAL APOLOGETICS

Classical apologetics, as the name implies, is the approach to apologetics that
has the deepest roots in the history of Christian apologetics, and in its explicit
modern form it remains a potent force today. Several strengths account for this
approach's perennial success.

Affirms the Universal Applicability of Reason

One of the great strengths of classical apologetics is its emphasis on the inescapable character of logic or reason. As Geisler observes, "Unless the law of
noncontradiction holds, then there is not even the most minimal possibility of
meaning nor any hope for establishing truth."[1] There can be no meaningful dis-

course without the fundamental laws of logic. The most basic of these is the law of noncontradiction (also known as the law of contradiction), according to which something cannot be both true and false at the same time and in the same respect. Although Christian apologists learned this and other principles of deductive logic from Greek philosophy, especially Aristotle, classical apologists rightly emphasize that adherence to these laws does not commit them to an uncritical acceptance of Aristotelian philosophy. Aristotle defined but did not invent logic.[2] R. C. Sproul observes that a number of twentieth-century thinkers rejected the law of contradiction on the theoretical level. In spite of this intellectual denial, "they all live their daily lives in the tacit assumption of the validity of the law. . . . Man cannot survive or function without assuming the validity of the law of contradiction."[3]

The importance and value of this emphasis on deductive logic is great. Logic is an enormously helpful tool for understanding and evaluating arguments, and is useful to the apologist in three ways. First, it is an indispensable tool for *checking the apologist's own arguments to make sure they are constructed properly*. Those we are seeking to persuade rightly dismiss illogical arguments, even if the conclusions happen to be true. This is because the same kinds of arguments could also be used to support falsehoods. Illogical arguments are therefore unreliable, and it is the function of logic to pinpoint where arguments go awry. We have a responsibility to present arguments to non-Christians that they cannot fairly reject as misleading or unreliable. Logic is the formal discipline that provides us with the intellectual tools that can make our arguments as reliable and truth-based as possible.

Second, logic is a powerful instrument for *exposing problems in arguments used against Christian beliefs*. Classical apologists are rightly confident that every argument raised against the Christian faith is in principle answerable; many of these are problematic simply because they are logically invalid. Since most non-Christians are capable of understanding at least some basic principles of logic, exposing logical fallacies in their arguments can help show them that their reasons for rejecting Christianity are misplaced. The value of reason in this regard is heightened because reason, unlike technical information from the sciences or personal religious experiences, is in principle universally available to all people. If they are willing, non-Christians of any culture and virtually any amount of education can be helped to recognize that their objections to Christianity depend on mistakes in thinking.

Third, the emphasis on logic is helpful in *commending the claims of Christ to intelligent non-Christians*. Too often unbelievers get the impression that Christianity is an irrational faith that requires people to suspend their critical reasoning faculties. Classical apologists work to overcome this stereotype and to reach out to the educated and intellectually oriented non-Christian with the message that the God in whom we believe is the God of reason and truth.

Raises Awareness of the Unavoidable Role of Worldviews

Classical apologists rightly emphasize that it is impossible to think about the world at large or about facts or experiences apart from some worldview. "Refusing to adopt an explicit worldview will turn out to be itself a worldview or at least a philosophic position."[4] Classical apologists recognize that facts are perceived in accordance with an interpretive framework, a way of looking at facts themselves and even of thinking about the concept of "fact." It is best, therefore, for people to be conscious and critical of the philosophy of life they have assumed, and to be willing to adopt a new model if it commends itself as a more reasonable alternative. Classical apologists encourage nontheists to try looking at the world through theistic glasses and see the difference it will make. This is not an exercise in futility because, as Geisler argues, "There are a limited number of mutually exclusive ways to view the whole of reality."[5]

This emphasis on worldviews is significant and valuable for two reasons. First, non-Christians are often unaware that they look at life through a specific set of worldview "glasses." Making them aware of this can *help non-Christians rethink some of their beliefs*. Second, non-Christians and Christians alike are often unaware that distinctive Christian beliefs typically seem odd or even absurd to non-Christians because they do not fit within their worldview. Comparing the two worldviews can *help non-Christians recognize the rationality of Christian beliefs given a theistic worldview*. Comparing the naturalist worldview with the Christian theistic worldview, for example, can help non-Christians understand why a miracle would seem reasonable and believable to a Christian even though it seems absurd to the naturalist. Once the naturalist understands that the real question is not whether miracles are possible but whether God exists, the apologetic discussion is placed on a much broader, and hence firmer, foundation of understanding.

Recognizes Common Ground with Non-Christians

The third major strength of the classical approach is its *ability to find common ground with non-Christians* in the principles of reason and in whatever truths they already believe. In this characteristic emphasis, classical apologists show themselves concerned with the practical task of communicating the gospel effectively to people of differing religious and philosophical beliefs. Non-Christians are shown respect when classical apologists commend them for recognizing specific truths even while seeking to convince them of the distinctive, saving truths of the Christian message. For example, classical apologists commend atheists for their rejection of superstition and their concern that religion not be used as a pretext for complacency or ignorance. Acknowledging the legitimate concerns and genuine insights of an unbeliever can be an effective means of building mutual respect and preparing the way for a candid discussion of the truth that the unbeliever still needs to hear.

POTENTIAL WEAKNESSES OF CLASSICAL APOLOGETICS

During the past two centuries the classical approach has come under increasing fire both from outside the church and from within. As the near consensus of the Christian worldview has been eroded and broken down by the onslaught of secularism and humanism in the West, many Christians have concluded that the classical approach has some significant problems, or at the very least limitations.

Let us first briefly mention some common criticisms of this approach that are based on clear and outright misunderstandings. Classical apologists do not claim that one must believe in God or in Christ on the basis of rational arguments to be justified in believing or to have a proper faith. What they maintain is that for such belief to be rational, there must be somewhere a rational grounding of that belief in truth—even if the believer may not be aware of that grounding or be able to articulate it. Likewise, classical apologetics does not substitute reason for faith. Classical apologists regard some of the beliefs essential to sound faith to be demonstrable by reason, but faith itself includes beliefs that reason cannot demonstrate. Moreover, faith is more than an assent of the mind to beliefs; it is also a response of the will to God, and this is something that reason cannot produce.

While such misplaced criticisms should definitely be set aside, we should give careful consideration to other concerns that critics have voiced about the classical approach. These criticisms do not apply to all classical apologists, but they do apply to some, and all of these criticisms explain why classical apologists generally do not limit themselves to a purely rational apologetic method. We will highlight three of these.

Overestimates the Adequacy of Reason as a Criterion for Truth

As valuable as reason or logic is in apologetics, many Christian apologists today express reservations about the primacy and comprehensive use of reason, and in particular deductive logic, in classical apologetics. We may distinguish three concerns under this general heading.

First, *logic, though universally necessary, is universally insufficient as a criterion of truth.* This is because at best deductive logic can only test the *falsity* of a worldview, and cannot actually determine that a worldview is *true.* This is because a deductive argument, even if formally correct or valid, is assured of arriving at a true conclusion only if the premises are true. Ultimately the premises of an apologetic argument must consist of facts derived from some source other than logical analysis. It is doubtful that any religiously significant truths can be proved using reason alone, apart from facts about the world or us. Application of the law of contradiction in critiques of worldviews may reveal flaws, but, as Montgomery argues, "the fallaciousness of another world-view never establishes the truth of your own."[6]

Now, classical apologists during the past couple centuries have recognized that apologetic arguments cannot proceed on the basis of reason alone. As we have explained, contemporary classical apologists such as Norman Geisler or Peter Kreeft or William Lane Craig are not rationalists in the older sense of the term. However, the concern raised here is still an important one, because once it is recognized that reason alone does not suffice as the criterion of truth, one must decide what other criteria will be used in apologetic argument. And this raises the second difficulty for the classical approach's attempt to find universally sufficient criteria for determining truth: there appear to be *no universally accepted criteria of truth that can be applied without already assuming the truth of a particular worldview.*

For example, most contemporary classical apologists employ some form of **combinationalism** (as Geisler has called it): testing for truth on the basis of internal coherence (logic) and external coherence (fact). Others add that whether a worldview is consistently livable or practicable must also be regarded as a test for truth. But these tests cannot be employed in a worldview vacuum. Those who employ them already have a worldview from within which they view some claims as coherent and others not, some statements as fact and others not, some ideas as livable and others not. Appeals to these tests can be misleading because one's perspective on what is reasonable, factual, and practical is largely determined by the worldview one has already espoused.

Recognizing this problem, Geisler, unlike most classical apologists, rejects combinationalism as a test for the truth of worldviews. He states that "when testing world views we cannot presuppose the truth of a given context or framework, for that is precisely what is being tested. Combinationalism cannot be a test for the context (or model) by which the very facts, to which the combinationalists appeal, are given meaning."[7] What is perceived as rationally satisfactory and empirically adequate is actually predetermined by the theistic or nontheistic worldview one has. According to Geisler, "Combinationalism has no way to know whether the model fits the facts best because the facts are all prefitted by the model to give meaning to the whole from the very beginning."[8]

Geisler's alternative is a dual test of unaffirmability and undeniability, which only requires the admission that something finite exists to proceed to a demonstrative proof of theism. This test, though, comes very close to establishing rationalism, or the use of deductive logic alone, as the supposedly sufficient criterion for determining the truth of a worldview—despite the fact that Geisler recognizes the inadequacy of rationalism. The real question is whether Geisler's argument for theism is sound and cogent, or persuasive.

Third, the emphasis on logical analysis has come under fire for *presuming that human reasoning is capable of recognizing truth about God*. Apologists and theologians outside the classical tradition often complain that classical apologetics assumes that God and his relation to the world are susceptible to logical analysis and description by finite minds. This assumption appears to fly in the face of God's infinitude and transcendence, and rigorous application of it would seem to call into question such doctrines as the Incarnation and the Trinity, as well as predestination (particularly as understood by Lutherans and Calvinists). Many Christians regard these doctrines as **paradoxes**—concepts that are beyond resolution by logical analysis even though they are not illogical. Even most classical apologists today, while denying that any Christian doctrine is illogical, would concede that the being of God is beyond our ability to comprehend. Moreover, even if it is possible for Christians to perceive the logical coherence of their beliefs about God, it does not follow that non-Christians will be able to perceive that coherence.

The classical approach assumes that the application of logical categories to God is a neutral, objective manner on which Christians and non-Christians can agree. Apologists outside the classical tradition question this assumption. There is, they insist, no epistemological neutrality.

For all these reasons, then, the primacy of logic is widely regarded as a potential weakness of the classical approach. Reason is a necessary but insufficient criterion of truth, and there is no universally agreed-upon set of criteria that can be applied from an objective standpoint outside one's own worldview. In addition, there is continuing debate among Christians about the applicability of logic to the being of God and his relation to the world.

Depends on Theistic Arguments of Debated Validity and Value

The theistic arguments of natural theology have inherent limitations that make them a dubious foundation for apologetics in the eyes of many Christian thinkers.

First, in the opinion of many Christian apologists, *there are reasons to question whether the traditional theistic proofs are sound*. Mark Hanna speaks for many when he writes:

> Comprehensive verificationism does not succeed because of the un-soundness of theistic arguments. Beginning with a mere concept of God, one cannot validly infer the extraconceptual or actual existence of God. Beginning with a finite world, one cannot deductively arrive at an infinite God. In spite of the great ingenuity expended in attempting to frame a sound theistic argument, none has escaped the charge of smuggling in question-begging assumptions. Although there are recurrent attempts to rehabilitate the classic theistic arguments (e.g., the cosmological argument by Norman Geisler and other Thomists, the ontological argument by Charles Hartshorne, the teleological argument by Richard Taylor), they are rejected by most philosophers.[9]

The claim that none of the theistic arguments is sound is perhaps the most critical objection to classical apologetics. If the truth of theism cannot be established as a philosophical starting point for presenting the evidences for Christianity, the classical model is fundamentally flawed. Of course, classical apologists maintain that at least one, and perhaps several, of the traditional arguments are sound. But it should be noted that even classical apologists critique one another's theistic proofs. For example, Geisler disputes the validity of the *kalām* cosmological argument, preferring a modified form of the Thomistic cosmological argument.[10] According to Geisler, the *kalām* argument cannot establish theism over either deism or pantheism, and therefore cannot establish the theistic worldview.[11] We are therefore faced with the difficulty of deciding which, if any, of the theistic proofs used in the classical tradition is a cogent basis on which to defend theism.

A second limitation is that, even if they are sound, *the theistic arguments are often exceedingly complicated and beyond the grasp of most people.* Thomas Aquinas himself recognized this limitation, but it has attained greater importance in a modern society impatient with abstract reasoning. Even sophisticated persons capable of following an abstract argument are likely to remain skeptical in the face of a complicated, multilevel philosophical theistic proof. Concerning Geisler's revised cosmological argument, for example, Whitcomb writes, "One must seriously question whether any sophisticated unbeliever would surrender to God after reading such an argument."[12]

Third, even if the arguments are sound, it has often been pointed out that *they do not lead to the personal God of Christian theism.* Hoover adds that an excessive preoccupation with the theistic proofs actually inhibits the religious life because it can turn one away from the true personal God to a philosophical construct.[13] This criticism does not apply to all apologists who employ the classical approach. Still, the danger must be conceded. Some people may indeed end up believing in God as the conclusion of an argument rather than as (to use Francis Schaeffer's phrase) the God who is *there.* In any case, intellectual acceptance of the theistic arguments must not be confused with faith in God. As a rule, classical apologists recognize this limitation on theistic proofs, but it is a point worth emphasizing.

Does Not Address the Personal Dimensions of Knowledge and Belief

Classical apologists are concerned, as a practical matter, to persuade non-Christians to believe in Christ, as is evident in their emphasis on finding common ground with unbelievers. On the other hand, common ground for classical apologists is typically understood as rational or intellectual. This focus is widely perceived as a weakness in the classical approach because it *overlooks the personal, nonrational factors that contribute to a person's knowledge and beliefs.*

As Thomas V. Morris has pointed out, "no world view, and in fact no human knowledge at all, is without dependence on the nonlogical or personal contributions of the knower."[14] Classical apologists are often charged with overlooking this fact and writing as though people reason in a way that is totally dispassionate, disinterested, nonpersonal, and mechanical.[15] When the "personal coefficients of logic"[16] are ignored, an apologetic system becomes abstract, theoretical, and impractical. Commitment to ultimate philosophical perspectives is not merely intellectual; it is also influenced by emotional and volitional factors. Few people can objectively put on another set of worldview glasses to see if they make more sense of the world than their own, as classical apologists ask them to do.

It may be unrealistic, for instance, to expect naturalists to be willing to make a radical shift in thinking by looking at the world through theistic glasses. Naturalists may look at the theistic worldview with prejudice because they assume it would commit them to a change in lifestyle if they accepted it. They may associate belief in God with unpleasant experiences they had in church as children, or with an abusive relationship with a religious parent. To extend the metaphor, many people are unwilling to try on the Christian worldview glasses because of how they think those glasses will affect *their* appearance. These factors are overlooked when objections to the theistic worldview, or to specifically Christian beliefs, are answered in a purely logical mode.

We should repeat the point that these potential weaknesses in the classical approach are not criticisms of all classical apologists. Most of the accomplished apologists in this tradition nuance their approach to overcome or at least ameliorate some or all of these difficulties.

The following table summarizes the major notable strengths and potential weaknesses in the classical model of apologetics.

Classical Apologetics	
Notable Strengths	*Potential Weaknesses*
Affirms the universal applicability of reason	Overestimates the adequacy of reason as a criterion for truth
Raises awareness of the unavoidable role of worldviews	Depends on theistic arguments of debated validity and value
Recognizes common ground with non-Christians	Does not address the personal dimensions of knowledge and belief

CONCLUSION

The classical model of Christian apologetics has some significant strengths. It emphasizes the importance of logic, the need for an interpretive framework or worldview from within which facts gain meaning, and the value of finding common ground with non-Christians.

On the other hand, the classical approach is beset by certain potential limitations, which are often raised as objections to the entire approach. Of these, three stand out. First, the arguments used in classical apologetics tend to treat their criteria for testing the truth of Christianity as neutral criteria that can be objectively and correctly employed by Christians and non-Christians alike to determine the truth. Such neutrality would appear to be impossible: people come to the table with different ideas already formed about what is reasonable, what is factual, and what is practical. Second, the soundness of arguments used to establish theism as the true worldview is debated, and even those found to be sound are too abstract and complex to help most people. Third, classical apologetics tends to overlook the nonrational, personal factors that affect people's beliefs.

In reaction to these and other difficulties, most Christian apologists today working from an essentially classical model moderate or qualify that approach. Thus the aforementioned weaknesses do not apply to all apologists who operate within the classical tradition.

On the other hand, other Christian apologists have sought to develop alternative approaches to defending the faith. In the next section we will consider the one that is most closely related to the classical approach, that of evidentialism.

For Further Study

Clark, Kelly James. *Return to Reason: A Critique of Enlightenment Evidentialism and a Defense of Reason and Belief in God*. Grand Rapids: Eerdmans, 1990. See chapter 1, "Proving God's Existence: Problems and Prospects" (15-54), for a critique of classical apologetics.

Corduan, Winfried. *No Doubt about It: The Case for Christianity*. Nashville: Broadman & Holman, 1997. Originally *Reasonable Faith: Basic Christian Apologetics* (1993). Popularly written introduction to apologetics by a philosopher. Corduan follows Geisler's method and argument very closely but also presents that apologetic in a more practical, people-oriented fashion. (Corduan was also co-author of the second edition of Geisler's *Philosophy of Religion*.)

Green, Michael, and Alister McGrath. *How Shall We Reach Them? Defending and Communicating the Christian Faith to Nonbelievers*. Nashville: Nelson, Oliver-Nelson, 1995. Practical manual for making apologetics in the classical tradition more people-sensitive.

Part Three

Evidentialist Apologetics: Just the Facts

Chapter 8

Apologists Who Emphasize Fact

In the modern period American evangelical apologetics has been dominated by the **evidentialist** approach. Its emphasis is on the presentation of Christianity as *factual*—as supportable or verifiable by the examination of evidence. This type of apologetic system, while acknowledging that indisputable and absolutely certain proof of Christianity lies beyond human reach, defends the truth claims of the faith as eminently reasonable. More specifically, evidentialist apologetics argues that these crucial truths can be shown to be highly probable. Rather than defending the faith in two stages, as does classical apologetics (first by defending theism, then by defending specifically Christian claims), evidentialism uses multiple lines of evidence to support Christian theism as a whole.

In this chapter we will examine the roots of evidentialist apologetics and consider briefly the thought of five modern evidentialists. We will give special attention to the apologetic system of the influential contemporary evidentialist John Warwick Montgomery.

HISTORICAL ROOTS OF EVIDENTIALISM

Evidentialist apologetics may from one perspective be viewed as a subtype of classical apologetics. Both approaches want to provide reasons for faith that are accessible to non-Christians. However, the evidentialist approach has over the past two centuries gradually emerged as a significantly different model of apologetics.

Defending against Deism

The impetus to the development of evidentialist apologetics was the rise of deism. By the early eighteenth century modern science seemed to be explaining more and more about the natural world, requiring God as an explanation for things less and less. Copernicus, Galileo, Kepler, Newton—these giants of science had completely changed the way modern people looked at the world. The enormous success of science encouraged many people to believe that eventually everything could be explained naturalistically, thus eliminating the need to appeal to the existence of a supernatural Creator to explain reality as we know it. Deism was, then, in effect a way station on the road to atheism: the deists allowed that God had created the world and initiated the processes governing it but denied that God was involved in the subsequent history of creation or of humanity.

To combat deism apologists began constructing arguments defending the supernaturalism of biblical Christianity that were modeled after the sciences. The idea was essentially to fight fire with fire—to show that a scientific approach to the Christian truth claims would vindicate their rationality. The dominant work of apologetics to appear in this context was Joseph Butler's *Analogy of Religion* (1736). We will return to Butler's apologetic in more detail shortly. Suffice it to say that the book was the most successful and popular work of apologetics for well over a century, and inspired a proliferation of apologetic works emphasizing inductive reasoning analogous to that used in science. Indeed, Butler can arguably be called the father of evidentialism, even though, as we will see, his apologetic was only a precursor to the evidentialist approach.

William Paley and Natural Theology

Butler's approach quickly came to dominate conservative Protestant apologetics, especially in English-speaking countries. As deism flourished and contributed in turn to the skepticism of Kant and Hume, apologists increasingly mounted their defense of Christianity on two fronts. On one front they countered the philosophical objections to the traditional cosmological and ontological arguments for God's existence with detailed, empirically based versions of the teleological argument, or the argument from design. This line of argument was sometimes called physico-theology or, more commonly, **natural theology**.

William Paley (1743–1805) presented a classic statement of this theistic argument in his *Natural Theology*.[1] The book begins by introducing and elaborating on Paley's famous analogy of the watch providing evidence of a watchmaker. The bulk of the book consists of a detailed discussion of the arrangement and functions of the various components of the bodies of animals and humans. Evidence from plants, the elements, and astronomy is also adduced. Paley argues that from the "contrivances" evident in nature, one may infer that God is one, personal, intelligent, omnipotent, omniscient, omnipresent, eternal, self-existent, spiritual, and good. In his conclusion he explains the purpose of this line of reasoning. Although he expects that most of his readers already believe in God, he suggests that when that belief is tested, it will be helpful "to find a support in argument for what we had taken upon authority."[2] Furthermore, studying nature in order to find evidence of God enhances our awareness of God's hand in everything around us. Finally Paley urges that the proof of God's existence furnished by natural theology should encourage us to be open to receiving as true whatever revelation God may choose to impart. "The true Theist will be the first to listen to *any* credible communication of divine knowledge." By "credible" Paley means a revelation "which gives reasonable proof of having proceeded from him."[3]

For Paley, then, Christianity must prove itself to be based on an authentic revelation. This leads us to the second front of evidentialist apologetics: its appeal to history. Such proof is to be found, according to Paley and other likeminded apologists, especially in historical evidences for the central biblical events. Paley presented a classic statement of these evidences in his 1794 book, *A View of the Evidences of Christianity*.

The Rise of the Legal Evidence Model

Paley's argument in *View* was representative of a century-long trend of apologists developing historical, inductive arguments defending the biblical miracles, and especially the resurrection of Jesus Christ.[4] The epistemological basis for such apologetic arguments was the British empiricism pioneered by the philosopher **John Locke** (1632–1704).[5] Locke's own approach to apologetics was classical in form,[6] but apologists after him often applied his empiricist approach to general knowledge to the defense of Christianity. Ironically, Locke's own thought was in some respects appreciated by the deists, since he strongly insisted that revelation claims should be tested by reason. He himself, however, concluded that the miraculous claims of Christianity were true.

In any case, in the eighteenth century Christian apologists adopted and expanded on Locke's strategy for defending the historical evidence for the resurrection of Jesus. **Thomas Sherlock**'s book *The Tryal of the Witnesses of the Resurrection of Jesus* (1729) set the tone for what followed. As the title indicates, Sherlock argued for the historicity of the Resurrection on the model of a court trial. The thrust of the apologetic case was simple: an impartial jury, examining the evidence as one would in a court of law, would have to conclude that Jesus rose from the dead.

Sherlock argued that the Resurrection was an historical event subject to verification by human investigation, "a thing to be judg'd of by men's senses."[7]

Numerous other apologetic writings in the eighteenth century argued in a similar fashion, emphasizing the evidences for Christianity. This legal-evidences apologetic tradition continued throughout the nineteenth century (and continues to this day). Another nineteenth-century advocate of this tradition was **Richard Whately**, an Irish theologian and churchman who sharpened the evidentialist approach in his famous book entitled *Historic Doubts Relative to Napoleon Bonaparte* (1849). The point of this book was that the skepticism of Hume regarding miracles such as the resurrection of Jesus, followed through consistently, would lead to skepticism regarding the existence of Napoleon (who had died in 1821). Whately also contributed a textbook on apologetics, *Introductory Lessons on Christian Evidences* (1850). A third figure of note was **Simon Greenleaf**, a Harvard professor of legal evidences who took Sherlock's approach to the Resurrection to new heights in *The Testimony of the Evangelists* (1874). Greenleaf's arguments continue to be read and cited by both scholarly and popular evidentialist apologists to this day, and his book was recently reprinted.

JOSEPH BUTLER

The Christian apologist who pioneered the evidentialist approach was **Joseph Butler** (1692–1752). In 1736 Butler published *The Analogy of Religion, Natural and Revealed, to the Constitution and Course of Nature*.[8] It was the most important work contributing to a radical shift in British apologetics away from metaphysical, rationalistic argumentation to a more scientific, empirical form of reasoning. Butler wrote it to refute the deistic claim that, while natural religion was valid, revealed religion—Christianity per se—was beset by various intellectual problems and could not be rationally believed. He argued that the problems raised for the Christian religion are analogous to problems in nature.

It is critical that Butler's argument be seen in its context. Butler used analogy not to prove Christianity true, and not to provide a foundation for revealed religion, but to answer the objection that revealed religion is irrational. In his introduction he explained that his argument deals with *probability*. He admitted that the imperfect character of probabilistic knowledge is irrelevant "to an infinite Intelligence. . . . But to us, probability is the very guide of life" (2). He then proposed to argue, by probabilistic reasoning, "that he who denies the Scripture to have been from God" because of its apparent difficulties might as well, "for the very same reason, deny the world to have been formed by him" (4). Thus Butler sought to show that the deist, who admits the creation of the world by God, is being irrational in denying the divine origin of the biblical revelation—or at the very least "to answer objections" against revelation.

Butler rejected the attempt, typified in French philosopher René Descartes, to develop a Christian worldview "without foundation for the principles which we assume," a project Butler characterized as "building a world upon hypothesis" (4). Rather, he took for granted the existence of God as "an intelligent Author of Nature, and *natural* Governor of the world" (5), and used arguments from analogy to answer deistic objections against the revealed religion of Christianity (8).

Butler's book is divided into two major parts, dealing with natural religion and revealed religion respectively. The first division corresponds roughly to arguing for a position common to some forms of deism and Christianity, while the second division presents an argument for what is distinctive to Christianity itself. More specifically, Part I deals with life after death, arguing for the rationality of believing that rewards and punishments will be meted out by God based on our conduct in this life. Part II argues from analogies with nature that revelation, like nature, will contain things that seem problematic but are nevertheless true and should be accepted. Butler argued, for example, that the lack of universality in the Christian revelation—the fact that it is not known to all human beings—is not a valid objection against its truth.

Only in chapter 7 of Part II did Butler offer positive evidences and arguments for Christianity. He began by arguing that biblical history should be presumed accurate in the absence of evidence to the contrary. He pointed out that Paul's epistles offer substantial evidence for the gospel, independent of the other apostles. And he noted that Christianity appears fairly unique in having been founded on the belief in miracles (in contrast especially to Islam, which does not view Muhammad as a miraculous figure). While admitting that none of these arguments is a proof by itself, Butler averred that taken cumulatively, they form a strong proof. Another line of evidence for the truth of Christianity is the fact of fulfilled biblical prophecy. Butler anticipated and responded to the objection that we are presently unable to understand all of biblical prophecy, pointing out that our inability in this matter does not invalidate our conclusion that some biblical prophecies have been fulfilled.

Butler was therefore frank in admitting that problems face the Christian who wishes to understand everything in the Bible and in Christian faith. But in his estimation these problems are minor and do not undermine the truth of Christianity. Rather, he found it remarkable that the Bible, written so long ago by so many writers over such a long period of time, is not viewed as more problematic than it is—that it has not been completely refuted and set aside.

Butler concluded *The Analogy of Religion* with a chapter emphasizing that he had been answering objections, not providing absolute proof. In fact, he wrote, "in this treatise I have argued upon the principles of others, not my own; and I have omitted what I think true, and of the utmost importance, because by others thought unintelligible, or not true" (249). By arguing on the principles of others Butler meant that, for the sake of argument, he had contended that even if the deists or other critics of Christianity were allowed certain principles or assumptions, their objections against the Christian revelation were still without force. He admitted that his positive arguments for Christian beliefs fell short of being demonstrative, but at the same time he thought they were "impossible . . . to be evaded, or answered" (251). "Those who believe will here find the scheme of Christianity cleared of objections, and the evidence of it in a peculiar manner strengthened: those who do not believe, will at least be shown the absurdity of all attempts to prove Christianity false" (251–252).

We conclude by emphasizing four points about Butler's method. First, his approach was empirical, not rationalistic, and the character of his conclusions was that of probability, not certainty. His dictum that "probability is the very guide of life" (2) is a classic expression of the evidentialist perspective. Finite human beings cannot expect to gain absolutely certain knowledge of the past, of the course of nature, or of any empirical reality.

Second, Butler employed this empirical, inductive, and probabilistic approach in a *defensive* mode of apologetic reasoning. His goal was not to prove Christianity true, but to prove that deistic charges that Christianity was irrational were unfounded.

Third, Butler candidly stated that he was attempting to respond to the deists on their own ground—"I have argued upon the principles of others, not my own" (249). Thus, one should not conclude that Butler was claiming that Christianity requires an empirical defense or that its truth cannot be accepted on other grounds.

Fourth, Butler assumed the existence of a God, an assumption he could make because his opponents granted it. He was therefore not claiming to mount a defense of Christianity that would withstand the scrutiny of the hard-line atheist.

By contrast, the main opposing worldview for twentieth-century evidentialists was indeed atheism, or at least some form of agnosticism or skepticism. In the remainder of this chapter we will profile the apologetic thought of four leading evidentialists from the twentieth century.

JAMES ORR

James Orr (1844–1913)[9] was a Scottish pastor and scholar who eventually became a noted professor of apologetics and theology in Glasgow during the early part of the twentieth century. His books were highly successful and popular defenses of Christian belief among evangelicals in English-speaking countries around the world.[10]

In his classic apologetic book, *The Christian View of God and the World as Centering in the Incarnation*, Orr sought to defend the Christian worldview by appealing to the facts. Orr, who endorsed Butler's argument in *The Analogy of Religion* (90),[11] emphasized that faith in Christ commits the believer to a whole theology and worldview that need to be defended: "He who with his whole heart believes in Jesus as the Son of God is thereby committed to much else besides. He is committed to a view of God, to a view of man, to a view of sin, to a view of Redemption, to a view of the purpose of God in creation and history, to a view of human destiny, found only in Christianity" (4).

Orr proposes to defend the Christian view of all these matters by an appeal to history, for it brings "all the issues into court at once. The verdict of history is at once a judgment on the answers which have been given to the theological question; on their agreement with the sum-total of the facts of Christianity; on the methods of exegesis and New Testament criticism by which they have been supported; on their power to maintain themselves against rival views; on how far the existence of Christianity is dependent on them, or bound up with them" (43–44). Note Orr's use of the courtroom metaphor popularized by apologists like Sherlock and Greenleaf; he speaks of bringing "issues into court" and of reaching a "verdict." The imitation of legal argument is typical of the evidentialist approach.

Contrary to a common stereotype of the evidentialist approach, Orr did not maintain that Christianity was to be proved by an appeal to bare or brute facts. The facts support Christianity because they are set in a context that includes speech expressive of the meaning of the facts:

The gospel is no mere proclamation of "eternal truths," but the discovery of a saving purpose of God for mankind, executed in time. But the doctrines are the interpretation of the facts. The facts do not stand blank and dumb before us, but have a voice given to them, and a meaning put into them. They are accompanied by living speech, which makes their meaning clear. . . . [T]he facts of Christianity, rightly understood and interpreted, not only yield special doctrines, but compel us to develop out of them a determinate "Weltanschauung." (22–23)

In Orr's view, belief in God and belief in Christ "stand or fall together" (65). "A genuine Theism can never long remain a bare Theism" (76). To be complete and stable, theism, or belief in God, must be held in the context of "the entire Christian view" provided in the biblical revelation (77). This revelation is absolutely necessary, because reason on its own cannot arrive at a Christian worldview. Reason can, however, give "abundant corroboration and verification" to the truth of the Christian revelation. This verification, while perhaps not demonstrative, at least is sufficient to show "that the Christian view of God is not *un*reasonable" (111). Orr is confident that the facts, properly presented, can be used to show that objections to Christianity are without merit. "The reason why Christianity cannot be waved out of the world at the bidding of sceptics simply is, that the facts are too strong for the attempt. The theories which would explain Christianity away make shipwreck on the facts" (234).

CLARK H. PINNOCK

Clark Pinnock is a well-known proponent of evidentialist apologetics whose approach to the defense of the Christian faith has been unusually diverse.[12] His *Set Forth Your Case* focuses on the philosophical and cultural movements that shaped twentieth-century thought in order to expose the inadequacy of non-Christian worldviews. In this book he decries rationalism and mysticism and espouses the epistemological alternative of empirical verifiability. Thus his apologetic system centers on the historical resurrection of Christ and the historical reliability of the Bible. Pinnock challenges the non-Christian "to suspend his prejudice against Christianity for the time it takes to examine fairly the evidence for the Christian faith, to take up a proven method for ascertaining the truth, the empirical method, and apply it to the biblical records."[13] Pinnock is confident that the person who does this will find a strong probable case for the truth of Christianity.

Pinnock's *Live Now, Brother* details the metaphysical and moral crisis in human values and offers as a solution the concept of grounding values in a supernatural revelation. He then presents the person and work of Christ, with special emphasis on the Resurrection as an historical fact to authenticate the Bible's revelatory claims. *A Case for Faith* offers a "comprehensive evidential picture" by developing five circles of evidence for the truth of the Christian faith: the pragmatic basis for faith (existential needs), the experiential basis (religious intuitions), the cosmic basis (rational scrutiny), the historical basis (historical evidence), and the community basis (moral necessities).

Like other evidentialists, Pinnock uses several lines of evidence as "reasonable probabilities" that combine together like "argumentative links in a legal brief" or strands in a rope.[14] He offers yet another metaphor: "Like legs of a table, each shaft of evidence does its part to support the weight of the case for Christianity. Because we are all culturally conditioned in different ways, it is inevitable that some of us will be more impressed with one evidential approach than another." Pinnock acknowledges that the knowledge gained through empiricism is only probable, but maintains that one cannot wait "until all uncertainty disappears before dealing with ultimate issues."[15] Probability, he writes, indeed falls short of the absolute certainty of mathematics, but "it is the sort of knowledge we are able to operate on in all the affairs of life, and it is adequate to provide us with a sound basis for the trustful certainty of faith."[16] Pinnock supports this position in contradistinction to presuppositionalism in "The Philosophy of Christian Evidences," a chapter in *Jerusalem and Athens*, where he writes that "a philosophy of Christian evidences which employs theistic argument and historical evidence is needed, lest the gospel be discredited as a grand and unwarranted assumption."[17]

Another major aspect of Pinnock's apologetic approach is a defense of biblical revelation, inspiration, and hermeneutics in view of the challenges of modern theology and higher criticism. For Pinnock the defense of the Bible as revelation must be carried out inductively, by examining the evidences and building up a doctrine of Scripture from the empirical facts about the Bible, as well as from biblical statements about inspiration. In his earlier works he utilized this inductivist approach to defend the traditional evangelical doctrine of biblical inerrancy.[18] In his later works he moved away from this conservative position and argued for a view of Scripture as "inerrant" only in a very loose sense. According to Pinnock, the doctrine of strict biblical inerrancy is flawed because it is based on deductions from the doctrine of inspiration rather than on an inductive study of what the Bible says about itself and of the actual phenomena of the biblical text.[19]

JOHN WARWICK MONTGOMERY

John Warwick Montgomery's numerous books and articles, years of teaching on the graduate level in the United States and France, and public debates with men like Bishop James Pike, Thomas J. Altizer, and Joseph Fletcher have earned him a prominent place as a Christian theologian, historian, lawyer, and apologist.[20] Montgomery influenced Josh McDowell, through whom evidentialist apologetics gained a wide popular audience. In the 1970s and 1980s Montgomery was the leading advocate of the evidentialist approach to apologetics.

Montgomery's apologetic system is strongly empirical, with an emphasis on the historical evidence for the resurrection of Jesus. He regards apologetics as a kind of evangelism designed to overcome objections to the saving message of the Gospels. He seeks to do this by grounding Christianity on historically verifiable truths beginning with a demonstration of the reliability of the Gospel records as primary historical documents. He calls historians to suspend disbelief and honestly examine the evidence without prejudging it on the basis of antisupernatural bias. This line of argumentation leads to the conclusion that Jesus' resurrection proves his divine claims to be true. Montgomery acknowledges that this kind of argument can provide only probable, not certain, conclusions, and that historical arguments, while they may provide objective grounding, do not necessarily produce subjective belief.

One of Montgomery's most recent articulations of his evidentialist apologetic was in an essay entitled "The Jury Returns: A Juridical Defense of Christianity."[21] He contrasts the appeals to self-validating faith experiences in Eastern religions with the factual verifiability of the Christian faith: "Christianity, on the other hand, declares that the truth of its absolute claims rests squarely on certain historical facts, open to ordinary investigation. These facts relate essentially to the man Jesus, His presentation of Himself as God in human flesh, and His resurrection from the dead as proof of His deity" (319).

Whereas elsewhere he employed "standard, accepted techniques of historical analysis" to argue for the truth of these facts, in this essay Montgomery urges the application of specifically "legal reasoning and the law of evidence" to the apologetic task (320). Recall the extensive use of the courtroom model in evidentialist apologetics going back to Thomas Sherlock and Simon Greenleaf and echoed by James Orr. Montgomery's case for Christianity begins with the reliability of the New Testament writings as historical documents. He quotes with approval Greenleaf and other legal scholars in support of the conclusion that "the competence of the New Testament documents would be established in any court of law" (322).

Given the authenticity and competency of the New Testament documents, Montgomery then defends their testimony to Jesus Christ. He cites a fourfold test for exposing or determining perjury from a legal text: (a) internal defects in the witness himself, that is, anything about the witness that would undermine his credibility; (b) external defects in the witness himself, that is, motives or reasons why the witness may be lying in this instance; (c) internal defects in the testimony itself, that is, inconsistencies in the witness's statements; and (d) external defects in the testimony itself, that is, inconsistencies between the witness's statements and other facts or testimonies from other witnesses.[22]

Montgomery applies this fourfold test within an evidentialist approach, and presents four reasons for concluding that the New Testament documents cannot be impugned with providing false testimony. (a) There is no reason to regard the New Testament writers as untrustworthy. (b) They had no motive to lie about Jesus, and indeed suffered greatly for their testimony to Jesus. (c) The Gospel accounts differ enough to be regarded as independent yet are not inconsistent with one another. (d) The New Testament accounts have been abundantly confirmed by archaeological and historical study (324–326).

Montgomery extends the juridical model even further. Had the New Testament writers tried to lie about Jesus, Montgomery argues that they would not have gotten away with it. The Jewish religious leaders function as "hostile witnesses" because of their inability to answer the apostles' claim that Jesus had risen from the dead (327, 330). Montgomery denies the charge that the New Testament writings are to be rejected as "hearsay"—secondhand information is often accepted in both civil and criminal cases, where that information can be evaluated in some way. And he points out that the New Testament contains statements indicating that the writers are offering eyewitness testimony (330).

The next stage in Montgomery's apologetic is his argument for the resurrection of Jesus as an historical event. We will discuss the evidentialist argument for the Resurrection in some detail in chapter 10. Here we draw attention to some key elements of Montgomery's presentation of that argument. The core is the "missing body" argument. If Jesus' body didn't rise from the dead, then someone must have stolen it (because an occupied tomb would have brought the Resurrection story to a grinding halt). But the Roman authorities would not steal the body because that might contribute to unrest; the Jewish authorities would not steal it because that would undermine their religious influence; and the disciples would not steal it and then lie about Jesus rising from the dead because that would get them into trouble with the Roman and Jewish authorities (precisely for the reasons just mentioned). By process of elimination, then, no one stole the body, and therefore the body must have been raised from the dead (331).

Admittedly such fantastic alternative explanations as Schonfield's *Passover Plot* (according to which Jesus arranged to be crucified and managed to survive the ordeal long enough to convince his disciples he had risen) are barely possible. "But legal reasoning operates on *probabilities*, not possibilities" (332). The fact that legal reasoning cannot produce absolute demonstrative proof is not a valid objection, even though if Jesus did rise from the dead we are expected to place absolute faith in him. In matters of fact, probability is unavoidable. "And the law in every land redistributes property and takes away liberty (if not life) by verdicts and judgments rooted in the examination of evidence and probabilistic standards of proof" (323).

Given that Jesus rose from the dead, can this fact alone establish the truth of Jesus' claims to deity? Montgomery stoutly answers in the affirmative, arguing that "the very nature of legal argument (judgments rendered on the basis of factual verdicts) rests on the ability of facts to speak for themselves" (335). He points out that the Resurrection did not occur in a factual vacuum, but was accompanied by Jesus' own explanation of its significance as the miraculous act of God.

Not only can Jesus' resurrection alone establish his deity, it can establish the existence of the Deity in the first place. The existence of God "then becomes the proper inference from Jesus' resurrection as he himself explained it—not a prior metaphysical hurdle to jump in order to arrive at the proper historical and evidential interpretation of that event" (336). This last comment is aimed at classical apologetics, which argues that the existence of God needs to be established before trying to show the truth and meaning of Jesus' resurrection. Montgomery, in fact, was one of the first evidentialists to self-consciously distinguish his apologetic method from the classical approach.

Although Montgomery is best known for his historical evidentialism, he has written very widely in apologetics and theology. One aspect of his apologetics that is not often noticed is his interest in a "literary apologetic" for the Christian gospel. Such an apologetic, he has argued, can draw from such fiction as *The Lord of the Rings* as pointers "to the fulfillment of mankind's longings in the factuality of the Gospel Story."[23]

RICHARD SWINBURNE

The diversity of evidentialist apologetics would not be well represented without some notice of the work of Richard Swinburne. From 1977 to 1981 Swinburne, a British philosopher, published a trilogy of books in defense of theism.[24] In 1989 he launched a four-book series defending specifically Christian beliefs.[25] These seven books constitute the most sophisticated evidentialist defense of Christianity to appear so far. Swinburne's plan, as he has explained, was "to use the criteria of modern natural science, analysed with the careful rigour of modern philosophy, to show the meaningfulness and justification of Christian theology."[26] In 1996 he published *Is There a God?* in which he offered a more popular-level statement of his apologetic. Swinburne summarizes his argument at the beginning of this book:

> Scientists, historians, and detectives observe data and proceed thence to some theory about what best explains the occurrence of these data. We can analyse the criteria which they use in reaching a conclusion that a certain theory is better supported by the data than a different theory—that is, more likely, on the basis of those data, to be true. Using those same criteria, we find that the view that there is a God explains everything we observe, not just some narrow range of data. It explains the fact that there is a universe at all, that scientific laws operate within it, that it contains conscious animals and humans with very complex intricately organized bodies, that we have abundant opportunities for developing ourselves and the world, as well as the more particular data that humans report miracles and have religious experiences. In so far as scientific causes and laws explain some of these things (and in part they do), these very causes and laws need explaining, and God's action explains them. The very same criteria which scientists use to reach their own theories lead us to move beyond those theories to a creator God who sustains everything in existence.[27]

Swinburne begins his case for Christianity with the question of the coherence of the Christian conception of God,[28] because if the notion of God is incoherent, there is no point in asking if there is enough evidence to justify belief in God's existence. His goal in this stage of his apologetic is to defend theism from a priori objections that would disallow in advance the marshaling of evidence for God's existence.[29]

Although Swinburne defends a form of theism, he finds it necessary to reject specific aspects of traditional or classical theism that he finds incoherent. Most significantly, he argues that God knows only what it is logically possible to know, and hence that God does not know all future events that depend on the free decisions of creatures. In keeping with this view, he denies that God is a "timeless" being, preferring to view God as everlasting.[30]

The most important fact about God's nature for Swinburne's argument is that, if God exists, he is what he is necessarily or essentially; his existence and nature are not dependent on anyone or anything else. "If, as theism maintains, there is a God who is essentially and eternally omnipotent, omniscient, and perfectly free, then he will be the ultimate brute fact which explains everything else."[31]

Swinburne's central apologetic argument is that the existence of this God is "significantly more probable than not."[32] He contends that the existence of God provides a simple, powerful explanation for what we already know.

> It remains passing strange that there exists anything at all. But if there is to exist anything, it is far more likely to be something with the simplicity of God than something like the universe with all its characteristics crying out for explanation without there being God to explain it. . . . The experience of so many men in their moments of religious vision corroborates what nature and history shows to be quite likely—that there is a God who made and sustains man and the universe.[33]

Swinburne admits that it is always possible to challenge this or that element of his or any other theist's argument. He points out, though, that this is also true in science, history, and politics. "But life is short and we have to act on the basis of what such evidence as we have had time to investigate shows on balance to be probably true."[34]

CONCLUSION

Although the five apologists profiled in this chapter are all identified with the evidential tradition pioneered by Joseph Butler, some distinct differences among them should not be overlooked. John Warwick Montgomery is perhaps the most thoroughly empiricist or inductivist of the five, by which we mean that inductive argument or factual investigation plays the most comprehensive role in his apologetic. He is also the only one of the five who is overtly critical of the classical apologetic tradition and its reliance on deductive argument. Yet even Montgomery rejects a pure empiricism.

James Orr, writing before the advent of distinctively Reformed apologetics, developed an approach that in some respects anticipated the presuppositionalist form of Reformed apologetics. Yet at its core, Orr's method is evidentialist. We will discuss the relationship of Orr's apologetic to Reformed apologetics in Part Four.

Evidentialism is, by its nature, rather eclectic. As Montgomery once remarked, "But just as there are numerous ways to skin a cat, so there are numerous ways to defend Christianity."[35] Evidentialists freely combine multiple lines of reasoning, often from widely different disciplines, in support of the Christian faith. Thus they often recast arguments from other apologetic approaches as elements in an overall evidential case for the truth of Christianity. Each evidentialist also tends to emphasize those types of evidences that are of special interest to him, and some evidentialists are more eclectic than others. Thus Montgomery emphasizes historical evidences while Pinnock emphasizes the importance of a variety of types of evidences.

In the following chapters we will examine the evidential approach in greater detail, drawing on the writings of these five apologists and others who follow in the evidentialist tradition.

For Further Study

Abraham, William J. "Cumulative Case Arguments for Christian Theism." In *The Rationality of Religious Belief: Essays in Honour of Basil Mitchell*, ed. William J. Abraham and Steven W. Holtzer, 17-37. Oxford: Clarendon, 1987. Exposition of Basil Mitchell's form of evidentialism, with some comparisons to Swinburne; for advanced readers.

Montgomery, John Warwick, ed. *Christianity for the Tough-Minded: Essays in Support of an Intellectually Defensible Religious Commitment*. Minneapolis: Bethany Fellowship, 1973. Essays by Montgomery, James R. Moore, Rod Rosenbladt, and others advocating an evidentialist apologetic and taking on such wide-ranging subjects as situation ethics, Buddhism, LSD, and the Resurrection.

Wainwright, William J. "The Nature of Reason: Locke, Swinburne, and Edwards." In *Reason and the Christian Religion: Essays in Honour of Richard Swinburne*, edited by Alan G. Padgett, 91-118. Oxford: Clarendon, 1994. Fruitful comparison of Swinburne's evidentialism with the thought of John Locke and Jonathan Edwards; for advanced readers.

Chapter 9

Evidentialist Apologetics: Faith Founded on Fact

The title of John Warwick Montgomery's best-known book, *Faith Founded on Fact*, well illustrates the methodological perspective of the evidentialist model of apologetics. Evidentialists believe that "the facts speak for themselves"—that the best approach to defending the Christian faith is simply to present the factual evidence for the crucial claims of Christ. This rather simple way of stating their position, of course, does not do justice to the sophisticated way that evidentialist scholars have developed a philosophy of fact to undergird the apologetic task. In this chapter, then, we shall consider in some detail the evidentialist system of apologetics in order to come to terms with the distinctive way it responds to the challenges facing the Christian apologist.

METHODS FOR DISCOVERING TRUTH

Evidentialism in Christian apologetics seeks to show the truth of Christianity by demonstrating its factuality. Whereas classical apologetics characteristically regards logic or reason as the primary criterion of truth, evidentialism characteristically assigns this priority to fact. (This difference can be understood largely as a matter of emphasis; of course, both classical apologists and evidentialists consider reason and fact to be both essential to apologetic argumentation.) The meaning of "fact" in evidentialism is quite broad. Bernard Ramm, for example, classifies the scope of Christian evidences under the three categories of *material fact* (historical events, documents, archaeological artifacts), *supernatural fact* (events or phenomena that can only be explained by "invoking the category of the supernatural"), and *experiential fact* (individual and social phenomena).[1] This empirical approach makes use of a wide variety of concrete evidences, although some, like the historical evidence for the resurrection of Christ, are more extensively developed and emphasized.

Two Kinds of "Evidentialism"

Evidentialism in evangelical Christian apologetics should be carefully distinguished from *epistemological evidentialism,* which adheres to W. K. Clifford's dictum that "it is wrong, everywhere, always, and for anyone, to believe anything upon insufficient evidence."[2] Clifford's maxim has rightly been questioned from a variety of perspectives. For one thing, the statement itself is not one for which we can even imagine what would constitute "sufficient evidence"; what would count for or against evidence for the maxim? Second, it establishes what we might call an *epistemology of suspicion:* the belief that we should consider all beliefs false unless proven true by sufficient evidence. But why should the burden of proof be placed on a belief rather than on its denial? If I believe that the world exists as a reality independent of my senses, I am perfectly right to adhere to this belief in the absence of reasons or evidence to the contrary.

Apologetical evidentialism does not assume epistemological evidentialism, and most if not all evidentialist apologists would reject Clifford's maxim. If we were to formulate a maxim for evidentialist apologetics, it would be something like this: it is wrong, everywhere, always, and for anyone, *to tell someone else* to believe something other than on the basis of evidence. In other words, evidentialism in apologetics places a certain burden of proof on the apologist to show non-Christians why it is rational to believe in Christ. At the same time, evidentialists claim that the truth of the Christian message cannot be successfully or properly denied without a fair consideration of the factual basis for the Christian truth claim. Henceforth when we refer to evidentialism, we are referring to the apologetic approach.

Although apologetical evidentialists generally do not subscribe to epistemological evidentialism, they sometimes do argue that people ought to have evidence or reasons for the beliefs they hold in matters of supreme importance. Dan Story, for example, contends, "If you and I are to bet our eternity on a particular religion, we had better have reasons for why we believe as we do."[3] The point here is to press non-Christians to inquire whether they have good reasons for believing what they believe instead of believing in Christ.

Priority of Fact and Induction

Although there are different varieties of evidentialist apologetics, they have several crucial aspects in common. First, *evidentialism is primarily inductive, rather than deductive, in its logical form.* Inductive arguments reason from as many facts, or data, as can be mustered to a conclusion that is shown to be supported in some way by the facts. By contrast, deductive arguments, such as those favored in classical apologetics, reason from as few facts, or premises, as are needed to a conclusion that is shown to follow from the facts. Evidentialism makes induction, rather than deduction, the primary form of apologetic argumentation.

We say "primarily" because deduction does play a role in evidentialist argument (as of course induction plays a role in classical apologetics), and it would be a mistake to characterize evidentialism as relying *solely* on inductive argument. Even John Warwick Montgomery, whose advocacy of empirical method is more thoroughgoing than perhaps any other noted evidentialist, denies that all knowledge is gained solely through inductive reasoning—a position known as **inductivism**. He recognizes that there is actually a complementary interplay of deduction and induction in investigative operations, as well as a second level of induction that C. S. Peirce called imaginative retroduction or **abduction**. This involves an interaction between concepts, hypotheses, and theories and facts, observations, and experiments through imagination and logic.[4]

Nevertheless, evidentialists insist that verification of the central claims of Christianity unavoidably involves induction. Moreover, at least some evidentialists are dissatisfied with the primarily deductive approach used in classical apologetics. They insist that a sound apologetic can and must consist primarily in an appeal to the facts. For Montgomery the facts take precedence over rationality and should be viewed as essentially self-interpreting. He explicitly rejects the claim that one must first establish the truth of a worldview and then view the facts within that worldview context. Rather, he insists, the facts determine the worldview.

> Facts are not made of wax, capable of infinite molding from the pressure of interpretive world-views. . . . Facts ultimately arbitrate interpretations, not the reverse, at least where good science (and not bad philosophy) is being practiced. . . . If one removes his nose from philosophical speculation and breathes the fresher air of societal and personal decision-making, he will find abundant illustration that facts must carry their own interpretations (i.e., must arbitrate among diverse interpretations of the data).[5]

More recently he reiterated this point in an essay defending a "juridical" approach to apologetics—one that adopts legal principles of evidence as the methodological basis for verifying the Christian truth claims. He argues that "the very nature of legal argument (judgments rendered on the basis of factual verdicts) rests on the ability of facts to speak for themselves."[6]

The priority assigned to factual evidence over against rational deduction does not mean that evidentialists are critical of reason or logic. According to Montgomery, "The law of contradiction and the logical thinking based upon it are not optional. They must be employed for any meaningful thought, theological or otherwise."[7] However, evidentialists are suspicious of logic employed in a speculative manner, and they emphasize that rational arguments are only as good as the facts with which they work. Logical coherence or consistency is at best a negative test for truth, because it is possible to construct a coherent worldview that is actually false. Montgomery observes that "the greatest of the world's madmen have held the most consistent delusions,"[8] and illustrates his concern in an amusing parable about a man who was convinced he was dead.

> His concerned wife and friends sent him to the friendly neighborhood psychiatrist. The psychiatrist determined to cure him by convincing him of one fact that contradicted his belief that he was dead. The fact that the psychiatrist settled on was the simple truth that dead men do not bleed, and he put the patient to work reading medical texts, observing autopsies, etc. After weeks of effort, the patient finally said: "All right, all right! You've convinced me. Dead men do not bleed." Whereupon the psychiatrist stuck him in the arm with a needle, and the blood flowed. The man looked with a contorted, ashen face and cried: "Good Lord! Dead men bleed after all!"[9]

Montgomery concludes that the moral of the story is "that if you hold unsound presuppositions with sufficient tenacity, facts will make no difference to you at all."[9] His solution to this problem is to urge people to abandon any presuppositions that would close their minds to potential facts, whether they be metaphysical assumptions that prejudge the possibility of certain kinds of facts or methodological assumptions that preclude the discovery of certain kinds of facts.

Moreover, some evidentialists have argued that logical coherence or consistency is from one perspective faulty even as a negative test for truth. They point out that assigning priority to rational deductive logic can actually undermine the apologist's position because of the paradoxical nature of central Christian teachings. Montgomery, a Lutheran, follows Martin Luther in asserting that Christianity involves antinomies. An **antinomy** is an apparently intractable contradiction between two ideas, both of which we have good reason to accept as true (for example, predestination and free will, or God as one Being and three Persons). Such humanly irresolvable paradoxes are to be believed, according to Montgomery, because we have evidence from Scripture that they are true, not because they pass the test of logical consistency.

In defense of the rationality of believing such antinomies, Montgomery points out that antinomies exist in science as well as in theology. He asserts that "to blast other systems for internal inconsistencies does not necessarily destroy them, since in a real sense life *is* bigger than logic (the paradoxical wave-particle character of light does not destroy the empirically established evidence of light's characteristics or the physics that investigate it—and the paradoxical character of the Trinity surely doesn't destroy the Biblical evidence for God's trinitarian nature or the validity of Christian faith in the Triune God!)."[10]

Probable Character of Evidentialist Arguments

Evidential apologists of all stripes hold in common a second crucial aspect: *the conclusions of the apologetic arguments they employ are shown to be probable rather than certain.* This follows from the inductive nature of the arguments typically employed. Inductive reasoning assembles facts and argues that a particular conclusion offers the best or most probable explanation of the facts. Such reasoning does not absolutely close the door on other possible explanations of the facts, and for that reason inductive arguments do not attain certainty for their conclusions.

This lack of certainty is one of the most commonly criticized aspects of the evidentialist approach. If one concludes that God probably exists, or that Jesus most likely rose from the dead, how does that provide an adequate basis for the absolute commitment of faith in Jesus Christ to which people are summoned by the gospel? Evidentialists respond to this complaint on two levels.

On one level they insist that the lack of rational certainty is dictated by the nature of the Christian message. For Montgomery the probabilistic character of apologetic argument is an unavoidable result of the fact that the Christian faith centers on historical events. While he admits that his evidential apologetic leads only to a "high level of probability," he points out that we never have absolute rational certainty in our knowledge of the real world.[11] His argument "is not a rational proof in the sense of a demonstration in pure mathematics or formal logic; rather, it is an empirical argument based upon the application of historical method to an allegedly objective event. Thus it provides no more than probable evidence for the truth of the Christian world view."[12] For Montgomery, apodictic certainty is possible only in deductive arguments that proceed from self-evident axioms. No arguments that appeal to facts from the real world can furnish mathematically certain conclusions. But while empirical proofs fall short of certainty, all factual decisions in life are based on such proofs. "Historians, and indeed all of us, must make decisions constantly, and the only adequate guide is probability (since absolute certainty lies only in the realms of pure logic and mathematics, where, by definition, one encounters no matters of fact at all)."[13] Probabilistic arguments for the truth of Christianity, then, "cannot be summarily dismissed just because a vital religious question is at issue."[14]

On another level, though, evidentialism affirms that a kind of certainty is possible. Evidentialists do not claim that the most or best we can ever say is that God "probably exists" or that Jesus "most likely" rose from the dead. For them, apologetic arguments are designed to *show* that their conclusions are *at least* probably true. That they are certainly true can also be known, according to evidentialists, but not by argument. Such certainty is a characteristic of faith and is made possible by the work of the Holy Spirit. There is no contradiction in claiming that something is probably true (on the basis of a particular argument) and also certainly true (on some other basis). After all, if something is certainly true, then it is also probably true—with the probability of 1, or 100 percent.

Content-Neutral Methods

The third point on which all evidential apologists agree is that *evidentialism seeks to employ methods that are in principle acceptable to non-Christians* as a means of convincing them of the truth of Christianity. These methods are modeled on those used by both Christians and non-Christians in various disciplines. The evidentialist goal is to avoid gratuitous or disputable assumptions about the nature of things. Montgomery, for example, prefers the empirical method because the truth-*discovering* presuppositions of empiricism assume as little as possible while providing optimal conditions for objective discovery. He rejects apologetic approaches that begin with dogmatic, truth-*asserting* presuppositions, whether of a philosophical theism (as in classical apologetics) or of the biblical Christian theism (as in Reformed apologetics).

Properly, we should start not with substantive, "content" presuppositions about the world (e.g., the axiom of revelation), which gratuitously pre-judge the nature of what is, but with heuristic, methodological presuppositions that permit us to discover what the world is like—and (equally important) what it is not like. Such are the *a prioris* of empirical method, which are not only heuristic but *unavoidably necessary* in all of our endeavors to distinguish synthetic truth from falsity.[15]

In other words, Montgomery begins with presuppositions of *method* rather than of substantive *content*, which already assume a body of truth.

Evidentialists believe it crucial to employ methods modeled on those of disciplines other than Christian theology or apologetics, so that non-Christians can understand and appreciate the validity of the arguments. As Montgomery puts it, "Objective empirical evidence for Jesus Christ and his message is the only truly valid Christian apologetic possible, for it alone is subject to the canons of evidence employed in other fields of endeavor."[16]

Montgomery himself uses both historical methods and legal or juridical methods. These methods are closely related, because in fact legal evidences are a form of historical inquiry, pursuing an accurate understanding of past events related to cases brought before a court. In the previous chapter we surveyed a recent articulation by Montgomery of a juridical model of evidentialist apologetics. We also noted that such apologists as Thomas Sherlock and Simon Greenleaf developed evidentialism with a heavy reliance on the legal evidence model. Francis Beckwith, a former student of Montgomery, also prefers the legal evidence approach, especially in its defense of belief in miracles. Beckwith notes that miracle claims rely heavily on eyewitness testimony, and the legal model is particularly useful in evaluating such testimony.[17] Lawyers and professors of law, most recently Berkeley law professor Phillip Johnson, have also used legal reasoning to evaluate the arguments for evolution.[18]

Another model of evidentialist apologetics makes use of the scientific method. Dan Story, a former student of Montgomery, speaks for many evidentialists when he expresses a preference for the scientific method, precisely because it makes the truth of the Christian position verifiable for all people. "Truth, if it is to be acknowledged and accepted by all people as universal truth, must stand up to critical scrutiny; it must be able to be tested." Such criteria as authority, common sense, rationalism, and pragmatism cannot be used to discover the truth, but only to confirm what we have already learned to be the truth. "We are left with only one remaining truth-test. It is the only valid and reliable way to determine truth: the scientific method. . . . The [naturalistic] scientific worldview is subject to many distortions that evolve out of its erroneous presuppositions. But I am suggesting that the *scientific method* for discovering truth is the most reliable method because *it alone can be tested.*"[19]

While Montgomery typically does not present apologetics as employing the scientific method per se, he does argue that an evidentialist apologetic is based on the same methodological assumptions as the scientific method. "In our modern world we have found that the presuppositions of empirical method best fulfil this condition; but note that we are operating only with the presuppositions of scientific method, not with the rationalistic assumptions of Scientism ('the Religion of Science')."[20]

These empirical presuppositions are threefold: (1) epistemologically, knowledge is possible; (2) metaphysically, the universe is regular; and (3) ethically, the results of empirical investigation will be reported honestly.[21] The evidentialist uses these presuppositions as methodological assumptions that justify the empirical investigation of the universe rather than (as in classical apologetics) as axioms or premises from which the theistic worldview is deduced.

The Postmodern Challenge to Evidentialism

Evangelical evidentialist apologetics seeks to present evidence for the truth of Christianity using methods of inquiry that are in principle acceptable to non-Christians. This methodological approach has come under frontal assault from postmodernism. In essence, postmodernism is a philosophical movement that is rooted in modernism but proclaims the bankruptcy of certain aspects of modern thought. In particular, it denies the modernist belief that there is an objective truth about the world that can be discovered using reason. According to postmodernists, truth is subjective, not objective. Our knowledge of reality is a construction that we build up as we look at the world through our eyes and through the assumptions and experiences of our communities. This is true whether we are reading the Bible, watching the news, hearing testimony and arguments in a criminal court case, studying history, or doing science.

The old rationalist, modernist ideal was of a single, objective method of gaining more and more complete and accurate knowledge of the real world in the disciplines of history, law, science, and theology. Postmodernists argue that this ideal is to be replaced by a methodological pluralism in which there is no one right way to look at the world. And therein lies the problem for evidentialism: if there is no universally recognized way of determining the truth, the evidentialist project of presenting evidences using the accepted methods of established disciplines cannot get off the ground because such accepted methods no longer exist. Objective methods of discovering truth cannot be used with people who believe that "truth isn't discovered, but manufactured."[22]

In general, evidentialists make common cause with classical apologists in rejecting outright the relativism and subjectivism of postmodernism, but both acknowledge that the rationalistic ideal of modernism deserves criticism as well. People cannot find out the truth about God or any other ultimate issue in life through human reasoning or investigation. The postmodernist is thus left with no way at all to attain ultimate truth. For the Christian, on the other hand, the failure of modernism leaves us with revelation as the only viable way to know the truth about God and his world.

Moreover, evidentialists, like classical apologists, stress the indispensability of reason as a means by which we are able to *recognize* God's revelation. While these apologists would deny that we can discover the truth about God on our own, they do contend that we can "discover" the truth of God's revelation by applying the methods of such established disciplines as law, history, and science to the facts of Christianity. In order to make this case classical apologists directly confront what they regard as the self-defeating, irrational character of postmodernism. That is, they argue that postmodernism is forced to make absolutist statements denying absolute truth.

Evidentialists endorse the criticism that postmodernism is self-defeating, but their chief objection to it is that in everyday matters people do not accept a pluralistic, relativistic view of truth. Virtually all people are outraged when neo-Nazi groups claim that the Holocaust never happened. So much for the postmodern claim that history is whatever people construct it to be! When the space shuttle *Challenger* exploded, no one would have been satisfied had NASA issued a statement claiming that the cause of the accident was different for different people; everyone demanded to know exactly what happened, and why. In short, evidentialists argue that while postmodernism may seem formidable in theory, in practice it may to a great extent be ignored when presenting the evidence for the truth of the gospel. Dan Story, for example, concludes:

The majority of people on the street still view the world through modernist eyes. Even people who openly endorse postmodernism and argue for relativism do not live consistently with this philosophy—especially when it conflicts with *their* self-interests.

Although religious pluralism and moral relativism are quickly becoming ingrained in modern culture, the majority of people still think in terms of absolutes and accept the reality of logic and reason. These people need their intellectual obstacles to faith removed.[23]

THE DEFENSE OF THEOLOGY

For evidentialists, apologetics is a discipline that seeks to present the factual evidence or basis for the Christian faith in its every aspect. They join all apologists in seeing the nature of apologetics as dictated by the nature of the Christian faith, but they argue that this means that Christianity requires an evidential apologetic. They offer two reasons, broadly speaking, for this assertion.

First, they contend that since the Bible itself is an historical object, its content can only be properly evaluated when objective history is taken seriously. Montgomery quotes with approval George I. Mavrodes's statement, "Whenever the Bible forms a link in an epistemological chain, then sensory contact with the Bible must form the very next link."[24] The inductive method is the "only entrée to verifiable knowledge of the external world,"[25] and the Bible is part of that world. Moreover, the essential and distinctive truth claims of the Bible are historical claims, assertions that specific events took place in the past. This simple fact forces inductive argument upon us.

Second, evidentialists contend that *apologetic arguments in Scripture are evidential*. Montgomery lists four types of these arguments: miracle (especially the Resurrection), fulfilled prophecy, inner experience or subjective immediacy, and natural theology (of an empirical kind).[26] In particular he points to the evidential use of the Resurrection in the Christian apologetic of the first-century church. The apostles argued for the truth of the Resurrection by appealing to known facts and eyewitness testimonies, and by correlating this empirical evidence with the Old Testament prophecies fulfilled by Christ's death and resurrection (for example, Acts 2:22–36; 26:26). On the basis of the apostolic testimony, those of us who did not personally witness the Resurrection ought nevertheless to believe it (John 20:24–29). In order to commend the apostolic testimony to people today, we must be prepared to give them credible reasons to accept that testimony.

Admittedly, an evidentialist apologetic cannot provide absolute proof or compel faith, but this, evidentialists argue, is as it should be. "Absolute proof of the truth of Christ's claims is available only in personal relationship with Him; but contemporary man has every right to expect us to offer solid reasons for making such a total commitment."[27] The apologetic task is not to construct a rational substitute for faith but to provide a factual ground for faith. Thus, although the facts cannot *compel* faith, they can leave people without a legitimate excuse for not coming to faith. Evidentialists recognize, as do all other apologists, that human beings in their sinfulness can reject the truth to which the facts point. But Montgomery warns, "If you reject Him it will not be because of a deficiency of evidence but because of a perversity of will."[28]

Evidentialist John A. Bloom expands on this idea that evidence does not compel faith by considering a number of perspectives on the question, "Why isn't the evidence clearer?"[29] Bloom argues that "the God of the Bible is not seeking to make His presence compellingly obvious" because then human beings would not express their moral and spiritual attitudes freely. Furthermore, "because men may distort data to their seeming advantage, they will tend to obscure any evidence which hints that there is an authority or power greater than themselves, especially one which they cannot control and to which they should be subject."[30]

Evidentialist apologetics seeks to correlate and interpret empirical facts to show that the Christian faith is true. In turn, evidentialists understand the task of theology to be that of building on the conclusion of the truth of Christianity by correlating and interpreting the facts of Scripture. Such theology itself has an apologetic function insofar as the theologian must critique theological systems that undermine the Christian truth claims by reinterpreting in corrupt forms the Christian message. Here the facts to which the evidentialist theologian appeals are the propositional statements of the Bible. This does not, from the evidentialist's perspective, represent a shift in method. The apologist appeals to facts *about* and *from* the Bible to show that Christianity is *true;* the theologian appeals to facts *of* the Bible to show what Christianity *means.*

In a paper entitled "The Theologian's Craft: A Discussion of Theory Formation and Theory Testing in Theology,"[31] Montgomery compares scientific and theological methodologies using Karl Popper's work on model formation. The theologian, in this view, engages in forming and testing theories concerning the divine, and the source of revelational data for this kind of model formation is Scripture.

These theological models must be repeatedly tested against the data of Scripture as interpreted through the application of a sound hermeneutic.

On the basis of this theological method, Montgomery critiques various non-Christian and sub-Christian teachings that deviate from historical Christianity. In the opening essay of *The Suicide of Christian Theology*, he traces the shift in Christian theology since the eighteenth century away from a revelatory base to current subjective uncertainty. After examining the influences of deism, naturalism, and humanism on early twentieth-century Protestant and Catholic modernism, he discusses Barth's attempt to restore Christian doctrine through a dialectic of yes and no and the subsequent developments in the theologies of Bultmann, Tillich, and the "death of God" movement. Montgomery then argues that "the only hope for a resurrected theology lies in a recovery of confidence in the historical Christ and in the Scriptures He stamped with approval as God's Word."[32] The "keystone" of this resurrected theology is "an unqualified acceptance of the resurrected Christ," whose reality is validated by the historical facts.[33]

The evidentialist insistence that theological models, as well as apologetic arguments, must be testable is not a mere abstraction. Evidentialists have demonstrated their willingness to reassess traditional theological models. Perhaps most notably, several leading evidentialists have argued that specific features of the classical view of God's nature as formulated by such theologians as Augustine and Thomas Aquinas need to be rethought or even abandoned. For example, Richard Swinburne contends that God exists everlastingly in time rather than in a timeless eternity.[34] He also holds that God is "omniscient" in the sense that He knows everything that it is logically possible to know—and that this qualification excludes future actions of free creatures, including human beings.[35] Clark Pinnock holds to essentially the same views.[36] William Lane Craig, whose apologetic approach is essentially classical but with strong evidentialist leanings, adopts a compromise or middle-ground position between classical theism and the neoclassical theism of Swinburne and Pinnock. In his view, God was outside time before He created the world, but since the beginning of the universe (which was the beginning of time itself) God has existed in time. Furthermore, Craig argues that God can and does know all future acts of free creatures because God knows what each person would do in every possible world.[37]

There are few evidentialists in the Reformed or Calvinistic theological tradition (which does include many classical apologists as well as adherents of a Reformed apologetic). Most evidentialists are Arminian (a variety of evangelicalism that is non-predestinarian); this was true of Joseph Butler and is true of Pinnock and Craig. James Orr, a notable evidentialist from a century ago, was Reformed, and significantly his apologetic method in certain respects resembles the Reformed apologetic tradition. John Warwick Montgomery is neither Arminian nor Calvinist; he is, rather, a conservative Lutheran. Without minimizing the differences, this puts Montgomery somewhat closer to the Reformed tradition than most other contemporary evidentialists.

CRITICAL USE OF PHILOSOPHY

Evidentialists generally disapprove of the kind of philosophical apologetics that seeks to construct a deductive system of proof for Christianity. This does not mean, however, that evidentialism is hostile to all philosophy. Indeed, in recent years some of the most influential evidentialists have been philosophers, notably Swinburne, profiled in chapter 8. Other philosophers who advocate an evidentialist apologetic include Francis Beckwith[38] and Douglas Geivett.[39] In addition, J. P. Moreland and William Lane Craig, two of the most influential contemporary evangelical apologists, are philosophers whose apologetic approach has affinities with both classical and evidentialist apologetics.

The difference between classical apologists and evidentialists may be identified from one perspective as the difference between two broad conceptions of the task of philosophy.[40] The **speculative** or **constructive** view of philosophy understands that task to be to construct a comprehensive view of knowledge, reality, and values. In this conception philosophy is a discipline of thought in its own right and yields knowledge not found in other disciplines. This view dominated Western philosophy for most of its history; it is the view of philosophy presupposed by the work of both Plato and Aristotle, and many if not most of the other great philosophers of the past. It fits naturally with the classical approach to apologetics, which has maintained a close relationship between apologetics and what is now known as philosophy of religion. Thomas Aquinas is the paradigm case of a Christian philosopher-apologist whose work utilized philosophy as a means to develop a comprehensive world-and-life view.

In the twentieth century a number of philosophers questioned this historic understanding of the task of philosophy. In its place they contended for the analytical or critical conception of philosophy, according to which the task of philosophy is to clarify the meaning of knowledge claims and to assess the rationality of those claims. In this conception philosophy is, strictly speaking, a "second-order" discipline that does not yield knowledge of its own but simply examines and clarifies the knowledge claims of other, "first-order" disciplines. For most philosophers who advocate this view, the primary (if not the only) first-order disciplines are the sciences, including both the natural sciences (physics, chemistry, biology, etc.) and the human sciences (psychology, sociology, history, etc.).

Evidentialists generally reject the constructive view and embrace the analytical or critical view, for in their apologetic the sciences provide the evidence for the truth claims of Christianity. The role of philosophy for evidentialists can be viewed both negatively and positively. Negatively, they view philosophy as useful for critiquing anti-Christian presuppositions and philosophies that prejudice people against the factual case for Christianity. Positively, some evidentialists also use philosophy to assess the evidential support for the Christian position of the knowledge produced by the sciences.

Montgomery himself provides a clear example of the negative use. He believes that contemporary analytical philosophy's verification principle (that to be meaningful, a claim must be verifiable) makes an "inestimable contribution to epistemology." The implementation of this principle means that "vast numbers of apparently sensible truth-claims can be readily identified as unverifiable, and time and energy can thereby be saved for intellectual pursuits capable of yielding testable conclusions."[41] Rational arguments for the truth of a religion, including many of the traditional arguments of the classical apologetical kind, are inadequate because they fall short of true verification. He contends that instead apologetics must focus on verifiable truth claims. "Objective empirical evidence for Jesus Christ and his message is the only truly valid Christian apologetic possible, for it alone is subject to the canons of evidence employed in other fields of endeavor."[42]

Since the evidence for Christianity must come from first-order disciplines such as history and science, the main role of philosophy for the evidentialist is to expose and critique what Montgomery calls "bad philosophy." Evidentialists critique non-Christian worldviews and philosophies, not primarily by demonstrating logical incoherence (as in classical apologetic critiques), but by showing that these systems of thought are resistant to or incompatible with the facts. Examples of such critiques can be found in *Christianity for the Tough-Minded*, a compendium that includes critiques by evidentialist apologists of a number of nontheistic positions in philosophy, science, ethics, religion, psychology, and literature.[43] These include the rationalistic humanism of Bertrand Russell, the evolutionary humanism of Julian Huxley, the agnosticism of Franz Kafka, and the objectivism of Ayn Rand, as well as existential psychology and fundamental Buddhism. Such critiques are designed to show how the Christian position makes better sense of the relevant scientific, moral, historical, and experiential data than the interpretations derived from alternate worldviews.

Although evidentialists commonly rely on philosophical reasoning to critique anti-Christian philosophies, some have used these same methods to mount the case for Christianity. Specifically, some evidentialist philosophers have employed modern philosophical analyses of inductive argument as tools for displaying the evidence for Christian truth claims.

Richard Swinburne employs a sophisticated formulation of probability theory (that he himself has further developed) in his apologetic for belief in God. He argues for the probability that God exists with the same criteria used in science to assess whether a particular hypothesis or theory is likely to be true, and identifies four such criteria. A good theory *has predictive power*: it leads us to expect certain things to occur which in fact do occur. Second, a good theory is simple—it does not needlessly multiply explanations. Swinburne has given much attention to arguing that simplicity is evidence of truth[44] and to defending the claim that God constitutes a simple explanation for everything.[45] Third, a good theory *fits our background knowledge*—it squares with things we already know. Fourth, a good theory *has explanatory power*—it explains things better than any rival theory. The more these four things are true of a theory, the more probable it is to correspond to reality.[46]

Swinburne argues that the theory that God exists meets these four criteria sufficiently to justify the conclusion that God probably does in fact exist. He seeks to make this case in a very formal way by defining the "probability" of a particular truth claim by way of a mathematically expressed theorem of confirmation theory known as **Bayes's theorem**. This theorem uses the following definitions as its building blocks:

$P =$ the probability that something is true
$h =$ the hypothesis or theory
$e =$ the evidence (that is, phenomena or observations to be explained)
$k =$ general background knowledge of the world

From these definitions, the following complex terms are derived:

P(h/k) =   prior probability of *h* (its probability before the evidence is considered)

P(e/k) =   prior probability of *e* (probability of the evidence itself if we do not assume *h*)

P(e/h.k) = probability of *e* if *h* is true, given *k* (the predictive power of *h*)

P(h/e.k) = probability of *h* in view of both *e* and *k* (the probability of *h*)

For a comprehensive explanation such as the claim that God exists, *P(h/k)*, or the prior probability of *h*, will be in effect the simplicity of the claim. Bayes's theorem runs as follows:

$$P(h/e.k) = P(e/h.k)/P(e/k) \times P(h/k)$$

Stated in layman's terms, Bayes's theorem holds that the more a truth claim can explain, the better it can explain things; and the simpler it can explain things, the more likely that truth claim is to be true. Evidentialists who use Bayes's theorem do so in order to present an objective, quantifiable measure of the probability that a truth claim is true.

Although most evidentialists use a less formal approach than Swinburne's, many agree with his use of the concept of explanatory power to give some rigor to the claim that the Christian position is supported by the evidence. Consider, for example, the apologetic developed by Douglas Geivett, who favors a cumulative-case approach that "proceeds from the general to the particular" (93).[47] This should not be confused with *reasoning* from the general to the particular, which is deductive reasoning. Geivett is speaking of reasoning inductively, beginning "with very general considerations that require explanation" and proceeding to "more particular features of this world." As the considerations become more specific and particular, the explanations or conclusions become correspondingly more specific and thus more complete (93–94). As a result, "the theistic conclusion comes to enjoy greater support as more and more features of reality are found to be best explained theistically. In this respect it is similar to the approaches of Mitchell and Swinburne" (95).

Geivett's argument is not only a cumulative-case argument, it is an "inference to the best explanation." As such it is based on premises that are in turn dependent "upon the inductive strength of various inferences." Moreover, "this argument gets its force from considerations of the comparative explanatory power of alternate hypotheses" (95). Here Geivett's position appears especially close to that of Swinburne.

The use of probability theory has enabled evidentialists to overcome certain arguments against the Christian faith that purport to show that Christian truth claims are inherently improbable. Francis Beckwith, for example, has urged that one must not use the concept of probability in such a way as to disallow any amount of evidence to establish the reality of a particular event. Even if an event is in and of itself less probable than other kinds of events, if there is sufficient evidence for the event in question it should be believed. Beckwith gives several examples. Reliable sources reported that on one occasion fifteen people all happened for different reasons to show up late to a church choir rehearsal, thus narrowly avoiding being in the church when it was accidentally destroyed in an explosion. A royal flush is an extremely rare poker hand, but if several competent witnesses see a player get such a hand it should be believed. A woman might commit only one murder in her life, but her defense attorney cannot contend that her *not* committing murder is so commonplace in her life that her committing murder must be regarded as a priori unlikely. Beckwith therefore urges that probability not be applied to unusual specific events, such as miracles, in a way that overrides the actual evidence for those events.[48]

In Swinburne's terms, Beckwith's point amounts to saying that the prior probability of *h* is only one of several factors in determining the actual probability of *h;* one must also factor in the explanatory and predictive power of *h* and its simplicity as an explanation of the evidence. Thus, even though a miracle is a highly improbable type of event, if accepting the report of a miracle will explain it a great deal better and more simply than any other explanation, one has rational grounds for concluding that the miracle probably did occur.

CHRISTIANITY VINDICATED BY SCIENCE

Up until the eighteenth century, apologetics was modeled on philosophy, which was generally deductive in form. "Philosophy" until that time was a much broader term than it is now, and included the study of the natural world (what was called "natural philosophy"). In turn, the word "science" was understood in its common Latin sense as *scientia*, knowledge. As disciplines of study became more specialized, the sciences emerged as distinct branches of knowledge increasingly differentiated from philosophy by their inductive, empirical method. It was natural, then, for apologists to begin modeling their apologetic after the increasingly successful disciplines of empirical science.

The technological revolutions of the nineteenth and twentieth centuries have made the coherence of the Christian worldview with modern science one of the most significant issues in Christian apologetics. A widespread disdain for and distrust of abstract reasoning in general and deductive philosophical argument in particular have brought the classical theistic arguments into disrepute. In place of these, Christian apologists have increasingly relied on empirical, scientific arguments for the existence of God and in defense of the biblical worldview. Such natural theologians as Joseph Butler and William Paley set the pattern for such arguments. For evidentialists, the traditional theistic arguments, if they are used at all, must be recast in empirical form and be used to build up a case for theism from the facts of nature or human experience. For example, in his *Systematic Theology* J. Oliver Buswell, Jr., drew on the "inductive probability reasonings" in Aquinas's theistic arguments to develop a modern defense of theism.[49] Richard Swinburne has reformulated as inductive, probabilistic arguments the cosmological and teleological arguments, as well as the arguments for God from mind and morality—all of which, except for the teleological, were classically formulated as deductive arguments.[50]

Although Montgomery's apologetic thrust is primarily historical, he also offers his own version of some of the theistic proofs. The fundamental argument for him is what Frederick C. Copleston called the argument from contingency. In essence, this states that existence cannot be accounted for without a meaningless infinite regress unless there is a being that contains within itself the reason for its existence, that is, a self-existent being. Montgomery, however, prefers a more concrete, empirical version of this argument. He uses the second law of thermodynamics to illustrate the contingency argument, maintaining that the entire universe can be viewed as a closed system that, left to itself, would go to a state of maximum entropy (disorder).[51] Without divine intervention, this irreversible process will lead to the heat death of the universe at a finite time in the future. Thus, if the universe were uncreated and eternal, it would already have reached maximum entropy. Montgomery adds that "this *a posteriori* argument from contingency is empirically grounded in testable experience; it is neither a disguised form of the highly questionable ontological argument, which asserts *a priori* that God's essence establishes his existence, nor an attempt at allegedly 'synthetic *a priori*' reasoning."[52]

Other Christian apologists, including an increasing number trained in the sciences, agree with Montgomery's approach of developing an inductive, evidential apologetic that appeals to scientific fact. Several of the essays in the Cornell Symposium volume *Evidence for Faith* represent this trend. Robert C. Newman, for example, in an article entitled "The Evidence of Cosmology," argues that the astronomical evidence is such that "the universe is most naturally understood as created." The theory that the universe is eternal (and therefore uncreated) is "controlled by other considerations than scientific data," and for that reason is less probable. It should be noted that the same weakness applies, in Newman's opinion, to the young-earth model of creationism that views the universe as only a few thousand years old. Both the eternal-universe model and the young-universe model begin with their presupposed doctrine and then "interpret the data to fit."[53]

A similar position is taken by the old-earth creationist Hugh Ross, an astronomer turned evidentialist apologist. As head of Reasons to Believe,[54] a parachurch ministry focusing on scientific apologetics, Ross has written a number of books advocating a scientifically oriented evidentialism.[55] In his apologetic the cosmological and teleological arguments are expressed in thoroughly scientific, rather than philosophical, terms. Ross argues that an apologetic that is not based firmly on the scientific as well as the biblical facts will not be effective in reaching educated non-Christians. He contends specifically that the young-earth form of creationism is so scientifically disreputable that its affirmation by many Christians discourages "a large segment of society from taking seriously the call to faith in Christ."[56] Given that "no contradiction can exist between the words of the Bible and the facts of nature," Ross concludes that any apparent conflicts between the two are due to misinterpretation of the Bible or the facts of nature, and that further research will resolve such apparent conflicts.[57]

In general, evidentialists tend to hold firmly to a realist view of science as a discipline that yields actual knowledge of the world corresponding to the way things really are. Unlike classical apologists, they tend to base arguments on scientific theories with great confidence. While they agree that science changes, they see its changes as primarily advances in knowledge. Thus evidentialists are rarely young-earth creationists; most hold to some form of old-earth creationism. They appeal primarily to the facts of nature to refute evolutionism on the scientists' own terms, rather than questioning the reliability of the scientific enterprise.

HISTORY AS THE MEDIUM OF REVELATION

It is in the area of history where most evidentialists seek primarily to ground their apologetic.[58] Swinburne is only a partial exception to this generalization. While he gives scant attention in most of his books to the historical evidence for Christianity, this is because he regards himself as a philosopher and not an historian. However, he does hold that a positive assessment of the historicity of the biblical miracles would increase the probability of theism. He also argues "that the testimony of many witnesses to experiences apparently of God makes the existence of God probable if it is not already on other evidence very improbable."[59] But this is essentially an historical argument.

The most basic reason evidentialists ground their apologetic in history is because the revelation of God they are seeking to defend is essentially historical. History is the medium of revelation; our knowledge of God comes from his acts in history. Since the Christian faith stands or falls on its claim that God has acted in history, apologists must make their defense at that point. For evidentialists this historical, testable character sets Christianity apart from other religions and is its greatest strength, as Montgomery explains:

> The historic Christian claim differs qualitatively from the claims of all other world religions at the epistemological point: on the issue of testability. Eastern faiths and Islam, to take familiar examples, ask the uncommitted seeker to discover their truth experientially: the faith-experience will be self-validating. . . . Christianity, on the other hand, declares that the truth of its absolute claims rests squarely on certain historical facts, open to ordinary investigation.[60]

The evidentialist appeal to historical facts should not be construed as naively expecting non-Christians to recognize the significance of the facts without resistance. Evidentialists emphasize that there is a subjective dimension to the interpretation of history. Specifically, they point out that persons holding implicitly or explicitly to philosophies of history that are inimical to the Christian worldview will not be open to the historical facts that verify that Christian worldview. They find it necessary, then, to subject such philosophies of history to critique, and to explicate a Christian philosophy of history. Swinburne's defense of theism fits here: his argument for the existence of God is concerned with showing not merely that there is a God but that this God providentially orders the world and history.[61]

On the other hand, evidentialists maintain that historical interpretation has an objective dimension as well, one presented by the facts that stubbornly refuse to fit into anti-Christian belief systems. The historical facts about Jesus Christ constitute the primary challenge to non-Christian philosophies of history, and these facts carry within themselves their own interpretation that the historian discovers, not imposes.

Evidentialists do recognize, then, that the religious beliefs and values of historians have a profound influence on their interpretation of historical events. In some cases what passes for "unbiased" history is "often no more than a mask covering presuppositions of a most gratuitous sort."[62] The solution to this problem, according to Montgomery, is not to abandon one's presuppositions, but to think about and be frank about them. History should be written from a definite point of view because "the most dangerous historians have not been those with definite convictions, but those who have been unaware of their convictions."[63]

Montgomery rejects the claim of historical relativists that the historian's own subjectivity defeats any attempt to obtain a genuinely objective view of the past.[64] He also rejects the claim of some neo-orthodox theologians, such as Rudolf Bultmann, that historical events have no meaning apart from the present spiritual experience of encounter with the Christ of faith. Montgomery argues that "if historical judgments cannot be anchored in the bedrock of objective reality, then the events which are the focus of those judgments become secondary and for all practical purposes useless."[65] In short, if Christ has not been raised in historical fact, our faith in Christ as the risen Savior is in vain (1 Corinthians 15:12–19).

Montgomery also defends an objective, evidential approach to biblical history against the criticisms of other apologists who reject the notion of historical events as self-interpretive. For example, he takes issue with Ronald H. Nash's claim that "there is no necessary connection between any alleged fact and its interpretation."[66] In contrast he asserts, "The conviction that historical facts do carry their interpretations (i.e., that the facts in themselves provide adequate criteria for choosing among variant interpretations of them) is essential both to Christian and to general historiography."[67] Elsewhere he writes that "a Christian philosophy of history has to begin with the assumption that there are objective events which do indeed carry their interpretation with them. This is true not only of the events of biblical history but of the events of history in general."[68] If historical facts were not objectively true or knowledge of them was not possible, the apostles could not have proclaimed Christ's resurrection as a truth to be accepted by all people.

After all, people whose worldview was inhospitable to such facts could simply dismiss the Christian historical claims as nonsense. The very fact that people's worldviews can and do change when they take seriously the factual claims of the gospel proves that there is an objective dimension to historical knowledge.

According to Montgomery, a Christian philosophy of history is needed if history is to be interpreted properly as to its ultimate significance. However, this Christian philosophy of history is not to be used as the basis on which the historical events of the New Testament are defended. Such an approach would be viciously circular. Rather, these principles of historiography are based on the verifiable reality of Jesus' death and resurrection and provide a guide for interpreting the rest of human history. In addition, the apologist must employ a Christian philosophy of history as a benchmark against which non-Christian presuppositions about history that distort or reject the gospel events can be exposed. That is, the evidentialist does not ask the non-Christian to accept these historiographical principles, but he does ask the non-Christian not to assume dogmatically principles that are at odds with a Christian view of history (for example, an antisupernatural assumption). Instead, he asks the non-Christian to examine the historical evidence fairly and be open to the philosophical implications of that evidence. As the non-Christian does this, he will find that God has revealed himself in and through history, particularly in the unique events of Christ's incarnate life, death, and resurrection.

EXPERIENCE FOUNDED ON EVIDENCE

Evidentialism recognizes the importance of experience in the Christian life. Christian faith is not merely an intellectual acceptance of facts about Christ, but is a personal experience of a relationship with Christ. But evidentialists generally hold that the Christian's experience is not self-validating. Robert Sabath, in a paper entitled "LSD and Religious Truth," makes the point with startling forcefulness:

> It cannot be emphasized too strongly that every psychological by-product of Christianity can be reproduced by LSD and by almost every other religion, including a sense of meaning in life, integration of personality, increased sensitivity to others, greater self-acceptance, psychological relief from anxiety and guilt feelings, tranquility and inner harmony. . . . The mere fact that a psychological event has taken place in one's brain cannot establish the truth of any metaphysical assertion. The assertion "God exists" does not follow from the assertion "I had an experience of

God" simply because experiences admit to radically different interpretations.[69]

The subjective experience of faith is for evidentialists a response to the objective revelation of God in his historical acts of redemption through Jesus Christ. Sabath continues:

> If God exists—the kind of personal creator God most Christians and theists talk about—he must exist independent of my subjective experience of him; his existence must therefore be validated by a criterion other than my own private experience. The uniqueness of Christianity is that there is such a criterion in the personal invasion of God himself into the public world of our objective experience. Christian existential experience is rooted in objective, external works of God himself, fleshing out his life in space and time in the person of Jesus Christ and showing himself to be God by his resurrection from the dead.[70]

Whereas apologists of other traditions tend to be critical of the apostle Thomas's demand to see and touch the resurrected body of Jesus before he would believe, evidentialists are often more sympathetic. They suggest that Christ's appearance to Thomas shows that God is quite willing to provide empirical evidence for the truth of the gospel, as Clark Eugene Barshinger's statement in *Christianity for the Tough-minded* illustrates:

> Christian believers have never been able to separate their religious experience from the positive assertions of Scripture regarding the nature and authority of Jesus Christ. Doubting Thomas is the prime example. He refused belief until he saw the evidence of the resurrection. When this evidence was provided, the religious experience became existential truth and he responded, "My Lord and my God." The existential Christian experience rests in the revealed truth of God embodied in the resurrected Christ and the authoritative Scripture.[71]

The purpose for which apologists present non-Christians with evidence, according to evidentialists, is to bring them to the point where they have a credible basis for believing the gospel. But the subjective experience and assurance of its truth come from the Holy Spirit when a person responds to the evidence and comes to faith. According to Montgomery, the evidence brings nonbelievers to a point of decision in which they have good grounds for "trying" Christianity; it does not "force" anyone to believe.

> The argument is intended, rather, to give solid objective ground for testing the Christian faith experientially. How is the test made? By confronting, with no more than "suspension of disbelief," the Christ of the Scriptures; for "faith comes by hearing and hearing by the word of God" and (said Christ) "whoever has the will to do the will of God shall know whether my teaching comes from God or is merely my own" [Romans 10:17; John 7:17]. The Scriptural Gospel is ultimately self-attesting, but the honest inquirer needs objective grounds for trying it, since there are a welter of conflicting religious opinions and one can become psychologically jaded through indiscriminate trials of religious belief. Only the Christian world-view offers objective ground for testing it experientially; therefore Christ deserves to be given first opportunity to make His claims known to the human heart.[72]

For Further Study

Montgomery, John Warwick. *The Shape of the Past: A Christian Response to Secular Philosophies of History*. Minneapolis: Bethany Fellowship, 1962. Reprint 1975. Reviews the history of historiography and sets forth a Christian philosophy of history.

_____. *Where Is History Going? Essays in Support of the Historical Truth of the Christian Revelation*. Minneapolis: Bethany Fellowship, 1969. Follow-up volume to *Shape of the Past*, presenting an historical defense of the Christian claims about Jesus Christ and critiquing the philosophies of history of Barth, Tillich, and others.

_____, ed. *Evidence for Faith: Deciding the God Question*. Cornell Symposium on Evidential Apologetics 1986. Dallas: Probe Books, 1991; distributed by Word Publishing. A collection of evidentialist essays: Part One defends an evidentialist approach to apologetics; Parts Two and Three discuss scientific evidences from cosmology and biology; Part Five contains John E. Hare's article "The Argument from Experience" (253-73).

Chapter 10

Presenting Evidence That Demands a Verdict

Of the four approaches profiled in this book, the classical and evidentialist approaches are the closest to each other. Indeed, many apologists, such as William Lane Craig, J. P. Moreland, and Richard Swinburne, cannot for various reasons be neatly placed into one approach rather than the other. One reason this is so is that the second "step" or stage of the classical apologetic uses many if not all of the very same arguments that are part of the evidentialist arsenal. That is, after showing that God exists, classical apologists turn to evidences showing that God has revealed himself in the Bible and incarnated himself in Jesus—and these evidences will be the same evidences that are crucial to most evidentialist apologetics. Another reason for the similarity between these two approaches is that evidentialism is by nature eclectic, and therefore evidentialists freely use classical apologetic arguments, including those used by the classical apologist to establish theism.

Despite the similarities between the two approaches, there are some differences that justify recognizing them as two distinct "families" or types of apologetics. As we have already noted, the main difference is that classical apologetics builds the case for Christianity in two stages: first the evidence for God (theism), and second the evidence for Christianity. The rationale for this approach is that the miracles of Christianity can be viewed as credible only within a theistic worldview. Evidentialists, on the other hand, think the case for Christianity can be most effectively presented using evidences for creation, for the historicity of Jesus and especially his resurrection, and other evidences in one "cumulative case" for Christian theism.

SCRIPTURE AS SOURCE

According to John Warwick Montgomery, "The final and best evidence of God's existence lies in his Word—in the triple sense of Christ, the gospel he proclaimed, and the Scripture that infallibly conveys it."[1] This statement nicely captures the spirit of the evangelical evidentialist apologetic. Rather than developing an apologetic for theism as preparation for considering the specific claims of Christ to reveal God to us and to reconcile us to God, the evidentialist views Christ and the Bible, in which we learn about Christ, as the best source for a Christian apologetic.

The first step for evidentialists such as Montgomery, then, is to defend the biblical writings, not as infallible Scripture, but as historically credible and reliable documents. Securing belief in God is not considered a prerequisite to taking this first step; only clearing away any methodological or philosophical assumptions that prejudge the question of the truth of the biblical narratives is necessary. So, for example, in his book *History and Christianity*, Montgomery details "four common errors" in the anti-Christian polemic of philosopher Avrum Stroll before beginning his apologetic proper: (1) Stroll relies almost exclusively on modern "authorities" of a radically rationalistic sort (17–18).[2] (2) Stroll ignores the evidence of the earliest primary documents, specifically the letters of Paul (18–19). (3) Stroll begs the question by assuming that the miraculous events reported in the Gospels could not have happened simply because they were miraculous (19–21). Note that Montgomery does not argue here that miracles are possible; he simply objects to the assumption that they are *im*possible. (4) Stroll engages in groundless historical speculation when he suggests that the Christian view of Jesus was the product of "messianic fever" in first-century Judaism (21–22).

Having cleared away these errors, Montgomery begins his positive case with this disclaimer: "We won't naively assume the 'inspiration' or 'infallibility' of the New Testament records and then by circular reasoning attempt to prove what we have previously assumed. We will regard the documents, even though today they are usually printed on fine India paper with verse numbers, only as documents, and we will treat them as we would any other historical materials" (25–26).

To assure his readers he is employing an unbiased method of treating the historical reliability of the New Testament, Montgomery chooses tests of reliability drawn from a textbook on English literary history by a military historian.[3] These are the bibliographical, internal, and external tests (26). Montgomery and other evidentialists use this threefold test regularly to defend the historical reliability of the New Testament.[4]

The **bibliographical test** seeks to determine whether the existing or extant copies of a document are reliable reproductions of the wording of the original document. Montgomery emphasizes that we have many more manuscript copies for the New Testament writings than for other ancient writings, and that the time gap between the earliest complete copies and the originals is smaller for the New Testament than for other ancient writings (26–29). "To be skeptical of the resultant text of the New Testament books is to allow all of classical antiquity to slip into obscurity, for no documents of the ancient period are as well attested bibliographically as the New Testament" (29).

The bibliographical test does not establish the factual accuracy of the historical narratives in the documents, only that the documents as we know them are substantially the same as they were when originally written. Accurate copies of fables would still be fables. But the claim is so often made that the New Testament writings arc unrcliablc bccausc of mistakes in the copying process that apologists find it necessary and helpful to point out the evidence for the textual reliability of the Bible.

The second and third tests address the historical reliability of the contents of the biblical documents. The **internal test** considers the claims of the writings as to their historicity and internal consistency. Here Montgomery and other evidentialists insist "that the benefit of the doubt is to be given to the document itself, not arrogated by the critic to himself" (29). Paul's writings claim to be written by Paul, and the Gospels, especially Luke and John, claim to be recording history based on eyewitness testimony (29–30). These claims should be accepted at face value as truthful unless and until evidence to the contrary is produced.

The **external test** asks whether the testimony of the biblical writings is corroborated or undermined by extrabiblical sources. Here Montgomery focuses on the Gospels. Luke's accuracy is confirmed by the archaeological and geographical investigations of William Ramsay toward the end of the nineteenth century (31–32). Second-century Christians who knew the apostles or their immediate disciples testified that the Gospels were based on eyewitness testimony. Thus Mark's Gospel was based on Peter's recollections; Matthew, himself an apostle, wrote his Gospel while the other apostles were still alive; Luke was written by Paul's traveling companion; and John the apostle wrote the Gospel bearing his name (32–34).

Montgomery concludes "that on the basis of the accepted canons of historical method . . . the New Testament documents must be regarded as reliable sources of information" (43). This line of argument "depends in no sense on theology. It rests solely upon historical method, the kind of method all of us have to use in analyzing historical data, whether Christians, rationalists, agnostics or Tibetan monks" (44).

Besides passing tests of general historical reliability, Scripture functions in more profound ways as the source of evidence for its own truth and the truth claims of Christianity. Evidentialists marshal evidences from a number of directions to build a cumulative case for the truth of the Bible. These evidences include the miracles of the Bible, the uniqueness of the Bible, and fulfilled prophecy. Later we will consider the evidentialist approach to the miracles of the Bible; here we will highlight the argument from fulfilled prophecy.

Fulfilled prophecy, while it has always had a place in apologetics,[5] has a distinctive use and emphasis in evidential apologetics, especially since the nineteenth century when books like Alexander Keith's *Evidence of the Truth of the Christian Religion Derived from the Literal Fulfilment of Prophecy* went through many editions.[6]

Evidentialists note that "fulfilled prophecy was part of the means of establishing Old Testament religion."[7] John Bloom, for example, quotes the Lord's challenge in Isaiah issued to idols and all false gods to prove themselves by predicting the future (Isaiah 41:21–23; 44:7–8), and comments: "The God of the Bible is calling for a rigorous test which involves the objective prediction of future events in human history. . . . Logically, we can reverse this challenge to other 'gods' and ask if the God of the Bible can predict the future Himself. If He can, and if no other religion can substantiate a similar claim, then we have an objective, historically testable verification that the God of the Bible alone exists."[8]

Bloom identifies four criteria that need to be satisfied in order to conclude that a genuine prophecy has been given. (1) It must be clear. (2) We must know that it was given before the event. (3) It cannot be fulfilled by the actions of the human person making the prediction. And (4) its content must be unusually specific or long range so as to make its fulfillment remarkable. Bloom then implicitly adds a fifth, namely, that the successful prediction must not be accompanied by a number of false predictions. Thus Jeane Dixon might be given some credit for predicting John F. Kennedy's assassination but for the fact that so many of her other predictions have failed.[9] Anyone making dozens of unlikely predictions year after year is bound to get a few of them right!

Evidentialists point to three clusters of fulfilled prophecies as evidence for the divine inspiration and truth of the Bible. First, the Old Testament contains numerous prophecies concerning the rise and fall of various nations and cities surrounding Israel, such as Egypt, Tyre and Sidon, Babylon, and Nineveh. There is some dispute about the details of the Tyre prophecy in Ezekiel 26, but evidentialists are confident that the chapter, properly interpreted, was dramatically and literally fulfilled.[10]

Second, evidentialists cite the existence and history of Israel as an amazing fulfillment of biblical prophecy.[11] Robert Newman tells the story of the skeptical Frederick the Great, who asked his court chaplain for a good argument for God, to which the chaplain replied, "The Jew, your majesty!"[12] The Bible predicts that the Jews would fall into idolatry and be chastised, yet would later be returned to the land. Evidentialists point out that nations have repeatedly tried to annihilate the Jewish culture and people and yet have failed; they see this as evidence of God's remarkable providential care for the Jewish people.[13]

Third, evidentialists are especially impressed by the fulfilled prophecies in the life, ministry, death, and resurrection of Jesus. The Gospels, especially Matthew, strongly emphasize the idea that Jesus fulfilled Old Testament prophecies. Evidentialists are aware of the common criticism that the Gospel writers take the Old Testament texts out of context, but they reply that this criticism is without merit. Newman points out various paradoxical features of Old Testament messianic prophecies that find their natural and obvious fulfillment in Jesus. The Messiah was to be a Jew who brought light to the Gentiles (Isaiah 42:6–7; 49:5–6). He was to be born a human son, yet he preexisted as God (Micah 5:2; Isaiah 9:6–7). He will be humble yet exalted (Daniel 7:13–14; Zechariah 9:9). He will suffer ignominiously yet be vindicated and exalted as universal ruler (Psalm 22; Isaiah 52:13–53:12). He will be both king and priest, offices kept separate in Judaism (Psalm 110).[14] Newman also cites prophecies indicating that the Messiah would come toward the end of the Second Temple period (ca. 515 B.C.–A.D. 70), making it impossible that any individual living after that time could be the Messiah (Haggai 2:3–9; Daniel 9:24–27).[15]

These three types of fulfilled prophecies in the Bible add up to an impressive array of evidences that evidentialists believe are unparalleled and should be quite convincing. The skeptic whose worldview excludes divine fulfillment of prophecy is advised that the evidence is sufficient to call such a worldview into question. So Newman concludes, "one would be a fool to keep appealing to accident when the evidence suggests one's worldview is faulty."[16] Fulfilled prophecy, then, not only provides evidence for the inspiration of the Bible, but for evidentialists it also contributes to the case for the theistic worldview.

Evidentialists are not alone in using fulfilled prophecy as part of their apologetic. However, while evidentialists use it to prove the existence of God, classical apologists generally do not. Norman Geisler, for example, states plainly: "Fulfilled prophecy does not prove the existence of God, but it does show that unusual events predicted in his Name that come to pass are evidence of his special activity."[17]

THE UNIQUENESS OF CHRISTIANITY

The apologist today is confronted with myriad religious options in almost every part of the world and a rising tide of religious pluralism. Faced with these realities, the evangelical apologist must be prepared to give a reason for claiming that Jesus Christ is the only Savior and that true knowledge of God can be found only in the Christian faith.

As we saw in Part Two, classical apologists generally approach this question by analyzing the worldviews of the major non-Christian religions. They contend that only theism, the belief that the world was created and is utterly dependent on an infinite yet personal Creator, is a philosophically viable worldview. From there they argue that of the major theistic religions (Judaism, Islam, and Christianity), Christianity is the true one (because it, not Judaism or Islam, is the fulfillment of the revelations given to Abraham and his people in the Old Testament). While evidentialists might find such an argument useful as a supplementary line of reasoning, their primary approach to this question is characteristically different.

Evidentialists confront the problem of religious pluralism on two levels. First, they argue that the belief that all religions are basically the same does not take seriously the facts about the different religions. For example, Montgomery criticizes Altizer's claim that the modern discipline of comparative religions has demonstrated "an underlying unity of thought between Eastern mystical religion and the Christian faith"[18] by noting that the famed comparative religions scholar Mircea Eliade, whom Altizer professes to follow, rejects this idea. Montgomery tells of a conversation he had with Eliade in which the renowned scholar agreed that "Christianity's unique, historical focus on a 'once-for-all' incarnation of God in Christ" sharply distinguishes it from mythical and mystical religions. Altizer's mistake "stems from his general disrespect for historical facts: he will not allow a given religion to speak for itself. . . . If Professor Altizer would let the facts speak for themselves, he would have to give up any hope of blending Eastern and Western religion."[19]

Other evidentialists make the same point in different ways. For example, Francis Beckwith objects to the Baha'i teaching that all the world's major religions were inspired by God. He compares the doctrines about God taught by Moses, Buddha, Confucius, Jesus, Muhammad, and other religious founders and finds them hopelessly contradictory. "God cannot be impersonal, personal, transcendent, polytheistic, pantheistic, monotheistic, able to beget, not able to beget, relevant, and irrelevant all at the same time. . . . Irreconcilable data gives us no knowledge of God whatsoever."[20]

Second, evidentialists maintain that Christianity has a solid claim to be the only true religion because it alone can produce testable evidence of God's activity in establishing Christianity in the first place. According to Montgomery, "What modern man insists on above all is a verifiable base for his faith, so that he can bring some order out of the conflicting welter of religious claims."[21] Christianity has miracles, fulfilled prophecies, and other evidences that the God of the Bible is the true God; other religions do not have these phenomena. For example, evidentialists emphasize that non-Christian religions do not even claim that their religious leaders were raised from the dead.[22] Beckwith observes, "a religion that is true would be one that defeats death, man's most detestable foe. Of all the religious leaders previously discussed, only one, Jesus of Nazareth, has conquered the Grim Reaper."[23]

THE CASE FOR GOD

Evidentialists, like classical apologists, seek to offer arguments for the existence of God on grounds that are in principle understandable and acceptable to non-Christians. However, they go about this task in a somewhat different way.

First, they generally subordinate the classical philosophical proofs for God's existence to a different place in their apologetic, and a few evidentialists even reject the philosophical proofs as invalid and unhelpful. Arnold Weigel is an extreme example of the latter: "In opposing the traditional rational proofs of God's existence, [Bertrand] Russell is destroying a straw man, not the Christian position. . . . A rational proof of God's existence is, moreover, actually inconsistent with the Christian faith."[24]

Much more commonly, though, evidentialists retain the philosophical proofs but do not treat them as sufficient to establish theism. Instead they rework the philosophical arguments into a cumulative case for theism that is predominantly inductive in character. Richard Swinburne, who exemplifies this approach, argues that the existence of God is a probable hypothesis because it is relatively simple and has significant explanatory power. Specifically, the theory that God exists helps explain the existence of the world (the cosmological argument), its order and basic beauty (the teleological argument), as well as human consciousness (the argument from mind) and morality (the moral argument).[25]

Likewise, William Lane Craig has developed the cosmological and teleological proofs into complex arguments combining philosophical reasoning with scientific evidence. Craig is perhaps best known for his articulation of the *kalâm* cosmological argument, a philosophical proof for God's existence based on the premise that the universe cannot exist without a beginning.[26] But he does not leave the argument there. Recognizing that the logical case against a beginningless universe is abstract and not intuitively obvious to all, he offers confirmation of the premise from the evidence for the big bang,[27] a lead other evidentialist philosophers and apologists have followed.[28] Big bang cosmology is a crucial aspect of the evidentialist apologetic of Hugh Ross, whose professional training was in astronomy.[29]

The argument may be briefly summarized here.[30] Scientists have observed that galaxies are moving away from us in all directions, and that the farther away they are the faster they are receding. This evidence shows that the universe is expanding. Scientists have also discovered a faint background radiation in the cosmos such as was predicted to exist if the universe had exploded into existence from an original single point. These and other observations have led the vast majority of scientists working in the field to embrace some form of big bang cosmology, according to which the universe had a beginning. This conclusion was not reached easily. An absolute beginning for all physical reality implies that the universe was caused to come into existence by something beyond the investigative competency of the natural sciences. This limitation provoked many scientists at first to resist the conclusion that the universe had a beginning. Scientists often operate by the ideal that everything can and should eventually be explained scientifically, and the big bang presents an apparent dead end to this ideal. Yet the vast majority of scientists have been won over to the big bang by the evidence.

Although most scientists admit that the universe had a beginning, many try to remain agnostic as to its cause. Scientists should not shy away from concluding that God created the universe if that is where the evidence leads, as Douglas Geivett, an evidentialist philosopher, has argued. "Even if the cause of the origin of the physical universe is not directly and empirically accessible, theoreticians fail in their capacity as scientists if they resist the conclusion to which the evidence leads, for the ideal objective of science is to explain all phenomena."[31]

The teleological argument has also been reworked into an evidentialist argument, and in fact has enjoyed something of a renewed respect in the past fifteen years or so. The argument is now commonly based on the so-called anthropic cosmological principle, or more simply the **anthropic principle**.[32] This term refers to the observation that numerous factors inherent in the universe appear to be just right for sustaining a universe in which life, including humanity, has even the possibility of existing. In other words, these are factors that must be just right—often within a very small range—for us to be here noticing them in the first place. This phenomenon is often called the "fine-tuning" of the universe. Again, Hugh Ross is a scientist-apologist who has given this argument a great deal of prominence,[33] though it is now widely used in evidentialist apologetics.[34] The following table summarizes just ten of the more than fifty factors that have been identified in the anthropic principle.[35]

In addition to scientific, empirical reworkings of the classical theistic arguments, most evidentialists emphasize the evidence for God's existence from his acts in history. Here we are again talking about fulfilled prophecy, miracles in general, and above all the resurrection of Jesus. For evidentialists, the main reason we know God exists is because he revealed himself in verifiable ways in history—ultimately and most definitively in Jesus. Montgomery makes this point in connection with an illustration used by the philosopher Antony Flew (who at the time was an atheist[36]). Flew asked us to imagine a situation in which we are told that an invisible gardener visits a garden every day and tends it. Should we believe the gardener exists despite the fact that every attempt to observe his movements fails? Montgomery comments: "The New Testament affirmation of the existence of God (the Divine Gardener in Flew's parable) is not a claim standing outside the realm of empirical testability. Quite the contrary: the Gardener *entered* his garden (the world) in the person of Jesus Christ, showing himself to be such 'by many infallible proofs' (Acts 1:3)."[37]

Cosmic and Geological Evidence of Design

Factor	If Greater	If Fewer
Strong nuclear force constant	No hydrogen	Nothing but hydrogen
Gravitational force constant	Stars burn out quickly	Stars don't produce heavy elements
Expansion rate of the universe	No galaxies form	Universe contracts before stars can form
Average distance between stars	Heavy elements spread too thin for rocky planets to form	Planetary orbits would be destabilized by nearby stars
Earth's surface gravity	Too much ammonia and methane in atmosphere	Not enough water in atmosphere
Earth's distance from sun	Too cold	Too hot
Earth's rotation period	Fierce winds	Temperature extremes from day to night
Thickness of earth's crust	Not enough oxygen in atmosphere	Volcanoes and earthquakes in much greater measure
Carbon dioxide level	Runaway greenhouse effect	Plants die
Ozone level	Too cold	Too hot

THE INDUCTIVE PROBLEM OF EVIL

As we saw in Part Two, classical apologists have responded at great length to "the problem of evil." As traditionally defined, this is a logical, or deductive, problem that presents a seeming contradiction in the theistic worldview. Specifically, the (deductive) problem of evil asks whether it is logically possible for an all-good, all-powerful God to exist simultaneously with a world he created and yet has evil in it.

While many modern skeptics continue to cite it in this deductive form, some nontheistic philosophers acknowledge that the problem of evil fails to prove a logical consistency in the theistic worldview. As classical apologists and philosophers have pointed out, an all-good and all-powerful God might choose to create a world in which evil would arise if God had some good reason for doing so. For example, it is at least logically possible that creating such a world was unavoidable if God was to create people with a moral capacity for making choices. But nontheistic philosophers have not been entirely satisfied with this defense. They argue that a much more difficult version of the problem still remains to be addressed. Granted (at least for the sake of argument) that it is possible that God created a world where evil exists, how likely is this to be in fact the case? This is the inductive or evidential problem of evil. Douglas Geivett explains the difference between these two versions of the argument.

> The logical problem of evil asks, Is it logically *possible* that God and evil coexist? Any answer to this problem must show that the existence of God is compatible with the fact of evil in the world. . . . The evidential problem of evil asks, Is it evidentially *plausible* that God and evil coexist? This objection has the following form: God must have a morally sufficient reason for allowing any evil that he allows; but there is much evil in the world for which we can imagine no morally sufficient reason, such that it is highly unlikely that God exists (61).[38]

Geivett's own response to the evidential problem of evil is based on the positive evidence for God's existence. If significant evidence can be presented to show that it is highly likely that God exists, then the burden of proof is on the person who would argue that God's existence is unlikely. Moreover, if on the basis of the evidence we conclude that God probably does exist, then, given that God is good and all-powerful, we may conclude that God is justified in permitting evil even if we do not know what his reason or reasons may be (61). "There is room for speculation about the mystery surrounding God's actual reasons for permitting evil. But failure to identify the actual reasons God has for permitting evil will touch the natural theologian's conclusion—God exists—*not at all*" (62). Once the theist concludes that God does exist and therefore must have a good reason for permitting evil, a problem of evil remains. This new problem is not whether God and evil both exist, but "*how* both can exist" (64). "The theist will have deflected the specific objection to the existence of God on the basis of evil *without even the most cursory analysis of evil* if the theist has produced a compelling argument for the existence of God on independent grounds" (64–65).

Another evidentialist who analyzes the problem of evil along inductive lines is John Hare. He notes that while any form of the problem is insufficient as a deductive proof of God's nonexistence, a more defensible version of the argument reasons "that the amount of evil we experience makes the existence of an omnipotent, omniscient, and omnibenevolent God *unlikely*" (238).[39] Hare goes on to note that the likelihood of God's existence will depend largely on whether, apart from the reality of evil, one sees good evidence for God's existence:

We are interested in how probable it is that God exists, given that there is a certain amount of evil. This depends, first, on how probable it is that God exists anyway. This is the so-called *prior probability* of the hypothesis. It also depends on whether this much evil is more likely to exist if God exists or if He does not. This is very roughly the *explanatory power* of the hypothesis. . . . Theists, in my experience, usually agree with atheists that the amount of evil in the world makes it harder to believe in a good God. But they have to be careful. For if theists agree that it is *much* harder, and they do not think that God's existence is, independent of evil, *much* more likely, they may be in an untenable position. (239–240)

After surveying recent attempts to deal with the evidential problem of evil and deeming them all inadequate, Hare suggests that the only viable solution may be what he calls a *"disjunctive explanation"* (245). That is, the explanation will have the following form: *x* (evil) is to be explained by either *a, b, c,* or some other factor. In other words, there is no one explanation for each instance of evil. Bad things happen for a variety of reasons: to develop and refine a person's faith and character, to bring about a revelation of God's glory, to experience suffering vicariously in someone else's place, to punish people for their own acts of evil, to alert people to physical dangers (biologically useful pain), to learn the consequences of evil, or to alert people to their need for salvation (248–250).

In an essay on the evidence from the fine-tuning of the universe for God's existence, Robin Collins argues that this positive argument for belief in God is much stronger than the inductive argument from evil against belief in God. In the case of the fine-tuning argument, we actually have good, objective data from which to derive a reasonable estimate of the probability of the universe just happening to be the kind capable of having and sustaining intelligent living beings. This is because the scientific data includes information about the universe as a whole (e.g., the universe's expansion rate, the universal forces of matter, gravity, and electromagnetism). In the case of the evidential argument from evil, we have no way to quantify the relative amounts of good and evil that have been and will be produced in the universe, and indeed have good reason to admit that we know about only a small fraction of the good and evil that have occurred and will occur in the universe. Collins concludes that "the relevant probability estimates in the case of the fine-tuning argument are much more secure than those estimates in the probabilistic version of the atheist's argument from evil."[40]

MIRACLES AS EVIDENCE FOR GOD

Evidentialists believe that miracles, like fulfilled prophecy, can be used in the verification of the supernatural. Whereas classical apologists tend to argue that one must first establish the existence of God in order to render miracles credible, evidentialists argue that miracles can actually serve as evidence for the existence of God. An excellent example of an evidentialist treatment of miracles may be found in the work of Francis Beckwith, particularly his monograph critiquing David Hume's argument against miracles.[41]

Beckwith defines the term miracle inductively or empirically rather than deductively: "A miracle is a divine intervention which occurs contrary to the regular course of nature within a significant historical-religious context" (7). That is, a miracle is (a) scientifically inexplicable, (b) religiously significant, and (c) supernaturally (or, divinely) caused.

Regarding the first-mentioned requirement, Beckwith denies that a miracle must be defined as an event that can be known to be *permanently* inexplicable scientifically. He contends that a miracle "is inexplicable in terms of *what we know about currently well-established scientific laws*" (9). This means that it is always possible, however slender the possibility, that an apparent miracle will turn out to be scientifically explicable. But Beckwith does not see this as a liability.

> Hence, the fact that one cannot find deductive validity for any scientific law only means that our judgments about events purporting to violate these laws cannot reach the point of apodictic certainty. Since no discipline dealing with empirical judgments can render such certainty (e.g., law, history, psychology, anthropology, archaeology, etc.), it should not bother the believer in miracles one bit that miracles cannot be demonstrated to be permanently inexplicable; scientific inexplicability in terms of currently well-established laws will do just fine. (9)

Beckwith also points out "that science's problem-solving capacity has been completely impotent in making any of the primary law-violating miracles of the Christian tradition scientifically explicable, e.g., resurrections, changing water into wine, walking through walls, levitating, multiplying fishes and loaves, instantaneously healing lepers, and walking on water" (10).[42]

Beckwith's second condition for an event to be regarded as a miracle is that it have an historical-religious significance. "Miracles are not just purposeless and bizarre scientific oddities, but occur in such a way that purpose is attached to them by virtue of when and why they occur." Beckwith illustrates his point with the case of a person who had apparently returned to physical life after having died. Suppose this person had claimed that he would do this and had offered a theological explanation for it, and suppose further that he claimed to be the culmination of his culture's theological expectations and prophetic predictions. "Within this religious context the physiological anomaly of a resurrection takes on a significance which would not have been present if this individual had 'just happened' to rise from the dead for no apparent reason" (11).

If an event is scientifically inexplicable and has historical-religious significance, Beckwith concludes that we are justified in concluding that the event was supernaturally caused. This assumes, of course, that we have already concluded that the event occurred at all. Ever since David Hume's critique of belief in miracles, answering skepticism about the rationality of believing any such events occur has been of crucial importance in Christian apologetics, and this problem is the focus of Beckwith's book.

Hume himself had enunciated the evidentialist principle that "a wise man . . . proportions his belief to the evidence" (32).[43] But Beckwith concludes that Hume did not live by this principle because he confused evidence with probability. He "failed to realize that the wise and intelligent person bases his or her convictions on evidence, not on Humean 'probability.' That is, an event's occurrence may be very improbable in terms of past experience and observation, but current observation and testimony may lead one to believe that the evidence for the event is good" (38). He gives several examples (discussed in chapter 9) to illustrate the point that the unusual or unlikely may be quite believable if the evidence is good enough.

Beckwith admits that one or several pieces of testimonial evidence would usually be insufficient evidence to conclude that a miracle had occurred.

> However, if the testimonial evidence is multiplied and reinforced by circumstantial considerations . . . and the explanation of the event as a violation connects the data in a simple and coherent fashion (just as we expect a natural law to do), and a denial of the event's occurrence becomes an ad hoc naturalism-of-the-gaps, I do not see why it would not be entirely reasonable to believe that this event has occurred (based on a convergence of independent probabilities). I believe that this ap-

proach retains a healthy Humean skepticism by taking into consideration the improbability of a miraculous event, but I also believe that it resists a dogmatic skepticism by taking seriously the possibility that one may have evidence for a miracle. (37)[44]

To Hume's argument that the miracle stories of differing religions cancel one another out, Beckwith replies that some miracle stories are of more profound significance than others, and that the most impressive and significant kind of miracle is resurrection from the dead.

> This type of miracle touches man at his deepest existential and personal level, and can be a source of hope, assurance, and peace of mind if the person who conquered death promises eternal life to those who follow his teachings. . . . And, of course, if the miracles of religion A and religion B are evidentially equal, and religion A claims to be ordained by the true God because the leader has the ability to instantaneously heal patterned baldness, while religion B appeals to the resurrection of its founder, then religion B has a qualitatively better miracle. (56, 57)

Beckwith also criticizes the argument that, even granting the occurrence of a miracle, one could not fairly infer the religious significance attributed to it, and answers this argument with a thinly veiled, abstract reference to the Resurrection:

> Suppose that a purported miracle-worker, C, says that he is God's chosen and that he will perform a miracle, R, a resurrection, at time t in order to confirm God's approval of his mission. . . . Given its human impossibility, its uniqueness (i.e., nobody who has made similar claims, except C, has ever performed R), C's claim that God is responsible for R, its existential and teleological significance (i.e., C performed R at a particular time t, not at any other time), and the religious context of the event (i.e., C performed R when his claims about himself hinged on the actuality of R occurring at time t), it becomes apparent that a particular message is being communicated through this event, namely, *C is God's chosen one.*
> . . . Furthermore, in light of the *converging* nature of the facts in this case, and the inference to a rational cause made eminently plausible by them, any appeals to *coincidence* or *freak accident* become entirely *ad hoc*, a sort of naturalism-of-the-gaps. (62–63)

Only at this point does Beckwith discuss God's existence. He believes a miracle can be identified as such without first establishing God's existence. Still, he recognizes that providing "good reason" to believe in a God capable of doing miracles "makes it more plausible to believe" that a particular event is a miracle (71). We see here a telling, even defining, difference between the evidentialist and the classical apologist. The evidentialist is not closed to using theistic arguments to make belief in God more plausible or acceptable. Unlike the classical apologist, though, he does not think such arguments are *necessary*. According to evidentialism, the historical evidence for God's intervention in space and time is sufficient of itself to establish God's existence.

After utilizing Craig's version of the *kalâm* cosmological argument in support of theism (73–84), Beckwith returns to Hume's argument against miracles, focusing now on modern reformulations and defenses of Hume's argument. In response to the skepticism of Antony Flew, Beckwith agrees with Montgomery that the Christian is prepared to exercise a modest skepticism as well, but not to the extent of being closed to the possibility of a miracle. Thus Beckwith quotes with approval Montgomery's statement that "we accept no miracles unless the primary evidence compels us to it" (100).[45] He notes that "most of the objections to the miraculous are pre-evidential. That is, they do not examine the evidence for particular miracles per se, but dispense with miracles in general prior to the examination of the evidence" (121). Again following Montgomery, Beckwith favors "the legal model of evaluating evidence" as the best method for determining whether to believe a particular miracle claim (122).

JESUS: THE EVIDENCE

Although some evidentialists focus their apologetic on the scientific evidence for creation, by far the majority concentrate on defending the claims of Jesus Christ, and the overwhelming focus of these defenses pertains to belief in his resurrection from the dead.

The two leading apologists writing on the Resurrection in the past twenty years or so have been Gary Habermas[46] and William Lane Craig.[47] Although Craig is a classical apologist, his position is in many ways compatible with evidentialism. And in fact, Habermas and Craig use very similar strategies in arguing for the reasonableness of believing that God raised Jesus from the dead.

First, Habermas and Craig develop a set of "core" facts that are rarely denied by modern biblical scholars or historians writing on the subject and for which good evidence exists. Their enumerations differ from one presentation to another, but the following facts appear again and again on the lists.[48]

1. Jesus was publicly executed and died on a Roman cross.
2. Jesus was buried in a tomb.
3. Jesus' tomb was discovered empty the Sunday after his burial.
4. Jesus' followers had no basis for hoping that he would be raised from the dead.
5. Women friends of Jesus had experiences of seeing Jesus alive from the dead.
6. Jesus' apostles had experiences of seeing Jesus alive from the dead.
7. The first Christians proclaimed in Jerusalem just weeks after Jesus' death that he had literally risen from the dead.
8. Paul, a persecutor of the Christians, converted to faith in Christ after an experience of seeing Jesus alive from the dead.

One may wonder why, if the vast majority of biblical scholars acknowledge these facts, so many of them question the Resurrection. Craig comments, "It may seem stupefying that while most New Testament critics who have written on these subjects accept the facts which, at least in my opinion, furnish inductive grounds for inferring the resurrection of Jesus, they do not themselves make that inference; but this is, in fact, the situation."[49] Craig himself bases his argument on facts admitted by this majority, "not because truth is determined by numbers, for it certainly is not; rather, it is precisely because . . . I am interested in convincing outsiders that I appeal only to facts which would be accepted by the broad spectrum of scholarship, not just by conservatives."[50]

Second, Habermas and Craig refute objections to each of these generally recognized facts and offer additional support for each of these planks of the argument. In practice the two facts most often disputed are the empty tomb and the first appearances of Jesus. The credibility of the empty tomb is defended by several considerations.[51] Paul's reference to Jesus' death, burial, and resurrection as part of the received tradition of the church (1 Corinthians 15:3–5) and the burial account in Mark (which itself is likely pre-Markan) show that the empty tomb was a part of the earliest church's understanding. The report of all four Gospels that women disciples of Jesus were the first to discover the empty tomb must be historical, since the chauvinistic men of that time were not likely to have invented such a detail. The fact that Jesus' tomb was not venerated as a shrine shows, again, that the earliest Christians believed the tomb to be empty. The report in Matthew 28:11–15 that the earliest Jewish explanation for the Resurrection story was that the disciples had stolen the body proves that Jesus had in fact been buried and the tomb was in fact empty. This is so, even if one is skeptical about Matthew's claim that the tomb had been guarded to prevent the body from being stolen—since no one would make up such a story if the tomb had not become empty.

The Resurrection appearances are shown to be authentic history for similar reasons.[52] Again, the accounts of the appearances, especially in 1 Corinthians 15:6–8, are too early to have arisen as myths or legends. We have Paul's firsthand testimony that he saw Jesus alive. The Gospel testimony that the first persons to see Jesus alive were women is self-evidently reliable. All these considerations are brought together by evidentialists to constitute a cumulative case showing that the Resurrection is the most probable, reasonable explanation of the facts.

Third, alternative, naturalistic explanations are examined and shown to be less plausible or factually based than the Resurrection. These explanations typically function as alternatives to one or more of the generally accepted facts adduced by Craig and Habermas. For example, the swoon theory, which holds that Jesus merely passed out on the cross and was revived after being left for dead in the tomb, attempts to overturn the fact of Jesus' death. John Dominic Crossan's theory that Jesus' dead body was left in a ditch or shallow grave and eaten by dogs is meant to circumvent the claim that Jesus was buried in a tomb. Evidentialists argue that such theories are either purely speculative or are based on misreadings of the New Testament writings, and that all fail to come to terms with significant factual evidence.

Fourth, the positive argument from these facts to the conclusion of the resurrection of Jesus is presented. It is argued that the *best explanation* of the facts is that Jesus did actually rise from the dead. Habermas writes: "In particular, when the early and eyewitness experiences of the disciples, James, and Paul are considered, along with their corresponding transformations and their central message, the historical Resurrection becomes the best explanation for the facts, especially because the alternative theories have failed. Therefore, it may be concluded that the Resurrection is a probable historical event."[53]

Craig makes the same point in somewhat more developed fashion:

> . . . I am employing inductive reasoning understood according to the model of inference to the best explanation. This model holds that there may be a number of reasonable explanations for a body of evidence, and that one is to choose from this pool of live options that explanation

which is the best, that is, which most successfully meets such criteria as having explanatory power, explanatory scope, and not being ad hoc. My claim is that the hypothesis "God raised Jesus from the dead" is the best explanation of the evidence discussed.[54]

Lastly, Craig and Habermas argue that the resurrection of Jesus in the context of his life and teachings verifies his claim to deity. Jesus' claim to be God would lack all credibility had he remained dead. The fact that he rose from the dead provides strong warrant for accepting his divine claims. On the other hand, the Resurrection would lack all significance if it had appeared in history merely as an anomalous or inexplicable event. As Habermas and his co-author Michael Licona observe, Jesus' life "created a context in which his resurrection from the dead would not be a surprise. He claimed that he was divine. He performed deeds that were interpreted as miracles. And he predicted his resurrection."[55] Instead, the Resurrection comes with an interpretive context of the supernatural acts and revelations of the God of Israel in the Old Testament and the supernatural works and claims of Jesus in his earthly ministry.[56] Here these and other apologists adduce evidence from the Gospels that Jesus did in fact claim to be deity. Jesus forgave sins that had not been committed against him; he made statements that the Jewish authorities understandably interpreted as blasphemous claims to deity; he spoke on the Law of God as if it was his to define and apply.

From the historical evidence for the Resurrection, then, evidentialists infer that God really did raise Jesus from the dead, and from this one point the whole of the Christian faith may potentially be defended. For if Jesus was raised from the dead, given the religious context of the event, then God evidently does exist. If God raised Jesus from the dead, then the true God is the God of Jesus Christ. He is the God of the Jewish people who inspired the Old Testament, who sent Jesus his Son into the world for our salvation, and who commissioned the apostles and their associates to establish the Christian church and to produce the New Testament.

For Further Study

Collins, Steven. *Championing the Faith: A Layman's Guide to Proving Christianity's Claims*. Tulsa: Virgil W. Hensley, 1991. A manual teaching evidentialist apologetics.

Geivett, R. Douglas. *Evil and the Evidence for God: The Challenge of John Hick's Theodicy.* Afterword by John Hick. Philadelphia: Temple University Press, 1993. Thoroughly evidentialist approach to the problem of evil, arguing that the positive evidence for God's existence from natural theology is essential to answering the problem.

Geivett, R. Douglas, and Gary R. Habermas, eds. *In Defense of Miracles: A Comprehensive Case for God's Action in History*. Downers Grove, Ill.: InterVarsity, 1997. Essays by leading evangelical apologists, many of whom are evidentialist or semi-evidentialist in their method (notably Beckwith, Craig, Geivett, Moreland, and Newman).

Chapter 11

Apologetics and the Interpretation of Fact

In this concluding chapter on evidentialist apologetics, we will summarize this model or paradigm for apologetics, illustrate its use in practical apologetic encounters, and then consider its major strengths and weaknesses.

THE EVIDENTIALIST MODEL

As explained in chapter 3, we are summarizing each model of apologetic system under two headings (metapologetics and apologetics) and six specific questions under each heading. Here we apply this analysis to the evidentialist model.

Metapologetic Questions

Metapologetic questions deal with the relation of apologetics to other forms of human knowledge. In chapter 9 we considered the evidentialist approach to answering questions about knowledge in general, theology, philosophy, science, history, and experience. Here we summarize our findings in that chapter.

1. On what basis do we claim that Christianity is the truth?

In broad terms we have distinguished the evidentialist approach from the classical approach in a number of ways. Classical apologetics is characteristically dominated by deductive reasoning and seeks to base its case on a foundation of select, rationally certain truths. Evidentialist apologetics is dominated by inductive, empirical reasoning and seeks to build its case from a mass of factual evidences. The classical approach typically launches its argument in two stages: the first seeks to prove the theistic worldview, while the second, building on the first, seeks to prove the specific, central claims of the Christian faith. The evidentialist approach typically involves one complex process of mounting a case for the truth of the whole of the Christian theistic faith, though almost always with the case turning on the evidence for Jesus' death and resurrection.

The two approaches make common cause in rejecting outright the philosophical movement known as postmodernism. Both emphasize the irrational nature of the relativism that is at the heart of the postmodernist agenda. Whereas classical apologists typically analyze postmodernism as a philosophy or worldview, though, evidentialists often treat it more as a cultural trend that at bottom is still modernist. Postmodernists are really not relativists; they have instead substituted a new set of absolutes or standards for the Judeo-Christian absolutes. In matters of ordinary fact, evidentialists find that most people today still operate on the assumption that the facts are objective, knowable truths. At least some evidentialists in this sense affirm that facts "speak for themselves."

Evidentialists do not believe, however, that factual evidence in and of itself produces faith, and in fact most of them deny believing that faith requires evidence; faith is based on the witness of the Holy Spirit. Evidentialists do maintain that what sets Christianity apart from other religions is that it is rooted in facts that are in principle verifiable on the basis of publicly accessible evidence.

2. What is the relationship between apologetics and theology?

Evidentialists view the relationship between apologetics and theology as one of defense and exposition of the same truth. That is, apologetics offers a reasoned defense of the Christian beliefs that are explained and defined in theology. Moreover, apologetics and theology utilize essentially the same method. Both reason inductively from the data or facts to conclusions using a method similar to what is used in the sciences. The apologist appeals to facts *about* and *from* the Bible to show that Christianity is *true;* the theologian appeals to facts *of* the Bible to show what Christianity *means*. Most evidentialists are not Reformed in theology; they run a gamut from moderately conservative, Arminian Protestants (for example, Swinburne, Pinnock) to very conservative Lutherans (Montgomery).

3. Should apologetics engage in a philosophical defense of the Christian faith?

Evidentialists view philosophy as a critical tool for understanding the implications of the sciences in matters beyond the sciences' direct competency. For example, while the sciences cannot examine God, they can examine the world he created and infer his existence from the evidence in the world. Thus evidentialists do use philosophy, but primarily as a means of clarifying concepts and analyzing the methods and reasoning used in discussing matters of theological significance in the light of natural science and of human history. For evidentialists, when philosophy seeks to construct positive answers to ultimate issues apart from facts, it is merely speculative.

4. Can science be used to defend the Christian faith?

Of the four apologetic approaches, evidentialism makes the most positive use of science. While evidentialists do not accept all conventional scientific theories uncritically, they tend to be more confident in their use of scientific information and theories to support theistic conclusions than the other approaches. They also tend to adhere to a realist view of science—typically assuming such a view without discussion. Some evidentialists are theistic evolutionists, but most are old-earth creationists.

5. Can the Christian faith be supported by historical inquiry?

While evidentialists tend to make confident and even enthusiastic use of science in apologetics, most of them base their apologetic primarily, and in some cases exclusively, on historical evidence. In their view the Christian faith in its essence involves belief that God has done certain things in history for our salvation, specifically in the death and resurrection of Jesus. They recognize that many people view historical knowledge as too subjective or uncertain to be the basis of faith. They admit that historical knowledge as such can never rise above probability, but contend that this is so with all knowledge of matters of fact, yet we base life-and-death decisions on such knowledge every day. Furthermore, they argue that there is plenty of evidence for the historicity of the central events of the Christian faith.

6. How is our knowledge of Christian truth related to our experience?

Evidentialists recognize that people have religious experiences. However, while they acknowledge that some of these are genuine encounters with God, they point out that such experiences are also common in non-Christian religions. Personal, subjective experiences are meaningful or helpful only to the persons experiencing them. If we are to commend the truth of Christianity to people, evidentialists conclude, we must appeal to publicly accessible facts. Testimonies of changed lives may help people see that Christianity is not *only* about events in the past, but the "evidence that demands a verdict" is to be found in history.

Apologetic Questions

Apologetic questions deal with issues commonly raised by non-Christians themselves. In chapter 10 we considered the approach evidentialism takes to answering questions about the Bible, Christianity and other beliefs, the existence of God, the problem of evil, the credibility of miracles, and the claims of Jesus Christ. Here we summarize our findings in that chapter.

1. Why should we believe in the Bible?

Most evidentialists begin their apologetic by presenting evidence, not for the inspiration of the Bible, but for its historical reliability. They emphasize the authenticity of the biblical text as it has been passed down through the centuries as well as the historical credibility of its contents. In particular they focus on the historical value of the Gospels and Paul's epistles as source material for information about Jesus' death and resurrection. They want to use this material to present their central apologetic argument, namely, that the historical facts show that Jesus rose from the dead. In turn, Jesus' resurrection will validate Jesus' teaching and, by extension, the teaching of the entire Bible.

Like classical apologists, then, evidentialists affirm that we believe in the Bible because we believe in the God revealed in Christ—not the other way around. But for evidentialists it is not necessary to convince people that a God exists before presenting evidence for the divine inspiration of the Bible. In addition to the historical argument outlined above, they appeal to fulfilled prophecy as evidence arising from the Bible itself for the existence of a God who knows the future.

2. Don't all religions lead to God?

The major premise of religious pluralism is that all religions are basically alike. Evidentialists attack this premise directly by appealing to the historically verifiable miracles of the Bible, especially the resurrection of Jesus, as proof of the uniqueness of Christianity. Whereas other religions represent mankind's best guesses, intuitions, or mystical religious experiences, none of which can be verified as based on truth, Christianity alone represents God's direct intervention into human history to redeem mankind.

3. How do we know that God exists?

Evidentialists typically do not reject the classical theistic proofs (other than the ontological argument, which most evidentialists reject). However, they do rework them into fact-based, evidentiary arguments to augment or replace the classical deductive, philosophical proofs. The cosmological and teleological arguments are the arguments of choice here, commonly articulated using the scientific evidence for the big bang (which proves the universe had a beginning) and for the intricate, delicate balance and design of the universe to sustain life. Evidentialists also point to miracles, fulfilled prophecy, and other evidences from the Bible to support belief in the existence of God.

4. If God does exist, why does he permit evil?

Classical apologists usually address the problem of evil in its most historically familiar form as a logical conundrum: How can God be all-powerful and all-loving, yet permit evil? Evidentialists may discuss the problem in this form, too, but they most characteristically deal with it as a matter of probability or evidence. That is, in more recent anti-theistic polemic the nontheist often adduces the great, often inexplicable evils of the world not as a logical disproof of God's existence, but as evidence showing God's existence to be improbable or unlikely. In turn, the evidentialist seeks to answer whether these evils really are evidence that "counts" against God's existence, and also whether there is sufficient evidence in favor of God's existence to counterbalance the evidence of evil. Evidentialists point out various reasons why certain evils may be present in the world, and argue that the positive evidence for God's existence is so great that the problem of evil does not make his existence unlikely.

5. Aren't the miracles of the Bible spiritual myths or legends and not literal fact?

To the question of whether miracles are myths or facts, evidentialists answer simply, look at the evidence. They agree that it is reasonable to be somewhat skeptical of miracle claims; they insist, though, that it is unreasonable to decide that no amount of evidence could ever warrant belief that a miracle had occurred. While belief in God certainly makes miracle claims somewhat more believable, one still must question such claims and determine if there is evidence for them. Moreover, evidentialists maintain that in some cases the evidence for a miracle is so great that even a person who does not already believe in God can and should recognize it as a miracle. Thus they think the evidence for miracles can provide rational grounds for belief in God's existence.

6. Why should I believe in Jesus?

Nearly all evidentialists view the resurrection of Jesus as the primary factual basis for faith in Jesus. It is Jesus' resurrection that vindicates his claim to be the Messiah, the Son of God, and that also reveals his death to have been a redemptive sacrifice for sins. The origin and history of the church would be unintelligible without the Resurrection. Other lines of evidence—for creation, for the historical reliability of the Bible, for the life and miracles of Jesus, for fulfilled prophecy in the Bible—supplement and converge on this point. Evidentialists argue that people should believe in Jesus because the facts show him to be what the Bible says he is.

The following table presents an overview of the evidentialist model of apologetics with these twelve questions in mind.

Issue		Position
Metapologetics	**KNOWLEDGE**	Fitting of the facts is the primary test of truth Postmodernism is unrealistic Spirit's witness is the ground of faith
	THEOLOGY	Apologetics and theology use scientific method Apologetics defends debated aspects of theology
	PHILOSOPHY	Apologetics uses philosophy's critical tools Methodological use of non-Christian philosophy
	SCIENCE	Freely accepts established theories Science and theology view same facts differently Typically old-earth creationism
	HISTORY	Objective view of history quite realizable Right view of history requires right method
	EXPERIENCE	Religious experiences possible but not reliable Test private experiences by public facts
Apologetics	**SCRIPTURE**	Scripture the source of evidence for apologetic Begin with reliability, conclude with inspiration Fulfilled prophecy proves inspiration, proves God
	RELIGIONS	Religious pluralism ignores gospel's factual basis Christianity makes uniquely verifiable claims
	GOD	Generally inductive proofs favored Design argument most common
	EVIL	Inductive problem of evil: Is theism likely? Evidence for God holds up despite evil
	MIRACLES	Miracles add evidence for a theistic worldview Miracles not to be believed unless good evidence
	JESUS	Jesus' resurrection can be proved historically False dilemma: Jesus of history or Christ of faith

EVIDENTIALISM ILLUSTRATED

In this second of four dialogues we will present in this book, a Christian named Joe becomes involved in a discussion with Sarah and Murali while riding a city bus. Joe is a researcher in the city's police crime lab. He has read a lot about, and talked with people of, various different religions, and is especially interested in the New Age movement. Joe likes a variety of apologetics authors, including John Warwick Montgomery. When he boards the bus, he sits in front of Sarah and Murali, who are already deep in conversation about a devastating earthquake that has been in the news.

Murali: In India, where I come from, most people believe that things like this happen because of karma. The people who died in the earthquake were meant to die, and they will come back in reincarnation to live again.

Sarah: Some people here in America believe that, too, but I don't. I don't think there's any life after death. When you die, that's it.

Murali: You may be right, although I hope not. I don't know what I think about this anymore. I don't think anybody really knows. Our religions help us feel better about life, and they may be right about there being life after death, but no one knows for sure.

Joe: Excuse me—I couldn't help overhearing what you were talking about. My name is Joe. May I say something?

Murali: Of course. I am Murali, and this is Sarah.

Joe: I think it is possible to know about life after death.

Murali: How?

Joe: Well, suppose someone died and then came back to life, and he was able to tell you about what lies beyond death and how we need to prepare for it. That would be one way to know.

Sarah: Yeah, but no one has ever done that.

Joe: Actually, someone has. Jesus Christ died and rose from the dead, and he has told us all about God and how we can live forever in God's presence.

Sarah: Oh, no. You're one of those Bible-thumping Christians. Murali, you gotta watch out for these guys. They're always going around saying that you have to believe in Jesus.

Joe: Guilty as charged, although I promise not to thump you with my Bible. I did bring one, though.

Murali: I have heard this before, of course, that Jesus rose from the dead. It is a beautiful story, but you don't take it literally, do you?

Joe: Again, guilty as charged. I certainly do take it literally. Jesus is not a mythical character. He was a real, flesh-and-blood man who lived almost two thousand years ago in a real place.

Murali: Yes, I'm sorry, I didn't mean to suggest that Jesus never lived. That is obvious. But the story of his coming back to life—why would you take that literally?

Joe: Well, for one thing, because the people who first told this "story" said that it really happened. They specifically denied that it was a made-up story.

Murali: When did they say that?

Sarah: Now you've gone and done it. He's going to start quoting the Bible at you.

Joe: You're right, Sarah, but I won't ask you or Murali to take the Bible's word for anything. In fact, I encourage you to examine the evidence to see whether what the Bible writers say about Jesus is true or not.

Murali: That seems fair.

Joe: In 2 Peter 1:16 the apostle Peter wrote, "For we did not follow cleverly devised tales when we made known to you the power and coming of our Lord Jesus Christ, but we were eyewitnesses of His majesty." You see, Peter is saying that the stories they told about Jesus were not made-up myths or fairy tales, but were eyewitness testimony. And you find this kind of statement throughout the New Testament.

Sarah: But everyone knows that these things were written down long after Jesus had died. Scholars say the Gospels were written about a hundred years after Jesus.

Joe: I'm curious about those scholars. But before I say anything about that, can we agree at least that the New Testament *claims* that the resurrection of Jesus is not a myth, but is an historical fact told to us by eyewitnesses?

Murali: That does seem to be what it claims, yes. At least in that one verse that you read to us.

Sarah: Well, I'm not convinced. How do you know that the Gospels claim to be historical fact?

Joe: A fair question. Let me give you a couple of easy examples. In Luke 1:1–4, Luke tells us that there were "those who from the beginning were eyewitnesses and servants of the word," and that these eyewitnesses had "handed down" to us what had happened. And Luke says that he "investigated everything carefully from the beginning" before writing it down, "so that you might know the exact truth about the things you have been taught." In other words, Luke says his Gospel is based on eyewitness testimony, and that he did historical research in order to write an accurate account. Now in the Gospel of John, it tells us that soldiers stabbed Jesus on the cross with a spear to make sure he was dead. The author then says in John 19:35, "And he who has seen has borne witness, and his witness is true; and he knows that he is telling the truth, so that you also may believe." So, the author of the Gospel of John claims to have been an eyewitness to the death of Jesus, as well as to many other things, of course.

Sarah: All right, I guess the Gospels, or at least those two Gospels, claim to be telling historical fact. But how can we be sure about anything they tell us? Like I said, they were written about a hundred years after the fact.

Joe: You did say that. But Sarah, the fact is that no biblical scholar says the Gospels were written a hundred years later. Jesus died in A.D. 33. The latest dates given by scholars put the Gospel of Mark around the year 70, about forty years after Jesus' death, and the Gospel of John around the year 100, or about seventy years after Jesus' death. And some biblical scholars, including the radical theologian John A. T. Robinson, have argued that all of the Gospels were written before the year 70. I have some literature on this subject that I can get for you if you're interested.

Murali: You seem to know what you're talking about. But even forty years is a long time. Isn't it possible that the story of Jesus developed over the years into the story we now have?

Joe: I don't see how, if John was himself an eyewitness, as he says he was. Besides, the Gospels aren't the earliest books of the New Testament. The epistles of the apostle Paul were written between about the years 50 and 65. In other words, Paul was writing about Jesus' resurrection less than twenty years after it happened. And Paul himself saw Jesus alive after his death.

Sarah: It's my understanding that some of those epistles weren't even written by Paul.

Joe: That is the opinion of many scholars today, but by no means all of them. But I'll tell you what. I'll stick to the epistles that all biblical scholars agree were written by Paul. For example, in Galatians, which was one of Paul's first epistles, he writes at length about the fact that he was a persecutor of the church until Jesus appeared to him and called him to be an apostle. And in 1 Corinthians 15, Paul says he and the other apostles all had the same message, which was that Jesus had died, had been buried, had been raised from the dead, and had appeared to them and to many others. So here we see proof that Christians had been proclaiming Jesus' resurrection as an historical fact from the very beginning of the church. It wasn't a myth that developed gradually over many years.

Murali: This is very interesting. I have never heard these facts before. But tell me, Joe: Are you saying that Paul and these other apostles actually saw Jesus alive from the dead? Could it be that what they experienced was some sort of vision? Perhaps they had a vision of Jesus in a higher state of consciousness, and they gained comfort and encouragement from that vision.

Joe: That's a good question. I think Paul is very clear about what he means. Let me read 1 Corinthians 15:3–4 to you. It says "that Christ died for our sins according to the Scriptures, and that He was buried."

Now, let me stop right there. Why do you suppose Paul mentioned Jesus' burial? Why would that be important?

Murali: Now it is your turn to ask a good question. I don't know. Perhaps he mentioned it to make the point that Jesus was really dead?

Joe: Excellent! I think you're exactly right. Now, the next thing Paul says is "that He was raised on the third day according to the Scriptures, and that He appeared." Let me stop there again. Paul says that Jesus died, and then he points to Jesus' burial as proof of that fact. Paul then says that Jesus was raised, and he points to Jesus' appearances as proof of his resurrection. When you take it all together, it's clear that Paul is talking about Jesus being raised physically from the grave. That's the whole point of mentioning Jesus' burial between his death and resurrection. Remember, Paul was a Pharisee, a Jewish rabbi, who had become a Christian. In his vocabulary, for a man to be buried and then to have been raised meant just one thing: the man's grave was empty and he was alive from the dead.

Sarah: You may be right; that may have been what Paul was saying. But why should we believe him? Why should we take his word for it?

Joe: What are the alternatives? If Jesus wasn't raised from the dead, why do you suppose Paul would say that he had been? Was he lying?

Sarah: No, I don't think he was lying. Maybe Paul had some kind of hallucination and thought he saw Jesus.

Joe: What about all of the others who saw Jesus? Paul mentions that Jesus appeared to Peter, the other apostles, and to more than five hundred people at one time. Were they all hallucinating?

Sarah: Well, I don't know if I take that five hundred number seriously.

Joe: I don't know why not. But let's leave them aside, if you like. Do you really think that Peter, James, and the other apostles all had hallucinations of Jesus? That doesn't seem very likely, does it?

Sarah: It seems much more likely than the idea that a dead man came back to life.

Joe: Normally, Sarah, I'd agree with you. But in this case, the idea that Jesus came back to life is much more likely to be true than that over a dozen men, some of whom loved Jesus, some of whom hated Jesus, all had hallucinations of Jesus alive from the dead. You see, if we heard that your aunt Edna or my cousin Jasper had died and come back to life, we'd probably dismiss the idea out of hand. After all, why should Aunt Edna or Cousin Jasper rise from the dead? There's no rhyme or reason to it. But with Jesus, there is a very good reason. Jesus claimed to be the Messiah. He claimed to have come to overcome sin and death for all humanity, and to bring eternal life. He is reported to have performed many miracles, including resuscitating people who had died. He was executed on Passover, a Jewish feast that celebrated God's deliverance of his people from bondage. Given all that we know about Jesus, his being raised from the dead makes perfect sense. God raised him from the dead to vindicate him as the Messiah and to bring to us the promise of eternal life if we trust in him.

Murali: You make an interesting case. But what you just said bothers me. You are saying, if I understand you correctly, that one must believe in Jesus to have eternal life. But I cannot accept the idea that God loves Christians but does not love Hindus or Buddhists or Muslims. Throughout the world for centuries people have killed each other because they were of a different religion. This intolerance is so destructive.

Joe: I certainly agree with you that it is terribly wrong to kill people because they are of a different religion. In fact, my religion considers such killing to be a grievous sin. We believe that God loves people of all nations and races, and it is our duty to tell them the good news of God's love for them in Jesus Christ.

Murali: But why must they believe in Jesus to have God's love? Surely God already loves them.

Joe: In a sense, you're right, of course. But there is a problem. We human beings—all of us, of whatever religion, or of no religion—are sinners.

Sarah: That's so judgmental.

Joe: Not at all. I'm not saying anything about you or anyone else that doesn't also apply to me. I'm a sinner, too. None of us is morally perfect, and all of us are alienated from God until we come to faith in Jesus Christ.

Murali: This idea of sin is difficult for me. But I see that my stop is coming up. I must go.

Sarah: Me, too. It's been interesting, Joe.

Murali: Yes, very.

Joe: Let me give you my phone number and e-mail address and you can contact me at your convenience if you decide you'd like to continue this discussion.

Murali and Sarah: Okay!

NOTABLE STRENGTHS OF EVIDENTIALIST APOLOGETICS

As we did with classical apologetics in chapter 7, we will here review the most common and important observations that have been made as to the notable strengths and potential weaknesses of the evidentialist apologetic model.

Recognizes That Probability Is Unavoidable

Evidentialists readily admit that the conclusions available through the inductive process of historical inquiry are probable, not certain. But they are quick to add that *no* decision in life is based on deductive certainty. Deduction can reveal whether a conclusion follows from specific premises, but it cannot tell us whether premises correspond to truth about the real world. In all matters of fact, we are dependent on human observation and human interpretation, both of which are fallible. Because we will never have *all* the facts, we can never arrive at absolute certainty from our analysis and interpretation of the facts. But this does not stop us from reaching conclusions and making decisions in law courts, scientific laboratories, or business meetings. William Dyrness observes that "it is inadmissible to ask more of a line of reasoning than it can possibly give. Historical judgments are based on available records. No historical data can ever be conclusive. In historical reasoning, therefore, we can expect only probability, and we must not be disappointed when we cannot have certainty. The uncertainty here is not with Christianity, but with the tenuous nature of historical argumentation."[1]

Even if the validity of inductive, probabilistic arguments is acknowledged, the way such arguments are developed is often questioned. For example, some critics regard the cumulative-case approach to argumentation, frequently used by evidentialists, as akin to a series of leaky buckets. Antony Flew put the point most succinctly: "If one leaky bucket will not hold water there is no reason to think that ten can."[2] This is not to say that Flew rejected all empirical argument. However, he distinguished cumulative arguments in which each element has real evidentiary value from those in which each element is really valueless. "We have here to insist upon a sometimes tricky distinction: between, on the one hand, the valid principle of the accumulation of evidence, where every item has at least some weight in its own right; and, on the other hand, the Ten-leaky-buckets-Tactic, applied to arguments none of which hold water at all."[3]

Richard Swinburne addresses the leaky-bucket objection head-on: "For clearly if you jam ten leaky buckets together in such a way that holes in the bottom of each bucket are squashed close to solid parts of the bottoms of neighbouring buckets, you will get a container that will hold water."[4] Douglas Geivett, though, worries that Swinburne's super bucket "can be expected, at best, to retard the leak," not to "prevent eventual drainage."[5] He distinguishes the approach of inference to the best explanation from the informal cumulative-case approach of Basil Mitchell and the rigorously formal use of confirmation theory by Swinburne to build a cumulative-case argument.

Some evidentialists prefer the analogy of a rope. Irwin H. Linton, in *A Lawyer Examines the Bible*, writes: "It is a commonplace that while one thread of a three stranded rope may possibly be broken, the three strands twisted together and each multiplying the strength of the others may produce a tensile strength beyond the power to overcome."[6] J. P. Moreland, an apologist whose approach straddles the classical and evidentialist models, states flatly that "the leaky bucket metaphor is the wrong one. A rope metaphor is more appropriate. Just as several strands make a rope stronger than just a few strands, so the many-stranded case for God is made stronger than would be the case with only a few strands of evidence."[7]

The leaky-bucket analogy is just that, an analogy. While it makes a valid point, it may have been overanalyzed a bit. Flew himself acknowledged that one may argue from an accumulation of evidence. His caution is one that many evidentialists take seriously. It does not overturn the fact that arguments designed to show that something is true in the real world will inevitably fall short of demonstrative, deductive proof.

Appealing Methods of Inquiry

One of the great strengths of the evidentialist approach is its use of methods of inquiry already familiar and acceptable to many non-Christians. As Mark Hanna acknowledges, evidentialism "recognizes the unavoidability of making use of ordinary ways of knowing in order to become aware of God's self-revelation in Scripture."[8] Since the goal of apologetics is to persuade people that Christianity is true, or at least that it is reasonable to believe it is true, arguments that employ strategies familiar to those being persuaded are so much more likely to be effective. And it is undeniable that evidentialist apologetics has enjoyed great success.

Evidentialists emphasize that daily communication between believers and unbelievers requires a commonly held logic and world of experience.[9] Without this commonality, communication and dialogue would be impossible.

Stresses the Factual Evidence

If the goal of Christian apologetics is to defend the truth of Christianity, and if truth is understood as correspondence with reality, then an apologetic that emphasizes the factual reality of Christianity is mandatory. Evidentialism is defined by the primacy it assigns to fact. Montgomery argues that the Christian doctrine of the Incarnation, which teaches that God entered the human sphere in the person of the God-man, repudiates any attempt to divorce "Christian facts" from secular, nonreligious facts.[10] Truth must be factually based, and Christian truth can be verified by objective, public evidence.

Evidentialists stress the importance of empirical content in the substantiation of the Christian worldview. They focus on the historicity of Christianity and approach the Bible as a primary historical document. Montgomery has made a particularly significant contribution in this regard. As Ronald H. Nash has stated, "No conservative theologian has done more to articulate the nature and importance of the relationship between Christian faith and history than John Warwick Montgomery."[11] Even some of his critics acknowledge the importance of his stress on empirical study and investigation of history.[12] For Montgomery, the historical Incarnation provides an answer to Flew's parable of the gardener, because "central to the Christian position is the historically grounded assertion that *the Gardener entered the garden:* God actually appeared in the empirical world in Jesus Christ and fully manifested his deity through miraculous acts in general and his resurrection from the dead in particular."[13]

Montgomery claims that if the Resurrection event is granted, it cannot be re-garded as trivial because of its profound implications for the universal problem of death.[14] The fact of the Resurrection and its meaning are conjoined in the context of Christ's own claims. "Christ's resurrection can be examined by non-Christians as well as by Christians. Its factual character, when considered in light of the claims of the One raised from the dead, points not to a multiplicity of equally pos-sible interpretations, but to a single 'best' interpretation (to an interpretation most consistent with the data), namely the deity of Christ (John 2:18–22)."[15]

Not all evidentialists agree with Montgomery that historical events are self-in-terpreting, but they agree that while facts do not create faith, they are essential for faith. R. N. Williams writes that a perceptual shift can take place in the logic of the whole situation that can move a person beyond the level of fact to an illumination of the facts from a new perspective. In this sense biblical miracles "were intended to conduct, not to compel, men to faith."[16] Fact does not force faith, but faith can-not be divorced from fact. Montgomery argues that the factual evidence leaves non-Christians with no excuse:

> Of course, sinful self-interest may tempt the non-Christian to avoid the
> weight of evidence, just as self-interest has so frequently corrupted in-
> vestigation in other purely secular matters. But selfish perversions of
> data or interpretation can be made plain in the area of revelational fact no
> less than in the nonrevelational sphere, for Christian revelation occurred
> in time—in the secular world. To miss this point is to miss the character
> of the Incarnation.[17]

POTENTIAL WEAKNESSES OF EVIDENTIALIST APOLOGETICS

Evidentialist apologetics has been widely criticized from a number of perspec-tives. We will consider here some of the most common and important criticisms identifying potential weaknesses in or challenges to the evidentialist approach.[18]

Assumes the Theistic Worldview

The principal objection to evidentialism from a classical apologetics perspec-tive is that it attempts to make a case for the theistic worldview on the basis of facts. According to both classical apologists and most Reformed apologists, this will not work; one must first have a worldview before one can interpret the facts in the world. As Geisler puts it, "facts and events have ultimate meaning only within and by virtue of the context of the world view in which they are conceived."[19] Geisler explains that

> evidence gains its meaning only by its immediate and overall context; and evidence as such cannot, without begging the question, be used to establish the overall context by which it obtains its very meaning as evidence. . . . it is a vicious circle to argue that a given fact (say, the resuscitation of Christ's body) is evidence of a certain truth claim (say, Christ's claim to be God), unless it can be established that the event comes in the context of a theistic universe.[20]

Geisler adds that meaning is not inherent in historical facts and events; meaning demands an interpretive context that is distinct from the facts and events.[21] Apologists from other perspectives agree that evidentialists tacitly assume the validity of the theistic worldview from the beginning.[22]

One possible response to this criticism is that it assumes that non-Christians will rigorously screen out any and all facts that do not fit consistently in their worldviews, regardless of the evidence. No doubt non-Christians do this a lot, but the evidentialist thinks that the facts can also undermine those false worldviews when the evidence is cogently presented.

Uses Hidden Presuppositions

It is the contention of evidentialists that metaphysical presuppositions can be minimized in apologetics. Batts asserts that "Montgomery rightly emphasizes that the historical method (the scientific method as applied to historical phenomena) assumes as little as possible and provides for the objective discovery of as much as possible."[23] But critics of evidentialism contend that evidentialists work with hidden presuppositions about the nature of reality. For example, in their scientific and historical arguments, evidentialists presuppose that there is a rational structure to the whole of reality.[24] The heuristic, methodological assumptions that knowledge is possible, that the universe is structured, and that the senses can be trusted cannot themselves be empirically substantiated.[25] Gordon Clark charges that Montgomery as an empiricist is as much a "dogmatist" on sensation as the presuppositionalist is on revelation; he cannot provide any evidence for his own first principle.[26] Carl F. H. Henry likewise states, "Empiricists always operate on presuppositions which they cannot prove by their own methodology."[27]

Montgomery admits that "a prioris must lie at the basis of every procedure," but says that "they should be kept to a minimum, and be as self-evident and beyond dispute as much as possible."[28] Because of this, Henry has commented that "Montgomery differs from the presuppositionalists he disowns only in the number and scope of the presuppositions he prefers for deciphering the meaning of history."[29]

Montgomery's presuppositions are not only epistemological but also metaphysical. "Metaphysical presuppositions are implicit in every epistemology, and epistemological presuppositions are implicit in every metaphysics."[30] It is therefore impossible to separate epistemological assumptions from metaphysical ones. The assumption that the mind can perceive reality, for example, is an assumption *about reality*, that is, a metaphysical assumption. Montgomery and all evidentialists unavoidably import Christian presuppositions into their apologetic methodology. Thom Notaro writes:

> [Pinnock and Montgomery] seem unaware that they, as believers, are sitting on a gold-mine of presuppositions. In the past they have dipped into that hidden treasure most noticeably when confronted with the question of biblical inerrancy, yet without admitting the cash-value of the presuppositional method. . . . all Christian apologists presuppose certain biblical commitments, regardless of whether they are willing to *call* them presuppositions. The wide discrepancy between Christian apologists arises from the varying degrees of consistency with which they honor those commitments in their apologetic method.[31]

Evidentialists are generally unmoved by these concerns. They freely acknowledge that evidential arguments require certain assumptions about the reality of our physical world, the ability of the mind to perceive reality, and the like. What the evidentialist wants is not to make arguments that are totally free of presuppositions but rather arguments that presuppose only what must be presupposed to know anything at all. This challenge to the evidentialist approach, then, identifies a real limitation of the approach but one with which evidentialists insist everyone must live in order to know anything or reason about anything.

Underestimates the Human Factor

Both classical and evidentialist apologists are often criticized for an excessive optimism in assuming that unbelievers are willing and able to examine the evidence for Christianity in an open, honest, and unprejudiced way. Empirically oriented apologists in particular are said to place too much confidence in the persuasive value of evidences and erroneously assume a stance of historical objectivity, forgetting that the significance of historical facts is in fact determined by one's presuppositional framework. For example, Henry declares that Pinnock's empirical method

> requires a herculean burden of demonstration that no evangelical theologian, however devout or brilliant, can successfully carry. For Pinnock seems to imply . . . that, without any appeal to transcendent divine revelation and by empirical considerations alone, the ordinary unregenerate man can be logically and inescapably driven to a Christian understanding of reality, and that any insistence on the invalidity of such empirical argumentation is due solely to volitional recalcitrance and not at all to empirical evidential deficiencies.[32]

Along similar lines, evidentialists are accused of unrealistically minimizing the effect of sin on unregenerate cognition and volition. According to critics, Montgomery and others overestimate the ability of the unbeliever, in Montgomery's words, to "understand the factual nature of the world and rationally interpret the data of his experience."[33] Hillman, for example, who is critical of both the presuppositional and evidentialist models, contends, "If it is true that Van Til emphasizes too greatly the inability of man to perceive truth, then it is also true that Montgomery's approach is too greatly weighted in favor of man's ability to understand and to respond to the truth of God."[34] Some evidentialists, however, acknowledge the effects of sin on human reasoning; they appeal to the common and special grace of God in overcoming these cognitive and volitional barriers.

The following table summarizes the major notable strengths and potential weaknesses that have been perceived in the evidentialist model of apologetics.

Evidentialist Apologetics	
Notable Strengths	*Potential Weaknesses*
Recognizes that probability cannot be avoided in apologetic arguments	Does not provide worldview context needed to assess probability
Uses methods of inquiry that are often appealing to non-Christians	Has hidden presuppositions in its application of the methods it uses
Emphasizes the importance of the factual evidence for Christianity	Diminishes the role of personal factors affecting perception of facts

CONCLUSION

So far we have examined two models of apologetics, the classical and evidentialist models. In some ways these two models are very similar. Both models attempt to make a case for the truth of Christianity that will be accessible to the non-Christian who follows the argument openly and honestly. The classical model is generally more rationalist while the evidentialist model is characteristically more empiricist. The classical model follows a two-step approach (prove theism, then prove Christianity on the assumption of theism), while the evidentialist model follows a cumulative-case approach (scientific and historical evidences combine to prove Christian theism). But the two strategies share a common understanding of the apologetic task: commending the Christian faith to non-Christians on the basis of truths that they already believe.

It is this very understanding of apologetics that is at the heart of many of the criticisms made of both models. Such an understanding, it has been urged, fails to take into account the great disparity between the Christian and non-Christian mindsets. The two models, many apologists now believe, both assume that Christianity can be proved to non-Christians on their own terms, without challenging their own most basic assumptions or presuppositions. To correct this faulty assumption, a third model of apologetics, which we call Reformed apologetics, has been developed. It is the Reformed approach that will be examined next.

For Further Study

Geisler, Norman L. *Baker Encyclopedia of Christian Apologetics*. Grand Rapids: Baker, 1999. See especially the article on "Historical Apologetics" (318-320) for an evaluation of the usual type of evidentialism.

Habermas, Gary R., and Antony G. N. Flew. *Did Jesus Rise from the Dead? The Resurrection Debate*. Edited by Terry L. Miethe. San Francisco: Harper & Row, 1987. An excellent example of an evidentialist in debate.

Part Four

Reformed Apologetics: God Said It

Chapter 12

Apologists Who Emphasize Revelation

With the decline throughout the twentieth century of the orthodox, super-naturalistic Christian worldview in American culture, it is understandable that many Christians have declared traditional apologetics a failure and have cast about for a new approach to defending the faith. In conservative Calvinistic or Reformed circles, several closely related apologetic systems have been developed as alternatives to both the classical and the evidentialist approaches. Most of these systems are known by the label **presuppositionalism**, although the term **Reformed apologetics** is more inclusive of the different systems to be considered here. The approach emphasizes the presentation of Christianity as *revealed*—as based on the authoritative revelation of God in Scripture and in Jesus Christ. Its most common forms find absolute and certain proof of Christianity in the absolute and certain character of the knowledge that God has and that he has revealed to humanity.

Because of his continuing importance for Christian theology and apologetics, and because there is considerable debate about his apologetic approach, we will begin by examining in some depth the apologetic thought of John Calvin. Following that we will discuss the modern roots of Reformed apologetics, and then consider the thought of four twentieth-century Reformed apologists.

JOHN CALVIN

The roots of Reformed apologetics actually go back prior to Calvin. Tertullian's sharp antithesis between Jerusalem and Athens may be cited as the clearest anticipation of the Reformed approach in the ante-Nicene fathers. The mature Augustine, as well as the medieval philosopher Anselm, both explicitly insisted on faith leading to understanding. Although Augustine and Anselm were part of the classical tradition of apologetics, there is a side to their thinking that prepared for and established some precedent for the Reformed approach.[1]

Still, it was John Calvin, the sixteenth-century Reformer, who provided the underpinnings of modern Reformed apologetics.[2] While it would be anachronistic to describe Calvin as a "Reformed apologist" in the technical sense used here, it is true that the Reformed approach is rooted in his theology. We begin our discussion of Calvin and apologetics by examining his most famous work, the *Institutes of the Christian Religion*.[3]

Basic to Calvin's distinctive approach to apologetics is his strong doctrine of human sin. In his view, our fall into sin has corrupted our entire being, including our mind: "the reason of our mind, wherever it may turn, is miserably subject to vanity" (2.2.25). Thus our reasoning is now not only limited, but suspect. For this reason Calvin insists that the pagan philosophical ideal of "reason alone as the ruling principle in man," the sole measure of truth and guide in life, be abandoned in favor of "the Christian philosophy" of submitting human reasoning to the Holy Spirit's teaching in Scripture (3.7.1). Calvin's rejection of any apologetic that is ultimately rationalistic is plain. Calvinists, following Calvin, have argued that the corrupting influences of sin on the human mind—what are often called the **noetic effects of sin** (from the Greek *nous*, "mind")—must be taken seriously in the apologetic task.[4]

This does not mean that Calvin endorses irrationality. However much Scripture may contradict the reasoning of sinful, unbelieving men, in reality what it presents for faith is consistent, coherent, and reasonable. It is "a knowledge with which the best reason agrees" (1.7.5). The problem that unbelievers have is not that they are rational—they aren't—but that they are ignorant of the truth.

Calvin's conviction that Christianity is the truth influenced even the plan and structure of his chief work, the *Institutes*. As Ford Lewis Battles has shown, the opening chapters of the work present a series of contrasts or antitheses between the false, ignorant religious beliefs of the unbelieving and the true knowledge that is essential to Christian faith.

True and False Religion in Calvin's *Institutes*[5]

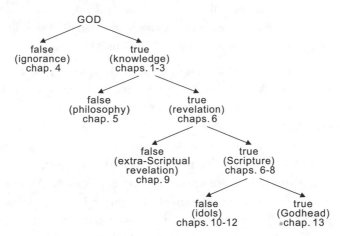

Modern interpreters are sharply divided on the question whether Calvin allowed for any sort of "natural theology" as part of a Christian apologetic.[6] Some things, however, are clear. According to Calvin, God ought to be known from the "sense of divinity" (divinitatis sensum) within every human being (1.3.1).[7] In addition, God "revealed himself and daily discloses himself in the whole workmanship of the universe" (1.5.1). Unfortunately, human depravity has rendered this internal and external general revelation incapable of creating a true knowledge of God, and humanity has corrupted the knowledge of God from natural revelation into idolatry or other forms of false worship (1.2.2; 1.10.3). As a result, Calvin concludes, natural revelation ends up giving fallen human beings just enough awareness of and information about God to render them without excuse for their unbelief (1.3.1; 1.5.14).

This negative judgment of the effect of natural revelation is the basis for what Alvin Plantinga has called "the Reformed objection to natural theology."[8] Ironically, in a sense Calvin seems to practice a kind of "natural theology" in book 1 of the *Institutes*. His argument—that human beings know there is a God from the sense of divinity and from the created works of nature—is drawn heavily from Cicero and other classical writers.[9] The argument is a "way of seeking God [that] is common both to strangers and to those of his household" (1.5.6), that is, to both non-Christians and Christians. This is different from traditional natural theology in that, for Calvin, all that can be safely inferred from the argument is that human beings, left to themselves, are incapable of viewing God's natural revelation correctly. Calvin goes on to argue that the true knowledge of God as Creator is to be learned in complete dependence on the special revelation of God in Scripture accompanied by the internal witness of the Holy Spirit (1.6–10).

Interpreters of Calvin generally agree that he had little use for the kinds of philosophical theistic proofs offered by Thomas Aquinas and other classical Christian apologists. In Calvin's view, rigorous philosophical proofs for God's existence are unnecessary because the evidences of God in nature are "so very manifest and obvious" that "no long or toilsome proof is needed to elicit evidences that serve to illuminate and affirm the divine majesty" (1.5.9). Moreover, because of our innate sense of divinity, the existence of God "is not a doctrine that must first be learned in school, but one of which each of us is master from his mother's womb and which nature itself permits no one to forget, although many strive with every nerve to this end" (1.3.3). Also, such arguments cannot produce faith, since in Calvin's teaching "the knowledge of faith consists in assurance rather than in comprehension" (3.2.14). For Calvin, faith must be characterized by an unshakable assurance that goes beyond what reasoned arguments can produce: "Such, then, is a conviction that requires no reasons; such, a knowledge with which the best reason agrees—in which the mind truly reposes more securely and constantly than in any reasons; such, finally, a feeling that can be born only of heavenly revelation" (1.7.5).

It follows, then, that we ought to "seek our conviction in a higher place than human reasons, judgments, or conjectures, that is, in the secret testimony of the Spirit" (1.7.4).[10]

Although Calvin questioned the value of theistic proofs, he did not question their validity. That is, he did not attempt to show that the Thomistic theistic proofs, or any other theistic arguments, were philosophically inadequate. He simply viewed them as of marginal value in producing the kind of assured knowledge of God that is characteristic of faith. For his purposes he preferred simple, concrete forms of the traditional theistic arguments. He offered short, simple proofs of "God's power, goodness, and wisdom" from the power and grandeur evident in nature and from the marvelous design of the human being (1.5.1–3). These proofs are essentially concrete forms of the teleological argument. Calvin also presented a simple cosmological argument, writing that "he from whom all things draw their origin must be eternal and have beginning from himself" (1.5.6). Thus Calvin used forms of the traditional theistic arguments.[11]

Much of what Calvin says about theistic proofs applies also to the issue of evidences for Christianity. Ultimately, according to Calvin, our faith is produced by and depends on the testimony of the Holy Spirit, not reason: "the testimony of the Spirit is more excellent than all reason" (1.7.4). There are many good arguments for the truth of Scripture, "yet of themselves these are not strong enough to provide a firm faith, until our Heavenly Father, revealing his majesty there, lifts reverence for Scripture beyond the realm of controversy. . . . But those who wish to prove to unbelievers that Scripture is the Word of God are acting foolishly, for only by faith can this be known" (1.8.13).

Since Scripture is God's Word, human reasoning of any kind cannot be used to judge the truth of Scripture; Scripture should not be subjected "to proof and reasoning." Rather, all human reasoning must be subjected to Scripture as from God: "Therefore, illumined by his power, we believe neither by our own nor by anyone else's judgment that Scripture is from God. . . . We seek no proofs, no marks of genuineness upon which our judgment may lean; but we subject our judgment and wit to it as to a thing far beyond any guesswork!" (1.7.5).

Calvin is not denying that "proofs" or "marks of genuineness" of the truth of Scripture exist. Rather, he is arguing that our ability to discover and verify such proofs or marks of genuineness by human reasoning should not be the foundation of our faith. To make such evidential arguments the basis of faith would be to place the authority of Scripture under the judgment of human reason.

Calvin allows for two legitimate uses of evidential arguments for the Christian faith. First, he teaches that they can be used to *confirm the truth of Scripture to believers*. We should not use them to try to produce faith in Scripture, and our assurance of faith must ever be sustained by the testimony of the Spirit to the divine truth of Scripture. Still, "once we have embraced" Scripture as God's Word, "those arguments . . . become very useful aids" (1.8.1). Indeed, the same arguments that can be used to answer the objections of critics can also be the means by which "the dignity and majesty of Scripture are . . . confirmed in godly hearts" (1.8.13).

Second, Calvin teaches that such arguments can have the apologetic purpose of *silencing critics of Scripture*. For the most part this means using evidential arguments to answer objections. He insists that there are many reasons, "neither few nor weak," by which Scripture can be "brilliantly vindicated against the wiles of its disparagers" (1.8.13).

He presents a very well developed apologetic for Scripture in book 1, chapter 8 of the *Institutes*. He defends the truth of Scripture by appealing to its antiquity and preservation, the candor of the biblical writings, fulfilled biblical prophecies, the preservation of the Jewish race as a miracle, the wisdom of the apostolic writings in contrast with their humble origins, the testimony of martyrs, and other evidences. He also defends the historicity of Moses and his miracles, the Mosaic authorship of the Pentateuch, and the reliability of the biblical texts (1.8.1–13).

Ramm summarizes Calvin's position on the vindication of the Christian worldview:

> Therefore the certification of the Christian faith is not to be found in the utterances of a proposed infallible Church; nor in rationalistic Christian evidences; nor in the appeals of philosophers to reason; nor is [*sic*] ecstatic experiences of the Holy Spirit. It is to be found in the knowledge of God as Creator and Redeemer; it is to be found in the union of Word and Spirit; it is to be found in special revelation centering on the person of Christ and affirmed by the inner witness of the Holy Spirit.[12]

Although Calvin's most famous writing is the *Institutes*, his apologetic method is actually set forth in greatest detail in a little-known work called *Concerning Scandals* (1550). In this work he discusses in detail how Christians should deal with the stumbling blocks or "scandals" that non-Christians present as objections to the biblical, Reformed gospel.

Perhaps his simplest recommendation in this book is that the response should take into consideration the person to whom it is being given. In particular, he suggests that we concentrate our efforts on answering people who are troubled by objections and can be helped, not those who are clearly using objections as excuses for their unbelief. "I shall address myself to those who are indeed troubled by scandals of that kind, but who are still curable."[13]

Calvin admits it is impossible to answer every objection to Christian faith (because of time constraints, if nothing else), and offers three points for dealing with this problem. (1) Read Scripture with the focus on going the way God's Spirit is leading us and on our relationship with Christ, and we will find that way to be "a plain, consistent way." (2) Do not try to be clever by overcomplicating questions that are difficult enough. (3) "Finally, if we find something that is strange and beyond our understanding, do not let us be quick to reject it."[14]

Calvin also instructs Christians to recognize the "root cause" of objections to "the fundamentals of the Christian religion" in the demonic deception that grips the entire non-Christian world, namely, the lie that God need not be feared, that non-Christians are not in danger of judgment because of their sin. Such persons need to be confronted with their own sinfulness and the holiness of God before they will see their need of Christ: "You may therefore talk about Christ, but it is to no purpose except with those who are genuinely humbled and realize how much they need a Redeemer, by whose mediation they may escape the destruction of eternal death."[15]

MODERN ROOTS OF THE REFORMED APPROACH

The modern roots of Reformed apologetics are to be found in two streams of Reformed or Calvinist theology: the Scottish Calvinist and Dutch Calvinist traditions.[16] In Scotland the stream of thought that is especially important for the rise of Reformed apologetics is known as Common Sense Realism, the key figure of which was Thomas Reid.[17]

Thomas Reid

Thomas Reid is not very well known today, but he played a very significant role in the history of modern thought, and philosophers have recently been giving his thought renewed attention.[18] Reid was one of David Hume's most famous and important critics in his home country of Scotland. According to Reid, Hume's skepticism was quite reasonable, given the guiding principles of Hume's philosophy. Rather than try to disprove Hume on his own terms, Reid sought to expose and refute the "principles" or underlying assumptions of his position. "His reasoning appeared to me to be just: there was therefore a necessity to call in question the principles upon which it was founded, or to admit the conclusion."[19]

Reid identified the faulty principle underlying Hume's philosophy as *rationalism*—the belief that all knowledge had to be justified by reason, or reasoning. This presupposition had led René Descartes to doubt the reality of everything outside his own doubting, and George Berkeley to deny the independent reality of anything other than minds and their ideas. Now this same rationalistic premise had led Hume to question the possibility of knowing things that our senses and memories plainly tell us are so.

In direct opposition to such varying forms of skepticism, Reid proposed a *principle of credulity*—namely, that we ought to accept as true that which our mind, our senses, and our memories tell us is so unless we have good reasons to disbelieve them. As Kelly James Clark helpfully explains, the rationalists and skeptics had operated on a kind of *"guilty until proven innocent"* principle of rationality. Reid, by contrast, proposed an *"innocent until proven guilty"* principle. The former held that any belief was to be treated as suspect until it could be definitively proved true; Reid held that any belief was to be treated as justified until it could be shown to be false.[20] We might put it this way: whereas the rationalists and skeptics made their motto "When in doubt, throw it out," Reid advocated as the proper epistemological motto "If it ain't broke, don't fix it."

Reid's principle of credulity is closely related to the *principles of common sense*, "certain principles which the constitution of our nature leads us to believe, and which we are under a necessity to take for granted in the common concerns of life, without being able to give a reason for them."[21] Even the skeptic who professes not to believe these principles acts as if they were true. "I never heard that any sceptic run his head against a post or stepped into a kennel, because he did not believe his eyes."[22]

According to Reid, the validity of the principles of common sense is ultimately grounded in our creation by God. "Common sense and reason both have one author; that almighty Author, in all whose other works we observe a consistency, uniformity, and beauty, which charm and delight the understanding: there must therefore be some order and consistency in the human faculties, as well as in other parts of his workmanship."[23]

As various scholars have pointed out, this does not mean that Reid thought one needed to believe in God in order to trust one's senses. In Reid's philosophy, belief in God provides a rational ground for belief in the reliability of one's senses. The person who believes in God will regard God's existence as "a good reason to confirm his belief" in the reliability of his senses. "But he had the belief before he could give this or any other reason for it."[24]

Reid, then, appears to stop just short of including belief in God among the "principles of common sense." God's existence is, for Reid, the necessary presupposition of those principles, but not one of the principles themselves. Reid's own approach to defending belief in God and in the Christian revelation would fit fairly comfortably in either the classical or evidentialist apologetic tradition.[25] He favors the design or teleological argument as the principal one confirming the existence of God, on the grounds that "design and intelligence in the cause may, with certainty, be inferred from marks or signs of it in the effect."[26] In his *Lectures on Natural Theology* (1780), Reid contends that, although the existence of God is "so evident" from everything around us that argument may seem superfluous, the design argument can be useful in answering skeptics.[27]

Reid's most distinctive argument for God's existence is the **argument from other minds**. We believe that the people we see around us have minds, Reid pointed out, even though we have no direct access to those minds. Yet there is no good reason to doubt what we all know is true, namely, that there are other minds. From this premise Reid argued that "if a man has the same rational evidence for the existence of a Deity as he has for the existence of his father, his brother, or his friend, this, I apprehend, is sufficient to satisfy every man that has common sense."[28]

Perhaps the most striking aspect of Reid's approach to apologetics is his contention that, confronted with a purported revelation from God such as that found in Scripture, "reason must be employed to judge of that revelation; whether it comes from God." Just as reason must be used to interpret the meaning of Scripture and to refute false interpretations of it, so also must it be used to determine whether Scripture really is revelation from God in the first place.[29]

Although Reid was a minister of the Church of Scotland and worked within the Calvinist tradition, there is reason to doubt that he held to strictly Calvinist theological beliefs. On the problem of evil, he took the position that evil exists because God permits people to abuse their power of "liberty" (or "free will," as most people would say today). As Paul Helm observed, this explanation assumes "a very mild form of Calvinism, to say the least."[30]

Because Reid employed the concept of "common sense" principles and held that our sense perceptions and memories should be assumed to correspond to reality and not be mere constructs of the mind, his epistemology became known as **Common Sense Realism**. This approach to knowledge was to play a significant role in the apologetics of the leading American evangelical seminary of the nineteenth century—Princeton.

Charles Hodge

Common Sense Realism greatly influenced American philosophy and theology in the nineteenth century,[31] notably at Princeton Theological Seminary.[32] In Part One we profiled the thought of one of Princeton's last great theologians, B. B. Warfield. The dominant theologian at Princeton a generation before Warfield was Charles Hodge, whose *Systematic Theology* is still often reprinted and widely respected.[33]

Hodge's indebtedness to the Common Sense Realist tradition is apparent from the opening pages of his work. In chapter 1, after defending the notion of theology as a science and disputing the validity of speculative and mystical approaches to it (1–9), he defends an inductive model of theology patterned after the natural sciences. He points out that the scientist "comes to the study of nature with certain assumptions," notably "the trustworthiness of his sense perceptions"; "the trustworthiness of his mental operations," such as memory and logical inference; and the certainty of such truths as "every effect must have a cause" (9).

According to Hodge, "The Bible is to the theologian what nature is to the man of science" (10). The theologian, like the scientist, "comes to his task with all the assumptions above mentioned." He must also "assume the validity of those laws of belief which God has impressed upon our nature," including "the essential distinction between right and wrong, . . . that sin deserves punishment, and other similar first truths, which God has implanted in the constitution of all moral beings, and which no objective revelation can possibly contradict." Not just any beliefs can be assumed as such "first truths of reason," though, or made "the source or test of Christian doctrines." The first truths must be universally and necessarily believed (10). Although the term *common sense* is not itself used here, Hodge's universal and necessary first truths represent essentially the same idea.

In chapter 2 Hodge argues for the necessity of a revealed theology. He distinguishes between natural theology, the knowledge of God gained from God's revelation in nature, and Christian theology, which is based on the Bible. Regarding the former, he seeks to avoid two extremes: "The one is that the works of nature make no trustworthy revelation of the being and perfections of God; the other, that such revelation is so clear and comprehensive as to preclude the necessity of any supernatural revelation" (21–22). Hodge's perspective here reflects his staunch Calvinism and is at least broadly in agreement with the approach taken by Calvin himself.

In the third chapter he discusses rationalism as a rival approach to the knowledge of God. Here Hodge is concerned first to refute deism, a form of rationalism that affirms the existence of a Creator God and yet denies any supernatural revelation from that God. Against the deists, he argues that such a revelation is possible and in fact has been supplied in Scripture, and he offers in support a fairly traditional battery of arguments, such as the unity of Scripture and fulfilled prophecy (37–38). In addition, he appeals to "the demonstration of the Spirit" by which people are convinced of the authority of God speaking in Scripture (39). Although Hodge's articulation of the evidences for the revelatory character of Scripture has been influenced by the evidentialist tradition, the general shape and direction of his thought closely follows that of Calvin's *Institutes*.

The second form of rationalism Hodge refutes is the variety that admits some revelation of God in Scripture but denies the absolute authority of Scripture. These rationalists will believe only those things in the Bible that they think they can comprehend and prove by reason. Hodge's leading criticism of this rationalism is that "it is founded upon a false principle," namely, that it is irrational to believe what one does not comprehend (40). Likewise, the dogmatic rationalism that claims to affirm the doctrines of Scripture on the basis of their fitting into a comprehensive philosophical system is also to be rejected on the "essentially false principle" of "the competency of reason to judge of things entirely beyond its sphere" (47). In line with the Common Sense Realist tradition, Hodge maintains that reason is competent in its sphere, as are our senses, but neither is competent to determine the truth about God:

> Nothing, therefore, can be more opposed to the whole teaching and spirit of the Bible, than this disposition to insist on philosophical proof of the articles of our faith. . . . There is no safety for us, therefore, but to remain within the limits which God has assigned to us. Let us rely on our senses, within the sphere of our sense perceptions; on our reason within the sphere of rational truths; and on God, and God alone, in all that relates to the things of God (48, 49).

Having examined and critiqued three versions of rationalism, Hodge sets forth what he understands to be the proper role of reason in Christian theology. At this point his affinity for the evidentialist approach comes to the fore. He points out, first, that revelation is a communication from God directed to the human mind, and therefore to human reason (49–50). He then affirms that "it is the prerogative of reason to judge of the credibility of a revelation" (50). "Christians concede to reason the *judicium contradictionis*, that is, the prerogative of deciding whether a thing is possible or impossible." And it is impossible, Hodge urges, for God to reveal anything that is morally wrong, self-contradictory, or contradictory to "any of the laws of belief which He has impressed upon our nature" (51).

Third, Hodge argues that "reason must judge of the evidence by which a revelation is supported" (53). In support of this position he reasons "that as faith involves assent, and assent is conviction produced by evidence, it follows that faith without evidence is either irrational or impossible." This evidence must be "such as to command assent in every well-constituted mind to which it is presented" (53). Hodge here seems to agree not only with a broadly evidentialist approach to apologetics, but with the strong epistemological evidentialism enunciated famously in Clifford's maxim.

Like Thomas Reid, then, Charles Hodge was a Calvinist whose thought had strong affinities with both the classical and the evidentialist approaches to apologetics. Nevertheless, certain aspects of their thought, especially in their epistemology, were preparing the way for a new and distinctively Reformed approach to apologetics.

Abraham Kuyper

Contributing also to the rise of Reformed apologetics was the tradition within Dutch Calvinist thought, originating primarily with Abraham Kuyper (rhymes with *hyper*). Dutch Calvinism was keenly concerned about the rise of **secularization**, the principled exclusion of faith from the ordinary activities of life, including the sciences, the arts, and politics.[34] The key figure in this stream of Reformed theology was Abraham Kuyper (1837–1920), an influential Dutch Calvinist theologian and politician.[35] The middle third of his most significant work, *Theological Encyclopedia*, has been translated into English as *Principles of Sacred Theology*.[36] In it Kuyper sought to keep two doctrines in balance, common grace and particular grace, both of which he understood to flow directly from Calvinist theology. **Common grace** in Calvinism is the doctrine that, despite the universality and incorrigibility of sin in the human race (what Calvinists call **total depravity**), God graciously preserves non-Christian individuals and societies from becoming as bad as they could be. According to Kuyper, the Calvinist explains "that which is good in fallen man by the dogma of *common grace*" (123). God "has interfered in the life of the individual, in the life of mankind as a whole, and in the life of nature itself by His common grace" (123). By common grace God is "making it possible for men to dwell together in a well-ordered society" (125). That is, common grace explains why non-Christians can hold down jobs, learn true things about the world, care for their families, and maintain order in society.[37] Through it non-Christians can also retain some awareness of God's existence and their need for God, as expressed in religion. "Sin, indeed, is an absolute darkening power, and were not its effect temporarily checked, nothing but absolute darkness would have remained in and about man; but common grace has restrained its workings to a very considerable degree; also in order that the sinner might be without excuse" (302).

Common grace, though, needed to be balanced by a second doctrine. Kuyper stressed that in spite of common grace, there is an **antithesis** between the regenerate and unregenerate that is grounded in the absolute antithesis between the two sets of principles to which Christians and non-Christians are fundamentally committed. The cause of this antithesis is the new birth, or regeneration, effected by God's **particular grace** through the work of the Holy Spirit in the Christian. "This 'regeneration' breaks humanity in two, and repeals the unity of the human consciousness." The result is "an abyss in the universal human consciousness across which no bridge can be built" (152).

In his *Lectures on Calvinism* Kuyper divides people into two groups, the normalists and the abnormalists. The former group thinks that the world is proceeding normally; the latter, that it is not. The latter recognizes regeneration as the only hope for humanity's return to normalcy; the former discounts the idea of regeneration because it sees no need for it.[38] Kuyper uses the Greek word *palingenesis* as a technical term to refer to regeneration and its effects. What both Christians and non-Christians have typically failed to understand, he maintains, is that all belief and knowledge, even in matters of science, and even for people who consider themselves nonreligious, are at root religious and depend on faith. The conflict is thus not between those who have faith and those who do not, but between those whose faith is rooted in palingenesis and is placed in the God of Scripture and those whose faith is rooted in their own fallen nature and is placed in something else.

Kuyper defines faith as "that function of the soul *(psuchē)* by which it obtains certainty directly and immediately, without the aid of discursive demonstration" (*Principles*, 129). It follows from this definition that faith is not based on observation or reasoning. "Faith can never be anything else but an immediate act of consciousness, by which certainty is established in that consciousness on any point outside observation or demonstration" (131). When people speak of the "ground" of one's faith, they are referring not to faith but to its content, "and this does not concern us now" (131). As the act of consciousness possessing certainty, faith "not only needs no demonstration, but allows none" (131–132). In all reasoning, Kuyper observes, one must "have a point of departure." Such "fixed principles introductory to demonstration" are known as *axioms*. Admitting the existence of axioms is a tacit admission that some things must be taken on faith. "To you they are sure, they are lifted above every question of doubt, they offer you certainty in the fullest sense, not because you can prove them, but because you unconditionally believe them" (136).

Kuyper accepted Calvin's view that the unregenerate have an innate knowledge of God that has been distorted by the destructive effects of sin on the intellect. Warning that "it will not do to omit the fact of sin from your theory of knowledge," he asserts that "it is plain that every scientific reproduction of the knowledge of God must fail, so long as this sense remains weakened and this impulse falsified in its direction" (113). Here again, Kuyper attempts to maintain two ideas in balance. On the one hand, following Calvin, and in agreement with such Calvinists as Hodge, he insists that there is a natural knowledge of God—a "natural theology"—reflected in non-Christian religion, however debased. "The purest confession of truth finds ultimately its starting-point in the seed of religion (*semen religionis*), which, thanks to common grace, is still present in the fallen sinner; and, on the other hand, there is no form of idolatry so low, or so corrupted, but has sprung from this same semen religionis. Without natural Theology there is no *Abba, Father*, conceivable, any more than a Molech ritual" (301).

On the other hand, Kuyper insists that this natural theology does the non-Christian no good; indeed, its development in non-Christian religion is completely unhelpful as a support for the Christian faith. "The Christian Religion and Paganism do not stand related to each other as the higher and lower forms of development of the same thing; but the Christian religion is the highest form of development natural theology was capable of along the positive line; while all paganism is a development of that selfsame natural theology in the negative direction" (302).

Lest we misunderstand Kuyper here, he does not mean that Christianity develops natural theology by rationally thinking out its implications. What he means is that in Christianity natural theology has been *supernaturally* developed by the miracle of special revelation. This special, saving revelation of God, necessitated by sin, can itself be received only through the miracle of palingenesis. "There is no man that seeks, and seeking finds the Scriptures, and with its help turns himself to God. But rather from beginning to end it is one ceaselessly continued action which goes out from God to man, and operates upon him, even as the light of the sun operates upon the grain of corn that lies hidden in the ground, and draws it to the surface, and causes it to grow into a stalk" (365).

Kuyper uses the case of us accepting someone's self-identification to illustrate the necessity of receiving God's revelation by faith in order to gain knowledge of God. After all, "no one is able to disclose the inner life of a man except *that man himself.* . . . Not observation, but *revelation,* is the means by which knowledge of the human person must come to you" (142). Analogously, Kuyper argues that we cannot know God apart from revelation, and that all attempts to produce religiously significant knowledge of God from our moral consciousness or from nature must fail.

> Against all such efforts the words of the Psalmist are ever in force: "In Thy light shall we see light," and also the words of Christ: "Neither doth any know the Father save the Son, and he to whomever the Son willeth to reveal *him.*" Presently your demonstration may have a place in your theological studies of the knowledge that is revealed, and in your inferences derived from it for the subject and the cosmos; but observation or demonstration can never produce one single milligramme of religious gold. The entire gold-mine of religion lies in the self-revelation of this central power to the subject, and the subject has no other means than *faith* by which to appropriate to itself the gold from this mine. He who has no certainty in himself on the ground of this *faith,* about some point or other in religion, can never be made certain by demonstration or argument. In this way you may produce outward religiousness, but never religion of the heart. (149)

There is some ambiguity here and elsewhere in Kuyper's thought concerning the possibility of rational arguments for the truths of faith. Here he seems to admit that such arguments might produce some recognition of the truth, but warns that such recognition will fall short of certainty and will not produce genuine faith from the heart. Such an admission is all the classical and evidentialist apologists typically claim for their arguments; the arguments are not thought to produce faith in any of the approaches to apologetics, but in the classical and evidentialist traditions they are thought to prepare the mind for faith. In general, Kuyper questions this view of apologetics, going so far as to conclude that apologetics has made matters worse. In the struggle between modernism and Christianity, he says, "Apologetics has advanced us not one single step. Apologists have invariably begun by abandoning the assailed breastwork, in order to entrench themselves cowardly in a ravelin behind it."[39] Elsewhere he admits that apologetics may have some value in removing difficulties or silencing critics, but he insists that it is useless to assist in bringing people to faith. Christian faith can be produced only by the internal witness of the Holy Spirit:

> This is the reason why the arguments for the truth of the Scripture never avail anything. A person endowed with faith gradually will accept Scripture; if not so endowed he will never accept it, though he should be flooded with apologetics. Surely it is our duty to assist seeking souls, to explain or remove difficulties, sometimes even to silence a mocker; but to make an unbeliever have faith in Scripture is utterly beyond man's power.[40]

Kuyper specifically takes issue with Hodge's teaching that theology should authenticate the character of Scripture as revelation. "He declares that the theologian must *authenticate* these truths. But then, of course, they are no *truths*, and only become such, when I authenticate them" (*Principles*, 318). Kuyper argues that the necessity of God's illumination of those who come to faith excludes any possibility of apologetic argument leading people to the Bible and from the Bible to God:

> At no single point of the way is there place, therefore, for a support derived from demonstration or reasoning. . . . What God Himself does not bear witness to in your soul personally (not mystically-absolutely, but through the Scriptures) can never be known and confessed by you as Divine. Finite reasoning can never obtain the infinite as its result. If God then withdraws Himself, if in the soul of men He bears no more witness to the truth of His Word, men *can* no longer believe, and no apologetics, however brilliant, will ever be able to restore the blessing of faith in the Scripture. *Faith*, quickened by God Himself, is invincible; *pseudo-faith*, which rests merely upon reasoning, is devoid of all spiritual reality, so that it bursts like a soap-bubble as soon as the thread of your reasoning breaks. (365, 366)

One of the chief defects of apologetics, according to Kuyper, is that the knowledge it produces is based on probabilities, not certainties. This is a problem because for Kuyper, as for Calvinists generally, certainty is of the essence of faith.

Indeed, as we have seen, for Kuyper faith is an incorrigible human capacity for certainty that still operates, though in a sinful direction, in the unregenerate. Apologetics, by seeking to produce knowledge not grasped by faith, actually undermines faith. "Faith gives highest assurance, where in our own consciousness it rests immediately on the testimony of God; but without this support, everything that announces itself as faith is merely a weaker form of opinion based on probability, which capitulates the moment a surer knowledge supersedes your defective evidence" (367–368).

Kuyper specifically takes issue with Hodge's belief that the special revelation of God in Scripture can and should be tested or validated using reason or natural revelation. Such a position fails to take into account the noetic effects of sin: "If special revelation assumes that in consequence of sin the normal activity of the natural principium [that is, human reason] is disturbed, this implies of itself that the natural principium has lost its competency to judge" (381). Kuyper suggests that asking man to judge the validity of special revelation using natural knowledge is akin to asking a psychiatric patient to judge the validity of the psychiatrist's method of treatment (381). Likewise, it is impossible to convince a person of the truth of the Christian position if he thinks his natural ability to determine truth is unimpaired. "Being as he is, he can do nothing else than dispute your special revelation every right of existence; to move him to a different judgment you should not reason with him, but change him in his consciousness; and since this is the fruit of regeneration, it does not lie with you, but with God" (383).

It follows, then, that apologetics as traditionally conceived must be abandoned. Negatively, Christians should seek to expose the anti-Christian religious root of all non-Christian thought. Positively, they should attempt to articulate and model the truth of Christianity to the world by living and working in every sphere of life according to biblical principles. As Kuyper puts it, "Principle must again bear witness against principle, world-view against world-view, spirit against spirit."[41] In order that *principle* must be arrayed against *principle,*" Kuyper insists, we must do more than merely offer objections to non-Christian systems of thought and arguments in defense of theism or a generic form of Christianity. Instead, against the comprehensive life system of modernism, "we have to take our stand in a life-system of equally comprehensive and far-reaching power."[42] Kuyper finds this comprehensive Christian life system in Calvinism.[43]

HERMAN DOOYEWEERD

Kuyper stimulated tremendous interest among Dutch Calvinist thinkers to work out a Christian philosophy that was faithful to Reformed theological principles.[44] His seminal ideas were developed into a full-fledged philosophy by others, notably **Herman Dooyeweerd** (1894–1977).[45] Dooyeweerd (pronounced *DOE-yuh-vair*) was Professor of Philosophy of Law at the Amsterdam Free University, an institution Kuyper founded, and also head of the Kuyper Institute in The Hague. He worked out his philosophy with the help of his brother-in-law, D. H. Theodor Vollenhoven, also a professor of philosophy at the Amsterdam Free University (specializing in the philosophy of history).

Dooyeweerd's magnum opus was a four-volume work originally published in 1935–1936 as *De Wijsbegeerte der Wetsidee* ("The Philosophy of the Law-Idea"). The title reflects his central contention that philosophical thought has an underlying religious root that is related to a transcendent origin and destiny of reality that he called the law-idea. This religious root gives unity to the cosmos in its various aspects or "law-spheres" (such as the biotic, the intellectual, and so forth). Because this law-idea relates to the unity of the cosmos, another name by which Dooyeweerd's philosophy is known is the **cosmonomic** (from *cosmos*, "world," and *nomos*, "law") philosophy.

De Wijsbegeerte der Wetsidee was published in a second edition in English in 1953–1957 with the title *A New Critique of Theoretical Thought*.[46] The English title is also fitting, because the goal of the book is to develop what Dooyeweerd called a **transcendental** criticism of theoretical thought, an idea that comes from Immanuel Kant, the Enlightenment philosopher whose most important work was entitled *Critique of Pure Reason*.[47] Putting the matter as simply as possible, in a transcendental critique one seeks to show what are the necessary preconditions or presuppositions of all knowledge. In his *Critique* Kant argued that both *dogmatism* (the unjustified assumption that human reason is competent to know everything) and *skepticism* (the hypercritical denial that human reason is competent to know anything) should be rejected. In their place Kant favored the method of *criticism*—seeking to discern both the competency and the limitations of human reason.[48]

Dooyeweerd's *New Critique* may be read largely as a critique and refutation of Kant's philosophy. He explains, "it can be said that our transcendental critique of theoretical thought has an inner connection with Kant's critique of pure reason, notwithstanding the fact that our critique was turned to a great extent against the theoretical dogmatism in Kant's epistemology" (1:118). According to Dooyeweerd, Kant recognized the need to avoid dogmatism but actually fell into it by assuming the autonomy of theoretical thought (1:35). That is, Kant assumed "that he could lay bare a starting-point in theoretical reason itself, which *would rest at the basis of every possible theoretical synthesis*" (1:49). To put it simply, Kant sought to use reason alone to critique reason. Dooyeweerd believes such a project impossible, even for well-meaning Christians—among whom he counts himself. "The great turning point in my thought was marked by the discovery of the religious root of thought itself, whereby a new light was shed on the failure of all attempts, including my own, to bring about an inner synthesis between the Christian faith and a philosophy which is rooted in faith in the self-sufficiency of human reason" (1:v). Note the Kuyperian themes of the religious root of all thought and the unavoidability of faith in all human thinking.

Kant's assumption that reason was competent to critique reason was based on the assumption that he could develop a theory of knowledge free of religious presuppositions. Kant's theory of knowledge presupposed a view of nature and freedom that was a "very religious basic motive" (1:89). By "religious basic motive," or ground motive as he also calls it, Dooyeweerd means "the central spiritual motive power of our thinking and acting,"[49] the most fundamental way of thinking about reality that moves people to think and act a certain way. A ground motive "gives content to the central mainspring of the entire attitude of life and thought" of a religious community (1:61). In other words, it is a basic root way of thinking from which various worldviews and systems of thought spring.

Dooyeweerd identifies four basic ground motives in Western thought. The Greek worldview, given concrete formulation by Aristotle, was rooted in a **dualism** of form and matter in which form represented the rationality of mind while matter represented the irrationality of brute fact. The biblical worldview was not dualistic, but was rooted in the motive of creation, fall, and redemption. The medieval worldview, associated especially by Dooyeweerd with Thomas Aquinas, utilized a half-Greek, half-biblical worldview based on a dualism of nature and grace. According to Dooyeweerd, traditional Christian apologetics has been dominated for centuries by this unbiblical nature-grace dualism. Finally, the modern, humanistic worldview (which Dooyeweerd relates especially to Kant) is characterized by a dualism of nature and freedom (1:61–63).[50]

All three nonbiblical worldviews, argues Dooyeweerd, despite their efforts to secure an autonomous rationality, lead to irrationality by absolutizing one aspect of creation and therefore rendering creation void of meaning. This inevitably results in a dualism in which one side is viewed as rational (form or nature) and the other side as irrational (matter, grace, or freedom). This internal incoherence is due to the fact that non-Christian thought invariably proceeds from one or another kind of **immanentism**, the hopeless belief that one can know ultimate reality using a standard found within one's immanent experience (rather like a goldfish trying to know the fishbowl from within it). Likewise, immanence philosophy refers to "all philosophy that seeks its Archimedean point in philosophic thought itself" (1:14). Exposing this immanentism is the task of a "transcendental" critique.

Only the Christian faith, Dooyeweerd argues, provides a true standpoint of transcendence from which created reality can be viewed. This standpoint involves an *arche* (the Greek word for beginning) and an **Archimedean point** (a metaphor drawn from the story of Archimedes, who claimed that from a point far enough above the earth and with the proper lever, he could move the earth). An *arche* is *"an origin which creates meaning,"* the transcendent origin of all meaning in the cosmos (1:9). An Archimedean point is a conceptual point from which a comprehensive philosophical view of the cosmos in all its aspects of meaning may be coherently held (1:11). The *arche* of the biblical ground motive is God as the Creator, the Origin of all created reality in all its aspects. The Archimedean point is Jesus Christ as the root of the new, redeemed humanity in whom regeneration (what Kuyper called palingenesis) has taken place.

The task of Christian philosophy, then, according to Dooyeweerd, is twofold. First, the Christian thinker is to expose the inadequacy of non-Christian worldviews by showing that they collapse into an untenable dualism with both rationalistic and irrationalistic tendencies. Second, the Christian is to commend the Christian worldview as the only one able to provide a secure footing for knowledge and ethics. In doing so, the Christian will confront non-Christians with their need to receive God's grace of redemption in Jesus Christ, through whom they will be regenerated and in whom they will find the ultimate reference point of meaning in life.

CORNELIUS VAN TIL

Arguably the most controversial apologist of the twentieth century was Cornelius Van Til (1895–1987), a Dutch-American Calvinist whose system of thought is often called presuppositionalism.[51] Van Til lived the first ten years of his life in Holland while Abraham Kuyper was at his height both as a Christian theologian and as a statesman. His family moved to Indiana and he later attended Calvin College and then Calvin Theological Seminary for a year. Both institutions were located in Grand Rapids, Michigan, and affiliated with the Christian Reformed Church, a Calvinist denomination populated primarily by Dutch immigrants. Van Til then transferred to Princeton Theological Seminary, the Calvinist institution where Hodge and Warfield had taught. He earned a master's degree from the seminary in 1925 and a doctorate in 1927 from Princeton University, where he studied under the idealist philosopher A. A. Bowman. In 1929 J. Gresham Machen founded Westminster Theological Seminary as a conservative alternative to Princeton Theological Seminary, which had been taken over by liberalism, and the next year brought Van Til to Westminster as its first professor of apologetics.[52] Van Til served in that capacity until his retirement in 1972, when he was named professor emeritus.[53]

Van Til has had an impact on Christian apologetics both inside and outside of strictly Calvinist theological circles. His many loyal followers have labored to promote his approach to apologetics, among whom we may especially mention Greg L. Bahnsen and John M. Frame as two of Van Til's star pupils who have proved able interpreters of their teacher. In addition to numerous scholarly publications on other matters, Bahnsen wrote many articles and books expounding and defending Van Til's apologetic, culminating in two important books published posthumously.[54] Frame taught apologetics for many years at Westminster Theological Seminary in California, a sister institution to the Philadelphia school, and has also written some of the best books on Van Til.[55] He is also one of the very few self-confessed "Van Tilians" to express significant disagreements and criticisms of Van Til's teaching on apologetics.

Van Til's students have also included some of the most influential apologists of a more broadly evangelical perspective, most notably Edward John Carnell, professor of apologetics at Fuller Theological Seminary, and Francis Schaeffer, one of the most popular evangelical teachers and writers of the twentieth century. Van Til did not, however, regard either of these students of his as sound proponents of a Reformed apologetic, and wrote extensive critiques of their apologetic thought.[56] Van Til has also stimulated enormous debate over apologetic method; most of the leading American evangelical apologists of the last forty years have interacted with his approach in their writings.[57]

Van Til has typically been characterized as abandoning the apologetic approach of Old Princeton for a Kuyperian approach. This is not so much incorrect as it is incomplete, as he essentially formed a creative synthesis of the two.[58] He made this especially clear in his book *Common Grace and the Gospel*. "So far as choice had to be made between the two positions, I took my position with Kuyper rather than with Hodge and Warfield. But there were two considerations that compelled me finally to seek a combination of some of the elements of each position."[59] These two considerations were that Old Princeton recognized the antithesis in its theology, if not fully in its apologetics, and that Old Princeton was right in insisting that "Christianity is capable of rational defense" (184).

Van Til, therefore, did not abandon Old Princeton's epistemology or apologetic concern. "But never have I expressed a basic difference with its theology or its basic epistemology" (155). He agreed with the Common Sense Realist view taught at Old Princeton that the validity of sense perception, logic, moral values, and the like was guaranteed to us by God's creation of us and of the world. He also agreed with Old Princeton that apologetics should offer proof for the Christian position. But he integrated this position with the Kuyperian doctrine of the antithesis. Common Sense Realism had held that non-Christians live in a God-created universe and thus operate on the basis of Christian presuppositions, whether they acknowledge it or not. For the Old Princetonians this meant that Christians might appeal to these shared presuppositions in traditional apologetic arguments. In Van Til's thinking, however, the Kuyperian doctrine of the antithesis indicated that the non-Christian so suppresses these presuppositions when thinking about matters of principle that no argument based on them will connect.

For Van Til traditional apologetics suffered from being founded on a faulty theological basis—either Roman Catholic, Arminian, or inconsistently Calvinistic. The last fault belonged to the apologetical tradition that had been the rule at Old Princeton. In Van Til's view, the great mistake of this tradition was in using rationalistic arguments that concluded that the truths of Christianity are *probably* true. Van Til thought probabilistic arguments detracted from the certainty of faith and the absolute authority of Scripture as the written word of God. Arguing that a Reformed or Calvinistic theology required an equally distinctive Reformed apologetic, Van Til called on the church to rethink its classical apologetical tradition and develop a radically biblical apologetic.

This apologetic would not attempt to prove or substantiate Christianity by a simple appeal to factual evidence, as though non-Christians were honest enough to examine the evidence fairly. Instead it would argue by presupposition. The first step in this approach is to show that non-Christian systems of thought are incapable of accounting for rationality and morality. Here the apologist is to show that ultimately all non-Christian systems of thought fall into irrationalism. The second step is to commend the Christian view as giving the only possible presuppositional foundation for thought and life.

Christian apologetics, then, is to argue by presupposition, as Van Til maintained in his major textbook on apologetics, *The Defense of the Faith*. "To argue by presupposition is to indicate what are the epistemological and metaphysical principles that underlie and control one's method."[60] For Van Til this is the *only* legitimate apologetic approach. There is no room in his approach for deductive arguments from premises granted by non-Christians to Christian conclusions. Nor is there any room for inductive arguments from facts granted by non-Christians and used as evidences to support Christian conclusions. The *only* legitimate type of apologetic argument is one that reasons indirectly and presuppositionally that unless Christianity is true, nothing can be known or predicated.

"There is, accordingly, but one thing that Christians can do," namely, challenge unbelieving assumptions.[61] The point of contact with non-Christian systems "must be in the nature of a head-on collision" (98–99). Van Til concludes *The Defense of the Faith* with a summary of his position, including the following statement:

> That the argument for Christianity must therefore be that of presupposition. . . . The best, the only, the absolutely certain proof of the truth of Christianity is that unless its truth be presupposed there is no proof of anything. Christianity is proved as being the very foundation of the idea of proof itself (298).[62]

For Van Til there was only one apologetic method—arguing by presupposition.

GORDON H. CLARK

Of the four twentieth-century Reformed apologists we are profiling in this chapter, the one whose thought seems least indebted to Abraham Kuyper is Gordon Haddon Clark (1902–1985).[63] Clark received a Ph.D. in philosophy from the University of Pennsylvania in 1929, where he taught philosophy until 1936. He then taught philosophy at Wheaton College, an evangelical liberal arts college near Chicago (1936–1943). During this period, most of his published works were professional philosophy textbooks and articles published by secular academic presses.[64]

Finding that he was too Calvinist for the broadly evangelical Wheaton, Clark resigned his position there and in 1945 was ordained as a teaching elder in the Philadelphia Presbytery of the Orthodox Presbyterian Church (OPC), a denomination he had helped J. Gresham Machen get started a decade earlier. Ironically, Clark was regarded as not Calvinist enough by Van Til, who led an effort to have his ordination revoked. Although the presbytery decided in Clark's favor, the controversy led to his departure from the OPC and completely soured relations between Clark's supporters and Van Til's, a situation that generally persists to this day.[65]

From 1945 to 1973 Clark served as chairman of the philosophy department at Butler University in Indianapolis. During this long period of his life he authored his most influential works of Christian philosophy and apologetics. After his retirement at Butler, he took a position at Covenant College in Lookout Mountain, Georgia (1974–1983).

Gordon Clark is one of the most influential advocates of a presuppositional approach to apologetics. Two of the many theologians and apologists greatly influenced by him were Carl F. H. Henry and Ronald H. Nash. Henry (1913–2003), a student of Clark at Wheaton, was one of the major leaders of evangelicalism in the second half of the twentieth century.[66] He helped establish Fuller Theological Seminary, was the first editor of *Christianity Today*, was a founding member of the Evangelical Theological Society and of the International Council on Biblical Inerrancy, and lectured around the world for World Vision International and Prison Fellowship. At the beginning of his magnum opus, the six-volume *God, Revelation, and Authority*, Henry enthusiastically made explicit his dependence on Clark's apologetic teaching.[67] Nash (1937–2006) was an evangelical philosopher also greatly influenced by Clark, though he expressed some disagreements with Clark's position. Nash edited a volume of essays in honor of Clark[68] and authored a number of important works in Christian apologetics and philosophy.[69]

Whereas Van Til's apologetic system may be described as a *transcendental* presuppositionalism, Clark's is best characterized as *deductive* presuppositionalism. The difference is subtle but important. According to Van Til, the apologist should argue that logic, truth, meaning, and value can be what they are only on the presupposition that the God of Scripture is real. Truth is found everywhere in God's world, but this truth can be known only because we are created in God's image and have been given the capacity to know God's truth. The transcendent God of Scripture provides a transcendental point of reference; it is from God that all truth comes and it is in the light of God that all truth is known.

By contrast, Clark maintained that all that could truly be known was to be found in Scripture itself. In his view, knowledge of truth requires deductive proof, and nothing can be deduced from the uncertain facts of the natural world or of the human mind. Furthermore, inductive reasoning is unreliable, because "all inductive arguments are formal fallacies" when judged by the canons of deductive reasoning, and so cannot be used to arrive at truth.[70] The only source of indisputable premises with which logic can work is the Bible. So, Clark argued, the infallible statements of Scripture provide the only source of certain knowledge, and only what the Bible actually says, or what can be logically deduced from those biblical statements, constitutes real knowledge.

The truth of the Bible as God's word is what Clark in his later works called his "axiom."[71] The idea of an axiom is most easily illustrated from geometry, where theorems, such as the Pythagorean theorem, are deduced logically from elemental facts of geometry called axioms. "But the axioms are never deduced. They are assumed without proof." Such starting points that are not demonstrable and not questionable are unavoidable, for without them one could never begin a process of proving anything.[72] According to Clark, "Every system of theology or philosophy must have a starting point."[73]

> The inference is this: No one can consistently object to Christianity's being based on an indemonstrable axiom. If the secularists exercise their privilege of basing their theorems on axioms, then so may Christians. If the former refuse to accept our axioms, then they can have no logical objection to our rejecting theirs. . . . Our axiom shall be that God has spoken. More completely, God has spoken in the Bible. More precisely, what the Bible says, God has spoken.[74]

Although the axiom of biblical revelation must be "accepted without proofs or reasons," its truth is shown by "its success in producing a system."[75] According to Clark, systems of thought that do not rest on the biblical axiom are inevitably inconsistent and incoherent. His apologetic therefore consists of two steps: showing that non-Christian philosophies are hopelessly inconsistent and incapable of accounting for morality and meaning, and showing that Christianity is internally consistent. At the end of his most celebrated book, *A Christian View of Men and*

Things, Clark sums up his thesis: "that Christian theism is self-consistent and that several other philosophies are inconsistent, skeptical, and therefore erroneous." In contrast to such philosophies as Marxism and humanism that Clark believes render history and morality meaningless, "it has been argued that Christianity is self-consistent, that it gives meaning to life and morality, and that it supports the existence of truth and the possibility of knowledge."[76] Likewise, at the end of his textbook on the history of philosophy, Clark suggests that "a choice must be made between skeptical futility and a word from God."[77]

Clark maintains, then, that nonbiblical systems of thought cannot provide an internally consistent worldview within which knowledge and morality have meaning. Of course, advocates of other systems of thought will deny this claim. In particular, advocates of religions that have their own dogmatic principle other than biblical revelation (for example, the Qur'an in the case of Islam) might object that their claimed revelation could just as well become one's axiomatic starting point. To all such counterarguments Clark simply responds: "Since all possible knowledge must be contained within the system and deduced from its first principles, the dogmatic answer must be found in the Bible itself. The answer is that faith is the gift of God. . . . The initiation of spiritual life, called regeneration, is the immediate work of the Holy Spirit. It is not produced by Abrahamic blood, nor by natural desire, nor by any act of human will."[78]

Ultimately, then, for Clark as well as for Kuyper, Dooyeweerd, and Van Til, we know that the God of the Bible is the true God because he has sovereignly chosen to illuminate our minds by the regenerating work of the Spirit.[79]

Because Van Til and Clark are so often compared, and because both are commonly called presuppositionalists, it will be helpful to review the differing versions of Reformed apologetics articulated by these two thinkers.

Van Til	Clark
Transcendental argument	Deductive argument
Scripture provides rational basis for scientific and historical knowledge	Scripture provides only rational source of knowledge; science and history are not valid sources of truth
Logic must be defined and understood on the basis of God's revelation in Scripture	Logic is the method by which we derive truth from God's revelation in Scripture
External consistency *with* Scripture as the test of truth	*Internal* consistency *of* Scripture as the test of *its* truth
Believers and unbelievers do not share a common reason	Believers and unbelievers share reason in common

ALVIN PLANTINGA

The one Reformed apologist profiled in this chapter who was still living at the beginning of the twenty-first century is Alvin Plantinga (b. 1932), chairman of the philosophy department at the University of Notre Dame and the director of its Center for Philosophy of Religion. He has served as president of both the Society of Christian Philosophers (which he helped found) and the American Philosophical Association. With Plantinga we have the advantage of two autobiographical pieces in which he tells us about his intellectual and spiritual pilgrimage and introduces his published work.[80] Our inclusion of Plantinga in this survey of Reformed apologists is controversial because of the significant differences between his views and those of the other apologists profiled here. However, the similarities are significant enough to support identifying his position as a variant form of Reformed apologetics.

Plantinga, the son of a philosopher, Cornelius Plantinga (Sr.), grew up in a Dutch-American home that was staunchly conservative and Calvinist. After a year at Calvin College, he won a scholarship to Harvard University, where he seems to have passed through his major crisis of faith. It disturbed him that so many of his professors and fellow students—including people that seemed smarter than him—did not believe in God. The crisis was resolved on a gloomy winter evening while he was out walking on the campus:

> But suddenly it was as if the heavens opened; I heard, so it seemed, music of overwhelming power and grandeur and sweetness; there was light of unimaginable splendor and beauty; it seemed I could see into heaven itself; and I suddenly saw or perhaps felt with great clarity and persuasion and conviction that the Lord was really there and was all I had thought. The effects of this experience lingered for a long time; I was still caught up in arguments about the existence of God, but they often seemed to me merely academic, of little existential concern, as if one were to argue about whether there really had been a past, for example, or whether there really were other people, as opposed to cleverly constructed robots.[81]

During a recess at Harvard, Plantinga visited his family and attended some classes from W. Henry Jellema, the professor from whom his father had learned philosophy in the late twenties and early thirties. Alvin was so taken by Jellema's teaching that he transferred back to Calvin to study under him (from 1951 to 1954). In Jellema's teaching on the history of philosophy, he argued that the rejection of Christianity and theism in modern philosophy did not result from intellectual objections but rather from a religious commitment antithetical to Christianity. "Jellema's way of thinking about these matters (as he said) goes back to Abraham Kuyper and other Dutch Calvinists" (54). Plantinga accepted this Kuyperian notion of the antithesis while carefully observing the qualification (which goes back to Kuyper himself) that this antithesis does not prevent non-Christians from getting some things right:

> Those who don't share our commitment to the Lord are in transition, just as we are. As Calvin says, there is unbelief within the breast of every Christian; but isn't there also belief within the breast of every non-Christian? The antithesis is of course real; but at any time in history it is also less than fully articulated and developed.[82]

Plantinga is not uncritical about the teaching he received at Calvin College. He confesses that at Calvin there

> was a sort of tendency to denigrate or devalue other forms of Christianity, other emphases within serious Christianity. . . . We Calvinists, we thought, were much more rigorous about the life of the mind than were fundamentalists, and as a result we were inclined to look down our Reformed noses at them. . . . Since the Enlightenment, we Christians have had real enemies to fight and real battles to win; why then do we expend so much time and energy despising or fighting each other? (57–58)

Plantinga did his graduate work in philosophy at the University of Michigan, where he took courses from William P. Alston and other noted philosophers. At Michigan the question he considered the most important in philosophy—"what is the truth about this matter?—was often greeted with disdain as unduly naïve."[83]

In the 1960s he taught philosophy at Calvin College with another of Jellema's students, Nicholas Wolterstorff. Through the Calvin Center for Christian Scholarship, the two developed close associations with other philosophers sympathetic to a Reformed approach to philosophy, including George Mavrodes, William Alston, and David Holwerda.

The New Reformed Epistemology

In 1982 Plantinga accepted a position at the University of Notre Dame, which, although Roman Catholic, had a very high concentration of evangelical graduate students in philosophy. The following year the university press released a book co-edited by Plantinga and Wolterstorff entitled *Faith and Rationality: Reason and Belief in God*.[84] The book contained articles by the editors and several other philosophers—Mavrodes, Holwerda, Alston, and George Marsden—from a year-long project at the Calvin Center on the subject "Toward a Reformed View of Faith and Reason." *Faith and Rationality* had an immediate and profound impact, not only on Christian apologetics, but also in the halls of academia. Plantinga's lengthy contribution "Reason and Belief in God," in particular, changed the direction of philosophy of religion in universities and colleges around the world. Books and articles appear every year discussing the merits of Plantinga's "Reformed Epistemology," as it has come to be known.

Plantinga's interest in philosophy has been and is largely apologetical. He suggests that "perhaps the main function of apologetics is to show that from a philosophical point of view, Christians and other theists have nothing whatever for which to apologize" (33). Three apologetical issues have concerned him: "the existence of certain kinds of evil, the fact that many people for whom I have deep respect do not accept belief in God, and the fact that it is difficult to find much by way of noncircular argument or evidence for the existence of God" (34). The second and third issues do not now greatly disturb him, "But the first remains deeply baffling" (34). His answer to the problem of evil is, like Thomas Reid's, an appeal to human free will (41–47). In this respect he differs from the other major Reformed apologists profiled in this chapter.

The first book Plantinga authored (he had already edited a couple books) was *God and Other Minds* (in 1967). The main argument of this work, as he explains in "Self-Profile," is "that belief in God and belief in other minds are in the same epistemological boat; since belief in other minds is clearly rational, the same goes for belief in God" (55).

Years later, Plantinga's assessment of his efforts in *God and Other Minds* was that it looked "like a promising attempt by someone a little long on chutzpah but a little short on epistemology."[85]

In 1974 Plantinga wrote "Is It Rational to Believe in God?," a precursor to his longer paper in *Faith and Rationality*. "There I argued that belief in God can be perfectly rational even if none of the theistic arguments work and even if there is no non-circular evidence for it; my main aim was to argue that it is perfectly rational to take belief in God as basic—that is, to accept theistic belief without accepting it on the basis of argument or evidence from other propositions one believes" (55–56). This idea of belief in God as "basic" is the core of Plantinga's new Reformed Epistemology.

Plantinga then turned to a question he found puzzling, namely, that Reformed Christians tended to view natural theology—"the attempt to prove or demonstrate the existence of God"—with suspicion, if not hostility. What is the reason for this (60)? Plantinga concluded that the Reformed thinkers were implicitly reacting against the underlying assumption of much natural theology, namely, the assumption of classical and modern foundationalism that the existence of God could not be among those beliefs that were properly basic (61). Moreover, Reformed thinkers were rejecting the claim that belief in God on the basis of evidence or proof was somehow superior to belief in God without such evidence or proof (that is, as basic). To explain why, Plantinga asks us to consider three analogies. The person who accepts $2 + 3 = 5$ because a computer that yields that equation has proved itself reliable in most instances he has been able to check, is not in a better position epistemically than the person who accepts as self-evident $2 + 3 = 5$ as basic. Nor is the person who, while walking around the Tower and observing pigeons flying around it, believes there are pigeons there only because it says so in the guidebook. The person depending on the computer for his acceptance of arithmetic and the person depending on the guidebook for his knowledge of the pigeons are both exhibiting what Plantinga labels a perverse approach to knowledge.

> The same thing may be said for the person who believes in the existence of her husband on the basis of the sort of evidence cited by an analogical argument for other minds. Belief in God on the basis of the sort of evidence furnished by the traditional theistic arguments (even supposing the arguments successful) is, according to the Reformed epistemologist, rather like these cases. It is not epistemically superior to taking belief in God as basic. The shoe, indeed, is on the other foot: the better of these two ways of accepting theistic belief is the latter. (62)

Plantinga puts the idea of belief in God as basic in a broader perspective by rehearsing Thomas Reid's argument against modern skepticism concerning sense perception. "Reid argues—correctly, I believe—that the deliverances of sense perception don't need justification or certification in terms of other sources of belief as introspection and self-evidence. . . . What Reid said about sense perception, Reformed thinkers have said about belief in God" (63).

Plantinga does not think the Reformed objection to natural theology renders apologetics suspect. In another article, in which he argues that apologetics should play a role in the Reformed tradition, he admits that some Reformed theologians have thought otherwise: "But isn't the very idea of apologetics, whether negative or positive, contrary to the basic Reformed insight of Kuyper and Dooyeweerd? If all thought has religious roots, then the thing to say about attacks on Christianity is just that they too have religious roots—*non-Christian* religious roots; thus they do not require an answer. Faith cannot reason with unbelief: it can only preach to it."[86]

Plantinga's answer is that apologetics is useful after all because people's condition and direction in life are complex and changing. Thus the Christian, according to Calvin, experiences doubt as well as the certainty of faith.[87] Negative apologetics can help Christians, then, by refuting the arguments that stir up doubts. Apologetics, both negative and positive, can also help non-Christians who are on their way to becoming Christians.[88]

Warranted Christian Belief

Plantinga's *magnum opus* is a three-volume series of books that develops his mature thinking regarding Christian epistemology. The first two books, *Warrant: The Current Debate* and *Warrant and Proper Function*, both published in 1993, surveyed the field of epistemology and proposed a theory of warrant. The third volume, *Warranted Christian Belief* (2000), refined Plantinga's theory and applied it to the defense of the reasonableness of Christian belief.[89] This landmark book deserves careful study by everyone interested in apologetic theory; here we will briefly summarize the argument of the book.[90]

Plantinga begins by saying that the question he will be addressing is whether Christian belief is "intellectually acceptable" for thinking people today (viii). Modern Western thought has posed two kinds of objections to Christian belief. First, *de facto* objections challenge "the truth of Christian belief" (viii); these include the problem of evil and the alleged incoherence of specific Christian doctrines such as the Trinity or the Incarnation (viii-ix). Second, *de jure* objections claim not that Christian belief is (necessarily) false but that it is somehow "not up to snuff from an intellectual point of view" (ix). Plantinga will argue that *de jure* objections to the effect that Christian belief is unjustified or irrational are not viable. "As I see it, if there are any real *de jure* objections to Christian belief, they lie in the neighborhood of warrant" (xi). Warrant is what makes a particular belief not only *true* but also *knowledge*; it is what separates a "lucky guess" and other types of true beliefs that are not knowledge from true beliefs in which we really *know* something.

Plantinga distinguishes both *de facto* and *de jure* questions from the question of whether there can "really be such a thing as Christian belief" (3). This question asks not whether Christian belief is true (*de facto*) or warranted (*de jure*) but whether it is really a belief at all. Plantinga has in mind here the claim credited (at least) to Immanuel Kant (chapter 1, pp. 3–30) and made by a variety of modern philosophers and theologians—of whom he discusses Gordon Kaufman and John Hick as examples—that if God exists our concepts could not apply or refer to him. Kaufman argues that God, if he exists, transcends all finite reality and so cannot be identified with anything we actually experience; Kaufman ends up concluding that the term "God," if it refers meaningfully to anything, is a symbol of the "cosmic forces" that make it possible for us to pursue human values. Hick argues that God—or, as he prefers, "the Real"—exists, and our religious language does refer in some way to the Real, but what it says about the Real is not "literally" true. Plantinga examines both of these positions and finds them self-defeating and unworthy of acceptance (chapter 2, pp. 31–63).

In the book *Warrant: The Current Debate*, Plantinga had argued that justification, coherence, rationality, and reliable faculties do not adequately distinguish knowledge from mere true belief. He retraces and augments this argument in chapters 3 and 4 of *Warranted Christian Belief*. In his earlier works *God and Other Minds* (1967) and "Reason and Belief in God" (1983), Plantinga says, he took it for granted "that this question of the rational justification of theistic belief is identical with, or intimately connected with, the question whether there are *proofs*, or at least *good arguments*, for or against the existence of God" (68).

> In *God and Other Minds*, I argued first that the theistic proofs or arguments do not succeed. In evaluating these arguments, I employed a traditional but wholly improper standard: I took it that these arguments are successful only if they start from propositions that compel assent from every honest and intelligent person and proceed majestically to their conclusion by way of forms of argument that can be rejected only on pain of insincerity or irrationality. Naturally enough, I joined the contemporary chorus in holding that none of the traditional arguments was successful. (I failed to note that no philosophical arguments of any consequence meet that standard; hence the fact that theistic arguments do not is of less significance than I thought.) (69)

The problem with such reasoning, Plantinga explains, is that it presupposes that a belief such as belief in God requires rational justification according to the canon of *evidentialism*: "that belief in God, if it is to be rationally acceptable, must be such that there is *good evidence* for it" (70). Plantinga traces this evidentialist approach to religious belief especially to John Locke (71–82). "*Evidentialism* is the claim that religious belief is rationally acceptable only if there are good arguments for it; Locke is both a paradigm evidentialist and the proximate source of the entire evidentialist tradition, from him through Hume and Reid and Kant and the nineteenth century to the present" (82).

Evidentialism is part of a larger epistemological tradition called **classical foundationalism**. According to foundationalism, there are two categories of beliefs: those that we believe "*on the evidential basis* of others" (82), and those "basic" beliefs that we accept without basing our acceptance on other beliefs (83). These basic beliefs are the "foundations" of one's entire belief system or "noetic structure." Hence, according to foundationalism, "every proposition is either in the foundations or believed on the evidential basis of other propositions." Plantinga considers this point "trivially true" and states, "This much of foundationalism should be uncontroversial and accepted by all" (83). However, the classical foundationalist goes further and specifies that only certain kinds of beliefs can be "properly basic"; these are usually specified to include propositions that are self-evident, incorrigible, or evident to one's senses (84). (By "evident to the senses" in this context is meant merely that we are experiencing certain sensory impressions; for example, that I am experiencing seeing something white.) This classical foundationalism is accompanied by "deontologism," the belief that humans have a duty or obligation to regulate their beliefs in accord with evidentialist strictures. The classic expression of this evidentialism is W. K. Clifford's essay "The Ethics of Belief" in which he argued that "it is wrong, always, everywhere, and for anyone to believe anything upon insufficient evidence" (89).[91] Plantinga devotes the rest of chapter 3 of *Warranted Christian Belief* to explaining why this classical foundationalism does not work as a *de jure* objection to Christian belief. The claim that only what is self-evident, incorrigible, or evident to the senses is itself none of those things, and therefore the claim is self-defeating (94–97). Moreover, accepting classical foundationalism would require us not to believe many of the things we actually believe, such as our memories, the reality of the external objects that we perceive through our senses, and the like (97–99). Since classical foundationalism is not a cogent position, Plantinga sees no reason why a person who has thought about the objections to Christian belief and remains convinced that Christianity is true would not be justified in that belief (99–102).

In chapter 4, Plantinga explores the notion that Christian belief is intellectually unacceptable because it cannot be shown to be "rational" in some sense (108–34). He finds this claim wanting as well. Clearly, there are millions of "rational" human beings who do in fact accept Christian belief (109), and it is not plausible to claim that in all of these persons their rational faculties are malfunctioning (110–13). Nor will it work to fault Christian belief for not being among "the deliverances of reason": many things that we believe do not fit in that category but are still perfectly acceptable beliefs (113–15).

In *Warrant and Proper Function*, Plantinga had argued that "proper function" constitutes warrant for our true beliefs. He fine-tunes this argument in chapter 5 of *Warranted Christian Belief*. The objections that such non-Christian thinkers as Freud and Marx (136–44) raise to Christian belief amount to saying "that there is something wrong with believing it" whether it happens to be true or not. "They are best construed, I think, as complaining that Christian belief is not produced by cognitive faculties functioning properly and aimed at the truth" (152). The *de jure* issue, then, is warrant, understood as proper function. "More fully, a belief has warrant just if it is produced by cognitive processes or faculties that are functioning properly, in an environment that is propitious for that exercise of cognitive powers, according to a design plan that is successfully aimed at the production of true belief" (xi).

Christian belief, on this definition of warrant, is warranted (assuming that it is true) because the cognitive process that produces Christian belief is the internal work of the Holy Spirit, restoring to proper function the *sensus divinitatis* or natural knowledge of God that all human beings have (xii; see chapters 6–10). Plantinga introduces this "model" of warranted Christian belief in chapter 6. He views the natural knowledge that God exists not as an inference from nature (which would constitute a kind of natural theology) but as "*occasioned*" by our observations of nature (175). "In this regard, the *sensus divinitatis* resembles perception, memory, and *a priori* belief" (175). Therefore, belief in God's existence arising from the *sensus divinitatis* and occasioned by our experience of the natural world is properly "basic" rather than inferred (176–79). The reason why so many people do not believe in God is that this *sensus divinitatis* no longer functions properly as the result of sin. Thus, "it is really the *unbeliever* who displays epistemic malfunction" (184). Looked at in this way, a "basic" belief in God is probably warranted if God exists though unwarranted if he does not (186–90). It turns out, then, that the *de jure* objection that Christian belief is unwarranted really depends on the *de facto* claim that it is false (190–91). "If I am right in these claims, there aren't any viable *de jure* criticisms that are compatible with the truth of Christian belief; that is, there aren't any viable *de jure* objections independent of *de facto* objections" (xii).

Plantinga elaborates and defends this model in chapters 7 to 10. Early in chapter 7, Plantinga explains his purpose:

> . . . I'll argue that many or most Christians not only can be but are both justified and internally rational in holding their external beliefs. External rationality and warrant are harder. The only way I can see to argue that Christian belief has these virtues is to argue that Christian belief is, indeed, true. I don't propose to offer such an argument. That is because I don't know of an argument for Christian belief that seems very likely to convince one who doesn't already accept its conclusion. That is nothing against Christian belief, however, and indeed I shall argue that if Christian beliefs are true, then the standard and most satisfactory way to hold them will not be as the conclusions of argument (200–201).

Plantinga then explores the concept of sin and its noetic effects, concluding with a rather technical discussion of the problems attending naturalism (227–39). Here Plantinga argues that naturalism is not only self-defeating (as he had argued in chapter 12 of *Warrant and Proper Function*) but also improbable.

To complete his account of Christian belief as warranted, Plantinga addresses the claim that Christian belief faces certain defeaters, warranted beliefs incompatible with Christian belief (chapter 11). Plantinga examines what he thinks are the three most important proposed defeaters for Christian belief—historical biblical criticism, postmodernist and pluralist objections to the exclusive truth claims of Christian belief, and the problem of suffering and evil (chapters 12–14)—and argues "that none of these succeed as a defeater for classical Christian belief" (xiii).

Plantinga's project in this book, then, can be viewed as "an exercise in apologetics and philosophy of religion," the purpose of which is to clear away the *de jure* objection "that Christian belief, whether true or not, is intellectually unacceptable" (xiii). His purpose is not to show that Christian belief is true but that, *if* it is true, then it is also warranted. In his closing paragraph, Plantinga makes it clear that he has not attempted to address the question of the truth of Christian belief:

> But *is* it true? This is the really important question. And here we pass beyond the competency of philosophy, whose main competence, in this area, is to clear away certain objections, impedances, and obstacles to Christian belief. Speaking for myself and of course not in the name of philosophy, I can say only that it does, indeed, seem to me to be true, and to be the maximally important truth (499).

CONCLUSION

Alvin Plantinga is clearly a different sort of Reformed apologist than Herman Dooyeweerd, Gordon Clark, or Cornelius Van Til. He represents what might be termed the "left wing" of Reformed apologetics, advocating in many respects a more classical approach to the field. By classifying Plantinga as a Reformed apologist, we are by no means glossing over the significant differences between his thought and that of the presuppositionalists.[92] Nevertheless, his indebtedness to the Kuyperian tradition and his advocacy of the idea that belief in God is properly basic position his apologetic in the Reformed type. We will discuss some of Plantinga's views further in the next two chapters, while giving more attention to presuppositionalism.

Dooyeweerd's philosophy is essentially a highly sophisticated development of Kuyper's position. Of the twentieth-century thinkers profiled here, he was closest to Kuyper both culturally and philosophically.

Clark combined the primacy of deductive logic, characteristic of the classical model, with a radical view of the Bible as furnishing the premises from which logic can derive conclusions qualifying as knowledge. The result is an unusually rationalistic form of Reformed apologetics.

Van Til is by far the most controversial of the major Reformed apologists of the twentieth century. He combined the apologetic tradition of Old Princeton (which drew from both classical and evidentialist approaches) with the anti-apologetic theology of Kuyper. He used the concept of a transcendental argument, which was at the heart of Dooyeweerd's philosophy, but employed it as an overtly apologetic argument. The result is a theory of apologetics that has been both highly influential and severely disputed. In the next two chapters we will give special attention to understanding Van Til in our analysis of the Reformed approach to apologetics.

For Further Study

Clark, Kelly James. *Return to Reason: A Critique of Enlightenment Evidentialism and a Defense of Reason and Belief in God*. Grand Rapids: Eerdmans, 1990. Excellent introduction to Plantinga's approach to apologetics.

Frame, John M. *Cornelius Van Til: An Analysis of His Thought*. Phillipsburg, N.J.: Presbyterian & Reformed, 1995. Excellent exposition of Van Til's thought, including chapters on his controversies with Gordon Clark and Dooyeweerd.

Hart, Hendrik, Johan van der Hoeven, and Nicholas Wolterstorff, eds. *Rationality in the Calvinian Tradition*. Christian Studies Today. Lanham, Md.: University Press of America, 1983. Contains essays on Calvin, Reid, and the Dutch Calvinists, and includes Plantinga's article on natural theology.

Chapter 13

Reformed Apologetics: Christianity in Conflict

One of Cornelius Van Til's many unpublished syllabi was an overview of the history of Christian apologetics entitled *Christianity in Conflict*.[1] The title aptly characterizes Van Til's view of apologetics in two ways. First, he saw apologetics as properly confronting unbelief in non-Christian thought. In this sense it stands at the point of conflict between Christianity and non-Christian religions and philosophies. But second, he argued that there was an internal conflict within Christianity over the method and approach to be used in apologetics. This conflict was and is between defending Christianity by the improper approach of accommodating it to the unbelieving presuppositions of non-Christian thought and defending it by the proper approach of challenging those unbelieving presuppositions. This twofold note of conflict is characteristic of the Reformed approach to apologetics, especially as practiced by Van Til, Gordon Clark, and their disciples.

BIBLICAL STANDARD FOR DEFINING TRUTH

Fundamental to classical apologetics and evidentialism are their respective approaches to epistemology, or the theory of knowledge. Putting the matter rather broadly, classical apologetics is indebted largely to the rationalist tradition in Western philosophy, while evidentialism is indebted to the empiricist tradition. Now this characterization immediately requires qualification. Few if any classical apologists have been pure rationalists, and few (though some) evidentialists have been thoroughgoing empiricists. Nearly all apologists of both approaches today would favor some epistemology that combined elements of rationalism and empiricism and avoided the extremes of both theories.

Reformed apologists, on the other hand, believe a different approach to epistemology is in order. They typically reject not only rationalism and empiricism but also any epistemology that seeks to combine the two theories, as all these epistemologies in their different ways treat human knowledge as self-sufficient or *autonomous*. That is, rationalism, empiricism, and other such epistemologies attempt to explain how human beings can gain knowledge *without reference to God and man's relationship to God*. According to Van Til, there are ultimately only two kinds of epistemologies: those that make all human knowledge dependent on God and those that do not. "In the last analysis we shall have to choose between two theories of knowledge. According to one theory God is the final court of appeal; according to the other theory man is the final court of appeal."[2]

Reformed apologists argue that when classical and evidentialist apologists seek to use a method that non-Christians can accept, they are actually seeking a method that assumes man's self-sufficiency to arrive at truth (since only a method based on that assumption would be acceptable to non-Christians). Van Til, for example, insists that the Christian should use a distinctive method of knowledge in keeping with his distinctive understanding of God as the source of all knowledge: "The question of method is not a neutral something. Our presupposition of God as the absolute, self-conscious Being, who is the source of all finite being and knowledge, makes it imperative that we distinguish the Christian theistic method from all non-Christian methods."[3]

Most Reformed apologists do not reject deductive and inductive reasoning as such. However, they typically do reject deductive and inductive *apologetic* arguments. For Van Til, a deductive apologetic argument would require agreement between the Christian and the non-Christian on the premises, and such agreement does not exist. Moreover, the use of reason is not the same for the two kinds of people. The appeal to reason in apologetics as traditionally carried out is therefore problematic, as Van Til explains: "'Reason' in the case of the non-Christian is employed by such as assume themselves to be self-sufficient, while 'reason' in the case of the Christian is employed by those who through regeneration have learned to think of themselves as creatures of God and of their task of life as keeping covenant with God."[4]

While Clark and Van Til disagree on the proper use of deductive logic in apologetics, both flatly reject inductive apologetic arguments because they conclude in probability rather than certainty. Van Til writes, "It is an insult to the living God to say that his revelation of himself so lacks in clarity that man, himself through and through a revelation of God, does justice by it when he says that God *probably* exists."[5]

Reformed apologists also warn against defending Christianity on the basis of an epistemology that does not provide a proper ground for deduction and induction. The proper ground cannot itself be epistemological, since one cannot ground an epistemology on an epistemology, but must be a *metaphysic*—a view of reality, or what is also known as a worldview. Thus Reformed apologists insist that apologetics ultimately involves a conflict between Christian and non-Christian worldviews. As Greg Bahnsen puts it, "every apologetic encounter is ultimately a conflict of worldviews or fundamental perspectives (whether this is explicitly mentioned or not)."[6]

Both Dooyeweerd and Van Til argue the necessity of employing transcendental reasoning to establish the ground of knowledge and meaning. As we saw in our profile of Dooyeweerd, a transcendental argument seeks to know what the conditions are that make knowledge possible; it seeks to give an account for what makes both deductive and inductive reasoning intelligible or meaningful in the first place. Unlike deductive and inductive reasoning, a transcendental argument does not begin from specific truth claims (premises or data) that must themselves be established before any conclusion can be drawn. Rather, it gives an account of what the necessary conditions must be for any truth claim, or even the *negation* of that truth claim, to be at all intelligible.[7] According to Van Til, only a transcendental argument can validly be used to prove the reality of God: "Now the only argument for an absolute God that holds water is a transcendental argument. A deductive argument as such leads only from one spot in the universe to another spot in the universe. So also an inductive argument as such can never lead beyond the universe. In either case there is no more than an infinite regression."[8]

Van Til also spoke of this transcendental argument as "reasoning by presupposition":

> To argue by presupposition is to indicate what are the epistemological and metaphysical principles that underlie and control one's method. . . . The method of reasoning by presupposition may be said to be indirect rather than direct. The issue between believers and non-believers in Christian theism cannot be settled by a direct appeal to "facts" or "laws" whose nature and significance is already agreed upon by both parties to

the debate. The question is rather as to what is the final reference-point required to make the "facts" and "laws" intelligible.[9]

Putting the question this way may seem to assume that non-Christians will agree on the need to have some consistent, intelligible view of facts and laws. As John Frame recognizes, not everyone actually agrees or even seems to care: "So the choice is this: either accept the God of the Bible or deny objective morality, objective truth, the rationality of man, and the rational knowability of the universe. Some might maintain that they don't care much about this. They might say that they can go on living happily enough without having a rational basis for thinking and acting."[10]

Elsewhere Frame observes that in contemporary thought a burgeoning movement called postmodernism self-consciously argues that there is no single rational basis for thinking and acting. Here is how he describes the movement:

> Every several years, one hears the claim that contemporary thought has become radically different from anything that has gone before. The latest claim of this sort is made for "postmodernism." We are told that thirty years ago or so, our culture rejected the rationalistic assumptions of the Enlightenment and came to recognize that "linear, scientific, objective" thinking is largely an expression of bias. Therefore, contemporary postmodern thought rejects all the assurances of the past and opens itself up to various non-Western, nonlinear influences, such as Eastern religions, occultism, and so on. It "deconstructs" language to lay bare its essential use—not as a means of rational communication from one mind to another, but as a means of social power, to control and oppress.[11]

Contemporary Reformed apologists like Frame agree with their classical and evidentialist counterparts that postmodernism is an unacceptable and irrational approach to knowledge. Unfortunately, from the Reformed perspective, traditional apologists tend to assume a modernist philosophy as the stance from which to refute postmodernism. That is, classical apologists treat postmodernism as the abandonment of the belief in absolute truth for the belief in the relativity of all beliefs—as if modernism were somehow preferable to postmodernism. Evidentialists criticize postmodernism on the grounds that it flies in the face of the facts—as if facts had meaning apart from the philosophical framework in which they are viewed.

Frame proposes that postmodernism be viewed in terms of Van Til's analysis of the history of non-Christian thought as the working out of a kind of dialectic between a rationalistic impulse and an irrationalistic impulse. If Van Til were alive today, Frame comments, "he would say that the 'new thinking' of our time is really nothing drastically different from what has been going on since the Garden of Eden. Essentially, it is rationalism and irrationalism."[12]

The rationalistic impulse is an expression of the desire by fallen human beings to subject all of reality, including God, to rational inspection and evaluation. Rationalism, in this broad sense, is the error of treating the human mind as capable in principle of determining what is true and what is right. It is the sin of seeking "the knowledge of good and evil" (Genesis 2:17; cf. 3:5, 22) as a knowledge measured by the human mind. The irrationalistic impulse expresses the desire by fallen human beings to be free of any final, determinative standard of truth and value. In this sense irrationalism is the error of denying that there is an objective, transcendent Origin determining for us what is true and what is right. It is the sin of seeking to "be like God" (Genesis 3:5), to be gods unto ourselves. According to Van Til, both impulses are constantly present to some extent in unbelieving thought:

> It was thus that man, in rejecting the covenantal requirement of God became at one and the same time both irrationalist and rationalist. These two are not, except formally, contradictory of one another. They rather imply one another. Man had to be both to be either. . . . In ancient philosophy the rationalistic motif seemed to dominate the scene; in modern times the irrationalist motif seems to be largely in control. But the one never lives altogether independently of the other.[13]

Frame applies this analysis of the history of unbelieving thought to the contemporary movement of postmodernism:

> The latest contemporary ideas are essentially no different from those of the ancient Greeks, the modern rationalists and empiricists, Kant, Hegel, and the others. Postmodernism, insofar as it is really a change from what has gone before, is a shift from a rationalist to an irrationalist impulse. Its rejection of "linear objectivity" is something we have seen before, among the Greek Sophists, in Hume's critique of objectivity, in Kant's

critique of metaphysics, and in Hegel's attempt to achieve truth through negation and synthesis.[14]

Frame suggests two lines of criticism that the apologist can fruitfully present when confronted with a non-Christian who claims not to care whether his life has a rational basis or who adheres to postmodernism or any other irrationalist philosophy. First, the apologist can point out that the irrationalist's attitude or profession is inconsistent with the way he normally lives. Second, the apologist can tell the irrationalist that in his heart he knows better:

> But if someone has resolved to live without logic, without reason, and without standards, we cannot prevent him. He will, of course, accept logic and rationality when he makes his real-life decisions, and so he will not live according to his theoretical irrationalism. In many apologetic situations, it is useful to point this out. But for a tough-minded irrationalist, logical inconsistency is not a problem. Still, at some level he knows he is wrong. God still speaks, around and in the unbeliever.[15]

THE VINDICATION OF REFORMED THEOLOGY

In the late nineteenth and early twentieth centuries, Presbyterian and Reformed churches struggled over encroaching modernism. A breach developed between those who defended historic Calvinism and those who moved in the direction of theological liberalism. But within the conservative Calvinistic camp, another rift developed over the way the Calvinistic position should be defended. While the "Old Princeton" school, including B. B. Warfield and Charles Hodge, advocated a classical approach to Christian apologetics, Dutch Calvinists such as Abraham Kuyper argued that such an approach was inconsistent with Reformed theology's Augustinian and Calvinistic roots. This is the heart of R. J. Rushdoony's later criticism of the Old Princeton apologetic method. "To believe that man can reason his way to the faith constitutes a form of Arminianism; it is an affirmation that the natural man *can* receive the things of the Spirit of God, and that he *can* know them (I Corinthians 2:14). To attempt to reason man into faith, or to appeal to a rationalistic apologetics is thus to set up reason rather than God as ultimate, because it asks the sinful and fallen reason of the natural man to assess and judge God."[16]

Similarly, Cornelius Van Til argues that Calvinistic theologians who follow the traditional method of apologetics derived from Arminian theologians (especially Butler) have allowed their apologetic to lag behind their theology.[17] He agrees with Warfield's theological position, especially on the inspiration of Scripture, but takes issue with his appeal to the reason of natural man because of its inconsistency with the implications of Reformed theology.[18] In the same way, he criticizes Hodge's use of the traditional method of apologetics and endorsement of reason as a means of evaluating a revelation.[19] Van Til instead follows Kuyper by beginning with the Christian theistic position rather than reasoning "to the full theistic position from a standpoint outside of it."[20] He contends that a choice must be made: a person can either use reason to stand in judgment of the credibility of the Christian revelation, or he can renounce his perception of himself as ultimate. Arminian apologetics follows the former course; Reformed apologetics takes the latter.

Van Til insists that it is "logically quite impossible for the natural man, holding as he does to the idea of autonomy, even to consider the 'evidence' for the Scripture as the final and absolutely authoritative revelation of the God of Christianity."[21] Apart from the Reformed faith, theology and philosophy "lead ultimately to a universe where chance is placed above God."[22] In short, Van Til maintains that the traditional method of apologetics compromises the biblical doctrines of God, revelation, man's creation in the image of God, and sin.[23] The fact that this method has been employed for so long by Reformed theologians has "stood in the way of the development of a distinctly Reformed apologetic."[24]

TOWARD A CHRISTIAN PHILOSOPHY

Reformed apologists of all the kinds surveyed in the previous chapter call for Christians to develop a Christian philosophy that is based on its own principles and is faithful to the Christian revelation. Alvin Plantinga, the most renowned Reformed philosopher of the past century, and representative of what we called the "left wing" of the Reformed apologetic tradition, will serve as our example here. In his paper "Advice to Christian Philosophers," he urges Christian philosophers to be more independent of the academic philosophy establishment, to display more integrity or wholeness in their work, and to be bolder in affirming their Christian perspective.[25] He points out that "the Christian community has its own questions, its own concerns, its own topics for investigation, its own agenda, and its own research program" (298). He also warns that Christian philosophers need to avoid becoming so enamored of contemporary philosophers that they fall into the trap of trying to express Christian concepts using alien ideas. He uses the philosopher Willard van Orman Quine as an example:

Quine is a marvelously gifted philosopher; a subtle, original, and powerful philosophical force. But his fundamental commitments, his fundamental projects and concerns, are wholly different from those of the Christian community—wholly different and, indeed, antithetical to them. And the result of attempting to graft Christian thought onto his basic view of the world will be at best an unintegral *pastiche;* at worst it will seriously compromise, or distort, or trivialize the claims of Christian theism. (299)

Plantinga encourages Christians engaged in philosophical work to be unabashed in expressing a distinctively Christian point of view. "And—and this is crucially important—the Christian philosopher has a perfect right to the point of view and pre-philosophical assumptions he brings to philosophic work; the fact that these are not widely shared outside the Christian or theistic community is interesting but fundamentally irrelevant" (299).

According to Plantinga, a Christian philosopher who stands resolutely on his principles will respond to philosophical challenges to Christianity differently than one who wants to accommodate Christianity to philosophy. Plantinga uses verificationism, the logical positivist movement, as an example. Many Christian philosophers and theologians, faced with the challenge of the verifiability criterion of meaning (according to which theological statements are meaningless), took the challenge far too seriously. All too often they tried to accommodate Christian theology to verificationism.

> What they should have said to the positivists is: "Your criterion is mistaken: for such statements as 'God loves us' and 'God created the heavens and the earth' are clearly meaningful; so if they aren't verifiable in your sense, then it is false that all and only statements verifiable in that sense are meaningful." What was needed here was less accommodation to current fashion and more Christian self-confidence: Christian theism is true; if Christian theism is true, then the verifiability criterion is false; so the verifiability criterion is false. (301)

Plantinga illustrates his point again with the problem of evil. Against those who press the reality of evil as evidence weighing against belief in God's existence, he replies that in ordinary reasoning such evidence is weighed along with the rest of what the person considering this evidence already believes and knows to be true. He then suggests that the Christian has every right to include the belief that God exists as a basic part of that body of truth that is already believed and possessed—in which case the reality of evil will not undermine the person's confidence that God exists.

> Perhaps the theist has a right to *start from* belief in God, taking that proposition to be one of the ones probability with respect to which determines the rational propriety of *other* beliefs he holds. But if so, then the Christian *philosopher* is entirely within his rights in starting from belief in God to his philosophizing. He has a right to take the existence of God for granted and go on from there in his philosophical work—just as other philosophers take for granted the existence of the past, say, or of other persons, or the basic claims of contemporary physics. (303–304)

If a Christian is asked what justifies his belief that God exists, one possible answer is that given by Augustine and developed by Calvin. God, Plantinga says, "has developed in humankind a tendency or nisus or disposition to believe in him," a disposition that remains universally present despite its suppression by sin (304, 305). "No doubt this suggestion won't convince the skeptic; taken as an attempt to convince the skeptic it is circular" (305). But that should not inhibit the theist from affirming this answer, since a Christian philosophy rightly takes its foundational principles as basic and builds on them.

> But this means that the Christian philosophical community need not devote all of its efforts to attempting to refute opposing claims and/or to arguing for its own claims, in each case from premises accepted by the bulk of the philosophical community at large. It ought to do this, indeed, but it ought to do more. For if it only does this, it will neglect a pressing philosophical task: systematizing, deepening, clarifying Christian thought on these topics. (312)

Much of what Plantinga says here will resonate with more conservative Reformed apologists. One key difference, though, is that he concludes that Christian philosophers ought to be prepared to argue their position based on premises acceptable to non-Christian philosophers, while not treating such arguments as primary or necessary justification for their position. For Van Til, on the other hand, as for most conservative Reformed apologists, it is impossible to find any premises acceptable to non-Christians from which the Christian position can be validly defended. Whereas Plantinga argues for the rational *respectability* of theism, especially Christian theism, Van Til argues for the rational *inescapability* of Christian theism (and *only* specifically Christian theism). "We as Christians alone have a position that is philosophically defensible."[26]

Van Til's view of philosophy may also be helpfully compared with that of Herman Dooyeweerd. Both of them agreed that the only true philosophy would emanate from what Dooyeweerd calls "a radical Christian starting-point." However, Dooyeweerd argues "that this Christian philosophy does not derive its fundamentals from theology in its scientific sense, and, therefore, should be sharply distinguished from the latter."[27] In the end this means that Christian philosophy does not derive its fundamentals from a study of the Bible. Dooyeweerd does encourage Christians to believe that philosophical thought can "be ruled by the central motive of Holy Scripture." However, this central or "spiritual basic motive is elevated above all theological controversies and is not in need of biblical exegesis, since its radical meaning is exclusively explained by the Holy Spirit operating in our opened hearts, in the communion of this Spirit."[28]

Van Til, on the other hand, argues against any hard-and-fast distinction between philosophy and theology. "Philosophy deals with no concepts that theology does not deal with. It is but a matter of terminology."[29] Both philosophy and theology are concerned with the subjects of being (metaphysics), knowledge (epistemology), and morality (ethics); they simply deal with them in different language. Moreover, the Christian philosopher, no less than the theologian or anyone else, must base his intellectual work, his arguments and conclusions, on the Bible. This does not mean, Van Til cautions, that philosophy is subordinate to theology; rather, both are subject to the Bible. The philosopher may, however, turn to the theologian for help in understanding the Bible, since that is the theologian's area of specialization. "The philosopher is directly subject to the Bible and must in the last analysis rest upon his own interpretation of the Word. But he may accept the help of those who are more constantly and more exclusively engaged in biblical study than he himself can be."[30]

CHRISTIANITY AGAINST FALSE SCIENCE

Both classical and evidentialist apologetics tend to accept the methods of modern science as basically valid and its findings as generally correct. The former tends to be more cautious in endorsing scientific theories than the latter, but both agree that Christianity can be shown to be consistent with science. Reformed apologetics calls this traditional assumption into question on the grounds that the nature, methods, and findings of science will in principle be different when practiced by non-Christians than when practiced by Christians. While Christianity is in agreement with the facts, non-Christians naturally view the facts in a way that is biased against the Christian faith.

The basic lines of this view of science were laid down by Abraham Kuyper in his *Principles of Sacred Theology*.[31] As we noted in the previous chapter, at the heart of Kuyper's teaching is the idea that regeneration, or palingenesis, effectively divides the human race into two kinds of people, the regenerate and the unregenerate. These two kinds of people "face the cosmos from different points of view, and are impelled by different impulses," resulting in "two kinds of *science*." The assumption of the absolute unity of science, therefore, "implies the denial of the fact of palingenesis, and therefore from principle leads to the rejection of the Christian religion" (154). Kuyper hastens to explain that "truth is one," and from that standpoint "science also can only be one" (155). What he means is that the regenerate and the unregenerate are building "two different structures, each of which purposes to be a complete building of science," yet they necessarily differ from one another because of their differing viewpoints on the world (156). Both edifices cannot be true; one must be regarded as ultimately false to the reality it seeks to reproduce.

Kuyper also emphasizes that the difference between the two sciences does not prevent overlap and even cooperation in some matters.

> First, because there is a very broad realm of investigation in which the difference between the two groups exerts *no* influence. For in the present dispensation palingenesis works no change in the senses, nor in the plastic conception of visible things. The entire domain of the more primary observation, which limits itself to weights, measures and numbers, is common to both. . . . Whether a thing weighs two milligrams or three, can be absolutely ascertained by every one that can weigh. (157)

It would, however, be a mistake to conclude that science is the same for both groups. Kuyper points out that measures and numbers constitute only the "*first and lowest* part" of science, representing "the foot of the ladder of scientific investigation" (157). As one moves up that ladder into the interpretation of such measures and numbers, one quickly begins to deal with matters where one's worldview affects one's interpretation. Thus it is really useless for a Christian to try to persuade a non-Christian that Christianity is scientifically true. The worldview of non-Christians dictates that they practice science and view the facts studied by science in a way that really assumes that Christianity is false. Kuyper concludes that traditional apologetics is misguided in its efforts to convince non-Christians that Christianity is scientifically credible:

> No polemics between these two kinds of science, on details which do not concern the statement of an objectively observable fact, or the somatic side of the psychical sciences, or, finally, a logical fault in argumentation, can ever serve any purpose. This is the reason why, as soon as it has allowed itself to be inveigled into details, and has undertaken to deal with things that are not palpable phenomena or logical mistakes, Apologetics has always failed to reach results, and has weakened rather than strengthens the reasoner. (160)

Kuyper's position, in sum, is that the usual characterization that modern discoveries and theories have resulted in a conflict between religion and science, or between faith and science, is mistaken. "Not faith and science therefore, but *two scientific systems* or if you choose, two scientific elaborations, are opposed to each other, *each having its own faith.*"[32]

Van Til's most extensive treatment of science appears in his book *Christian-Theistic Evidences*, in which he begins by defining such evidences as "the defense of Christian theism against any attack that may be made upon it by 'science.'" He takes "the word science in its current meaning," including both "the results of science, both real and imaginary," and "the methodology of science." The thesis of Van Til's book is "that it is only upon Christian presuppositions that we can have a sound scientific methodology." It is because science typically proceeds on the basis of assumptions or presuppositions that are inimical to the Christian faith that it reaches conclusions that are at variance with the teachings of the Bible. "The chief major battle between Christianity and modern science is not about a large number of individual facts, but about the principles that control science in its work. The battle today is largely that of the *philosophy* of science."[33]

For Van Til, the fundamental premise of a true philosophy of science must be the biblical view of the world as created and providentially ruled by God. "Scripture teaches that every fact in the universe exists and operates by virtue of the plan of God. There are no *brute facts* for God." Modern science, on the other hand, "takes for granted the ultimacy of brute facts."[34] By "brute facts" he means the idea that facts are random bits of information that are not necessarily related in any fixed or given way and may therefore be known by the human interpreter apart from an interpretive context.[35] They are not to be confused with *objective* facts, the existence of which Van Til affirms.[36] The idea of brute facts presupposes that facts are random occurrences in a universe operating according to chance rather than the determined plan and purpose of God. Thus modern science is principially committed to the presupposition that the God spoken of in Scripture (particularly as understood in Reformed theology) does not exist.

Not surprisingly, then, Van Til concludes, "It is fatal to try to prove the existence of God by the 'scientific method' and by the 'appeal to facts' if . . . the scientific method itself is based upon a presupposition which excludes God."[37] Rather than trying to prove God by science, the apologist should argue that the validity of science depends on God. Science seeks to discover the coherence, unity, and uniformity in nature. But the assumption that there is uniformity in nature is at odds with viewing nature as a mass of brute facts waiting for the scientist to correlate and interpret them as he sees fit. The uniformity of nature presupposes a transcendent origin of nature in the singular mind of God, who created the world and made the facts of nature what they are according to his design.

> Our argument as over against this would be that the existence of the God of Christian theism and the conception of his counsel as controlling all things in the universe is the only presupposition which can account for the uniformity of nature which the scientist needs. But the best and only possible proof for the existence of such a God is that his existence is required for the uniformity of nature and for the coherence of all things in the world.[38]

Thus Christian apologists or scientists should not entertain as valid possibilities scientific theories that exclude God and debate such theories on a factual level, as if the matter were open to interpretation. Instead, they should insist that any theory that is inconsistent with the necessary presupposition of all scientific theory, the existence of the sovereign God, is self-defeating and irrelevant.

> Over against this contention that theoretically any hypothesis is as relevant as any other, we place the Christian position which says that no hypotheses which exclude the necessary existence of the triune God of Scripture can be relevant to any group of facts. There is only one absolutely true explanation of every fact and of every group of facts

in the universe. God has this absolutely true explanation of every fact. Accordingly, the various hypotheses that are to be relevant to the explanation of phenomena must be consistent with this fundamental presupposition.[39]

For example, Van Til argues that the theory of evolution should be rejected as irrelevant: "If one offers the hypothesis of biological evolution as the explanation of man's appearance on the earth, we reply that the hypothesis is irrelevant. Our further study of the factual material is no more than a corroboration of our assertion of the irrelevancy of this hypothesis." He makes clear that while the "factual material" can and should be studied, the Christian should conduct such study on the assumption that any and all facts must confirm what we know from Scripture is the true interpretation of the facts. "*We appeal to facts, but never to brute facts. We appeal to God-interpreted facts.*"[40]

We should not overlook the importance of Van Til's teaching on science for creationism. One of the founders of contemporary creationism was John C. Whitcomb, Jr., whose book *The Genesis Flood*, co-authored with Henry M. Morris, is really the primary text of the movement. More specifically, this book is commonly regarded as marking the beginning of the contemporary scientific creationist movement that defends a young earth, a global Flood, and geologic catastrophism in defense of a literal interpretation of Genesis.[41] Whitcomb based his view of the relationship between science and Scripture on a form of Van Til's apologetic system.[42] Like Van Til, Whitcomb and other young-earth creationists emphasize the impossibility of scientific theories without religious presuppositions. They argue that both creationism and evolutionism should be seen as essentially religious in character, an assessment that is characteristic not only of Van Til but of the entire Kuyperian tradition. Like Van Til, young-earth creationists affirm the priority of biblical teaching to scientific investigation. In their view the Bible speaks both more authoritatively and more clearly about such questions as the age of the universe than science should or can. Young-earth creationists also understand the radical effects of the Fall on human thought to extend to affect science in a substantial way.

Van Til himself appears to have been broadly supportive of the creationist movement, although his treatment of creation did not focus on such questions as the age of the universe.[43] He did criticize Philo for his view that "the Mosaic account of the origin of the world and of the days of creation must not be taken as historical but allegorical."[44]

We should also note the highly controversial view of science advocated by Gordon Clark. As mentioned in the previous chapter, Clark rejected inductive argument as fallacious when used as a means of knowing truth, favoring instead an exclusive use of deductive logic working from premises known to be true. True to this epistemology, in his book *The Philosophy of Science and Belief in God* Clark reviews the history of science in order to show that science does not and cannot arrive at truth. This is not to say that Clark thinks we cannot ascertain facts about the physical world; rather, there is a sense in which science cannot *explain* any of the facts it describes. "Does science explain anything? . . . Surely we want to know more than the path of the planets and the acceleration of a freely falling body. Facts such as these are interesting and important. But a statement of fact is not an explanation: It is the very thing that needs to be explained. Viewed in this light, science explains nothing."[45]

Worse still, according to Clark, science's descriptions of nature in the form of laws or mathematical formulas are not descriptions of the way things actually are in the real world. Rather, they are mathematical idealizations. For example, the law of the pendulum, which "states that the period of the swing is proportional to the square root of the length," assumes a perfect pendulum in a perfect environment (57). "Only an ideal pendulum, an imaginary pendulum, only a non-existing pendulum is described by the Newtonian law" (58). And this is true for all such scientific laws describing physical processes in mathematical form. Clark does not mince words: "Therefore, all the laws of physics are false" (60).

Science depends heavily on the use of inductive argument. So much the worse for science, according to Clark. Recall that his form of presuppositionalism regards the Bible's truth as axiomatic and assumes the validity of deductive reasoning as a means of drawing inferences from the Bible. This emphasis on deduction carries through to his view of science. The argument form implicit in all claims of verification of scientific laws through experimentation, according to Clark, is the following.[46]

> *If hypothesis H is true, then experiment E will produce the results R.*
>
> *Experiment E does produce the results R.*
>
> *Therefore, hypothesis H is true.*

Clark comments, "Obviously, this argument is the fallacy of asserting the consequent; and since all verification must commit this fallacy, it follows that no law or hypothesis can ever be logically demonstrated" (71). This fallacy is a mistake in deductive reasoning of the following form:

If A, then B.

B.

Therefore, A.

In logic the *A* is called the antecedent and the *B* the consequent. The fallacy of affirming the consequent is the mistake of thinking that if the consequent is true, the antecedent must be true. To see that this is not so, consider the following example:

If it rained, the driveway will be wet.

The driveway is wet.

Therefore, it rained.

With a moment's reflection one can easily imagine other circumstances that might have caused the driveway to become wet (for example, someone just washed the car). Arguments of this form, then, are deductively invalid. According to Clark, this is also true of all claims that experiments have verified scientific hypotheses. He concludes "that the violation of logic can be justified only on the ground that scientists are not interested in the literal truth of their laws. . . . What is needed now is not so much a new science, but a new philosophy of science" (72).

On the basis of this line of reasoning, Clark favors a form of the philosophy of science known as **operationalism**, a version of **nonrealism**, according to which science does not progress toward a greater and more accurate knowledge of the "real" world. According to operationalism, science consists in descriptions of the *operations* performed by the scientist and not the actual entities or realities studied or hypothesized. For Clark "the most certain truth of physics is that physics is not true—not true as an account of what nature is and how nature works" (79). "Electrons and light waves are not physically existing things; they are elements of a set of instructions on how to operate in a laboratory" (90).

In Clark's apologetic, operationalism completely undermines any attempt to use science to disprove creation or any other aspect of Christian doctrine. If science is not a means for gaining knowledge about nature but is instead a method developed "to utilize nature for our needs and wants" (93), then science cannot overturn what we know about God's activity in the creation of nature. If science is not *true*, it cannot prove Christianity false. Since science is a discipline that develops protocols for performing operations in a laboratory, its "laws" are not literal descriptions of reality that do not change. Rather, they are conventions that can and are frequently discarded for new ones. "Therefore anti-Christian arguments based on science always depend on premises that will soon be discarded" (102).

For Clark, then, science really is irrelevant to Christian apologetics. Noting that even Einstein acknowledged that science can never enable us to know the real nature of things, Clark concludes: "From this the further conclusion follows that science can never disprove the truth of Christianity. It can never prove or disprove any metaphysical or theological assertion" (109).

Presuppositionalists who follow Van Til instead of Clark generally assume a realist view of science, yet heavily qualify their realism in light of their conviction that non-Christian science fails to interpret the real world properly. In making this distinction two Van Tilians in particular, Vern Poythress and John Frame, have drawn on the work of the nonrealist philosopher of science Thomas Kuhn. In Kuhn's landmark book *The Structure of Scientific Revolutions*, he argued that science progresses as communities with shared paradigms, or ways of viewing the world, replace their paradigms in sudden revolutions or "paradigm shifts." These occur under the pressure of internal criticism from within the scientific community as scientific renegades propose rival paradigms to account for information not well integrated into the old paradigm.[47] Poythress in particular has found a number of useful and valid insights in Kuhn's work. The Reformed claim is that there are rival sciences rooted in the different paradigms, or worldviews, of the Christian and non-Christian scientific communities. Poythress also suggests that Christians progress in their understanding of science, and indeed of theology, by considering rival paradigms (for example, alternative theological formulations on controversial doctrinal questions). Both Poythress and Frame, while distancing themselves from Kuhn's relativistic and outright nonrealistic view of science, consider him useful in helping people understand the critical role that presuppositions play in apologetics.[48]

REVELATION AS INTERPRETING HISTORY

The way Reformed apologists view science carries over into how they view history and the use of historical evidences in apologetics. We will speak briefly of the views of Kuyper and Clark, then give Van Til's more complex position more in-depth attention.

Kuyper had no real use for historical evidences. In his view, apologetic arguments in support of the Christian faith are constrained by the fact that in every single point of contention, the antithesis between the Christian and non-Christian view of knowledge and of the world is ultimately at issue. "Scarcely has a single step been ventured in the way of such a controversy before it is felt on both sides that the acknowledgment of a different opinion on this one point would unsettle one's entire life- and world-view." The naturalist, therefore, cannot concede one miracle without forfeiting his position. He will answer the argument from miracles by denying their very possibility; he will answer the argument from prophecy by claiming that all apparent prophecies must have been written after the fact.[49]

Given Clark's thoroughgoing rejection of all empirical, inductive arguments as resting on deductive fallacies, one would assume that he rejected all historical arguments supporting the Bible and Christian truth. Actually, though, that would be something of an overstatement. First of all, Clark agreed that evidences have their place; he simply denied that they could serve as positive arguments for the truth of Christianity. "Certainly there is a place for evidences in the propagation of the Christian faith. Certainly the resurrection of Jesus should be preached and the testimony of the eye witnesses recounted. But after we have published abroad His wonderful name, and after we have declared our faith, the auditors may ask us a reason. Apologetics therefore has its place too, but in the temporal order it is a later place."[50]

Clark saw only a limited, negative purpose for such argumentation, that of answering objections. Apologetics must go beyond these matters to the underlying, foundational issues:

> The Christian reply to a rationalistic rejection of revelation should not concern itself too much with archaeological evidence that the Bible is historically accurate. Spinoza, to be sure, was an early member of the long line of higher critics who delighted to find blunders in the Old Testament. . . . But Spinoza's argument was that an historical narrative, even if perfectly accurate, is valueless in religion. A Christian reply therefore must be directed against the epistemology that underlies Spinoza's statement. The important question is not whether or not the Bible is true, but whether or not all knowledge is deducible by reason, i.e., by logic alone.[51]

For Clark, historical argument cannot prove Christianity true; at best it can answer arguments purporting to show that it is false. Clark denies that one can logically reason from the fact of the Resurrection (assuming a non-Christian can be persuaded to agree to that fact) to the truth of the Christian belief about Jesus.

> Suppose Jesus did rise from the grave. This only proves that his body resumed its activities for a while after his crucifixion; it does not prove that he died for our sins or that he was the Son of God. While this line of anti-Christian argument contains certain misstatements, none the less the inference in the last sentence is valid. The resurrection, viewed purely as an isolated historical event, does not prove that Christ died for our sins, not only because Lazarus also rose from the dead, but also because sin is a notion which requires a particular view of God and the universe, and on such questions archeology and history are incompetent.[52]

Van Til's position is more complex, and there has been much controversy about its actual import. On the one hand, his critics routinely complain that his method negates any value for historical evidences and arguments in apologetics, and they can cite a number of passages from his writings that would seem to support their contention. On the other hand, his defenders insist that he had a positive place for historical argument and evidences in his apologetic. They too cite supportive passages from his writings.

The most often cited such passage appears in *The Defense of the Faith*. In it Van Til quotes at length from an article in which he responded to criticisms of his apologetic by J. Oliver Buswell, Jr., a well-known evidentialist. Van Til explains how his approach differs from the traditional one. (a) He says he takes the Bible as absolutely authoritative and bases his apologetic, and indeed his whole philosophy of life, on its teachings. (b) He argues that God's revelation of himself both in nature and in Scripture is objectively clear, so that people are utterly without excuse for their failure to believe in God. This leads him to reject any kind of apologetic that stops short of that conclusion. In particular, he objects to formulating theistic arguments in such a way that they conclude that God *probably* exists. (c) He does not deny that fallen human beings can reason or understand truth. What he does deny is that their reason and understanding can be intelligible apart from the creation of human beings in God's image. He therefore objects to an apologetic that seeks neutral ground between Christians and non-Christians.[53] The fourth and final way Van Til's apologetic differs from the traditional is:

(d) Implied in the previous points is the fact that I do not artificially separate induction from deduction, or reasoning about the facts of nature from reasoning in an *a priori* analytical fashion about the nature of human-consciousness. I do not artificially abstract or separate them from one another. On the contrary I see induction and analytical reasoning as part of one process of interpretation. I would therefore engage in historical apologetics. (I do not personally do a great deal of this because my colleagues in the other departments of the Seminary in which I teach are doing it better than I could do it.) Every bit of historical investigation, whether it be in the directly Biblical field, archaeology, or in general history, is bound to confirm the truth of the claims of the Christian position. But I would not talk endlessly about facts and more facts without ever challenging the non-believer's philosophy of fact. A really fruitful historical apologetic argues that every fact *is* and *must be* such as proves the truth of the Christian position.[54]

While this frequently quoted statement must, of course, be given full weight in interpreting Van Til, it must be read in light of everything else that he says about evidences and apologetics. The last sentence is key: historical apologetics should argue that every fact *must* prove Christianity. And how, for Van Til, is this to be done? Van Til leaves no doubt. Christian evidences must show that apart from Christ's interpretation of man in Scripture, man's speech is meaningless.[55] Non-Christian interpretations of the facts or evidences are not to be refuted primarily by a study of the facts but by dismissing them as irrelevant. "For the non-Christian any sort of hypothesis may, at the outset of an investigation, be as relevant as any other. . . . But for one who holds that the facts are already part of an ultimately rational system by virtue of the plan of God it is clear that such hypotheses as presuppose the non-existence of such a plan must, even from the outset of his investigation, be considered irrelevant."[56]

Recall that this is how Van Til asserted that scientific hypotheses should also be treated. Study of the facts can at best corroborate the Christian position; *proof* is to be found in the transcendental or presuppositional argument that unless Christianity is true there are no intelligible facts to be studied in the first place. He illustrates this point with the Resurrection: "*God's self-existence is the presupposition of the relevancy of any hypothesis.* If one should seek to explain the claim of the disciples of Jesus that their Master's body was raised from the tomb by offering the hypothesis of hallucination, we reply that the hypothesis is irrelevant. Our further study of the factual evidence in the matter is no more than a corroboration of our assertion of the irrelevancy of such an hypothesis."[57]

Van Til flatly disallows any attempt to reason apologetically by a direct appeal to the facts,[58] because the non-Christian can always toss the facts "in the bottomless pit of pure possibility." For example, he can allow that the Resurrection took place as merely an unusual event, while rejecting the Christian understanding of that event as God's miraculous vindication of his Son. "You see that the unbeliever who does not work on the presupposition of creation and providence is perfectly consistent with himself when he sees nothing to challenge his unbelief even in the fact of the resurrection of Christ."[59]

The basic difference between the approaches to historical evidences of presuppositionalists on the one hand and classical and evidentialist apologists on the other hand is that the former reason *transcendentally* about the facts while the latter reason *inductively* about them. Consequently, presuppositionalists claim that their apologetic argument yields absolute certainty for their knowledge of the historical facts of the Bible, whereas traditional apologetic arguments yield only probability. Presuppositionalists, in fact, consistently criticize apologetic arguments that conclude that this or that biblical event or claim is "probably" true. To the criticism that historical investigation by its very nature cannot rise above probability in its findings, Greg Bahnsen makes the following telling reply:

> This kind of criticism [against probabilistic arguments] is often answered by saying that historical facts (especially miraculous ones), just because they are such, cannot be known with any more than a high degree of probability. Such an opinion is contrary to God's inspired word, however. Peter proclaimed this historical event (and miracle): "Let all the house of Israel therefore *know with certainty* that God has made him Lord" by raising Jesus from the dead (Acts 2:24, 36). He did not say that it was highly probable that Christ rose from the dead, but rather that it was "not possible" that death could hold him (v. 24).[60]

Bahnsen's defense of the presuppositionalist rejection of probabilistic apologetic arguments makes it clear that his approach to historical evidences does not proceed inductively. That is, we do not "know with certainty" that God raised Jesus from the dead because we have studied the historical evidence inductively. We know it with certainty because if we were to deny it, we would implicitly be denying the Christian theistic revelation, apart from which we have no coherent basis for knowing anything in history.

We may summarize the distinctive approach taken by Reformed apologetics to historical evidences by comparing it with the two approaches already covered. Evidentialists argue that one can make a case for God's action in history by examining the evidence for those events using critical historical methods that do not assume that God exists. Classical apologists disagree; they maintain that one must first establish theism as true and, on that basis, examine the evidence for God's actions in history. Reformed apologists take the classical objection to evidentialism one step further: not only is it necessary to establish the truth of theism in order to see God's actions in history for what they are, it is necessary to establish the truth of *Christian theism*. But this is really the same as saying that the historical evidence cannot be the basis of any kind of empirical apologetic argument for the truth of Christianity. At most the historical evidence can be adduced as confirmation within the perspective of a full-orbed Christian worldview.

In short, Reformed apologists argue that we cannot use history to prove theism (as in evidentialism) or even to prove revelation to those who accept theism (as in classical apologetics). Rather, we must use revelation to prove theism and the true meaning of history.

THE PROBLEM WITH EXPERIENCE

Classical apologists appeal to the pervasiveness of religion and religious experiences (of all kinds) throughout human history and in all cultures to show that human beings have an incorrigible need to relate to a source of transcendence. This argument aims at proving that some kind of God must exist. Evidentialists commonly take a different approach in view of the fact that vastly different religions claim rather similar religious experiences. For them Christianity is unique because it offers objective, verifiable evidence for its religious claims, which are then known with certainty through the experience of Christian faith. They therefore invite non-Christians to examine the evidence for Christianity in order to see that there are objective grounds for "trying" Christianity experientially.

Reformed apologists take yet another approach to the relation of experience to apologetics, basic to which is the Reformed understanding of the "total depravity" of unredeemed humanity. According to the Reformed doctrine, unredeemed human beings are still in God's image, and yet that image is thoroughly darkened by sin. Non-Christian religion, in this view, in some way bears witness to the reality of God's image in man, yet at the same time is a completely unreliable source of knowledge about God. The only way human beings can come to know God truly is to experience the illuminating effects of regeneration by the Holy Spirit through faith in Christ.

On the basis of this understanding of the creation and fall of mankind, most Reformed apologists avoid basing apologetic arguments on religious experiences in general. But neither do they appeal to the experience of regeneration as the basis of an apologetic argument. Rather, they typically contend that the rational faculties of Christians are enabled through regeneration to recognize and believe the truth about God. In other words, the experience of regeneration is the cause, not the ground, of Christian belief.

According to Reformed apologists, the condition of the unregenerate mind precludes finding common ground with the unregenerate in shared beliefs or principles of thinking. This is because the unregenerate mind is committed in principle to thinking about everything in such a way as to avoid acknowledging their spiritual darkness and need for redemption in Christ. However, Reformed apologists do acknowledge another kind of common ground, or what is often called a point of contact, between Christians and non-Christians: the image of God that is in both of them. Because all people are still in God's image, they have within them, albeit suppressed by sin, an awareness of God to which appeal may and should be made in apologetics.

Both Clark and Van Til share this understanding of the point of contact. We quote first from Clark's defense of apologetics in his critique of Karl Barth's theological method: "But Reformed theology, while denying a common epistemological ground, has always asserted a common psychological or ontological ground. Believer and unbeliever alike, though their philosophic axioms and theorems are totally incompatible, bear in their persons the image of God from creation."

By "a common epistemological ground" Clark means the idea of non-Christians and Christians sharing the same approach to knowledge. For Clark the only sound approach to knowledge is to accept the Word of God in Scripture as absolute truth. The "common psychological or ontological ground" is the image of God that exists in both Christian and non-Christian. The mind and being of the unregenerate is still created in God's image. As a result, non-Christians still know and think some truth. Thus, Clark continues: "This image consists of or at least includes their ordinary rational ability as human beings and as an exercise of this rationality certain minimal theological and moral principles. These beliefs, dimly and inconsistently held, often submerged and repressed, can be thought of as a point of contact for the Gospel."

Although believers and unbelievers do not agree on the axiomatic starting point for knowledge of the truth, unbelievers do recognize some truth because they still bear God's image. Clark speaks of this recognized truth as "beliefs, dimly and inconsistently held, often submerged and repressed." That is to say, non-Christians do in some fashion believe some truth about God, but they may not be aware of it and may on the surface appear to believe something quite different. These beliefs, despite these difficulties, may be used in apologetics as the point of contact:

> Apart from the supernatural agency of the Holy Spirit, these beliefs could never develop into a belief in the Gospel nor even into a knowledge of the Gospel. But in the series of psychological experiences, with all the many and great differences from individual to individual, these elementary beliefs can be used by the Holy Spirit to produce an acceptance of the message preached. Thus there is no inconsistency in denying a common axiom while asserting a common psychological or ontological "ground" or "point of contact."[61]

Turning to Van Til, we find at first much the same understanding of the point of contact. "Disagreeing with the natural man's interpretation of himself as the ultimate reference-point, the Reformed apologist must seek his point of contact with the natural man in that which is beneath the threshold of his working consciousness, in the sense of deity which he seeks to suppress."[62]

For Van Til, as for Clark, the sense of deity (Calvin's *sensus divinitatis*) is a function of the image of God that is present in both the unregenerate and the regenerate. Like Clark, he contends that the truth about God is still present in the unregenerate, though "beneath the threshold of his working consciousness," due to its suppression in sin. However, he does not apply the image of God as the point of contact in the same way as Clark: "And to do this the Reformed apologist must also seek a point of contact with the systems constructed by the natural man. But this point of contact must be in the nature of a head-on collision. *If there is no head-on collision with the systems of the natural man there will be no point of contact with the sense of deity in the natural man.*"[63]

Thus, for Van Til the point of contact is not one of *agreement* with what the unbeliever thinks, but of *disagreement*, for the position the unbeliever professes and thinks is at odds with what he knows in his heart. "All men, even after the fall, know, deep down in their hearts, that they are creatures of God; that they should therefore obey, but that they actually have broken, the law of God." But because they are in rebellion against God, "all men seek to suppress this truth, fixed in their being, about themselves."[64] The result is that, outwardly, non-Christians refuse to believe in the true God, while inwardly, at the core of their being, they really know that he is God and are unable to escape this knowledge entirely. "Psychologically there are no atheistic men; epistemologically every sinner is atheistic."[65] According to Van Til, an apologetic argument can appeal to this point of contact by reasoning in a transcendental argument that unless man is made in the image of God, nothing in our experience makes sense. "A truly transcendental argument takes any fact of experience which it wishes to investigate, and tries to determine what the presuppositions of such a fact must be, in order to make it what it is."[66]

Reformed apologists, then, like Clark and Van Til, do not appeal to specific experiences to validate or provide evidence for theism or Christianity. Rather, they appeal to the universal experience or condition of humanity as both created in God's image and fallen in sin. They argue that confronting the unbeliever with the truth about his created and sinful condition is a necessary part of presenting the gospel of redemption from sin. They then look to the work of the Holy Spirit in regenerating those God has chosen to redeem as the experience by which the unbeliever will be able to recognize the truth about his fallen condition and gratefully repent of his epistemological rebellion. As Van Til explains, the Reformed apologist recognizes that apologetic argument will not convert or regenerate anyone, but at the same time he engages in apologetics in the expectation that God will use it as part of the experience leading to regeneration. "The miracle of regeneration has to occur somewhere, and all that we are arguing is that we must ask where it is that the Holy Spirit will most likely perform this miracle. And then there can be no doubt but that the likelihood is in favor of that place where the non-theist has to some extent seen the emptiness and vanity of his own position."[67]

For Further Study

Clark, Gordon H. *A Christian View of Men and Things: An Introduction to Philosophy*. Grand
    Rapids: Eerdmans, 1952; reprint, Grand Rapids: Baker, 1981. One of Clark's most respected works, presenting his approach to history, science, religion, epistemology, and other areas of thought.

North, Gary. *Foundations of Christian Scholarship: Essays in the Van Til Perspective*. Vallecito,
    Calif.: Ross House, 1976. Collection of thoughtful essays on a Van Tilian approach to

various academic disciplines, including psychology, history, mathematics, apologetics, philosophy, and theology.

Notaro, Thom. *Van Til and the Use of Evidence*. Phillipsburg, N.J.: Presbyterian & Reformed, 1980. An influential, short book arguing that Van Til had a positive view of evidences.

Chapter 14

Taking Every Thought Captive

Reformed apologetics is an approach to defending the faith that differs significantly from traditional apologetics. Nevertheless, Reformed apologists do seek to provide a reasoned defense of the gospel. The apostle Paul described his ministry as "destroying speculations and every lofty thing raised up against the knowledge of God, and . . . taking every thought captive to the obedience of Christ" (2 Corinthians 10:5). Reformed apologists commonly understand their ministry as continuing Paul's mandate. They staunchly oppose the idea of neutrality in any area of thought, insisting that Jesus Christ is Lord over science, philosophy, theology, and apologetics. The title of John Frame's book *Apologetics to the Glory of God* nicely captures the spirit of Reformed apologetics.

The distinctive theological and philosophical assumptions of Reformed apologetics lead its advocates to equally distinctive approaches to such issues as the existence of God and the problem of evil. In general, Reformed apologetics, especially as articulated by such conservative apologists as Gordon Clark and Cornelius Van Til, may be fairly characterized as *offensive*. The term is susceptible of two senses here, and actually both apply. Objectively, Reformed apologetics seeks to take the initiative and show that unbelieving thought is irrational, not merely that faith is plausible or reasonable. In this sense "offensive" contrasts with a "defensive" approach to apologetics. Van Til was not shy about using martial metaphors to express this approach (as Paul also did in speaking of "taking every thought captive"). For example, Van Til could write:

> Apologetics, like systematics, is valuable to the precise extent that it presses the truth upon the attention of the natural man. The natural man must be blasted out of his hideouts, his caves, his lurking places. Neither

Roman Catholic nor Arminian methodologies have the flame-throwers with which to reach him. In the all-out war between the Christian and the natural man as he appears in modern garb it is only the atomic energy of a truly Reformed methodology that will explode the last *Festung* [fortress] to which the Roman Catholic and the Arminian always permit him to retreat and to dwell in safety.[1]

Subjectively, Reformed apologists warn that the gospel will be personally offensive to non-Christians. Apart from the enlightenment of regeneration, unbelievers take offense at the message that they are spiritually dead, at enmity with a holy God, helpless to redeem themselves, and therefore utterly dependent on the grace of God to save them through faith in Jesus Christ. Reformed apologists warn that an apologetic that fails to make the offense of the gospel clear is neither faithful nor effective. This does not mean that Reformed apologists think it is appropriate to speak to non-Christians in a harsh manner. Van Til expressed the distinction with the Latin saying *suaviter in modo, fortiter in re*, "gentle in how, strong in what" we say.

SCRIPTURE AS FOUNDATION

Clark and Van Til both insisted on the necessity of presupposing the divine inspiration and absolute truth of Scripture, not only in theology but also in apologetics. For them the divine authority of Scripture is the beginning, not the conclusion, of the apologetic case for Christianity. As with other aspects of their thought, Clark and Van Til worked out this presuppositional view of biblical authority in somewhat differing ways.

Clark's view is disarmingly simple on one level, but it should not be dismissed as simplistic. Every system of thought, he contends, must rest on one or more axioms, fixed assumptions that need not and cannot be demonstrated, and from which all other elements of the system are derived. Since this is unavoidable, there can be no objection in principle to Christianity being based on such an axiom. Clark puts forward as the proper axiomatic foundation of Christianity the proposition that the Bible is God's word. "Our axiom shall be that God has spoken. More completely, God has spoken in the Bible. More precisely, what the Bible says, God has spoken."[2]

There is a very close relation between Scripture, God, and logic in Clark's axiom, which is brought out very clearly in a postscript to his textbook on logic. In one of his most controversial views, Clark suggests that the Greek word *logos* in John 1:1, usually rendered "Word," can also be rendered "Logic."[3] (Earlier in the same book [page x] he suggests the rendering "Wisdom.") The whole verse may then be properly translated, "In the beginning was Logic, and Logic was with God, and Logic was God." Clark points out that the word *logos* carried an intellectualist connotation in much of its usage and argues that his rendering no more depersonalizes the preincarnate Christ than does "the Word." Clark wishes to make two points with this surprising interpretation of John 1:1. First, irrationality has no place in Christianity. If Logic is God, then we ought to think logically about God and not retreat into mysticism. Second, though, logic is not an independent standard of truth to which God himself must conform, but is rather an expression of the eternal nature of God. "The law of contradiction is not to be taken as an axiom prior to or independent of God. The law is God thinking" (121).

Clark then turns to the relation of God to Scripture. He denies that the Bible should be thought of essentially "as a material book, with paper contents, and a leather binding." Rather, "the Bible expresses the mind of God. Conceptually it is the mind of God, or, more accurately, a part of God's mind. . . . The Bible then is the mind or thought of God" (124). Clark is not denying that the material books bearing the title "the Bible" exist. He is arguing that these many printed volumes are representations of the one body of truth communicated from the mind of God to us. That body of truth is the singular reality that is meant when we speak of *the* Bible.

Since Logic is of the essence of God, presumably "if God has spoken, he has spoken logically" (125). Scripture, then, is eminently logical and contains numerous instances of various kinds of logical arguments.

The fact that Scripture is logical and expresses the mind of God makes it the proper axiom, according to Clark. He explains why neither logic nor God per se should be made the axiom. The law of contradiction (which Clark regards as the base principle of logic) is essential for knowledge, but by itself "is not sufficient to produce knowledge" (126). Clark recognizes that a contentless logic is meaningless; it is order without anything to be placed in order. He acknowledges that it may seem more reasonable to make God the axiom of one's system, but to speak of "God" without specifying which God is also useless. He cites the pantheistic system of Spinoza, who made God his axiom—but defined God as Nature. "Hence the important thing is not to presuppose God, but to define the mind of the God presupposed. Therefore the Scripture is offered here as the axiom" (127).

As we have seen, Van Til's apologetic was a transcendental presuppositionalism, whereas Clark's was a deductive presuppositionalism. Van Til does not seek to build a system of thought deductively from an initial axiom or axioms. For him the presupposition of all thought is not a logical axiom but a transcendent reality that makes all thought possible, meaningful, and intelligible. This presupposition is not Scripture per se, nor is it God as an abstract concept (generic theism); rather, it is the God who speaks in Scripture (*Christian* theism). The closeness with which God and Scripture are associated allows Van Til to speak sometimes of God, sometimes of Scripture, and sometimes of Christian theism as the presupposition of all intelligibility. In fact, he asserts that it makes very little difference which one of these we treat as our "starting point."

> We know nothing but such facts as are what the book, the authoritative revelation of God, says they are. And we challenge unbelievers by saying that unless the facts are what the Bible says they are, they have no meaning at all.[4]

> Christian theism must be presented as that light in terms of which any proposition about any fact receives meaning. Without the presupposition of the truth of Christian theism no fact can be distinguished from any other fact. . . . It is the actual existence of the God of Christian theism and the infallible authority of the Scripture which speaks to sinners of this God that must be taken as the presupposition of the intelligibility of any fact in the world.[5]

> So also it makes very little difference whether we begin with the notion of an absolute God or with the notion of an absolute Bible. The one is derived from the other. They are together involved in the Christian view of life. . . . The Bible must be true because it alone speaks of an absolute God. And equally true is it that we believe in an absolute God because the Bible tells us of one.[6]

In Van Til's view, the Bible is God's authoritative revelation of the truth that must be the truth if we are even to make sense of speaking of the Bible or anything else as true or not. Given this view of the Bible, it follows that the Bible cannot be rationally subjected to any tests or criteria of reason to determine or validate its claim to authority.

In the first place it must be affirmed that a Protestant accepts Scripture to be that which Scripture itself says it is on its own authority. Scripture presents itself as being the only light in terms of which the truth about facts and their relations can be discovered. . . . So we cannot subject the authoritative pronouncements of Scripture about reality to the scrutiny of reason because it is reason itself that learns of its proper function from Scripture.[7]

In a section of his book *Warranted Christian Belief*, Plantinga discusses "Proper Basicality and the Role of Scripture."[8] Christian belief, he argues, is properly basic and immediate. "It doesn't proceed by way of an argument from, say, the reliability of Scripture or of the church.... Instead, Scripture (through the work of the Holy Spirit) carries its own evidence with it; as Calvin says, it is 'self-authenticating'" (259). After quoting Calvin on this point, Plantinga elaborates further: it is not that the Holy Spirit convinces us that the Bible is true, and we then infer that if something is taught in the Bible it must be true. (Note here how different Plantinga's view is from Clark's, for whom the truth of the Bible is the axiom from which all Christian beliefs are to be inferred.) Rather, as we read or hear what Scripture says, the Holy Spirit convinces us that what we have just read or heard (the teaching or report given in Scripture) is true (260). Plantinga comments further that Scripture is not 'self-authenticating' by way of its truth-claims being a priori self-evident or by way of its providing evidence or proof of its accuracy (260–61). They are, however, 'self-evident' in an "extended sense," in that they are properly basic, like memory beliefs, neither a priori self-evident nor accepted a posteriori on the basis of other evidences or reasons, but warranted immediately in themselves.

> Scripture is self-authenticating in the sense that for belief in the great things of the gospel to be justified, rational, and warranted, no historical evidence and argument for the teaching in question, or for the veracity or reliability or divine character of Scripture (or the part of Scripture in which it is taught) are necessary. (262)

Plantinga's view of Scripture has affinities with both Reformed apologetics and (as we shall see later) fideism. Like Clark, Van Til, and other conservative Reformed apologists, Plantinga affirms that Scripture is self-authenticating and that Christian faith comes through reading or hearing the Scripture as God's self-authenticating truth. Like fideists, on the other hand, Plantinga holds that the work of the Holy Spirit authenticates the concrete, central truths of Scripture, not neces-sarily the truth of every part of Scripture. According to Plantinga's model, "the central truths of the gospel are self-authenticating in this way; the same does not (necessarily) go for the rest of what the Bible teaches" (261 n. 38).

ANTITHESIS BETWEEN CHRISTIAN AND NON-CHRISTIAN RELIGION

The exclusive truth claims of Christianity are widely rejected today in favor of religious pluralism—the belief that the different religions of the world all are valid paths and none of them is to be regarded as true to the exclusion of the oth-ers. Classical apologists argue that this view is false because the different world religions are logically incompatible. Evidentialists argue it is false because non-Christian religions are not supported by the facts of history and science, while Christianity enjoys strong factual support.

Reformed apologists characteristically find these approaches inadequate. A typical Van Tilian critique would run along the following lines. The classical ap-proach assumes that Christians and non-Christians share the same understanding of what is logically possible, and the evidentialist approach assumes that they share the same understanding of what kinds of facts are even possible, as well as what kinds are religiously significant. Reformed apologists favor a more head-on approach, which we may summarize in two points. First, it is characteristic of Reformed apologetics to contend that religious pluralism is self-defeating; any criticism of religious exclusivism actually presupposes its truth. (In practice clas-sical and evidentialist apologists can and sometimes do make the same point.) Second, at bottom there are really only two kinds of religion: the one that makes God ultimate (Christianity), and the ones that do not (all the other religions).

We begin with the first point, one made across the spectrum of the Reformed approach to apologetics (and by some other apologists as well). For a recent no-table statement of the view that religious pluralism is self-defeating, we refer to an article by Alvin Plantinga.[9] He observes that as a Christian he finds himself holding to religious views that he realizes are not held by everyone. These beliefs may be distilled to two:

(1) The world was created by God, an almighty, all-knowing, and perfectly good personal being (one that holds beliefs; has aims, plans, and inten-tions; and can act to accomplish these aims)

(2) Human beings require salvation, and God has provided a unique way of
   salvation through the incarnation, life, sacrificial death, and resurrection
   of his divine son. (192)

As Plantinga observes, people disagree with his position in three ways. Some
affirm (1) but not (2); these are non-Christian theists such as Jews and Muslims.
Some affirm neither (1) nor (2) but agree that there is a transcendent reality to
which human beings need to be properly related; these are members of nontheistic
religions such as Hinduism and Buddhism. Finally, some affirm neither (1) nor (2)
and also believe in no transcendent reality; these are naturalists or atheists (192).

In contrast to these three avowed non-Christian views, the affirmation of both
(1) and (2) as true implies "that any propositions, including other religious beliefs,
that are incompatible with those tenets are false." This position is what Plantinga
calls **exclusivism** (194), and its denial is termed **pluralism**.

Exclusivism as used here refers to the claim that only the Christian religion is
true. In a narrower sense the term also refers to the claim that only the Christian
religion is *salvific*, that is, that only those who believe in Christ will be saved.
Exclusivism in the narrow sense presupposes exclusivism in the broader sense.
On the other hand, it is possible to hold that Christianity is exclusively true while
denying that it is exclusively salvific.

Plantinga identifies two basic kinds of objections to exclusivism, moral and
epistemic. The moral objections complain that exclusivism is arrogant, imperi-
alistic, oppressive, and the like, while epistemic objections characterize it as irrational or unjustified. Plantinga observes that these objections do not purport
to question the truth of (1) or (2); "they are instead directed to the *propriety* or
rightness of exclusivism" (195).

In the face of the moral objections, Plantinga further qualifies his definition of
exclusivism. Someone who sincerely thought there were arguments that would
convince most or all honest people of the truth of his position would presumably
not be arrogant to think so. Plantinga proposes to exclude such persons from the
category of exclusivists. An exclusivist thus affirms both (1) and (2), but also affirms (3) that they know of no arguments that would necessarily convince most
or all other people of the truth of (1) and (2). Plantinga's answer to the charge that
exclusivists, thus defined, must be arrogant is to show that the accusation would
have to apply equally to the critic of exclusivism. "These charges of arrogance
are a philosophical tar baby: get close enough to them to use them against the
exclusivist, and you are likely to find them stuck fast to yourself" (197–198). He

shows this by considering the alternatives. The person who denies the truth of both Christianity and other religions actually disagrees with or rejects the religious views of even more people than the person who affirms the truth of Christianity and denies the truth of other religions (198). The person who professes to abstain from either believing or rejecting the Christian religion ("the abstemious pluralist") implicitly disagrees with both those who believe and those who avowedly reject Christianity (198–199).

Plantinga considers several forms of epistemic objections to exclusivism. The charge that exclusivism is unjustified really turns on whether beliefs (1) and (2) are true, since, if they are, it follows quite simply that denials of (1) and (2) are false (202–203). But Plantinga goes the extra mile and asks whether exclusivism is justified even if we are aware of other religious beliefs that seem to be as reasonable for their adherents to believe as Christianity is for us (204–205). His answer is that the Christian is still justified in affirming an exclusivist position. In affirming Christianity "she must still think that there is an important difference: she thinks that somehow the other person has *made a mistake*, or *has a blind spot*, or hasn't been wholly attentive, or hasn't received some grace she has, or is in some way epistemically less fortunate" (205). Plantinga admits that, in principle, he could be wrong, but points out that he cannot avoid that risk by withholding all belief, since it might be a mistake to view all religions as on a par. "Again, there is no safe haven here, no way to avoid risk" (205).

Plantinga's handling of the popular accident-of-birth argument is particularly interesting. According to this argument, the exclusivist is unwarranted in thinking that his religious beliefs are true and alternative beliefs false, because most people's religious beliefs (including the exclusivist's) are a function of where they were born and who their parents were. Plantinga responds that "this argument is another philosophical tar baby" that will apply equally to the pluralist (211). "Pluralism isn't and hasn't been widely popular in the world at large; if the pluralist had been born in Madagascar, or medieval France, he probably wouldn't have been a pluralist" (212). Plantinga concludes that we can apparently infer nothing at all about whether a religious belief is warranted from the so-called accident of birth.

Van Til also considers the accident-of-birth argument in his apologetic tract *Why I Believe in God*. He contends that such an argument results in a stalemate and cannot then be used to determine what is true. He contrasts his upbringing in a devout Calvinist home with the imagined upbringing of his fictional non-Christian listener in a pluralistic home:

> Shall we say then that in my early life I was conditioned to believe in
> God, while you were left free to develop your own judgment as you
> pleased? But that will hardly do. You know as well as I that every child
> is conditioned by its environment. You were as thoroughly conditioned
> *not* to believe in God as I was to believe in God. So let us not call each
> other names. If you want to say that belief was poured down *my* throat,
> I shall retort by saying that unbelief was poured down *your* throat. That
> will get us set for our argument.[10]

Having shown that neutrality on religious questions is not an option, conservative Reformed apologists such as Van Til and Clark go on to show why Christianity must be regarded as the true religion. Clark's strategy in *A Christian View of Men and Things* is to argue that only on the grounds of Christian theism can one avoid skepticism. The first part of his argument focuses on showing that naturalism "leads to inconsistency, despair, or suicide," and that only "theistic presuppositions" can provide a basis for history, politics, and ethics. But he recognizes that this argument, if not fully developed, may seem to leave the door open to other forms of theism.

> But the fact that naturalism has proved intolerable does not of itself im-
> ply that the particular Christian presuppositions underlying the whole
> of the present volume are the only principles capable of supporting a
> satisfactory worldview. If theism is indeed necessary to the intelligibil-
> ity of history, possibly Mohammedan theism or some other form would
> function as well as or even better than Christian theism. There has not
> been much argument so far to rule out such a possibility.[11]

Clark is not here conceding that Islam might conceivably constitute a workable, or even superior, form of theism compared to Christianity.[12] Rather, he is speaking pedagogically about the limitations of what he has made clear in the book up to this point. He goes on to outline a basic strategy for responding to the challenge of Islam and other non-Christian forms of theism: "Apparently the best general procedure for one who wishes to recommend Christian theism is to show that other forms of theism are inconsistent mixtures. If some of their propositions should be carried to their logical conclusions, naturalism and eventually skepticism would result; whereas if justice is to be done to possible interpretations of other of their assertions, Christianity would have to be assumed."[13]

Apologists following Van Til's method insist on what they see as an even more radical response to the challenge of other religions, both theistic and nontheistic. Bahnsen sets up the parameters as follows:

> In dealing with the advocates of other religions, the Christian apologist should use the presuppositional method in the same way that he would use it with atheists and materialists. That is, he makes an internal exami-nation of the worldview that is offered by whatever religious devotee he is having the dialogue with. The fact that the opposing religionist speaks formally of "God" (or "gods") is not a difficulty here, for he must define his specific concept of deity. . . . The use of religious vocabulary does not change the applicability of the indirect method of disproving non-Christian presuppositions.[14]

The basic approach here is to show that there is an antithesis between Christianity and all non-Christian religions, fundamental to which is that Christianity alone presents us with an absolute and personal God. John Frame has pointed out that the conception of an absolute personal God is virtually unique to Christianity. Most world religions throughout history have been ei-ther pantheistic or polytheistic. "Pantheism has an absolute, but not a personal absolute. Polytheism has personal gods, but none of these is absolute."[15] Insofar as Judaism and Islam adhere to the concept of God as absolute personality, they show indebtedness to the biblical revelation. Frame also points out that non-Christian religions tend to obscure or deny the biblical conception of God as both transcendent and immanent (concepts somewhat parallel to the concepts of God as absolute and personal). Only if God is understood as both transcendent and immanent (in the orthodox sense of those terms) is the Creator properly distinguished from the creature. "And non-Christians of all persuasions radi-cally deny the biblical Creator-creature distinction."[16] Atheists deny it outright, pantheists dissolve it, and liberals redefine it.

Bahnsen's analysis complements Frame's. He argues that most of the world's religions "cannot even offer epistemological competition to the Christian world-view." They teach "that there is no god, or no personal God, or no god who is omniscient, sovereign, etc."—that is, no god who is absolute, to use Frame's term. Lacking the conception of a personal, sovereign God who is all-knowing and can reveal truth to us, these religions can have no "epistemological authority." They are simply the products of human opinion.[17]

World religions and cults that confess "a personal deity and a verbal revelation" may seem to offer Christianity some competition, but they "are usually poor imitations of Christianity (using 'borrowed capital') or Christian heresies (departing from biblical teaching in a crucial way). Ordinarily, the best tactic is to reason with the advocates of these groups from Scripture, refuting their errors from the Scripture itself."[18] In the process some extrabiblical authority will typically be revealed. As for Islam, Bahnsen argues that "it can be critiqued internally on its own presuppositions." Thus the Qur'an both affirms the words of the Bible and contradicts the Bible. It teaches the utter impossibility of using language to speak about Allah but then uses language to speak about Allah. It teaches that God is holy but that God accepts worshipers whose sins have not been atoned.[19]

In sum, Reformed apologists answer the challenge of religious pluralism in two ways. First, they explain that there is nothing arrogant or unreasonable about believing that one's religious beliefs are true and therefore that other beliefs are false. Indeed, it is unreasonable to say anything else. Second, particularly conservatives such as Clark and Van Til argue that only Christian theism presents a worldview or a transcendent point of reference in terms of which knowledge and ethics are possible or intelligible. On that basis, they conclude that non-Christian religions, though there is much good in them, are basically false.

BELIEF IN GOD AS BASIC

Apologetics in the modern period has been dominated by the concern to provide reasons, whether in the form of proof or evidence, for belief in the existence of God. Increasingly in modern philosophy the assumption became more and more prevalent that the burden of proof was on the theist to show good reasons for believing in God, not on the nontheist to show good reasons for disbelieving in God. This assumption reached its classic formulation in Antony Flew's often discussed article "The Presumption of Atheism."[20] The Reformed apologist seeks to end this trend, and even to turn the tables around. Greg Bahnsen offers a particularly forceful rebuttal to the atheist presumption:

> The issue of the burden of proof is often misconstrued. If we are arguing over something whose existence or nonexistence has no bearing on the intelligibility of our experience and reasoning (say, unicorns), then un-

derstandably the burden of proof rests on those who affirm its existence; without evidence, such things should be dismissed as figments of their imagination. But the existence of God is not on this order. God's existence would have tremendous bearing on the possibility of man knowing anything at all, having self-conscious intelligence, properly interpreting his experiences, or making his reasoning intelligible—even making sense out of what we call "imagination." In this special case, the burden of proof in the argument between a theist and an antitheist would shift to the person denying God's existence, since the possibility and intelligibility of that very debate is directly affected by the position taken.[21]

One important Reformed apologist who focuses on removing the burden of proof from the theist (though not on transferring the burden of proof to the nontheist, as Bahnsen urges) is Alvin Plantinga. His most famous contention is that the Christian (or other theist) is warranted in believing in God's existence whether or not he can offer supporting arguments or evidences for his belief. As Plantinga puts it, belief in God is properly basic. We introduced his position in chapter 12. Here we will consider this particular idea in more depth, since it is often misunderstood. In what follows, we will be summarizing many of the key points in Plantinga's paper "Reason and Belief in God" in *Faith and Rationality*.[22]

According to Plantinga, a belief is **basic** if a person holds it without basing it on some other belief, that is, if it is not inferred from other beliefs. A belief is **properly basic** if the person holding it is in some significant way warranted in doing so. Several important implications of Plantinga's notion of basicality need to be understood.

First, a belief may be basic for a person at one time but not at another. For example, a person who believes that a man committed a murder on the basis of a detective's investigative report might come to hold that belief as basic after viewing a tape of the incident. Likewise, a person who believes in God on the basis of rational arguments for God's existence might later come to hold that belief as basic after having a religious experience (as happened to Plantinga).

Second, a belief may be properly basic for one person but not for another. For example, a person who witnessed a murder may hold as a basic belief that the defendant committed the murder (simply because he saw it happen), while a person on the jury who agreed would not be able to hold that belief as basic. Likewise, one person might believe that Jesus rose from the dead based on the testimony of the apostles in the New Testament, while the apostles themselves held that belief as basic because they saw and touched the risen Jesus.

Third, the fact that a belief is basic for someone does not mean it is *groundless*. For example, a person's belief that he sees a tree is basic because it is not inferred from other beliefs; but it is not groundless, because it is grounded in his immediate experience of seeing the tree. Likewise, a person who holds as a basic belief that God exists might do so because he had a religious experience; that experience, then, would be the ground of the belief. Plantinga insists that belief in God can be properly basic for him without being groundless (78–82).

Fourth, Plantinga's claim that belief in God can be properly basic does not imply that just any belief can be basic. This is what he calls "the Great Pumpkin objection": "What about the belief that the Great Pumpkin returns every Halloween? Could I properly take *that* as basic?" (74). Plantinga's answer is no, because that belief would have nothing to ground it, and there is no reason why anyone should consider such a belief basic (74–78).

Fifth, the idea that a belief is properly basic is to be distinguished from two other concepts. To say that a belief is basic is not a statement about the degree of confidence or certainty with which it is held. The firmness with which a person holds a specific belief is not directly related to whether that belief is basic for him. One may hold different basic beliefs with varying degrees of firmness—for example, being more confident that $2 + 3 = 5$ than that one had eggs for breakfast this morning. One may even be more confident of some nonbasic beliefs than of some basic beliefs—for example, being more confident that $21 \times 21 = 441$, a belief held from computing it using other math facts, than that one had eggs for breakfast last Saturday (49–50).

Sixth, it is possible to abandon beliefs that one held as basic beliefs, even as properly basic. Any argument or information that removes the ground for acceptance of a belief is called a **defeater**. A person who sees what looks exactly like a bowl of fruit on a table may hold as a basic belief that he sees a bowl of fruit. Later, if a trusted friend informs him that the bowl contained imitation fruit made of plastic, he will likely abandon his belief, even though it was properly basic. In this case the trusted friend's testimony constitutes a defeater. The person who holds a basic belief that God exists is not thereby closed to evidences or reasons that might be raised against it. Such evidences or reasons "constitute potential defeaters for justification in theistic belief," and they will become real defeaters for the person who is made aware of the arguments but has nothing with which to "defeat the defeaters." According to Plantinga, "Various forms of theistic apologetics serve this function (among others)" (84). Plantinga, then, is supportive of apologetics, both negative (answering defeaters) and positive (offering positive arguments).

Most Reformed apologists are critical of natural theology and the traditional theistic proofs on the basis of a simple contention: the arguments don't work. Plantinga is one of the few in this tradition who have defended some of the traditional proofs, albeit in reconstructed form. In his 1974 book *God, Freedom and Evil* he examines and sets aside the cosmological and teleological arguments as unsuccessful.[23] He then considers the ontological argument, contending that Kant's criticism of it can be overcome and the argument restated in a form that is sound yet not necessarily persuasive to everyone. "What I claim for this argument, therefore, is that it establishes, not the *truth* of theism, but its rational acceptability."[24]

Kelly James Clark, a Reformed epistemologist who studied under Plantinga, may fairly be described as ambivalent toward arguments for God's existence. In the book *Five Views on Apologetics*,[25] Clark expresses admiration for William Lane Craig's defense of the *kalām* cosmological argument but cautions against claiming too much for this or other theistic arguments. The *kalām* argument, for example, proves at most that some timeless being created the universe, but tells us little about what such a being is like. "We cannot conclude, based solely on this argument, that *theism* is true" (86). Nor is it clear that the argument can be combined with other arguments to prove theism. Clark argues that there are brilliant, rational people who look at the same evidence and draw opposite conclusions, some (like Richard Swinburne) in favor of theism while others (like J. L. Mackie) in favor of atheism. Furthermore, the success of our arguments "depends not only on the logic of the argument but on the will (including the passions, values, and emotions) of the people involved" (88). In his concluding remarks, though, Clark affirms that "theistic arguments and the like are part and parcel of apologetics.... The kind of arguments that one might offer are the very ones offered by Craig" (366, 372). Clark would offer such arguments not to show that theism or Christianity is true but to show that Christianity is not an unreasonable choice of belief:

> Perhaps demonstrating that Christian belief is at least as rational as its alternatives is the best that can be expected of apologetics.... I wish Reformed epistemology and/or theistic arguments could do more than

establish that belief in God is rationally permissible, but I'll settle for rational permissibility. That way I can know that my faith is not blind. I may be taking a leap in the dim, but it is not a leap in the dark (372, 373).

The more conservative wing of the Reformed apologetic tradition is troubled by this modest conclusion. An argument that concludes merely that belief in God is reasonable would seem to imply, or at least leave open the possibility, that nonbelief in God is also reasonable. Both Gordon Clark and Van Til adamantly rejected this idea. At the same time, they were more radical in their criticisms of the theistic arguments as traditionally formulated, as was Dooyeweerd.

Most of the modern philosophical criticisms of the traditional theistic proofs stem from the attacks on those proofs by David Hume and Immanuel Kant. In general, Reformed apologists endorse Hume's and Kant's criticisms, with Dooyeweerd being especially appreciative of Kant's critique of the Thomistic proofs, particularly cosmological arguments based on causality. He explains his rejection of such proofs as follows:

> Take for instance the notorious antinomy of natural theology with its no-
> tion of the "unconditioned ultimate causality of God" proceeding from
> the impossibility of a *regressus in infinitum* in the empirical causal rela-
> tions. This notion lands us in an insoluble contradiction with man's per-
> sonal accountability for his actions, since it makes God the ultimate term
> of a series of causes and effects which must be conceived as continuous
> and leaving no single hiatus in the causal chain.[26]

Thus the Thomistic cosmological argument creates an "antinomy between 'causality' and normative responsibility of man."[27] In other words, if we say there must be a God because the universe must have a cause, we have created an irresolvable contradiction. This is because the cosmological argument commits us to a causal determinism in which all events from the beginning of time to its consummation are causally determined, including our own personal decisions. Dooyeweerd agrees with Kant that if we reject the idea that our decisions are causally determined, then we cannot endorse the causal cosmological argument. If we are to avoid the antinomy identified by Kant, we must see God not as "the ultimate cause" but as "the Origin of causality in the temporal coherence and radical unity of all its modal aspects." In doing so we will have to acknowledge that this Origin is beyond our comprehension: "For human thought it is absolutely impossible to form a defined concept of causality in the supertemporal fulness of meaning or in the sense of God's creative act. Impossible, because human thought is bound within the limits of the temporal coherence of meaning."[28]

Gordon Clark's criticisms of the theistic proofs are fundamentally similar, though worded very differently. Clark's major contention is simple: "The cosmological argument for the existence of God, most fully developed by Thomas Aquinas, is a fallacy. It is not possible to begin with sensory experience and proceed by the formal laws of logic to God's existence as a conclusion."[29]

More specifically, Clark contends that the cosmological argument is circular in form and at best warrants the conclusion that the universe had a cause along the lines of Aristotle's "Unmoved Mover," not that the universe was created by a transcendent personal Creator.[30] He acknowledges the skeptic David Hume as the source of these criticisms, and suggests that Christians should thank Hume for disabusing them of an embarrassingly fallacious apologetic. Clark then explains Hume's three major criticisms of the teleological or design argument (which Clark subsumes under the cosmological argument). First, the argument is fallacious if it is pressed to prove that God is more than a Master Architect; from the design of the universe it cannot be validly inferred that God is infinite in wisdom or power. Second, Clark follows Hume in arguing from the causation and design of the parts of the universe that the whole universe must have been caused or designed. In other words, he contends that the cosmological and teleological arguments commit the logical fallacy of composition (assuming that what is true of the parts will be true of the whole). Third, he agrees with Hume that the design argument, to be fair and consistent, would have to take into account the great amount of evil and chaos in the world as we know it as well as the good and order. But then it would seem that we could not validly infer an all-good and all-powerful God from the world as it now stands.[31] Clark concludes that the argument "is worse than useless. In fact, Christians can be pleased at its failure, for if it were valid, it would prove a conclusion inconsistent with Christianity."[32]

Although Clark eschews the cosmological argument and other attempts to prove God's existence using reason, it seems that he does offer arguments in support of belief in God. Ronald Nash has argued that Clark in effect offers two types of justification for the affirmation of God's existence. One is an argument from coherence in which Clark seeks to demonstrate that only the position that all things depend on God provides metaphysical consistency. In this respect, the implications of the Christian worldview can be critically compared with those of contending worldviews, and the most promising first principle can be chosen. The second form of justification stems from the nature of truth. Here Nash understands Clark to be arguing that "whatever knowledge man may derive of God from nature is possible only because man possesses an a priori knowledge of God which enables man to recognize God in nature. Just as man can know the world because he comes to the world equipped with a set of innate ideas, so man can know God in nature because there is an a priori knowledge of God present in the soul. If man sees God in nature, it is because he already knows God in his mind."[33]

A similar pattern appears in Van Til's discussions of the question of arguments for God's existence. He frequently speaks positively of theistic proofs, but in his view the traditional formulations of these proofs are invalid and theologically compromised. "I do not reject 'the theistic proofs' but merely insist on formulating them in such a way as not to compromise the doctrines of Scripture."[34]

Properly formulated, the several theistic proofs really reduce to one, namely, the indirect, presuppositional proof. Van Til says explicitly that "the true method" of proving God's existence "must be the indirect method of reasoning by presupposition. . . . But this God cannot be proved to exist by any other method than the indirect one of presupposition."[35] Theistic proofs "have absolute probative force" if formulated on a Christian basis, assuming creation and providence, but they are "not demonstrable" in the sense that they do not proceed by "pure deduction of one conclusion after another from an original premise that is obvious. Such a notion of demonstration does not comport with the Christian system."[36] "To be constructed rightly, theistic proof ought to presuppose the ontological trinity and contend that, unless we may make this presupposition, all human predication is meaningless."[37] Van Til puts the matter most clearly in the following passage:

> The true theistic proofs undertake to show that the ideas of existence (ontological proof), of cause (cosmological proof), and purpose (teleological proof) are meaningless unless they presuppose the existence of God. . . . The theistic proofs therefore reduce to one proof, the proof which argues that unless *this* God, the God of the Bible, the ultimate being, the Creator, the controller of the universe be presupposed as the foundation of human experience, this experience operates in a void. This one proof is absolutely convincing.[38]

Van Til favors this way of formulating the theistic proof because it avoids the specter of apologetic arguments that conclude merely that God probably exists or that it is reasonable for people to believe in God. "True reasoning about God is such as stands upon God as upon the emplacement that alone gives meaning to any sort of human argument. . . . I hold that belief in God is not merely as reasonable as other belief, or even a little or infinitely more probably true than other belief; I hold rather that unless you believe in God you can logically believe in nothing else."[39]

Van Til generally makes a sharp distinction between natural revelation and natural theology. Natural revelation is God's activity of making himself known to us in nature and in the *sensus divinitatis* that we have within us; natural theology is man's attempt to reason his way to a knowledge of God apart from revelation (both natural *and* biblical).[40] In one passage he seems to speak of a legitimate natural theology that, "standing upon the basis of faith and enlightened by Scripture, finds God in nature."[41] But here he is clearly summarizing the teaching of Herman Bavinck, using Bavinck's own terminology.[42] Van Til stoutly rejected seeking to formulate an argument for God's existence that was not based on divine revelation, specifically in Scripture. He held that the proper ideal was enunciated by Bavinck, even if he did not always live up to that ideal, "that theology must be built upon the Scriptures only. There must be only one principle in theology."[43]

Ironically, though, as with Clark, some apologists have argued that Van Til really did formulate a kind of natural theology argument after all. The fact that it is a *transcendental* argument does not disqualify it as a natural theology argument as well. Gilbert Weaver summarizes Van Til's theistic argument in this way:

> There are only two alternatives: either the Sovereign God of Scripture is ultimate, whose will determines whatsoever comes to pass, or Chance is ultimate. (There can be no combination of these, for says Van Til, as Hume has shown, if any degree of chance is allowed it always becomes the final and ultimate principle of explanation.) If there is no such God, then Chance is ultimate and there is no meaning in anything: thoughts, words, events or what have you follow each other in a random, meaningless order. Speech fails, and one cannot even *discuss* God, let alone which view solves the most problems, or any other subject.[44]

Although Scripture is mentioned in passing here, the argument is not taken from Scripture itself and does not seem to depend on it in any clear way. It would seem to take the following form:

A. Either an absolute sovereign God is ultimate, or Chance is ultimate.

B. If Chance is ultimate, then there is no meaning.

C. But there is meaning.

D. Therefore, Chance is not ultimate.

E. Therefore, an absolute sovereign God is ultimate.

This would seem to qualify as a natural theology argument in the usual sense of the term. Bernard Ramm labeled Van Til's theistic proof "the epistemological argument," and David Diehl similarly referred to it as Van Til's "epistemic argument."[45] Diehl admits that Van Til explicitly denies that he is doing natural theology or offering an argument based on premises to which Christians and non-Christians are both agreed. "Nevertheless, for all practical purposes Van Til does admit the laws of logic as common ground, i.e. he uses the same laws of logic that non-Christian philosophers use; and he seeks to show by these laws that non-Christian metaphysical positions cannot explain human knowledge or cosmic rationality and that only Christian theism can."[46]

Diehl acknowledges that Van Til believes himself dependent on Scripture for his idea of God; Van Til did not arrive at his conception of God by rational argument. But this autobiographical fact does not alter the character of the argument Van Til offers to non-Christians as a rational ground for believing in his God. "But I contend that any appeal to our God-given human intelligence to show the evidence for God in the creation or in human experience in general is an exercise in natural theology, i.e. a theological exercise independent of Scripture, however dependent upon Scripture one's thinking may have been prior to this in gaining a proper theistic perspective."[47]

Van Til's transcendental argument can be related to the traditional theistic proofs in another way. William Lane Craig, in a response to an essay by John Frame presenting the presuppositional approach, contended that Frame's version of the argument was not transcendental at all but was, rather, "what medievals called *demonstratio quia*, proof that proceeds from consequence to ground."[48] That is, when Frame argues that God is the necessary presupposition of all meaning, he is reasoning from consequence (meaning) to ground (God), that which makes the consequence a reality. In his reply Frame suggested that all transcendental arguments can be viewed as reasoning from consequence to ground and that "many traditional types of arguments can be steps toward a transcendental conclusion." Whereas other presuppositionalists, such as Greg Bahnsen, sharply distinguish transcendental argument from all other types,[49] Frame does not.[50]

THE THEOLOGICAL PROBLEM OF EVIL

In general, classical apologists have focused on the deductive problem of evil (how can there be evil if God exists?) while evidentialists have focused on its inductive counterpart (how likely is it that God exists in light of how much evil there is?). Reformed apologists have not entirely ignored these dimensions of the problem—Plantinga, in fact, has given a great deal of attention to developing a response to the inductive problem of evil—but the dimension that concerns most Reformed apologists is what we call the **theological problem of evil**. This arises specifically within a Calvinist (and to some extent Augustinian) theological context, in which a strong doctrine of divine sovereignty in human history and in salvation is taught. We may pose the problem as follows: How can God be absolutely sovereign over all that happens (including sin) and yet not be held responsible or liable for sin? Or, to put the matter more pointedly: How can God be the author of all and not be the author of sin?

Actually, the question can be restated as a particular version of the deductive problem. (Indeed, Reformed apologists usually do state it in its deductive form, with the Calvinist notion of God as sovereign implicit.) In the usual deductive form the problem is stated as follows: How can God be all-knowing, all-powerful, and all-good, and yet evil exist? The Reformed version introduces the concept of sovereign control or foreordination into the problem, as follows: How can an all-good God foreordain everything that happens, and yet evil exist?

As mentioned above, Plantinga (like Thomas Reid) advocates a version of the free-will defense as the solution to the deductive problem, and in this respect is not typical of the Reformed apologetic approach. Clark and Van Til both held frankly and adamantly to a doctrine of divine determinism, understanding it to be necessitated by the biblical doctrines of the nature of God and of salvation. Their solution to the problem of evil is essentially that of Calvin himself, and more particularly that found in the Westminster Confession of Faith (1647), the standard Protestant confession recognized by conservative Presbyterians and the basis of instruction at Westminster Theological Seminary, where Van Til taught for half a century. The key text from the confession is the following (3.1): "God from all eternity did, by the most wise and holy counsel of his own will, freely and unchangeably ordain whatsoever comes to pass; yet so as thereby neither is God the author of sin, nor is violence offered to the will of the creatures, nor is the liberty or contingency of second causes taken away, but rather established."

A related portion (5.1–4) reads as follows:

I. God, the great Creator of all things, doth uphold, direct, dispose, and govern all creatures, actions, and things, from the greatest even to the least, by his most wise and holy providence, according to his infallible foreknowledge and the free and immutable counsel of his own will, to the praise of the glory of his wisdom, power, justice, goodness, and mercy.

II. Although in relation to the foreknowledge and decree of God, the first cause, all things come to pass immutably and infallibly, yet by the same providence he ordereth them to fall out, according to the nature of second causes, either necessarily, freely, or contingently.

III. God, in his ordinary providence, maketh use of means, yet is free to work without, above, and against them, at his pleasure.

IV. The almighty power, unsearchable wisdom, and infinite goodness of God so far manifest themselves in his providence that it extendeth itself even to the first fall, and all other sins of angels and men, and that not by a bare permission, but such as hath joined with it a most wise and powerful bounding, and otherwise ordering and governing of them, in a manifold dispensation, to his own holy ends; yet so as the sinfulness thereof proceedeth only from the creature, and not from God; who, being most holy and righteous, neither is nor can be the author or approver of sin.[51]

Clark and Van Til pick up and emphasize several elements of the confession's teaching on God's sovereignty and the problem of evil. First, both clearly affirm that God is the cause of everything. Van Til affirms the confession's statement that God ordains everything that happens (3.1) and comments, "This is what I mean when I say that God is the ultimate cause back of all things."[52] Clark is startlingly clear that this includes sin: "Let it be unequivocally said that this view certainly makes God the cause of sin. God is the sole ultimate cause of everything. There is absolutely nothing independent of him."[53]

Second, both apologists explain God's causal relation to the universe as the *ultimate* cause. In qualifying their use of the term *cause* they are following the confession, which distinguishes between God as the "first cause" and other, "second causes." Likewise, Van Til notes, Calvin had distinguished between "*remote* and *proximate* causes," teaching that God was the remote cause of everything but not the proximate cause.[54]

Third, this distinction between God as the ultimate or first cause and other causes as secondary or proximate allows Clark and Van Til to deny that God is "the author of sin" (as the confession puts it, 3.1) while affirming that God is the ultimate cause of sin. That is, God is not regarded as actually committing the sin, doing the sin, or in any way culpable for the sin, because he is not the proximate or immediate, direct cause of the sin. This explanation is what John Frame calls the "indirect cause" defense against the problem of evil. It is somewhat surprising to find Frame, a conservative Presbyterian and a Van Tilian, criticizing this explanation as both unbiblical and inadequate.[55] His main objection, though, is the usual concern about this theory: it is difficult to understand how standing back in the causal chain from an act of sin, but ultimately and intentionally causing it to come about, would relieve the causal agent (in this case, God) from responsibility and even culpability for the sin.

Fourth, both Van Til and Clark can characterize their understanding of divine sovereignty as a form of determinism. Clark criticizes Calvinists who are squeamish about describing their position as such: "Some Calvinists prefer to avoid the word *determinism*. For some reason it seems to them to carry unpleasant connotations. However, the Bible speaks not only of predestination, usually with reference to eternal life, but it also speaks of the foreordination or predetermination of evil acts. Therefore, deliberate avoidance of the word *determinism* would seem to be less than forthright."[56]

It seems reasonable to conclude that Clark embraces a strong doctrine of causal determinism in which God is the first or ultimate cause. Van Til's position is similar but somewhat nuanced by comparison. He is surprised that J. Oliver Buswell, a Calvinist, would criticize theological determinism. Van Til does complain, though, that "in opposing determinism you [Buswell] do not carefully distinguish between fatalism and Calvinism."[57] Elsewhere Van Til makes it clear that he rejects a physical, causal determinism. "The Calvinist notion of divine sovereignty has nothing to do with the philosopher's notion of physical, causal determinism. I have developed at length in other places the covenantal, exhaustively personalist view of providence which is clearly part of Calvin's thought."[58]

Clark and Van Til, then, follow both Calvin and the Westminster Confession in arguing that the theological problem of evil cannot be resolved by denying God's absolute sovereignty as the ultimate cause of all that exists and all that happens. At the same time, though, they insist that the problem has a rational solution. Responsibility for sin devolves on the one who actually commits the sin—the person who is its immediate, direct, or proximate cause. God cannot be held culpable or liable for the sins committed by his creatures.

Behind the indirect-cause defense as employed by these Reformed apologists is the conviction that apart from God, *nothing* could have meaning. Either God or Chance is ultimate. If sin did not arise by God's foreordained plan, then it arose by Chance. Clark and Van Til thus argue that anything less than a consistent theological determinism dethrones God as the ultimate source of meaning. Reformed apologists, and Reformed Christians in general, do not find this position troubling, but encouraging. That God is the ultimate cause of all that happens, including sin, means that even the worst that men can do is part of a rational, morally praiseworthy purpose and plan of God. It means, to put it in biblical language, that what sinful people mean for evil, God means for good (Genesis 50:20), and that indeed God can and does work all things together for the good of those who love him (Romans 8:28).

MIRACLES AS REVEALED BY GOD

In classical apologetics, once it is established that God exists and *could* do miracles, the historical evidence in the Bible may be fairly considered to determine whether God *did* in fact do miracles. In evidentialism, the evidence that miracles have occurred is potent and may be part of (even the primary part of) a case for the existence of the God of the Bible.

Reformed apologists object to both approaches. They do agree that one must be convinced that God exists in order to take the biblical miracles seriously, but they reject the idea of using an inductive method to determine whether the biblical miracles have occurred. As we saw in the previous chapter, they argue that biblical revelation provides the only rational context in which knowledge of history is even possible. For Clark, we need revelation to know what God has done in history for us because the empirical study of history cannot yield true knowledge. For Van Til, we need revelation in order to have the proper worldview perspective from which to study history. Both apologists agree that since miracles are special acts of God in which he reveals himself and his purposes, one cannot really accept the biblical miracles for what they are without accepting the revelation of which they are an integral part.

According to Van Til, the real, underlying reason non-Christians object to the biblical miracles is that they imply the existence of a God who is sovereign over all natural law and all fact—and therefore sovereign over *them*. The biblical miracles also presuppose that something is wrong with the human condition (sin) that God is acting to correct in an extraordinary way (redemption). They are thus an affront to non-Christians. "We would have to interpret the idea of scientific 'law' as being subservient to that of the biblical account of sin and redemption controlled by the fiat of the sovereign God. This cannot be, and we will not have it!"[59]

One of David Hume's main objections to the argument from miracles was that it depends on *reports* of miracles, not on direct personal observation or experience of miracles. Hume argued that if all we have are persons reporting that they witnessed a miracle, it is always more reasonable to doubt the truthfulness or reliability of the persons reporting the alleged miracle than to believe that a miracle actually occurred. Reformed apologists typically agree that a report of a miracle must be viewed very differently from a personal experience of a miracle. For example, to evidentialist John Warwick Montgomery's claim that we should base our apologetic on miracles because the apostles did, Bahnsen replies that "Christian apologists are not in the same position as Christ or the apostles with respect to presenting empirical evidence. Their hearers were presented with miracles, while our hearers are presented with reports of miracles. This important difference has tremendous epistemological implications for the way in which a person defends, or even can defend, the person and claims of Christ."[60]

Reformed apologists also criticize the traditional historical argument for the resurrection of Jesus, and typically offer at least two related criticisms. First, they argue that the historical argument, insofar as it seeks to prove the Resurrection without presupposing the truth of Christianity, is fallacious. For example, no matter how well preserved the biblical text is or how soon it was written after the events it reports, the skeptic is only being consistent in rejecting its reliability when it reports miracles such as Jesus' resurrection. Bahnsen also argues that unbelievers would be inconsistent with their principles if they were not to view the resurrection of Jesus as highly improbable. "The traditional apologist appeals to 'probability,' yet from his own experience the unbeliever knows how extremely improbable a resurrection is."[61]

Second, Reformed apologists argue that the skeptic can always agree that Jesus may have risen from the dead but then suggest that it doesn't prove that he is God incarnate. In one of his most famous illustrations, Van Til presented a dialogue in which Mr. Grey, a Christian using a traditional apologetic, sought to convince Mr. Black, a non-Christian, that Jesus rose from the dead. Mr. Grey's strategy was to try to convince Mr. Black of the truth of the Resurrection as an historical fact separate from its theological significance. Here is Mr. Black's reply: "To tell you the truth, I have accepted the resurrection as a fact now for some time. The evidence for it is overwhelming. This is a strange universe. All kinds of 'miracles' happen in it. The universe is 'open.' So why should there not be some resurrections here and there? The resurrection of Jesus would be a fine item for Ripley's *Believe It or Not*. Why not send it in?"[62]

Van Til offers an explanation:

> For Mr. Black, history is something that floats on an infinitely extended and bottomless ocean of Chance. Therefore he can say that anything may happen. Who knows but that the death and resurrection of Jesus as the Son of God might issue from this womb of Chance? . . . Now the Evangelical does not challenge this underlying philosophy of Chance as it controls the unbeliever's conception of history. He is so anxious to have the unbeliever accept the possibility of God's existence and the *fact* of the resurrection of Christ that, if necessary, he will exchange his own philosophy of fact for that of the unbeliever. Anxious to be genuinely "empirical" like the unbeliever, he will throw all the facts of Christianity into the bottomless pit of Chance. Or, rather, he will throw all these facts at the unbeliever, and the unbeliever throws them over his back into the bottomless pit of Chance.[63]

The only way out of this apologetic nightmare, according to Van Til, is to challenge the unbeliever's philosophy of fact and to present the Resurrection, along with all other facts, as meaningful only in the context of Christian theism. "But I would not talk endlessly about facts and more facts without ever challenging the non-believer's philosophy of fact. A really fruitful historical apologetic argues that every fact is and must be such as proves the truth of the Christian theistic position."[64]

JESUS: THE SELF-ATTESTING CHRIST OF SCRIPTURE

In the 1971 volume *Jerusalem and Athens*, a collection of essays examining Van Til's philosophy and apologetic, Van Til was invited to present his own position, which he called "My Credo."[65] This essay is rightly regarded as his clearest statement of his apologetic approach. The thrust of the essay is that Christ should be viewed and honored as *self-attesting*. Thus he opens with this statement: "The self-attesting Christ of Scripture has always been my starting-point for everything

I have said" (3). He explains, "Jesus asks me to do what he asked the Pharisees to do, namely, read the Scriptures in light of this testimony about himself" (4). Christ's own word about himself, his self-attestation, is the basis on which we are to believe in him.

Van Til then explains the place of Scripture in his view of Christ as self-attesting. For him the Bible is, in essence, "a letter" from Christ himself, written through helpers who "wrote what he wanted me to know" (5). As a Protestant, Van Til is convinced that the Bible, as Christ's letter to us, must also be viewed as self-attesting. The problem with Roman Catholic and non-Reformed evangelical theologies is that to varying degrees (Catholics more, evangelicals less) they compromise this self-attesting authority of Christ speaking in Scripture. None of them "have a view of Scripture such that the Lord Christ speaks to man with absolute authority. The self-attesting Christ of Scripture is not absolutely central to these theologies. Just so, he will not be central in any apologetic form to defend them" (10).

Even Reformed theologians, Van Til found, typically defended the self-attesting Christ "with a method which denied precisely that point!" (10). He therefore sought to develop "a Christ-centered apologetic" that would focus "on the self-attesting Christ of Scripture" (10, 11), and found its basis in Calvin's understanding of Christ as *autotheos*, "God himself" (14). This is a particularly emphatic way of designating Christ as God that eliminates any vestiges of subordinationism in the Trinity. That Christ is *autotheos* implies that Christ's own identification of himself is self-authenticating.

> If Christ is who he says he is, then all speculation is excluded, for God can swear only by himself. To find out what man is and who God is, one can only go to Scripture. Faith in the self-attesting Christ of the Scriptures is the beginning, not the conclusion of wisdom! It was, therefore, not until the fully developed trinitarian theology of Calvin, which says that Christ is authoritative because *autotheos*, that there was therewith developed a truly Christian methodology of theology and of apologetics. (15)

Given this understanding of Christ as self-attesting, Van Til resolutely rejects any method of apologetics that would seek to base the truth about Christ on reasons or proofs that could be recognized as such by the non-Christian on his own terms. "Rather the Christian offers the self-attesting Christ to the world as the only foundation upon which a man must stand in order to give any 'reasons' for anything at all" (18).

The first plank of Van Til's proposal "for a consistently Christian methodology of apologetics," then, is "that we use the same principle in apologetics that we use in theology: the self-attesting, self-explanatory Christ of Scripture" (21).

For Further Study

Clark, Gordon H. *Religion, Reason and Revelation*. Nutley, N.J.: Craig Press, 1961; 2nd ed. Jefferson, Md.: Trinity Foundation, 1986. Notable for Clark's treatment of the relationship of faith and reason, his critique of the cosmological argument, and his argument for a deterministic solution to the problem of evil.

Plantinga, Alvin, and Nicholas Wolterstorff, eds. *Faith and Rationality: Reason and Belief in God*. Notre Dame, Ind.: University of Notre Dame Press, 1983. Includes Plantinga's landmark essay "Reason and Belief in God," in which he discusses theistic arguments, the problem of evil, and the nature of rationality.

Westminster Theological Journal 57, no. 1 (fall 1995). Special issue marking the centennial of Van Til's birth with a number of excellent, relevant articles by Bahnsen, Frame, and other advocates of Van Til's apologetic.

Chapter 15

Apologetics and the Authority of Revelation

In this concluding chapter on Reformed apologetics, we will summarize this model or paradigm for apologetics, illustrate its use in practical apologetic encounters, and then consider its major strengths and weaknesses. Because of the diversity of methods within this tradition, we will focus on Gordon Clark and Cornelius Van Til, with special emphasis on Van Til.

THE REFORMED APOLOGETICS MODEL

As explained in chapter 3, we are summarizing each model of apologetics under two headings (metapologetics and apologetics) and six specific questions under each heading. Here we apply this analysis to the Reformed model.

Metapologetic Questions

Metapologetic questions deal with the relation of apologetics to other forms of human knowledge. In chapter 13 we considered the approach taken in Reformed apologetics to answering questions about knowledge in general, theology, philosophy, science, history, and experience. Here we summarize our findings in that chapter.

1. On what basis do we claim that Christianity is the truth?

Classical apologists seek to demonstrate the truth of Christianity by establishing the theistic worldview using primarily deductive reasoning, and then to show that Christianity is the most coherent or well-supported theistic religion. Evidentialists seek to build a cumulative case for Christianity through historical and scientific evidences, using arguments that are primarily inductive in form. Reformed apologists consider both approaches flawed.

Gordon Clark agrees with classical apologists in making deduction primary—in fact, he regards it as the only proper form of reasoning—but he faults them for trying to infer God's existence and nature from the empirical facts of nature and history. According to Clark, for deduction to produce meaningful results, one must proceed from an axiom that is beyond proof or argument and from which a coherent view of reality and morality can be sustained. Clark finds only one such axiom to be available—that Scripture is God's word.

Van Til considers deductivism an inadequate philosophy of logic but agrees that apologetics cannot rest on an inductive examination of facts either. His solution is to show through transcendental reasoning the foundation on which both deduction and induction rest; only Christian theism provides this foundation, or presupposition. Human reasoning and ethical judgments presuppose a God who is supremely rational and good and who made human beings in his image. The fact that people in their natural state do not recognize this image is proof that it has been darkened by sin. If we are to have our rational and moral faculties restored, we need a divine work of regeneration, that is, we need what Christ offers us in his work of redemption. Thus knowledge, reason, and ethics, if they are to be rationally grounded, presuppose the whole of Christian theism.

Reformed apologists do not expect non-Christians to be converted as a direct result of this argument. Only regeneration, a work of the Holy Spirit, can convert a person. Indeed, only regeneration can enable a person to acknowledge the truth that the apologist is presenting.

For many classical apologists, at least some foundational truths of the Christian faith, such as the existence of God, may be regarded as "provable" in a fairly strict sense, approaching logical or rational certainty. In evidentialism the truths of Christianity may be "proved" only in the same sense that other factual claims can be proved—with some degree of probability, stopping short of rational certainty. Reformed apologetics seeks to prove Christianity as well, but in a different way. Essentially, Reformed apologists argue *from the impossibility of the contrary*—that unless Christianity is true, there is no way to prove anything. In this approach, as Van Til emphasizes, everything proves Christianity true, and the proof is absolute and irrefutable.

Contemporary Reformed apologists agree with their classical and evidentialist counterparts that postmodernism is an unacceptable and irrational approach to knowledge. Unfortunately, as Reformed apologists see things, traditional apologists tend to assume a modernist philosophy as the stance from which to refute postmodernism. Thus classical apologists treat postmodernism as the abandonment of the belief in absolute truth (whatever one happens to think that it is!) for the belief in the relativity of all beliefs. Evidentialists criticize postmodernism on the grounds that it flies in the face of the facts, as if facts had meaning apart from the philosophical framework in which they are viewed. Reformed apologists suggest that postmodernism should be viewed as simply the current form of unbelieving philosophy, with the pendulum having swung from an unbelieving rationalism (modernism) to an unbelieving irrationalism (postmodernism).

2. What is the relationship between apologetics and theology?

Reformed apologists agree with evidentialists, over against classical apologists, that apologetics and theology deal with the same subject matter and should use essentially the same method. However, they disagree with the inductive, empirical method advocated by evidentialists. According to Reformed apologists, in a consistently Reformed method the truth of Scripture should be presupposed in both theology and apologetics, and specific truths deduced from the statements or propositions given in Scripture. Van Til qualifies this dogmatic method of apologetics, though, by introducing the transcendental argument. In brief, this argument seeks to show that what has been deduced from Scripture must be true if anything we claim to know other than what is deduced directly from Scripture is to be intelligible. By way of contrast, Clark's thoroughgoing deductivism leads to the conclusion that human beings really cannot know anything that is not in Scripture or deducible from Scripture.

3. Should apologetics engage in a philosophical defense of the Christian faith?

Classical apologists seek to articulate Christian theism using methods and presuppositions taken from non-Christian philosophy (say, that of Plato or Aristotle) as a way of commending Christianity to non-Christians on their own terms. They believe that arguments for theism and other elements of the Christian faith can be developed using philosophy. Evidentialists prefer to see philosophy essentially as a critical tool for clarifying concepts and presuppositions and for analyzing the methods used in science and other disciplines, including theology.

Reformed apologists, on the other hand, call for the development of a distinctively Christian philosophy that is based on methods and presuppositions taken from Scripture. This philosophy will essentially present the same truths as Christian theology but in different terminology.

4. Can science be used to defend the Christian faith?

Whereas classical apologists cautiously relate the Christian view of creation and nature to the findings of science and evidentialists make such comparisons enthusiastically, Reformed apologists are generally highly critical of modern science. Rather than seeing the resolution of any potential conflict between science and theology in philosophical scrutiny (classical apologetics) or further study of the facts (evidentialism), Reformed apologists see an irresolvable conflict between believing science and unbelieving science. They argue that the non-Christian proceeds from a standpoint of faith in the ultimacy of chance, whereas the Christian proceeds from a standpoint of faith in the ultimacy of God.

This view of science has led most Reformed apologists to endorse the young-earth form of creationism. Clark's denigration of all inductive reasoning as fallacious leads him to hold to a nonrealist view of science, specifically operationalism, which views science as descriptive of operations in the laboratory, not of nature itself. Some apologists who follow Van Til also draw on the work of nonrealists, notably that of Thomas Kuhn, to show that scientific theories presuppose an interpretive community working from an agreed set of assumptions. However, these Van Tilian apologists in the end accept a heavily qualified realism.

5. Can the Christian faith be supported by historical inquiry?

Reformed apologists are critical of inductive historical arguments in apologetics, especially as practiced in evidentialism. Clark rejects induction outright. Van Til does not, but he does criticize apologetic arguments that use inductive reasoning to defend the biblical truth claims. Both apologists criticize such arguments because their conclusion is that Christianity, or some part of Christianity, is probably true. Van Til insists that apologetic argument should reason transcendentally that unless the facts are what God in Scripture says they are, there is no rational ground for finding any meaning or significance in facts at all.

6. How is our knowledge of Christian truth related to our experience?

Classical apologists appeal to the near universality of religious belief and the desire for religious experience as proof that there is a transcendent source of personal meaning that all human beings need. Evidentialists appeal to the objective facts of history as the basis on which non-Christians should be encouraged to pursue the experience of a relationship with Christ; testimonies of changed lives are offered as supplemental evidence that such experiences are real. Reformed apologists object to both approaches because they treat Christianity as one of many forms of religious experience (even if the only *true* form). They argue that the proper method is to appeal to the image of God that is in all people, and to point out its obscurity within the non-Christian, as proof of the need of regeneration. Rather than seeking proof of God in "religious" experiences, Van Til argues that we should contend that attributing meaning to any and every experience presupposes the existence of God.

Apologetic Questions

Apologetic questions deal with issues commonly raised by non-Christians. In chapter 14 we considered the approach taken by Reformed apologists to answering questions about the Bible, Christianity and other beliefs, the existence of God, the problem of evil, the credibility of miracles, and the claims of Jesus Christ. Here we summarize our findings in that chapter.

1. Why should we believe in the Bible?

In both classical and evidentialist apologetics, the apologetic argument first establishes the existence of God and his revelation in the crucified and risen Jesus Christ, and culminates in the inspiration of the Bible. Reformed apologists (specifically presuppositionalists) turn the argument around: the Bible should be believed as the starting point for all knowledge. For Clark this is because knowledge requires an axiomatic starting point, and the Bible provides one. For Van Til the Bible should be the starting point in a transcendental sense. That is, the apologist should argue that unless the God who speaks in Scripture is real, human knowledge is without an intelligible basis.

2. Don't all religions lead to God?

Classical apologists argue that religious pluralism is irrational because the different religions have different worldviews and different conceptions of God. Evidentialists argue that religious pluralism does not consider the fact that only Christianity offers verifiable factual evidence of God taking the initiative to make himself known to us. Reformed apologists generally consider these points to be basically correct but inadequate (and they would warn against inviting non-Christians to verify these claims on their own terms).

They respond to religious pluralism with two basic points. First, it is really a nonexistent position; the religious pluralist is actually assuming an exclusivist stance based on some religious perspective, stated or unstated. Second, Reformed apologists such as Clark and Van Til argue that only Christian theism presents a worldview or a transcendent point of reference in terms of which knowledge and ethics are possible or intelligible. Non-Christian religions make man or chance ultimate; Christianity alone makes God truly ultimate and alone presents the means (in Christ's redemptive work) by which sinful man can come to recognize and honor God as the absolute personal Creator.

3. How do we know that God exists?

Classical apologists advocate one or more of the theistic arguments, which prove the existence of a God. Evidentialists typically rework these arguments into fact-based, evidentiary forms. Reformed apologists uniformly contend that these arguments are unnecessary and that belief in God can be (or even should be) a properly basic belief. They also usually argue that the theistic proofs in both their deductive and inductive forms are logically flawed. For Clark this means that theistic proofs such as the cosmological argument should simply be abandoned. Van Til, on the other hand, advocates reworking them into one proof that is transcendental, rather than deductive or inductive, in form. That proof is that unless God is presupposed, there is no accounting for the world, its order, or moral standards.

4. If God does exist, why does he permit evil?

Classical apologists focus on the deductive problem of evil: How can God be all-powerful, all-knowing, and all-loving, yet evil exist? Their usual answer is that God permits evil because of the greater good resulting from creating beings with free will. Evidentialists characteristically deal with the inductive problem of evil: Does the great amount of evil count as significant evidence against God's existence? They argue in effect that the positive evidence for God's existence more than counterbalances the negative evidence of evil.

Reformed apologists generally object to the free-will defense because it conflicts with the biblical view of God's sovereignty. (Plantinga is a notable exception.) They also take exception to the evidentialist approach of weighing evidence for and against God's existence: on a Reformed view of things, *everything* in God's world must count as evidence for God's existence. The reality of God must be presupposed even to make the judgment that something is evil.

Conservative Reformed apologists such as Clark and Van Til stoutly defend the Calvinist teaching that God foreordains everything that happens. They argue that God is not liable for sin because, although he is the ultimate cause of everything, he is not the direct or proximate cause of sin. Clark unabashedly describes his position as determinism. Van Til adheres to a form of theological determinism but rejects physical determinism, emphasizing that the ultimate cause is the transcendent person of God.

5. Aren't the miracles of the Bible spiritual myths or legends and not literal fact?

To the question of whether miracles are myths or facts, the classical apologist answers: look at the worldview of which those miracles are a part. The evidentialist answers simply, look at the evidence. The Reformed apologist essentially sides with the classical apologist here, but takes the point one step further: look at the *whole* worldview of which the miracles are a part. Theism in the abstract does not prove that miracles have occurred. The biblical miracles are to be believed because they are part of God's self-revelation to us. Reformed apologists criticize the evidentialist argument for the resurrection of Jesus for failing to challenge the skeptic's philosophy of fact and evidence. Even if a non-Christian were convinced that Jesus rose from the dead, Reformed apologists suggest, he could always dismiss it as an unusual chance event.

6. Why should I believe in Jesus?

Van Til's answer to this question is disarmingly simple: because Jesus is God. To put it more fully, since Jesus is God, what he says about himself in Scripture (which is Christ's own word to us) carries its own authority and is self-validating. There is no higher standard by which the self-identification of God can be made. The foundation of our apologetic, then, should be the self-attesting Christ of Scripture.

The table on the following page presents an overview of the Reformed model of apologetics with these twelve questions in mind.

REFORMED APOLOGETICS ILLUSTRATED

In this, the third of four dialogues we will present in this book, a Christian named Cal becomes involved in a discussion with Sarah and Murali while stranded at an airport during a snowstorm. Cal teaches world history at a Christian high school and has done a lot of reading in Reformed theology, and is especially interested in biblical ethics. He is a staunch Calvinist and an advocate of the Reformed apologetic of Cornelius Van Til. When Cal sits down next to Sarah and Murali, they are already bemoaning their flight delay.[1]

Issue		Position
Metapologetics	**KNOWLEDGE**	Coherence with revelation is the test of truth Postmodernism is irrationalist form of modernism Spirit's witness is the origin of faith
	THEOLOGY	Apologetics and theology both based on Scripture Apologetics presupposes the truth of theology
	PHILOSOPHY	Apologetics confronts unbelieving philosophy Christians should develop a Christian philosophy
	SCIENCE	Rejects theories that are viewed as unbiblical Believers and unbelievers view facts differently Typically young-earth creationism
	HISTORY	Objective truth about history given in Scripture Right view of history based on revelation
	EXPERIENCE	God's image in man is the point of contact Test all experiences by Scripture
Apologetics	**SCRIPTURE**	Scripture the foundation of apologetics Begin with self-attesting Scripture Scripture gives the only coherent worldview
	RELIGIONS	Religious pluralism is self-refuting Christianity presents uniquely absolute God
	GOD	Traditional theistic proofs are rejected Transcendental or epistemic argument for God
	EVIL	Theological problem of evil: Did God cause sin? Evil can be deemed such only if God exists
	MIRACLES	Miracles are part of Christian theistic worldview Miracles are revealed in God's self-attesting Word
	JESUS	Jesus is the self-attesting Christ of Scripture Jesus should be believed because he is God

Sarah: I can't believe we're stuck here. If this storm doesn't lift soon, I'm not going to get home in time for Christmas.

Murali: Things like this happen. It can't be helped.

Sarah: My mother always told me that everything happens for a reason. Well, I'd like to know what the reason is for this.

Murali: In the religion of my people, we are also taught that everything happens for a reason, but we are not able to see it.

Sarah: Do you still believe that?

Murali: I don't know. I'd like to believe it, but it is hard sometimes.

Sarah: Well, I can't believe it anymore. There are too many terrible things that happen in this world for no good reason.

Cal: Excuse me, but is it all right if I join in the discussion? My name is Cal, and I would greatly enjoy passing the time with you.

Murali: Certainly. My name is Murali, and this is Sarah.

Cal: Glad to meet both of you. I heard what you were talking about, and I do believe that everything happens for a reason.

Sarah: Really? So, what's the reason for our flight delay?

Cal: Well, of course, the immediate reason is that the airport officials have made the decision, with which I of course agree, not to allow any planes to take off during this snowstorm.

Sarah: We all understand that. But I think what Murali was saying was that there was some kind of cosmic reason for everything—some kind of overall purpose that explains why bad things like this happen. Do you think there's any such reason for our flight delay?

Cal: I'm sure there is.

Sarah: Well, what is it?

Cal: I don't know what the specific reason is for this particular situation. There may be many things going on as a result of this flight delay that we know nothing about that will result in some good. But I know that good will be accomplished because of it. If we knew everything that was happening right now, and everything that was going to happen as a result of this flight delay, we would be able to see that great good was going to be the end result.

Murali: As I said, I would like to believe this very much. But we do not know everything that is happening or that will happen. How can we know that everything will work out for good?

Cal: Because there is Someone who does know everything that is happening and that will happen, and he is the one who has a plan to work everything out for good.

Sarah: Don't tell me, let me guess—God, right?

Cal: Right!

Sarah: Well, I personally have a hard time believing in God.

Cal: That's quite understandable. In fact, in a sense that's why this plane delay has happened.

Sarah: What? Are you saying God is punishing me because I don't believe in him?

Cal: That's not exactly my point. My point is that all of the difficult, painful, and bad things that happen to us happen because all of us—the entire human race—have failed to believe in God, to honor him as our Creator and King. And God has ordained that things like this happen in part as a way of bringing to our attention the fact that we need to be restored to a right relationship with him.

Murali: In the Hindu religion in which I was raised, we are taught that difficult things happen to us because of the law of karma. We are taught that such things help us on our way toward spiritual perfection in the cycle of reincarnation.

Cal: It sounds like you don't believe that anymore.

Murali: I am unsure. Again, I would like to believe that there is some reason for the things that happen. I respect your right to your religious opinion, as I respect the religion of my family and my country. But I do not think anyone's opinion is better than anyone else's.

Cal: I agree that none of us has the right to claim that our own religious opinion is better than anyone else's. However, what I have been telling you is not my opinion. It is what God himself says about the matter in the Bible.

Murali: I respect the Bible, and I know that it comforts many people. I have no problem with you saying that you have found your answer there. I'm sure your answer is true for you. But I cannot agree that any one religion is the truth. I believe that there are many valid religions and all of them express truth about God as they understand it.

Cal: But in expressing that opinion, Murali, you are actually saying that my view is *wrong*.

Murali: How can that be? I have just said that I think your view is one of many truths.

Cal: But that's just the problem. Basic to my answer to the problem of evil is the belief that there is only one truth, because there is only one true God. What I am trying to tell you is that he has determined what is true and false and what is right and wrong, and that if it's not his answer, then it's the wrong answer. So if you say that my answer is not the *only* right answer, you're actually saying that it is the wrong answer.

Murali: But this is so intolerant, for you to claim that only your answer is God's answer.

Cal: Actually, that's not what I said. What I said is that *God's* answer is the one that we should accept as the only true answer. My answer is just my best attempt to explain God's answer. I don't see how it is intolerant for me to say that we should accept God's explanation for things.

Sarah: But you're assuming that God exists.

Cal: You're exactly right. I am assuming or presupposing that God exists.

Sarah: But isn't it unreasonable just to assume that God exists? I don't think it's reasonable to believe in God without proof.

Cal: Actually, I do have proof. I have it on the highest authority that God exists. You see, God has spoken. He has revealed himself in Scripture, which is God's word.

Sarah: So you believe in God because you believe in the Bible, but you believe in the Bible because it's God's word. That's a textbook case of circular reasoning. My philosophy professor told me that there were people that argued like this, but you're the first person I've met who did.

Cal: I understand your objection, but in the nature of the case I don't think circular reasoning can be avoided here. Let me ask you something. What is my name?

Sarah: Cal. Why?

Cal: How do you know?

Sarah: You told us that was your name.

Cal: Exactly. And you believed me, correct?

Sarah: Well, sure. Why not? I mean, you would know, wouldn't you?

Cal: Absolutely. And God knows who he is, too.

Murali: I'm afraid I don't follow.

Cal: Here's what I'm saying. If I tell you my name, you will normally accept what I say without question unless you have some reason to be suspicious. If you did have reason to question my identity, you could try to find confirmation from some higher authority. For example, you could ask to see my driver's license to see if the state concurs with my self-identification. But in the case of God, there is no higher authority one can consult to confirm that he is speaking. If God—the true God—speaks, his word will be self-attesting or self-validating. And we have such a self-attesting word from God in Scripture.

Murali: But what makes your scripture self-attesting? After all, there are many religions with many scriptures. Why cannot God be speaking through them, too?

Cal: Actually, most of the world's religions do not have a scripture that even professes to be the word of the self-attesting God. They may have scriptures that speak about various gods, but the scriptures do not even claim to be the word of an absolute, personal, self-attesting God. None of the Eastern religions have such scriptures, for example.

Sarah: What about Islam? The Muslims have the Qur'an, and it claims to be dictated by God to Muhammad.

Cal: Islam is about the only other religion that even makes a similar claim for its scripture. But in fact, historically Islam is a derivative religion that depends on what Muhammad took from the Jews and Christians he encountered in Arabia. Islam officially claims that its god is the same God as the God of the Bible. The question is whether God actually spoke through Muhammad. Since the Qur'an contradicts the Bible on several crucial points, its claim to be God's word must be rejected.

Sarah: But why should we accept your claim that the Bible is God's word? Why can't we simply dismiss that as your opinion? Can't you offer us some kind of proof?

Cal: I can, but it may not be the kind of proof you want. The proof that the Bible is God's word is that if you don't accept what it says as the truth, you will not be able to give an account of anything you think you know to be true. In fact, every reason you can possibly give against belief in the Bible in one way or another really assumes the truth of what it says.

Sarah: Huh? That doesn't make any sense. Can you explain that?

Cal: Let me try. Why don't you tell me why you don't believe in the God of the Bible.

Sarah: That's easy; it's just what we were talking about before. The God of the Bible is supposed to have created everything, which means he created evil, or at least created the creatures that became evil. He is supposed to be all-powerful, which would mean that he could stop evil anytime he wants to. He is supposed to be all-loving, which would mean that he'd want to stop evil right away, maybe even before it got started. But evil has been around for a long time, and God hasn't done anything to stop it. So it seems that either God doesn't exist at all, or that if he does exist he either isn't all-powerful or he isn't all-loving. Which is it?

Cal: Actually, in a kind of backwards way your argument proves that the God of the Bible must exist.

Sarah: How can that be?

Cal: Well, the argument as you have stated it assumes that there is such a thing as evil. But how do you determine what is evil and what is not? Calling things "evil" assumes that there is a standard of good that transcends the world or the human race. That standard of good is God. So your argument against God's existence is self-contradictory, because you're saying that there cannot be a Being who is the standard of goodness because there are departures from that standard of goodness in the world.

Sarah: Why do we have to believe in a God to recognize something as evil? Are you saying that atheists or agnostics can't tell right from wrong? That's pretty insulting.

Cal: No, actually I'm saying the opposite. I'm saying that you are quite correct in seeing evil in the world. But that evil wouldn't be *evil* if there were no God. What we call evil would just be stuff that happens that we don't like, or at least that some of us don't like. Atheists and agnostics can and do recognize much evil for what it is. They are right to regard ignorance, superstition, murder, child abuse, and the like as evils. Atheists are like people who can tell right away when a fine painting has been spoiled by vandalism, but who don't believe that an artist produced the painting. What I am saying is that if there is no God, then these things aren't really evils; they're just things we don't like.

Murali: You have raised some interesting points. But I see now that the snowstorm is lifting and they are getting ready for us to board our plane.

Sarah: We still don't have a good reason why God would want our flight to be delayed.

Cal: I don't know that I agree. Perhaps one of the many good things God was doing was setting things up so that we would have this discussion. Murali, do you have a copy of the Bible?

Murali: Actually, no, I don't think I do.

Cal: If you give me your address, I'd be happy to send one to you at no cost or obligation. After all, you can't hear God speaking in Scripture if you never read it.

Murali: That is most kind of you. I would be happy to receive a Bible.

Sarah: I've already got one—two, actually.

Cal: I hope that you will read it again and consider what we've talked about. Thanks for letting me horn in on your discussion.

NOTABLE STRENGTHS OF REFORMED APOLOGETICS

Reformed apologetics is really the newest of the four approaches discussed in this book, and it is easily the most controversial and misunderstood. But even most of its harshest critics have recognized some of its strengths, which are considerable. We will highlight just a few of them.

Links Apologetics and Theology

Reformed apologists have made a powerful case for recognizing that apologetics inevitably presupposes theology. That is, the apologist has a specific understanding of Christian theology that informs his method as well as the substance of his defense of the Christian faith.

Consider first the substance of apologetic argument. One's specific theological convictions will unavoidably affect the substance of one's answer to the perennial apologetic issue of the problem of evil. If one does not believe in free will, then clearly one cannot (or at least should not!) use the free-will defense as part of one's theodicy.

Theological perspectives also affect apologetic method. If one believes that all human beings have an inner sense of divinity by which they really know that God exists, whatever they may tell themselves or others, that will affect how one argues for God's existence. For example, the apologist who has this view of the unregenerate is not likely to agree to shoulder the burden of proof on the question of God's existence.

Reformed apologists have demonstrated that it is impossible to present a generic apologetic for "mere Christianity" that does not assume a specific theological stance. C. S. Lewis (whose primary apologetic work bore the title *Mere Christianity*) clearly wrote from an Anglican theological perspective. However much he might have liked to represent all Christian traditions, in fact his views on a variety of issues were quite specific and came out in his apologetics. Lewis held, for example, to a strong doctrine of free will. Apologists ignore or gloss over such theological matters to the detriment of their efforts.

Raises Epistemological Awareness

Probably the central and most distinctive aspect of Reformed apologetics is its emphasis on reckoning with the epistemological dimensions of belief and unbelief. Reformed apologists have forced apologists of other approaches to become more aware of their own epistemological framework as well as those of the non-

Christians they are seeking to convince. This epistemological consciousness-raising has a number of elements.

First, Reformed apologists have made a forceful case for recognizing that there is an epistemological divide between Christians and non-Christians. Although this divide must be properly qualified (and Reformed apologists are not always careful in this regard), in principle Christians and non-Christians are committed to radically opposed assumptions about knowledge. Christians recognize that our knowing faculties have been corrupted by sin and need restoration through the regenerating and sanctifying work of the Holy Spirit. Non-Christians generally do not recognize this situation. Christians regard God as knowable yet incomprehensible to human beings. This is a difficult balance for most non-Christians, who tend either to view God as utterly beyond knowing (a view shared ironically by agnostics and mystics) or to insist that God must be rationally comprehensible to us (a view shared, again ironically, by atheists, many theological liberals, and some cultists).

Second, Reformed apologists have made apologists of all approaches more aware of the role that presuppositions play in human thought in general and in religious thought in particular. It is not so much the stated assumptions or beliefs as the unstated presuppositions that prevent non-Christians from taking Christianity seriously. Reformed apologists have taught us to look beneath the surface of what the non-Christian is saying, to look for the hidden or unarticulated belief or attitude that is driving the position he is actually articulating.

Third, Reformed apologists rightly emphasize that a discussion of only facts may prove fruitless if the non-Christian's philosophy of fact is not challenged. There is likely little use in trying to debate the scientific evidence for creation versus evolution with a non-Christian who assumes that science must look at all the facts from an assumption of naturalism.

Fourth, Reformed apologists should be heeded when they warn apologists to be careful not to compromise their own commitments epistemologically when defending the faith. For example, there is much to be said for avoiding the line of reasoning that the evidence for God's existence outweighs the evidence against it. Surely in God's world, even marred by sin, there cannot be any real evidence against God's existence.

Offers Strong Rational Challenge to Unbelief

All orthodox Christian apologists agree that apologetic arguments in and of themselves cannot produce conversion. Still, assuming apologetics has any value or utility in evangelizing non-Christians, some arguments are surely better than others. And the transcendental argument used by Van Til has a great deal to commend it.

First, from a Christian point of view the premise of the argument surely must be regarded as true. God is the presupposition of all meaning, knowledge, logic, fact, and moral value and judgment. It is because God exists that all these things are what they are, and it is because we were created in God's image that these things can be intelligible to us.

Second, the transcendental argument is applicable in any context and in relation to any question. Classical and evidentialist apologetics require some familiarity with specific philosophical arguments or with various bits of information, and tend to plow over the same ground repeatedly. Van Til's transcendental argument, on the other hand, maintains that any and every fact is intelligible only on the presupposition of a rational, absolute, and personal Creator whose universe reflects his nature. The argument may even be used in response to a direct denial of some aspect of Christian truth, because it points to the conditions that make affirming or denying any particular truth claim meaningful and intelligible.

Third, the transcendental argument puts non-Christians on the defensive. The burden of proof is laid on them to give an alternative account of the rational ground of meaning or morality. They are confronted with their philosophical prejudice against Christianity and their need for a changed attitude toward the God of the Bible.

These strengths are only some of the reasons why apologists of all traditions should seek to learn from the Reformed apologists.

POTENTIAL WEAKNESSES OF REFORMED APOLOGETICS

First let us consider a common misunderstanding about Reformed apologetics: it is not a kind of fideism. In Part Five we will explore this approach to apologetics in depth, but here we simply point out that fideism denies that there can or should be any rational argument given directly in support, defense, or vindication of the Christian faith. Now, admittedly some Reformed apologists at times sound fideistic. As we have emphasized throughout, the four approaches highlighted in this book do not usually appear in "pure form" in the work of specific, real-life apologists. Just as those who identify themselves as classical apologists sometimes reason like evidentialists and vice versa, those who consider themselves to be Reformed apologists sometimes reason like fideists and vice versa. Moreover, arguably Abraham Kuyper, the father of the Reformed apologetic tradition, had strong fideistic leanings and could with justice be labeled a fideist.

On the other hand, it is a fact that the twentieth-century Reformed apologists profiled here have vigorously repudiated fideism in name and substance. Plantinga denies that reasons are necessary, but he does not deny that they can be used. Clark is routinely castigated for his rationalism, a criticism that is hard to reconcile with his being a fideist. In fact, he argues for the truth of Christianity on the grounds of its uniqueness as a coherent system of knowledge. Van Til insisted against Kuyper specifically that the Christian faith can and should be defended rationally, and developed his transcendental, presuppositional argument as a method for doing just that within a staunchly Calvinistic perspective.

The main reason for the frequent charge that Reformed apologists are fideists is that they often characterize the argument for Christianity as *circular*. Critics of the Reformed approach typically charge that this argument is fallacious. William Lane Craig, for example, writes: "As commonly understood, presuppositionalism is guilty of a logical howler: it commits the informal fallacy of *petitio principii*, or begging the question, for it advocates presupposing the truth of Christian theism in order to prove Christian theism." However, Craig goes on to acknowledge that "at the heart of presuppositionalism" is its "epistemological transcendental argument."[2] This is the argument that Christian theism must be true because it alone makes all meaning possible. At its best, then, the Reformed approach does not beg the question of the truth of Christianity. Its argument is "circular" only in the sense that it seeks to show that ultimately all argument and proof are possible because the God of which Christianity speaks does exist.

Although the charge of fideism is generally inappropriate, the Reformed apologetic approach is susceptible to some significant potential weaknesses or deficiencies. These problems may not all apply to every Reformed apologist, and it may be that Reformed apologetics can be developed or nuanced to overcome all of these difficulties. In any case, there are some reasonable concerns that various critics have expressed and that are worthy of serious consideration. We will highlight three of those here.

Assumes a Rigidly Dogmatic Calvinism

Advocates see the Calvinistic stance of Reformed apologetics as its great strength—and it may be—but it may also be viewed with some justice as its major weakness. The problem here is not the specific theological affirmations distinctive to Calvinism that play a role in the Reformed apologetic. The problem, rather, is the tendency among Reformed apologists to engage in relentless critique of other Christian theologians and apologists—even other Reformed apologists—on exceedingly narrow grounds, sometimes to the relative neglect of actual engagement with non-Christian thinkers.

The pursuit of "consistent Calvinism" has been something of a perennial in the conservative American Calvinist tradition, and has in general been unhealthy. The protracted war of words between Van Til and Clark in the 1940s and beyond is just one of the sorrier examples. Both sides continue to this day to maintain that their champion was grossly misrepresented—and, by our estimation, both sides are right.

While apologists cannot avoid adopting specific theological points of view, they can avoid the excessive dogmatism and party spirit that has marked the conservative wing of the Reformed apologetic tradition. We should mention that in recent years apologists in this tradition have begun to overcome this weakness. John Frame and Vern Poythress have both written books emphasizing the need for Christians of varying theological perspectives to learn from one another.[3] Frame's major book on Van Til strongly criticizes the "movement mentality" among many Van Tilians and offers some trenchant criticisms of Van Til's writings.[4] William Edgar, a professor at Westminster Theological Seminary, has argued that Van Til and Francis Schaeffer were not as far apart as Van Til himself seems to have thought.[5] These writings offer encouraging signs that the Reformed apologetic movement may be maturing out of this particular weakness.

Underestimates the Power of Facts

Reformed apologists rightly stress the importance of challenging the philosophy of fact presupposed by non-Christians. However, they overstate the case when they maintain that facts alone cannot persuade non-Christians to embrace a Christian worldview and faith. The truth is that one valid and effective way of challenging people's faulty philosophy of fact is to confront them with facts that do not fit their philosophy. This is essentially what evidentialists seek to do by arguing empirically and inductively in defense of biblical miracles and fulfilled prophecies.

In this connection we would suggest that non-Christians are rarely willing to accept the "bare fact" of the resurrection of Jesus and then relegate it to the realm of the unexplained, as Van Til so often claimed. The vast majority of atheists, skeptics, and advocates of Eastern and New Age religious perspectives who have written about the Resurrection either deny that it occurred or claim there is no way to know what happened. Defenders of alternative religions and philosophies— even ones that conceivably might make a place for it—nearly always refuse to admit that the Resurrection was an historical fact. The reason is obvious: even non-Christians with a strong worldview of their own recognize that the resurrection of Jesus as an historical fact cannot be isolated from its context as the decisive vindication of Jesus as the Jewish Messiah and the Lord and Savior of the Christian church. We think this pattern shows that presenting the facts supporting the Resurrection can itself go far to bursting the bubble of non-Christian worldviews.

Places Excessive Restrictions on Apologists

Following up on the point just made, Reformed apologists unnecessarily limit themselves in the kinds of apologetic arguments they can and will use. Both Clark and Van Til refuse to use any sort of inductive, empirical argument for Christianity. Van Til acknowledges the legitimacy of induction, but refuses to allow it any real place in apologetics. He claims the only valid proof for Christianity is the transcendental proof.

One of the assumptions underlying this narrow approach is the idea that any apologetic argument that concluded with an affirmation that some aspect of biblical faith was probably true would be dishonoring to God. After all, how can we say that God *probably* exists, or that Jesus *probably* rose from the dead? But this objection implicitly assumes that the apologist is asserting that God's existence or Jesus' resurrection is *merely* probable. An argument that concludes that, based on this or that specific set of facts, the swoon hypothesis is highly improbable is not asserting that in fact it might be true. Likewise, an argument that concludes that the Resurrection is, for a specific set of reasons, the most probable explanation does not imply that one cannot be certain about the Resurrection in some other way.

Reformed apologists contend that the theistic proofs as traditionally formulated are logically flawed. Perhaps they are, but then again perhaps they are not. Hume and Kant critiqued the arguments from avowedly non-Christian presuppositions. Perhaps the arguments can be (and already have been) developed in ways that overcome the skeptical philosophers' criticisms. Ultimately, of course, all theistic arguments that are sound must be grounded in assumptions and presuppositions that are true because this is God's world. But that does not make the arguments unsound.

The following table summarizes the major strengths and weaknesses in the Reformed model of apologetics.

Reformed Apologetics	
Notable Strengths	*Potential Weaknesses*
Establishes close relationship between apologetics and theology	Assumes a narrowly dogmatic form of Calvinism
Inculcates awareness of epistemological factors in belief	Underestimates the value of empirical argument in apologetics
Presents strong rational challenge to unbelief	Limits apologists to a restrictive and rather abstract apologetic

CONCLUSION

Reformed apologetics is a relatively new, dynamic tradition that offers some forceful and surprising ways of defending the Christian faith. However, certain aspects of the movement's history and theology make it difficult sometimes for Reformed apologists to avoid falling into fideism. Yet, as we have seen, Reformed apologetics represents a distinct approach to defending the faith that appeals to rational standards and is characteristically opposed to fideism.

But what exactly is fideism, and why even consider it in a book on different approaches to apologetics? We will explore these questions in the next major part of this book.

For Further Study

Geehan, E. R., ed. *Jerusalem and Athens: Critical Discussions on the Philosophy and Apologetics of Cornelius Van Til*. Nutley, N.J.: Presbyterian & Reformed, 1971. Essays discussing the pros and cons of Van Til's position, including frequently discussed critiques by Herman Dooyeweerd, John Warwick Montgomery, and Clark Pinnock.

Nash, Ronald H., ed. *The Philosophy of Gordon H. Clark*. Philadelphia: Presbyterian & Reformed, 1968. Essays by and about Clark, including critiques of his position by Nash and others.

Sproul, R. C., John Gerstner, and Arthur Lindsley. *Classical Apologetics: A Rational Defense of the Christian Faith and a Critique of Presuppositional Apologetics*. Grand Rapids:

Zondervan, Academie, 1984. Popular book criticizing Van Til's apologetic method as fideistic; see Frame, *Cornelius Van Til: An Analysis of His Thought*, 401-422, for a reply.

Part Five

Fideist Apologetics: By Faith Alone

Chapter 16

Apologists Who Emphasize Faith

In a long-running feature on the PBS television series *Sesame Street*, four pictures are placed on the screen, three of which are identical or of the same kind of object and one of which is different. Accompanying the pictures, a song (which most will undoubtedly remember!) ran, "One of these things is not like the other; one of these things just doesn't belong. . . ."

One could make a strong case that counting fideism as one of four major approaches to apologetics is a case of "one of these things just doesn't belong." After all, fideism, as the term is usually used in this context, utterly rejects the whole idea of apologetics. So why treat it as a kind of apologetics?[1]

Greg Bahnsen, arguing strenuously that Cornelius Van Til was not a fideist, cites a number of definitions of the term *fideism* to support his conclusion.[2] For example, Alan Richardson defined it as "a pejorative term for subjectivist theories which are based upon religious experience and which undervalue reason in theology."[3] To Van Harvey it is the doctrine that "Christian assertions are matters of blind belief and cannot be known or demonstrated to be true."[4] With definitions like these, no wonder hardly any Christian writer will admit to being a fideist. Yet the term is applied to a wide range of Christian thinkers. We would be speaking only somewhat facetiously if we defined it as "the position of someone whose critique of the use of reason in apologetics seems more extreme than ours."

C. Stephen Evans advances the discussion considerably in a recent book entitled *Faith Beyond Reason*. He argues that we should distinguish irrational fideism from what he calls responsible fideism. *Irrational fideism* denies that we can or should think rationally or logically about matters of faith. Any attempt to give a reasoned account of the Christian faith is dismissed as illegitimate or impossible or both. *Responsible fideism* offers (paradoxical as it may sound) a *reasoned* case for viewing faith as justified even though what it believes is above, beyond, or in some sense against reason. Evans even describes this position as *rational fideism*, a term that neatly contrasts this approach with irrational forms of fideism.[5]

We recognize that Evans's definitions are unusual and that most people who use *fideism* will probably continue to use it as a term of reproach. Nevertheless, we suggest that there exists a distinct approach to apologetics that we may helpfully designate fideism. From this point forward, unless we specify otherwise we will use the term to refer to this "responsible" or "rational" fideism as the fourth major type or approach to apologetics.

As here defined, **fideism** (pronounced *FID-ee-ism* or sometimes *fi-DAY-ism*) is an approach to apologetics that argues that the truths of faith cannot and should not be justified rationally. Or, to look at it another way, fideists contend that the truths of Christianity are properly apprehended by faith alone. The word *fideism* derives from the Latin *fide* (pronounced *FI-day*), meaning "faith," and so in a general sense means a position that assigns some kind of priority to faith. Although fideists often speak of Christian truth as "above" or "beyond" or even "against" reason, they do not maintain that the truths of Christianity are actually irrational. Rather, by "reason" they mean *human* reason or rationality, the use of reason by the human mind. Essential to the case for fideism is the belief that some truths of Christianity are beyond our capacity to understand or express in a logically definitive fashion.

Although fideists deny that human reason can prove or justify Christian beliefs, they do *not* conclude that we should offer no answer to the apologetic questions and challenges posed by non-Christians. The irrationalist may rebuff such challenges with non-replies like "Just believe," but this is not what we mean by fideism. Rather, fideists answer those apologetic challenges by explaining *why* reason is incompetent to provide a satisfactory answer and then showing that faith does provide a way to deal with the problem.

Since critics of Reformed apologetics so often equate it with fideism, we should briefly explain where the two approaches diverge. Apologists of both traditions agree that Christian truth claims cannot be justified or verified on the basis of assumptions or methods of reasoning *acceptable to non-Christians*. Reformed apologists, though, contend that these truth claims are internally consistent and that they can show them to be rational from within a Christian system of thought, based on certain key Christian assumptions. All the Reformed apologists we discussed in Part Four make this claim, including Cornelius Van Til and Alvin Plantinga, whom Evans classifies as fideists.[6] But we argue that it is just this claim to be able to produce a rational Christian system that thinkers best described as fideists reject. It is their contention that the truths of Christianity at their core present us with a "paradox" that no amount of rational analysis can eliminate *even for Christians*.

Apologists of all other schools of thought regard fideism as diametrically opposed to the very idea of apologetics—and most fideists themselves would agree. From this perspective, fideism can have nothing to offer apologetics. However, in our opinion there are three reasons why apologists need to consider seriously the claims that fideists make. First, fideism is an increasingly influential perspective in Christianity, including among evangelicals. For good or for ill, Christian apologists need to be familiar with fideism. Second, fideists do offer reasoned arguments for Christian faith, though of a very different kind from the sorts of arguments we have considered so far. This leads us to the third reason: we suggest that apologists of all approaches can learn quite a bit from fideism even while criticizing it.

In this chapter, we will examine the roots of fideist apologetics and consider briefly the thought of five influential fideist apologists. We will pay special attention to the apologetic system of the nineteenth-century fideist Søren Kierkegaard.

HISTORICAL ROOTS OF FIDEISM

Like evidentialism and Reformed apologetics, fideism is a modern development. However, its roots extend back into the early church. The church father most commonly cited as a precursor to fideism was **Tertullian** (ca. 160–220),[7] whose *Apologeticum* was for Latin Christians what Origen's *Contra Celsum* was for the Greek believers. Tertullian presented in many respects a fairly traditional apologetic, citing fulfilled biblical prophecies and historical evidences for the resurrection of Jesus in support of the Christian faith. But he is most famous for his repudiation of Greek philosophy. "What indeed has Athens to do with Jerusalem?" he asked, with the implied answer, nothing. "Away with all attempts to produce a mottled Christianity of Stoic, Platonic, and dialectic composition!"[8]

Tertullian's position has often been summarized in the formula *credo quia absurdum* (I believe because it is absurd), but he never made this statement.[9] What he said (that has been misrepresented using that formula) was that the seeming foolishness of the Christian position proves that human beings did not invent it: "The Son of God is born; it does not shame, because it is shameful. And the Son of God is dead; it is altogether believable, because it is foolish [*ineptum*]. And having been buried, he rose again; it is certain, because it is impossible."[10]

This argument appears repeatedly in the writings of modern fideists: the moral and spiritual impossibility of human beings inventing the teaching that we need to be saved from sin through the atoning death and resurrection of God incarnate proves that the teaching originated from God. Note that this is, in its own way, a kind of apologetic argument. It may be paradoxical but it is not irrational.[11]

Tertullian's rejection of philosophy was not, then, a rejection of logic, critical reasoning, or of the consideration of philosophical issues, but of the pagan philosophies that took their point of departure in human speculations. Indeed, Tertullian in his *Apology* could appeal to Stoic philosophers and poets (much as did the apostle Paul in Acts 17:28) to show that even pagans occasionally recognized truths about God. What Tertullian rejected was the project of *syncretism*—the attempt to combine or mix together Christianity with pagan philosophies to make Christianity more palatable.

MARTIN LUTHER

The fideist approach to apologetics, though by no means limited to one theological or denominational camp, is most deeply rooted in the Lutheran tradition. Not surprisingly, key aspects of fideism can be traced back to Martin Luther himself.[12] We are not classifying Luther as a fideist, but rather saying that key elements of fideism have their seed in the views of the German Reformer.

Einar Billings's dictum that the test of a correct understanding of Luther is whether it can be reduced "to a simple corollary of the forgiveness of sins"[13] is relevant to a discussion of Luther's view of apologetics. For Luther forgiveness of sins is a gift of God through faith alone, a gift needed by all human beings because of their bondage to sin. This spiritual bondage is so radical that the human mind is simply incapable of knowing anything significant about God and his will or about understanding the liberating truth of the gospel apart from the work of the Holy Spirit.

In this context, Luther takes a very dim view of human reason. In the temporal affairs of human beings in the kingdom of earth, "the rational man is self-sufficient." But in the eternal issues of life in the kingdom of heaven, "nature is absolutely stone-blind" and human reason is completely incompetent.[14] Worse, reason is an enemy of God, "the devil's whore," whom Luther nicknames "Frau Hulda." Reason was responsible for the distortion of the gospel by the Scholastics, who had tried to reconcile the gospel with Aristotle. For Luther, Aristotle was "the stinking philosopher" (*rancidi philosophi*, one of Luther's more *polite* descriptions of Aristotle),[15] "that noble light of nature, that heathen master, that archmaster of all masters of nature, who rules in all of our universities and teaches in the place of Christ."[16]

Some of what Luther says about apologetic issues overlaps the views of both classical and Reformed apologetics. Non-Christians can, Luther admits, by their reason know that there is a God. Natural reason "is aware that this Godhead is something superior to all things" and recognizes "that God is a being able to help"; indeed, such knowledge "is innate in the hearts of all men." This innate knowledge Luther calls a "general" knowledge of God, one for which the universality of religion and worship (in all its corrupt forms) provides "abundant evidence." By this general knowledge, all people know "that God is, that He has created heaven and earth, that He is just, that He punishes the wicked, etc." The light of natural reason even "regards God as kind, gracious, merciful, and benevolent." But "that is as far as the natural light of reason sheds its rays." This knowledge does them no good, since reason "does not know who or which is the true God" and cannot know "what God thinks of us, what He wants to give and to do to deliver us from sin and to save us." Luther calls such knowledge the special, proper, or particular knowledge of God.[17]

Worse still, what God has done for human beings—becoming incarnate, dying and rising from the dead—seems quite unreasonable to them. "All works and words of God are contrary to reason."[18] The use of syllogistic reasoning in theology will inevitably lead to falsehood, even when the premises are true and the form of reasoning logically valid. "This is indeed not because of the defect of the syllogistic form but because of the lofty character and majesty of the matter which cannot be enclosed in the narrow confines of reason or syllogisms. So it [the matter] is not indeed something contrary to, but is outside, within, above, before, and beyond all logical truth."

Luther concludes, "God is not subject to reason and syllogisms but to the word of God and faith."[19] This view of reason has important implications for the usefulness of apologetical appeals to the natural realm. Since logic is inapplicable to God and the central claims of Christianity, no arguments can be given for the gospel of grace from the natural realm or from reason. The gospel must be heard from the Word, and its sole argument is that God has spoken. Attempts to defend it utilizing reason (in its arrogant mode) will only succeed in subverting it. "Let us not be anxious: the Gospel needs not our help; it is sufficiently strong of itself. God alone commends it."[20]

BLAISE PASCAL

Blaise Pascal was a Catholic mathematician and writer whose thought has attracted much interest in recent years. Although he was not a fideist, his position anticipates the fideist model of apologetics in significant respects.[21] Although his *Pensées* ("Thoughts") consists of scattered fragments of the apologetic treatise he never wrote, it is one of the most remarkable apologetic works ever penned. In it Pascal chose to avoid metaphysical theistic proofs and provided a trenchant analysis of the paradoxes of the human condition and the interplay between faith and reason.[22]

Pascal's *Pensées* begins with a discussion of the dynamics of human thought. He notes that some people's minds are more intuitive, while others are more mathematical; both ways of thinking are important (1). Some people's thinking emphasizes precision, while others' emphasizes comprehension (2). Pascal therefore urges a sensitivity and respect for the differences in the way people think. Instead of telling them they are wrong, he recommends acknowledging where they are right and then showing them another side of the issue, so as to avoid unnecessary offense (9). The goal is to help them discover the truth for themselves, rather than forcing it on them: "People are generally better persuaded by the reasons which they have themselves discovered than by those which have come into the minds of others" (10). We can do this only if we "put ourselves in the place of those who hear us" (16). What line of reasoning we will then use depends on what is perceived to be the difficulty. "For we always find the thing obscure which we wish to prove, and that clear which we use for the proof" (40).

In number 60 Pascal summarizes what were evidently to be two major points developed in his work. The first part he entitles "Misery of man without God" or "That nature is corrupt. Proved by nature itself," and the second part "Happiness of man with God" or "That there is a Redeemer. Proved by Scripture." Later he will note that "the Christian faith goes mainly to establish these two facts, the corruption of nature, and redemption by Jesus Christ" (194).

He begins his discussion of man's misery without God by urging his readers to "contemplate the whole of nature in her full and grand majesty," and in doing so they will find that nature "is the greatest sensible mark of the almighty power of God" (72). Those seeking to understand everything, to comprehend the totality of the world, have acted "with a presumption as infinite as their object" (72). Pascal further warns that every aspect of human nature contributes to human error. "The senses mislead the reason with false appearances, and receive from reason in their turn the same trickery which they apply to her; reason has her revenge. The passions of the soul trouble the senses, and make false impressions upon them" (82). Reason, therefore, as valuable as it is, cannot be fully trusted, since it is "blown with a breath in every direction" (82).

Although the will does not create belief, it "is one of the chief factors in belief" because it can influence the mind to look at things according to the likes and dislikes of the person (99). Motivated by self-love, we hate the truth and wish to hide the truth about ourselves from others (100). But we betray our unhappiness in the pursuit of diversions: "If our condition were truly happy, we would not need diversion from thinking of it in order to make ourselves happy" (165).

If people hate the truth about themselves, it follows that they hate religion even while fearing that it is true. The apologetic task is to overcome this hatred of truth: "To remedy this, we must begin by showing that religion is not contrary to reason; that it is venerable, to inspire respect for it; then we must make it lovable, to make good men hope it is true; finally, we must prove it is true" (187). In this remarkable statement Pascal refers to three of the functions of apologetics (see chapter 1): as defense ("showing that religion is not contrary to reason"), as offense or proof ("we must prove it is true"), and as persuasion ("we must make it lovable").

So far Pascal has argued in a manner fairly close to the classical approach to apologetics, but his argument is about to take a new turn. In number 194 he argues for the importance of seeking the truth, of considering questions of ultimate purpose. God has given "visible signs" to make it possible for people to find him, but has "disguised" them so that only those really seeking him will succeed (cf. 430). Many people claim to have tried to learn the truth but are really indifferent and have made at best a casual effort. They then abandon the quest, comforting themselves with the notion that the truth in these matters is unknowable and unimportant. Such carelessness in the most important issues of life, Pascal says, moves him "more to anger than pity." People who deny the existence of a God to whom they are accountable and pretend to be self-sufficient and happy, are not being honest with themselves or others. "Let them at least be honest men, if they cannot be Christians."

To show atheists and other skeptics that they need to consider the Christian position seriously, Pascal offers the following argument: "If there is a God, he is infinitely incomprehensible." From this premise it follows that nothing in this world can prove God, for God is beyond anything in this world. "Who then will blame Christians for not being able to give a reason for their belief, since they profess a religion for which they cannot give a reason?" It is of the essence of the Christian religion that God is beyond our reason, and thus that Christianity "is a foolishness, *stultitiam*"; atheists who ask for proof are then asking for something that would *disprove* Christianity. One is therefore faced with a choice, to believe or not to believe. "A game is being played at the extremity of this infinite distance where heads or tails will turn up. What will you wager?" (233).

Pascal then offers his famous "wager argument": "Let us weigh the gain and the loss in wagering that God is. Let us estimate these two chances. If you gain, you gain all; if you lose, you lose nothing. Wager then without hesitation that He is." The person who wagers that God exists can find God in the experience of a changed life. "Endeavor then to convince yourself, not by increase of proofs of God, but by the abatement of your passions. . . . Learn of those who have been bound by you, and who now stake all their possessions" (233). Contemporary philosophers have given the wager argument considerable attention, and there has been much debate about its significance and validity.[23] In the context of his *Pensées*, Pascal's wager appears to be a recommendation to unbelievers to *try* the Christian faith—to enter into the experience of the faithful as a way to faith. If we refuse to believe and act unless we have certainty, Pascal reminds us, we will "do nothing at all, for nothing is certain" (234).

Pascal regards attempts "to prove Divinity from the works of nature" in arguments with unbelievers to be counterproductive. Although believers rightly see God's handiwork in nature, arguments that appeal to nature to prove God to unbelievers "give them ground for believing that the proofs of our religion are very weak" (242). Scripture never reasons in the manner that "There is no void, therefore there is a God" (243). "There are three sources of belief: reason, custom, inspiration. The Christian religion, which alone has reason, does not acknowledge as her true children those who believe without inspiration. It is not that she excludes reason and custom. On the contrary, the mind must be open to proofs, must be confirmed by custom, and offer itself in humbleness to inspirations, which alone can produce a true and saving effect" (245).

Faith, then, comes only from God. "Faith is different from proof; the one is human, the other is a gift from God" (248).

Pascal attempted to chart a course between "two extremes: to exclude reason, to admit reason only" (253). To make faith contrary to the senses would be to exclude reason; to limit it to the senses would be in effect to admit reason only (265). Likewise, to limit ourselves to reason would mean the elimination of mystery, while to ignore reason would result in absurdity: "If we submit everything to reason, our religion will have no mysterious and supernatural element. If we offend the principles of reason, our religion will be absurd and ridiculous" (273). "The heart has its reasons, which reason does not know" (277). These "reasons" of the heart are irreducible first principles, analogous to the axioms of mathematics. Such principles are intuited, not deductively derived. "And it is as useless and absurd for reason to demand from the heart proofs of her first principles, before admitting them, as it would be for the heart to demand from reason an intuition of all demonstrated propositions before accepting them" (282). Rather than seek to prove such first principles, "reason must trust these intuitions of the heart, and must base them on every argument" (282).

In the central and most distinctive arguments of the *Pensées*, then, Pascal appears as a precursor to what C. Stephen Evans calls a responsible fideism.[24] It would be a mistake, though, to view him as a thoroughgoing fideist; as we have seen, his apologetics contains aspects of the classical approach. Although he denies that faith rests on proofs, he affirms that proofs *are* available and offers a brief list of a dozen such proofs. These include the establishment of the Christian religion despite its being contrary to human nature; the changed life of a Christian; the biblical miracles in general; the miracles and testimonies of Jesus Christ, the apostles, Moses, and the prophets; the Jewish people; the biblical prophecies; and other evidences (289). The rest of the *Pensées* elaborates on these evidences or proofs. These proofs provide confirmation of the claims of Jesus Christ in Scripture: "Apart from Jesus Christ, we do not know what is our life, nor our death, nor God, nor ourselves. Thus without the Scripture, which has Jesus Christ alone for its object, we know nothing" (547). The voice of God is clearly heard in Scripture, and for Pascal, the Christ of Scripture is the real proof of Christianity.

SØREN KIERKEGAARD

Søren Aabye Kierkegaard (1813–1855) lived a relatively short life, during which he was not widely known outside his native Denmark. Yet in the twentieth century he became one of the dominant influences in Western philosophy and theology. Kierkegaard (pronounced *KEER-kuh-gore*) is generally regarded as the father of both religious and atheistic existentialism. His thought profoundly influenced such theologians as Karl Barth, Emil Brunner, and Reinhold Niebuhr. Brunner, in fact, hailed him as "the greatest Christian thinker of modern times"[25] as well as "incomparably the greatest Apologist or 'eristic' thinker of the Christian faith within the sphere of Protestantism."[26] Brunner's description of Kierkegaard as an "Apologist" will surprise those who are used to thinking of fideism and apologetics as mutually exclusive.[27]

Like many profound thinkers, Kierkegaard is often cited but rarely understood. Perhaps it would be best to say that the project of understanding Kierkegaard is still under way. He is the subject of an unending stream of books and articles analyzing his life and thought in minute detail.[28] Scholars interpret his thought in radically different ways; such diversity exists among interpreters sympathetic to Kierkegaard as well as among those critical of him. Evangelicals generally view Kierkegaard negatively in light of his role in the rise of modern existentialism and neoorthodox theology.[29] While not denying the problematic aspects of his thought, our focus will be on explaining what many Christian thinkers have found of positive value in Kierkegaard in order to understand the appeal of fideism.

Kierkegaard's writings need to be interpreted in the context of his life experiences.[30] More so than most theologians or philosophers, he wrote out of the intensity of his own spiritual journey.

Two individuals dominated Kierkegaard's life, and his relationships with them are profoundly mirrored in his writings. The first was his father, Michael Pedersen Kierkegaard, an extremely strict and pious man overwhelmed with guilt. As a child Michael had cursed God, and for this and other reasons he feared his family was under a divine curse. In midlife he began reading seriously in theology and philosophy, an interest he passed on to Søren, the youngest of his seven children. Two of Søren's brothers died while he was a young child, and his mother died when he was a young adult, seemingly proving the elder Kierkegaard's fear valid. (In the end, only one member of the family, Peter, outlived Søren.) A year after his mother died, Søren rebelled against his father and sought his escape in a life of wanton pleasures. His conduct was so colorful that he became the inspiration for a character in a novel written by Hans Christian Andersen, Søren's childhood classmate and Denmark's other famous nineteenth-century son. The prodigal son eventually realized the emptiness of that path and returned home to his father, who died soon thereafter (in 1838). Søren followed his father's passion for theology and philosophy, completing his graduate studies with a dissertation entitled "The Concept of Irony, with Continual Reference to Socrates" (1841).

The second person of life-changing importance for Kierkegaard was Regina Olsen, a young woman of fourteen he had met during his prodigal days. In 1840 Søren became engaged to her, and he immediately regretted it. The following year he broke off the engagement, feeling that God had called him to a life of solitude and internal suffering. Kierkegaard never married, and he carried his love for Regina to his grave.

During the next seven years Kierkegaard wrote most of the books for which he is now well known, including *Either/Or* (1843), *Fear and Trembling* (1843), *Philosophical Fragments* (1844), *Stages on Life's Way* (1845), and *Concluding Unscientific Postscript to "Philosophical Fragments"* (1846). He wrote these books under pseudonyms such as Johannes de Silentio ("Johnny Silent") and Johannes Climacus ("Johnny Climax"). To this day there is considerable debate as to whether or to what extent these pseudonymous "authors" actually spoke for Kierkegaard. What is clear is that his use of the pen names was part of his method of, as he called it, "indirect communication." This seeks to communicate ideas not by directly asserting or arguing for them, but by speaking in such a way as to provoke people to think about those ideas and come to embrace the truth "on their own," as we sometimes say. It is interesting that Hans Christian Andersen is famous for his own method of indirect communication, namely, his popular children's stories.

Two primary sources will guide our interpretation of Kierkegaard's pseudonymous writings. First, he wrote voluminously in journals and other unpublished papers, and often indicates there his agreement or disagreement with something attributed in his books to one or another fictional writer or speaker. We will be referring to these materials frequently in discussing his position on various apologetic issues.[31]

Second, he capped off seven years of literary output, during which he produced his major writings, with a book that was not written under a pseudonym: *The Point of View for My Work as an Author. A Direct Communication: A Report to History* (1848). As the title indicates, this book was "a direct communication," setting forth plainly how his earlier writings should be interpreted. Those writings seemed to be largely "aesthetic" at first, becoming more "religious" toward the end. However, Kierkegaard insists that "the religious is present from the beginning," and he denies being "an aesthetic author who with the lapse of time has changed and become a religious author."[32] Between the strongly aesthetic writings and the later overtly religious writings was his *Concluding Unscientific Postscript*, which centered on "the problem of the whole authorship: how to become a Christian."[33] Kierkegaard goes on to explain that in his day virtually everyone was considered a Christian, and yet Christendom fell woefully short of the true Christianity of the New Testament. In such a situation, he realized, he could never get people to see the problem by attacking their status as Christians directly. "If it is an illusion that all are Christians—and if there is anything to be done about it, it must be done indirectly, not by one who vociferously proclaims himself an extraordinary Christian, but by one who, better instructed, is ready to declare that he is not a Christian at all. . . . A direct attack only strengthens a person in his illusion, and at the same time embitters him."[34]

Kierkegaard took just this approach in *Concluding Unscientific Postscript*, in which his pseudonymous author, Johannes Climacus, explicitly disavowed being a Christian.[35] We see here a kind of "apologetic" at work, but an unusual one in that its purpose is not to convert people of other religions to Christianity but to convert people of the Christian religion to authentic Christian faith. Kierkegaard viewed himself ideally called to this work because he himself struggled to become a Christian.

The ancient Greek philosopher Socrates had troubled Athens with his message that the Athenians did not really know what they thought they knew; he had claimed to be wiser than the rest of them only in that he knew that he didn't know. Socrates sought to communicate this message indirectly by acknowledging his ignorance and asking his fellow Athenians to share their wisdom with him. Likewise, Kierkegaard (who had written his thesis on Socrates) troubled Copenhagen with his message that the people of Christendom thought they were Christians but were not. He communicated this message by acknowledging that he himself was not a Christian in the true sense of the word and by raising questions designed to bring those who were confident of their own Christianity face-to-face with the problem.

After 1848 Kierkegaard wrote fewer books, as he apparently saw his primary mission as already fulfilled. Two of his most notable publications during this last period of his life, *The Sickness unto Death* (1849) and *Training in Christianity* (1850), were written under the pseudonym Anti-Climacus ("Anticlimax"), suggesting that in these works he was correcting or balancing some of the things he had published under the pseudonym of Johannes Climacus. The central point of *Training in Christianity* epitomizes his message: to be a believer in Christ, a true Christian, is not to know that Christ lived in the past but is instead to live as a contemporary of Christ in the present. In 1854 and 1855, he published a flurry of articles and pamphlets protesting the self-assurance of the establishment church. These writings, later published as a book entitled *The Attack upon "Christendom,"* took Kierkegaard's nominally Christian culture to task not so much for failing to live up to the ideal of Christianity as for failing to have the humility to admit that it fell short. Kierkegaard evidently burned himself out in the effort, falling ill and dying in 1855.

Kierkegaard is commonly, and we believe rightly, described as a fideist. However, the context in which he advocated a fideistic approach to the truth of Christianity is all-important. He was sharply opposed to the traditional defenses of Christian orthodoxy because he believed they led only to a conceited sense of intellectual triumph among philosophers and theologians and distorted the essence of the Christian faith. "If one were to describe the whole orthodox apologetical effort in one single sentence, but also with categorical precision, one might say that it has the intent to make *Christianity plausible.* To this one might add that, if this were to succeed, then would this effort have the ironical fate that precisely on the day of its triumph it would have lost everything and entirely quashed Christianity."[36]

A "plausible," nonparadoxical, inoffensive Christianity is not, Kierkegaard insisted, the Christianity of the New Testament. When Christianity is reduced to a set of propositions that can be demonstrated by rationalistic and historical argumentation, the dimension of personal encounter, inner suffering, and decisive response to truth is lost. Kierkegaard's intention was to bring people to the realization that becoming a Christian requires more than membership in the church or assent to a doctrinal formula. "My intention is to make it difficult to become a Christian, yet not more difficult than it is, and not difficult for the obtuse and easy for the brainy, but qualitatively and essentially difficult for every human being, because, viewed essentially, it is equally difficult for every human being to relinquish his understanding and his thinking and to concentrate his soul on the absurd."[37]

If becoming a Christian is not more difficult for the obtuse than for the brainy, then it cannot depend in any way on following the rational arguments traditionally used to prove that Christianity is true. In fact, Kierkegaard concludes that such arguments actually become obstacles to genuine faith, because they obscure the radically scandalous and personally challenging nature of the Christian message.

Although Kierkegaard opposed traditional apologetics, he offered a kind of "indirect" apologetic for Christianity in keeping with his method of indirect communication. C. Stephen Evans has identified four basic apologetic arguments in Kierkegaard's *Philosophical Fragments*.[38]

The "no human author" argument. In setting forth the Christian position as a "thought experiment," Johannes Climacus (Kierkegaard's pseudonymous author) presents it as hypothetical or imagined, to which his interlocutor objects that the position is already well known. Climacus admits this, but suggests that while he cannot take credit for it, no other human being can either; it is not something anyone would make up (65–66).[39] "Everyone who knows it also knows that he has not invented it." From this "oddity" Climacus concludes that the lack of any human author demonstrates its truth: "It tests the correctness of the hypothesis and demonstrates it" (66).[40] There is some uncertainty as to what this claim that no one would invent is. Evans suggests that in context Climacus's point is that the idea that human beings are spiritually dead and incapable of overcoming this problem "is not one that could 'naturally' occur to any human being, but can only be known after God has revealed it" (67).

The argument from the uniqueness of the Incarnation. The second apologetic argument is very much like the first. Climacus's "poem" about God becoming a man in order to be our Teacher and Savior is again shown not to be his invention or the creation of any other human being; it must have come from God himself (67).[41]

The argument from offense. Those who hear the story of the Incarnation and disbelieve it are always offended at it, a fact that Climacus takes as confirmation of its truth. The absurdity of the Incarnation is viewed as an objection and an offense by the unbeliever (68), but Climacus views the reaction of being offended as "an indirect testing of the correctness of the paradox" (68–69).[42] Evans explains that since we would expect people to find the Incarnation absurd and offensive, the fact that they do is indirect confirmation of its truth. "A person who wanted to make up a story would make up something much more plausible" (69).

The argument of the book as a whole. Evans contends that the argument of the book as a whole is that the Christian doctrine of the Incarnation is a plausible idea. This interpretation of Kierkegaard is certainly ironic, given his emphatic condemnation of attempts to make Christianity plausible. "Chapter 1 argues that any genuine alternative to Socrates will have God as our teacher." That is, either we follow a great human teacher or we follow God as teacher. Chapter 2 argues that God can be our teacher ultimately only if he gives himself in love by becoming one of us. Chapter 3 argues that natural theology (rational proofs of God's existence) is a failure, and therefore that if we are to know God, he must reveal himself. "Chapters 4 and 5 . . . imply that historical apologetics is pointless" because faith is produced by an encounter with God and cannot be grounded on argument or evidence. Unbelievers are offended by the Incarnation, not because it supposedly lacks evidence but because they find it absurd (70–72).

Evans's reading of *Philosophical Fragments* shows that we must be careful not to read too much into Kierkegaard's rejection of apologetics. On the one hand, Kierkegaard rejected attempts to make Christianity "plausible" in the sense of making it into an intellectual system to which one might comfortably give assent. True Christianity always requires leaving our "comfort zone." On the other hand, Kierkegaard offered constructive suggestions for ways to show indirectly that Christianity is true while retaining its radical, life-changing character. Ironically, he turns the fact that Christianity is not "plausible" (in the intellectually comfortable sense) into an indirect argument for the truth of Christianity. Kierkegaard was thus far from advocating a thoughtless, uncritical, or irrational faith. What he advocated was a careful thinking about faith that recognized that faith was not itself merely a matter of thought. There is, to be sure, a naive and irrational fideism that waives all questions and squelches all doubts with a demand to "just believe," but this is not the kind exemplified by Kierkegaard. Indeed, from his perspective it is the nominal Christian who assumes he is a Christian because of his baptism, doctrinal belief, church membership, morality, or even piety that has failed to think seriously and clearly about the Christian faith.[43]

KARL BARTH

Karl Barth (1886–1968) is widely regarded as the most important and influential theologian of the twentieth century. Admittedly other theologians of the century were more radical, or more conservative; "Barthianism," so called, never did amount to much in the way of a coherent movement (which is just as Barth would have liked it); and outside scholarly settings Barth's name (pronounced *BART*) is not particularly well known. But Barth forged a new approach to theology that continues to challenge and inspire theologians of all perspectives. His importance can best be seen by a review of his life and work.[44]

Barth's Early Theological Development

Barth was the son of Fritz Barth, a conservative Swiss theologian, and was educated in leading German universities during the first decade of the twentieth century under such renowned liberal theologians as Adolf von Harnack and especially Johann Wilhelm Herrmann.[45] As the pastor in Safenwil, a small Swiss town, Barth found the liberal theology he had learned in Germany difficult to preach. The bankruptcy of liberalism became overwhelmingly clear to him in the light of his German professors' support (along with that of numerous other German intellectuals) for the policy of Kaiser Wilhelm II in World War I (1914–1918). Liberalism, he realized, accommodated Christianity to the culture rather than confronting or challenging the culture.[46] In 1919 Barth published his commentary on Romans (*Der Römerbrief*), sounding the message that God is known only in his self-revelation as the God who transcends history and culture. "God is God," Barth protested against his former professors. In the often-quoted words of Karl Adam, a Roman Catholic theologian writing in 1926, Barth's commentary on Romans fell like "a bomb on the playground of the theologians."

Der Römerbrief is a kind of "transitional fossil" in the evolution of Barth's theology. It signaled a break with the old liberalism and sounded some of the characteristic themes of Barth's theology, but it did not articulate a stable alternative to liberalism. His theology was now in transition, retaining fundamental assumptions and elements of liberalism even while he was seeking to pull away from it. He began almost at once to rewrite the entire commentary even while reviewers were hailing the first edition as the charter of a new theological model. This theology was sometimes called the "theology of crisis" because of its emphasis on the judgment (Greek, *krisis*) of God's revelation against culture, or "dialectical theology" because of its emphasis on the antithesis or polar opposition between God and humanity. The two best-known theologians who associated themselves with this theology, Rudolf Bultmann and Emil Brunner, found over the years that they could not follow Barth's continued movement in a more conservative theological direction. The common practice of classifying these three theologians as "dialectical" or "neo-orthodox" tends to obscure the radical differences between Barth and others identified by those labels. In later years Barth actually disavowed the term "dialectical theology." He summed up his theological position during the early

1920s in an often quoted statement from his preface to the second edition (1922) of *Der Römerbrief*:

> I know that I have laid myself open to the charge of imposing a mean- ing upon the text rather than extracting its meaning from it, and that my method implies this. My reply is that, if I have a system, it is limited to a recognition of what Kierkegaard called the "infinite qualitative dis- tinction" between time and eternity, and to my regarding this as having negative as well as positive significance: "God is in heaven, and thou art on earth." The relation between such a God and such a man, and the relation between such a man and such a God, is for me the theme of the Bible and the essence of philosophy. Philosophers name this KRISIS of human perception—the Prime Cause: the Bible beholds at the same cross-roads—the figure of Jesus Christ.[47]

About the same time that Barth was finishing the second edition of *Der Römerbrief*, he began his academic teaching career. He held teaching positions at three German universities—Göttingen (1921–1925), Münster (1925–1930), and Bonn (1930–1935). While he was at Bonn, Adolf Hitler came to power in Germany, and once again Barth found it necessary to protest the accommoda- tion of the church and its theology to German nationalistic ideology. He was the principal drafter of the Barmen Declaration (1934), which affirmed the lordship of Jesus Christ over all individuals and nations. The following year Barth, forced to give up his chair at Bonn and expelled from Germany, accepted a position at the University of Basel in his native Switzerland, where he remained until his retirement in 1962.

During his years teaching in Germany, Barth wrestled to come to terms with both the teachings of the Bible and the theological heritage of the church's his- tory. His mentors from 1910 to 1920 had been Harnack, Herrmann, and the father of theological liberalism, Friedrich Schleiermacher; during the 1920s they were Luther, Calvin, and Anselm. While his theology increasingly inclined toward the views of Luther and Calvin,[48] his theological method was shaped through his dis- tinctive reading of Anselm. In *Anselm: Fides Quarens Intellectum* (1931), Barth challenged the conventional interpretation of Anselm's theology as an attempt to establish the rationality of Christianity apart from revelation. Rather, Barth argued, Anselm himself stated that his method was one of "faith seeking under- standing" *(fides quarens intellectum)*, that is, of a person who has already accepted God's revelation in faith then seeking to articulate a rational understanding of the meaning of that revelation. This does not mean that Anselm was not concerned to reach the unbeliever. But Barth's take on Anselm's method of communicating the Christian faith to unbelievers is a surprising one:

> Perhaps Anselm did not know any other way of speaking of the Christian *Credo* except by addressing the sinner as one who had not sinned, the non-Christian as a Christian, the unbeliever as a believer, on the basis of the great "as if" which is really not an "as if" at all, but which at all times has been the final and decisive means whereby the believer could speak to the unbeliever. Perhaps desiring to prove, he did not really remain standing on this side of the gulf between the believer and non-believer but crossed it, though on this occasion not in search of a truce as has been said of him and has often happened, but . . . as a conqueror whose weapon was the fact that he met the unbelievers as one of them and accepted them as his equal.[49]

Here we see the heart of Barth's fideistic understanding of apologetics. He did not advocate irrationalism—no one could, using Anselm as a model! On the other hand, he insisted that Anselm did not seek a rationally based accommodation to or compromise with unbelief. Instead, Barth interpreted Anselm as taking the paradoxical approach of humbly identifying himself with unbelievers in their astonishment at the Christian message in order to conquer them with its truth. The apologist is not to seek a "neutral" common ground between Christian and non-Christian on which both can reach a "truce." Nor is he to remain triumphantly on Christian ground, demonstrating the truth of Christianity to his own satisfaction while ignoring the perspective of the non-Christian. He is rather to present Christian truth as the answer to questions that he asks right along with the non-Christian.

Barth's *Church Dogmatics*

In the preface to the second edition of the book, Barth commented that his interpretation of Anselm was "a vital key, if not the key," to understanding the method that was increasingly informing his theology.[50] Barth's discovery of this Anselmic method led him to do with his already-begun systematic theology what he had done earlier with his commentary on Romans: start over from the beginning. In 1927 he had published what was supposed to be the first volume of a series entitled *Christian Dogmatics in Outline*. Through his continued immersion in the church's theological heritage, and especially his study of Anselm, he became convinced that he needed to redo the dogmatics. The new series was entitled *Church Dogmatics*, and it was to dominate Barth's work for the rest of his life. At the beginning of the first volume, published in 1932, he made explicit his change of method:

> This means above all that I now think I have a better understanding of many things, including my own intentions, to the degree that in this second draft I have excluded to the very best of my ability anything that might appear to find for theology a foundation, support, or justification in philosophical existentialism. . . . In the former undertaking I can only see a resumption of the line which leads from Schleiermacher by way of Ritschl to Herrmann. And in any conceivable continuation along this line I can see only the plain destruction of Protestant theology and the Protestant Church.[51]

Barth published the *Church Dogmatics* in installments in German from 1932 until 1959, with a volume "fragment" published in 1967, the year before Barth's death. Ironically, Barth never finished his magnum opus, a reminder of his own teaching that a perfect or complete human theological system is unattainable in this life.

An understanding of the *Church Dogmatics* as a whole is essential to understanding Barth's statements relating to apologetics in their context. This poses a considerable challenge because of the work's length, depth, and creative approach.[52] Its plan called for five volumes organized around the affirmation that the church's dogma, or authoritative teaching, is a witness to the revelation of the triune God. Barth was to explicate this teaching by considering, in turn, the Word of God as revelation (volume I), the one God who reveals himself (II), and his revelation in the Father as Creator (III), in the Son as Reconciler (IV), and in the Holy Spirit as Redeemer (V). The volumes ran so long that Barth published them in parts and even half-parts, so that the first four volumes consisted of thirteen weighty books (and Barth did not quite finish volume IV and was unable to start volume V).

In volume I, *The Doctrine of the Word of God* (1932, 1938), Barth argues that theology is properly understood as the church's critical examination of its speech about God in the light of God's own revelation in the Word of God. This Word is God himself, revealing himself as the triune God, preeminently in the Incarnation of the Word in Jesus Christ, the Son, and in the outpouring of the Holy Spirit (I/1, chapters 1–2). (We will consider Barth's teaching in these opening pages of the *Church Dogmatics* in somewhat more detail in chapter 17.) This personal self-revelation is communicated to us in Scripture, which as the witness to God's revelation becomes the written Word of God. In turn, the church communicates its understanding of God's revelation witnessed in Scripture to the world, and as it does so the church is preaching the Word of God (I/2, chapters 3–4). (We will have more to say about Barth's view of Scripture in chapter 18.)

Volume II, *The Doctrine of God* (1940, 1942), is a volume of obvious relevance to apologetics. Barth begins by arguing that the true God is the one who is known to us exclusively at his initiative, by his revealing of himself to us in the Word of God. This means that natural theology is an utterly futile and irrelevant path to the knowledge of God. The God known to us by revelation is the absolutely perfect, personal God who freely loves us (II/1, chapters 5–6). Furthermore, this God has chosen to make himself known graciously and redemptively to mankind in Jesus Christ, who is ultimately God's chosen one. God's command to us is a call to union with and conformity to the character of Jesus Christ, so that Christian ethics must be grounded in the Christian gospel and doctrine of God (II/2, chapters 7–8).

Volume III, *The Doctrine of Creation* (1945–1951), expounds the Christian conception of the world and of mankind as created by God, a work appropriately credited especially to the Father. A Christian knows God as Creator not as an abstract truth but as defining our relationship to God as creatures who have fallen in sin and are in need of the grace we receive in Jesus Christ. This knowledge comes only by faith in God's revelation of himself as Creator in Scripture. The biblical account of creation is neither unhistorical myth nor humanly constructed history, but is instead a theological account focusing on the meaning of creation for our knowledge of God. That meaning is that the purpose of creation was to create the setting for the covenant of grace between God and mankind (III/1, chapter 9). God's purpose for creating man is seen concretely in Jesus Christ. In his incarnation Jesus perfectly embodied man's intended relationship to God and to his fellow man. He also perfectly exhibited man's wholeness as creatures consisting of an integrated unity of body and soul. Finally, Jesus Christ perfectly realized God's purpose for man as creatures living in time. By his birth into our world of time, and by his death and resurrection, Jesus shows himself to be the Lord of time (III/2, chapter 10). Throughout time God as Lord providentially rules over creation to ensure the fulfillment of his covenant of grace with mankind. Again, this providence can be known only by faith in God's revelation. God's providence includes his acting through the agency of angels, since he is Lord of heaven as well as of earth (III/3, chapter 11). God's providential rule over creation does not negate human responsibility, which was perfectly revealed in Jesus Christ. That responsibility is to love God and others, with respect for one's own life and with focused commitment to one's calling (III/4, chapter 12).

In volume IV, *The Doctrine of Reconciliation* (1953–1959), Barth focuses on what God has done in Jesus Christ to fulfill the covenant of grace for mankind in its estrangement from God. Christ's reconciling work is considered in terms of the three classic offices of priest, king, and prophet (IV/1, chapter 13). We learn what sin truly is from God's judgment against it in Jesus Christ, who took our judgment so that we might be freed from it. This justification is received by faith alone because it is accomplished in and by Christ alone as our Priest. In his resurrection Jesus Christ is exalted as King on our behalf, and his deity is made known to us through the testimony of the Spirit. The exaltation of the risen Jesus Christ as Lord at once pronounces judgment against sinful man and the assurance of exaltation to God's purpose for man (IV/2, chapters 14–15). To the truth of this reconciliation Jesus Christ is himself the true Witness, the Prophet in whom God's Word is personally embodied as well as definitively spoken. In turn, Christians are called to bear witness to the truth of Jesus Christ individually and as the church (IV/3, chapter 16). In baptism Christians make their initial witness to God's reconciling grace in Jesus Christ (IV/4, "Fragment").

From our regrettably abbreviated summary of the *Church Dogmatics*, we would highlight two crucial themes or motifs in Barth's theology that are characteristic of fideism in Christian apologetics. First, we can know God and the truth about us in relation to God only by faith in his revelation. By faith alone we know that God is real, that he is absolutely personal and a perfect being, and that he created and providentially cares for us. Likewise, by faith alone we know that God purposes for us to live in relationship with him for eternity, that we are sinners deserving of his judgment, and that Christ died and rose again to make God known to us in grace. We see here Luther's principle of justification by faith alone theologically applied to all our knowledge of and about God, an application that calls into question traditional apologetic methods.

Second, our knowledge of and about God is gained directly from Jesus Christ through the Holy Spirit and only indirectly from Scripture. Rather than basing Christian knowledge on the Bible as the foundation of a rational worldview, as in various forms of Reformed apologetics, Barth bases Christian knowledge on Jesus Christ as the embodiment of God and of God's purpose for mankind. Thus it is in Christ that we come to know God's reality and perfection, his purpose and will for mankind; it is in Christ that we come to know that we are sinners deserving judgment, and that instead we are called to be saints preserved from judgment by grace. Scripture mediates this knowledge of God by its witness to Jesus Christ, not by providing a rational philosophical or theological system.

Assessing Barth

Barth's theology has been highly controversial among evangelicals, particularly in the English-speaking world. Widely disparate assessments of the meaning and soundness of his theology have been defended.[53] Some evangelicals have been mildly critical of Barth,[54] others enthusiastic in their appreciation of Barth,[55] and still others sharply critical of what they perceive as Barth's thoroughly unorthodox theology.[56] Given the diversity of opinion and the complexity of many of the criticisms of Barth, we cannot enter into this debate here, but can only offer some general observations.

First of all, Barth clearly intended his theology to be evangelical Protestant in character. He himself expressly stated that to be his intention, and differentiated his theology from both Roman Catholicism and liberal Protestantism (*CD* I/1, xiii-xv), both of which he described as heresy (I/1, 34).

Second, although Barth espoused an evangelical Protestant position, the soundness of his theology has been widely questioned by conservative evangelicals. On the one hand, Barth affirmed the doctrine of the Trinity, the centrality and uniqueness of Christ as God incarnate, the redemptive death and resurrection of Christ, and the grace of God as all-determining in our reconciliation to God. On the other hand, evangelicals have vigorously questioned his orthodoxy on each of these issues.[57]

Third, Barth's theological legacy is clearly problematic for evangelicals in some important respects. Although assessments of his view of Scripture vary significantly, everyone agrees that he denied the inerrancy of Scripture as well as its character as "propositional" revelation (I/2). Barth's teaching on this subject seems to have helped create the "neo-evangelical" view of Scripture as theologically authoritative but factually errant.[58] His explanation of evil in terms of "nothingness" and of God's "non-willing" (III/3) is speculative and unbiblical, and it undermines the reality of sin. Along the same lines, although Barth affirmed the reality of a final judgment (II/2; IV/3), his affirmation is weak and leaves the door open to universalism, the heresy that all individuals will ultimately be saved.[59]

Finally, Barth himself recognized a significant divide between his theology and that of conservative Protestants. Although he considered himself Reformed, he distanced himself from traditional Calvinism. "I betray no secret in alluding to the fundamental (and, if I may say so, mutual) aversion which exists between the 'historical' Calvinism that follows in the footsteps of A. Kuyper and the Reformed theology represented here."[60]

Although Barth was not soundly evangelical, he represents an important and influential voice in Christian theology. As such, his view of apologetics is deserving of careful attention, especially because some contemporary evangelicals are emulating his approach. One such evangelical is Donald G. Bloesch.

DONALD G. BLOESCH

Donald G. Bloesch is an unfamiliar name to most evangelicals, but he is becoming ever more widely known and respected as one of America's leading evangelical theologians.[61] He is an excellent example of a contemporary evangelical who advocates a fideist approach to apologetics.

Bloesch was born in Indiana in 1928. His father was a pastor in the Evangelical Synod of North America, a denomination with German and Swiss theological roots, and a close friend of Reinhold Niebuhr (1892–1971), who went on to become one of America's most influential 'neo-orthodox' theologians.[62] Bloesch remained in his father's denomination, which eventually merged with others to form the United Church of Christ in 1957. After attending the denomination's Elmhurst College, he attended Chicago Theological Seminary and then the University of Chicago Divinity School. He read works by Kierkegaard, Barth, and other modern theologians, and was especially impressed by Barth. At the same time, his involvement with InterVarsity Christian Fellowship convinced him of the need for an evangelical faith. Bloesch received his doctorate after writing a dissertation entitled "Reinhold Niebuhr's Re-evaluation of the Apologetic Task" (1956). In his estimation Niebuhr's approach, while it made some good criticisms of traditional apologetics, was itself too rationalistic.

The year following the completion of his doctorate, Bloesch began teaching at the University of Dubuque Theological Seminary in Iowa. Ironically, he was hired in the expectation that, as a University of Chicago graduate, he would be more liberal than Arthur C. Cochrane, a professor at Dubuque who followed Barth. Bloesch taught at Dubuque until his retirement in 1992.

Bloesch's writings during the 1960s focused on renewal in the church. The one notable exception was *The Christian Witness in a Secular Age* (1968), in which he examined the apologetic thought of nine twentieth-century theologians, beginning with Barth and including Niebuhr and other more liberal theologians.[63] The concluding chapter is entitled "Beyond Apologetics: A Restatement of the Christian Witness" (120–135). As the title suggests, the approach Bloesch favors here is heavily indebted to Barth. He defines apologetics as "the attempt to make the faith plausible to the world of unbelief on the basis of a criterion held in common with unbelief" (121). He bases his rejection of such apologetics on Luther's teaching that man is in bondage to sin (121). He quotes Barth, Calvin, and Pascal to support the conclusion that the gospel cannot be correlated with man's searching in culture and religion (122). Again he quotes Kierkegaard and Luther in support of the assertion "that God's truth is beyond the reach of man's conception and perception," even for Christians, for whom "God remains hidden even in the act of revelation" (122–23). "With Barth we contend that revelation must be proclaimed, not defended or even recommended in the sense of trying to heighten its value" (126). According to Bloesch, apologetics is "the attempt to compel a man by rational means to assent to the truth of faith" (130). In place of such "religious imperialism" he advocates "gospel evangelism," a presentation of the message that people need to believe in Christ for salvation (130–31).

While Bloesch rejects apologetics as traditionally conceived "as a preparation for and validation of the Gospel," he acknowledges that "there is an element of truth in the traditional apologetic enterprise which must not be lost" (132). Apologetics is needed to clarify our own understanding of the gospel so that we can be sure that what we are preaching is indeed the gospel and not a message accommodated to the culture (132–33). "This is apologetics in the context of faith seeking understanding. . . . Apologetics, as I now try to define it, is oriented not about a defense of the faith but rather about the heralding and explication of the message of the Bible" (133). Like many Christians today, Bloesch considers the rational, explanatory function of apologetics to be of value to Christians seeking to understand what they believe, rather than of use for convincing non-Christians that the Bible's message is reasonable.

Bloesch followed up *Christian Witness* with *The Ground of Certainty* (1971).[64] In this book, dedicated to his colleague and mentor Arthur C. Cochrane, Bloesch explored issues in the relation of theology to philosophy, concluding with a chapter entitled "Faith and Reason" (176–203). According to Bloesch, Martin Luther "illustrates the position of evangelical fideism." Luther "saw faith as standing in contradiction to reason" (178). By contrast Pascal, who "might be considered a representative of fideism in the Catholic Church . . . did not see faith as contrary to reason: rather faith goes beyond reason" (179). (Our own assessment, explained earlier in this chapter, is that Luther and Pascal were not fideists but anticipated certain elements and emphases of fideism.) Kierkegaard is another thinker whom Bloesch cites as a fideist. For Kierkegaard, Bloesch points out, human reason finds that "the revelation of God in Christ is an absolute paradox, and even faith cannot fully penetrate this mystery" (181). These thinkers stand in sharp contrast to Charles Hodge and Gordon Clark, whom Bloesch cites as examples of rationalistic Calvinists (182–185). Finally, Bloesch commends Karl Barth's "noteworthy and fresh contribution to the subject." Following Anselm and the Reformers, Barth understands that "faith is prior to human reasoning, but in itself it is rational, not suprarational" (185). However, Bloesch does fault Barth for minimizing the "mystical dimension of faith" and overemphasizing its cognitive dimension (187). Bloesch places himself in this fideist tradition, with some qualification:

> My position is much closer to fideism than to rationalism in that I see faith as determining reason and not vice versa. I stand in that tradition which includes Forsyth, Kierkegaard, Pascal, Edwards, Luther, Calvin, Irenaeus and also Paul the Apostle. Some Christian mystics (Bernard of Clairvaux and John of the Cross), as well as luminaries of neo-orthodoxy like Emil Brunner and Karl Barth, evangelical Calvinists such as Martyn Lloyd-Jones, and neo-Lutherans like Helmut Thielicke and Gustav Wingren, also belong to some degree to this general tradition. (187)

Bloesch continued to publish major works of theology that have deeply influenced a generation of evangelical theologians. His writings in the 1970s included a work on Barth's doctrine of salvation[65] and a two-volume textbook on systematic theology, *Essentials of Evangelical Theology*, a pioneering work in the new progressive form of evangelicalism sometimes called neoevangelicalism.[66] Over the years he has continued to nuance his position as one closer to fideism than to rationalism, yet in some ways not simply identified with either. Thus in his 1983 book *The Future of Evangelical Christianity*, he affirmed "a pressing need to transcend the cleavage between fideism and rationalism." Faith is "a rational commitment," but reason cannot provide the basis for or even prepare the way for faith.[67] A pure fideism would involve "beginning with a leap of faith," whereas the proper method is to begin neither with faith nor with reason but with revelation.[68] Consistent with the Lutheran roots of fideism, Bloesch warns that evangelical rationalists such as Norman Geisler, by allowing that unbelievers could respond properly to the light of nature before receiving the light of the gospel, are in effect allowing intellectual works to contribute to salvation.[69]

In 1992 Bloesch retired from his teaching post at Dubuque and published the first volume of *Christian Foundations*, a seven-volume series of systematic theology textbooks.[70] In the first volume he labels his position "fideistic revelationalism, in which the decision of faith is as important as the fact of revelation in giving us certainty of the truth of faith. . . . This is not fideism in the narrow or reductionist sense because our faith has a sure anchor and basis in an objective revelation in history" (21). Later in the book Bloesch returns to this distinction: "What I espouse is not fideism but a faith that is deeper than fideism, for it is anchored in the supreme rationality that constitutes the content and object of faith" (203). He again calls for the affirmation of a theological method that goes beyond the polarity of fideism and rationalism. Here fideism is typified, not by Luther, Pascal, Kierkegaard, and Barth, whose writings are said to evince only "a fideistic thrust," but by Jacques Ellul. This is because Ellul views faith as "an illogical venture" devoid of intellectual or cognitive content (57).[71]

> While rationalism holds to *credo quia intelligo* (I believe because I understand) and fideism to *credo quia absurdum est* (I believe because it is absurd), evangelical theology in the classical tradition subscribes to *credo ut intelligam* (I believe in order to understand). In this last view faith is neither a blind leap into the unknown (Kierkegaard) nor an assent of the will to what reason has already shown to be true (Carl Henry), but a venture of trust based on *evidence that faith itself provides*. (58, emphasis added)

Note that fideism is here implicitly defined as the position of believing despite not having any understanding of what it is one believes. Again, this would seem to fit Stephen Evans's category of irrational fideism, as distinguished from rational or responsible fideism, which does recognize a cognitive and even rational dimension to faith. Bloesch carries his understanding of fideism through consistently when, in terms reminiscent of his conclusion in *Christian Witness*, he writes: "My position is probably closer to fideism than to rationalism; yet it is not really fideism, for it is based not on a venture into the unknown, necessarily fraught with uncertainty, but on the divine-human encounter, which expels all doubt. We know really and truly because we are known by God" (61).

Bloesch's reticence to embrace the term *fideism* is understandable, given its widespread negative and pejorative use. But we would suggest that any apologetic method that denies that reason can demonstrate the truth of Christianity, even on Christian principles, and that grounds faith "on evidence that faith itself provides," as Bloesch puts it, is rightly called fideism.

CONCLUSION

Very often *fideism* is used as a pejorative label to censure views of faith and reason that are "to the left" of the person applying the label. Not surprisingly, hardly anyone will confess to being a fideist. Using the term in this way would appear to render it a subjective judgment rather than a useful description of a particular position. Alternatively, many people define fideism as the view that faith is irrational. Admittedly some people do think this is the case, but such a view is hard to find among serious theologians or apologists, for the obvious reason that serious-minded persons do not wish to be irrational. Making matters worse, Christian thinkers are often far too quick to deem another Christian's position irrational. Several of the thinkers profiled in this chapter, notably Kierkegaard and Barth, as well as Reformed apologists such as Cornelius Van Til, are frequently and unjustly labeled irrationalists.

We suggest, then, that it is time to rehabilitate the term *fideism* and use it to refer to an approach to apologetics that not only exists as more than a caricature or an extreme, but is also in fact highly influential. As we have seen, there is a significant tradition in Christian theology taking a distinctive approach to faith and reason that runs from Martin Luther to Kierkegaard, Barth, and Bloesch (among others). A comparable approach was also taken by the Catholic thinker Pascal, who is, if it is possible, more popular among Protestants today than among Catholics. This theological tradition has developed in modern times into a distinct approach to apologetics that we call fideism. While neither Luther nor Pascal were fideists, their views—especially those of Luther—helped to prepare the way for the development of fideism.

Like Reformed apologists, these fideists argue that the traditional apologetic method of trying to defend Christianity as reasonable on the basis of principles acceptable to non-Christians is unbiblical and unworkable. Unlike Reformed apologists, though, fideists hold that Christianity cannot be shown (at least directly) to be reasonable even as a Christian system based on Christian principles. Rather than try to show non-Christians that Christianity is *reasonable*, these opponents of traditional apologetics urge us to try to show them that Christianity is *faithful*—that is, faithful to God and to his revelation in Jesus Christ. How this approach transforms the apologetic task will be spelled out in more detail in the following two chapters.

For Further Study

Hughes, Philip Edgecumbe, ed. *Creative Minds in Contemporary Theology*. 2d ed. Grand Rapids: Eerdmans, 1969. Excellent collection of essays on major theologians of the first half of the twentieth century, including Barth.

Lønning, Per. *The Dilemma of Contemporary Theology: Prefigured in Luther, Pascal, Kierkegaard, Nietzsche*. Oslo: Universitetsforlaget, 1962; New York: Humanities Press, 1964.

Pelikan, Jaroslav. *From Luther to Kierkegaard: A Study in the History of Theology*. St. Louis: Concordia, 1967. One of Donald Bloesch's professors offers an insightful study demonstrating Kierkegaard's theological connection to Luther.

Chapter 17

Fideist Apologetics: Reasons of the Heart

The term *fideist apologetics* strikes many apologists as an oxymoron (like *square circle* or, as the old joke goes, *military intelligence*); one can advocate fideism or apologetics, but not both. Actually, while some fideists attack apologetics without qualification, some of the thinkers we are considering as fideists do not. What they attack is apologetics as usual—apologetics as traditionally practiced. In their own way, though, fideists do offer a reasoned argument for Christian faith, even if they are loath to call it a "defense" or an "apologetic."

Look at it this way. If explaining how Christian faith relates to human knowledge and to questions about matters of faith constitutes apologetics, then fideists do engage in apologetics. In this chapter we will consider the approach they take to relating the Christian faith to human knowledge in general; to the disciplines of theology, philosophy, science, and history; and to human experience.

DIVINE CALL TO OBEY THE TRUTH

The three approaches to apologetics we have already considered all view truth essentially as a body of factual, propositional knowledge corresponding to reality. Where they differ is in their preferred or basic method of validating this truth and commending it to others. Thus classical apologists prefer deductive, rational tests for determining truth; evidentialists prefer inductive, empirical methods used in the sciences and other disciplines; and Reformed apologists typically appeal to the Bible as the standard of truth, sometimes employing a transcendental method of reasoning to demonstrate its truth.

Fideists consider these approaches to knowledge of the truth of Christianity inadequate for two basic reasons. First, they take a different approach, not merely to how we can know or validate the truth, but more fundamentally to what is meant by *the truth*. For fideists, the truth accepted by Christians is fundamentally not some body of knowledge, but Somebody to know. In other words, the truth is ultimately a person, Jesus Christ (compare John 14:6), and it is not merely *about* the person of Jesus, but Jesus himself is the truth. As fideists rightly insist, the essence of Christian faith is not simply *knowledge about* Christ but *knowing* Christ, that is, knowing him personally. And it is just this aspect of Christianity that they argue renders traditional apologetics not merely inadequate but worse than useless. For if we know God personally in Christ, of what use are arguments proving his existence? If we have a personal relationship with the living Christ, will we not be offended at the suggestion that we need to provide evidence for his resurrection?

Kierkegaard, for example, compares the person who engages in the "defense of Christianity" to a person who professes to be a lover and offers "three reasons" for the greatness of his beloved (*JP* 474, 1:188). "There is an unholy inversion in all this business of having to prove everything first. I wonder if it would ever occur to anyone really in love to prove the blessedness of love with three basic reasons? But the fact is that men no longer believe—alas, and so they want to help themselves with the artificial legs of a little scientific scholarliness" (*JP* 1358, 2:102–103).

He ridicules the Augustinian idea of faith as an intellectual belief that falls short of and aspires to knowledge or understanding: "Christianly, faith is at home in the existential—God has not made his appearance in the character of an assistant professor who has a few axioms which one must first believe and afterward understand" (*JP* 180, 1:71). Faith should rather be understood as the "purely personal relationship between God as personality and the believer as *existing* personality" (*JP* 180, 1:72).

This emphasis on the personal dimension of faith is characteristic of fideism. Donald Bloesch writes, "The object of faith is neither true propositions (as in rationalism) nor an experience of the ineffable (as in mysticism) but the living Word of God who is revealed as well as hidden in the mystery of his self-disclosure in biblical history. . . . And the object of faith is not a propositional formula or a rational, ethical ideal but the living, redeeming God incarnate in Jesus Christ, attested nowhere more decisively than in Holy Scripture."[1]

Kierkegaard admits that an unbeliever might be helped by some reasons as he moves from unbelief to faith, but he insists that these will be unusable once he has made the personal commitment of faith. In fact, he will not or should not use them even to help other unbelievers make the same commitment:

> My development, or any man's development, proceeds in this way. Perhaps he does begin with a few reasons, but this is the power stage. Then he chooses; under the weight of responsibility before God a conviction comes into existence in him through God. Now he is in the positive position. Now he cannot defend or prove his conviction with reasons; it is a self-contradiction, since reasons are lower. No, the matter becomes more fully personal or a matter of personality: his conviction can be defended only ethically, personally—that is, by the sacrifices which he is able to make for it, the fearlessness with which he holds on to it. (*JP* 3608, 3:663–664)

We see here a major theme in fideist writings, and especially in Kierkegaard: the only real "apologetic" or defense of the Christian faith that a believer has to offer is his life. Consistent with this viewpoint, Kierkegaard argues that apologetics errs in treating the symptom of unbelief, intellectual doubt, while ignoring the real disease—disobedience and rebellion against God. "It is claimed that arguments against Christianity arise out of doubt. This is a total misunderstanding. The arguments against Christianity arise out of insubordination, reluctance to obey, mutiny against all authority. Therefore, until now the battle against objections has been shadow-boxing, because it has been intellectual combat with doubt instead of being ethical combat against mutiny" (*JP* 778, 1:359).

"Faith's conflict with the world is not a battle of thought with doubt, thought with thought. . . . Faith, the man of faith's conflict with the world, is a battle of character" (*JP* 1129, 2:14; cf. 1154, 2:25). Kierkegaard quotes with approval Pascal's statement, "The reason it is so difficult to believe is that it is so difficult to obey" (*JP* 3103, 3:418). Bloesch agrees, stating that "the basic problem in evangelism is not just lack of knowledge of the gospel—it is lack of the will to believe."[2] Karl Barth also views faith as essentially a response of obedience to the truth. Faith is "knowledge of the truth solely in virtue of the fact that the truth is spoken to us to which we respond in pure obedience."[3]

The personal, ethical, and relational factors involved in genuine faith, then, constitute one type of consideration that leads fideists to reject traditional apologetics. The second consideration is the nature of the object of faith. Not only is Christian faith trust in a person rather than mere intellectual agreement with a position, but it is also trust in a person whose nature defies rational validation. Specifically, Christian faith is trust in God, the God who became incarnate in Jesus Christ. We have here, according to fideists, triple trouble for apologists. For one thing, God in his intrinsic divine being is beyond our understanding. God is infinite, eternal, transcendent Being, and as such beyond the scope of our finite logical analyses. Second, the Christian revelation of this God shows him to be triune—Father, Son, and Holy Spirit—and this triunity of God eludes our logical powers of comprehension. Third, compounding the problem of God's own nature as the transcendent, triune God is the fact that God, in the person of the Son, has incarnated himself as immanent, finite man. And he, though omnipotent God, became incarnate in weakness, poverty, and obscurity, climaxing in his death on the cross.

According to fideists, these basic, essential truths of the Christian message show us that God, as the object of our faith, is beyond understanding and beyond proof. Some fideists have even said that God is *against* understanding, meaning not that he is actually illogical or irrational in his being and acts, but that he contradicts man's best reasoning. Knowing God is not like knowing another human being, about whom we may learn additional factual information, and thus begin closing the gap in our knowledge about that person. Rather, true knowledge about God consists in knowing that he is beyond our comprehension. As Kierkegaard explains:

> The rule for the relationship between man and humanness is: the more I think about it, the better I understand it. In the relationship between man and God, the rule is: the more I think about the divine, the less I understand it. . . . As a child I think I am very close to God; the older I become, the more I discover that we are infinitely different, the more deeply I feel the distance, and in *casu:* the less I understand God, that is, the more obvious it becomes to me how infinitely exalted he is. (*JP* 77, 1:29–30)

Kierkegaard explicitly uses the formula "faith against understanding" in this connection: "God cannot be the highest superlative of the human: he is qualitatively different. From this at first comes incomprehensibility, which grows with the development of man's understanding—and thereby *faith, which believes against understanding*, is again potentiated" (*JP* 77, 1:30, emphasis added).

Barth quotes with approval Luther's assertion that "we must not regard reason or its work when we speak of faith and God's work. Here God worketh alone and reason is dead, blind, and compared to this work an unreasoning block" (*CD* I/1, 245).[4] He also agrees with Luther's assertion that the Christian faith is "counter to all reason" (*CD* I/1, 246).[5] Barth warns that theology cannot claim to resolve the apparent contradictions it contains: "Even the minimum postulate of freedom from contradiction is acceptable by theology only when it is given a particular interpretation which the scientific theorist can hardly tolerate, namely, that theology does not affirm in principle that the 'contradictions' which it makes cannot be resolved" (*CD* I/1, 9).

Fideists believe it is impossible to construct a rational "system" in which all reality, including God and his world, is located, and thus their response to postmodernism is different from that of the other approaches. The classical apologist, evidentialist, and Reformed apologist all agree that it is possible and desirable for us to have a worldview (or more precisely, a God-and-world view), a systematic view of all reality, that is logically coherent as well as comprehensive. Thus, each approach is committed to refuting the postmodernist doctrine that a comprehensive, "objective" view of the world is unattainable. In varying ways each seeks to show that Christianity, and it alone, offers a true and satisfying worldview that meets these criteria, to show that the Christian faith offers a systematic view of reality that can and should be accepted by all people. But the fideist thinks such an approach is ill-advised. Rather than advocating Christianity as the true worldview, fideists argue that we should advocate Christ as the true Word.

Gregory A. Clark makes this point in a recent essay entitled "The Nature of Conversion: How the Rhetoric of Worldview Philosophy Can Betray Evangelicals."[6] He contends that "when evangelicals articulate their faith in terms of worldviews, they make philosophy foundational to their theology, and this philosophy prevents them from grasping the literal message of Scripture" (202). Clark points out that the concept as well as the term *worldview* originate from Immanuel Kant, who used the German *Weltanschauung* to refer to the view that a human being has of the world through the imposition of structures that originate from the human mind (205–207). Throughout the nineteenth century and into the twentieth, the term has been used to refer to human constructions of reality that cannot be affirmed to correspond with reality. Even evangelicals who use the term commonly claim that the Christian worldview should be accepted because it is the most coherent and livable of all the worldviews, a claim that stops short of asserting an actual correspondence between the Christian worldview and reality (208).

To show that this worldview approach to explaining and defending Christianity can betray evangelicals, Clark uses as a case study Jesus' statement in John 14:6, "I am the way, and the truth, and the life." We can understand why Jesus claims to be the way and the life, but what can He mean by claiming to be the truth? Clark suggests that Jesus' claim here does not fit well with the standard evangelical worldview philosophy. In that model, conversion must be described as exchanging one worldview for another. But Jesus did not say that his worldview was the way, truth, and life, as He should have "if Christianity is a worldview and conversion to Christianity is a conversion to a Christian worldview." Jesus' words call us to convert, not from one worldview to another, but "from worldview philosophy to Jesus" (215). "The best case for Christianity, then, is not the coherence and comprehensiveness of its worldview. Jesus himself is the most persuasive case for Christianity" (218).

The question remaining is how a person becomes convinced that Jesus is someone to whom he can and ought to be committed in a personal relationship of absolute faith. The fideist's answer is: through the testimony of the Holy Spirit. The focus of this testimony is not on the truth of Scripture as a source of propositional revelation, as is characteristic of the other three approaches, but rather on the person of Jesus Christ as the personal revelation of God, to which Scripture is the authoritative, Spirit-inspired, and Spirit-illuminated witness as God's written Word. Fideism, then, of the type we are considering here, is a staunchly trinitarian position. Fideists view the objective revelation of God in the incarnate Son and the subjective revelation of God in the indwelling Spirit as inseparably united. Kierkegaard wrote:

> There is only one proof for the truth of Christianity—the inward argument, *argumentum spiritus sancti.*

> I John 5:9 intimates this: "If we receive the testimony of men" (this is all the historical proofs and considerations) "the testimony of God is greater"—that is, the inward testimony is greater. And then in verse 10: "He who believes in the son of God has the testimony in himself." (*JP* 3608, 3:664)

Bloesch repeatedly emphasizes the complementary roles of the Word and the Spirit in *A Theology of Word and Spirit*. In the foreword he explains: "When I speak of the Word and Spirit, I am not thinking primarily of a book that receives its stamp of approval from the Spirit, though I affirm the decisive role of the Spirit in the inspiration and illumination of Scripture. I am thinking mainly of the living Word in its inseparable unity with Scripture and church proclamation as this is brought home to us by the Spirit in the awakening to faith."[7]

As fideists see it, the use of rational arguments to support or defend the Bible detracts from the true role and character of the testimony of the Holy Spirit. Where this testimony is understood as a subjective experience enhancing our confidence in the message of Scripture, or serving as one proof among many, it tends to fade into the background. Barth argued that Calvin, despite his strong affirmation of the Spirit's testimony, laid the groundwork for this development by allowing rational proofs a place in his theology:

> The unarmed power of the one ground that in the Bible God has attested Himself to be God and still does so, came more and more to be regarded, as it was never meant to be regarded in the 16th century, as the power of a particular spiritual experience, which at some point we have to have of the Bible. But on this understanding, it could not have the force of a real ground. Calvin had seen in it only the power of an objective proof. But it was now suspected to be only subjective and in the strict sense not a proof at all. Therefore the witness of the Holy Spirit necessarily retired and finally disappeared behind the rational proofs which Calvin had treated only as luxuries. (*CD* I/2, 536–537)

MAKING THEOLOGY PERSONAL

If we cast about in Kierkegaard's writings for a single sentence that expresses the essence of his position, a good candidate would be this assertion: "But Christianity is not a doctrine; it is an existence-communication" (*JP* 517, 1:212). The statement is found repeatedly in his journals, and he even calls it his "thesis": "Here I come again to my thesis—Christianity is not a doctrine but an existence-communication" (*JP* 1060, 1:463). We get a better idea of what he means when he explains that because "Christianity is not a doctrine . . . but an existential-communication," Christianity can be presented only by "existing" as one in whom Christianity is "reduplicated" (*JP* 484, 1:191). In Christianity God makes his existence known to us by communicating or sharing himself with us in the Incarnation, in such a way that our own existence or life is changed. Kierkegaard's point is that

Christianity in its essence is the impartation not of a doctrinal system but of a new life in relationship to God in Christ.

It follows that the traditional goal of systematic theology, namely, to attain a theological system in which we can understand as much as possible of what we believe, needs to be radically revised. As we have seen, Kierkegaard and other fideists vigorously deny that we can attain a comprehensive, rational system within which to understand the mysteries of the faith. Here is Kierkegaard's proposal for a new guiding principle for theology, or dogmatics: "A dogmatic system ought not to be erected on the basis: *to comprehend faith*, but on the basis: *to comprehend that faith cannot be comprehended*" (*JP* 3564, 3:635).

According to fideists generally, the purpose of theology should be seen as the faithful exposition of the gospel in all its ramifications, not as the construction of a rational system of doctrine. The theologian's fidelity to the gospel will entail leaving the apparent contradictions or paradoxes of the Christian faith as they are rather than trying to resolve them logically.

Fideists who reject apologetics outright, at least in name, obviously consider the question of the relation between apologetics and theology to be pointless. Perhaps the most traditional account of this relation by a fideist is given by Donald Bloesch, who complains, "Too often in the past, apologetics occupied the central role in Roman Catholic and Reformed theology." Bloesch flatly rejects the classical view of apologetics as a discipline in some way preliminary to or preparatory for theology. But he does not advocate abandoning apologetics. The church, he says, needs "to recover dogmatics as the central task in theology, though not to the exclusion of apologetics," which should "be seen as a branch of dogmatics, the branch that seeks to combat the attacks upon the faith from its cultured despisers."[8]

The most distinctively fideist account of the relation of apologetics to theology, and one of the most magisterial treatments in church history, is found in the second section (part of the first chapter) of Karl Barth's *Church Dogmatics*. Here Barth explains why he distinguishes prolegomena—that branch of dogmatics that considers the method and presuppositions of theology—from apologetics. He notes that various theologians in his day and earlier were arguing that prolegomena was necessary now because of the widespread denial of the basic assumptions of dogmatics stemming from rationalism and naturalism. Emil Brunner, he observes, "proposes to give to this preparatory dogmatic discipline the name of eristics rather than apologetics." But Barth questions himself whether he does not "make out the older apologetics to be worse than it was" by characterizing it as a defensive self-justification before the world, in order to claim that Brunner avoided apologetics. "Would it not be clearer to accept the name apologetics without apology?" (*CD* I/1, 27).

Barth rejects this rationale for dogmatic prolegomena on three grounds. (1) Theology has always been done in the face of widespread rejection of its presupposition of God's revelation; the modern situation is not as different as Brunner and others have supposed. They argue that theology faces a more difficult task in a culture generally skeptical of religion than it did in a highly religious, if pagan, culture (as in the early church). To the contrary, Barth insists, the Christian revelation claim has always been at odds with non-Christian thought, whether religious or skeptical. "Knowledge of the revelation believed in the Church does not stand or fall with the general religious possibility that is made easier by the ancient view of things and more difficult by the modern" (*CD* I/1, 28).

(2) To do dogmatic prolegomena as a means of justifying God's revelation is to abandon the dogmatic task for another; it is to stop speaking as the church. Barth objects to framing the epistemological question as "How is human knowledge of revelation possible?" because such a question implies that there is some question about "whether revelation is known." Rather, the epistemological question is, "What is true human knowledge of divine revelation?" This question presupposes that revelation itself creates man's knowledge of that revelation—which for Barth is the crucial point (*CD* I/1, 29).

(3) Barth argues that the desire to make theology responsible and up to date cannot be satisfied by engaging in the negative task of refuting unbelief, but only by engaging in its own proper and positive task of articulating the witness of faith. As Bromiley helpfully and succinctly puts it, "theology which does its own job will be the best apologetics."[9] Barth himself put it in almost the very same terms in another work late in his life: "Dogmatics will always have an apologetic side. In a certain sense all dogmatics is apologetics, namely, in the sense it is setting the limits. But God's revelation defends itself. . . . The best apologetic is a good dogmatics. Truth will speak for itself."[10]

Theology should refuse "to be drawn into discussion of its basis, of the question of the existence of God or of revelation." Dogmatics cannot produce an effective apologetic by trying to defend faith, but only by presenting a faithful witness of faith to God's self-revelation (*CD* I/1, 30).

There can be no question, of course, that with the Christian Church generally dogmatics, too, has everywhere to speak in the antithesis of faith to unbelief and therefore apologetically and polemically. But there has never been any effective apologetics or polemics of faith against unbelief except that which is not deliberately planned, which simply happens as God Himself acknowledges the witness of faith. There are three reasons why all planned apologetics and polemics have obviously been irresponsible, irrelevant and therefore ineffective.

Barth then presents his three objections to intentional apologetics. "*(a)* In such apologetics faith must clearly take unbelief seriously. Hence it cannot take itself with full seriousness. Secretly or openly, therefore, it ceases to be faith." That is, apologetics as prolegomena either overtly or covertly treats unbelieving assumptions as serious options. "*(b)* In all independently ventured apologetics and polemics there may be discerned the opinion that dogmatics has done its work." That is, Barth contends that apologetics is a distraction of the theologian from his actual task, that of articulating the church's witness to God's revelation.

> *(c)* An independent eristics at least runs the risk that once its task is completed dogmatics will think that its conflict with unbelief has been brought to an end in the form of such prolegomena, and that it will thus lose the necessary awareness of the constant exposure to assault of all its statements. In other words, dogmatics may well come to act as an eristics which is *praenumerando* assured, and thus be guilty of a genuine Chinese Wall mentality, the building of the Great Wall of China being obviously a thoroughly eristic enterprise. (*CD* I/1, 30–31)

That is, eristics, as an independent effort preceding dogmatics, implies that dogmatics can then proceed without concern for unbelieving thought.

> Theology is genuinely and effectively apologetic and polemic to the extent that its proper work, which cannot be done except at the heart of the conflict between faith and unbelief, is recognised, empowered and blessed by God as the witness of faith, but not to the extent that it adopts particular forms in which it finally becomes only too clear to the opposing partner that it is either deceiving him when it proposes to deal with him on the ground of common presuppositions, or that it is not quite sure of its own cause in so doing. Either way, there can be no shattering of the

axiom of reason along these lines, but only as theology goes its own way sincerely and with no pretence. Apologetics and polemics can only be an event and not a programme. (*CD* I/1, 31)

If the purpose of dogmatic prolegomena is not to engage in an intentional apologetic discussion with unbelief outside of a faith position, then what is its purpose? According to Barth, it is to give an account of the path of knowledge properly taken by dogmatics, over against alternative accounts vying within the church. That is, its purpose is to oppose not the avowed unbelief of those outside the church, but the materially defective faith of those within the church. Prolegomena, in short, deals with heresy. The two main heresies Barth identifies are Roman Catholicism and Protestant modernism, over against which he favors what he considers to be an evangelical theology (*CD* I/1, 31–34).

CRITIQUING THE GOD OF THE PHILOSOPHERS

The inability of human reason to make a rational, coherent account of the paradoxes of the Trinity and especially the Incarnation exposes a serious limitation for philosophy. Fideists do not necessarily reject philosophy outright, but they do cordon it off from theology in the sharpest possible way. Moreover, they reject the project of developing a "Christian philosophy," whether conceived as a foundation, companion, or product of Christian theology.

This fideist view of philosophy was clearly anticipated by Martin Luther. The seeming irrationality of the gospel message cannot, Luther concludes, be overcome by developing a superior philosophy. Rather, Luther insists that philosophy must be completely separated from theology, lest the gospel that theology seeks to propound be corrupted. "Philosophy deals with matters that are understood by human reason. Theology deals with matters of belief, that is, matters which are apprehended by faith."[11] Ironically, this distinction is itself a Scholastic one, going back to Albert the Great and Thomas Aquinas himself. Some later Scholastics, notably Robert Holcot (a student of the famous Ockham), took this distinction so far as to maintain that "a proposition may be false in theology and true in philosophy, and *vice versa*."[12] Luther comes close to this view, arguing that Catholic theologians who insisted "that truth is the same in philosophy and theology" were really teaching "that articles of faith are subject to the judgment of human reason." In opposition to this approach, Luther maintains that such truths as the doctrine of the Incarnation are true "in theology," but "in philosophy" they are "impossible and absurd." For Luther the bottom line is that "God is not subject to reason and syllogisms but to the word of God and faith."[13]

A sharp opposition between what philosophers can speculate about God and what God has himself revealed is characteristic of fideism. Pascal is well known for his personal motto (which he carried on his person for years):

> "God of Abraham, God of Isaac, God of Jacob," not of philosophers
> and scholars.
> Certainty, certainty, heartfelt, joy, peace.
> God of Jesus Christ.
> God of Jesus Christ.[14]

There is some evidence in Kierkegaard's writings that he was not opposed to philosophy per se. "Johannes Climacus" in *Concluding Unscientific Postscript*, while criticizing philosophical speculation, hastens to add that within its proper sphere, philosophy served a very beneficial function. "All honor to philosophy, all praise to everyone who brings a genuine devotion to its service."[15] What Kierkegaard does, though, is use the critical tools of philosophy to show that philosophy cannot be used to prove or defend the rationality of Christianity. Philosophy has its uses, but it cannot help us in our relationship with the living God: "Philosophy is life's dry-nurse, who can take care of us—but not suckle us" (*JP* 3252, 3:500). Kierkegaard scholar Peter Rhode observes: "Using the subtlest weapons of logic and philosophy . . . Kierkegaard performed the feat of demonstrating the impotence of logic and philosophy to deal with the ultimate problems of existence. This demonstration is really his title to fame."[16]

Kierkegaard roots his rejection of Christian philosophy or philosophical theology in the paradox of the Incarnation. "Philosophy's idea is mediation—Christianity's, the paradox" (*JP* 3072, 3:399). He asserts that "because all Christianity is rooted in the paradox, one must accept it (i.e. become a believer) or reject it (precisely because it is paradoxical), but above all one is not to think it out speculatively, for then the result is definitely not Christianity" (*JP* 3083, 3:403–404). At one point he stated emphatically, *"Philosophy and Christianity can never be united"* (*JP* 3245, 3:496). Echoing Luther and the Scholastic dualism between philosophy and theology, Kierkegaard comments in a note: "Compare the scholastic thesis: 'Something can be true in philosophy which is false in theology'" (*JP* 3245, 3:497).

For Kierkegaard, the philosophy of the German thinker Georg W. F. Hegel (1770–1831) epitomized the attempt to formulate a conceptual scheme by which all reality could be ordered. Hegel sought to deduce all categories of reality from an original abstract category of being, and maintained that there is a metaphysical continuity between God and man. He reinterpreted the New Testament concept of the Incarnation in symbolic terms to fit his philosophical system. Kierkegaard comments: "Thus there is no philosophy which has been so harmful to Christianity as Hegel's. For the earlier philosophies were still honest enough to let Christianity be what it is—but Hegel was stupidly impudent enough to solve the problem of speculation and Christianity in such a way that he altered Christianity—and then everything went beautifully" (*JP* 1619, 2:226–227).

Kierkegaard was impressed enough with Hegel's intellectual brilliance. His claim was not that Hegel had done a poor job of giving a philosophical account of Christianity, but that the whole enterprise was an improper use of reason. His assertion that "Hegel was stupidly impudent" is a judgment on the ethics of Hegel's use of reason, not an evaluation of his mental ability. Thus in another place Kierkegaard could write: "If Hegel had written his whole logic and had written in the preface that it was only a thought-experiment, in which at many points he still steered clear of some things, he undoubtedly would have been the greatest thinker who has ever lived. As it is he is comic" (*JP* 1605, 2:217).

Kierkegaard's critique of Hegel, which we cannot explore here, is one of his major contributions to the history of Christian thought. Indeed, at least one author has spoken of it as an exercise in Christian apologetics:

> Quite in the spirit of Pascal, Kierkegaard has used reason to teach us reason's limits, to show that there is nothing more irrational than the pretenses of the autonomous human reason, and thus to bring us to "the borders of the marvellous." That is, to prepare us for the reception of divine revelation—a revelation not volatilized, as in the case of theological liberalism, nor made synonymous with an evolutionary process culminating in the State, as in Hegel, but a revelation uniquely focused in the God-Man and in the Church his coming created. Kierkegaard's attack on Hegel is, therefore, equally an apology for the Christian faith.[17]

CHRISTIANITY AND THE REALITY BEYOND SCIENCE

We have emphasized that fideists, while disavowing the use of reason to defend or prove Christianity true, are not thereby irrationalists. This is demonstrable from the view of science most fideists take. They do not reject science, and generally do not dispute the findings of mainstream science. Rather, they argue that the findings of science in principle can neither confirm nor disprove the truth of Christianity. They generally hold to some form of **complementarianism**, according to which science and theology deal with different questions, perhaps even different subject matters, so that as a matter of principle neither discipline can properly yield results in conflict with the other.

The foundations of this approach appear in the writings of Kierkegaard. As he himself acknowledged, modern science was beginning to call into question some things found in Scripture (at least, as they were commonly understood), although he died before the modern conflict heated up over evolution. In the main, Kierkegaard scolded people for giving too much reverence to science and consequently expecting Christianity to be validated by science. He spoke of this trend as "a curious misunderstanding, a consequence of the deification of the scholarly and the scientific—namely, this desire to apply the scientific also to the portrayal of the existential" (*JP* 1058, 1:461). Kierkegaard decried the exaltation of science at the expense of theology:

> Once upon a time all the other branches of knowledge drew their prestige from Christianity, from theology: a natural scientist, a physician, etc.— for him to be a doctor of theology as well was a recommendation. Alas, men have turned this almost completely around. The fact that Pascal was a famous mathematician is almost a benefit to Christianity, because of that people feel that they can listen to and reflect on what he says. Alas, what a change. (*JP* 3118, 3:423)

A scientific approach to matters of the spirit is positively dangerous, Kierkegaard warns, indicating that while science deals with the physical, it is incompetent to deal with the spiritual:

> Many admirers . . . believe that carrying out investigations microscopically is synonymous with scientific earnestness. . . . But all such scientificalness becomes especially dangerous and corruptive when it wants to enter into the realm of the spirit. Let them treat plants, animals, and

stars that way, but to treat the human spirit in this way is blasphemy, which only weakens the passion of the ethical and of the religious. (*JP* 2809, 3:242–243)

Not only is he not interested in natural theology, he actually sees anything along that line as offensive and negating of genuine faith:

> To me there is something repulsive when a natural scientist, after having pointed to some ingenious design in nature, sententiously declares that this reminds us of the verse that God has counted every hair of our heads. O, the fool and his science, he has never known what faith is! Faith believes it without all his science, and it would only become disgusted with itself in reading all his volumes if these, please note, were supposed to lead to faith, strengthen faith, etc. (*JP* 2810, 3:246)

Admitting that there appear to be scientific errors in Scripture, Kierkegaard asks us to imagine a revelation given in our time. Assuming that we acknowledge that modern science is not perfect and that many of its current notions will one day be set aside, he suggests that a revelation given to us today would not concern itself with correcting such scientific errors. Rather, it "will speak about natural phenomena in exactly the same way we do, for there is no time to waste on such matters, and the teacher (God) is not like a conceited human teacher who wants to show what he knows" (*JP* 2823, 3:253).

> At present natural science shows that a whole range of ideas about natural phenomena found in Holy Scripture are not scientifically defensible: ergo, Holy Scripture is not God's Word, is not a revelation.

> Here theological scholarship gets into trouble, for the natural sciences are perhaps right in what they say—and theological scholarship is also eager to be a science, but then it loses the game here, too. If the whole thing were not so serious, it would be extremely comical to consider theology's painful situation, which it certainly deserves, for this is its nemesis for wanting to be a science. (*JP* 2823, 3:252)

In general, fideists are open to theistic evolution as an explanation of origins, though not all fideists actually embrace evolutionary theory. They tend to read Genesis 1 as a poetic, theological account of origins, relating the truth of what occurred in prehistory, but in a nonliteral narrative. Karl Barth, for example, treats Genesis 1–3 as "a legitimate non-historical and pre-historical view of history, and its non-historical and pre-historical depiction in the form of saga." By *saga* he means a narrative of historical truth conveyed using a nonhistorical genre or form; saga in this sense is to be sharply distinguished from myth, in which a fictional narrative symbolizes nonhistorical truth. "In what follows I am using saga in the sense of an intuitive and poetic picture of a pre-historical reality of history which is enacted once for all within the confines of space and time" (*CD* III/1, 81).

Donald Bloesch exemplifies a moderate application of the fideistic position to matters of science. "The Bible is a document concerning not science, history or religion as such but a divine-human encounter, which we find above all in Jesus Christ. . . . The biblical culture is prescientific, but the truth that the Bible attests is suprascientific."[18] Like apologists of other approaches, though, Bloesch reserves judgment on whether Scripture is actually contradicted by the physical facts. "I readily grant that forms of expression in Scripture may conflict with science, but science is not the final norm, for scientific theories are constantly in flux."[19] Bloesch is serious about this critical view of science, for he commends fundamentalists for their "opposition to the myth of evolution, which continues to beguile earnest Christians seeking a satisfactory rational explanation of the origin of species."[20] But he also criticizes fundamentalists for insisting on interpreting the Bible to teach a young earth in the teeth of the scientific evidence.[21]

REVELATION AS TRANSCENDING HISTORY

While fideism opposes the other three apologetic approaches considered in this book, it is arguably most opposed to evidentialism. The evidentialist project of persuading non-Christians to put their faith in Christ on the basis of factual evidence—especially historical evidence—strikes the fideist as a most foolhardy undertaking. While rumblings against such an approach were sounded before him, Kierkegaard raised the first loud, clear cry against basing Christian belief on historical argument.

The issue is raised, but not directly answered, in *Philosophical Fragments* (1844). A brief, simplified overview of this important work will make clear the approach taken in fideism to historical apologetics. The question is posed on the title page of the work: "Can a historical point of departure be given for an eternal consciousness; how can such a point of departure be of more than historical interest; can an eternal happiness be built on historical knowledge?"[22]

The book opens, though, with a more general question: "Can the truth be learned?" (9). From this question Kierkegaard (or his pseudonymous author Johannes Climacus) develops throughout the first two chapters a "thought experiment." In it he represents the Incarnation as the coming into the world of God himself to be our Savior and Teacher—a Savior to bring us back to acceptance of the truth and a Teacher to actually communicate it (9–36). Such a God become man would be the "absolute paradox," one that is an offense to man (37–54).

In chapter 4 Climacus points out that even a contemporary of this hypothetical "god," that is, the God-man, could not base his faith in him on his knowledge of the historical facts. Even a contemporary would not know every historical detail about the God-man, and even if he did, that would not make him a follower (55–71, especially 59). In an "Interlude" Climacus argues that the passage of time does not make the historical "necessary" (72–88). As Kierkegaard wrote elsewhere: "Contemporaneity or noncontemporaneity makes no essential difference; a historical point of departure (and this it is also for the contemporary, the historical, that the God exists—that is, exists by having come into the sphere of actuality)—for an eternal decision is and remains a leap" (*JP* 2354, 3:20).

In the fifth and final chapter, Climacus considers the position of "the follower at second hand" (89–110). No matter how increasingly probable the evidence for the coming of the God-man might seem with the passing of time and the unfolding consequences of his coming, the sheer improbability of "the absolute paradox" overwhelms the positive evidence for it (94–95). The only way for a person to become a follower of the God-man is for him to "receive the condition" from the God-man directly. But in that case the person has this faith "at first hand," and cannot be considered a follower at second hand (100). No amount of historical knowledge derived from those who did receive faith at first hand from the God-man will make faith reasonable, because "its absurdity completely absorbs minor matters." What matters is the humanly unbelievable, paradoxical fact that God became a man, not the relatively believable facts of the circumstances surrounding his coming.

> Even if the contemporary generation had not left anything behind except these words, "We have believed that in such and such a year the god appeared in the humble form of a servant, lived and taught among us, and then died"—this is more than enough. The contemporary generation would have done what is needful; for this little announcement, this world-historical *nota bene*, is enough to become an occasion for some-

one who comes later, and the most prolix report can never in all eternity become more for the person who comes later. (104)

Kierkegaard makes the same point elsewhere, writing more directly about faith and historical knowledge about Christ:

> It is nonsense that the significance of historical details should be decisive with respect to faith in Him who is present with one and with whom one speaks daily and to whom one turns. . . . Yet Christ is actually treated as if He were merely a historical figure who lived 1,800 years ago. . . .

> A merely historical person, a human being, is present only historical-ly—therefore every detail is of great importance. It certainly does not help me to pray to Socrates: what I am to know about him I must learn from history or shape it out of my own head. But Christ is present in an entirely different way. Once again it is seen how strict orthodoxy re-ally downgrades Christ. For however paradoxical it is, it is true and it is Christian that with regard to Christ the historical details are not nearly so important as with Socrates and the like, simply because Christ is Christ, an eternally present one for He is true God. (*JP* 318, 1:133–134)

Throughout *Philosophical Fragments* up to this point, Climacus has coyly avoided any direct reference to Jesus or to Christianity, speaking entirely hypo-thetically. At the very end of the book he admits that his interest is in Christianity, and comments that he will deal with the question more concretely in a sequel, if he ever gets around to writing it.

> As is well known, Christianity is the only historical phenomenon that despite the historical—indeed, precisely by means of the historical—has wanted to be the single individual's point of departure for his eternal consciousness, has wanted to interest him otherwise than merely his-torically, has wanted to base his happiness on his relation to something historical. No philosophy (for it is only for thought), no mythology (for it is only for the imagination), no historical knowledge (which is for mem-ory) has ever had this idea—of which in this connection one can say with all multiple meanings that it did not arise in any human heart. (109)

Here we have, as C. Stephen Evans has pointed out, an indirect apologetic argument for the truth of Christianity: it is not something anyone would make up. From the impossibility of arriving at faith via the historical evidence because of the absurdity of the Incarnation to the human mind, Kierkegaard, through Climacus, slyly infers that the very absurdity of the idea, in the light of its uniqueness, suggests its divine origin.[23]

The sequel to which Climacus refers at the end of *Philosophical Fragments* was produced just two years later as *Concluding Unscientific Postscript to "Philosophical Fragments"* (1846).[24] In his introduction Climacus explains that how an historical point of departure can be the basis of eternal happiness is *not* a question "about the truth of Christianity but about the individual's relation to Christianity" (15). He will consider the question of the truth of Christianity, but only as a prelude to the critical question of how one can receive the benefits of that truth: "The objective issue, then, would be about the truth of Christianity. The subjective issue is about the individual's relation to Christianity. Simply stated: How can I, Johannes Climacus, share in the happiness that Christianity promises?" (17).

Climacus here indicates in outline form the plan of the book: in the first part he will consider the objective question of the truth of Christianity; in the second part he will consider the subjective issue of the individual's relation to Christianity. Part One turns out to be by far the shorter portion of the book (19–57). Here Climacus argues that every effort to secure a knowledge of the truth of Christianity through reason not only fails to attain faith, but in fact undermines it. For example, even if every historical problem relating to the Bible could be resolved, the person acquiring such knowledge would be no closer to faith: "Faith does not result from straightforward scholarly deliberation, nor does it come directly; on the contrary, in this objectivity one loses that infinite, personal, impassioned interestedness, which is the condition of faith, the *ubique et nusquam* [everywhere and nowhere] in which faith can come into existence" (29).

Under the most ideal conditions, historical knowledge can never produce certainty. "If all the angels united, they would still be able to produce only an approximation, because in historical knowledge an approximation is the only certainty—but also too little on which to build an eternal happiness" (30).

Part Two of the *Concluding Unscientific Postscript* is divided into two sections. In the first Climacus interacts with the thought of **Lessing**, who alerted Kierkegaard to the problem of historical knowledge and faith (61–125). Gotthold

Ephraim Lessing (1729–1781) was an Enlightenment thinker who introduced some of the earliest works of liberal biblical criticism. He is best known for his axiom, which Kierkegaard quotes and discusses at length, *"that contingent historical truths can never become a demonstration of eternal truths of reason"* (93). Kierkegaard had alluded to this axiom with his question on the title page of *Philosophical Fragments*, quoted earlier, and which he asked again toward the beginning of this book (15). Working from a deistic assumption that all essential religious truths had the character of necessary truths of universal reason, Lessing concluded that the historical events of the life of Jesus could not prove religious truth. He could not see how one could reason from the occurrence of a past event, even a reported miracle, to a conclusion about God or eternal issues. Climacus quotes Lessing's conclusion: "That, that is the ugly broad ditch that I cannot cross, however often and however earnestly I have tried to make the leap" (98). **Lessing's ditch,** as this principle came to be known, plays a prominent part in Kierkegaard's critique of historical apologetics. Elsewhere, writing in his own name, Kierkegaard makes it clear that he thinks Lessing raised a critical issue: "This [an historical point of departure for an eternal consciousness] is and remains the main problem with respect to the relationship between Christianity and philosophy. Lessing is the only one who has dealt with it. But Lessing knew considerably more what the issue is about than the common herd of modern philosophers" (*JP* 2370, 3:27).

Although Kierkegaard accepts Lessing's premise that one cannot base eternal or necessary truths on contingent historical fact, he rejects his conclusion that the historical aspect of Christianity is nonessential. This is because Kierkegaard rejects the idea that the truths of Christianity are timeless truths that existed before Christianity itself. Such an idea treats Christianity as an abstract system of truth. "But Christianity is an historical truth; it appears at a certain time and a certain place and consequently it is relevant to a certain time and place" (*JP* 1635, 2:232). If one rigorously maintains that Christianity existed as a timeless abstract truth before Christianity itself came into existence, "then the essence of Christianity is enervated, because in Christianity it is precisely the historical which is the essential; whereas with the other ideas this is accidental" (*JP* 1635, 2:233).

Where Kierkegaard follows Lessing is in affirming that truths bearing on one's eternal happiness cannot be held on the basis of historical knowledge. He insists that "even if it were the surest thing in all history, this does not help; no *direct* transition from the historical can be made as the basis for an eternal happiness." The person who would turn to Jesus Christ for his eternal happiness "must beware of taking the wrong turn into scientific rummaging and reconnoitering to see if it is historically entirely certain" (*JP* 73, 1:27). Instead, a person must "choose" to "venture" his whole life on the historical person of Jesus Christ. "This is called *venturing*, and without venturing faith is an impossibility." Unlike Socrates, who wagered his whole life on his own inherent immortality, the Christian is wagering his whole life on another, on Jesus Christ. "Thus the historical is the occasion and still also the object of faith" (*JP* 73, 1:28).

The second section of the second part of *Concluding Unscientific Postscript*, and by far the largest portion of the work, is taken up with "the subjective issue" of an individual actually becoming a Christian in light of the problem raised by Lessing (127–616). At the risk of oversimplification, we may say that Kierkegaard's burden here, as really throughout the work, is to show that people who imagine themselves to be Christians because they have accepted the Gospel reports about Jesus and assented to the Christian doctrine are deceived. Recall that Kierkegaard saw his primary mission as awakening the nominally Christian culture of Denmark to the fact that being a Christian was not the automatic, easy thing they took it to be. The issue here is not the apologetic problem of persuading non-Christians that Jesus rose from the dead or even that He was God incarnate. Rather, the problem is persuading people who affirm those truths that their affirmations do not make them genuine Christians. Climacus asserts that "the difficulty is to become Christian, because every Christian is Christian only by being nailed to the paradox of having based his eternal happiness on the relation to something historical" (578). Thus, Climacus concludes, "The present work has made it difficult to become a Christian" (587).

The thrust of Kierkegaard's efforts in these and other works is not so much to provide the positive answer to how one becomes a Christian—he struggled with this question for himself to the end of his life—but to expose the fraudulent character of nominal Christianity. Fideists following Kierkegaard have sought to build on his insights and to develop answers to his searching questions. Chief among these in the twentieth century was Karl Barth, who gave considerable attention to the relationship between faith and history. Barth fully agrees with Kierkegaard's critique of Lessing's reduction of Christianity to timeless, universal ideas:

> The revelations attested in the Bible do not purport to be manifestations of a universal or an idea which are special by nature but which can then be comfortably compared with the idea and understood and evaluated in their particularity.

Because this is not the case, the philosophy of religion of the Enlightenment from Lessing by way of Kant and Herder to Fichte and Hegel, with its intolerable distinction between the eternal content and the historical "vehicle," can only be described as the nadir of the modern misunderstanding of the Bible. (*CD* I/1, 329)

Barth affirms that revelation reaches man in history and is therefore an historical event, but cautions that it is not "historical" in the Enlightenment sense of something that could be recognized and proved by a neutral observer:

Historical does not mean historically demonstrable or historically demonstrated. Hence it does not mean what is usually called "historical" *(historisch)*. We should be discarding again all that we have said earlier about the mystery in revelation if we were now to describe any of the events of revelation attested in the Bible as "historical" *(historisch);* i.e., apprehensible by a neutral observer or apprehended by such an observer. What a neutral observer could apprehend or may have apprehended of these events was the form of revelation which he did not and could not understand as such. It was an event that took place in the human sphere with all the possibilities of interpretation corresponding to this sphere. In no case was it revelation as such. . . . The "historical" element in the resurrection of Christ, the empty tomb as an aspect of this event that might be established, was not revelation. This "historical" element, like all else that is "historical" on this level, is admittedly open to very trivial interpretations too. (*CD* I/1, 325)

Barth contends that "we have to speak about an indirect *identity*" between revelation and the Bible. In this regard he warns against "modern theological historicism," which seeks "to penetrate past the biblical texts to the facts which lie behind the texts," in which facts, rather than in the text of the Bible itself, revelation is found (*CD* I/2, 492). The attempt to subject the Bible to historicist canons "was a mistake from the very first," even when the intent was to vindicate the Bible's truth rather than to challenge it. Reading the Bible in this way was a mistake because it meant reading it as something other than what it is. The Bible does not purport to be a collection of sources from which the revelation given to Israel can be extracted using neutral historical methods. "We cannot therefore put the question of truth in the direct way that it was arbitrarily thought it should be put" (*CD* I/2, 493).

This is not to say that historical scholarship does not have its place; but its place is in illuminating the meaning of the texts, not in sifting through them to find an alleged truth behind them. "All relevant, historical questions must be put to the biblical texts, considered as witnesses in accordance with their literary form." The answers to these questions are valuable so long as they are not being used in the service of "the foolish end of mediating an historical truth lying behind the texts. The historical truth which in its own way biblical scholarship does have to mediate is the true meaning and context of the biblical texts as such. Therefore it is not different from the biblical truth which has to be mediated" (*CD* I/2, 494).

In review, fideists deny that we can lead people to faith in Christ through presentations of the empirical, historical evidence. Such historical apologetics will always fall short of certainty and will fail to engage the revelatory character of the events. But fideists do not deny that the central events of the Christian gospel occurred in real history, nor do they minimize the importance of those events. Their claim is that their significance as revelation is beyond the competence of historical scholarship, and so must be grasped by faith alone.

FAITH IS EXPERIENCE

Reformed apologetics and fideism are often confused because of their similar demand that faith be placed firmly in God's revelation without reliance on any reasoning. Both also speak of God's revelation as "self-attesting," which adds to the similarities. However, one significant difference between the two approaches is found in their view of faith. For fideists, faith is also in some sense self-attesting. That is, fideists believe that faith is, or carries with it, its own evidence or basis of assurance. Kierkegaard states this idea rather plainly: "Away with all this world history and reasons and proofs for the truth of Christianity: there is only one proof—that of faith. If I actually have a firm conviction (and this, to be sure, is a qualification of intense inwardness oriented to spirit), then to me my firm conviction is higher than reasons: it is actually the conviction which sustains the reasons, not the reasons which sustain the convictions" (*JP* 3608, 3:663).

In saying that faith is its own proof, Kierkegaard does not mean that simply believing, in and of itself, is self-attesting. Remember that for him faith is not mere intellectual assent but a passionate commitment to Jesus Christ, which must be the result of a person's despairing of self and turning in helplessness to Christ. "There is only one, and quite rightly pathological, proof of the truth of Christianity—when the anxiety of sin and the burdened conscience constrain a man to cross the narrow line between despair unto madness—and Christianity" (*JP* 503, 1:201–202). Thus the faith that is its own proof is the faith that expresses itself in a person's life in such a way that there can be no doubting one's relationship with Christ. "According to the New Testament, is there not only one proof, only one thing that convinces—the fact that one's life expresses it?" (*JP* 3580, 3:646). "A witness is a person who directly demonstrates the truth of the doctrine he proclaims—directly, yes, in part by its being truth in him and blessedness, in part by volunteering his personal self and saying: Now see if you can force me to deny this doctrine. . . . But a teacher! He has proofs and arguments—but he stands outside, and the whole thing becomes ridiculous, all the objections triumphant" (*JP* 4967, 4:558–559).

Kierkegaard points out that others in the past have held up the changed lives of Christians as proof of Christianity. (The argument is still often used.) Unfortunately, he is rather pessimistic about its validity, since so few professing Christians really live the authentic, transformed life spoken of in the New Testament: "This is, after all, an apologetic for Christianity. He [Savonarola] proves the truth and divinity of Christianity by the transformation which occurs to those who become Christians—the proud become humble, the voluptuous chaste, etc. . . . Such an apologetic in our time would be a satire on us Christians" (*JP* 3842, 4:9–10).

Donald Bloesch advocates a nuanced approach to the place of experience in Christian faith. His main concern is to avoid both objectivism and subjectivism and to find a basis of certainty that "is neither subjective nor objective." This basis is God's revelation: "The ground of certainty is God speaking through the objective event and the subjective experience."[25] Bloesch's view derives from P. T. Forsyth:

> What Christians have is not self-certainty but "soul-certainty" (Forsyth), or even better, God-certainty. It is not the fact of our experience but the fact *which* we experience that shapes and determines Christian faith (Forsyth). . . . What Forsyth says is quite sound: "We have not two certitudes about these supreme matters, produced by authority *and* experience, but one, produced by authority *in* experience; not a certitude produced by authority and then corroborated by experience, but one produced by an authority active only in experience, and especially the corporate experience of a Church."[26]

Here we see that evangelical fideism seeks to uphold the objective revelation of God as the ground of our confidence or certainty, but at the same time views the inner assurance of faith produced by the Spirit as closely integrated with that objective ground.

For Further Study

Bloesch, Donald G. *The Ground of Certainty*. Grand Rapids: Eerdmans, 1971. Programmatic articulation of an evangelical fideist approach, discussing faith and reason, theology, philosophy, and experience.

McLaren, Brian D. *Finding Faith: A Self-Discovery Guide for Your Spiritual Quest*. Grand Rapids: Zondervan, 1999. Maryland pastor and leader in the Willow Creek movement presents a fideist apologetic aimed at seekers.

Chapter 18

Calling People to Encounter God in Jesus Christ

In the preceding two chapters we have profiled the thought of noted fideists in church history and surveyed their approach to relating apologetics to human knowledge and experience. While not irrationalists, fideists seek to present the Christian faith without compromise and without succumbing to the rationalism that they think characterizes what is usually called apologetics.

Advocates of other approaches may still, though, wonder at classifying fideism as a type of apologetics. Do fideists even attempt to provide meaningful answers to common objections to the Christian faith? Do they seek to give a reason for the hope that is within them (1 Peter 3:15)? In this chapter we will see that the answer to these questions is yes.

SCRIPTURE AS WITNESS

If there is an aspect of the fideist approach that especially troubles evangelicals, it is its view of Scripture. Fideists, seeking to center their faith, theology, and apologetics on Jesus Christ, tend to distinguish between Jesus Christ as *the* Word of God and Scripture as a "witness" to the Word of God, or of Scripture "becoming" God's Word in its witness to Jesus Christ. In some cases they deny the inerrancy of Scripture as part of their polemic against a bibliolatrous centering of the Christian faith in Scripture.

Arguably, as with other aspects of fideism, the fideist view of Scripture owes something to Martin Luther. Specifically, while Luther viewed the entirety of Scripture as God's Word, he tended to "grade" the different parts of the Bible depending on the extent to which they were centered on Christ and the gospel of justification through faith in Christ. Thus a higher value or esteem was placed on Paul's epistles than on the rest of the New Testament, and a sharp contrast was drawn between law (which dominates the Old Testament) and grace (which dominates the New Testament). Luther went so far as to question the inclusion of the epistle of James in the canon of the New Testament. This stratification of the Scriptures is often described as having a **canon within the canon**. While most theologians today (including many Lutherans) eschew this approach to Scripture, it survives in popular and even scholarly reading of Scripture. In addition, the classical form of dispensationalist theology, still popular in many circles, applied much the same principle to Scripture. In dispensationalism all parts of the Bible are equally Scripture and equally inspired, but some parts (especially Paul's epistles) are more directly applicable to the church in this dispensation.

Fideists tend to apply a similar principle to Scripture. For them the purpose of Scripture is to witness to Jesus Christ as the one, living Word of God. Aspects or statements of the Bible that do not contribute to that function need not be accepted as true, and certainly should not be defended.

Kierkegaard found evidence of a fideist approach to Scripture in Luther:

> In the sermon on the Gospel for Easter Monday, in the final passage, Luther makes the distinction: You have the right to argue the Bible, but you do not have the right to argue the Holy Scriptures. This is the old view that something may be true in philosophy which is not true in theology. The Bible and Holy Scriptures are the same book, to be sure, but the way in which it is regarded makes the difference.

> Here as everywhere we must pay attention to the qualitative leap, that there is no direct transition (for example, as from reading and studying the Bible as an ordinary human book—to taking it as God's word, as Holy Scripture), but everywhere a *meiabasis eis allo genos*, a leap, whereby I burst the whole progression of reason and define a qualitative newness, but a newness *allo genos*. (*JP* 2358, 3:22)

The Bible as the Bible, as a collection of books with a literary and textual history, can be studied, analyzed, debated, and even, for some fideists, critiqued. The Bible as Scripture, on the other hand, as the authoritative canon of writings bearing witness to God's reconciliation of mankind to himself through Jesus Christ, must be accepted by faith as beyond argument or debate. Notice that for Kierkegaard, as for Luther, Scripture is "God's word." To characterize Kierkegaard's view of Scripture as merely a witness to God's Word and not actually God's Word would be incorrect. On the other hand, the fact that the same book can be viewed either as the Bible or as Scripture implies that, for Kierkegaard, the divine character of Scripture is in some way dependent on the context in which it is viewed. This is evidently why he is not uncomfortable with the presence of apparent errors in the Bible:

> Up until now we have done as follows: we have declared that Holy Scripture is divine revelation, inspired, etc.—ergo, there must then be perfect harmony between all the reports down to the last detail; it must be the most perfect Greek, etc. . . . Precisely because God wants Holy Scripture to be the object of faith and an offense to any other point of view, for this reason there are carefully contrived discrepancies (which, after all, in eternity will readily be dissolved into harmonies); therefore it is written in bad Greek, etc. (*JP* 2877, 3:275; similarly *JP* 3860, 4:18)

Note that Kierkegaard affirms that the apparent errors in Scripture will be resolved in eternity. This qualification should be kept in mind when considering passages from his writings like the following:

> Take all the difficulties in Christianity which free-thinkers seize hold of and apologists want to defend, and see, the whole thing is a false alarm. The difficulties are simply introduced by God in order to make sure that he can become only the object of faith (although it is necessarily implicit in his essence and in the disproportion between the two qualities: God and man). This is why Christianity is a paradox; this explains the contradictions in Scripture, etc.

> But the intellectual approach wants to put everything into a direct relation—that is, wants to abolish faith. It wants to have direct recognizability, wants to have the most absolute harmony throughout Scripture, and then it will believe Christianity, believe that the Bible is the Word of God—that is, it will not believe. It has no inkling of God's sovereignty and what the requirement of faith means.

> The apologists are just as stupid as the free-thinkers and are always shifting the viewpoint of Christianity. (*JP* 1144, 2:21–22)

The basic fideist distinction between Scripture as witness and Christ as the One to whom Scripture witnesses is found in Kierkegaard. "The Holy Scriptures are the highway signs: Christ is the way" (*JP* 208, 1:84). "He was the Scriptures given life" (*JP* 342, 1:143). This distinction was developed greatly by Karl Barth. According to Barth, it is as the Bible engenders faith in God revealing himself that it functions as or is the Word of God. That is, God's Word is an event, the event of God speaking through the human words of Scripture. It is not up to us to make the Bible to be God's Word; rather, that is what God in his sovereign grace does. "The Bible is God's Word to the extent that God causes it be His Word, to the extent that He speaks through it" (*CD* I/1, 109). "It does not become God's Word because we accord it faith but in the fact that it becomes revelation to us" (*CD* I/1, 110). Because God's revelation is an event, the Bible "is not in itself and as such God's past revelation. As it is God's Word it bears witness to God's past revelation, and it is God's past revelation in the form of attestation" (*CD* I/1, 111). Barth accepts "direct identification of revelation and the Bible" only in the dynamic sense, stressing that as the Bible becomes God's Word it also becomes revelation. "Thus in the event of God's Word revelation and the Bible are indeed one, and literally so" (*CD* I/1, 113). Note, then, that Barth can accept a dynamic identity between the Bible and God's Word.

Barth says "we distinguish the Bible as such from revelation" by describing it as a witness to revelation. At the same time, he hastens to add that "the Bible is not distinguished from revelation" in that "it is for us revelation by means of the words of the prophets and apostles written in the Bible." Thus the Bible is revelation mediately, not immediately. "A real witness is not identical with that to which it witnesses, but it sets it before us" (*CD* I/2, 463). No denigration of Scripture is meant by this distinction; after all, Barth can speak of Jesus Christ as the true *Witness* and of the *witness* of the Holy Spirit to Jesus Christ. With the qualification that the book of Scripture is valued because in it the Holy Spirit witnesses to Jesus Christ, Barth can even affirm that Christianity is a religion of the Book: "If in reply it is asked whether Christianity is really a book-religion, the answer is that strangely enough Christianity has always been and only been a living religion when it is not ashamed to be actually and seriously a book-religion" (*CD* I/2, 494–495).

According to Barth, the Christian's faith that the Bible is the written Word of God has no logically prior ground. The authority of Scripture, because it is the Word of God, is self-attesting. Barth frankly accepts the circularity of this position:

> We have to admit to ourselves and to all who ask us about this question that the statement that the Bible is the Word of God is an analytical statement, a statement which is grounded only in its repetition, description and interpretation, and not in its derivation from any major propositions. It must either be understood as grounded in itself and preceding all other statements or it cannot be understood at all. The Bible must be known as the Word of *God* if it is to be *known* as the Word of God. The doctrine of Holy Scripture in the Evangelical Church is that this logical circle is the circle of self-asserting, self-attesting truth into which it is equally impossible to enter as it is to emerge from it: the circle of our freedom which as such is also the circle of our capacity. (*CD* I/2, 535)

CHRISTIANITY: NOT ANOTHER RELIGION

Among evangelicals, it is popular to affirm that Christianity is not a religion but a relationship with Jesus Christ. This saying nicely captures the view of religion taken by fideists, with one qualification: they generally acknowledge that a religion named Christianity exists, but insist that it comes under the same judgment as all other religions.

Like apologists of other approaches, fideists affirm that Christianity is unique among other religions and that Jesus Christ is the only Savior. Kierkegaard affirms quite simply that "Christianity is still the only explanation of existence which holds water" (*JP* 1052, 1:457), and offers two main arguments for why it is superior to all other religions. First, and somewhat surprisingly, Christianity is superior because it alone tells the truth about man's tragic standing as a sinner. "And this is the very proof of Christianity's being the highest religion, that none other has given such a profound and lofty expression of man's significance—that he is a sinner. It is this consciousness which paganism lacks" (*JP* 452, 1:179). The fact that Christianity offends many people in its assessment of the human condition is for Kierkegaard just as important as the fact that many are attracted to it. "The double relationship in Christianity is the very thing that demonstrates its absolute truth, the fact that it goads just as intensely as it attracts" (*JP* 455, 1:179).

Second, Kierkegaard points out that Jesus Christ, alone among all the founders of the major world religions, made himself the supreme issue. "All other religions are oblique; the founder steps aside and introduces another who speaks; therefore, they themselves belong under the religion—Christianity alone is direct address (I am the truth)" (*JP* 427, 1:172).

In two different sections of the *Church Dogmatics*, one toward the beginning and the other near the end, Barth developed a fideist account of the exclusive claims of Jesus Christ in the context of religious pluralism. Ironically, he traces the liberal denial of the uniqueness of Christ to the excessive rationalism of some orthodox Protestant scholars of the early eighteenth century. He summarizes the import of their teaching as follows.

> Human religion, the relationship with God which we can and actually do have apart from revelation, is not an unknown but a very well-known quantity both in form and content, and as such it is something which has to be reckoned with, as having a central importance for all theological thinking. It constitutes, in fact, the presupposition, the criterion, the necessary framework for an understanding of revelation. It shows us the question which is answered by revealed religion as well as all other positive religions, and it is as the most satisfactory answer that the Christian religion has the advantage over others and is rightly described as revealed religion. The Christian element—and with this the theological reorientation which had threatened since the Renaissance is completed—has now actually become a predicate of the neutral and universal human element. Revelation has now become a historical confirmation of what man can know about himself and therefore about God even apart from revelation. (*CD* I/2, 289–290).

From the roots of this rationalistic view of religion and revelation eventually emerged the destructive developments typified in the thought of Wolff, Kant, Schleiermacher, Strauss, Feuerbach, Ritschl, and Troeltsch. "All these more or less radical and destructive movements in the history of theology in the last two centuries are simply variations on one simple theme . . . that religion has not to be understood in the light of revelation, but revelation in the light of religion" (*CD* I/2, 290–291). Barth concludes that the roots of liberalism and relativism in modern Protestantism are in the rationalism of the orthodox Protestant tradition (*CD* I/2, 291–292).

Against the rationalistic account of the relation of revelation to religion, Barth argues that religion is actually in antithesis to revelation.

> Because it is a grasping, religion is the contradiction of revelation, the concentrated expression of human unbelief, i.e., an attitude and activity which is directly opposed to faith. It is a feeble but defiant, an arrogant but hopeless, attempt to create something which man could do, but now cannot do, or can do only because and if God Himself created it for him: the knowledge of the truth, the knowledge of God. We cannot, therefore, interpret the attempt as a harmonious co-operating of man with the revelation of God, as though religion were a kind of outstretched hand which is filled by God in His revelation. Again, we cannot say of the evident religious capacity of man that it is, so to speak, the general form of human knowledge, which acquires its true and proper content in the shape of revelation. On the contrary, we have here an exclusive contradiction. In religion man bolts and bars himself against revelation by providing a substitute, by taking away in advance the very thing which has to be given by God. (*CD* I/2, 302–303)

On the basis of this view of religion, Barth concludes that in a sense *no* religion is true. "Religion is never true in itself and as such. The revelation of God denies that any religion is true, i.e., that it is in truth the knowledge and worship of God and the reconciliation of man with God" (*CD* I/2, 325). On the other hand, in another sense Christianity is the true religion, but only because God in his grace makes it so.

> The abolishing of religion by revelation need not mean only its negation: the judgment that religion is unbelief. Religion can just as well be exalted in revelation, even though the judgment still stands. It can be upheld by it and concealed in it. It can be justified by it, and—we must at once add—sanctified. Revelation can adopt religion and mark it off as true religion. And it not only can. How do we come to assert that it can, if it has not already done so? There is a true religion: just as there are justified sinners. If we abide strictly by that analogy—and we are dealing not merely with an analogy, but in a comprehensive sense with the thing itself—we need have no hesitation in saying that the Christian religion is the true religion. (*CD* I/2, 326)

Barth's statement here makes explicit a pun or play on words noted by Geoffrey Bromiley in the title of this section, "The Revelation of God as the Abolition of Religion." Bromiley observes "that the word abolition is used here for the German *Aufhebung*, which in good Hegelian fashion can mean elevating as well as abolishing. Barth undoubtedly has this double meaning in mind."[1] Here Barth expounds that double meaning: the revelation of God elevates or exalts religion paradoxically at the same time that it abolishes religion; it does this by establishing a new religion that has as its central affirmation that God has judged sinners and their religion and now offers them a new standing of righteousness by grace. Thus Christianity is unique in its self-criticism. Rather than proclaiming itself to be the best or greatest religion, the highest achievement of man's spiritual quest, Christianity proclaims all religion, even that of its own adherents, to be under the judgment of unbelief: "We must insist, therefore, that at the beginning of a knowledge of the truth of the Christian religion, there stands the recognition that this religion, too, stands under the judgment that religion is unbelief, and that it is not acquitted by any inward worthiness, but only by the grace of God, proclaimed and effectual in His revelation" (*CD* I/2, 327).

Barth finds this judgment on the Christian religion expressed in 1 Corinthians 13, which, he says, "we shall best understand if for the concept 'love' we simply insert the name Jesus Christ."

> The chapter summarizes the whole religious life of a Christian community at the time of Paul: speaking with tongues, prophecy, knowledge of mysteries, a faith that removes mountains, giving all one's goods to the poor, martyrdom in the flames to close—and of all this it is said that it helps the Christian not at all, absolutely not at all, if he has not love. For love alone never fails. . . . At the very heart of the apostolic witness (which accepts the Christian as the true religion) Christianity could not be more comprehensively relativised in favour of revelation, which means a crisis even for the religion of revelation. (*CD* I/2, 330–331)

Toward the end of the *Church Dogmatics* Barth explains why the church is not arrogant to claim that Jesus Christ is the only self-revelation of God. Regarding whether there might not be other valid, prophetic sources besides the one Word of God incarnated in Jesus Christ and witnessed in Scripture, Barth replies with the first statement of the Barmen Declaration of 1934: "We reject the false doctrine that the Church can and must, as the source of its proclamation, recognise other events and powers, forms and truths, as the revelation of God outside and alongside this one Word of God" (*CD* IV/3/1, 86). He then explains that the intent of this statement is to exalt Christ, not to commend the church.

> The statement that Jesus Christ is the one Word of God has really nothing whatever to do with the arbitrary exaltation and self-glorification of the Christian in relation to other men, of the Church in relation to other institutions, or of Christianity in relation to other conceptions.

> It is a christological statement. It looks away from non-Christian and Christian alike to the One who sovereignly confronts and precedes both as *the* Prophet. (*CD* IV/3/1, 91)

Barth points out that the prophets of the Old Testament and the apostles of the New were just as aware of the plurality of religions in their cultures as we are of this plurality in ours. Yet none of them ever left a trace of the idea that these extra-biblical religions represented alternative revelations (*CD* IV/3/1, 92–93).

Barth then raises the question of the basis on which we affirm that Jesus Christ is the one Word of God, to which he proposes a counterquestion:

> Hence, if anyone asks concerning the basis of our statement, we must put the counter-question whether he sees and realises that Jesus Christ actually shows Himself to be the one Prophet of God. This is the question to which we must make answer to ourselves and others. The revelation of God vouches for its uniqueness as it does for itself as such. If Jesus Christ is the one Word of God, He alone, standing out from the ranks of all other supposed and pretended divine words, can make Himself known as this one Word. (*CD* IV/3/1, 103–104)

As Isaiah 40 sets forth the incomparable deity of Yahweh, all we can and should really do is to explicate what it means that Jesus Christ is the one Word of God (*CD* IV/3/1, 105). We do that by pressing the uniqueness of Jesus Christ as the Word of God. No other word reveals the omnipotent grace of God and his love for all mankind in providing full justification and sanctification in a once-for-all event (*CD* IV/3/1, 107–108). We are to press the point that it is not Christianity, the church, or even the Bible that cannot be compared with other words, but rather it is Jesus Christ who is incomparably the Word (*CD* IV/3/1, 108).

This does not mean that we are engaging in apologetics. Or if so, it is only the apologetics which is a necessary function of dogmatics to the extent that this must prepare an exact account of the presupposition, limits, meaning and basis of the statements of the Christian confession, and thus be able to give this account to any who may demand it. . . . In relation to the content of the Word spoken in Jesus Christ, we have tried to describe and explain this basis. The fact remains, however, that it can only speak for itself and show itself to be the basis of our statement. Without counting on the Holy Spirit as the only conclusive argument, even the prophet of the Exile who advanced those arguments and proofs could not have undertaken to proclaim the uniqueness of Yahweh among the gods of the nations. (*CD* IV/3/1, 109)

TO KNOW GOD IS TO KNOW GOD EXISTS

Fideists approach the question of the knowledge of God from the starting point that God is personal. To prove that God exists is insulting, because He is someone we already know personally, and unreasonable, because God by his nature transcends our world and is beyond proof. Rather than try to prove that God exists, fideists urge Christian apologists to call on non-Christians to hear God revealing himself personally to them in his Word.

In some important ways, Blaise Pascal's *Pensées* anticipated a fideistic approach to knowing God. We reviewed his argument in some detail in chapter 16; we will simply summarize the main points here. According to Pascal, God has given "visible signs" to make it possible for people to find him, but has "disguised" them so that only those really seeking him will succeed (*Pensées*, 194).[2] These signs, therefore, are not rational proofs, nor can they be made the basis of such proofs. After all, if God does exist, he "is infinitely incomprehensible"; if he is beyond our rational understanding, he is beyond our rational proof. Atheists who ask for proof are asking for something that would *disprove* Christianity. It is in this context that Pascal offers his famous "wager argument": if we believe in God and he does not exist, we lose nothing; if we believe in God and he does exist, we gain everything (233). This argument appears to be a recommendation to unbelievers to take the Christian faith seriously enough to try it. As unbelievers are awakened to the need to take God seriously, some will be brought to faith by the grace of God. "Faith is different from proof; the one is human, the other is a gift from God" (248).

Something like Pascal's wager appears also in the thought of Kierkegaard, according to whom a person must "choose" to "venture" his whole life on the historical person of Jesus Christ. "This is called *venturing*, and without venturing faith is an impossibility." Unlike Socrates, who wagered his whole life on his own inherent immortality, the Christian is wagering his whole life on another, on Jesus Christ (*JP* 73, 1:28).

Because of his view of God as wholly other than the world, Kierkegaard believed that natural theology and rational proofs of the existence of God were entirely invalid. Like Hume, he objected that an infinite God cannot be deduced from a finite world.[3] Faith in God can neither be rationally certain nor empirically evident; revelation is paradoxical and requires a leap of faith.

> For whose sake is it that the proof is sought? Faith does not need it; aye, it must even regard the proof as its enemy. But when faith begins to feel embarrassed and ashamed, like a young woman for whom her love is no longer sufficient, but who secretly feels ashamed of her lover and must therefore have it established that there is something remarkable about him—when faith thus begins to lose its passion, when faith begins to cease to be faith, then a proof becomes necessary so as to command respect from the side of unbelief.[4]

In the beginning of his *Philosophical Fragments*, Kierkegaard sought to expose the fallacious arguments in the standard demonstrations of God's existence. "For if the God does not exist it would of course be impossible to prove it; and if he does exist it would be folly to attempt it."[5]

An additional objection to theistic proofs stems from the personhood of God. God must be approached in the humility of subjection and submission, not in the arrogance of rational speculation. This is one of the recurrent themes in *Concluding Unscientific Postscript:*

> So rather let us mock God, out and out, as has been done before in the world—this is always preferable to the disparaging air of importance with which one would prove God's existence. For to prove the existence of one who is present is the most shameless affront, since it is an attempt to make him ridiculous. . . . But how could it occur to anybody to prove that he exists, unless one had permitted oneself to ignore him, and now

makes the thing all the worse by proving his existence before his very nose?

Instead, the only appropriate "proof" of God's existence is an expression of submission: "one proves God's existence by worship . . . not by proofs."[6]

Like other fideists, Barth grounds his objections to natural theology, or theistic proofs, on the nature of God. For example, he argues that the fact that God created everything else that exists *ex nihilo* (out of nothing) puts God beyond all arguments based on analogies to cause-and-effect relationships in nature:

> Moreover, we have no analogy on the basis of which the nature and being of God as Creator can be accessible to us. We know originators and causes. We can again extend the series into the infinite. . . . But creation means that our existence and existence generally as distinct from God are opposed to nothing, to non-existence. Creator means one who alone exists, and everything else only as the work of His will and Word. Creator means: *creator ex nihilo*. But within the sphere of the ideas possible to us, *creatio ex nihilo* can appear only as an absurdity. (*CD* II/1, 76).

In addition, Barth objects to natural theology because it is incompatible with the doctrine of grace. He argues that grace does not merely reconcile us to God, it enables us to *know* God: "It [the church] must not withhold from the world, nor must it confuse and conceal, the fact that God is knowable to us in His grace, and because in His grace, only in His grace. For this reason it can make no use of natural theology with its doctrine of another kind of knowability of God" (*CD* II/1, 172).

THE PERSONAL PROBLEM OF EVIL

The problem of evil is one of the most famous puzzles in the history of human thought. For fideists, that is exactly what the "problem" is with the "problem of evil": it has been treated as an intellectual puzzle, a kind of apologetical Rubik's Cube. The real issue, they say, is whether people will trust God. When people ask how God can be all-powerful and all-loving and still allow evil, the unvoiced question they are almost always posing is, How can I trust God? or, Why should I trust God?

Fideists typically answer this question in two ways. First, they argue that in a sense the question is inappropriate and shows that people have not really come to terms with what it means for God to be *God*. Luther, for example, urged people to avoid speculating about the matter: "Let, therefore, his goodwill be acceptable unto thee, oh, man, and speculate not with thy devilish queries, thy whys and thy wherefores, touching on God's words and works. For God, who is creator of all creatures, and orders all things according to his unsearchable will and wisdom, is not pleased with such questionings."[7]

According to Kierkegaard, it is unthinkable to blame God for anything, and no proof of his goodness is needed. "For this reason Christianity cannot answer the question: Why? For in the absolute sense, 'Why?' cannot be asked. The absolute is the absolute" (*JP* 486, 1:193).

> The best proof that there is a just providence is to say: "I *will* believe it whatever happens." All proof is foolishness, a kind of double-mind-edness which by two paths (the objective and the subjective) wants to arrive simultaneously at the same point. The believer says to himself: "The most detestable of all would be for you to allow yourself, in any ever so hidden thought, to insult God by thinking of him as having done wrong. Therefore, if someone wishes to write a big book to justify or indict God—as far as I am concerned, I will believe. Where it seems that I might be able to understand, I will still prefer to believe, for it is more blessed to believe—as long as we human beings live in this world, understanding easily becomes something imagined, a chummy importunity—and where I cannot understand, yes, there it is blessed to believe." (*JP* 1117, 2:9)

Likewise, Barth held that God gave Job no answer to the problem of suffering, but simply asked Job to trust him: "He [God] does not ask for his understanding, agreement or applause. On the contrary, he simply asks that he should be content not to know why and to what extent he exists, and does so in this way and not another. He simply asks that he should admit that it is not he who plans and controls" (*CD* IV/3/1, 431).

Second, and in some tension with the claim that no answer should be given to the problem, some fideists do offer a reply to the question of why we should trust God, to wit: in Christ's suffering and death God has shown his trustworthiness beyond anything we have a right to have expected. Barth repeatedly gives this answer in his *Church Dogmatics:*

The New Testament answer to the problem of suffering—and it alone is the answer to the sharply put query of the Old Testament—is to the effect that One has died for all. (*CD* I/2, 109)

Thus even when we think of man in this negative determination, we still think of him as the one whom God loved from all eternity in His Son, as the one to whom He gave Himself from all eternity in His Son, gave Himself that He might represent him, gave Himself that He might bear and suffer on His behalf what man himself had to suffer. (*CD* II/2, 165–166)

If the created world is understood in light of the divine mercy revealed in Jesus Christ, of the divine participation in it eternally resolved in Jesus Christ and fulfilled by Him in time; if it is thus understood as the arena, instrument and object of His living action, of the once for all divine contesting and overcoming of its imperfection, its justification and perfection will infallibly be perceived and it will be seen to be the best of all possible worlds. (*CD* III/1, 385)

Barth takes this answer one step further. Rather than trying to justify God to the unbelieving world by constructing speculative, rational arguments, the church needs to show in its own response to human suffering that it is a people who know and trust God.

We do not believe if we do not live in the neighborhood of Golgotha. And we cannot live in the neighborhood of Golgotha without being affected by the shadow of divine judgment, without allowing this shadow to fall on us. In this shadow Israel suffered. In this shadow the Church suffers. That it suffers in this way is the Church's answer to the world on the question of a "theodicy"—the question of the justice of God in the sufferings inflicted on us in the world. (*CD* II/1, 406)[8]

MIRACLES AS GOD REVEALING HIMSELF

The fideist approach to miracles may be understood by comparing it to the approach taken in Reformed apologetics, in which the biblical miracles are problematic to non-Christians because they do not accept the Bible as God's self-attesting revelation. For Reformed apologists revelation is essentially verbal: God communicates truth to us in propositional form, and included in this truth is the fact that God has done certain miracles for our redemption. The apologetic task, then, becomes to present God's revelation in Scripture as his self-attesting Word, and belief in the biblical miracles will follow.

The fideists' approach differs in this respect: for them God's revelation is not essentially verbal, but active. It is what God does, particularly in Jesus Christ, that reveals God to us. Of course, part of what God does in Christ is to speak, and fideists do not deny that revelation includes a verbal aspect. But the point is this: in fideism one does not believe in the reality of miracles because God has revealed that they have happened; rather, one believes because in those very miracles one realizes that God is revealing himself. In Reformed apologetics miracles are believed because God reveals them; in fideism, because in them God reveals himself.

Barth articulates this view of miracles in the *Church Dogmatics*. He defines miracle as "an attribute of revelation":

> In the Bible a miracle is not some event that is hard to conceive, nor yet one that is simply inconceivable, but one that is highly conceivable, but conceivable only as the exponent of the special new direct act of God in time and in history. In the form in which it acquires temporal historical actuality, biblically attested revelation is always a miracle, and therefore the witness to it, whether direct or indirect in its course, is a narrative of miracles that happened. Miracle is thus an attribute of revelation. (*CD* I/2, 63–64)

Barth clearly did not think miracles should be accepted simply because they are in the Bible. He makes this point explicitly when, following on the above-cited passage, he asserts that the believer in God's revelation in Christ might conceivably question some of the miracle stories in the Bible:

> The fact that the statement "God reveals Himself" is the confession of a miracle that has happened certainly does not imply a blind credence in all the miracle stories related in the Bible. If we confess the miracle, we may very well, at least partially and by degrees, accept additional light from the miracles as necessary signs of the miracle. But even if we confess the miracle, why should we not constantly find this or that one of the miracles obscure, why should we not constantly be taken aback by

them? It is really not laid upon us to take everything in the Bible as true *in globo*, but it is laid upon us to listen to its testimony when we actually hear it. A man might even credit all miracles and for that reason not confess *the* miracle. (*CD* I/2, 65)

Years later Barth was asked about this statement. His comments were, in part, as follows: "I only say that we do not have to accept all the miracles *in globo*. I did not speak of excluding any miracle. There is *one* great miracle that is reflected in all the miracles. . . . We cannot reason: the Bible tells us the truth; the Bible tells us of miracles; therefore we must accept the miracles. No, the Bible tells us of *the* miracle of revelation. . . . We do not believe in miracles, but in God."[9]

JESUS: THE CHRIST OF FAITH

Fideists believe Jesus Christ needs no defense. They believe He is personally self-attesting: as people encounter Jesus Christ (through the witness of Scripture and the church), they are won to faith in him by the power of the love and grace of God that he embodies. To the question "Why should I believe in Jesus Christ?" the fideist answers simply, "Get to know him and you'll see." According to Karl Barth, for example, the life of Jesus is self-interpreting and self-validating. Since the history of Jesus' life is the history of God's revelation of himself in Jesus, the very history of that revelation in Jesus' life reveals the meaning of Jesus' life. This implies that "all verification of its occurrence can only follow its self-verification, all interpretation of its form and content its self-interpretation. His history is a question which gives its own answer, a puzzle which contains its own solution, a secret which is in process of its own disclosure." (*CD* IV/3/1, 46–47)

Although fideists oppose traditional sorts of arguments designed to prove or defend rationally that Jesus is the risen Christ and Son of God, they do employ indirect arguments in keeping with Kierkegaard's practice of "indirect communication." For example, in Kierkegaard's *Philosophical Fragments*, Climacus's "poem" about God becoming a man in order to be our Teacher and Savior is shown not to be Climacus's invention or the creation of any other human being; it must therefore have come from God himself.[10] Those who hear the story of the Incarnation and disbelieve it are always offended at the absurdity of it, a fact that Climacus takes as indirect confirmation of its truth.[11] Stephen Evans corroborates this view: "A person who wanted to make up a story would make up something much more plausible."[12]

Barth also indirectly argues that Jesus Christ must be the person attested in Scripture because no human being could ever have invented the story. He reminds his readers that he is "speaking of the Jesus Christ attested in Scripture," who "is not then the creation of free speculation based on direct experience." The biblical picture of Jesus "is not a picture arbitrarily invented and constructed by others. It is the picture which He Himself has created and impressed upon His witnesses." We know who he is because in rising from the dead he has "shown Himself to be who He is. . . . If there is any Christian and theological axiom, it is that Jesus Christ is risen, that He is truly risen. But this is an axiom which no one can invent. It can only be repeated on the basis of the fact that in the enlightening power of the Holy Spirit it has been previously declared to us as the central statement of the biblical witness" (*CD* IV/3/1, 44). As the living, risen Lord, Jesus Christ takes the initiative to make us known to him. "We are first known by the One whom we may know, and it is only then that we may know and believe and confess" (*CD* IV/3/1, 45).

Having affirmed that Jesus' life is a revelation of God, and that it is such in fulfillment of the Old Testament (*CD* IV/3/1, 48–71), Barth asks the apologetic question: "Hitherto we have presupposed and maintained that the life of Jesus Christ as such is light, that His being is also name, His reality truth, His history revelation, His act Word or Logos. We have simply ascribed to Him what the Bible calls glory and therefore His prophetic office. On what ground and with what right may we do this?" (*CD* IV/3/1, 72).

Barth elaborates on the question: Are we merely ascribing these things to Jesus after the fact, placing our own value judgment on him, describing him in categories of our own thought? For Barth the key to responding to these questions is to ask, "Who is it who puts these questions?" But this question implies and calls for another:

> But the question which we really ought to put first is whether we should decide, whether we are in any way competent, whether we can imagine that we have some light of our own which constrains and qualifies us, ever to put such questions. Is there any place from which we are really able to ask whether Jesus Christ is the light, the revelation, the Word, the Prophet? Is there any place where we are really forced to ask this for the sake of the honesty and sincerity which we owe ourselves? To ascribe to ourselves a competence to put such questions is *ipso facto* to deny that

His life is light, His work truth, His history revelation, His act the Word of God. (*CD* IV/3/1, 73)

According to Barth, it makes no sense for someone who believes in Christ as the Truth to try and prove or defend that belief.

> Let us suppose that someone does really presuppose and maintain that the existence of Jesus Christ is light, truth, revelation, Word and glory, and thinks that it is obviously reasonable and incumbent to confess this. Can it ever enter his head to think that he should justify himself in this matter, adducing proofs to convince himself and others, or to assure himself that he is really right, that what he does is necessary or at least possible? (*CD* IV/3/1, 74)

Barth is content, then, simply to present Jesus Christ as He has revealed himself to us and to explain what Christians believe about Christ. Ultimately Jesus Christ by the Spirit is the one who convinces us and others that He is who He claims to be. Barth admits frankly that in the end the Christian presentation of the claims of Christ will be circular:

> The point of our whole exposition is positively: *Credo ut intelligam*, and polemically: "The fool hath said in his heart, There is no God." As we have put it, the declaration of the prophecy of the life of Jesus Christ is valid as and because it is a declaration concerning the life of Jesus Christ. But is not this begging the question? Are we not arguing in a circle? Exactly! We have learned from the content of our presupposition and assertion, and only from its content, that because it is true it is legitimate and obligatory, and in what sense this is the case. (*CD* IV/3/1, 85–86)

For Further Study

Brown, Colin. *Miracles and the Critical Mind*. Grand Rapids: Eerdmans, 1984. Detailed historical study of miracles in Christian and non-Christian thought, written from a generally fideist perspective.

Rodin, R. Scott. *Evil and Theodicy in the Theology of Karl Barth*. Issues in Systematic Theology 3. New York: Peter Lang, 1997. Thorough study of Barth's treatment of the problem of evil.

Chapter 19

Apologetics and the Subjectivity of Faith

In this concluding chapter on fideism, we will summarize this model or paradigm for apologetics, illustrate its use in practical apologetic encounters, and then consider its major strengths and weaknesses.

THE FIDEIST MODEL

As explained in chapter 3, we are summarizing each model of apologetic system under two headings (metapologetics and apologetics) and six specific questions under each heading. Here we apply this analysis to the fideist model.

Metapologetic Questions

Metapologetic questions deal with the relation of apologetics to other forms of human knowledge. In chapter 17 we considered the approach taken in fideism to answering questions about knowledge in general, theology, philosophy, science, history, and experience. Here we summarize our findings in that chapter.

1. On what basis do we claim that Christianity is the truth?

Fideists argue that the only proper ground on which to claim that Christianity is the truth is that God has personally revealed himself in Christ. Christianity is essentially not a body of knowledge or a worldview, but a personal relationship with God in Christ. Faith in Christ is created and sustained by the witness of the Holy Spirit to Christ. Fideists argue that the other apologetic approaches are wedded to modernist notions of rationality, as seen in their efforts to develop Christianity into a comprehensive "worldview."

2. What is the relationship between apologetics and theology?

According to Karl Barth, who is representative of a mature fideism in this regard, the best apologetics is a good dogmatics, or Christian theology. That is, the best way to persuade people to believe in Christ is to give an accurate witness to the meaning of God's revelation in Christ and its significance for our lives. Apologetics should not be viewed as a separate discipline establishing the truth or the possibility of theology, as in classical apologetics.

3. Should apologetics engage in a philosophical defense of the Christian faith?

Fideists adamantly oppose the philosophical defense of the Christian faith. Apologists should study philosophy in order to contrast the way of philosophy with the way of faith, which are diametrically opposed. Christianity is not an intellectual system to be rationally defended, but a relationship with God in Christ to be personally experienced.

4. Can science be used to defend the Christian faith?

According to fideism, science can neither support the truth of Christianity nor undermine it, because science and theology deal with different questions. As a consequence, fideists tend to be open to theistic evolution, though not all fideists actually accept evolutionism.

5. Can the Christian faith be supported by historical inquiry?

It is a major characteristic of fideism that historical apologetics is firmly rejected. Historical argument can at best end in approximate knowledge and probability, an inadequate basis for the certainty of faith. Christ is objectively revealed in Scripture, but it is not possible or desirable to seek an objective account of the details of Jesus' historical life.

6. How is our knowledge of Christian truth related to our experience?

According to fideists, in some sense faith is self-attesting, because it is produced by the work of the Spirit. Thus our experience of genuine faith can be the basis of our confidence in the truth about Christ. This does not mean that the truth or even our assurance of the truth has no objective basis, since God has objectively revealed himself in Christ, but that without the subjective dimension of faith the objective revelation is not recognizable as such.

Apologetic Questions

Apologetic questions deal with issues commonly raised by non-Christians. In chapter 18 we considered fideist responses to questions about the Bible, Christianity and other beliefs, the existence of God, the problem of evil, the credibility of miracles, and the claims of Jesus Christ. Here we summarize our findings in that chapter.

1. Why should we believe in the Bible?

Actually, for fideists our faith is not in the Bible, but in Christ, to whom the Bible as Scripture gives reliable witness. We believe the Bible insofar as and because in it we encounter Jesus Christ, the living Word.

2. Don't all religions lead to God?

Fideists argue that no religion, not even Christianity considered as such, leads to God. It is in a personal relationship with Jesus Christ that we are reconciled to God, not in religion. By God's grace the religion of Christianity bears witness to Christ and is in that sense the only true religion.

3. How do we know that God exists?

To put it simply, fideists argue that we know that God exists only if we know God personally; and we come to know God personally only in Jesus Christ. They reject all attempts to prove that God exists.

4. If God does exist, why does He permit evil?

Fideists contend that we are really not in a position to know or understand why God has permitted things to happen as they have, but such knowledge is not really what we need. What we need is to know that we can trust God. Knowing that God is God really is to know that God is trustworthy; and we come to know God's goodness and love in Jesus Christ, whose suffering and death definitively reveal God's concern for our plight.

5. Aren't the miracles of the Bible spiritual myths or legends and not literal fact?

Fideists argue that we should not try to prove that miracles are possible or that they have happened; nor should we believe in miracles merely because they are reported in the Bible. Rather, we believe that miracles have occurred because in those miracles we see fleshed out *the* miracle of God's revelation of himself in Jesus Christ.

6. Why should I believe in Jesus?

Fideists reject any and all direct apologetic arguments for belief in Jesus. On the other hand, they do typically employ indirect arguments for belief in Jesus, notably that the Christian message about Jesus is something no human would ever have invented. Ultimately, though, fideists urge non-Christians to read the New Testament and meet Jesus there. As with any person, the best and only way to know the truth about Jesus is to get to know him personally.

The following table presents an overview of the fideist model of apologetics with these twelve questions in mind.

Issue		Position
Metapologetics	KNOWLEDGE	Faithfulness to revelation is the test of truth Postmodernism exposes modernism in apologetics Spirit's witness to Christ produces faith
	THEOLOGY	Good theology is the best apologetics Apologetics cannot prepare for or justify theology
	PHILOSOPHY	Apologetics confronts all philosophy Christians should oppose, not develop, philosophy
	SCIENCE	Science neither supports nor undermines faith Science and theology ask different questions Typically theistic evolutionism
	HISTORY	Christ objectively revealed in Scripture Faith cannot be based on historical knowledge
	EXPERIENCE	Christianity to be experienced, not defended Experience of faith is self-validating
Apologetics	SCRIPTURE	Scripture needs no defense Begin with Christ, not from Scripture as such Scripture gives faithful witness to Christ
	RELIGIONS	Christianity is relationship with Christ, not religion Christ unique among religious leaders
	GOD	All direct theistic proofs are rejected God known in encounter, not in argument
	EVIL	Personal problem of evil: How do I trust God? God shows his goodness in Christ's suffering
	MIRACLES	Miracles are credible to those who know God Miracles are God revealing himself
	JESUS	Jesus is self-attesting Christ witnessed in Scripture Jesus is someone no human could invent

FIDEISM ILLUSTRATED

In this fourth and final dialogue of the book, a Christian named Martina becomes involved in a discussion with Sarah and Murali while shopping at the mall. The three of them, along with others, have stopped to watch a news bulletin on a television in the department store. The bulletin announces that a lone gunman has killed several people at a local high school. As Martina stands next to Sarah and Murali, the three of them discuss the shocking story.

Murali: How can people do things like this? What's wrong with the world today?

Martina [speaking softly]: I am.

Sarah: Come again?

Martina: I'm sorry. I guess that must have sounded strange. My name's Martina. What's yours?

Sarah: I'm Sarah.

Murali: My name is Murali. What did you mean by saying "I am"?

Martina: I was thinking of G. K. Chesterton's answer to your question. The London *Times* once invited correspondence from readers in answer to that same question, "What's wrong with the world today?" Chesterton wrote a letter in reply that read, "Dear Sirs: I am. Yours respectfully, G. K. Chesterton."

Murali: But what does it mean? Surely he didn't blame himself for all the problems of the world.

Martina: No. But he was saying that the source of all the world's problems was just as much in him, and it is just as much in me, as it was in that teenager who killed all those people.

Murali: And what is that source?

Martina: Sin.

Sarah: Oh, brother. You're saying that the world is a mess because we're all a bunch of sinners?

Martina: Well, yes, we are—myself included. Aren't you?

Sarah: No, I don't consider myself a sinner.

Martina: Why not?

Sarah: Because for there to be sin, there'd have to be a God.

Martina: You're quite right about that.

Sarah: But I don't believe in a God.

Martina: Then how do you explain the sin that is within us all?

Sarah: I just told you, I don't think there is sin in us all. I mean, we're not all like that sicko. I certainly don't have that kind of hatred that would make me want to kill innocent people.

Martina: So you think that for all people to be sinners, sin would have to show itself in the same way in all people?

Sarah: Uh—well, no, that's not what I meant.

Martina: So perhaps sin shows itself in me, or in you, in a different way than the way it shows itself in a mass murderer.

Sarah: I don't think so. I don't think I have any sin in me at all.

Martina: What about the mass murderer? Is there sin in him?

Sarah: No, because nothing is sin unless there's a God.

Martina: Then the fact that you and Murali and I are relatively decent, moral people in comparison to the mass murderers of the world is beside the point. If no one is a sinner, then even the worst of us is not a sinner. And if sin is determined in relation to God, then we might all be sinners in his eyes.

Murali: But why would He consider us sinners, if we're good people?

Martina: Perhaps the two of you are thinking of sin in terms of overtly immoral and even criminal behavior, like stealing and murder. But those kinds of things are only symptoms of sin.

Sarah: What is sin, then?

Martina: There are many ways to define sin, but my favorite way is to say that sin is falling short of embodying God's glorious character— the perfect, infinite love of God. You see, sin is not merely doing forbidden things like stealing, but it's also the failure to do good things like giving generously and sacrificially to others.

Murali: That sounds like a beautiful and noble definition to me. It is a way of challenging us all to strive to be better persons.

Martina: Actually, it's no such thing.

Murali: How can you say that? If we all fall short of this ideal, should we not all strive to come closer to it?

Martina: No. Let me explain. Suppose you were being chased on foot by an army of soldiers bent on killing you, and you came to the edge of a cliff. The only way to safety is to jump half a mile across a canyon to the other side. Could you do it?

Murali: No.

Sarah: No one could.

Martina: Exactly. Would you try?

Murali: I guess not. Oh, I see. You're saying that the love of God is so far beyond our capacity that it is pointless for us to strive to meet that ideal.

Martina: Exactly.

Murali: It seems to me that you're taking this idea rather literally.

Martina: How else should I take it?

Murali: All of the religions of the world employ beautiful myths that inspire us to transcend the normal limitations of our material existence. They all have different ways of saying the same thing: that we must reach beyond ourselves.

Martina: And have you done that?

Murali: Well—I'm trying in my own way, as are we all, are we not?

Martina: But if we're all trying, is that good enough? Remember, you asked what's wrong with the world. Apparently some of us aren't trying, or trying isn't good enough, or both.

Murali: You have a point. I guess I would have to say that some of us aren't trying.

Martina: But why should any of us need to try?

Murali: I don't understand your question.

Martina: Why isn't transcending the normal limitations of our material existence, as you put it, as natural to us as breathing, or eating? If that is what we should all do, why is it so hard—why does it seem to be an unattainable ideal? Or, to return to your question, what's wrong with the world? Why aren't *we* the way *we're* supposed to be?

Murali: That is a very good question. I suppose that is what all of the religions try to explain with their myths.

Martina: And are any of their answers correct?

Murali: I don't think anyone can say that one religion's answer is more correct than that of any other religion. I think every religion is helpful to those who believe it.

Martina: But if we can't say that our religion's answer is correct, then we are admitting that its answer to the question of what is wrong with the world is unreliable. If that's the case, how can the religion be trusted to make things better?

Sarah: That's a good question. I don't think any religion is the answer. I think we need to grow up and stop believing in myths.

Martina: I couldn't agree with you more, Sarah. We shouldn't believe in myths, and religion is not the answer.

Sarah: But I thought you said that our problem was sin. Isn't that a religious concept?

Martina: Yes, indeed. Religion can point out the problem and also point to the true solution. But religion itself is not the solution.

Sarah: Then what is?

Martina: Since we can't solve our sin problem, the only way it could ever be solved is for God to solve it for us. And that's what He did in Jesus Christ.

Sarah: Whoa. I thought you said that the solution wasn't a religion. But Christianity *is* a religion.

Martina: In one sense, you're quite right. If by Christianity you mean the doctrines, rituals, buildings, moral codes, organizations, and so on that together constitute the world religion known as Christianity, then, yes, Christianity is a religion. But in that sense Christianity won't solve the problem any more than any other religion. In fact, as I'm sure you will agree, sometimes Christianity as a religion has made things worse.

Sarah: I'm so glad to hear you say that. I get so tired of Christians thinking that their religion is better than everyone else's religion.

Martina: Actually, I think it is, too.

Murali: There you go again! You seem to delight in contradictions.

Martina: I would prefer to call them paradoxes. They only seem contradictory to us because they challenge our way of thinking about life. You see, I think Christianity is better than other religions for only one reason: God has mercifully used Christianity to point to the true solution that no religion, not even Christianity, can provide.

Murali: And that solution is?

Martina: As I said, that solution is what God has done for us in Jesus Christ. Through Jesus becoming a human being and suffering and dying for us on the cross, He overcame sin for us.

Murali: I have always thought of the story of Christ as a wonderful myth, not as literal fact.

Martina: And myths can be wonderful stories. But while the story of Christ makes a wonderful fact, it makes a terrible myth.

Murali: Why do you say that?

Martina: Because the whole point of the story is that God has done for us what we could not do for ourselves. If that isn't actual fact, then God has not really done anything for us, and we are left in our hopeless state. That's what the apostle Paul meant when he said that if Christ has not been raised from the dead, we are still in our sins and our faith is in vain.

Sarah: But how do you know that it *is* a fact?

Martina: Because God has revealed himself in Jesus Christ, and by his Spirit He has led me to receive that revelation and to know that it is true.

Sarah: All that tells me is that you've had an experience that convinces you that it's true. That's not an argument that can convince *me*.

Martina: Of course not. You asked me how *I* knew it was true. That's different from asking for an argument that could convince *you*.

Sarah: Do you have such an argument?

Martina: I don't know. I'm not sure that arguments ever convince anyone to put their faith in Christ. That would be like a child asking for a reason to trust her mother.

Sarah: Then why should I believe in Christ?

Martina: Well, Sarah, the best way I know to learn to trust someone is to get to know that person. You can get acquainted with Jesus by reading the Bible, especially the Gospels. Have you read the Gospels?

Sarah: Yes, as a child I heard all the stories about Jesus, and in college I took a course on the Bible. We learned about the origins of the Gospels—that they probably weren't written by Matthew, Mark, and so on, and how they were composed from earlier sources like "Q."

Martina: Oh, my, that's not what I meant. Reading the Gospels as ancient documents to be analyzed and dissected may be a legitimate activity in its own right, but you'll never come to faith in that way. That would be like performing literary source criticism on a love letter in order to get to know your beloved better. No, you need to read the Gospels as a way of getting to know Jesus. Listen to what He says. Look at how He handles various situations. Ask yourself, is this someone I can trust? Is this someone who perfectly embodies the love of God? That's the way you need to read the Gospels.

Sarah: So, what you're saying is that we should believe in Jesus because the Bible says so. You're saying that we should just accept whatever is in the Bible.

Martina: Not at all. I do not believe in Jesus because I believe in the Bible. I believe the Bible because, as I read it, I find Jesus there. I believe the Bible because it speaks to me about Jesus and produces within me a confidence in Jesus and a love for Jesus that cannot be explained away. I believe the Bible because, as I read it, I realize that what it says about Jesus could never have been made up by human beings.

Murali: I have never heard the Bible explained in this way before. I have always found Jesus to be an intriguing figure. I think I will try to read the Gospels and see if what you say is true.

Martina: That's wonderful.

Sarah: I don't know if I buy any of this, but you've given me something to think about.

Martina: That's a start!

STRENGTHS OF FIDEISM

Fideism has some surprising strengths as an approach to apologetics, which we may summarize here.

The Personal Factor

Fideism rightly and helpfully emphasizes the personal dimensions of apologetics. God is a personal being, and apologetics should be done in a manner that respects that fact. Too often God is treated as an intellectual construct rather than a real person. God's revelation is ultimately and primarily a revelation of God himself, in which his purpose is to make himself known to us. Moreover, the purpose of apologetics is to persuade people, and they are persons, too, with problems and needs. Answers to unbelievers' objections that overlook the personal stake they have in the questions are likely to have little or no impact.

Humble View of Human Reason

Fideism takes very seriously the limitations of human reason and knowledge. The goal of constructing a systematic, comprehensive view of reality that is stated or implied in many works of Christian philosophy, apologetics, and theology suggests a kind of intellectual pride. Fideists rightly criticize an excessive reliance on powers of human reasoning and the acquisition of factual knowledge. Our problem is not that we lack intelligence or information, but that we lack the courage and honesty to accept the truth.

Centered on Christ

Fideism centers the Christian witness in apologetics where it should be—on the person of Jesus Christ. In Christ we have God's answer to our ignorance of God and to the problem of evil and suffering. Our mission is to call people to faith in Christ, not in the Christian religion, not in a Christian philosophy, and not in a system of Christian theology. Moreover, fideists are right in insisting that what unbelievers need most is simply exposure to the power of the person of Jesus Christ. As people read the New Testament, they do encounter Christ as the personal, gracious, and formidable God that He is. Apologetics certainly needs to retain this Christ-centered approach.

WEAKNESSES OF FIDEISM

We have had occasion throughout our discussion of fideism to dispel some of the most common misconceptions about the fideist position. Three points bear repeating before we identify some of the weaknesses in this approach to apologetics.

First, fideism is not an inherently irrationalist position. It is not irrational to claim that human reason is incapable of constructing a logically coherent account of such mysteries as the Trinity and the Incarnation. It is not irrational to use reason to show that reason has its limits in matters of faith.

Second, fideism is not pure subjectivism. That is, fideism does not deny objective reality or the objective character of God's revelation. This is a point repeatedly emphasized by such fideists as Karl Barth and Donald Bloesch, but it also applies to Kierkegaard, who asked, "Is there, then, nothing objective in Christianity or is Christianity not the object of objective knowledge? Indeed, why not? The objective is what he is saying, he, the authority" (*JP* 187, 1:75). Various evangelical scholars, including some leading apologists, agree that Kierkegaard was not a relativist. For example, Douglas Groothuis, who teaches philosophy and apologetics at Denver Seminary, points out that Kierkegaard "took the idea of 'truth as true for him' to mean what engaged him at the deepest levels of his heart, not in the sense that he could customize truth to fit his whims."[1] Fideists argue that the objective dimension of revelation must be united with the subjective dimension of the work of the Spirit within us if that revelation is to be seen for what it is.

Third, fideism is not opposed to all apologetics. Fideists often speak as if it were, but in fact fideists practice a kind of indirect apologetics of their own. Apologetics can be defined as the practice of giving reasoned answers to questions people ask about the truth of Christianity. On the basis of that definition, fideism is clearly a form of apologetics.

Fideism does have some serious weaknesses, though, which should also be noted. And here we do not speak of these weaknesses as merely "potential," as we did for the other three approaches, since these weaknesses do seem to be endemic if not intrinsic to fideism. Our focus here will be on weaknesses common to fideism, not on the theological problems or apologetic deficiencies associated with individual thinkers. So, for example, although we are critical of various aspects of Karl Barth's theology, the weaknesses identified here are those that characterize most fideists in modern times, including Kierkegaard, Barth, and Bloesch.

Undervalues Propositional Knowledge

Fideists routinely pit the personal kind of knowledge against the propositional kind. But there is no reason or need to do this. Propositional knowledge about God is a poor *substitute* for personal knowledge of God, but it can be a good *vehicle* to such personal knowledge. Indeed, propositional knowledge about God is given to us in Scripture.

Moreover, the fideist depreciation of propositional knowledge seriously compromises the apologetic task. Non-Christians have factual questions about the Christian faith, and these often are fair and important questions that need to be answered on the level that they are asked.

Now, we see no reason why a rational fideism of the sort discussed, for example, by C. Stephen Evans, *must* necessarily depreciate propositional knowledge. The fideist is right in saying that saving knowledge of God is personal knowledge— the knowledge of a person whom we love—and not mere knowledge of factual statements or propositions. But the one does not exclude the other. Still, modern fideists so commonly deny or diminish the possibility and value of propositional knowledge about God that we must recognize their doing so as a real weakness of the fideist approach.

Overstated Criticism of Reason and Knowledge

As we have said, fideists are right to point out the severe limitations of human reasoning powers and human knowledge. Unfortunately, they typically overstate these criticisms. As a result, fideism underestimates the role that reason and knowledge commonly play in people coming to faith. Scripture uses various kinds of arguments and appeals to factual knowledge to challenge unbelief and to encourage faith. It is true that we cannot expect to resolve all intellectual problems raised against Christianity, but we can resolve many of them adequately. It is also true that we cannot produce definitive, absolute proof for Christianity that will be fully convincing to all people, but that is never what Christian apologists have claimed to be doing. In short, fideist objections to apologetics as traditionally conceived are based on misunderstandings or missteps in reasoning.

Again, much of what fideists say is salutary and does not require such overstated criticisms of apologetics. It ought to be possible to take a humble view of human reason and knowledge without denying their validity and importance. Indeed, some fideists have themselves been extremely sharp thinkers and impressively knowledgeable.

Unnecessarily Critical View of the Bible

Fideism tends, unnecessarily, to undermine confidence in the Bible. Fideists are generally too quick to accept the theories of liberal biblical criticism or other fields of knowledge that seem to call into question the accuracy of the Bible. It is not necessary to depreciate the Bible in order to exalt Christ. Advocating belief in biblical inerrancy is not necessarily rationalistic, since inerrantists freely admit our inability to resolve all apparent difficulties in the Bible.

The following table summarizes the major notable strengths and widespread weaknesses in the fideist approach to apologetics.

Fideism	
Strengths	*Weaknesses*
Emphasizes the personal dimension of God and his revelation	Pits the personal against the propositional
Takes seriously the limitations of human reason and knowledge	Underestimates the role of reason and knowledge in faith
Centers the Christian witness in apologetics on Christ	Unnecessarily undermines confidence in the Bible

CONCLUSION

Fideism is in some ways a powerful and insightful approach that comes to age-old apologetic issues in a fresh and often surprising way. However, it also has some serious weaknesses that undermine the apologetic task considerably. We have argued that the insights of fideism can be incorporated into apologetics. It is clear, though, that a full-bodied apologetic will have to draw from one or more of the other approaches as well.

For Further Study

Evans, C. Stephen. *Faith Beyond Reason: A Kierkegaardian Account*. Reason & Religion. Grand Rapids: Eerdmans, 1998. Discusses fideism in Pascal, Kant, Kierkegaard, Barth, and others, with suggestions for applying fideism in apologetics.

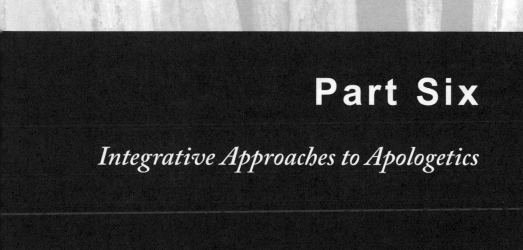

Part Six

Integrative Approaches to Apologetics

Chapter 20

Apologists Who Favor Integration

In the twentieth century, as the debates over apologetic approaches and methods sometimes seemed to overshadow the apologetic task itself, some apologists sought to develop an approach that combines or integrates elements of more than one approach. These apologists typically believe that the most effective apologetic will utilize more than one line of argument in defense of the Christian faith.

In a brief comment in one of his essays, C. S. Lewis mentions four kinds of "evidence" corresponding to our four basic types of apologetics: "And in fact, the man who accepts Christianity always thinks he had good evidence; whether, like Dante, *fisici e metafisici argomenti* [physical or metaphysical arguments, i.e., theistic proofs favored by classical apologetics], or historical evidence [preferred by most evidentialists], or the evidence of religious experience [emphasized by many fideists], or authority [the basis for most forms of Reformed apologetics], or all these together."[1] It is the last-mentioned possibility—using all of these approaches to commend Christian faith to others—that we shall consider in the remainder of this book.

We begin in this chapter by considering the thought of five modern apologists favoring some form of integrative approach.

PRECURSORS OF INTEGRATIVE APPROACHES

As we have seen throughout this book, few Christian thinkers exhibit a "pure" form of any one of the four approaches we have discussed. This is especially true of apologists before the modern era; few if any pre-modern apologists can be categorized simply as belonging to one of the four approaches. The classical approach, as the name suggests, is most deeply rooted in the history of Christian apologetics prior to the modern period. But, as advocated today, it has developed through its interplay with the other three approaches.

Most of the great apologists of the premodern period anticipate in some way one or more of the alternatives to what is now known as the classical model. This can be seen by the fact that modern apologists from different approaches may find aspects of their approach in the same premodern apologist.

Augustine, for example, is claimed as a forerunner by classical apologists, especially though not exclusively because in his earlier writings he made extensive use of arguments for God's existence. Warfield saw him as a forerunner of classical apologetics and of Reformed theology.[2] Reformed apologists, though, find Augustine on a trajectory leading toward their approach in his later writings, in which the authority of Scripture and the sovereignty of God are given special emphasis.

Thomas Aquinas is claimed as a forerunner of the classical approach because of his emphasis on Aristotelian, deductive reasoning. Yet he is also claimed as a precursor to the evidentialist approach because his "five ways" are all based on observed characteristics of the world, and because he insisted that apologetic arguments based on reason could only yield probable conclusions. And surprisingly, C. Stephen Evans has argued that he can also be read as adhering to a kind of moderate, rational fideism, on the grounds that he "clearly affirms that faith requires some beliefs that are above reason."[3]

Anselm of Canterbury is usually classified as a classical apologist because of his use of deductive, a priori reasoning in his ontological proof for God's existence and in his argument for the necessity of the Incarnation. But Karl Barth's thoughtful reinterpretation of his apologetic concludes that, for Anselm, "faith leading to understanding" means that only from within the standpoint of faith can the meaning and significance of the Christian doctrines be understood.

Of course, all Reformed apologists claim John Calvin as the forerunner of their apologetic tradition. Yet most also admit that in some ways he remained part of the classical tradition, notably in chapter 8 of book 1 of the *Institutes*, where he presented a traditional line of arguments defending the reliability of the Bible and its supernatural claims. This aspect of Calvin's theology has enabled classical apologists of a Reformed theological persuasion, such as B. B. Warfield and R. C. Sproul, to defend their approach as consonant with his.[4] Non-Reformed advocates of classical apologetics, such as Norman Geisler, also claim Calvin for their tradition.[5] Barth also cites Calvin in support of his version of fideism, again acknowledging that Calvin sometimes fell back on traditional apologetics.

Blaise Pascal has been cited here and elsewhere as an early advocate of what later developed into fideism. As we noted in our analysis of his *Pensées*, however, in much of his argumentation Pascal advocated traditional apologetics, especially of a kind characteristic now of evidentialist apologetics.

These examples (many more could be given) illustrate that it is usually a mistake to speak of premodern apologists as consistent advocates of any one of the four approaches, especially the three nonclassical ones. They may also be cited in support of considering whether an approach that combines or integrates the four model approaches is desirable and achievable.

In the second half of the twentieth century, as the varying approaches began to gain greater distinctiveness and debates about their relative merits began to take place, several apologists attempted to develop a comprehensive approach that incorporated more than one of these models. Most often the focus was on developing a rapprochement between classical or evidentialist apologetics on the one side and Reformed apologetics, especially presuppositionalism, on the other. Four of the apologists we consider in this chapter took up that challenge. Recently C. Stephen Evans has sought to integrate fideism with the classical and evidentialist approaches; our chapter will conclude with a review of his approach.

EDWARD JOHN CARNELL

One of the first Christian apologists to advocate an approach that was partly presuppositional and partly evidentialist was Edward John Carnell (1919–1967). Indeed, Gordon Lewis's summary of Carnell's approach suggests that he sought to integrate all four of the approaches we have considered:

> From Cornelius Van Til at Westminster Theological Seminary he took his starting point, the existence of the triune God of the Bible. However, this tenet is not an unquestioned presupposition for Carnell, but a hypothesis to be tested. His test of truth is threefold. At Wheaton College in the classes of Gordon H. Clark, Carnell found the test of non-contradiction. The test of fitness to empirical fact was championed by Edgar S. Brightman at Boston University where Carnell earned his Ph.D. The requirement of relevance to personal experience became prominent dur-

ing Carnell's Th.D. research at Harvard University in Sören Kierkegaard and Reinhold Niebuhr.[6]

Here we see respectively the approaches of Reformed apologetics (Van Til), classical apologetics (Clark, because of the emphasis on logic), evidentialism (Brightman, an unorthodox philosopher[7]), and fideism (Kierkegaard). Note that these are not the same "four distinctive and harmonious approaches" that Lewis earlier says are incorporated into Carnell's approach: "facts, values, psychology, and ethics."[8] Those four approaches stem from the four points of contact that dominate Carnell's four major apologetics treatises: reason (*An Introduction to Christian Apologetics* [1948]), values (*A Philosophy of the Christian Religion* [1952]), justice (*Christian Commitment: An Apologetic* [1957]), and love (*The Kingdom of Love and the Pride of Life* [1960]).[9] Carnell himself described these four approaches in *Kingdom of Love*: "In my own books on apologetics I have consistently tried to build on some useful point of contact between the gospel and culture. In *An Introduction to Christian Apologetics* the appeal was to the law of contradiction; in *A Philosophy of the Christian Religion* it was to values; and in *Christian Commitment* it was to the judicial sentiment. In this book I am appealing to the law of love."[10]

Carnell was a professor at Fuller Theological Seminary from its founding in 1948 until his untimely death from an overdose of sleeping pills in 1967, to which he was evidently addicted as a result of clinical depression. (He was also president of the seminary from 1954 to 1959.) His emotional turmoil perhaps made him identify more sympathetically with Kierkegaard, and in fact he was one of the first American evangelicals to write a book about Kierkegaard's thought.[11] As the sequence of titles cited previously suggests, with the passing of time Carnell came to place increasing emphasis and priority on the experiential and ethical dimensions of faith. However, his apologetic method remained essentially unchanged.[12]

Carnell and Classical Apologetics

Carnell held a mixed view of what we are calling the classical approach to apologetics. On the one hand, he strongly emphasized the fundamental undeniability of deductive logic. The "law of contradiction [better known as the law of noncontradiction] is so basic . . . that it cannot be demonstrated. The only proof for the law is that nothing is meaningful without the law's being presupposed" (*Introduction*, 57).[13] Here Carnell uses a transcendental argument to prove the validity of the first principle of deductive logic in the same way that Van Til used one to prove the existence of the God of the Bible. Carnell's argument, though, is another way of stating the argument—basic to classical apologetics—that logic must be valid because its denial is self-defeating.

On the other hand, Carnell rejected the idea that the theistic worldview could be deductively proved. The Bible offers no formal proof for God because "nothing significant is known of God until a person directly experiences him through fellowship" (*Philosophy*, 275). Aristotle's "unmoved mover," an impersonal God with which man cannot have fellowship, typifies what is wrong with formal proofs for God (*Philosophy*, 278–84). Thomas Aquinas's five proofs for God, though deductively formulated (*Introduction*, 126–28), really assume an empiricism that cannot validly prove God's existence. Carnell endorses Hume's criticisms of these arguments: the empirical cannot prove the transcendent; the finite cannot prove the existence of the infinite; the diverse effects cannot prove that there is only one divine Cause; the design in the universe cannot prove an absolutely good and perfect Designer (*Introduction*, 129–39).

In his later works Carnell rejects Aquinas's five proofs, not because they are invalid (he does not say they are or are not), but because they "are spiritually vapid. . . . The conclusion 'God exists' evokes no more spiritual interest than the conclusion 'Europe exists.'" A person who is convinced by such proofs may believe in God (James 2:19). "But he certainly does not believe very profoundly, for a profound knowledge of God presupposes a profound knowledge of sin. . . . A wretched man can intellectually assent to God's existence, but only a man of character can spiritually approach God's person" (*Commitment*, ix).

CARNELL AND EVIDENTIALISM

Carnell is much more sympathetic to the evidentialist approach. This is especially evident in the first part of *An Introduction to Christian Apologetics*. In the preface to the fourth edition, he explains the point of the book: "This is the foundation thesis upon which this system of Christian apologetics is built: In the contest between the rational and the empirical schools of thought, a Christian must pitch his interests somewhere between the two extremes" (*Introduction*, 7).

Carnell finds this middle path in **systematic consistency**, the internal lack of contradiction in one's belief combined with the external agreement with all the facts of one's experience (56–62). (Although Carnell does not say so specifically, the concept comes from Brightman.)

According to Carnell, systematic consistency is the proper criterion by which Christianity may be proved true. He views Christianity as a hypothesis to be proved in much the same way a scientist would seek to prove a theory by showing its systematic consistency in accounting for all the data. Christianity, for this purpose, is reduced to "one hypothesis—the existence of God Who has revealed Himself in Scripture." This one hypothesis "can solve the problems of personal happiness, present a rational view of the universe, and give a basis for truth" (107).

In showing that the Christian hypothesis satisfies the requirement not only of "horizontal self-consistency" (108–109) but also "vertical fitting of the facts" (109), Carnell acknowledges "the fact that proof for the Christian faith, as proof for any world-view that is worth talking about, cannot rise above rational probability" (113). Christianity at its core is about historical facts (especially Jesus' death and resurrection), and such facts cannot be proved with rational certainty (113–14). Carnell does not think this lack of rational certainty is a hindrance to faith; he contends that the believer who has an inner certainty and probable argument is better, not worse, off than the believer who has an inner certainty only. "One may be morally certain that God exists, and pray with full assurance, though the objective evidence is but rationally probable" (120).

The argument as we have summarized it to this point seems to place Carnell in the evidentialist tradition. Christianity is a hypothesis to be tested according to rational criteria of internal coherence and external fitting of the facts; the correlation of the hypothesis with the external facts will result at best in a conclusion of probability, not deductive certainty. Carnell even invites a critical comparison of the Bible with the historical facts: "Accept that revelation which, when examined, yields a system of thought which is horizontally self-consistent and which vertically fits the facts of history. . . . Bring on your revelations! Let them make peace with the law of contradiction and the facts of history, and they will deserve a rational man's assent. A careful examination of the Bible reveals [!] that it passes these stringent examinations *summa cum laude*" (178).

According to Carnell, the Christian proves the validity of the hypothesis that the God of the Bible exists "in the same way that the scientist proves the law of gravity." That is, he shows that this assumption, or hypothesis, is "horizontally self-consistent" and that it "vertically fits the facts of life" (355). Here again, Carnell's approach draws heavily on the evidentialist tradition, which self-consciously models apologetics after science.

The same method appears in Carnell's later books, including *Christian Commitment*. In an important passage in that book, he states the basis on which the Christian "system" is to be considered verified and worthy of belief. *"Systems are chosen or rejected by reason of their power to explain areas of reality that a particular person finds important. . . . Systems are verified by the degree to which their major elements are consistent with one another and with the broad facts of history and nature. . . .* Christianity is true because its major elements are consistent with one another and with the broad facts of history and nature" (*Commitment*, 285–86).

Finally, an evidentialist method is explicit in the following passage from *The Kingdom of Love and the Pride of Life:*

> A Christian is willing to accept the philosophy of evidences that men of ordinary intelligence accept when they go about their daily business. For example, such men believe that there was a man called Abraham Lincoln, and they believe because they feel that the evidences are sufficient. Historical claims are neither established nor refuted by science and philosophy. They can only be judged by the sort of common sense that takes pleasure in submitting to things as they are. (*Kingdom*, 148)

CARNELL AND REFORMED APOLOGETICS

If we were to stop at this point, we would seem to have presented a convincing case for classifying Carnell as an evidentialist. But we have passed over certain aspects of his argument that do not fit this model. Returning to his first and most influential work, *An Introduction to Christian Apologetics*, we find that the "hypothesis" that the God of the Bible exists is not treated as a typical scientific or historical hypothesis. Because this is not merely one hypothesis among many in a system, but "the ultimate postulate" (*Introduction*, 89), the Christian hypothesis is actually "an assumption" that the Christian says must be made in order to have a proper knowledge of reality (91). Assumptions are inevitable in daily life and in science, which cannot avoid making worldview assumptions about the nature of knowledge, reality, and ethics (91–94). Carnell anticipates the criticism that he is arguing in a circle and replies that circular reasoning about ultimates is unavoidable:

The Christian begs the question by assuming the truth of God's existence to establish that very existence. Indeed! This is true for establishing the validity of any ultimate. The truth of the law of contradiction must be assumed to prove the validity of that axiom. Nature must be assumed to prove nature. Strict demonstration of a first postulate is impossible, as Aristotle pointed out, for it leads either to infinite regress or to circular reasoning. (101–102).

The above statement would seem to require some qualification of Gordon Lewis's claim that "Carnell does not regard this starting point [of the God of the Bible] an axiom or an unquestionable presupposition."[14] Carnell, in fact, describes his starting point as an axiom that, like the law of noncontradiction, must be assumed in order to be proved. This is precisely what Van Til and others mean by a "presupposition."

It is true, though, that Carnell did not regard his axiomatic starting point as "unquestionable." (Depending on what this means, neither did Van Til.) But if the existence of the God of the Bible is an ultimate assumption that cannot be demonstrated, how can it also be treated as an hypothesis to be questioned or tested? Carnell solves this problem by distinguishing the *logical* starting point of the Christian system, which would be the triune God of the Bible, from the **synoptic starting point**, the conceptual point from which the logical starting point can be proved (*Introduction*, 124–25). But this raises the question of a suitable synoptic starting point.

Carnell first considers whether such a starting point can be developed using an empirical method, as in the natural theology typified by Aquinas's five proofs for God's existence (126–28). As we have seen, he rejects this approach (129–39). Oddly, he holds these arguments to the standard of rational or deductive demonstration, despite having made a good case for the legitimacy of fact-based apologetic arguments that can only yield probable conclusions.

Carnell continues in similar fashion to critique "Thomistic empiricism," concluding that "there are fewer difficulties which attend Christian rationalism than attend Christian empiricism" (151). By "Christian rationalism" Carnell does not mean the kind of rationalism that seeks to establish all knowledge on the foundation of logic and self-evident truths. Rather, he means a position that accepts the idea that the human mind possesses some knowledge of God a priori as a result of our creation in God's image (151 n. 20). It is in this innate knowledge of God that Carnell locates his synoptic starting point. We have, he argues, innate knowledge of the true, the good, and the beautiful, and of the self as existent and finite; only the existence of the God who made us with this innate knowledge can account for it (153–68). In knowing truth, for example, he says "we know what God is, *for God is truth.*" "This argument for God does not constitute a demonstration; rather, it is an analysis. By the very nature of the case, a fulcrum able to support the weight of a proof for God would have to be God Himself. God gets in the way of all demonstration of Deity, for His existence is the *sine qua non* for all demonstration. Proof for God is parallel to proof for logic; logic must be used to prove logic" (159).

In other words, the proof for God is a transcendental argument—the very kind championed by Van Til and other presuppositionalists in his tradition. Yet at the same time Carnell denies that this argument constitutes a "demonstration of Deity." Van Til, on the other hand, strongly claimed that the transcendental argument constituted an absolutely sound and irrefutable demonstration of God's existence.

With knowledge of these innate truths, Carnell does allow that nature can in a sense furnish knowledge of God, but only in a heavily qualified sense. On the grounds that one of the innate truths we possess is the knowledge of God, he concludes: "Because we *know* God's existence and nature in our heart, we *recognize* Him in His handiwork" (169). Once we realize our innate knowledge of God, we will recognize God in all his works. The evidences that served as the basis of the Thomistic proofs can be recognized as evidence of God only if we already know that God exists and what he is like. "This is not a formal demonstration of God's existence: it is simply proof by coherence. The existence of God is the self-consistent hypothesis that the mind must entertain when it views all of the evidence which experience provides" (170).

Unfortunately, because of sin people do not know God and do not recognize him in his works (171–72). This fact necessitates God acting to reveal himself to us in a special way; but how shall we recognize God's revelation among all the pretenders? Here Carnell returns to his affirmation of systematic consistency as the test of truth (178). Here and in the rest of the book, though, he shows that it is only a test *retrospectively.* That is, having accepted the "hypothesis" of the God of the Bible as the key to our worldview, we can examine this hypothesis and see that it does account for truth, ethics, and beauty, for the human self and the natural world. Carnell does not propose that non-Christians can or should, from their perspective, apply the test of systematic consistency to determine if Christianity is true.

So, in a later chapter Carnell argues that, while Christians and non-Christians are able to communicate with each other, there is no "common ground between Christianity and non-Christianity" viewed as systems (211–12). Specifically, there is no metaphysical common ground between the Christian and non-Christian. "God is the logical starting point for the Christian, and non-God is the logical starting point for the non-Christian" (215). This is a crucial point of agreement with Van Til, Clark, and other Reformed apologists.

In Carnell's concluding chapter he explains that the basic philosophical problem is the question of the unifying meaning or significance of the many facts of our experience—the problem of "the one and the many" (353–54). This problem played a major role in Van Til's philosophy and apologetic as well.

> But by the one assumption, the existence of the God Who has revealed Himself in Scripture, the Christian finds that he can solve the problem of the one within the many, and so make sense out of life. . . . Christ, as Creator, is the Author of the many, and, as Logos, is the principle of the One, the Author of the meaning of the many. . . . Christ *is* the truth, for He is the Logos, the synthesizing principle and the true meaning of all reality. (354)

The presuppositionalist aspect of Carnell's apologetic is most prominent in his first work, but it does surface in his later works as well. For example, he wrote that "defending Christianity by an appeal to evidences that are accessible to human self-sufficiency" was "futile" (*Commitment*, viii). The qualification here of his own appeal to evidences is one that Reformed apologists have insisted is essential.

Apologists outside the Reformed apologetic tradition tend to identify Carnell as a presuppositionalist. Norman Geisler, for example, says "Carnell was hypothetical or presuppositional . . . in his approach, in contrast to a classical apologetic method."[15] Presuppositionalists themselves, on the other hand, have offered strikingly varied evaluations of Carnell's apologetic. Van Til himself wrote against it, arguing that Carnell had really adopted the traditional method of apologetics. One of Van Til's most famous illustrations is a mock three-way dialogue between "Mr. White" (a Reformed apologist), "Mr. Black" (a non-Christian), and "Mr. Grey" (a traditional apologist). Mr. Grey was modeled on Carnell.[16] Van Til acknowledges that "Carnell frequently argues as we would expect a Reformed apologist to argue," but continues, "By and large, however, he represents the evangelical rather than the Reformed method in apologetics."[17] Van Til draws attention to what we have identified as the "evidentialist" thread in Carnell's apologetic to document his charge.

Greg Bahnsen strongly supports Van Til's assessment of Carnell. According to Bahnsen, "the heart of the matter" is that Carnell's "synoptic starting point" is "the *epistemological* criterion of systematic consistency for testing truth-claims," and this criterion is utilized as an epistemological common ground between Christians and non-Christians.[18] This interpretation would seem to be incorrect: Carnell's synoptic starting point is the innate knowledge of God all human beings have by virtue of their creation in the image of God (*Introduction*, 151–68).

John Frame takes a rather different view of Carnell. He notes that Carnell's *Introduction* "is, from a Van Tillian perspective, a curious volume. It is highly eclectic, hard to pin down as to its specific apologetic approach. Carnell uses a lot of language that is recognizably, even distinctively, Van Tillian. . . . There is also language, both in this book and in Carnell's other writings, that almost seems intended to offend Van Til."[19] Frame documents some of the veiled swipes Carnell took at Van Til's approach, as well as Van Til's unveiled, sharp criticisms of Carnell. He then seeks to isolate the real issues dividing the two apologists, concluding that Carnell made "serious errors of presentation" by speaking of systematic consistency as a test of truth, even of Scripture. The result is an unclear and misleading exposition of apologetics that, while intending to uphold a presuppositional stance, compromises that stance. But Frame also concludes that Van Til had "rather drastically overstated" the problems with Carnell's apologetic.[20]

Carnell and Fideism

Although Carnell was by no means a fideist, in his later works he drew heavily from and expressed great appreciation for Kierkegaard, while at the same time critiquing his fideist position. In *A Philosophy of the Christian Religion* Carnell proposes "to trace through a set of typical value options in life," giving reasons why in each case one ought to move up to the higher value commitment, the highest of which is faith in Christ (*Philosophy*, 5). This line of reasoning is reminiscent of Kierkegaard's "stages" in which people move from lower to higher forms of religious commitment. Carnell explains that he is not attempting a direct proof of Christianity here, but the indirect proof that if Christianity is not true, despair would seem to be the result: "It is not an attempted demonstration of Christianity in the conventional sense. The nearest that proof will be enjoyed is in the establishing of a dialectic of despair as the alternative to the Christian option. But in the last analysis there is no proof of any pudding apart from the eating" (45).

Kierkegaardian themes abound here, and they are developed throughout the book. Logical positivism, which claims that we can have no knowledge of the transcendent realities studied in metaphysics or the transcendent values studied in ethics (133–78), must be rejected because in fact no one can live as if such values are unreal. "When an epistemology forces us to deny in theory what we must live by in fact, it is as inadequate as it is inconsequential" (178). Rationalism, however, is not the answer either, because it settles for knowledge of things instead of the higher knowledge of persons, that is, relational knowledge or fellowship (179–224). The gods of the philosophers are unsatisfying; deism, pantheism, and the finite God of Brightman and others all fail to yield a God with whom we can have fellowship and in whom we can fully trust (286–323). The only truly satisfying knowledge of God is to be found in Jesus Christ. "Christ is Immanuel: God with us. And the proof is an examination of the life he lived and the death he died" (324).

Despite the strong affinities of this line of reasoning with the thought of Kierkegaard, Carnell argues that personal knowledge of God is not to be found in *existentialism*. Locating the way to knowledge of God in subjectivism has the unacceptable consequence of rejecting an objective grounding of that knowledge in evidence (449–507). Here Carnell focuses explicitly on Kierkegaard, explaining where he agrees and disagrees with the melancholy Dane. Rather than "a subjective 'leap' of faith," the Christian's response to the gospel is a "cordial trust in Jesus Christ [that] is always grounded in reasonable evidences. . . . Knowledge by acquaintance is still an act of rationality" (449). A person can properly have fellowship with God "only when he is first rationally convinced that it is *God* whom he is fellowshiping with" (450).

On the other hand, besides truth as reality itself and truth as "systematic consistency or propositional correspondence to reality," Carnell identifies a "third locus of truth" (450): correspondence to the perfect character of God, a correspondence embodied, as he says in John 14:6, absolutely in Jesus Christ (451–52). Carnell acknowledges that Kierkegaard "is a powerful apologist of the third locus of truth" (457). But while Kierkegaard's defense of truth as inward character is "profoundly convincing," Carnell questions his "attempt to secure inward truth by opposing it to objective evidences" (473). In doing so, he laid the foundation not only for neo-orthodox theology but also for atheistic existentialism (480–500). "Existentialism has ended in complete metaphysical nihilism" (500).

In *Christian Commitment* Carnell expands on the third locus of truth. Besides ontological truth (what is) and propositional truth (accurate statements about what is), there is "the third kind of truth," which is *"truth by personal rectitude"* (*Commitment*, 14–16). This kind of truth requires in turn a "third method of knowing," which Carnell calls *"knowledge by moral self-acceptance"* (22). He acknowledges that he learned of this third way from Kierkegaard: "It is a pleasure to acknowledge my indebtedness to Kierkegaard" (73). But Kierkegaard, in his zeal to oppose the formalism of Hegel's system, went too far by attacking systematic consistency and advocating absurdity as the precondition of faith. "Whatever else faith may be, it is at least a 'resting of the mind in the sufficiency of the evidences'" (76).

Despite his criticism of Kierkegaard's rejection of systems, by the end of the book he is issuing some cautions about systems himself. "Whenever a systematic theologian becomes too systematic, he ends up falsifying some aspect of revelation. It is extremely difficult, if not impossible, to coax all the data of Scripture into neat harmony" (285). No system that human beings can construct will be without problems.

Carnell concludes by insisting that "apologetics *has* its limits. . . . God is a living person, not a metaphysical principle. Evidences may point to God, but God himself must be encountered in the dynamic of personal fellowship. Only the Holy Spirit can illuminate the evidences" (302).

Carnell and Integration

As we have seen, Carnell's apologetic has strong connections to three of the four apologetic approaches. The Reformed and evidentialist approaches dominate *Introduction to Christian Apologetics*; Carnell's synthesis of them is augmented by elements of fideism in his subsequent works. Not surprisingly, he refused to pigeonhole his own approach into any specific camp. "There is no 'official' or 'normative' approach to apologetics. At least I have never found one. The approach is governed by the climate of the times. This means, as it were, that an apologist must play it by ear" (*Kingdom*, 5).

According to Carnell, the practical significance of this fact is that today Christian apologetics must emphasize moral and spiritual evidences over the more traditional kinds of evidence.

> Since apologetics is an art and not a science, there is no "official" way to go about defending the Christian faith. The defense must answer to the spirit of the times. . . . The climate of our modern world is dynamic and existential. People speak of Kierkegaard's "individual," of "confrontation" and "crisis." This is why we have sought to impress the contemporary mind with evidences drawn from man's marvelous powers of moral and rational self-transcendence. (*Commitment*, vii-viii)

Francis A. Schaeffer

Francis August Schaeffer IV (1912–1984) was one of the most beloved Christian apologists of the twentieth century. His influence was so great that *Newsweek* once called him "the guru of fundamentalism."[21] There are many reasons for Schaeffer's popularity, but two stand out.

First and foremost, Schaeffer embodied the ideal of an apologist who sought to "speak the truth in love" (Ephesians 4:15). He talked to people, showed a genuine interest in them, and in his teaching on apologetics emphasized the importance of approaching non-Christians with compassion as individuals in God's image. L'Abri, his retreat center in the Swiss Alps that has been duplicated in several countries, was a place where people in spiritual and intellectual anguish could go and be heard and helped.

Second, Schaeffer inspired evangelical Christians to broaden their approach to apologetics beyond the usual disciplines of philosophy, theology, science, and history—which have dominated our own discussion in this book—to encompass ethics and the arts. "Cultural apologetics" touches most people more profoundly than traditional forms, because it connects with them in those areas of life in which personality is more deeply involved.

Francis Schaeffer[22] grew up in a blue-collar family in Germantown, Pennsylvania, a suburb of Philadelphia. The son of liberal Presbyterians, he read the Bible as a teenager and was surprised to find that it contained answers to the most momentous questions in life. He gave his life to Christ and decided, against his father's wishes, to pursue the ministry. While in college he began spending Sunday afternoons teaching children at a nearby African-American church. While visiting home on one occasion, he attended his family's church, where a guest minister was openly attacking the Bible and the deity of Christ. Schaeffer stood up to protest, and then a young woman named Edith Seville also stood up and offered an intelligent defense of the Christian position. Edith, the daughter of missionaries to China, introduced Francis to the apologetic writings of J. Gresham Machen and other professors at Westminster Theological Seminary whom she had met in her parents' home.

After college Francis married Edith and enrolled at Westminster Seminary in 1935. There he studied under Cornelius Van Til, who was still developing his presuppositional system of apologetics. The following year the newly formed Presbyterian Church in America (now known as the Orthodox Presbyterian Church), which Machen had founded after he was ousted from the mainline Presbyterian church, suffered a split. The splinter group, which was called the Bible Presbyterian Church, favored a premillennial eschatology and differed in other ways from the more staunchly Calvinist parent body. Schaeffer transferred to the new group's Faith Theological Seminary. He was a member of its first graduating class in 1938 and became its first ordained minister, serving as a pastor for several years in Pennsylvania and Missouri. In St. Louis he and Edith established Children for Christ, which eventually became a worldwide ministry.

In 1948 the Schaeffers moved to Switzerland to serve as missionaries. Postwar Europe was in spiritual crisis, and in 1951 Francis experienced his own spiritual crisis, reexamining the truth claims of Christianity and gaining a more profound realization of the importance of holiness and love in the Christian life. During the next few years young people began coming to Schaeffer's home to discuss their doubts and to learn about Christianity. As they returned home, they spread the word, and soon the Schaeffers found themselves engaged full-time in a ministry of personal evangelism and apologetics from their home, which they called *l'Abri* ("the Shelter"), to people from all over the world.

Beginning in the 1960s Francis was invited to speak at conferences and at leading colleges and universities in Europe and America. Out of his lectures were developed his most influential books, beginning with *Escape from Reason* and *The God Who Is There*, both of which were published in 1968 by InterVarsity Press. Schaeffer regarded these two books and the 1972 book *He Is There and He Is Not Silent* as a trilogy that formed the foundation of his published work. He published ten other books during this period, and went on to publish six more in the next four years, culminating in *How Should We Then Live?* (1976). This book, which was also made into a film series, offered a sweeping overview of the history of culture and the different worldviews that emerged from the ancient Greeks, the early Christian church, the medieval church, the Renaissance and Reformation, and the modern West.

Schaeffer published just two more books, and because of them he is remembered as a prophetic voice of protest as much as he is an apologist or evangelist. In *Whatever Happened to the Human Race?* (1979), co-authored with C. Everett Koop, Schaeffer lamented the evil of abortion in America and warned that euthanasia was not far behind. Schaeffer was one of the principal figures who made abortion a central issue for American evangelicals during the last two decades of the twentieth century. In *A Christian Manifesto* (1981) he warned that America had moved so far away from a Christian worldview that Christians might find themselves in situations where they had to practice civil disobedience. Some evangelicals in the pro-life movement concluded that the time Schaeffer had spoken about had arrived, and that belief led to the practice of civil disobedience in their protests at abortion clinics.

These last two books were written and published while Schaeffer was battling cancer. Realizing that his life was coming to an end, he reedited his books into a five-volume set published in 1982 entitled *The Complete Works of Francis A. Schaeffer.*[23] His final literary effort was *Great Evangelical Disaster*, published just before he died in 1984. In this book he delivered a stinging indictment of the state of the evangelical church in America, warning that ethical and theological compromise was becoming the order of the day.

Schaeffer's apologetic method has been the subject of considerable debate, and was even while he was alive. Near the end of his life he commented ruefully, "I have been mystified at times about what has been said concerning 'Schaeffer's apologetics'" (1:176). Within three years of his death, four major books appeared evaluating his thought and offering markedly different analyses of his apologetic approach.[24] This diversity may best be explained on the view that Schaeffer had developed a distinctive apologetic that has important affinities with more than one of the four standard approaches.

Schaeffer and Classical Apologetics

Schaeffer distinguished his approach from classical apologetics but did not criticize that approach. As he saw it, classical apologetics was effective because most non-Christians accepted the elemental laws of logic and the reality of absolutes (though not the true absolute of God). Modern man's lack of confidence in logic and his relativistic view of truth make it ineffective to conduct apologetics without challenging such epistemological issues. "The use of classical apologetics before this shift took place was effective only because non-Christians were functioning, on the surface, on the same presuppositions, even if they had an inadequate base for them. In classical apologetics though, presuppositions were rarely analyzed, discussed or taken into account" (1:7).

Schaeffer's apologetic retained some elements of the classical model. As in classical apologetics, he advocated a two-stage defense that moves from God as Creator to Christ as Savior. "We must never forget that the first part of the gospel is not 'Accept Christ as Savior,' but 'God is there'" (1:144). Modern people are lost in two senses: they are "lost evangelically" in the sense that they are sinners without Christ, but they are also "lost in the modern sense" that their lives are without meaning. "This lostness is answered by the existence of a Creator. So Christianity does not begin with 'accept Christ as Savior.' Christianity begins with 'In the beginning God created the heavens (the total of the cosmos) and the earth.' That is the answer to the twentieth century and its lostness. At this point we are then ready to explain the second lostness (the original cause of all lostness) and the answer in the death of Christ" (1:181).

Schaeffer's argument for the existence of a Creator is most fully set out in *He Is There and He Is Not Silent*. His starting point in this book, which argues for "the philosophic necessity of God's being there and not being silent," is basically the same as in the cosmological argument. "No one said it better than Jean-Paul Sartre, who said that the basic philosophic question is that something is there rather than nothing being there" (1:277). As in classical apologetics, Schaeffer analyzes this question in terms of the basic alternative worldviews and the answers they give to the question of existence or being.

One might conclude "that there is no logical, rational answer—all is finally chaotic, irrational, and absurd" (1:280). Schaeffer points out that any attempt to express this view is self-defeating: one cannot make a meaningful statement about all being meaningless, or communicate the idea that there is nothing to communicate (1:281). So this is really a non-answer to the problem.

The possible answers to why something rather than nothing is there boil down logically to four. "(1) Once there was absolutely nothing, and now there is something; (2) everything began with an impersonal something; (3) everything began with a personal something; and (4) there is and always has been a dualism" (2:10;

cf. 1:282–284). The first answer is actually quite rare once the point is pressed that the beginning must be from an absolute nothing—what Schaeffer calls "*nothing nothing*" (1:282). One is reminded of Norman Geisler's version of the cosmological argument in which he emphasizes that "nothing comes from nothing." Schaeffer also dismisses dualism as an answer, since it inevitably reduces to one of the other two remaining options (1:284 n. 1; 2:10).

By far the most popular answer among non-Christians is that everything began from some impersonal beginning. Often this is articulated as *pantheism*, but Schaeffer argues that this term is misleading because it smuggles in the idea of a personal God ("theism") when in fact the pantheist actually holds to an impersonal view of the beginning. He prefers to call this answer "*pan-everythingism*" (1:283). Pan-everythingism is thus the same view, whether it is expressed in mystical religious terms or in modern scientific terms in which everything is reduced to fundamental physical particles. This view founders because it leaves us with no basis for attributing purpose or meaning to anything, including man: "If we begin with an impersonal, we cannot then have some form of teleological concept. No one has ever demonstrated how time plus chance, beginning with an impersonal, can produce the needed complexity of the universe, let alone the personality of man. No one has given us a clue to this" (1:283).

As Clark Pinnock points out, this appears to be "a rudimentary form of the teleological argument."[25] Schaeffer's argument here broadens beyond the usual confines of both the cosmological and teleological arguments, integrating into one argument the need to account for the origin of diversity, meaning, and morality as well as being.

This leaves as the only remaining possible answer that ultimately everything owes its existence to "a personal beginning" (1:284). This is an answer that gives meaning to ourselves as persons (1:285). This personal beginning cannot be finite gods (they are not "big enough" to provide an adequate answer), but must be a personal-infinite God (1:286–287). Schaeffer here follows a strategy similar to that employed by Geisler: set forth the basic worldviews (atheism, dualism, pantheism, finite theism, theism) and show that all of them except theism are irrational. As in classical apologetics, Schaeffer concludes that a worldview in which everything was created by an infinite-personal God is the *only* worldview that provides a rationally adequate answer to the question of why there is something (1:288).

We may represent the structure of Schaeffer's argument as follows:

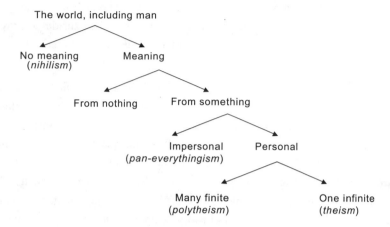

The world, including man

- No meaning (*nihilism*)
- Meaning
  - From nothing
  - From something
    - Impersonal (*pan-everythingism*)
    - Personal
      - Many finite (*polytheism*)
      - One infinite (*theism*)

The similarities to the cosmological argument are apparent. It is with some justice that Robert L. Reymond calls it "the old cosmological argument of Thomas in new garb."[26] In addition, the argument is structured using the law of noncontradiction as the basic principle, a feature characteristic of the classical approach.

Schaeffer and Evidentialism

While few if any students of Schaeffer would conclude that the classical model dominated his approach to apologetics, some do contend that he is properly identified as an evidentialist. Reymond includes Schaeffer (as well as Carnell) in his chapter on "empirical apologetics." He recognizes that Schaeffer's apologetic has presuppositional elements (of which Reymond approves), but concludes that he compromised that approach by using "an empiricist verification test of truth."[27]

There is indeed some basis for interpreting Schaeffer as advocating a verificational approach to defending Christian belief. The premise here is that Scripture deals with not only "religious" matters "but also the cosmos and history, which are open to verification" (1:120). He suggests "that scientific proof, philosophical proof and religious proof follow the same rules."

After the question has been defined, in each case proof consists of two steps:

A. The theory must be noncontradictory and must give an answer to the phenomenon in question.
B. We must be able to live consistently with our theory. (1:121)

Christianity is proved by the fact that it, and it alone, "does offer a nonself-contradictory answer which explains the phenomena and which can be lived with, both in life and in scholarly pursuits" (1:122).

A couple of key elements of the evidentialist approach are present in this passage. First, Schaeffer claims that proof in apologetics should follow the same rules as in science. Second, he specifies that for a theory to be considered proved it must not only be logically self-consistent but also consistent with the "phenomenon in question."

Schaeffer invites non-Christians to examine the Christian worldview in the light of every kind of phenomenon, including nature, history, human nature, culture, and ethics, confident that Christianity will be proved consistent with the facts. We can only do this, he contends, if we "have faced the question, 'Is Christianity true?' for ourselves" (1:140). On the basis of John 20:30–31 Schaeffer affirms, "we are not asked to believe until we have faced the question as to whether this is true on the basis of the space-time evidence." Likewise, the prologue to Luke's Gospel (Luke 1:1–4) shows that its "history is open to verification by eyewitnesses" (1:154). Schaeffer argues that if we deny that the Scriptures are "open to verification," we have no basis to say that people should choose to believe Christianity rather than something else (1:259). Christianity, he affirms, offers to modern man "a unified answer to life on the basis of what is open to verification and discussion" (1:263).

The non-Christian who denies that God can speak to us as he has done in the Bible must, Schaeffer warns, "hold to the uniformity of natural causes in the closed system, against all the evidence (and I do insist it is against the evidence)" (1:325). Such a presupposition is not "viable in the light of what we know. . . . It fails to explain man. It fails to explain the universe and its form. It fails to stand up in the area of epistemology." On the other hand, Schaeffer affirms that the Christian presupposition that God can and has spoken to man is reasonable in light of what we already know. "In my earlier books and in the previous chapters of this book we have considered whether this presupposition is in fact acceptable, or even reasonable, not upon the basis of Christian faith, but upon the basis of what we know concerning man and the universe as it is" (1:326).

Schaeffer therefore invites people to consider both the closed-system and open-system views of the universe, "and to consider which of these fits the facts of what is" (1:326). This "is a question of which of these two sets of presuppositions really and empirically meets the facts as we look about us in the world" (1:327).

Gordon Lewis argues that we need to distinguish between an inductive, empirical approach, exemplified by Montgomery, Pinnock, and others, and a verificational approach, exemplified above all by Carnell. According to Lewis, Schaeffer employed such a verificational method. "The *verificational*, or scientific, method addresses a problem by starting with tentative hypotheses. . . . Then the verification method subjects these hypotheses to testing and confirmation or disconfirmation by the coherence of their account with the relevant lines of data."[28]

We would contend that Lewis's verificationalism is just as much a type of evidentialism as the inductivism of such apologists as Montgomery and Pinnock. Few if any evidentialists operate according to the naive inductivism that supposes the apologist can begin with only the bare facts and no epistemology or hypothesis as to how the facts are to be explained. As we saw when we analyzed evidentialism, its essential feature is not a pure inductivism but an approach to justifying truth claims based primarily on empirical facts.

There is, however, one major difference between Schaeffer's apologetic and both Lewis's verificationalism and other forms of evidentialism. All evidentialists agree that the Christian apologetic properly concludes with the claim that the Christian beliefs defended have been shown to be probable, not certain. To be sure, Lewis argues that Schaeffer did hold to this probabilistic understanding of apologetics, even if he did not articulate it as clearly as he might: "No, Schaeffer's conclusion is not justified by a technically logical implication, but by a highly probable practical necessity, given the alleged lack of other hypotheses to test and the improbabilities of the non-Christian options. . . . A more precisely worded verificationalist like Trueblood or Carnell would state the point in terms of probabilities."[29]

However, Lewis's interpretation is rather difficult to sustain in the light of some specific statements Schaeffer made about probability.

> Those who object to the position that there are good, adequate, and sufficient reasons to know with our reason that Christianity is true are left with a probability position at some point. At some point and in some terminology they are left with a leap of faith. This does not mean that they are not Christians, but it means that they are offering one more probability to twentieth-century relativistic people to whom everything is only probability. They are offering one more leap of faith without reason (or with the severe diminishing of reason) to a generation that has heard a thousand leaps of faith proposed in regard to the crucial things of human life. I would repeat that what is left is that Christianity is a probability. (1:181)

Note that according to Schaeffer, if one concludes that reason can only show that Christianity is probable, the lack of certainty that results must be compensated with "a leap of faith." Clearly, Schaeffer saw this as unacceptable. By "good, adequate, and sufficient reasons" he did not mean arguments sufficient to convince one that Christianity was likely or probably true, but sufficient "to *know* with our reason that Christianity is true" (emphasis added). Apologists must maintain that Christianity is not merely the best answer to the big questions of life, but that it is the *only* answer.

Schaeffer's rejection of probability and his frequent reference to presuppositions suggest that he might have some affinity with presuppositionalism, to which we turn next.

Schaeffer and Reformed Apologetics

Like Carnell, Schaeffer was a student of Van Til, and like Carnell, he is commonly identified as a presuppositionalist by classical and evidential apologists and as an evidentialist by Reformed apologists. On the one hand, Schaeffer sometimes seems to express himself as only a presuppositionalist would. For example, speaking of the growing difficulty of communicating the gospel in a relativistic culture, Schaeffer states in a subheading, *"Presuppositional Apologetics Would Have Stopped the Decay"* (1:7). The question, of course, is what Schaeffer meant by "presuppositional." On the other hand, Schaeffer denied being either a presuppositionalist or an evidentialist: "I'm neither. I'm not an evidentialist or a presuppositionalist. You're trying to press me into the category of a theological apologist, which I'm not. I'm not an academic, scholastic apologist. My interest is in evangelism."[30]

The issue, though, is not in what setting Schaeffer employs his apologetic method, but rather what that apologetic method is. For that reason the above answer (which, it should be noted, was an off-the-cuff reply to a question in a public meeting) is less than satisfying. Still, it is clear enough that Schaeffer was unwilling to be classified as a presuppositionalist without qualification, and that fact should be taken into account. Evidently what he meant was that he did not wish to limit himself exclusively to the presuppositional approach. On one occasion he met with Van Til and Edmund Clowney, then president of Westminster Seminary, in Clowney's office to discuss their differences. Clowney reported that Schaeffer agreed with Van Til at every turn, even praising Van Til's summary of his apologetic as "the most beautiful statement on apologetics I've ever heard. I wish there had been a tape recorder here. I would make it required listening for all l'Abri workers."[31]

Schaeffer seems to have been indebted to at least *three* streams of Reformed thought. The first is the theology of Old Princeton. Forrest Baird (who seems generally critical of this influence) has pointed out that Schaeffer followed Hodge and the other Old Princetonians in their emphasis on the inerrancy of Scripture, their critical stance toward revivalism and pietism, and their opposition to liberalism.[32]

The second is the analysis of Western history and culture produced by the Kuyperian philosopher Herman Dooyeweerd, according to whom the biblical "ground motive" of creation-fall-redemption was supplanted in medieval thought by an irrational dualism between nature and grace. The biblical motive was revived in Reformation theology, the rejection of which led to the irrational dualism in modern thought between nature and freedom.[33] This analysis of the history of Western thought underlies Schaeffer's own sweeping treatments, notably in *The God Who Is There*, *Escape from Reason*, and *How Should We Then Live?*

Schaeffer's use of Dooyeweerd's analysis is creative and distinctive: according to Schaeffer, the modern dualism eventually broke down and resulted in modern man crossing what he calls **the line of despair**. This line represents the transition from a culture in which people lived "with their romantic notions of absolutes (though with no sufficient logical basis)" to one in which many people have abandoned belief in absolutes and so have despaired of finding any rational basis for meaning or purpose in life. "This side of the line, all is changed" (1:8).

Europe before 1890 and the

U.S. before 1935

The line of despair_____

Europe after 1890

U.S. after 1935

Schaeffer qualifies this schema, explaining that the shift across the line of despair "spread gradually" in three ways. First, it spread from one geographical area to another—from the Continent to Britain to America. Second, it spread from one segment of society to another—from the intellectuals to the workers to the middle class. Third, it spread from one discipline to another—from philosophy to the arts to theology (1:8–9).

Schaeffer argues that modern man, having crossed the line of despair, takes a leap of faith to affirm that life has meaning and purpose because human beings cannot live without such meaning (1:61). This "leap" results in a two-storied view of the world. The "downstairs" is the world of rationality, logic, and order; it is the realm of fact, in which statements have content. The "upstairs" is the world of meaning, value, and hope; it is the realm of faith, in which statements express a blind, contentless optimism about life (1:57–58, 63–64). *"The downstairs has no relationship to meaning: the upstairs has no relationship to reason"* (1:58). The downstairs is studied in science and history; the upstairs is considered in theology (1:83–85). According to Schaeffer, this two-storied view of the world is what makes liberal theology possible: the liberal excuses theological statements from any normal expectation that they will satisfy rational criteria of meaning and truth because they are upper-story statements.

The third stream of Reformed influence on Schaeffer is the presuppositional apologetics of Van Til.[34] While Van Til himself seems to have regarded his influence on Schaeffer as less than adequate, there is clear evidence that Schaeffer learned a great deal from him. Recently William Edgar—who was converted to Christ in a conversation with Schaeffer at L'Abri, later studied apologetics under Van Til, and is now a professor of apologetics at Westminster Seminary—argued that Schaeffer was much closer to Van Til's position than Van Til recognized.[35] He notes that both apologists

- emphasized presuppositions,
- argued that non-Christians could not give a unified account of reality,
- opposed both rationalism and irrationalism but not rationality,
- diagnosed man's ignorance of the truth as a moral rather than a metaphysical problem,
- advocated an indirect method of apologetics in which one assumes the non-Christian's position for the sake of argument, and
- affirmed both divine sovereignty and human responsibility.[36]

But Edgar also sees two crucial differences between the two. The first is Schaeffer's emphasis (which we have previously considered) that Christianity's consistency with the way things are provides verification of its truth. Edgar agrees with Van Til that in this regard Schaeffer was naively assuming that non-Christians agree with Christians as to the way things are and as to what is consistent with things as they are. However, Edgar qualifies this criticism by suggesting that Schaeffer's intent was not to concede to non-Christians that they had an adequate understanding of the way things are, but to acknowledge that by God's "common grace" non-Christians are enabled to express some truth.[37]

Second, according to Edgar, "presuppositions" are not understood in Schaeffer's system in the same way as in Van Til's. This is a more important question, since if Schaeffer means something different by the term *presuppositionalism* he cannot properly be termed a presuppositionalist in Van Til's line.

Edgar points out that for Van Til the unbeliever's presuppositions in every age and culture are radically different from those of believers. For Schaeffer, on the other hand, premodern unbelievers and believers had the "shared presupposition" that there are absolutes. Modern unbelievers no longer share this presupposition with believers, now that they have crossed "the line of despair."[38] However, this is not exactly what Schaeffer says. He says that before the line of despair, "everyone [that is, all non-Christians] would have been working on much the same presuppositions, which *in practice seemed to accord with* the Christian's own presuppositions" (1:6, emphasis added). Note that Schaeffer does not actually say that non-Christians had the *same* presuppositions as Christians, but that their presuppositions "in practice seemed to accord" with those of Christians. What Schaeffer appears to be saying is that non-Christians and Christians before the line of despair had different presuppositions, but in practice these did not seem to interfere with communication in the way the non-Christian presupposition of relativism does today.

Edgar also repeats Van Til's criticism that for Schaeffer a presupposition "is nothing much more than a *hypothesis*, or a starting point." That is, Edgar understands Schaeffer to view Christian presuppositions as hypotheses regarded as possibly true and subject to verification rather than, as Van Til held, transcendental truths to be defended by showing "the impossibility of the contrary." Edgar writes, "At bottom, then, Schaeffer's view of presuppositions does not allow him truly to be transcendental. Rather, he uses presuppositions as a kind of adjunct to various traditional methods in apologetic argument."[39]

What Van Til and Edgar identify as a weakness in Schaeffer's apologetic, Gordon Lewis identifies as a strength. As we saw earlier, Lewis also understands Schaeffer to present the Christian position as a tentative hypothesis verified by its internal and factual coherence. Schaeffer's emphasis on the verifiability of Christianity does lend some support to this interpretation. However, in general he presented Christianity as anything but a tentatively held position. His consistent claim is that no one can even make sense of being, truth, rationality, knowledge, personality, or morality on any other basis than that of the infinite-personal God revealed in the Bible. "No one stresses more than I that people have no final answers in regard to truth, morals or epistemology without God's revelation in the Bible" (1:184).

For Schaeffer the (transcendentally) necessary truth of Christianity is not incompatible with its verifiability. Although Christianity is absolutely true, non-Christians must still move in their minds from rejection of Christian presuppositions to acceptance of them. When Schaeffer assures non-Christians that they are not expected to believe and accept those presuppositions until they have verified them, by "verify" he means precisely to look and see that Christianity does give the only adequate answers to the big questions.

Schaeffer and Fideism

Like most conservative evangelicals, Francis Schaeffer was very critical of the philosophy of Kierkegaard and the theology of Barth and contemporary neoevangelicals. In particular, he frequently criticized the Kierkegaardian notion of a "leap" of faith. The index to Schaeffer's complete works lists over fifty references to the term in the foundational trilogy of books, and it appears sporadically throughout the other volumes (5:555). One might expect, then, that he would have little or no affinity for the fideist approach to apologetics. Yet in fact there is a strong element of fideism (as we have defined it) in Schaeffer's method.

First of all, it is worth noting that Schaeffer qualified his criticisms of both Kierkegaard and Barth. Kierkegaard is an important figure because he is the father of both secular and religious existentialism (1:14–16). Yet his writings, Schaeffer observed, "are often very helpful," and Bible-believing Christians in Denmark still use them (1:15). "I do not think that Kierkegaard would be happy, or would agree, with that which has developed from his thinking in either secular or religious existentialism. But what he wrote *gradually led* to the absolute separation of the rational and logical from faith" (1:16, emphasis added).

Likewise, Schaeffer acknowledged that Barth did not agree with much of what neo-orthodox theologians taught in his wake. "But as Kierkegaard, with his leap, opened the door to existentialism in general, so Karl Barth opened the door to the existentialist leap in theology" (1:55). Elsewhere Schaeffer expresses "profound admiration for Karl Barth" because of his "public stand against Nazism in the Barmen Declaration of 1934" (5:189).

While Schaeffer's theology and theory of apologetics differ significantly from those of the fideists, his method of apologetics has some striking similarities. Like both Pascal and Kierkegaard, Schaeffer sought to dislodge his hearers from their comfortable delusions through indirect argument. The delusions were different— Kierkegaard mainly combated nominal Christianity, Schaeffer mainly struggled against atheism and liberalism—but the goal was the same.

The key to Schaeffer's "method" is to find what he calls "the point of tension" (1:129–135). The basis of this method is the principle that "no non-Christian can be consistent to the logic of his [non-Christian] presuppositions." That is, people cannot live in a way that is consistent with unrealistic presuppositions about the world in which they live or about themselves. "Non-Christian presuppositions simply do not fit into what God has made, including what man is. This being so, every man is in a point of tension. Man cannot make his own universe and live in it" (1:132). "Therefore, the first consideration in our apologetics for modern man, whether factory-hand or research student, is to find the place where his tension exists. We will not always find it easy to do this" (1:135). We will have to invest ourselves in the person, get to know him, and help him discover the point of tension between his theory and his life. This point of tension is the place from which we can begin to communicate with him.

In order to enable the non-Christian to see the point of tension, we must help him realize the logical implications of his presuppositions. This means that we should not start out by trying to change his mind about his presuppositions, but rather to think more deeply about them. "We ought not to try first to move a man away from the logical conclusion of his position but toward it" (1:138). We must do this cautiously and lovingly. "Pushing him towards the logic of his positions is going to cause him pain; therefore, I must not push any further than I need to" (1:138–139). Exposing the point of tension entails what Schaeffer memorably termed "taking the roof off" (1:140), the "roof" being whatever rationale the non-Christian uses to excuse the disparity between what he believes and how he lives. The Christian must lovingly "remove the shelter and allow the truth of the external world and of what man is, to beat upon him" (1:140). The non-Christian must be helped to see his need before he is ready to accept the solution: "*The truth that we let in first is not a dogmatic statement of the truth of the Scriptures, but the truth of the external world and the truth of what man himself is*. This is what shows him his need. The Scriptures then show him the real nature of his lostness and the answer to it. *This, I am convinced, is the true order for our apologetics in the second half of the twentieth century for people living under the line of despair"* (1:140–141).

Schaeffer's reference to "the truth of the external world" should not be construed as a call for empirical investigation into nature or history as a means of establishing rational evidence for the truth of Christianity. While he does not seem to have been opposed to such lines of argument, that is not the direction he is taking here. Rather, he is saying that we need to confront the non-Christian with the truth about the world in which he lives and about what he is and what has gone wrong. This line of argument proves *directly* that we have a need but cannot identify or prove what the solution to that need is. For Schaeffer the answer to our need is only *indirectly* supported or verified by the argument, insofar as the answer given in Scripture—reconciliation with God through Jesus Christ—can be shown to meet the need.

Schaeffer's apologetic method shows affinities to fideism in its focus on the human condition and need as the point at which non-Christian beliefs are critiqued and the truth of the Christian faith is presented. Schaeffer also sounds a fideist note when he warns fellow Christians that a valid and effective apologetic must include the practice of the truth and not merely its rational defense.

> Christian apologetics must be able to show intellectually that Christianity speaks of *true truth;* but it must also *exhibit* that it is not just a theory. . . . The world has a right to look upon us and make a judgment. We are told by Jesus that as we love one another the world will judge, not only whether we are His disciples, but whether the Father sent the Son [John 13:34–35; 17:21]. The final apologetic, along with the rational, logical defense and presentation, is *what the world sees* in the individual Christian and in our corporate relationships together. (1:163, 165)

> There must be an individual and corporate exhibition that God exists in our century, in order to show that historic Christianity is more than just a superior dialectic or a better point of psychological integration. (1:189)

We may summarize those aspects of Schaeffer's apologetic that resonate with fideism as follows: (1) the non-Christian must be shown that he cannot consistently live with his non-Christian presuppositions, and (2) the Christian must show that he can live consistently with his presuppositions.

Schaeffer and Integration

Schaeffer's formal method of apologetics was shaped primarily, though not exclusively, by Reformed apologetics, including the presuppositionalism of Van Til. However, his actual argument for the existence of the God of the Bible closely follows the classical approach, and he affirmed the verifiability of biblical Christianity in terms compatible with some forms of evidentialism. The practical application of his apologetic, on the other hand, assumes the central fideist contention that the truth must be lived and not merely affirmed.

It is no wonder that Schaeffer avoided being labeled an advocate of any one school of apologetic theory. He did believe there were some guiding principles that should be followed, but he rejected the idea of an apologetic system that could be applied in all cases. He emphasizes that in evangelism and apologetics "we cannot apply mechanical rules. . . . We can lay down some general principles, but there can be no automatic application." Thus "each person must be dealt with as an individual, not as a case or statistic or machine" (1:130). "I do not believe there is any one apologetic which meets the needs of all people. . . . I do not believe that there is any one system of apologetics that meets the needs of all people, any more than I think there is any one form of evangelism that meets the need of all people. It is to be shaped on the basis of love for the person as a person" (1:176, 177).

DAVID K. CLARK

David K. Clark is an American evangelical who was raised in Japan, where he became acquainted firsthand with the Eastern philosophies that have since become prevalent in the United States. He studied philosophy of religion and apologetics under Norman Geisler at Trinity Evangelical Divinity School, where he received his master's degree. While studying for his doctorate at Northwestern University, he wrote a short book entitled *The Pantheism of Alan Watts*, for which Geisler wrote the foreword. Watts (1915–1973) was an Anglican priest who had left the church and devoted himself to advocating a Westernized form of Zen Buddhist philosophy.[40] Clark's doctoral dissertation extended his study of the mysticism of pantheistic religion.[41] He is now a professor of theology at Bethel Theological Seminary in Saint Paul, Minnesota.

Clark and Geisler's Classical *Apologetics in the New Age*

In 1990 Clark co-authored a book with Geisler critiquing pantheism. *Apologetics in the New Age*,[42] of which Clark was the primary author, is based squarely on

Geisler's apologetic method. The first of its two parts describes five different varieties of pantheism, while the second evaluates New Age pantheism, beginning with a summary of themes common in New Age belief, after which it proceeds to the critique proper. The critique begins by analyzing pantheism as a worldview and discussing the criteria for evaluating a worldview. Clark and Geisler first explain why a simple factual (or evidential) evaluation is inadequate. "Since facts are not entirely neutral with respect to world views, a theist and a pantheist may not even agree as to what the facts are. Therefore, straightforward appeal to facts as such cannot be decisive in choosing between two macroscopic world views" (135).

They then consider the view that there is no way to judge between competing worldviews. The premise of this view is "that every criterion for criticizing or defending world views grows out of a particular system of thought. On this view, for example, theism has certain principles and pantheism has others. When theistic criteria are used, theism is confirmed and pantheism disconfirmed. When pantheistic ones are used, the opposite occurs. . . . The argument becomes circular, and the choice of criteria is arbitrary" (136).

While admitting that "many criteria do depend on world views," such as the criterion of agreement with the Bible within Christianity, Clark and Geisler affirm "that at least some criteria are independent of world view" (137). At this point they appear to disagree with at least some versions of Reformed apologetics. But they go on to acknowledge that some people who hold a different worldview deny any rational principles in common with Christians, and suggest that such persons will "reveal by their actions or words a necessary dependence on or implicit assumption of these rational criteria." For example, "even while rejecting such criteria, pantheists implicitly affirm them in their actions" (137). This is an insight with which Reformed apologists, especially in Van Til's school of thought, will readily agree, although they apply it in a different way.

Clark and Geisler then present two different, overlapping sets of rational criteria for evaluating worldviews. Citing David L. Wolfe, they briefly endorse the four criteria of *consistency*, or lack of contradiction; *coherence*, "the presence of genuine unity and relatedness"; *comprehensiveness*, or agreement with "large ranges of experience"; and *congruity*, or close, natural fitting of the facts. The first two criteria amount to rationality, while the second pair constitutes empirical adequacy (137–38).[43] "In addition to these basic logical criteria, we will also use the tests of unaffirmability and actual undeniability. . . . We assume as basic principles that what is unaffirmable must be false and what is actually undeniable is true" (138). These two criteria are the basis of Geisler's classical apologetic method as set forth in his book *Christian Apologetics*.

Clark and Geisler go on to offer several specific objections to pantheism, closing with the point that "pantheism is unaffirmable and self-defeating" (155). They follow up with an analysis and critique of pantheistic views of knowledge, rationality, and good and evil, concluding that the New Age worldview is irrational and that such irrationality is unjustifiable. In their closing chapter they discuss how Christians should engage in apologetics with pantheists. "We believe it is helpful in apologetic conversations to seek to join forces with the dialog partner in a cooperative journey toward truth. If possible, it is helpful to set the stage in such a way that the battle is not between you and me, but between us and falsehood. You and I together are doing our best to root out what is false and find what is true" (225).

Throughout their book Clark and Geisler clearly follow the classical model of apologetics. In their concluding chapter, though, they warn that an apologist must use the arguments against pantheism in a way that is appropriate for the person to whom he is responding. "Apologetics is a concrete business. It means talking to people, individuals, not answering generic arguments that all persons in a class have in common. . . . It provides tools, raw materials, from which individual answers are shaped to meet particular needs of particular persons at their particular level" (226, 227).

Clark expanded on this point just three years later (1993) in another book, this one bearing his name alone.

Clark's *Dialogical Apologetics*

In *Dialogical Apologetics: A Person-Centered Approach to Christian Defense*,[44] Clark does not abandon the classical model, but he does deny it exclusive validity.

Clark begins by identifying three ways of relating faith and reason that are options for Christians. One may hold to a *faith without reason*, or at least a faith that is as isolated from reason as possible, in the tradition of Tertullian and Barth (6–7). One may affirm a *faith supported by reason*, as did Thomas Aquinas (7–9). Or one may hold to *reason dependent on faith*, following Calvin (9–11). The first and third options are what we have called fideism and Reformed apologetics respectively, while the middle option includes both classical and evidentialist apologetics. According to Clark, the disagreements are due in large part to differences in the way apologists have understood the words *faith* and *reason* (11–16). He favors the view that faith and reason "operate reciprocally" (23). "Minimum knowledge precedes the exercise of saving faith. But faith makes possible a fuller understanding and acceptance of God's truth. And richer knowledge in turn can deepen faith" (23–24). Clark does not equate this answer with any of the three mentioned above, and seems to think of it as a different answer. However, in fact he has restated the position taken in both classical and evidentialist apologetics. Augustine and Aquinas both held to this view of faith and reason; so do apologists like Norman Geisler and John Warwick Montgomery today.

In a later chapter Clark offers a parallel analysis of the relationship between conceptual schemes and facts. At one extreme, one may hold that "facts determine schemes" on the assumption that we can approach theoretical questions in a neutral fashion. At the other extreme, one may hold that "facts are at the mercy of conceptual schemes so no rational choice between paradigms is possible." Clark deems the first extreme rationalistic and the second fideistic. Between the two is "soft rationalism," the view that "facts are influenced by perspectives, yet facts and reasons can help determine the rational merits of competing points of view" (82). To determine which worldview is to be believed, one must employ rational criteria. Clark here repeats Wolfe's four criteria of consistency, coherence, comprehensiveness, and congruity (85–86), but not Geisler's two criteria of unaffirmability and actual undeniability. Instead he advocates a "cumulative case approach" to testing competing worldviews, specifically citing Joseph Butler in support (87). "Soft rationalism, therefore, follows this general principle: *the world view that most naturally explains wide ranges of evidence is the best*" (88). The evidence in support of Christianity includes the evidence of cosmology, the nature of human beings, ethics, religious experience, and the historical evidence for Jesus, especially the Resurrection. "The cumulative case approach posits the Christian world view as the best explanation for this network of evidence" (89). He continues: "Such an argument achieves only probability. But a cumulative case argument for one of a limited number of alternatives does have a certain strength: the conclusion does not stand or fall with any one point. All the apologetic eggs are not in one evidential basket" (90).

This would seem to be a quite explicit statement of evidentialism. However, Clark qualifies his advocacy of this approach. Since people are different, they will respond to apologetic arguments differently, and this implies that some arguments will be more effective with a particular individual than other arguments (98–99).

This is the basis of what Clark calls "dialogical apologetics": "Each of the major apologetic methods advanced among evangelical Christians today includes epistemological underpinnings that are partly right. But each also exaggerates its strong points in relation to other facets of a balanced apologetic. Dialogical apologetics recognizes and incorporates the strengths found in four traditional apologetic alternatives" (103).

These four alternatives correspond almost exactly to the four approaches discussed in this book. "Existential approaches to apologetics stress the uniqueness and convicting appeal of Christian experience." Pascal, Kierkegaard, and Barth exemplify this approach (103), which we have called fideism (with Pascal described as a precursor to fideism, not as a fideist himself). As we saw, it is somewhat misleading to define all of these thinkers' approach as stressing experience (though Kierkegaard certainly did). Fideists claim not "that experience stands on its own" (104), but rather that God's revelation stands on its own and must be believed even though it is beyond our ability to prove or comprehend.

"Presuppositional apologetics emphasizes special revelation as the starting point for apologetics" (104). Calvin, Kuyper, Van Til, Carnell, and Schaeffer all have contributed to or elaborated on this approach (105). Clark understands Van Til to have taught that Christians and non-Christians share "no common point of view, rational principles, or experiential facts" on which Christians can build an argument (105). He finds Schaeffer's "milder presuppositionalism" more workable as an apologetic because it assumes that there is at least common ground on the principle that "world views that make sense of human life and experience are better than those that do not" (106). Ironically, Schaeffer himself contended that the major apologetic challenge at the end of the twentieth century was the fact that many non-Christians no longer agreed that worldviews *need* to "make sense" (at least, not *rational* sense).

"Evidential apologetics . . . stresses the accumulation of biblical and historical evidence" (106). Paley, Montgomery, and Josh McDowell represent this approach (106–107). As we have seen, Clark's own approach has much in common with this model. Indeed, he identifies weaknesses, not in evidentialism itself, but in "naive evidentialists" who think "that facts speak unambiguously for themselves. The influence of points of view on interpretations of fact is lost on most evidentialists" (107). Such a criticism does not apply to leading evidentialists like Montgomery, though, who give considerable attention to exposing antisupernaturalist assumptions in non-Christian thought.

"Classical apologetics emphasizes a two-phase defense" in which theism is first proved "as the best world view" and multiple evidences are then used to prove that Christianity is "the best form of theism." C. S. Lewis, Geisler, Craig, and Moreland are all noted twentieth-century advocates of this approach (108). Classical apologists rightly emphasize the need to establish theism in order to place the evidences in their right worldview context. On the other hand, Clark says, "some are too rigid" in insisting that theism must first be accepted before examining any of the evidences for Christianity. He suggests that the distinction between the two stages of the apologetic be retained, while allowing people to "wander back and forth between the two stages as they assess the total cumulative weight of the case for Christianity." Some classical apologists also tend to demand rational certainty in an argument before it can be viewed as useful. "But shorn of such overstatement, classical apologetics . . . resembles the epistemology I favor" (109). Clark therefore is a classical apologist who, like Craig, incorporates significant elements of evidentialism in his approach.

According to Clark, dialogical apologetics is not merely a fifth view that combines elements of the previous four, "but a *second class or category of views*. The first group of options (the four positions) is, in theory, content-oriented. But dialogical apologetics is person-oriented both in practice and in theory" (109–110). It corrects certain false assumptions that commonly underlie all four of the standard approaches. "First, each tends to assume that proof is either absolute or useless" (110). On this basis classical apologists insist on arguments with deductive certainty while fideists reject rational apologetics because such arguments are invalid. Here again, Clark's position reflects evidentialist influence.

Clark denies the typical assumption of the four approaches that there is only "one correct epistemology" that "is right for all persons," arguing instead that while truth is one, human ways of coming to know that truth are varied. Likewise, he denies "that there is only one right way to practice apologetics" (111). The debate over the one right apologetic method "is exciting stuff for the apologetics junkie," but it searches for a method to reach an "unbeliever-in-the-abstract" rather than real, live unbelievers. "I have never talked with an unbeliever-in-the-abstract. When I am speaking with the man on the Bower Street bus, I try to find out what *he* knows and work from there. If knowledge is person-centered, then my apologetic should start with what *this man* believes" (111).

It is true that some apologists favor one form of apologetic argument, based on a single epistemological model of how a person should or can know that

Christianity is true. This is especially the case for Van Til, who reduced all apologetic arguments to the one transcendental argument that there can be no meaning or rationality or value in anything apart from the God who has been revealed in Scripture. But most apologists, while advocating a single epistemological theory, have allowed that different arguments can be useful in persuading people to believe. The approach that is most open to a variety of arguments is evidentialism. If one advocates a cumulative-case approach using evidence from various areas of knowledge and experience, then one might easily and naturally be interested in using both inductive and deductive arguments, and even the transcendental argument of Van Til—as long as it is viewed as one argument among many.

Here again, Clark's classical approach is moderated by elements of evidentialism. Thus he goes on to describe dialogical apologetics as "a rational enterprise in that it seeks to build a reasoned, probabilist, holistic, cumulative case for Christianity" (113). Where he distinguishes his approach is more in strategy than in epistemology: the arguments and evidences are to be used with due sensitivity to the differences among persons to whom the apologist is speaking. "Dialogical apologetics encourages a strategy of dialogue with unique persons in which an apologist uses all the tools in the toolbox to move particular individuals toward an intellectual acknowledgment of the Christian world view and a heartfelt commitment of life and soul to the Savior that this world view declares" (114).

C. STEPHEN EVANS

C. Stephen Evans (1949—)[45] is a Christian philosopher who has specialized throughout his career as an interpreter of Kierkegaard. In fact, Evans's work has encouraged evangelicals to reconsider the sharply critical view they have typically held toward the Danish thinker.

Evans grew up in Atlanta, Georgia, during the turbulent civil rights era. His father was a bus driver and his mother was a schoolteacher; both were from poor families in rural, Depression-era Georgia. He and his family attended very conservative Baptist churches; their principal church home, he later learned, excluded blacks from membership at the time. At a Christian school he attended, however, he was taught that segregation was wrong. Stephen read books by C. S. Lewis and other Christian authors while still in high school, and from early on showed an intellectual bent. He attended Wheaton College in Chicago, where he studied philosophy under Stuart Hackett and Arthur Holmes. Here he found his "privileged calling," as he terms it, of being a Christian philosopher. Hackett's philosophy emphasized the need for an epistemology that integrated rational and empirical dimensions of knowing, and Holmes's teaching emphasized the value of diverse schools of thought in philosophy. Their teaching informs Evans's own effort to integrate diverse approaches to Christian philosophy and apologetics.

From Wheaton, Evans went to Yale, where he earned his doctorate and also wrote his first book,[46] a response to Kierkegaard and other existentialist writers. It was later revised and published as *Existentialism: The Philosophy of Despair and the Quest for Hope*.[47] At Yale he developed an appreciation for both the analytic approach to philosophy dominant in England and America and the existentialist approach that was more prevalent on the Continent.

As he was finishing up his doctorate, he was offered a teaching post at Trinity College in Deerfield, Illinois, a suburb of Chicago. After two years there he accepted a position at his alma mater, Wheaton College, in 1974. During his early years there he decided to focus his research on a single philosopher, and chose Kierkegaard. On the advice of Howard and Edna Hong, who were overseeing the translation of Kierkegaard's works into English, Evans spent nine months in Denmark learning the language and culture and researching the thought of Kierkegaard.

In 1984 he accepted a position at Saint Olaf College, a Lutheran school in Minnesota, two years later succeeding Howard Hong there as professor of philosophy and curator of the Howard and Edna Hong Kierkegaard Library. During his twelve years at Saint Olaf, he became a renowned Kierkegaard scholar, publishing numerous articles and four academic books on him. He also became more widely known among evangelicals as a philosopher and apologist with such popular books as *Philosophy of Religion* (1985) and *The Quest for Faith* (1986).[48] In 1994 he moved to Grand Rapids, Michigan, where he is now professor of philosophy at Calvin College. He is also a member of the International Scholarly Committee of the Kierkegaard Research Centre at the University of Copenhagen in Denmark.

Evans, Classical Apologetics, and Evidentialism

In Evans's recent works on apologetics, he advocates a broadly evidentialist approach that incorporates what he regards as the valid insights of Reformed apologetics and of fideism. It should be noted that he usually views what we are calling classical apologetics as a variety of evidentialism. So, for example, in one of his most recent books, *The Historical Christ and the Jesus of Faith*, he classifies as a prominent type of "evidentialist apologetics" what he calls "the two-stage strategy." In this approach, one first argues for the existence of God, relying primarily on natural theology, and then argues that the Bible and its events, preeminently the resurrection of Jesus, constitute the true revelation of that God. Evans classifies Thomas Aquinas as "a classical example" of this strategy (233).[49] The "five ways" show that God exists, while the Christian miracles confirm the truth that Christianity, and not (especially) Islam, is the true revelation of God (233–35).

Evans also identifies Joseph Butler (235) and William Paley (235–36) as proponents of this approach—with some justification, for they are transitional figures leading up to the modern evidentialist approach. He also cites C. S. Lewis as an example of an apologist using the two-stage strategy, although his specific arguments at the two stages are somewhat different. In *Mere Christianity* Lewis appeals to the moral argument to prove God's existence, then employs the Trilemma argument to press the claims of Christ to be God (236). Evans appears to endorse these examples of the classical approach as legitimate variations on an evidential apologetic.

That Evans is an evidentialist is clear from the way he approaches theistic proofs. In an article defending natural theology, he argues that rather than abandoning theistic arguments we should frame them evidentially.

> Natural theology, conceived as part of an apologetic enterprise, does not need to lead to a complete view of God. It needs only to discomfit the atheist and agnostic, suggest the plausibility of thinking there is something transcendent of the natural order, something that has some of the characteristics of the Christian God. . . . Taken collectively they [the arguments] provide a cumulative case for the reasonableness of believing in God which is powerful for him who has ears to hear and eyes to see.[50]

This is the same approach he takes in his popular introduction to apologetics, a revision of *The Quest for Faith* entitled *Why Believe?* He urges critics of the theistic arguments to consider "the possibility that the arguments might have great force if taken collectively" (19).[51] Using the standards of proof in different kinds of court cases as an analogy, he argues that the level of proof should not be set beyond all possible or even all reasonable doubt, but rather at the level of "the preponderance of the evidence" (20).

A "clear and convincing proof" in this context is defined in terms of "a high probability." This seems to me to be the kind of "reasonable case" we ought to strive for in religious matters as well. We ought to strive to make a judgment that is in accord with "the preponderance of the evidence" and that seems highly likely or probable. . . . Trying to look for a single isolated argument on either side to serve as a "proof" is therefore a mistake. Rather, each side here will present a range of facts, drawn from many areas of human experience, to show that the "preponderance of evidence" is on its side. (20–21, 23)

Evans proposes, then, "to show that a reasonable 'cumulative case' can be made for a particular kind of religious faith: Christianity. Drawing on philosophy, personal religious experience, and historical evidence, I will try to show that we have very good reasons to think that the Christian faith is true" (24). This is an explicit and standard formulation of the evidentialist approach.

Evans continues to develop his apologetic in a fairly conventional evidentialist fashion. Noting that non-Christians cannot be expected to accept the Bible as inspired, he suggests that we "put aside, then, as question-begging, any assumption that the Bible is inspired by God. . . . Let us simply decide to treat the Bible as a historical document" (69). The New Testament documents consistently present Jesus as divine, and yet they were written too soon after Jesus for the attribution of deity to be a later accretion (69–70). As historical documents, they are worth taking seriously (70–71). They purport to be and are written in the genre of history, not mythology (71–72). The speculative theories of even the most skeptical scholars acknowledge that there is some historical truth in the Gospels (72–73).

According to Evans, the most plausible explanation for the early Christians' belief that Jesus was God is that he claimed that he was, as the Gospels clearly attest (74–75). Given that Jesus made this claim for Himself, it is difficult to deny his deity, since the alternative is to think Him a liar or insane (75–76). Jesus' followers were convinced of his deity by his resurrection from the dead (76). Evans acknowledges that some readers will deny this on the grounds that all miracles are impossible, but he asks such readers to "try to suspend judgment temporarily and keep an open mind on the question as to whether miracles occur." After all, he points out, "there is impressive evidence of Jesus' resurrection for those who approach the evidence with an open mind" (76). This evidence consists of the empty tomb, the testimony of eyewitnesses, and the changed lives of Jesus' followers (76–77). "If the resurrection did not occur and the witnesses made up the story, it is hard to see why they would be willing to suffer and die for such a concoction. Pascal puts the point bluntly: 'I prefer those witnesses that get their throats cut'" (77).

Although the evidentialist approach is clearly present in his writings, Evans is critical of a pure evidentialism that attempts to defend Christianity on the basis of an inductivist epistemology. In *The Historical Christ and the Jesus of Faith*, he faults an inductivist evidentialism for holding to an Enlightenment view of objectivity. Actually, Evans finds "two opposite difficulties, which may appear in fact to cancel each other out," in the evidentialist approach (32).[52]

> Both problems relate to the underlying Enlightenment ideal of objectivity that this type of defence of the narrative embodies. The essence of this strategy is to claim that an objective, neutral historical study of the Gospels confirms the basic reliability of the narrative. The proponents agree with the sceptical critics that the Gospels must be studied as "ordinary historical documents" by "ordinary historical means" and with no "special pleading." (32–33)

The problem here, Evans argues, is that "ordinary historical documents" do not report supernatural events or the messages of "divinely authorized messengers." He wonders if it would not be "special pleading" to take such reports seriously (33).

> A look at the practices of historical critics, as well as theoretical accounts of what historical method involves, makes it evident that many scholars would claim that ordinary historical methods do require such a bias against the supernatural. If that is the case, then defending the historicity of the narrative using "ordinary" historical methods will necessarily be a losing battle. This raises the question as to whether the defenders of the narrative have essentially given away the contest by accepting the terms of the engagement of their opponents. (33)

Evans's other objection to this evidentialist approach is that the apologists are not really as objective as they claim to be. Rather than being truly willing "to follow the evidence wherever it leads," they are simply marshaling the evidence to defend a conclusion they have already reached. "It does not follow from this that their readings are mistaken or unjustified, but it does suggest that presuppositions play a larger role than those committed to an 'inductive' method would allow" (34).

Evans and Reformed Apologetics

Evans has given little attention to the Reformed apologetics of Gordon Clark or Cornelius Van Til. However, consistent with his move in 1994 to Calvin College, in recent years he has expressed strong support for crucial aspects of the "new Reformed epistemology" associated especially with Alvin Plantinga.

In chapter 9 of *The Historical Christ and the Jesus of Faith*, entitled "Epistemology and the Ethics of Belief" (202–230), Evans endorses the Reformed epistemologists' approach to religious knowledge. Following Plantinga as well as William Alston, he articulates and supports "a broadly externalist account" of knowledge and proposes to apply this epistemology "in investigating the epistemological status of historical religious claims" (222). What this means and how it applies to apologetics is best seen from chapter 11, "The Incarnational Narrative as Historical: Grounds for Belief" (259–82), where Evans discusses "the Reformed account" of "incarnational knowledge" (260). By "incarnational narrative" Evans means the basic story line about Jesus, and by "incarnational knowledge" he means a person's knowledge that the story of Jesus is true.

The Reformed confessions (260–61) and Calvin (261–62) taught "that we gain certain knowledge that the Bible is from God by the internal testimony of the Holy Spirit in our hearts" (261). This does not mean that there is no evidence of the Bible's truth, but only that the believer's confidence or belief is not based or grounded on that evidence (261). According to Evans, this Reformed view seems fideistic only because it is often interpreted in the context of an internalist epistemology. The **internalist** says that a true belief constitutes knowledge when it is justified by *factors internal to the knower*. Specifically, one's belief must be based on good evidence of which one is aware (263). If we assume this understanding of epistemological justification, we can interpret the Reformed view of the testimony of the Holy Spirit in one of two ways. We might interpret it to mean that the Spirit enables people to see what is or should be obvious, namely, that the Bible is true (263), or that the testimony of the Holy Spirit is itself an experience that constitutes "internally available evidence" (264). But the truth of the Bible is not always obvious even to believers, and an internal experience seems to be a weak form of evidence.

"Rather than dismiss the Reformed view as bad apologetics," Evans concludes that we should interpret it as assuming an externalist account of knowledge. The **externalist** says that a true belief constitutes knowledge when it is justified by *facts external to the knower*. "At bottom the externalist says that what properly 'grounds' a belief is the relationship of the believer to reality" (264). Externalists differ in the way they explain justification. But they all agree that "what makes a true belief knowledge is a relation between the knower and the objective world; knowledge requires us to be so oriented to that world that our beliefs can be said to 'track' with that world, to use Robert Nozick's suggestive phrase" (265).

Assuming some form of externalism, then, Evans concludes that if his belief that the incarnational narrative is true is the result of the testimony of the Spirit, and if the Spirit's testimony generally produces true beliefs, then his belief is justified (268). "If a belief in the truth of the incarnational narrative is formed as a result of the Holy Spirit, and if beliefs formed in such a manner are usually true, then the testimony of the Holy Spirit produces knowledge" (274). This work of the Spirit is not to be equated with the believer's experience of that work, but is in essence whatever the Holy Spirit does, and however he chooses to do it, to bring a person to faith. This process may or may not include the use of evidence (268–269). The "subjective feeling of certainty" is not the ground of the belief, but is rather the result of the Spirit's work in bringing the person to embrace that belief (269).

Evans concludes that the primary purpose of Reformed epistemology is not to convince unbelievers that Christianity is true, but rather to help Christians understand how their belief qualifies as knowledge.

> The primary purpose of telling the Reformed story is not to persuade or convince someone of the truth of Christian faith; it is not at bottom a piece of apologetics, though in some cases it could function in that way. Rather, it is a story Christians tell when they wish to understand how God has given them the knowledge they believe he has given them. . . . The purpose of the evidentialist story is primarily apologetics, though the doubters to be convinced may be within as well as outside the Church. This task must not be understood as the task of providing a once-and-for-all justification of faith, one that would be convincing to any rational person in any time or place, but as the task of persuading or convincing particular groups of people by responding to particular objections and appealing to particular beliefs already held. (284)

Evans and Fideism

As we might expect of a scholar who has devoted years to the study of Kierkegaard, Evans's approach to apologetics draws heavily on the fideist tradition. Indeed, in his book *Faith beyond Reason* Evans takes the unusual stance among evangelical philosophers and apologists of viewing fideism as a rational and valuable perspective.

The fideist element in his apologetic may be illustrated from his book *Why Believe?* One way he adopts a fideist position is in his assessment of the value of theistic arguments. He views them neither as rigorous deductive proofs of theism (as in classical apologetics), nor as showing that theism is a probable or most probable position (as in evidentialism), nor as reducible to a single transcendental proof (as in Van Til's version of Reformed apologetics). Rather, he concludes that natural theology arguments should be viewed as bringing to people's attention *natural signs*, elements of nature that function as signs, pointers, or clues to God's reality. Such signs do not constitute *proof*, but they are not therefore valueless (73).[53] The arguments that present such signs are the traditional theistic arguments, but the clues exhibited by those arguments are "recognizable by the simple as well as the learned" (74).

Evans finds three "clues" of God's reality in three "fundamental mysteries . . . the mystery of the physical universe, the mystery of a moral order, and the mystery of human personhood" (31). The traditional theistic arguments explicate these clues, or "calling cards," as he also calls them (32–60). "A calling card is of course not an end in itself. It is a sign that someone has called on us and may call again. We should then be on the lookout, not merely for more clues, but for God himself. And for the person who has met God, the calling cards may look insignificant indeed" (63).

A second fideistic element of Evans's apologetic is that it is centered on an appeal to non-Christians to approach Jesus in the Gospels as a person to know. People do not become Christians "merely by considering evidence or arguments" (78) because, first, "there is a gap between an intellectual recognition of who Jesus is and a commitment to him." Many people agree that Jesus is God but do not live as if that were true. Second, people draw different conclusions from the evidence, as they did in the first century, because they differ "in their own response to Jesus as a person" (78). In turn, people tend to respond in faith to Jesus if they think of themselves as in great need, whereas people who think they are fine as they are tend to be most offended by Jesus (79).

The final challenge then to anyone who is seriously interested in Christianity is to go to the New Testament and meet the Jesus who is pictured there. Think about this Jesus, his life, his message, his death, and his resurrection. Think about your own failings and your own deepest needs and desires. Think as honestly as you can, and see if this Jesus creates in you a response of faith and trust as you get to know him. Perhaps you will discover that God has spoken to you. (80)

How this approach relates to answering apologetic challenges is illustrated by Evans's handling of the problem of evil. For Evans, the problem is solved through pointing to God's proven trustworthiness. "Our evidence for this is simply our total knowledge of God's character. God loves us, God cares about us, and God honors his commitments" (103). We know this to be true about God primarily because he has demonstrated his love and character in Jesus. "For Jesus is God in human form, a God who not only tells us he cares about our sufferings, but shows us he cares" by his life, death, and resurrection (103).

The implication of this for those who wonder whether God has a reason for allowing evil is clear. They do not need a philosophical argument. Rather they need to get to know God and understand his character. They need to be pointed to Jesus. . . . Christian philosophers have given strong refutations of the claims of atheists to have disproved God's existence on the basis of evil. However, the best answers Christians can ultimately give to the problem of evil are two. First, they can point to Jesus, who reveals God's goodness and love and suffers with us. Second, they can follow Jesus' example by working against suffering, and suffering with those who suffer. (103, 104)

A third way Evans follows the fideist tradition is in his use of the paradoxical argument that it is the incredible character of the Christian message that shows its divine origin.

If Peter and John and Paul and the other apostles wanted to invent a new religion, they could hardly have hit on doctrines less plausible to their hearers. To the strictly monotheistic Jews they proclaimed that Jesus was the Son of God and that Jesus and his father were both God. To the rationalistic Greeks they proclaimed that Jesus, lock, stock, and body, had risen from the dead and that his followers would someday experience this same resurrection. . . . The very preposterousness of their teachings is a sign that they were proclaiming what they had experienced as true and were convinced was true. (124)

Note the similarity of Evans's argument here to Tertullian's "I believe because it is foolish" argument. Evans continues by asking critics of the mysteries of the Bible to imagine what it would be like if God were to reveal truth to us. "What would we expect such a revelation to contain? Commonsense advice such as 'Dress warmly in cold weather'?" (125). Sound moral wisdom is a more reasonable expectation, but it would hardly be proof of divine revelation. "If God were going to give humans a special revelation, it should contain some truth that humans would be unable to discover on their own. Otherwise, why would he bother? In other words, we would expect a genuine revelation from God to contain mysteries" (125). "Christian doctrines are not philosophical theories to be logically proven. . . . Christians have usually insisted that the basic mysteries of the faith are *above* reason, but not *against* reason. That is, although we cannot fully understand them or prove their truth, they do not contradict what *is* known to be truth" (126).

Evans on Integration

Evans discusses the integration of diverse approaches to apologetics explicitly in *The Historical Christ and the Jesus of Faith*. Specifically, he states that he will assess the viability of "two different types of theological accounts of how knowledge of the incarnational narrative is possible. . . . These two accounts are an evidential model, that understands knowledge of the story as derived from ordinary historical evidence, and what I shall term the Reformed account, that describes the knowledge as the product of the work of the Holy Spirit within the life of the person." As we have seen, Evans includes classical apologetics with evidentialism. He will conclude that "a combined account provides the best picture of how such religious historical knowledge is possible" (25).[54]

Evans personally thinks "there is genuine force in a cumulative case argument for God's existence of the type Swinburne provides . . . though I would prefer to speak in terms of plausibility rather than probability" (240–41). But such arguments seem to be generally ineffective in persuading those who do not already believe. "The evidentialist offers a case that is supposed to be based on objective evidence, evidence that would be generally accepted. Such a case is supposed to show that Christians do know what they claim to know. It appears in the end, however, that the claim that this objective evidence is objectively good evidence is not itself a claim that is generally accepted" (241).

Evans concludes that the evidentialist argument can still be used, but the evidentialist will have to acknowledge that there is "a subjective dimension to the claimed objective case" (241). In other words, he will have to acknowledge that not everyone will see the evidence in the same way. "An Enlightenment foundationalism that demands foundational evidence that is completely certain and completely objective, accessible to all sane, rational beings, certainly will find the evidentialist case wanting. However, since in the previous chapter we found such an epistemology to be itself wanting, this by no means rules out such evidentialist arguments as having any value" (244).

Evans denies that these considerations prove Swinburne's argument to be valueless. Rather, he suggests that we can make the historical case and then, "if the historical basis of the case is attacked, one possible response is to view the concessions made to the more sceptical forms of historical criticism as only made *for the sake of argument*" (249).

> There is apologetical value in accepting, for the sake of argument, the conclusions of one's opponents. If I can get my opponent to see that some belief I wish to defend follows from her own premises, then I have been successful. So one can see the value of accepting, for the sake of argument, fairly sceptical accounts of the New Testament. One can then argue, "See, even on your account of the historical status of the New Testament, the conclusions I wish to defend can be derived." However, once we have put aside Enlightenment epistemologies that demand an evidential base of highly certain facts, we must recognize that this argumentative technique implies no general necessity to accept the views of one's opponents about such matters. (251–52)

Evans suggests that we view evidentialist apologetics and the testimony of the Holy Spirit, not as rivals, but as complementary. "On the assumption that the process whereby the Spirit produces belief can include the evidential story, it is perhaps best not to speak of the Reformed and evidential stories as distinct, rival accounts, but as accounts that are given for different purposes or that perhaps reflect different emphases" (288).

Evans suggests "several possible ways the two accounts can complement each other" (288). "First, and most obvious, one might simply see the two accounts as applying to two different groups of people" (289). Evans points out that this seems to be the actual state of affairs: some people come to faith without any conscious consideration of evidence, whereas others come to faith through a process that includes rational reflection on the evidence (289).

"A second possibility is to see the two types of account as applying to different *levels* of knowledge." Here Evans invokes William Alston's distinction between first-order knowledge, or *knowing* something, and second-order knowledge, or *knowing that we know* it, which he had discussed earlier (277–80). Evans suggests that we may possess first-order knowledge of the truth about Jesus as the result of the work of the Spirit (which may or may not involve evidence). "Our second-order knowledge that we have this first-level knowledge could be seen, in some cases though not necessarily for all, as based on a more traditional evidential case" (290). Not every believer will need evidentialist arguments to have second-order knowledge, but those with intellectual doubts may find it necessary to examine the evidence for their beliefs to make such second-order knowledge secure (290). Admittedly, such second-order knowledge would then be subject to possible objections, as all evidentialist arguments are. "However, it is important to remember that on this suggestion it would only be the second-level knowledge of a particular group that would be threatened in this way; the people in question as well as ordinary believers may still know what they know, whatever problems may beset philosophical and theological arguments designed to show that they do know what they know" (291).

Moreover, the objections may not be troubling even to second-order knowledge, since the objections will not have force with everyone (291).

> There is such a thing as failing to respect the evidence. But there is no looking at the evidence that is not a looking from a particular point of view. Hence evidence that is not appreciated by everyone can still be recognized as good evidence, once the Enlightenment ideal of certainty has been set aside. Of course the believer may be wrong; others will claim this is the case. But that is a necessary feature of being epistemologically finite. (292–93)

Third, Evans suggests that the two accounts can both play a role in resolving doubt in the mind of a believer. *General doubt* about whether I really know that I know can be resolved by an appeal to "the 'circular' kind of justification" that reminds me that what I believe is certainly true because it was revealed by God in the Bible. *Specific doubts* engendered by "defeaters"—arguments that, if accepted, would disprove or call into question some aspect or even the whole of my Christian belief—can be resolved by evidentialist type arguments (293), which are especially suited as a "rebuttal, or 'defeater for the defeater'" (294). Evidential arguments that seem weak or flawed when viewed as providing the sole basis for our knowledge of Christian truth can be perfectly sound as rebuttals (295–96).

> We should of course remember that apologetic arguments do not have to convince anyone, much less everyone, in order to be successful. There are many other goals for such arguments, that could be summarized under the rubric of "softening up" the intended audience, such as lessening the grip of various objections, removing certain barriers that make it impossible fairly to consider faith, producing a disposition to hear with a more open mind or to seek to hear more about the faith, and many more. (295)

Fourth, Evans discusses ways the evidentialist account can be strengthened by integrating it with the Reformed account. The incommensurability of evidential argument with the absolute commitment of faith can be resolved by rejecting the idea that the "degree" of belief (whatever that means) must be proportional to the degree of evidence. One could argue that faith should be rooted in some evidence—a kind of "threshold" requirement—while denying that faith must be weaker or stronger depending on the amount of evidence—the "proportionality requirement" (298). The firmness or tenacity with which a Christian believes can be attributed to the work of the Spirit rather than indexed to the varying strength of one's evidential case (299). The other major problem for evidentialism is the fact that evidential arguments depend greatly on prior assessments of the relative probability of specific assumptions of the argument. Evans suggests that the Reformed account can help here by assuring the evidentialist that his view is correct (because assured by the testimony of the Spirit) even if he cannot convince any or all nonbelievers that his assessment of those probabilities is correct. "If the believer's knowledge is rooted in a process (the work of the Holy Spirit) that is a truth-conducive ground, then whether the knowledge in question is basic or evidentially mediated, it can qualify as knowledge, *regardless of whether the believer can produce an argument that will satisfy some particular opponent.* Being justified or warranted in a belief is one thing; being able to justify a belief to someone else is another" (300).

Perhaps the central thesis of Evans's model for integrating the evidentialist and Reformed traditions is that apologetics and religious epistemology are not identical enterprises. "Apologetics is a vital enterprise, but it is not identical with the task of gaining a reflective understanding of how the knowledge is gained" (305–306). Understanding how one came to believe "is by no means the same thing as having an answer to a challenger or enquirer" (306). For Evans, the Reformed approach generally has more value in understanding how we come to faith, while the evidentialist approach generally has more value in functioning as a means through which we come to faith.

JOHN FRAME

John M. Frame (1939—) is an exceptional apologist in the Van Til tradition. Among Van Til's leading interpreters, Frame alone has offered a critical, creative interpretation of presuppositionalism that makes room for many of the traditional kinds of apologetic arguments criticized by Van Til.

Frame was converted to Christ as a teenager.[55] He went to Princeton University and majored in philosophy in the late 1950s, the heyday of the analytic philosophy school that is still dominant in many English and American departments of philosophy. The thinkers who most influenced him in college, though, were Christian apologists, especially C. S. Lewis, J. Gresham Machen, and above all Cornelius Van Til. After he finished at Princeton, Frame studied under Van Til at nearby Westminster Theological Seminary (1961–1964). From there he went to Yale, where he received a master's degree in philosophy. After teaching for some time at Westminster, he became professor of apologetics and systematic theology at Westminster's sister school, Westminster Theological Seminary in California (located in Escondido, a suburb north of San Diego). After many years there, Frame became Professor of Systematic Theology and Philosophy at Reformed Theological Seminary in Orlando, Florida.

The foundational book for Frame's apologetic method is *The Doctrine of the Knowledge of God* (1987).[56] In it he develops an epistemological theory that he calls **perspectivalism**, in which he seeks to integrate rational, empirical, and subjective aspects of human knowledge on the basis of a Reformed theology of knowledge and revelation. In summarizing Frame's system, we will be citing primarily from this book. In *Apologetics to the Glory of God* (1994), he applied this perspectivalism directly to apologetics.[57] In addition, he has written two books applying a perspectival model to ethics.[58] Frame's colleague Vern S.

Poythress, a professor of New Testament at Westminster in Philadelphia, has likewise applied perspectivalism to systematic theology and to hermeneutics.[59] Poythress's book *Symphonic Theology: The Validity of Multiple Perspectives in Theology* (1987)[60] was published the same year as Frame's *Doctrine of the Knowledge of God*. Poythress, in fact, contributed greatly to the development of Frame's perspectivalism, as Frame himself acknowledges in several places (194, 216, 328, 360).

Most modern epistemologies seek to correlate or balance two principles or aspects of human knowledge: the *subject*, or knower, and the *object*, or the known. According to Frame, subject and object cannot be properly correlated without relating them to a third aspect of knowledge, the *norm*, or standard of knowledge. Epistemological theories err if they seek to locate that norm in the subject or object, because in fact God, who created both the subject and object, is the source of the norms of human knowledge. Thus perspectivalism is an explicitly theistic epistemology, one in which God's norms for human knowledge must be taken into account in order to understand how we know what we know.

There are, then, three perspectives in all human knowledge, which Frame calls the existential, situational, and normative perspectives. All three are equally basic aspects of knowledge, and epistemologies that champion one at the expense of the others will be inadequate. So, when the **existential** perspective, which considers the knowing subject or self, is absolutized, the result is *subjectivism*. The **situational** perspective considers the object of knowledge, the world; *empiricism* results when this perspective is absolutized. The **normative** perspective considers God's laws of thought that govern how we know; when the laws of logic (here viewed as the supreme norm of thought) are absolutized as the only perspective on knowledge, the epistemological theory of *rationalism* is the result (62–75, 89–90, 107–122, 162–63, 250–51). Note that the three epistemologies criticized in Frame's perspectivalism correspond to the three non-Reformed approaches to apologetics: fideism tends to subjectivism, evidentialism is based on some form of empiricism, and classical apologetics tends to rationalism.

The solution is not simply to add these three approaches together: "Combining one bankrupt epistemology with another leads nowhere" (122). Rather, one should see each as a partial and interdependent perspective on the whole of knowledge. None is absolutized because the one absolute in knowledge is God, who alone as the Creator can "guarantee that the three elements will cohere" (110).

John Frame's Three Perspectives on Human Knowledge[61]

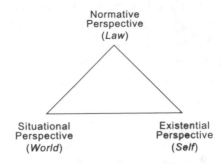

Normative
Perspective
(*Law*)

Situational
Perspective
(*World*)

Existential
Perspective
(*Self*)

What makes perspectivalism not only explicitly theistic but in fact a *Christian* epistemology is that Frame includes the revelation of God in Scripture as basic to the normative perspective. Rather than viewing logic alone as the norm of human knowledge, as in rationalism, Frame agrees with Van Til that all human knowledge depends on God's revelation. This does not mean the normative perspective *is* Scripture, but that in it all knowledge is viewed from the perspective of its accord with Scripture (163). Logic, on the other hand, is considered part of the situational rather than the normative perspective, because logic "is subordinate to Scripture, which is our ultimate law of thought." Logic is thus viewed as a discipline that uncovers information or facts to be used in interpreting Scripture (243).

Frame and Reformed Apologetics

Although Frame views himself as "Van Tilian," he is critical of the "movement mentality" that many of Van Til's students and followers exhibit. As early as 1976 he was calling in print for "constructive critical analysis" of Van Til's thought.[62] As we will see, this call was not mere lip service; Frame has gone on to publish several books in which he pointedly criticizes Van Til's writings and makes his own creative proposals for building on Van Til's achievement.

Basic to Van Til's apologetic was the assumption of Reformed or Calvinist theology as the best exposition of the teachings of Scripture. While Frame agrees with this assessment, he is uncomfortable with the dogmatic way Van Til applied Reformed theology. Van Til judged evangelical theologians, even other Reformed theologians, to have deviated from fundamental biblical truths if they strayed from what he regarded as the true understanding of Calvinism. As Frame notes, "Van Til tended to put the worst possible construction on the statements of non-Reformed writers," and, we may add, nonpresuppositional Reformed writers. Frame, on the other hand, tends to find as much truth as he can in writers of different points of view, and to try to give them "the benefit of the doubt."[63] Nevertheless, Frame himself acknowledges that, in *Doctrine of the Knowledge of God*, he was dogmatic enough "to assume Reformed theology without argument" (xv).

Since we referred frequently in Part Four to Frame's exposition of Van Til's system, a brief summary of the main points of his position will suffice here to make his broad agreement with Van Til clear. Since presuppositions are unavoidable in all human thinking, there can be no such thing as "neutrality" in the sense of an absence of commitment toward some view of truth and reality. Moreover, since fact and interpretation of fact are interdependent, there is no such thing as "brute fact," or uninterpreted fact (71–73, 99–100, 140–41). Thus non-Christians cannot be neutral with respect to Christianity, nor can they be shown facts that will in and of themselves prove Christianity true. They hold presuppositions that are alien to Christian faith, and they interpret all facts in light of those presuppositions (87–88, 125–26).

Presuppositions are not only intellectually unavoidable, they are also ethically obligatory. We have an obligation to believe the truth, and God holds all people accountable for believing falsehood. For Frame, this is just another way of asserting that God is the Lord of all human thought, an idea to which his subtitle, *A Theology of Lordship*, alludes (see also 11–21, 40–48). Therefore, basic to the Christian's message to unbelievers must be, at least implicitly, a call to repentance of intellectual sins, including the acceptance of unbiblical presuppositions (63–64, 73–75, 108–109, 149, 248).

Frame also agrees with Van Til that the triune God who reveals Himself in Scripture is the necessary and true presupposition of all truth, knowledge, and moral judgment. Thus he endorses Van Til's method of taking the non-Christian's position and showing by a *reductio ad absurdum* that it is at bottom irrational and incapable of justifying his claims to knowledge (359–63).

Frame and Classical Apologetics

Despite Frame's basic commitment to the presuppositional model, he interprets it broadly enough to accommodate significant elements of classical apologetics. This may be seen most directly in his handling of the question of arguments for God's existence. For Van Til, all apologetic argument must be transcendental: it must argue that unless Christianity is presupposed as true, nothing is intelligible. So, all theistic proofs reduce to the one transcendental proof that God is the necessary presupposition of everything. For Frame, by contrast, the transcendental argument functions in one of three perspectives of what he calls "offensive apologetics" (359–63).

In his later textbook on apologetics, Frame elaborates on theistic arguments. He denies Van Til's charge "that the traditional arguments necessarily conclude with something less than the biblical God." For example, the teleological argument does not imply that God is *merely* a designer; the cosmological argument does not imply that God is *merely* a first cause.[64] Nor does he think it proper to criticize an argument "because it fails to prove every element of Christian theism. Such an argument may be part of a system of apologetics which as a whole establishes the entire organism of Christian truth." Not even Van Til's transcendental argument can prove at once the entirety of Christian theism.[65]

Frame also points out, as we suggested in our discussion of Van Til's view of theistic proofs, that the indirect form of argument Van Til favors can be converted to a direct argument.

> In the final analysis, it doesn't make much difference whether you say "Causality, therefore God" or "Without God, no causality, therefore God." Any indirect argument of this sort can be turned into a direct argument by some creative rephrasing. The indirect form, of course, has some rhetorical advantages, at least. But if the indirect form is sound, the direct form will be too—and vice versa. Indeed, if I say "Without God, no causality," the argument is incomplete, unless I add the positive formulation "But there is causality, therefore God exists," a formulation identical with the direct argument. Thus, the indirect argument becomes nothing more than a prolegomenon to the direct.[66]

Frame and Evidentialism

Frame also builds bridges between presuppositionalism and evidentialism, giving a more respectful assessment of evidential apologetic labors than is typical of Van Til or his other advocates. He grants that specific evidentialist arguments can be useful and appropriate. "It is quite proper to point out that the resurrection of Christ is as well attested as any other historical fact. It is legitimate to ask why the apostles were willing to die for the belief that Christ had risen. It is legitimate to examine the alternate (unbelieving) explanations for the resurrection reports and to show how implausible they are" (353).

The last sentence here stands in tension with Van Til's position on alternative explanations for the resurrection of Jesus. According to Van Til, one must argue that such explanations are not merely "implausible" but *irrelevant: "God's self-existence is the presupposition of the relevancy of any hypothesis.* If one should seek to explain the claim of the disciples of Jesus that their Master's body was raised from the tomb by offering the hypothesis of hallucination, we reply that the hypothesis is irrelevant. Our further study of the factual evidence in the matter is no more than a corroboration of our assertion of the irrelevancy of such an hypothesis."[67]

Presumably one could argue that a hypothesis was both irrelevant and implausible, so Frame is not necessarily contradicting Van Til. Yet there can be no question but that Frame's approach makes a concession to more traditional historical apologetics that goes beyond Van Til and fits with his approach only with some stretching.

Basic to the evidentialist model of apologetics is the use of empirical arguments that end in conclusions deemed probable based on the evidence. Van Til flatly rejected such arguments in apologetics; the apologist, he maintained, must conclude that the Resurrection certainly occurred, not that it probably occurred. While agreeing in substance with Van Til's position here, Frame again seeks to broaden the presuppositional model to include some sort of probability. He points out that even if we regard some matters of faith as certain, not every factual matter pertaining to God's revelation in Scripture will be known to us with certainty. "Even if our faith were perfect, there would still be some matters relevant to theology about which, because of our finitude, we could have only probable knowledge. For example, I doubt that even an unfallen Adam, living in the present, could know with absolute certainty the author of Hebrews. . . . Butler was right when he said that many of our decisions in life are based on probability rather than absolute certainty" (136).

Frame goes on to assert that Butler went wrong because he said "that our belief in Jesus Christ for salvation is only a matter of probability" (136). Actually, Butler does not seem to have said this. For Butler and evidentialists following him, our ability to demonstrate facts about Jesus using historical methods of inquiry could never rise above probability, but this leaves open the possibility of the Christian having certainty about Christ from another source (say, the work of the Holy Spirit). Even this qualified statement about probability, though, would seem to be unacceptable to Frame. Based on the New Testament teaching that sinners have no excuse not to repent, Frame concludes, "Thus the evidential argument is demonstrative, not merely probable. The evidence compels assent; it leaves no loophole, no room for argument." He admits that an empirical argument generally "can never justify more than a probable confidence in its conclusion" (142). The Christian evidential argument attains certainty, though, for several reasons:

a. Empirical arguments are normally probabilistic because they utilize only *some* facts, but the Christian argument is that God reveals himself in "*all* the facts of experience."
b. "The very concept of probability presupposes a theistic world view."
c. The Holy Spirit's testimony can accompany the evidence and produce certainty.
d. "The Christian evidential argument is never *merely* evidential," but is always part of a "broadly circular" argument presenting the evidence in the light of Christian presuppositions. (143).

We should point out that these factors do not really address the point about empirical arguments reaching probable conclusions. Any specific evidential argument must be based on specific evidences, or selected facts, not on the whole of reality *(a)*. The argument that the concept of probability presupposes theism is not an evidential argument at all, but a worldview or presuppositional argument *(b)*. The testimony of the Holy Spirit does not alter the logical structure of empirical reasoning, and so is irrelevant to the question of the force of an evidential argument *(c)*. Finally, an argument that "always" presents evidence within a "broadly circular" presuppositional argument is really not an empirical argument, but an argument from the logical coherence of the evidence with the Christian system of thought *(d)*.

Frame takes more or less the same position in *Apologetics to the Glory of God*, but moves slightly closer to endorsing probabilistic arguments in apologetics. He suggests that it can be legitimate to formulate arguments in which, because of our imperfect understanding of the subject matter, we are not able "to convey adequately the absolute truth of God's evidence." "To do so, and to use the word probably in this connection, is not to say that the revealed evidence for God is merely probable; it is rather to say that one portion of the evidence, not well understood by a particular apologist, yields for him an argument which is at best possible or probable."[68]

Evidentialists should have no trouble agreeing with Frame here. They would simply go one step further and assert that in the nature of things, *no* "particular apologist" has or can have enough information about *any* "one portion of the evidence" to produce an argument that yields absolute certainty for its conclusion. In other words, because apologists are finite human beings with limited knowledge, they cannot produce empirically grounded arguments that show a 100 percent probability, or absolute certainty, for their conclusions.

Frame and Fideism

One of the three perspectives in Frame's perspectival epistemology is called the *existential* perspective. It is thus natural to ask whether Frame's treatment of this perspective integrates fideistic elements into his apologetic. It seems that it does. According to Frame, the Lordship of God consists of three perspectivally related aspects that correspond to the three epistemological perspectives. They are *authority*, in which he establishes the norms for his people; *control*, in which he rules over every situation of his people; and *presence*, in which God is personally related to the people themselves (15–18). Thus the existential perspective takes into account that coming to faith is a matter of a human person coming into a restored relationship with the God who is always present. We may illustrate these three perspectives as follows:

John Frame's Three Perspectives on God's Lordship

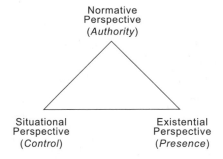

Normative
Perspective
(*Authority*)

Situational
Perspective
(*Control*)

Existential
Perspective
(*Presence*)

Frame's development of the existential perspective confirms its correlation with fideism. We are responsible not merely to agree intellectually with the truth, but to "live in truth, walk in truth, do the truth. . . . To know is to respond rightly to the evidence and norms available to us" (149). The apologist should challenge non-Christians, then, not merely to accept the doctrines of Christianity, but to act on the Christian message. One famous fideistic formulation of this challenge is Pascal's Wager, which Frame defends against several objections (356). "Faith is a lot like wagering, after all—not that Christianity is uncertain or like a throw of the dice! But the Christian's certainty is not the kind of certainty envisaged by rationalist philosophers, either. . . . Think again of the example of Abraham, who ventured in faith, though many objections to God's promise stared him in the face. In the midst of questions and unresolved difficulties, we follow God" (357).

In addition, Frame agrees with fideists when he writes, "One of the strongest (i.e., *most persuasive*) arguments is Christian love" (357). Apologetics without love and godly character poses a serious danger. Commenting on the famous apologetics text in 1 Peter 3:15–16, Frame writes: "It is interesting that Peter does not urge apologists to be intelligent and knowledgeable (although such qualities are certainly helpful), but to lead consistently godly lives. He gives us a practical standard for a discipline we are inclined to regard as theoretical. . . . If our life contradicts our doctrine, then our apologetics is hypocritical and loses credibility."[69]

Frame and Integration

Frame does not explicitly argue for integrating different apologetic approaches, but his handling of the approaches and his own epistemology imply a concern to bring them closer together. He explicitly denies that there is only one correct method in apologetics. "Indeed, there are as many methods in apologetics as there are apologists, persons needing Christ, and topics of discussion" (347). He qualifies this statement later by saying that "in some respects all of our methods should be alike" (355), but this does not negate the point.

Perspectivalism, in which the justification of Christian knowledge is refracted into three perspectives, is a model for integrating the different apologetic approaches. There is some ambiguity, though, as to how Frame's three perspectives correlate with the four apologetic approaches we have been discussing. As we have seen, when he critiques non-Christian epistemologies, he identifies rationalism, empiricism, and subjectivism as three extremes resulting from absolutizing the normative, situational, and existential perspectives respectively. Rationality, empirical reality, and subjective experience must all be used under the authority of God's revelation in Scripture. In his own Christian epistemology, though, rationality is assigned not to the normative but to the situational perspective, and Scripture is said to be the focal point for the normative perspective.

Further complicating the matter, in his book on apologetics Frame relates the three perspectives to apologetics in yet another way. Constructive apologetics, or apologetics as proof, is the normative perspective; offensive apologetics, or apologetics as offense, is the situational; and defensive apologetics, or apologetics as defense, is the existential.[70] We may understand what Frame means from his application of the schema to the rest of the book. Apologetics as proof centers on the proof for Christianity from God's own normative revelation, confirmed by arguments for God's existence and for the truth of the gospel (chapters 3–5). Frame's arguments here draw from presuppositional, classical, and evidential apologetics, and so this perspective cuts across the lines of the apologetic models we have drawn. Apologetics as defense focuses on responding to arguments thought to disprove Christianity; Frame focuses on the principal such argument, the problem of evil (chapters 6–7). Again one finds classical and presuppositional arguments here, as well as arguments common in more than one apologetic approach. Finally, apologetics as offense focuses on the critique of unbelieving thought; the argument here is characteristically presuppositional but is largely paralleled in classical and evidentialist apologetics (chapter 8).

CONCLUSION

All the apologists profiled in this chapter have made significant efforts to develop an approach to apologetics that makes good use of alternative approaches. They represent a growing number of evangelical apologists who believe that apologetics ought to incorporate elements traditionally distributed among the four approaches.

Typically, these apologists integrate two or more approaches by expanding one approach to absorb elements (usually not the whole) of the others. So, for example, David K. Clark is really a classical apologist with a broad enough understanding of that method to include the other approaches (especially evidentialism), using the important principle that the utility of arguments is person-relative. C. Stephen Evans is really an evidentialist in his apologetics and a broadly Reformed epistemologist in his theology of revelation and faith. John Frame is (as he maintains) a presuppositionalist with a broadened understanding of that approach to include the others viewed as perspectivally related.

We suggest that this practice of expanding or enriching one apologetic approach by incorporating elements of other approaches is just what apologists should do. We doubt that it is possible, or even desirable, to formulate a "fifth" apologetic system that would wholly combine and thus supersede the four basic approaches. Rather than striving to produce the perfect single apologetic system or method or model that all apologists should use, we think Christians should start from the best approach they know and augment or refine it using whatever they can from other approaches. In the remaining chapters of this book, we will elaborate on this proposal.

For Further Study

Hanna, Mark M. *Crucial Questions in Apologetics*. Grand Rapids: Baker, 1981. Presents an approach called "veridicalism" as an alternative to presuppositionalism and traditional apologetics.

Mayers, Ronald B. *Balanced Apologetics: Using Evidences and Presuppositions in Defense of the Faith*. Grand Rapids: Kregel, 1996. Originally published as *Both/And: A Balanced Apologetic*. Chicago: Moody Press, 1984. Argues that a sound apologetic must maintain a "dialectical balance" between the rational/presuppositional and the empirical/evidential aspects of apologetics.

Chapter 21

Contending for the Faith: Apologetics and Human Knowledge

The apologists profiled in the preceding chapter differ significantly on various matters of apologetic method. But unlike most (not all) of the apologists considered in the earlier parts of this book, Carnell, Schaeffer, David Clark, Evans, Frame, and the like are not particularly troubled by those differences. While they have worked, or are working, to develop the best apologetic they can, they see much value in the fact that there are different apologetic methods.

In the closing chapters of this book, we will discuss ways of integrating the four major approaches to apologetics. Let us be clear at the outset what we are and are not advocating.

First, we are not advocating a kind of "fifth approach" that would supposedly incorporate elements of the four basic approaches to create a new, superior approach to apologetics. We do not suggest that apologists abandon their approach to apologetics for a new, improved model. On the other hand, we do claim that apologists can improve their apologetic by learning from other approaches (and indeed that many apologists already do so).

Second, we are not arguing that all four approaches as they have historically been practiced are equally sound approaches to apologetics. In particular, we do not think that fideism, as represented by such modern thinkers as Kierkegaard, Barth, and Bloesch, is an adequate metapologetic. As we explained toward the end of Part Five, the weaknesses of fideism are significant and deeply rooted. Still, we think fideists bring often-neglected considerations to the apologetics table and that we can all learn from them and by doing so enrich our own apologetics.

(Again, many apologists have already been doing so.) We also maintain that fideism can be developed into a sounder and more robust apologetic, though doing so requires more of an "overhaul" than in the other three approaches. We also recognize that many apologists will regard one or more of the other two approaches as deficient in some way (e.g., evidentialists may view Reformed apologetics as inadequate, and vice versa). They may continue to regard each other's approaches as inadequate while still enriching their own apologetic through interacting with other approaches.

We do not claim, then, to be offering definitive proposals for integrating the different approaches to apologetics. If we succeed in helping to advance the discussion over integration and to stimulate others to do a better job than we do here, we will be gratified.

PERSPECTIVAL APPROACHES TO DEFENDING TRUTH

In the preceding chapter we noted that John Frame utilizes the schema of three perspectives in two somewhat disparate ways. When analyzing non-Christian epistemologies, he identifies rationalism, empiricism, and subjectivism as imbalanced theories of knowledge due to their lopsided elevation of logic, fact, and the person. As we pointed out, these three epistemologies correspond to classical, evidential, and fideist apologetics. On the other hand, when setting forth his own Christian epistemology, he moves logic to the same perspective occupied by facts or evidence and places revelation or Scripture under the "normative" perspective. Scripture as normative in knowledge is, of course, the crucial and distinctive claim of presuppositionalism.

We suggest, then, that Frame's perspectivalism can be adapted to encompass and correlate the four approaches to apologetics (see above table). One way to do this is to interpret the three perspectives as describing the **immanent aspect** of knowledge, and then to identify revelation as the **transcendent aspect** of knowledge. Logic, facts (evidence), and faith are the basis of three related perspectives on the way we receive God's truth; God's Logos (the Word), God's acts, and God's Spirit are the basis of three related perspectives on the way God reveals truth to us. We use our capacities for reason (the mind), sense, and choice (the will) to receive God's revelation; in turn, God, by his Spirit, creates faith within us in response to his revelation.

Transcendent and Immanent Perspectives in Knowledge

Reformed Apologetics

God's Logos
(*Scripture*)

God's Acts	God's Spirit
(*Miracle*)	(*Illumination*)

Revelation: Transcendent Aspect

Evidential *Apologetics*	**Situational** **Perspective**	**Normative** **Perspective**	**Existential** **Perspective**	*Fideist* *Apologetics*

Reception: Immanent Aspect

Facts	Faith
(Sense)	(Heart)

Logic
(Reason)

Classical
Apologetics

Some comments on this schema are in order if its significance is to be properly understood. First of all, a perspective is, as in Frame's system, a way of viewing the whole. For example, the work of God's Spirit in illumination causes us to think differently (logic), to see the facts differently (evidence), and to respond to God differently (faith). Our reason, perception of reality, and faith stance (whether believing or unbelieving) are always inseparably related in our knowledge. We use our reason to reflect on and interpret the teachings of Scripture, the redemptive acts of God reported in Scripture, and the illuminating work of the Holy Spirit enabling us to appreciate and accept the truth of Scripture.

Second, while all these perspectives are involved in knowledge, certain of them are inevitably primary in specific experiences of knowing. The nominal Christian who intellectually assents to the truth of Scripture and espouses a Christian worldview experiences the illuminating work of the Holy Spirit primarily as engendering the willingness to trust in the God revealed in that Scripture and articulated in that worldview. The Christian biblical scholar studying the date of the Exodus views the matter primarily through the situational perspective of the factual evidence (though other perspectives, such as his acceptance of Scripture as normative, play a role). The non-Christian who has been taught that the problem of evil poses a logical contradiction within the Christian worldview experiences challenges to this conclusion primarily through the normative perspective of reason (though other perspectives, such as his willfully unbelieving stance, again play a role). *Apologists need to identify which perspective is primary in any specific discussion with an individual and address the question at hand from that perspective.*

For example, in talking with a non-Christian about the problem of evil, the Christian may find that the non-Christian's difficulty centers on the loss of a loved one and the subsequent difficulty in believing that God loves him. In that situation the apologist should address the issue primarily as a matter of gaining confidence in God as a person who loves him, not as a logical difficulty to be solved. Here apologists of any approach may find that the fideist way of handling the question may be the most effective. On the other hand, some non-Christians are very troubled by the logical conundrum but not by a specific experience of their own. In that case the apologist should be sure to address the issue primarily, at least at first, as a matter of showing the non-Christian that the reality of evil does not disprove God's existence. Here Plantinga's free-will defense, Geisler's greater-good defense, or some similar philosophical argument may be most effective.

Third, the transcendent and immanent aspects of knowledge are united in the situational and existential perspectives in a way that it is not true in the normative perspective. God's acts in the world are both miraculous (the transcendent aspect) and factual (the immanent aspect). The work of God's Spirit within a person may be described both as illumination (transcendent) and the creation of faith (immanent). By contrast, Scripture and human reason are not two aspects of the same reality. The result is that an integrative view of the three transcendent perspectives and the three immanent perspectives results in four basic approaches to knowledge, not six. These four approaches appear as the four "corners" of the table and correspond to the four approaches to apologetics analyzed in this book.

Fourth, an apologetic argument could in theory start from any one of the four "corners" and be persuasive; at the same time, no one approach is guaranteed to be a successful or most effective starting point in all apologetic contexts. This generalization follows from the points just made: some perspectives are primary in one situation and not in others. On the other hand, because each perspective relates to the whole, a sound, comprehensive, and effective apologetic method can begin from any of the four approaches as long as it takes a broad enough view of the other approaches.

Broadening the Classical Approach

Let us illustrate our claim here by examining how each approach might appropriate the crucial insights of the other approaches in light of the above schema. We begin with classical apologetics. In the standard model one first constructs a rational argument or arguments for theism as the best worldview. Having established theism, one then presents the evidence for the distinctive claims of Christianity, which will be viewed without worldview prejudice.

This classical model can incorporate the evidentialist approach by agreeing that the two steps mutually support each other. That is, the arguments for theism make more plausible the arguments for such Christian claims as the resurrection of Jesus or fulfilled prophecy, while good evidence for the Resurrection or fulfilled prophecy can also be considered evidence for theism.

The classical model can also be broadened to include the Reformed approach. As we have pointed out, the transcendental argument for the existence of God functions much like the traditional theistic proofs, and could be used as the foundational theistic proof in which all the more traditional proofs are grounded. That is, the theistic arguments that appeal to causation, order and design, morality, human rationality, and so on can be grounded in the transcendental argument that they would have no meaning if an absolute, transcendent God did not exist. Classical apologists can also use the "new Reformed epistemology," assuring non-Christians who already confess the existence of God that they are rational to do so even if they are unprepared to prove his existence. The apologist may then present the evidence that God has revealed himself in Christ and in the Bible, noting that the validity of any appeal to evidence to establish facts assumes a rationality and order in the universe that is not self-explanatory.

Finally, the classical model can even encompass the approach taken in fideism. Before presenting rational proofs for God's existence, the classical apologist can get to know a non-Christian's beliefs about God. If the non-Christian recognizes that there must be some kind of God, the apologist might do better to bypass arguments for theism and ask if the non-Christian would like to know God personally. He can always circle back to the theistic proofs if, in further discussion, it becomes clear that the non-Christian firmly espouses an alternative worldview. Then, after explaining why God can be known only in Jesus Christ, the apologist can present evidences supporting Christ's supernatural existence as needed.

As we saw in the previous chapter, David K. Clark is a classical apologist who integrates the other three approaches in much the way sketched here. One could make a plausible case for classifying Clark as either a classical apologist or evidentialist due to the way he splits the difference between them. Clark also encourages apologists to draw upon the strengths of existential approaches (i.e., fideism) and presuppositionalism, especially the "milder" form advocated by Francis Schaeffer.

Broadening the Evidentialist Approach

Given the nature of the evidentialist approach to apologetics, it may have the easiest task integrating the other three approaches into its own. Since evidentialists tend to favor a multi-pronged or cumulative-case argument for Christianity, incorporating arguments from the other three approaches is for the evidentialist largely a matter of adding to its repertoire. C. Stephen Evans is an example of an evidentialist who has given substantial attention to integrating insights from both Reformed epistemology and fideism into his apologetic (see above, chapter 20).

Most evidentialists already use some of the theistic arguments favored by classical apologists for defending theism. The difference is that the evidentialist prefers to use such arguments as part of a broader case for Christianity, rather than divide apologetic arguments into those that support mere theism and those that support Christianity given a theistic worldview. Evidentialists should have no trouble acknowledging that for some people, at least, certain evidence-based arguments work better once a case for theism has been made.

Evangelical evidentialists do not, as we explained in our treatment of their approach to apologetics, affirm the Enlightenment form of "evidentialism," the epistemological claim that no belief can be rational unless the one holding the belief can back it up with sufficient evidence. From this perspective, the evidentialist and the Reformed apologist can make common cause. There is nothing to prevent evidentialists from agreeing with Plantinga that evidence is not needed for belief in God because it is properly basic—and then turning around and presenting such evidence for those who have not yet recognized that fact. (Again, some evidentialists, like Evans, already do just that.) Evidentialists can also agree with presuppositionalists in Van Til's line that God is the necessary presupposition of all evidence, fact, inference, and probability—and then turn around and offer evidential arguments in support of Christian belief. Some evidentialists have already added Van Til's transcendental argument to their "collection" of evidences.

Evidentialists need not *always* present a direct historical argument for the reasonableness of belief in the Resurrection to those who doubt it. They can instead offer an indirect argument based on the apparent absurdity in first-century Judaism of claiming that a crucified man (the presumed object of God's curse) was the Messiah and the lack of any expectation of the Messiah dying and rising again (he was rather expected to bring death to the pagans and resurrection to departed Israelites). The very apparent absurdity of this belief proves that human beings did not concoct the story. This is an argument that classical and Reformed apologists should also be able to use.

Broadening the Reformed Apologetics Approach

John Frame is an example of an apologist in the tradition of Van Til (the presuppositional wing of Reformed apologetics) who has broadened his approach to include what are from his perspective valid aspects of the other approaches (for what follows, see chapter 20). The central (and in a sense *only*) apologetic argument for Van Til is the transcendental argument that reason, fact, and value (and so forth) can have no coherent meaning except on the presupposition of the existence of the God revealed in Scripture. Van Til sharply distinguished this "indirect" argument for God's existence from the "direct" theistic arguments of classical apologetics, which he rejected. Frame, on the other hand, acknowledges that Van Til's indirect, transcendental argument can be "converted" into a direct argument of the classical type.

Frame also has room for the inductive, historical arguments typical of evidentialism. Whereas Van Til objected to arguments that concluded that Christian beliefs (such as the Resurrection) were probably true, Frame objects only if apologists conclude that those Christian beliefs are merely or only or at best probable. Thus, a Frame-type presuppositionalist should be able to use arguments for the reality of the God of the Bible from fulfilled prophecies, the historical evidence for Jesus' resurrection, and the like.

Reformed apologetics and fideism are in some ways not that far apart, and in Frame's thought certain key emphases of fideism are given a significant role. Frame's recognition of an "existential perspective" in knowledge leads him to affirm that the truth is something we do, not just something we believe. One of our strongest arguments for Christianity is love, without which our apologetics is hypocritical and ineffective.

Broadening the Fideist Approach

If evidentialism is the apologetic approach most conducive to integrating elements of the other three approaches, fideism is undoubtedly the approach least conducive to such integration. After all, fideism historically has been a reactionary way of thinking that has repudiated apologetics as traditionally understood. Of the apologists who favor integration discussed in the previous chapter, none can fairly be classified as a fideist.

In our opinion, what fideism needs above all is to abandon its false dichotomies. Fideists typically argue that revelation and the knowledge of God are personal rather than propositional. In fact, they are both. God has revealed himself both propositionally in Scripture, the written Word of God, and personally in Jesus Christ, the living Word of God. Propositional or factual knowledge *about* God can lead to personal knowledge *of* God. Of course, reading the Bible and learning doctrinal propositions about God will be useless if we fail to put our trust in the Lord Jesus and encounter the living God about which the Bible speaks. On the other hand, trusting in Christ would have little if any meaning or practical effect in our lives if we did not know anything *about* Christ.

Fideists argue that the gospel is an affront to human reason and therefore cannot be defended using human reason. Their argument amounts to another false dichotomy, between the gospel as contrary to human reason and the gospel as consistent with human reason. The dichotomy is a false one because it depends both on the humans doing the reasoning and on what we mean by reasoning. Human beings by their own wisdom are incapable of discovering God in order to know him (1 Cor. 1:21), but this does not mean that those endowed with human wisdom cannot recognize in retrospect ways in which God makes himself known. The gospel is "foolishness" to Greeks (vv. 22–23), but it is also divine wisdom, not foolishness, to those Greeks who are called by God (v. 24). It is reasonable to expect that God will be beyond our reasoning capacity to comprehend; thus we do not need to choose between Christianity being reasonable and beyond reason, since both are true.

If fideists abandon these false dichotomies, they will find that they can make good use of the apologetic arguments of the other three approaches. The classical apologists' arguments for theism can be used by such fideists as "signs" or pointers to the God who is beyond our comprehension (as indeed a God who transcends time and space and yet is immanently present and at work in creation surely is). There is nothing stopping a fideist from presenting such arguments to those who ask for reasons to believe that God exists—and then hastening to say that what the nonbeliever really needs, once he recognizes that God exists, is to get to know God personally. A fideist should also have no trouble affirming that belief in God is properly basic (as Reformed epistemologists argue) while insisting that belief or disbelief in God is primarily (not exclusively) a matter of the will. As we have already pointed out, fideists argue "indirectly" for the truth of the resurrection of Jesus by arguing that the idea is so contrary to conventional wisdom that it could not have been invented. It is a short step from that argument to a more traditional historical argument for the Resurrection as employed in both evidentialist and classical apologetics.

As we stated at the beginning of this chapter, fideism as it has historically been understood requires the most significant reconstruction if it is to be amenable to integration with the other three apologetic approaches. Fideists and non-fideists alike may conclude that giving up its usual dichotomies (personal v. propositional, living Word v. written Word, against reason v. agreeing with reason) would leave something unrecognizable as fideism. They may be right. What we think is a safe assertion is that an apologetic approach that is oriented from the "existential perspective" of the work of God's Spirit in bringing an individual to the point of choosing to believe can be broadened to include significant elements of more conventional apologetics. The Holy Spirit can and does use rational arguments, presentation of factual evidence, and appeals to the authority of God's self-revelation as means to engender faith, just as he uses the proclamation of the gospel and the faithful lives of Christians. Just as we sometimes need to use arguments to persuade a rebellious child to go home to the parents who love him, it is sometimes necessary to use arguments to persuade nonbelievers that they are estranged from God and need to be reconciled to him.

Test Case: Postmodernism

The utility of an integrative approach may be illustrated by considering how Christian apologists should respond to the challenge of postmodernism. It turns out that all four approaches make a valuable point on this. The classical apologist correctly observes that *postmodernism is self-refuting*. This observation, once understood, is enough to prove that postmodernism or any other relativistic philosophy is false. However, some people simply are not moved by this argument. The fact that postmodernism is irrational will not bother someone who embraces irrationality as good and proper. The postmodernist may reply that rationality and consistency are abstract notions; what matters is that the belief in the objectivity and absoluteness of truth has run aground.

At this point the evidentialist makes another good point: *postmodernism is unrealistic;* it doesn't fit the facts. In the real world (and there is one) there are objective facts, many of which can be known to be such, some of which remain out of our sure grasp because of lack of information. We all expect the bank's records of our deposits, withdrawals, and fees to match our own—and we assume that someone is in error if there is a discrepancy and that a review will resolve the question definitively. We may disagree about what happens to a human being after death—whether humans have souls that exist as personal, incorporeal entities after physical death—but that does not mean that all answers are equally true. This line of response is quite sound. Again, though, the postmodernist may complain that the apologist is once again assuming what he claims to prove—that what is real to one person is always real to another. He may even charge the apologist with laboring under the modernist delusion of objective truth.

Here Reformed apologists can make some very helpful points. The "new Reformed epistemologist" may say, in response to the charge of modernism, that the belief in objective truth is not the peculiar notion of modernism, but is a properly basic belief. The person who believes in objective reality and objective truth can no more stop believing in them than he can stop believing that he had, say, orange juice for breakfast. The presuppositionalist will go even further and turn the charge around. *Postmodernism is itself an irrationalist development within modernism.* The problem with modernism was not that it was rational; it was that it undermined the very foundation of rationality by denying that truth and reason are grounded in God. It was a short step from the modernist claim that human beings impose the rational categories of their own mind on the world to the postmodernist claim that each community of human beings, and in the end each human being individually, imposes a distinct point of view on the world. The presuppositionalist, then, shows the postmodernist that his supposed liberation from modernism is no such thing.

The evangelical fideist, while not necessarily disagreeing with the other three approaches, looks at postmodernism from the other end. Rather than looking for ways to refute it, he is more likely to ask what we can learn from it that will make our apologetic more viable. Fideists may even agree with postmodernists that some contemporary forms of apologetics operate under hidden modernist assumptions. The apologist should take this concern seriously. While we should not abandon our belief in absolute truth and the objectivity of reality, we ought to acknowledge that all human knowledge—even the knowledge that Christians have from reading the Bible—is partial, imperfect, and held from a limited point of view. In Scripture we have absolute truth presented to us, but we do not have absolute knowledge of that absolute truth.

The four responses to postmodernism described here are typical of the four basic apologetic approaches. Yet some apologists already use two or more of these strategies in their responses to postmodernism. Such "integration" is already happening as apologists of differing methods interact with one another and learn from one another. What we are advocating here is not something radically new; we simply encourage apologists to do consciously and systematically what many if not most apologists already do.

APOLOGETICS AND THEOLOGY

To some extent the differences among the four approaches to apologetics reflect differing theological roots. Just as the four approaches are not neatly divided camps, though, apologists advocating the four approaches do not fall neatly into four theological camps. That said, however, there is a pattern that confirms the distinctiveness of the four approaches.

Generally, classical apologetics has been most dominant in Catholic theology and among apologists influenced by Catholicism, including Anglicans of a more Catholic bent. This is what one would expect given the formative contribution to the classical model by Thomas Aquinas. Thus some of the leading classical apologists have been the Anglican writer C. S. Lewis, the Catholic philosopher Peter Kreeft, and Norman Geisler, who studied philosophy at Loyola University. Of course, classical apologetics has been widely influential among Christians of most theological traditions and denominations.

Evidentialists tend to be evangelicals who are non-Calvinist or "Arminian" in their theology. This was true of Joseph Butler and John Locke, and it is true of Clark Pinnock and Richard Swinburne. William Lane Craig, a classical apologist with strong evidential leanings, is staunchly Arminian in his theology. John Warwick Montgomery, our paradigm example of an evidentialist, is neither Calvinist nor Arminian, but a conservative Lutheran. It is surely no accident that theological traditions that downplay or deny human certainty about one's salvation also downplay or deny the possibility of rational certainty in apologetic argument. Arminians and Lutherans believe that Christians should be reasonably confident of their salvation but should not expect to be absolutely certain of it; likewise, many apologists from these traditions believe that Christians can make a reasonable case for Christianity, but not one that achieves absolute or deductive certainty.

Reformed apologists, as the name implies, tend to be staunchly, even dogmatically, Reformed or Calvinist in theology. While not all Calvinists espouse Reformed apologetics (e.g., R. C. Sproul is a classical apologist), most if not all Reformed apologists are Calvinists or have deep Calvinist theological roots. John Calvin's theology anticipated and inspired this approach. More specifically, what we have called Reformed apologetics has been dominant in Dutch Reformed circles: Abraham Kuyper, Herman Dooyeweerd, Cornelius Van Til, and Alvin Plantinga all had Dutch Reformed roots. Just as Reformed theology emphasizes personal assurance of salvation based on the certainty of God's sovereign purpose and his promise in Scripture, so also Reformed apologetics, especially of the presuppositional type, argues that God's sovereign word in Scripture should be regarded as the basis for certain knowledge.

We have traced the roots of fideism to Martin Luther. Again, not all Lutherans are fideists (Montgomery is Lutheran and the paradigm evidentialist), but most if not all modern fideists have roots in the Lutheran theological tradition. While Luther was the father of the Reformation, his theology was by far the most "Catholic" of the Reformers. The thinker who really laid the foundation for modern fideism was the Lutheran philosopher Søren Kierkegaard. In the twentieth century fideism emerged in developed form as the approach favored by Protestants seeking a middle way between liberalism and conservative evangelicalism, or fundamentalism. Karl Barth is the dominant figure; an American evangelical who favors a moderate fideism is Donald Bloesch. While all the major evangelical traditions affirm justification by faith alone *(sola fide)*, in Luther's theology it was the primary principle. Fideists apply the doctrine to apologetics, arguing that a person's faith cannot be based on arguments without implicitly basing justification on one's having had the good sense to accept the arguments.

If integration is regarded as the unification of diverse strands of apologetic thought into one comprehensive system, the diverse theological systems from which the different apologetic approaches arise pose a roadblock to that ideal. Three factors need to be borne in mind here. First, there is and will be no perfect theology this side of the Second Coming—and at that point theology, as a formal discipline, will give way to immediate knowledge (1 Corinthians 13:9–12). Likewise, the search for a perfect apologetic is the search for something that does not and will not exist. Second, in some cases the different theological systems are talking past one another, and it is possible to bridge such gaps. The same is true for the different apologetic approaches. Third, it is perfectly legitimate to maintain that some of the positions taken in a theological system are simply wrong. For example, most evangelicals will insist that Barth's rejection of biblical inerrancy was unnecessary and misguided. Likewise, criticism of specific positions taken in one or more apologetic approaches is to be expected.

Rather than seek a unified theological and apologetical system that assimilates all four approaches into one "super-approach," it may be more realistic and fruitful to adopt one of the four and broaden it in light of the other three. Just as Calvinists should articulate Calvinist theology in such a way that it does full justice to the biblical truths emphasized by Arminians, so Reformed apologists should articulate their approach in such a way that it makes full use of the insights and sound arguments originating from the other approaches.

That brings us to the relationship between theology and apologetics. The classical apologist tends to view apologetics as *prolegomena* (establishing the foundations of theology); the evidentialist as *polemics* (defending debated aspects of theology); the Reformed apologist as *part of theology;* and the fideist as *persuasive theology*. We would suggest that there is truth in all these views. The end goal of apologetics is to persuade non-Christians to believe in Christ. What might be called the *science* of apologetics is the branch of theology that studies matters relating to apologetics and develops apologetic arguments. While all of theology can and should inform apologetics, there is a great deal of overlap between the science of apologetics and that of prolegomena. The *art* or practice of apologetics applies what is learned in the science of apologetics. It seeks to present Christianity persuasively, and so implicitly accepts the entire range of Christian theology as its subject matter. However, in practice apologetics focuses on a limited range of issues—those necessary for a person to be persuaded to believe in Christ and begin his Christian life (including his theological development). In fact, apologetics really is necessary only where objections to Christianity or some aspect of its claims are challenged by the non-Christian.

APOLOGETICS AND PHILOSOPHY

The different views of philosophy characteristic of the four major approaches are to some extent a reflection of the fact that the meaning and scope of philosophy has changed over the centuries. In ancient and to some extent medieval usage, philosophy was understood largely in the speculative or constructive sense. It included logic, epistemology, ethics, metaphysics, theology, and even some of what is now studied in the natural sciences. This scope has narrowed in modern times with increased specialization, and many twentieth-century philosophers preferred to understand philosophy as a method of analysis and critique, not as a systematic view of reality.

Classical apologetics historically appealed to substantive ideas in ancient Greek philosophy, whether Aristotelian or Platonic, to support Christian ideas. Reformed apologetics, especially in the traditions of Dooyeweerd, Gordon Clark, and Van Til, has been extremely critical of classical apologetics for this very reason. The evidentialist attempt to use philosophical methods derived from non-Christian thought, but not the ideas, is likewise rejected because methods of knowing presuppose ideas about knowledge and reality. Reformed apologists urge Christians to develop a distinctively Christian philosophy on the basis of a distinctively Christian epistemology as an antidote to non-Christian thought. Fideists, while agreeing that non-Christian philosophy should be critiqued rather than used, reject the idea of developing a Christian philosophy, at least as the word *philosophy* is commonly understood.

The problem with these four approaches to philosophy is that they all assume an all-or-nothing point of view. Some ideas in non-Christian philosophy happen to be true—here the classical approach can proceed on safe ground—but others are, of course, wrong, and Reformed apologists and fideists are right to criticize them. Some methods of reasoning may be useful and reliable; others may not be. And apologists of other approaches should be able to agree with fideists that Christianity should not be reduced to a philosophy. Christ calls us to a relationship with God, in which developing a philosophy can be a part of what we do; but the fideist is right in pointing out that no human philosophy can neatly answer all questions or avoid paradox.

CHRISTIANITY AND SCIENCE

Various philosophers of science have observed that there are four basic models of the relationship between science and religion, or science and theology. Ian Barbour describes them as conflict, independence, dialogue, and integration. Both scientific materialists and Christian fundamentalists illustrate the conflict model. Karl Barth is one of several thinkers mentioned who view science and religion as independent. Thomas F. Torrance is mentioned among a very diverse group that advocates some kind of dialogue model. Richard Swinburne is a noted Christian philosopher advocating integration of science and religion (or theology).[1] These four models clearly correspond to the Reformed, fideist, classical, and evidentialist approaches to apologetics.

Other philosophers have picked up Barbour's analysis. John Haught rearranged his last two categories somewhat and relabeled the four ways as conflict, contrast, contact, and confirmation.[2] In their book *Reason and Religious Belief*, Michael Peterson and three other philosophers discuss whether religion and science conflict, are independent, interact in dialogue, or can be integrated.[3]

In his article "Science and Religion: Towards a New Cartography," David N. Livingstone argues that, broadly speaking, there are "four maps of the science-religion landscape, four ways of thinking about how the 'encounter' can best be plotted."[4] These four maps are conflict, competition, cooperation, and continuity. The competition map sees the conflict as one between scientists and theologians, not between science and theology (a position similar to classical apologetics). The cooperation map emphasizes the support theology has given to science historically (as in evidentialism). The conflict map sees the conflict as between secularized science and dogmatic theology (a view characteristic of Reformed apologetics). The continuity map sees the debate as really about the ground or basis of cultural values (as in fideism).

The all-or-nothing assumption characteristic in the debate over philosophy in apologetics is evident with science as well. Almost all the apparent conflicts between science and theology are really between what *some* scientists and *some* theologians say. That means, however, some scientific theories really do conflict with some Christian teachings. The fideist is right to suggest that *some* scientific theories deal with questions of a different type than in theology, but this way of handling apparent conflicts goes only so far. For example, the conflict between Genesis and modern science on the age of the universe may be only apparent, due perhaps to more being read into Genesis on the subject than is actually there. On the other hand, the theory that human beings evolved from nonhuman creatures is simply not reconcilable with Genesis.

Where there is real possibility of conflict, there is also real possibility of agreement and therefore of confirmation. The evidentialist is justified, then, in looking for support for the biblical teaching on creation from scientific evidence. But the classical apologist often is wise in exercising some caution in endorsing modern scientific theories as confirmation of Christianity. Indeed, in this respect we would suggest that the classical approach is in the strongest position from which to incorporate the legitimate perspectives of the other approaches.

REVELATION AND HISTORY

One of the clearest areas of disagreement among the four approaches is in their views of history. The classical apologist argues that a right view of history requires *the right worldview*, namely, theism. The evidentialist contends that it requires *the right method*, namely, an empirical method that makes minimal assumptions about what is historically possible. The Reformed apologist contends that it requires *the right revelation*, namely, God's word in Scripture. The fideist rejects the whole idea of faith being based on historical knowledge; Kierkegaard and Barth affirmed that God had acted in history but denied that historical study could lead to the knowledge of God's action in history.

A perspectival view of historical knowledge in relation to faith can surely see some validity in all four approaches. The miracle claims of the Bible ultimately make no sense unless the God of the Bible exists. In this respect both the classical and Reformed apologists are right. But it does not follow that a person must first accept a theistic worldview, or the Bible as God's revelation, to recognize the evidence for biblical miracles as persuasive. Some people are actually persuaded to believe in the God of the Bible on the basis of the historical evidence for the biblical miracles, especially the Resurrection. Such individuals typically are neither convinced theists nor convinced atheists prior to examining the evidence. Admittedly, avowed atheists or dogmatic agnostics (those who maintain that no one can prove or know that God exists) will resist such evidence and discount it at every turn. But they are just as likely to resist theistic arguments or appeals to biblical authority as they are historical arguments for the biblical miracles.

Evidentialists often claim that the historical or legal evidence methods they use to defend the Resurrection and other miracles are neutral with respect to the theistic worldview. Apologists of other approaches are highly critical of this claim, and with some justice. In the end, any measure of the probability of a miraculous explanation, or any judgment that a miracle is the "best explanation," must assume or include some assessment of the likelihood of a God who could and would do such a miracle. The evidentialist must therefore ask the nontheist to agree, for the sake of considering the historical argument, to regard the existence of God as a serious possibility—by assigning, say, a 0.5 probability to God's existence. In other words, the evidentialist argument must run something like this: "The best explanation for this event, if God's existence is granted as a serious possibility, is a miracle; therefore, this event constitutes evidence for God's existence."

Reformed apologists like Van Til also make a valid point when they observe that the methods of historical inquiry or legal evidence presuppose that certain things are so—things that can only be true because God exists. For example, the evidentialist methods assume that the universe is an orderly place in which the laws of probability have meaning and applicability from one situation to another. Such an assumption is true because God has created the universe as an orderly place. But the validity of the Reformed apologist's point here does not invalidate the empirical argument. One can reason transcendentally from the validity of sense perception, logic, the order of nature, etc., to the existence of God as the One who makes such assumptions intelligible. But one can also reason inductively from the evidence for miracles to the likelihood of a supernatural Being who can do such things.

Finally, the fideist raises a legitimate concern when he observes that belief in the historicity of a miracle is not the same as faith in the God who did the miracle. But surely this point can be, not merely conceded, but wholeheartedly affirmed without abandoning arguments in support of belief in the miracle. The crucial point here is that belief in the historicity of, say, the Resurrection is a *necessary* but not *sufficient* condition for faith. A person who has faith in Jesus to save him from his sins must believe that Jesus really rose from the dead (Romans 10:9–10); a dead man cannot do anything for us. But of course, merely agreeing with this fact does not constitute faith; one must act on this belief by calling on Jesus for salvation (Romans 10:11–13).

APOLOGETICS AND EXPERIENCE

Let us begin with the heart of the fideist perspective: Christian apologetics can be credible only when apologists are credible Christians. A hypocritical apologist does more damage to the reputation of the Christian faith than do hypocrites in most other positions in the church. But credibility includes both moral and intellectual dimensions. Without at all diminishing the importance of the personal side of evangelism and the apologetic value of demonstrating the truth of Christianity through actions and not mere arguments, the case for Christianity cannot be made to rest on Christians. After all, the message of the Christian apologist is that Christ *saves sinners*. Apologists need to be candid about their own failures, their own need for mercy and forgiveness, and at the same time show that faith in Christ makes a difference in their lives.

Presuppositionalists make a valuable point here: no Christian lives completely consistent with his Christian principles (because of the remaining sinful corruption of his human nature), but no non-Christian lives completely consistent with his non-Christian principles either (because of common grace). The atheist who expresses outrage at moral atrocities is acting inconsistently with his principles. Ultimately, experience cannot be the test of truth, although *relevance* to experience can be regarded as one way in which truth can be verified.

While moral failure reflects poorly on the church's message, so does intellectual failure. The anti-intellectual pietism that characterizes so much of evangelical and Pentecostal Christianity today does not serve the church's message well. The church's witness needs to include both piety and apology.

The classical apologist argues that the universality of the religious impulse, the universal desire for transcendence, proves that a transcendent God who can satisfy that desire exists. This argument is not undermined by the failures of Christians. If anything, such failures prove that what all people, including Christians, need is not mere religion, but *God*.

For Further Study

Boa, Kenneth D., and Robert M. Bowman, Jr. *An Unchanging Faith in a Changing World: Understanding and Responding to Critical Issues that Christians Face Today*. Nashville: Thomas Nelson, Oliver-Nelson, 1997. Includes chapters discussing how Christians should view science, postmodernism, and other contemporary challenges to the Christian faith.

Erickson, Millard J. *Postmodernizing the Faith: Evangelical Responses to the Challenge of Postmodernism*. Grand Rapids: Baker, 1998. After surveying the views of David Wells, Thomas Oden, Francis Schaeffer, Stanley Grenz, and others, Erickson proposes that evangelicals responding to postmodernism take their cue largely from Schaeffer.

Groothuis, Douglas. *Truth Decay: Defending Christianity against the Challenge of Postmodernism*. Downers Grove, Ill.: InterVarsity, 2000. Forceful critique of postmodernism, especially indebted to Francis Schaeffer but also drawing on the thought of apologists of diverse approaches (e.g., C. S. Lewis, J. P. Moreland, and Blaise Pascal).

Pearcey, Nancy R. *Total Truth: Liberating Christianity from Its Cultural Captivity*. Foreword by Phillip E. Johnson. Wheaton, Ill.: Crossway Books, 2004. Pearcey, who studied under Schaeffer at L'Abri, is the Francis A. Schaeffer Scholar at the World Journalism Institute and a senior fellow at the Discovery Institute (which promotes Intelligent Design theory). Pearcey's book encourages Christians to foster a biblical worldview, especially in matters of science and culture.

Chapter 22

Reasons for Hope: Integrating Diverse Arguments in Apologetics

We have argued that the four major approaches all have value, and that each can incorporate insights of the others if they are developed in a sufficiently broad fashion. The real test of this claim is whether the diverse arguments favored by these approaches can be used together in some way.

SCRIPTURE AS TRUTH

While all four models view Scripture as revealing truth from God, they differ in how they approach persuading non-Christians to accept that truth. Classical apologists tend to view Scripture as the *subject* of apologetics: the purpose of apologetics is to present an argument that concludes with the divine authority of Scripture. Evidentialists seek to conclude their argument in the same way, but they typically begin by viewing Scripture as the *source* of apologetics; that is, the argument uses Scripture as an historical source of facts or evidences from which the central claims of Scripture concerning Jesus Christ can be defended. Reformed apologists, especially in the tradition of Clark and Van Til, argue that Scripture should be viewed as the *standard* of apologetics: it lays down the theological basis and ground rules for apologetics, and the apologist must present it as the self-attesting authority or standard for all truth. Fideists view Scripture as the *story* of apologetics: it should not be defended, but instead should be used to tell the self-attesting story of Jesus Christ.

Four Perspectives on Scripture

REFORMED APOLOGETICS

Scripture as
Self-Attesting Authority

EVIDENTIALISM Scripture as
Factually Verified Story

Scripture as
Self-Attesting Story **FIDEISM**

Scripture as
Rationally Validated Story

CLASSICAL APOLOGETICS

Reformed and classical apologetics, both of which make a normative perspective primary, view Scripture as the authority to which apologetics points. The difference is that Reformed apologetics views Scripture's authority as self-attesting, and therefore in need of no validation such as is offered in classical apologetics. But surely these two perspectives are reconcilable. To say that Scripture does not need rational validation is not the same as saying that it does not or cannot have rational validation. Likewise, to say that apologetics should offer rational validation for Scripture is not to assert that Scripture is not self-attesting. Rather, the classical apologist can (and often does) view his apologetic argument as helping people recognize Scripture as the divinely inspired and therefore self-attesting Word of God. Moreover, the presuppositional argument is itself a kind of rational validation: to argue that Scripture provides the only coherent or intelligible basis for affirming truth, meaning, or moral values is an indirect form of validation.

Both evidentialism and fideism emphasize Jesus Christ as the authority and Scripture primarily as presenting the story of Jesus Christ. (Obviously, all four views regard Jesus and Scripture as authoritative; we are talking about the primacy of their authority in relation to apologetic argument only.) The difference parallels that between classical and Reformed apologetics: the evidentialist recounts as factually verifiable the story of One whose supernatural life was immanent in history, while the fideist recounts as self-attesting the story of One whose supernatural life transcended history. Both perspectives are true. The fideist claim that Jesus is his own best witness is not contradicted or undermined by appealing to factual evidences as secondary witnesses to Jesus.

MYTH, TRUTH, AND RELIGION

Two related questions have concerned us in discussing the different approaches to the plurality of religions. The first is the basis on which Christianity should be said to be unique; the second is the basis on which it should be distinguished from myths. The classical apologist argues that Christianity offers a *uniquely coherent worldview;* myths are the incoherent expressions of the human need for a coherent revelation from God. The evidentialist argues that it offers a *uniquely verifiable historical claim*, unlike the timeless, groundless stories in mythology. The Reformed apologist argues that it confronts us with a *uniquely authoritative God*; the gods of myths are either personal but merely superhuman, and therefore lacking absolute authority, or infinite but impersonal, and therefore lacking any authority. Only the God of the Bible is an absolute authority, and only such a God can be the source and ground of moral absolutes. The fideist argues that Christianity confronts us with a *uniquely compelling Man;* the Jesus of the Gospels puts the heroes of myths and legends to shame by the sheer force of his real yet unparalleled humanity.

Four Perspectives on the Uniqueness of Christianity

Here is one aspect of apologetics where the four approaches are most clearly compatible. Superficially, fideism seems to contradict the other three approaches by claiming that we should not defend Christianity as a religion but instead characterize it as a call to a relationship with God in Jesus Christ. In fact, the other three approaches seek to defend not the historical religion of Christianity, but the belief in the authoritative "call" found in Scripture. The different ways in which they tend to frame their defense are complementary, not contradictory.

GOD WHO MAKES HIMSELF KNOWN

For many apologists, the dominant question in apologetics is how one should seek to persuade non-Christians to believe in God. And it is here that the four approaches often seem furthest apart, though we think needlessly so. Classical and evidentialist apologists generally favor deductive and inductive proofs for God's existence, while Reformed apologists and fideists generally reject such proofs. However, in their place the latter two use *indirect* arguments for the existence of God. Reformed apologists argue that belief in God is properly basic (Plantinga), or that God's existence is as necessary a presupposition to make sense of the world as the most fundamental principles of logic (Van Til). Fideists argue that God can be known only in an existential or personal encounter in Jesus Christ, yet even they typically cannot resist offering an indirect argument for the reality of the God revealed in Christ. The very paradoxical nature of the God revealed in Jesus, the offense to our reason and sense of propriety that the Christian gospel evokes, is proof that it was not of human invention but of divine revelation.

Four Perspectives on Arguments for God's Existence

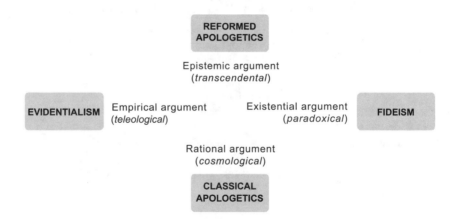

There is no reason why all these arguments might not be useful, either together or separately in different contexts. Fideists and Reformed apologists usually criticize the classical and evidential arguments because they cannot prove God; all they can prove is an infinite Ground of Being or a finite Designer (or Designers). We believe such objections can be largely overcome by combining the arguments in a cumulative case, as most classical and evidentialist apologists today do. But in any case, the apologist need not and usually does not claim that any one of these arguments, or even all such traditional arguments combined, proves everything that needs to be known about God. The purpose of theistic proofs is more modest: to establish the reasonableness of belief in the kind of God spoken of in Scripture, so that the non-Christian will be convinced to take the miraculous and revelatory claims of the Bible more seriously.

Evidentialist arguments for God are also commonly criticized for concluding merely that God probably exists. Faith, it is pointed out, must believe that God *is*, not that he "probably" is (Hebrews 11:6). But this criticism again asks too much of the arguments. To assert that a specific argument shows that God probably exists is not to assert that God's existence cannot be known as a certainty on some other basis. A person who concludes that God probably exists, based for example on the teleological or design argument, has not thereby arrived at faith—but no evidentialist would ever suggest that he had. But such a person is now confronted with the necessity of coming to a final conclusion and understanding about God. He now realizes that he must take seriously the possibility that God does exist and that he has revealed himself. The argument thus serves a valuable purpose, even though it does not yield the definitive certainty that is the property of faith.

Indeed, no argument can produce faith. This is just as true of the transcendental argument of Cornelius Van Til as it is of the design argument of William Paley or the cosmological argument of Norman Geisler. Even arguments that formally produce absolutely or deductively certain conclusions do not create or constitute faith.

Four Perspectives on the Ontological Argument

REFORMED APOLOGETICS

Alvin Plantinga
To understand what God is,
is to know that God necessarily exists

EVIDENTIALISM

Terry Miethe
The idea of God is
further evidence
of God

Karl Barth
Faith recognizes
God's being as
necessary

FIDEISM

R.C. Sproul
The nonexistence of infinite being,
that is, God, is inconceivable

CLASSICAL APOLOGETICS

Not only can different arguments be useful in persuading people to come to faith in God, but the same argument can be useful from different perspectives. We illustrate this with the ontological argument, which enjoyed something of a revival during the last third of the twentieth century. Surprisingly, it is possible to find advocates of all four approaches who find apologetic value in the ontological argument. According to R. C. Sproul and his co-authors in *Classical Apologetics*, it proves that the nonexistence of infinite being, or God, is inconceivable.[1] Terry Miethe, an evidentialist, has argued that the ontological proof is one of several that should be considered as evidence for God's existence.[2] Alvin Plantinga, the lead architect of the "new Reformed epistemology," has developed a very sophisticated restatement of the argument. His main contention seems to be that once a person understands the concept of God, implicit in that understanding is the logically certain existence of God. As a Reformed apologist, though, Plantinga recognizes that people generally do not come to belief in God via such an argument; he is therefore focusing on proving that God, if he exists, must be a necessary being.[3] Finally, Karl Barth has argued that Anselm's ontological argument is at bottom an affirmation of "faith seeking understanding." The believer in God, reflecting on the nature of God, comes to understand that God cannot not exist.[4]

SOLUTIONS TO THE PROBLEMS OF EVIL

The perspectival relationship among the four approaches is perhaps most easily seen in the "problem of evil" or, as we have seen, *problems* of evil, for there are several, not just one. Thus the integration of the four approaches here is essentially a matter of seeing them as contributing answers to different questions.

Classical apologetics focuses on resolving the *deductive* problem of evil: Is theism, which affirms both the existence of an all-loving, all-powerful God and the reality of evil, *coherent?* The classical model can include several explanations for a yes answer to this question, but they generally amount to this: the reality of evil does not contradict the existence of God if God has a good enough reason for allowing evil. Evidentialism focuses on answering the *inductive* problem of evil: Is theism, in view of the amount and kinds of evil that exist, *likely?* The evidentialist responds that evil does not make God's existence unlikely because it cannot counterbalance the significant evidence for God. Reformed apologetics (specifically presuppositionalism) focuses on the *theological* problem of evil that is particularly applicable to Reformed theology: If God is not to blame for evil, can he really be *sovereign?* Reformed theologians and apologists answer yes and typically argue that God's sovereign control over creation and history should not be construed as a mechanical or linear cause-and-effect determinism. Fideists focus on the *existential* or personal problem of evil: In light of the evils in the world God created, is God really *trustworthy?* They base their affirmative answer on God's personal, sacrificial involvement in the consequences of evil through the suffering and death of his Son Jesus Christ.

Four Perspectives on the Problem of Evil

REFORMED APOLOGETICS

Theological problem:
Is God sovereign?

EVIDENTIALISM   Inductive problem: Existential problem: FIDEISM
                  Is theism likely?   Is God trustworthy?

Deductive problem:
Is theism coherent?

CLASSICAL APOLOGETICS

As Steven Cowan has rightly pointed out, apologists need to "address all of these different aspects of the problem of evil."[5] Historically, however, apologists who advocated one of the four basic approaches to apologetics have tended to focus only on the one corresponding question. (Evidentialists, perhaps more than other apologists, have often addressed two or more of these questions.) What we are recommending here is that apologists explicitly recognize the importance of all four questions and overtly address all of them using the insights of apologists of different approaches.[6]

MIRACLES AS SIGNS

The question that has dominated discussions about miracles in apologetics for the past century or longer is this: Are miracles serviceable as elements of an apologetic, or are they difficulties for which an apologetic is needed? The answer, we would suggest, is both. For those who believe in God, or at least are open to belief in God, a well-attested miracle can be the basis of a persuasive argument that God has acted and revealed himself in a special way. To those who do not believe in God and are resistant to the idea of a miracle-working God, miracle stories are a major type of stumbling block to faith.

Four Perspectives on Miracles

```
                    ┌──────────────┐
                    │  REFORMED    │
                    │ APOLOGETICS  │
                    └──────────────┘

                   Biblical miracles
                    are prophetical

┌───────────────┐  Specific miracles      Christ's miracles   ┌──────────┐
│ EVIDENTIALISM │  are probable           are paradoxical     │ FIDEISM  │
└───────────────┘                                             └──────────┘

                     Miracles in
                  general are possible
                    ┌──────────────┐
                    │  CLASSICAL   │
                    │ APOLOGETICS  │
                    └──────────────┘
```

Classical apologists typically focus on showing that miracles in general are possible. Given that a Creator God exists, such a God could do miracles, and they would not contradict or violate natural law. Evidentialists typically focus on showing that specific miracles in light of the evidence are probable. They contend that well-documented miracles can count as evidence for a theistic worldview. Reformed apologists typically argue that the biblical miracles are prophetical. That is, miracles are part of God's authoritative, self-attesting revelation. (Reformed apologists tend to be more skeptical of modern miracles than most other apologists.) Fideists typically argue that miracles are paradoxical. They reveal a God who transcends the humanly possible and who, while not violating natural law, contravenes our natural expectations. To those who by grace know God to be the infinite, personal God revealed in Jesus Christ, such paradoxical events will be just the sort of thing they would expect from God.

It is apparent that the four approaches differ on the relation of miracles to apologetics at least in part because they focus on different questions about miracles. To establish that miracles are possible, one must first establish that God exists. However, to show that a specific miracle most likely occurred, one need not establish that God exists, but only that God's existence is as likely as not. But it would be a mistake to think that every person who believes that miracles have occurred believes each miracle on the basis of an assessment of the evidence for that specific miracle. If a Christian is convinced that the Bible is God's unerring Word, he will believe the biblical accounts of Elijah's altar being consumed by fire (1 Kings 18) or of Jesus raising Lazarus from the dead (John 11) simply because the Bible reports them. (It is unlikely that any empirical evidence could be marshaled to show that these miraculous events most likely occurred.) Yet the same Christian might express confidence in other biblical miracles, such as the resurrection of Jesus, on the basis of historical argument. Finally, the fideist's characterization of the miracles of Christ as paradoxical alerts us to the difference between showing that a miracle story is reasonable and showing that it will seem reasonable to the non-Christian. While the classical apologist rightly argues that if God exists we might expect him to do miracles, the fideist also is right to argue that if God does miracles they will likely not be what we expected.

JESUS: THE ANSWER

Christian apologetics in all four approaches is at heart about Christ; its goal is to present reasons why people should trust in Jesus Christ as their Savior and Lord. An apologetic that is not in some way focused on Christ is therefore deficient. However, the four approaches focus on Christ in different and complementary ways. Evidentialism and fideism tend to emphasize the work of Jesus Christ as Savior, while classical and Reformed apologetics tend to emphasize the person of Jesus Christ as Lord.

Four Perspectives on Jesus Christ and Apologetics

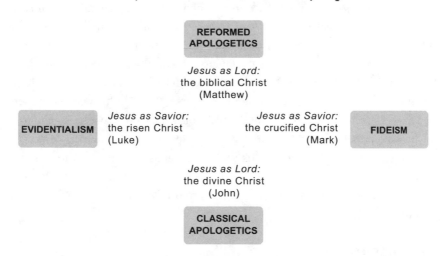

Remarkably, the four approaches emphasize perspectives on Jesus that correlate quite well with the different emphases of the four Gospels. Classical apologists argue that given the existence of God, Jesus Christ's claim to be God is extremely difficult to deny, and they naturally emphasize his more explicit claims to deity in the Gospel of John. Evidentialists argue that the evidence for Jesus' life, death, and resurrection provides compelling reasons to believe that he is the risen Savior. Most evidentialists appeal to Luke's explicit claim to be writing an historical account (Luke 1:1–4) and the emphasis in his Gospel and its sequel, the book of Acts, on the multiple witnesses to Jesus' resurrection. Reformed apologists, specifically presuppositionalists, argue that we should believe in Jesus Christ because he is revealed in the self-attesting Word of God in Scripture. They emphasize that Jesus' life, miracles, death, and resurrection did not occur in a vacuum, but were part of God's redemptive plan revealed prophetically in the Old Testament. The Gospel of Matthew, of course, is well known for the Old Testament quotations that punctuate its narrative and announce Jesus' fulfillment of messianic expectations. Finally, fideists argue that it is in the paradox of the powerful Messiah coming to serve, suffer, and die on the cross that Jesus reveals the love and mercy of God. This is indeed the focus of the Gospel of Mark: Jesus casts out demons, performs healings, speaks with authority, and yet in humility and seeming weakness allows himself to be crucified.

Just as the four Gospels present complementary portraits of Jesus Christ, so the four approaches emphasize complementary truths about Jesus that can be used to persuade people to believe. The complementary nature of these approaches is beautifully suggested by Jesus' discourse in John 5. Jesus' own witness to himself, while right and compelling, is not sufficient to establish the validity of his claim to be God's Son (verses 30–31). Jesus' works bear witness that his claim to be sent by the Father is true (verse 36). Of course, his works eventually included his death and resurrection. Ultimately, though, the final authoritative witness to Jesus is that of God the Father, given in Scripture (verses 37–47). The witness of mere men such as John the Baptist is not the basis on which Jesus' claim is validated, but it is nevertheless useful because it may help persuade some people (verses 33–35). The apologist's witness is like John the Baptist's: faith is not to be based on his arguments, but they may be helpful in pointing people to the truth about Jesus. Apologists are not the light, but they are privileged to be witnesses to the light (cf. John 1:8).

For Further Study

Peterson, Michael, William Hasker, Bruce Reichenbach, and David Basinger, eds. *Philosophy of Religion: Selected Readings*. 2d ed. New York: Oxford University Press, 2001. Collection of essays and excerpts from Christian and non-Christian thinkers on theistic arguments, the problem of evil, miracles, and other subjects of apologetic interest.

_____. *Reason and Religious Belief: An Introduction to the Philosophy of Religion*. 3d ed. Oxford and New York: Oxford University Press, 2003. Textbook survey of the same subjects covered in their *Readings*. Both books are especially strong in Christian philosophy from classical and Reformed perspectives.

Chapter 23

Speaking the Truth in Love: Perspectives on Apologetics

Integrating the different approaches is not merely a matter of comparing the arguments and looking for ways of harmonizing them. While we have suggested a holistic way of looking at the four approaches, we have also emphasized that we are not proposing a "new approach" or a comprehensive system that definitively unites them. Indeed, we doubt that this is possible or even desirable. In this final chapter we suggest some reasons why the diversity of apologetic approaches is unavoidable and may actually be a good thing.

ONE BODY, MANY GIFTS: HOW APOLOGISTS DIFFER

It is too easy to assert that some people are gifted to be apologists and others are not. While true, this observation is one-sided and does not go to the heart of the issue. Some Christians are indeed gifted and called by God to an ongoing and formal ministry of apologetics. But in a sense, all Christians are called to participate in this ministry. In Philippians, for example, the apostle Paul can say both that he was "appointed for the defense of the gospel" (Philippians 1:16) and that the Philippian Christians supported and shared with him "in the defense and confirmation of the gospel" (1:7). The apostle Peter instructed the whole church scattered throughout the region to be "always . . . ready to make a defense" to those who asked for the reason for their hope in Christ (1 Peter 3:15).

When Christians think about having different gifts, they often consider the overtly supernatural gifts that Paul discussed in 1 Corinthians 12–14. However, those chapters are notable by their exceptional nature and by the fact that Paul's focus was on correcting abuse and downplaying the importance of such gifts. While God does work in overtly supernatural ways among Christians as the Holy Spirit wills (1 Corinthians 12:11), the primary and regular way God gifts his people was and is not overtly supernatural. Instead, God's main ministry gifts to the church are the Spirit-motivated and Spirit-enhanced use of natural abilities that are sanctified and consecrated to God's service through faith. The apostles themselves are noteworthy examples: Peter was already an adventurous, outspoken man before Pentecost, and thus a natural leader. Paul was a sophisticated rabbinical student knowledgeable in Scripture and the Greek culture, and so brought considerable natural gifts, training, and experience to his ministry as the apostle to the Gentiles.

Consider Paul's list of gifts given by God to the members of Christ's body, the church, in Romans 12: prophecy, serving, teaching, exhorting (or encouraging), giving, leading, and showing mercy (verses 6–8). Most (possibly all) of these gifts are not abilities that some individuals have in abundance and others have not at all. They are functions that all Christians are expected to exercise according to their ability, recognizing that some people are exceptionally gifted in one and other people in another. (Prophecy may be the one exception; we leave this question to the side here.) Certainly, all Christians are expected to serve one another (Galatians 5:13), encourage one another (1 Thessalonians 5:11; Hebrews 3:13), give to one another (Acts 20:35), and be merciful to one another (Matthew 5:7; James 3:17). Most adult Christians find themselves in positions where they must lead and teach, whether children or younger men and women, or in other places of responsibility (cf. Ephesians 6:4; Titus 2:2–3). Yet some believers will be especially gifted for each of these normal functions of the Christian life.

Just as there are different gifts, there are different kinds of apologists. The two most basic kinds, in terms of regular ministries needing support from the church, are evangelists and teachers (cf. Ephesians 4:11). Some apologists are evangelist-apologists whose ministry is directed primarily to people *outside* the church, while others are teacher-apologists whose ministry is directed primarily to people *inside* the church. The former naturally and properly tend to use arguments that are persuasive to unbelievers, while the latter just as properly tend toward arguments that build on assumptions commonly taken for granted by the Christians they are teaching. Of course, all apologists engage in some evangelism and some teaching; we are talking about emphases and special callings.

Regarding the gifted functions in Romans 12, Christians have different strengths in which they can best use their apologetics. Some are most effective when encouraging others using apologetic insights. Some are effective in imparting apologetic concepts to others in a formal instructional setting (that is, teaching). Some are gifted to organize and lead others in the practice of apologetics.

There are other ways Christians engaged in apologetics differ from one another. But these differences can also be found among non-Christians. We will now consider these differences.

ONE WORLD, MANY INDIVIDUALS: HOW PEOPLE DIFFER

Human beings differ from each other in myriad ways. They come from different parts of the world, speak different languages, are taught in different educational systems. They grow up listening to different songs, reading different books, meeting different people. Apologists will tend to gravitate toward certain approaches because of their background and experience. It is no accident that evangelical scientists tend to be evidentialists or that evangelical artists tend to be fideists. Of course, such observations are generalizations, but they do point up factors that Christians engaged in apologetics need to consider. Thoughtful apologists will want to think about the factors that might influence their preference of one approach over another, other than the specific arguments they think warrant that approach.

In addition, apologists should use common sense and try to match their apologetic to the person with whom they are speaking. Technical distinctions that are important in the academic study of apologetics usually have no place in presenting apologetics to one's neighbor, schoolmate, co-worker, or family member. Someone with a scientific bent who wants empirically based evidence should be offered such evidence, even while being told that empirical facts alone cannot settle questions about God. Someone who is clearly struggling emotionally due to personal experiences should usually not be met with the cosmological or transcendental argument (though words of comfort might implicitly make points similar to those defended with those arguments).

Much attention has been given during the past half-century or so to analyzing the differences in attitude, aptitude, and related basic personality characteristics among people. Since psychology is still very much in its infancy, these studies should be regarded as suggestive, not settled fact. Still, they offer interesting and significant insights into the differences among Christian apologists.

In *Conformed to His Image*, one of us (Ken Boa) explained how the natural differences in people's spiritual, psychological, and physical inclinations provide some insight into why Christians gravitate toward different approaches to spirituality. For example, Christians tend to place a premium on theological renewal, personal renewal, social transformation, or inner transformation. An excessive focus on one of these four aspects of the Christian life results in rationalism, pietism, moralism, or quietism respectively.[1]

ONE PROCESS, MANY STAGES: HOW APOLOGETIC NEEDS DIFFER

One of the main reasons apologists often suppose that there is only one right approach is the assumption that an apologetic must move, or at least point, a person from rank unbelief to sound belief. The standard paradigm apologetic encounter is that of a Christian trying to convince an avowed atheist that the absolute truth is that God exists, is triune, views human beings as sinners deserving judgment, became incarnate in Jesus of Nazareth, redeemed us from our sins, and inspired an inerrant Bible. This is a tall order, and the notion that an apologetic is invalid if it does not meet this standard is enough to discourage all but the extremely confident.

The validity of the apologetic does not depend on its success, but on its utility in facilitating success through the hidden illuminating work of the Holy Spirit within non-Christians. On this premise, we favor the view that an apologetic is valid and valuable if it provides the basis for a non-Christian moving at all closer to embracing the Christian faith. People are indeed either dead in sins or born again, lost or found, unjustified or justified. But they may be closer or further away from crossing over from life to death, depending on what they believe or do not believe. People are typically not standing still: they are generally either moving toward faith or toward unbelief. A person who did not believe that a God exists but has now accepted that fact through hearing an apologetic argument has moved in the right direction. (Of course, factors other than what a person believes can affect the direction he is moving, but those fall outside the province of apologetics.)

It may be, then, that some apologetic approaches are more useful at certain points along the spectrum than at others.

Common Questions from Unbelief to Faith	Possible Apologetic Arguments
It doesn't matter to me if God exists or not.	Pascal's Wager: If God exists, it matters! (F)
God may be real to you, but he's not to me.	Is Jesus real enough for you? (F) You live every day as if God exists. (R)
How do you know there is a God?	Without God, there is no meaning. (R) No other worldview makes sense. (C) There are many lines of evidence. (E)
The stories in the Bible are hard to believe.	If God exists, nothing is too hard for him. (C)
Why must we believe in the God of the Bible?	God fulfilled prophecy and did miracles. (E)
How do we know Jesus rose from the dead?	The tomb was empty and people saw Jesus. (E)
Wasn't Jesus just a great prophet?	Great prophets don't claim to be God. (C)
Why is Christianity alone the truth?	The God of Christianity is the only true God. (R) Christ is the truth; Christianity points to him. (F)
I'd like to believe, but I'm not sure.	Read the Gospels and get to know Jesus. (F)
C: *Classical*; E: *Evidential*; F: *Fideist*; R: *Reformed*	

Thus, speaking very broadly and generally, we would suggest that elements of the fideist approach are most valuable at the extreme ends of the process of a person moving intellectually from unbelief to faith. This is because fideism is strongest in dealing with the personal or volitional dimension of apologetic questions. The Reformed approach is strongest in exposing the irrationality of unbelief (vital early in the process) and affirming the exclusivity of the Christian truth claims (vital near the end of the process). The classical and evidential approaches are strongest in defending specific truth claims that tend to be questioned in the middle of the process.

Stages Toward Faith	Dominant Approaches
Disinterested/ignorant	Fideism
Skeptical	Reformed apologetics
Confused	Classical apologetics
Has specific objections	Evidentialism
Has general objections	Classical apologetics
Is checking for a way out	Reformed apologetics
Has lingering doubts	Fideism

Of course, we are not suggesting that unbelievers always pass through this entire process before becoming convinced. Nor are we claiming that the different approaches only have utility at the stages indicated. We simply want to suggest that the different approaches have been developed at least partly because they tend to be more potent at different stages of a non-Christian's movement toward conviction. Moreover, as we argued in the preceding two chapters, each of the four approaches can be broadened to include elements of the other approaches.

ONE FAITH, MANY QUESTIONS:
HOW APOLOGETIC PROBLEMS DIFFER

We have already seen that apologetics deals with a variety of questions and suggested that different approaches are more effective with certain kinds of questions than others. This is true even when on a superficial level the questions seem to be on the same subject. We saw in the last chapter that the so-called problem of evil actually includes four distinct problems that are characteristically and most effectively addressed by the four different apologetic approaches (the deductive, inductive, theological, and existential problems of evil). Non-Christians can ask if a claim makes sense (for example, "Are miracles possible?"), what evidence supports it ("How do we know it happened?"), what it proves about God ("How do we know that God did it?"), or why it is significant for us ("Why does it matter to me if it happened?"). These questions correspond to the classical, evidentialist, Reformed, and fideist approaches respectively.

Approach	Typical Question	The Point	Apologetic Argument
Classical	"Are miracles possible?"	What it means	Miracles are coherent in a theistic worldview.
Evidential	"How do we know it happened?"	Why it's true	The crucial biblical miracles are well attested facts.
Reformed	"How do we know that did God it?"	What it proves	The miracles are found in God's authoritative word.
Fideist	"Why does it matter to me?"	Why it matters	The miracles show that God cares and that we need faith.

Many apologists already address more than one of these questions. For example, a classical apologist views the first question as relevant in the first step of a classical apologetic (establishing theism) and the second question as relevant in the second step (providing evidence for Christianity as the true theism). Both classical and evidentialist apologists view the third question as answered at the end of the apologetic argument (when the inspiration of Scripture is concluded from the testimony of the miraculously vindicated Jesus Christ). Reformed apologists can and do answer the first question in essentially the same way as a classical apologist would. All apologists can address the fourth question and would give essentially the same answer. Again, integration is already happening: what we hope to encourage is more deliberate, systematic efforts at integrating the insights and answers of other approaches into one's apologetic. One of the benefits of doing so is that we will be able to answer a broader range of questions more successfully.

METAPOLOGETICS: FOUR APPROACHES

	Classical	Evidential	Reformed	Fideist
GROUND	Reason	Fact	Revelation	Faith
FORM	Rational	Empirical	Transcendental	Paradoxical
PERSPECTIVE	Normative (immanent)	Situational	Normative (transcendent)	Existential
PRECURSORS	Anselm Aquinas	Joseph Butler William Paley	John Calvin Thomas Reid	Martin Luther Søren Kierkegaard
20TH CENT. ADVOCATES	C. S. Lewis Norman Geisler	J. W. Montgomery Richard Swinburne	Cornelius Van Til Alvin Plantinga	Karl Barth Donald Bloesch
GOSPELS	John	Luke	Matthew	Mark
GOD	God exists	God has acted	God has spoken	God loves me
KNOWLEDGE	Internal coherence Faith is reasonable Use rational tests to assess truth claims and to choose a worldview	External coherence Faith is not unreasonable Use sound methods for arriving at truth by discovering and interpreting facts	Fidelity to Scripture Unbelief is unreasonable God, as revealed in Scripture, is foundational for all knowledge of truth	Fidelity to Christ Faith is not known by reason alone Truth about God is found in encounter with Him, not in thinking about Him
THEOLOGY	Apologetics as prolegomena Catholics, broadly evangelicals	Apologetics as polemics Evangelical Arminians	Apologetics as part of theology Calvinists, especially Dutch	Apologetics as persuasive theology Lutherans, neoevangelicals
PHILOSOPHY	Apologetics uses philosophy's ideas	Apologetics uses philosophy's tools	Apologetics confronts false philosophy	Apologetics confronts all philosophy
SCIENCE	*Consistency model*: Show that science properly interpreted is consistent with the Christian faith Typically generic creationism	*Confirmation model*: Use science to give factual confirmation of the Christian faith Typically old-earth creationism	*Conflict model*: Show that true science depends on the truth of God's revelation Typically young-earth creationism	*Contrast model*: Show that science deals with physical matters, faith deals with the personal Typically theistic evolutionism
HISTORY	Objective view of history difficult but possible Right view of history requires right worldview	Objective view of history quite realizable Right view of history requires right method	Objective truth about history given in Scripture Right view of history based on revelation	Christ objectively revealed by the Spirit in Scripture Faith cannot be based on historical knowledge
EXPERIENCE	Religious experience not irrational Test experiences by worldview	Religious experience may not be reliable Test experiences by facts	God's image in man is point of contact Test experiences by Scripture	Experience faith, don't defend it Experience of faith is self-validating

APOLOGETICS: FOUR APPROACHES

	Classical	**Evidential**	**Reformed**	**Fideist**
SCRIPTURE	Scripture is subject of apologetics	Scripture is source of apologetics	Scripture is standard of apologetics	Scripture is story of apologetics
	Rationally verified authority of God	Factually verified story about Christ	Self-attesting authority of God	Self-attesting story about Christ
	First, theism; second, Christ; third, Scripture as attested by Christ	First, historicity of Scripture; second, Christ and theism; third, inspiration	First, Scripture's divine claims; second, irrationality of all alternatives	First and always, Scripture as witness to Christ
	Fulfilled prophecy proves inspiration if God exists	Fulfilled prophecy proves inspiration, which proves God	Fulfilled prophecy presupposes inspiration	Fulfilled prophecy is God's advance witness to Christ
RELIGIONS	Disprove the worldviews underlying other religions	Present the unique factual, miraculous character of the Christian religion	Present the antithesis between Christian and non-Christian principles	Explain that the Christian faith is not a religion, but a relationship
GOD	Show that theism is the only or most rational worldview	Use various lines of argument and evidence to build a case for theism	Show that God's existence is basic or foundational to all knowledge & proof	Explain that knowing God is a relational matter
	Cosmological, moral arguments most common	Design argument most common	Epistemic argument most common	All direct proofs are rejected; argument from paradox used
EVIL	Deductive problem of evil: Is theism inconsistent?	Inductive problem of evil: Is theism likely?	Theological problem of evil: Is God sovereign over evil?	Existential problem of evil: Can God be trusted despite evil?
	Freewill defense: evil result of free choice of creatures	Natural theology defense: evidence for God holds up	Compatibilist defense: God not direct cause of evil	*Theologia crucis:* God shows his goodness in Christ
MIRACLES	Miracles in general are possible	Specific miracles are probable	Biblical miracles are prophetical	Christ's miracles are paradoxical
	Miracles, credible in theistic worldview, are credentials of special revelation	Miracles provide evidence for theism in the context of biblical history	Biblical miracles are credible to those who accept the Bible's authority	Miracles, external and internal, are given by God in response to faith
JESUS	Examine alternative views of Jesus to show that none can be rationally held	Detail evidence for Jesus' resurrection, fulfilled prophecies, and the like	Present Jesus' claim to be God as his self-attesting Word confirmed by Spirit	Call people to meet God's love in Jesus. Jesus is someone no human could invent

CONCLUSION

The apostle Paul affirmed that there is "one body and one Spirit, just as also you were called in one hope of your calling" (Ephesians 4:4). Sometimes Christians allow their differences to obscure the unity that Paul affirmed. The church is one body, but it has many and varied members. We are empowered by one Spirit, but he has gifted us in different ways. We have one hope, but that hope can be articulated in many different ways to persuade others to respond to the Spirit's call to join us in that hope.

In this book we have emphasized the complementary ways in which different approaches to apologetics can be fruitfully related to one another. In doing so, we have sought to represent each approach at its best and in the most sympathetic manner possible. This means that we have often passed over some of the egregious errors and faults that can be found in the apologetic arguments and teaching of the very human, very imperfect apologists whose views we have discussed. (We hope others will do the same for us!) At the same time, we have drawn attention to some of the most important weaknesses that attend each of the major approaches, along with their perennial strengths. We handled the approaches in this way to underscore the fact that all of us can learn from other approaches.

In presenting an integrative analysis of apologetic systems, there is a real danger that we will be misconstrued as claiming to present yet another approach as the best or most complete approach to apologetics. We have therefore stated repeatedly that we are not advocating a "fifth" approach or proposing a system for definitively integrating all four basic approaches. Nor do we imagine that what we have said here is or should be the last word. We have our own pronounced tendencies and limited points of view, as do all apologists. Some of us are inclined to see issues in terms of *either/or*, emphasizing the dichotomies, the watershed issues, and the unbridgeable differences between points of view. Others of us are inclined to see issues in terms of *both/and*, emphasizing the commonalities, the qualifications to be made on both sides of a debate, the potential for reconciliation between seemingly opposed points of view. We confess to being persons, and apologists, of the latter kind. But we do not claim that our viewpoint in this regard is better—only that it is a needed voice to balance the viewpoints of the either/or temperament. In other words, we apply our "both/and" even to the need for the contributions of both the single-approach polemicists and the multiple-approach integrationists.

There are, after all, issues on which Christians must take a decisive stand for truth and against error, insisting that one is *either* upholding the truth *or* advocating error. Either one affirms that all facts are what they are ultimately because this is God's world, or one denies that God is the sovereign Lord of creation. Either one affirms that Jesus Christ rose physically from the dead in real space-time history, or one denies this cornerstone truth of the Christian faith. Either one affirms that the Bible is God's Word, communicating revealed truth just as God willed, or one undermines the church's foundational source for its worship, its practice, its doctrine, and its apologetics. Either one affirms that God is known savingly only in Jesus Christ, or one erroneously encourages people to believe that there is hope for them outside a relationship with Jesus Christ as their Lord and Savior. The multiplicity of ways that these truths have and can be defended should not be allowed to obscure the fact that these are the nonnegotiable principles for which all sound Christian apologetics must contend.

For Further Study

Boa, Kenneth D. *Conformed to His Image: Pathways to Spiritual Formation*. Grand Rapids: Zondervan, 2001. Applies insights into varying personalities and varying periods of church history to the question of why people follow different approaches to spiritual growth.

Afterword

Joining the Discussion

We hope that *Faith Has Its Reasons* has whetted your appetite for learning more about the great apologists of the past two millennia and for thinking more deeply about the issues introduced in this book. To that end, we invite you to visit us online and to find out about opportunities for further reflection and study.

Ken Boa is the founder and president of Reflections Ministries. Its mission is to provide safe places for people to consider the claims of Christ and to help them mature and bear fruit in their relationship with him. The ministry's web site (http://www.KenBoa.org) features a variety of resources for Christian apologetics.

Rob Bowman is the founder and president of the Center for Biblical Apologetics. Its mission is to revolutionize Christian apologetics by bringing together the best resources available and by working to fill in the gaps where good resources still don't exist. The ministry's web site (http://www.biblicalapologetics.net) includes an apologetics resource network and an online discussion forum dedicated to the issues covered in *Faith Has Its Reasons*.

As Christians, we rejoice to know a living God whose word is faithful and true, whose revelation is both eminently reasonable and wonderfully beyond our comprehension, whose incarnation in Jesus of Nazareth left a trail of evidence confirming his entrance into our space and time history, and whose presence gives our lives meaning, purpose, value, and hope. Truly, the Christian faith has a rich treasure of reasons to share with each other and to offer to anyone who will listen. Let's not keep it to ourselves!

Appendix
Categorizing Apologetic Methods

In this book we have identified, described, and compared four approaches to apologetics. The rationale for this fourfold analysis is given briefly in chapter 3 and developed throughout the book, but especially in chapters 21–23, where we compare the four approaches. In this appendix we will compare this analysis to the way other writers have analyzed apologetic thought into different approaches, models, or methods.

BERNARD RAMM

One of the earliest attempts to discuss the diversity of approaches to apologetics in a comprehensive way was Bernard Ramm's 1953 book *Types of Apologetic Systems*,[1] which was issued in a revised edition in 1962 as *Varieties of Christian Apologetics*.[2]

Ramm classifies apologetic systems into three types and identifies three representatives of each type, each of which is given a chapter. The first type stresses the subjective immediacy of religious experience as the grounds for confidence in its truth. The truth about God is found through "existential encounter" with Him, not in proofs or arguments. Ramm identifies Blaise Pascal, Søren Kierkegaard, and Emil Brunner as representatives of this type.

The second type stresses natural theology and appeals to reason as the starting point of apologetics. These apologists seek to prove Christianity the same way scientists seek to prove their theories. Ramm identifies Thomas Aquinas, Joseph Butler, and F. R. Tennant as examplary apologists of this type.

The third type stresses revelation as the foundation of human knowledge of the truth of the Christian faith. Apologists of this type argue that the proper role of reason in apologetics is to explicate God's revelation, not to prove it. In *Types*, the earlier edition, Ramm identified Augustine, Cornelius Van Til, and Edward John Carnell as representatives of this type. In *Varieties*, Ramm dropped the chapters on Van Til and Carnell (both of whom were still alive) and substituted chapters on John Calvin and Abraham Kuyper.

The system stressing subjective immediacy of religious experience is obviously the same as what we are calling fideism. Pascal was by our account a precursor to fideism and Kierkegaard is the paradigm example of a fideist. Brunner is in our view a mediating figure between fideism and the classical approach, as is illustrated in his famous debate with Karl Barth over natural theology (which Brunner defended against Barth).

Ramm's system stressing revelation is essentially the same as what we call Reformed apologetics. Calvin, Kuyper, and Van Til are key figures in the development of this approach. Augustine is widely regarded as a precursor to the Reformed approach by its advocates, though not by its critics; but then, virtually all Christian apologists wants to claim Augustine as a forebear. Carnell, as we argued in chapter 20, integrated Reformed and evidentialist apologetics (and in his later works introduced some elements of fideism as well).

Ramm's type that stresses natural theology includes both classical and evidentialist apologetics. Butler and Tennant clearly fall into the evidentialist tradition (Butler as a pioneer, Tennant as a modern proponent), while Aquinas can be viewed as a precursor to it. On the other hand, Aquinas set the standard for the classical approach, so much so that some of its most notable modern advocates (such as Norman Geisler and Peter Kreeft) are avowed Thomists. As we have noted before, the classical and evidentialist approaches are very close, which explains why Ramm could treat them together. We distinguish them because in the twentieth century evidentialism emerged as a distinct alternative in its methodology to the classical approach.

GORDON LEWIS

Probably the best known textbook surveying the different apologetic methods is Gordon Lewis's 1976 book *Testing Christianity's Truth Claims: Approaches to Christian Apologetics*.[3] The structure of the book is illuminating. After an introductory chapter, Lewis offers one chapter each on five apologists followed by four chapters on Carnell. The purpose of the book is to show that what Lewis calls Carnell's "verificational approach" brings together the valid elements of the other approaches. They are, Lewis says, "like separate pieces of a stained glass window" that Carnell "sought to put . . . back together" (176). In an appendix Lewis reviews more briefly the thought of ten other apologists.

Lewis's first apologist is J. Oliver Buswell, Jr., whom he describes as advocating "pure empiricism." His approach, according to Lewis, uses "the test of objective evidence" (45). Buswell falls clearly within the evidentialist approach we have identified. Lewis's bibliography at the end of the chapter includes many works by John Warwick Montgomery (our main exemplar of evidentialism), whose approach is surveyed in the appendix and likened to Buswell's.

Next, Lewis examines "rational empiricism" as a system that employs "the test of objective evidence and logical thought-forms" (76). Although the chapter title identifies Stuart Hackett as the primary exemplar, Lewis divides his attention equally between Hackett and Floyd E. Hamilton. Oddly, in the appendix he characterizes Norman Geisler's approach as "most similar to that of the pure empiricists" (311), though in Lewis's defense it should be noted that Geisler was in the early stages of his career at the time (his book *Christian Apologetics* appeared in 1976, the same year as Lewis's book). In our analysis Hackett, Hamilton, and Geisler are all advocates of the classical approach.

In the following two chapters Lewis considers the "rationalism" of Gordon H. Clark, who used "the test of logical consistency" (100), and the "biblical authoritarianism" of Cornelius Van Til, who used "the test of scriptural authority" (125). Clark makes logic primary and argues that the Bible provides the only logically consistent system of knowledge, while Van Til makes the Bible primary and argues that our use of logic must be subordinated to the Bible. Lewis emphasizes the differences between their two methods, which are indeed quite significant. We have treated them as variations of the same Reformed approach, however, because both argue on the basis of Reformed theology that apologetics must start from the Bible as the ultimate authority for knowledge. Clark's system, after all, is just as much one of "biblical authoritarianism" as Van Til's.

Lewis turns next to the "mysticism" of Earl E. Barrett as an example of a system utilizing "the test of personal experience" (151). Warren C. Young is also cited at length as an advocate of this approach. These two apologists are not well known today, but they were evangelical professors at Midwest schools in the mid-twentieth century who emphasized personal encounter with God in their apologetics. They may be regarded in our classification as fideists.

In the remainder of the book Lewis expounds on Carnell's approach and argues that it combines the strengths of the other approaches. In the appendix Francis Schaeffer (296–300), Os Guinness (300–301), Clark Pinnock (301–304), Arthur Holmes (319–326), Bernard Ramm (327–31), and C. S. Lewis (331–38) are profiled and said to take an approach similar to Carnell's.

Lewis's analysis of the major types of apologetic systems is quite similar to ours. If Clark and Van Til are treated as variations of the Reformed approach, his book covers the evidentialist, classical, Reformed, fideist, and integrationist approaches.

NORMAN GEISLER

In his 1999 magnum opus, *Baker Encyclopedia of Christian Apologetics*, Geisler includes an article on apologetic types.[4] He warns against trying "to make logically exhaustive categories of apologetic systems," but his main objection is to dividing apologetic systems into only two categories such as evidential and non-evidential (41). He also notes that apologetic types overlap. We certainly agree with these observations. Our four approaches are not exhaustive of all positions, since, as we have pointed out repeatedly, most apologists combine elements of two or more approaches. The four approaches are like the four points on a compass (with an indeterminate number of possible directions) or the three primary colors (with an indeterminate number of possible colors).

Having made his qualifications, Geisler proceeds to identify five types of apologetics. The first is *classical apologetics*, which "is characterized by two basic steps: theistic and evidential arguments" (41). As we do, Geisler identifies B. B. Warfield, C. S. Lewis, William Lane Craig, Peter Kreeft, and himself as proponents (42).

Geisler distinguishes *evidential apologetics* from *historical apologetics*. The former adduces evidence eclectically from a variety of fields to make an overall case for Christianity, and is represented by William Paley and Josh McDowell (42). The latter "stresses historical evidence as the basis for demonstrating the truth of Christianity" and is represented by John Warwick Montgomery and Gary Habermas. Geisler acknowledges that historical apologetics can be viewed as belonging "to the broad class of evidential apologetics"; what makes it distinctive is the priority it assigns to historical evidence (43).

Another type that Geisler discusses is *experiential apologetics*, which emphasizes self-authenticating religious experiences, both mystical and existential.

Proponents include Søren Kierkegaard and Karl Barth (43). This type is obviously identical to fideism.

Finally, Geisler discusses *presuppositional apologetics* as a type that "affirms that one must defend Christianity from the foundation of certain basic assumptions" (44). He distinguishes four subtypes: revelational (Cornelius Van Til, Greg Bahnsen, John Frame), rational (Gordon Clark, Carl Henry), systematic consistency (Edward John Carnell), and practical (Francis Schaeffer). This type is a large part of what we have called the Reformed approach.

In sum, Geisler's analysis of the types of apologetic systems is essentially identical to ours.

FIVE VIEWS ON APOLOGETICS

Finally, we consider the analysis offered by Steven B. Cowan in a book he edited entitled *Five Views on Apologetics*.[5] In his Introduction, Cowan questions the value of classifying approaches to apologetics according to their religious epistemologies (as in Gordon Lewis's book), suggesting that "the apologetic approaches that derive from these epistemologies, for all practical purposes, do not differ" (10). He thinks classifying apologetic approaches according to their view of faith and reason, as Bernard Ramm did, is somewhat better, but in the end he concludes that such an analysis also is inadequate (11–13). Instead, he prefers to classify approaches according to "the criterion of argumentative strategy"—the "distinctive types or structures of argument" used to make the case for Christianity (14). Cowan identifies the "Big Four" methods to be the classical, evidential, cumulative case, and presuppositional methods, with Reformed epistemology as a new and dramatic alternative (15–20).

Ironically, the submissions by the five authors chosen to represent these five methods undermine Cowan's analysis somewhat. William Lane Craig argues in favor of "classical apologetics," a two-step approach: first offer evidence for the existence of God, and then offer evidence that this God has revealed himself in Jesus (25–55). Gary Habermas presents "evidentialist apologetics" as a "one-step" approach that adduces historical evidence to show that God exists and has revealed himself in Jesus, focusing on the evidence for the resurrection (91–121). Paul Feinberg contends for "cumulative case apologetics," which seeks to draw upon a variety of arguments for God's existence, historical evidences, and other kinds of evidence to show that Christianity is the best explanation for everything that we know (147–72).

During the back-and-forth discussions among these three authors it becomes clear that very little separates their methods. In theory Craig's approach is a "two-step" method while the approaches of Habermas and Feinberg are narrower and broader versions of a "one-step" method. Yet Craig also views his approach as a cumulative case method, and both Habermas and Feinberg acknowledge the value of arguments for God's existence other than the historical argument. Little wonder that Craig sees the other two approaches as variations of the classical approach, while Habermas and Feinberg see Craig as an evidentialist.

The other two views are from our analysis the "left" and "right" wings of the Reformed approach. John Frame's "presuppositional apologetics" is a kinder, gentler version of the approach pioneered by Cornelius Van Til. He contends that no apologetic is adequate that does not set forth the God of Christianity as revealed in Scripture as the necessary presupposition of all thinking and of all knowledge (207–231). Frame finds so much of value in the traditional methods, though, that the spokesmen for all three of those methods conclude that he does not really have a distinct apologetic system or approach.

Kelly James Clark's "Reformed Epistemology apologetics" is, by contrast, a more strident version of the philosophical apologetic developed by Alvin Plantinga. His main contention is that the Christian is rational to believe in God with or without being able to offer arguments in support of that belief. All four of the other participants agree with this point. Clark affirms that some of the traditional apologetic arguments may have value but emphasizes their limitations, arguing that they are generally ineffective in persuading non-Christians (265–84).

Craig speaks for most if not all of the authors when, in his closing remarks, he observes, "What we are seeing in the present volume is a remarkable convergence of views, which is cause for rejoicing" (317). With this sentiment, we fully agree.

Our own view is that apologetic approaches can be fruitfully classified according to both religious epistemology and method, since there is typically a close correlation between the two. Of course, as we have stressed numerous times, individual apologists tend to vary from one another in many ways, so that no "taxonomy" of apologetic approaches will neatly or perfectly classify every apologist. The general validity of the fourfold analysis we have used in this book may be confirmed, however, by comparing the resulting classifications with those of the other studies we have reviewed here.

Four Approaches: A Comparison Chart

	Classical	Evidential	Reformed	Fideist
Ramm	Reason		Revelation	Experience
Lewis	Rational empiricism	Pure empiricism	Rationalism and Revelational Authoritarianism	Mysticism
Geisler	Classical	Evidential and Historical	Presuppositional	Experiential
Cowan	Classical	Evidential and Cumulative Case	Presuppositional and Reformed Epistemological	-----

Bibliography

Abraham, William J. "Cumulative Case Arguments for Christian Theism." In *The Rationality of Religious Belief: Essays in Honour of Basil Mitchell*, edited by William J. Abraham and Steven W. Holtzer, 17-37. Oxford: Clarendon, 1987.

Adams, Edward. "Calvin's View of Natural Knowledge of God." *International Journal of Systematic Theology* 3 (2001): 280-92.

Adams, Marilyn McCord. "*Fides Quaerens Intellectum:* St. Anselm's Method in Philosophical Theology." *Faith and Philosophy* 9 (1992): 409-435.

_____. "Philosophy and the Bible: The Areopagus Speech." *Faith and Philosophy* 9 (1992): 135-149.

Ahlstrom, Sydney E. "The Scottish Philosophy and American Theology." *Church History* 24 (1955): 257-272.

Alexander, Loveday. "The Acts of the Apostles as an Apologetic Text." In *Apologetics in the Roman Empire: Pagans, Jews, and Christians*, ed. Mark Edwards, Martin Goodman, and Simon Price, in association with Christopher Rowland, 15-44. Oxford and New York: Oxford University Press, 1999.

Anselm. *Anselm of Canterbury*. Translated and edited by Jasper Hopkins and Herbert Richardson. 4 vols. New York: Edwin Mellen Press; London: SCM, 1974-1976.

_____. *Saint Anselm: Basic Writings*. Translated by S. N. Deane. Introduction by Charles Hartshorne. La Salle, Ill.: Open Court, 1962.

Aquinas, Thomas. *Summa Contra Gentiles*. Translated by Anton C. Pegis. Notre Dame, Ind., and London: University of Notre Dame Press, 1975.

_____. *Summa Theologiae: Latin Text and English Translation, Introduction, Notes, Appendices and Glossaries*. London: Blackfriars, 1974.

_____. *The Summa Theologica*. Translated by the Fathers of the English Dominican Province. Revised by Daniel J. Sullivan. 2 Vols. Great Books of the Western World, vols. 19-20. Chicago: Encyclopaedia Britannica, 1952.

Ashcraft, Richard. "Faith and Knowledge in Locke's Philosophy." In *John Locke: Problems and Perspectives*, ed. John W. Yolton, 194-223. New York: Cambridge University Press, 1969.

Asiedu, F. B. "Anselm and the Unbelievers: Pagans, Jews, and Christians in the *Cur Deus Homo*."
    Theological Studies 62 (2001): 530-48.

Aucker, W. Brian. "Hodge and Warfield on Evolution." *Presbyterion* 20 (1994): 131-142.

Augustine. *Confessions*. Translated by Henry Chadwick. New York: Oxford University Press, 1991.

_____. *The Confessions; The City of God; On Christian Doctrine*. Great Books of the Western
    World, vol. 18. Chicago: Encyclopaedia Britannica, 1952.

_____. *The Works of Saint Augustine: A Translation for the 21st Century*. Edited by John E.
    Rotelle. In multiple volumes. Brooklyn: New City Press, 1990—.

Ayers, Robert H. *Language, Logic, and Reason in the Church Fathers: A Study of Tertullian,
    Augustine, and Aquinas*. Altertumswissenschaftliche Texte und Studien 6. Hildesheim:
    Georg Olms, 1979.

Bahnsen, Greg L. *Always Ready: Directions for Defending the Faith*, ed. Robert R. Booth. Atlanta:
    American Vision; Texarkana, Ark.: Covenant Media Foundation, 1996.

_____. "The Encounter of Jerusalem with Athens." *Ashland Theological Bulletin* 13 (1980): 4-
    40. Reprinted in Greg L. Bahnsen, *Always Ready: Directions for Defending the Faith*, ed.
    Robert R. Booth, 235-276. Atlanta: American Vision; Texarkana, Ark.: Covenant Media
    Foundation, 1996.

_____. "Machen, Van Til, and the Apologetical Tradition of the OPC." In *Pressing Toward
    the Mark: Essays Commemorating Fifty Years of the Orthodox Presbyterian Church*, ed.
    Charles G. Dennison and Richard C. Gamble, 259-294. Philadelphia: Committee for the
    Historian of the Orthodox Presbyterian Church, 1986.

_____. "Socrates or Christ: The Reformation of Christian Apologetics." In *Foundations of
    Christian Scholarship: Essays in the Van Til Perspective*, ed. Gary North. Vallecito,
    Calif.: Ross House, 1976.

_____. *Van Til's Apologetic: Readings and Analysis*. Phillipsburg, N.J.: Presbyterian &
    Reformed, 1998.

Baird, Forrest. "Schaeffer's Intellectual Roots." In *Reflections on Francis Schaeffer*, ed. Ronald W.
    Ruegsegger. Grand Rapids: Zondervan, 1986.

Balch, David L. "The Areopagus Speech: An Appeal to the Stoic Historian Posidonius against Later
    Stoics and the Epicureans." In *Greeks, Romans, and Christians: Essays in Honor of
    Abraham J. Malherbe*, ed. David L. Balch, Everett Ferguson, and Wayne A. Meeks, 52-
    79. Minneapolis: Fortress, 1990.

Balfour, Ian "Tertullian on and off the Internet." *Journal of Early Christian Studies* 8 (2000): 579-85.

Barbour, Ian G. *Religion and Science: Historical and Contemporary Issues*. San Francisco: Harper
    San Francisco, 1997.

Barker, Stephen F., and Tom L. Beauchamp, eds. *Thomas Reid: Critical Interpretations*.
    Philadelphia: University City Science Center, 1976.

Barnard, Leslie W. *Justin Martyr: His Life and Thought*. Cambridge: Cambridge University Press, 1967.

Barnberg, Stanley W. "Our Image of Warfield Must Go." *Journal of the Evangelical Theological Society* 34 (1991): 229-41.

Barnes, Timothy D. *Tertullian: A Historical and Literary Study*. Rev. ed. Oxford: Clarendon; New York: Oxford University Press, 1985.

Barr, James. *Biblical Faith and Natural Theology*. Gifford Lectures 1991. Oxford: Clarendon Press, 1992.

Barrow, John D., and Frank J. Tipler. *The Anthropic Cosmological Principle*. Oxford: Oxford University Press, 1986.

Barshinger, Clark Eugene. "Existential Psychology and Christian Faith." In *Christianity for the Tough-minded: Essays in Support of an Intellectually Defensible Religious Commitment*, ed. John Warwick Montgomery, 165-172. Minneapolis: Bethany Fellowship, 1973.

Barth, Karl. *Anselm:* Fides Quaerens Intellectum: *Anselm's Proof of the Existence of God in the Context of His Theological Scheme*, trans. Ian W. Robertson. 2nd ed. London: SCM; Richmond: John Knox, 1960.

_____. *Church Dogmatics*, ed. Geoffrey T. Bromiley and Thomas F. Torrance. 4 Vols. (in parts). Edinburgh: T. & T. Clark, 1936-1977.

_____. *The Epistle to the Romans*, trans. Sir Edwyn Hoskyns. 2nd ed. London: Oxford University Press, 1933; 6th ed., 1980.

_____. *How I Changed My Mind*. Introduction and Epilogue by John D. Godsey. Richmond: John Knox, 1966; Edinburgh: Saint Andrew Press, 1969.

_____. *Karl Barth's Table Talk*, ed. John D. Godsey. Scottish Journal of Occasional Papers. Richmond: John Knox, 1963.

_____. "The Principles of Dogmatics according to Wilhelm Herrmann." In *Theology and Church*, ed. Louise Pettibone Smith, 238-71. New York: Harper & Row, 1962.

Barth, Markus. "My Father: Karl Barth." In *How Karl Barth Changed My Mind*, ed. Donald K. McKim, 1-5. Grand Rapids: Eerdmans, 1986.

Basinger, David, and Randall Basinger, eds. *Predestination and Free Will: Four Views*, by John Feinberg, Norman Geisler, Bruce Reichenbach, and Clark Pinnock. Downers Grove, IL: InterVarsity Press, 1986.

Battenhouse, Roy W., ed. *A Companion to the Study of St. Augustine*. New York: Oxford University Press, 1955.

Battles, Ford Lewis. *An Analysis of the "Institutes of the Christian Religion" of John Calvin*. Assisted by John R. Walchenbach. Phillipsburg, N.J.: P & R, 2001. Originally published in 1976.

_____. *The Apologists*, Study Outline 1. Allison Park, Pa.: Pickwick, 1991.

_____. *Augustine: City of God*, Study Outline 9. Pittsburgh: Ford Lewis Battles, 1973.

_____. *Interpreting John Calvin*, ed. Robert Benedetto. Grand Rapids: Baker, 1996.

Batts, Martin. "A Summary and Critique of the Historical Apologetic of John Warwick Montgomery." Th.M. thesis, Dallas Theological Seminary, 1977.

Bauman, Michael, David Hall, and Robert Newman, eds. *Evangelical Apologetics*. Camp Hill, Penn.: Christian Publications, 1996.

Beanblossom, Ronald E. and Keith Lehrer, eds. *Thomas Reid: Inquiry and Essays*. Indianapolis: Hackett, 1983.

Beattie, Francis R. *Apologetics; or, The Rational Vindication of Christianity*. 3 vols. Richmond: Presbyterian Committee of Publications, 1903.

Beck, W. David. "A Thomistic Cosmological Argument." In *To Everyone an Answer: A Case for the Christian Worldview: Essays in Honor of Norman L. Geisler*, ed. Francis J. Beckwith, William Lane Craig, and J. P. Moreland, 95-107. Downers Grove, Ill.: InterVarsity Press, 2004.

Becker, Siegbert W. *The Foolishness of God: The Place of Reason in the Theology of Martin Luther*. Milwaukee: Northwestern Publishing House, 1982.

Beckwith, Francis J. *Baha'i*. Minneapolis: Bethany House, 1985.

_____. *David Hume's Argument against Miracles: A Critical Analysis*. Lanham, Md.: University Press of America, 1989.

_____. "History and Miracles." In *In Defense of Miracles: A Comprehensive Case for God's Action in History*, ed. R. Douglas Geivett and Gary R. Habermas, 86-98. Downers Grove, Ill.: InterVarsity, 1997.

Beckwith, Francis J., , eds. *To Everyone an Answer: A Case for the Christian Worldview: Essays in Honor of Norman L. Geisler*. Downers Grove, Ill.: InterVarsity Press, 2004.

Behannon, Woodrow. "Benjamin B. Warfield's Concept of Religious Authority." Th.D. diss., Southwestern Baptist Theological Seminary, 1964.

Berkhof, Hendrikus. *Two Hundred Years of Theology: Report of a Personal Journey*, trans. John Vriend. Grand Rapids: Eerdmans, 1989.

Berkouwer, G. C. *General Revelation*. Studies in Dogmatics. Grand Rapids: Eerdmans, 1955.

_____. *The Triumph of Grace in the Theology of Karl Barth*, trans. H. R. Boer. Grand Rapids: Eerdmans; London: Paternoster Press, 1956.

Beversluis, John. *C. S. Lewis and the Search for Rational Religion*. Grand Rapids: Eerdmans, 1985.

Bitar, Byron. "Augustine, Natural Theology, and General Revelation." Paper presented to the Evangelical Theological Seminary annual convention, 1997.

Bloesch, Donald G. *The Christian Witness in a Secular Age: An Evaluation of Nine Contemporary Theologians*. Minneapolis: Augsburg, 1968; reprint, Eugene, Ore.: Wipf & Stock, 2002.

_____. *Essentials of Evangelical Theology*. 2 vols. San Francisco: Harper & Row, 1978, 1979; 2 vols. in 1, Peabody, Mass.: Hendrickson, 2006.

_____. "Evangelical Rationalism and Propositional Revelation." *Reformed Review* 51 (1998) 169-81.

_____. "The Finality of Christ and Religious Pluralism." *Touchstone* 4, 3 (1991) 5-9.

_____. *The Future of Evangelical Christianity: A Call for Unity amid Diversity*. Garden City, NY: Doubleday, 1983.

_____. *God the Almighty: Power, Wisdom, Holiness, Love*. Downers Grove, Ill.: InterVarsity Press, 1995.

_____. *The Ground of Certainty: Toward an Evangelical Theology of Revelation*. Grand Rapids: Eerdmans, 1971; reprint, Eugene, Ore.: Wipf & Stock, 2002.

_____. *Holy Scripture: Revelation, Inspiration and Interpretation*. Downers Grove, Ill.: InterVarsity Press, 1994.

_____. *Jesus Christ: Savior and Lord*. Downers Grove, Ill.: InterVarsity Press, 1997.

_____. *Jesus Is Victor! Karl Barth's Doctrine of Salvation*. Nashville: Abingdon, 1976.

_____. "Karl Barth: Appreciation and Reservations." In *How Karl Barth Changed My Mind*, ed. Donald K. McKim, 126-30. Grand Rapids: Eerdmans, 1986.

_____. *A Theology of Word and Spirit: Authority and Method in Theology*. Downers Grove, Ill.: InterVarsity Press, 1992.

Bloom, John A. "Truth Via Prophecy." In *Evidence for Faith: Deciding the God Question*, ed. John Warwick Montgomery, 173-192. Cornell Symposium on Evidential Apologetics, 1986. Dallas: Probe Books, 1991; distributed by Word Publishing.

_____. "Why Isn't the Evidence Clearer?" In *Evidence for Faith: Deciding the God Question*, ed. John Warwick Montgomery, 305-317. Cornell Symposium on Evidential Apologetics, 1986. Dallas: Probe Books, 1991; distributed by Word Publishing.

Boa, Kenneth D. *Augustine to Freud: What Theologians & Psychologists Tell Us about Human Nature*. Nashville: Broadman & Holman, 2004.

_____. *Conformed to His Image: Pathways to Spiritual Formation*. Grand Rapids: Zondervan, 2001.

Boa, Kenneth D., and Larry Moody. *I'm Glad You Asked*. 2nd ed. Wheaton, Ill.: Victor, 1994.

Boa, Kenneth D., and Robert M. Bowman, Jr. *20 Compelling Evidences that God Exists*. Colorado Springs: Victor, 2005.

_____. *An Unchanging Faith in a Changing World: Understanding and Responding to Issues that Christians Face Today*. Nashville: Thomas Nelson, Oliver, 1997.

Bock, Darrell L. "Athenians Who Have Never Heard." In *Through No Fault of Their Own? The Fate of Those Who Have Never Heard*, ed. William V. Crockett and James G. Sigountos, 117-124. Grand Rapids: Baker, 1993.

Boice, James Montgomery. *Witness and Revelation in the Gospel of John.* Exeter: Paternoster, 1970.

Bolich, Gregory. *Karl Barth and Evangelicalism.* Downers Grove, Ill.: InterVarsity, 1980.

Bos, Abraham P. "Augustine (354-430)." in *Bringing into Captivity Every Thought:* Capita Selecta *in the History of Christian Evaluations of Non-Christian Philosophy*, ed. Jacob Klapwijk, Sander Griffioen, and Gerben Groenewoud, 49-66. Christian Studies Today. Lanham, Md.: University Press of America, 1991.

Bouwsma, William J. *John Calvin: A Sixteenth Century Portrait.* New York: Oxford University Press, 1988.

Bowman, Robert M., Jr. *Jehovah's Witnesses.* Zondervan Guide to Cults and Religious Movements. Grand Rapids: Zondervan, 1995.

_____. *Orthodoxy and Heresy: A Biblical Guide to Doctrinal Discernment.* Grand Rapids: Baker, 1991.

Boyd, Gregory A., David Hunt, William Lane Craig, and Paul Helm. *Divine Foreknowledge: Four Views.* Downers Grove, Ill.: InterVarsity, 2001.

Bradshaw, David. "Faith and Reason in St. Anselm's *Monologion.*" *Philosophia Christi* 4 (2002): 509-17.

Bratt, James D. *Dutch Calvinism in Modern America: A History of a Conservative Subculture.* Grand Rapids: Eerdmans, 1984.

_____. "In the Shadow of Mt. Kuyper: A Survey of the Field." *Calvin Theological Journal* 31 (1996): 51-66.

Bristley, Eric D. *A Guide to the Writings of Cornelius Van Til, 1895-1987.* Chicago: Olive Tree Communications, 1995.

Broadie, Alexander. *The Tradition of Scottish Philosophy: A New Perspective on the Enlightenment.* Edinburgh: Polygon; Savage, Md.: Barnes & Noble, 1990.

Bromiley, Geoffrey W. *Introduction to the Theology of Karl Barth.* Grand Rapids: Eerdmans, 1979.

_____. "Karl Barth." In *Creative Minds in Contemporary Theology*, ed. Philip E. Hughes, 27-62. 2nd rev. ed. Grand Rapids: Eerdmans, 1969.

Brown, Colin. *Christianity and Western Thought: A History of Philosophers, Ideas, and Movements*, vol. 1, *From the Ancient World to the Age of Enlightenment.* Downers Grove, Ill.: InterVarsity, 1990.

_____. "Glossary of Technical Terms." In *The New International Dictionary of New Testament Theology*, ed. Colin Brown, 49-72. Grand Rapids: Zondervan, 1975.

_____. *Karl Barth and the Christian Message.* Downers Grove, Ill.: InterVarsity, 1967.

_____. *Miracles and the Critical Mind.* Grand Rapids: Eerdmans, 1984.

Bruce, Alexander Balmain. *Apologetics; or, Christianity Defensively Stated*, 3rd ed. Edinburgh: T. & T. Clark, 1892.

Bruce, F. F. *The Defense of the Gospel in the New Testament*. Rev. ed. Grand Rapids: Eerdmans, 1977.

_____. "Paul's Apologetic and the Purpose of Acts," *Bulletin of the John Rylands Library* 69 (1986-87): 379-93.

Brümmer, Vincent. *Transcendental Criticism and Christian Philosophy: A Presentation and Evaluation of Herman Dooyeweerd's "Philosophy of the Cosmonomic Idea."* Franeker: T. Wever, 1961.

Brunner, Emil. *The Christian Doctrine of God*, trans. Olive Wyon. Philadelphia: Westminster, 1950.

_____. *Truth as Encounter*. Philadelphia: Westminster, 1964.

_____, and Karl Barth. *Natural Theology*, trans. Peter Fraenkel. London: Geoffrey Bles, Centenary Press, 1946; reprint, Eugene, Ore.: Wipf & Stock, 2002.

Burson, Scott R., and Jerry L. Walls. *C. S. Lewis and Francis Schaeffer: Lessons for a New Century from the Most Influential Apologists of Our Time*. Downers Grove, Ill.: InterVarsity, 1998.

Burtt, Edwin A. *Types of Religious Philosophy*. New York: Harper & Row, 1939.

Busch, Eberhard. *Karl Barth: His Life from Letters and Autobiographical Texts*, trans. John Bowden. 2nd rev. ed. Philadelphia: Fortress, 1976.

Bush, L. Russ, ed. *Classical Readings in Christian Apologetics, A.D. 100-1800*. Grand Rapids: Zondervan, Academie, 1983.

Buswell, J. Oliver, Jr. *A Systematic Theology of the Christian Religion*. 2 Vols. Grand Rapids: Zondervan, 1972.

Butler, Joseph. *The Analogy of Religion*. Introduction by Ernest C. Mossner. Milestones of Thought. New York: Frederick Ungar, 1961.

Calvin, John. *Concerning Scandals*, trans. John W. Fraser. Grand Rapids: Eerdmans, 1978.

_____. *Institutes of the Christian Religion*, ed. John T. McNeill, trans. Ford Lewis Battles. Library of Christian Classics, vols. 20-21. Philadelphia: Westminster, 1960.

Carnell, Edward John. *The Burden of Søren Kierkegaard*. Grand Rapids: Eerdmans, 1965.

_____. *Christian Commitment: An Apologetic*. New York: Macmillan, 1957; reprint, Grand Rapids: Baker, 1982.

_____. *An Introduction to Christian Apologetics: A Philosophic Defense of the Trinitarian-Theistic Faith*. Grand Rapids: Eerdmans, 1948; 4th ed., 1953.

_____. *The Kingdom of Love and the Pride of Life*. Grand Rapids: Eerdmans, 1960.

_____. *A Philosophy of the Christian Religion*. Grand Rapids: Eerdmans, 1952.

Carson, D. A. "Athens Revisited." In *Telling the Truth: Evangelizing Postmoderns*, ed. D. A. Carson, 384-98. Grand Rapids: Zondervan, 2000.

Carter, Alan. "Is the Wager Back On? A Response to Douglas Groothuis." *Philosophia Christi* 4 (2002).

_____. "On Pascal's Wager; or Why All Bets Are Off." *Philosophia Christi* 3 (2001).

Catherwood, Christopher. *Five Evangelical Leaders*. Wheaton, Ill.: Harold Shaw, 1985.

Chadwick, Henry. *Augustine*. New York: Oxford University Press, 1986.

_____. *Early Christian Thought and the Classical Tradition: Studies in Justin, Clement, and Origen*. Oxford: Clarendon, 1966.

_____. "Justin Martyr's Defence of Christianity." *Bulletin of the John Rylands Library* 47 (1965): 275-297.

Chang, Curtis. *Engaging Unbelief: A Captivating Strategy from Augustine & Aquinas*. Downers Grove, Ill.: InterVarsity Press, 2000.

Chappell, Vere, ed. *The Cambridge Companion to Locke*. New York: Cambridge University Press, 1994.

Charles, J. Daryl. "Paul before the Areopagus: Reflections on the Apostle's Encounter with Cultured Paganism." *Philosophia Christi* 7 (2005): 125-40.

Chenu, M.-D. *Toward Understanding Saint Thomas*. Translated by A.-M. Landry and D. Hughes. Chicago: Henry Regnery, 1964.

Chesterton, G. K. *Orthodoxy*. Image Books. Garden City, N.Y.: Doubleday, 1959 [1903].

_____. *St. Thomas Aquinas*. Garden City, N.Y.: Image Books, 1956.

Chung, Sung Wook. *Admiration & Challenge: Karl Barth's Theological Relationship with John Calvin*. New York: Peter Lang, 2002.

Clark, David K. *Dialogical Apologetics: A Person-Centered Approach to Christian Defense*. Grand Rapids: Baker, 1993.

_____. "Miracles in the World Religions." In *In Defense of Miracles: A Comprehensive Case for God's Action in History*, ed. R. Douglas Geivett and Gary R. Habermas, 199-213. Downers Grove, Ill.: InterVarsity, 1997.

_____. *The Pantheism of Alan Watts*. Downers Grove, Ill.: InterVarsity, 1978.

_____. *The Relation of Tradition to Experience in Mysticism*. Ann Arbor: University Microfilms, 1982.

_____, and Norman L. Geisler. *Apologetics in the New Age: A Christian Critique of Pantheism*. Grand Rapids: Baker, 1990.

Clark, Gordon H. "Apologetics." In *Contemporary Evangelical Thought*, ed. Carl F. H. Henry. Great Neck, N.Y.: Channel Press, 1957.

_____. "The Bible as Truth." *Bibliotheca Sacra* 114 (1957): 157-170. Reprinted in *God's Hammer: The Bible and Its Critics*, 24-38. 2nd ed. Jefferson, Md.: Trinity Foundation, 1987.

_____. *A Christian Philosophy of Education*. Grand Rapids: Eerdmans, 1946.

_____. *A Christian View of Men and Things: An Introduction to Philosophy.* Grand Rapids: Eerdmans, 1952; reprint, Grand Rapids: Baker, 1981.

_____. *God's Hammer: The Bible and Its Critics.* 2nd ed. Jefferson, Md.: Trinity Foundation, 1987.

_____. *In Defense of Theology.* Milford, Mich.: Mott Media, 1984.

_____. *Karl Barth's Theological Method.* Philadelphia: Presbyterian & Reformed, 1963.

_____. *Logic.* 2nd ed. Jefferson, Md.: Trinity Foundation, 1988.

_____. *The Philosophy of Science and Belief in God.* 3rd ed. Jefferson, Md.: Trinity Foundation, 1996.

_____. *Religion, Reason and Revelation.* Nutley, N.J.: Craig Press, 1961. 2nd ed. Jefferson, Md.: Trinity Foundation, 1986.

_____. *Thales to Dewey: A History of Philosophy.* Boston: Houghton Mifflin, 1957; reprint, Grand Rapids: Baker, 1980.

_____. *Three Types of Religious Philosophy.* Nutley, N.J.: Presbyterian & Reformed, 1977.

_____. *The Trinity.* Jefferson, Md.: Trinity Foundation, 1985.

Clark, Gregory A. "The Nature of Conversion: How the Rhetoric of Worldview Philosophy Can Betray Evangelicals." In *The Nature of Confession: Evangelicals and Postliberals in Conversation,* ed. Timothy R. Phillips and Dennis L. Ockholm, 201-218. Downers Grove, Ill.: InterVarsity, 1996.

Clark, Kelly James. *Return to Reason: A Critique of Enlightenment Evidentialism and a Defense of Reason and Belief in God.* Grand Rapids: Eerdmans, 1990.

Clifford, Ross. "Justification of the Legal Apologetic of John Warwick Montgomery: An Apologetic for All Seasons." *Global Journal of Classical Theology* 3, 1 (March 2002). Accessed online at < http://www.trinitysem.edu/journal/toc_v3n1.html >.

Clifford, William Kingdon. "The Ethics of Belief." In *Lectures and Essays,* ed. Leslie Stephen and Frederick Pollock. Vol. 2. London: Macmillan, 1879. Reprinted in *An Anthology of Atheism and Rationalism,* ed. Gordon Stein, 277-292. Buffalo: Prometheus Books, 1980.

Clough, Charles A. "Biblical Presuppositions and Historical Geology: A Case Study." *Journal of Christian Reconstruction* 1, no. 1 (summer 1974): 35-48.

Clouser, Roy A. *Knowing with the Heart: Religious Experience and Belief in God.* Downers Grove, Ill.: InterVarsity, 1999.

_____. *The Myth of Religious Neutrality: An Essay on the Hidden Role of Religious Belief in Theories.* Notre Dame, IN: University of Notre Dame Press, 1991.

Coleman, Francis X. J. *Neither Angel nor Beast: The Life and Work of Blaise Pascal.* New York: Routledge & Kegan Paul, 1986.

Collins, Robin. "A Scientific Argument for the Existence of God: The Fine-Tuning Design Argument." In *Reason for the Hope Within*, ed. Michael J. Murray, 47-75. Grand Rapids and Cambridge, U.K.: Eerdmans, 1999.

Collins, Steven. *Championing the Faith: A Layman's Guide to Proving Christianity's Claims*. Tulsa: Virgil W. Hensley, 1991.

Colyer, Elmer M., ed. *Evangelical Theology in Transition: Theologians in Dialogue with Donald Bloesch*. Downers Grove, Ill.: InterVarsity, 1999.

Copan, Paul. *"True for You, but Not for Me": Deflating the Slogans that Leave Christians Speechless*. Minneapolis: Bethany House, 1998.

_____, and William Lane Craig. *Creation Out of Nothing: A Biblical, Philosophical, and Scientific Exploration*. Grand Rapids: Baker Academic; Leicester, England: Apollos, 2004.

Copan, Paul, and Ronald Tacelli, eds. *Jesus' Resurrection: Fact or Figment? A Debate on the Resurrection between William Lane Craig and Gerd Lüdemann*. Downers Grove, Ill.: InterVarsity, 2000.

Copleston, Frederick C. *Aquinas*. Harmondsworth, U.K.: Penguin Books, 1957.

Corduan, Winfried. *No Doubt about It: The Case for Christianity*. Nashville: Broadman & Holman, 1997. Originally *Reasonable Faith: Basic Christian Apologetics* (1993).

Corey, M. A. *God and the New Cosmology: The Anthropic Design Argument.* Lanham, Md.: Rowman & Littlefield, 1993.

Cowan, Steven B. Review of *Faith Has Its Reasons* (1st ed.), by Boa and Bowman. *Philosophia Christi* 6 (2004).

_____, ed. *Five Views on Apologetics*. Counterpoint series. Grand Rapids: Zondervan, 2000.

Craig, William Lane. *Assessing the New Testament Evidence for the Historicity of the Resurrection of Jesus*. Studies in the Bible and Early Christianity, vol. 16. Lewiston, N.Y.: Edwin Mellen Press, 1989.

_____. "Classical Apologetics." In *Five Views on Apologetics*, ed. Steven B. Cowan, 26-55. Counterpoint series. Grand Rapids: Zondervan, 2000.

_____. "Colin Brown, *Miracles and the Critical Mind*: A Review Article." *Journal of the Evangelical Theological Society* 27 (1984): 473-85.

_____. *The Cosmological Argument from Plato to Leibniz*. New York: Macmillan, 1980.

_____. "Did Jesus Rise from the Dead?" In *Jesus Under Fire*, ed. Michael J. Wilkins and J. P. Moreland, 141-176. Grand Rapids: Zondervan, 1995.

_____. *Divine Foreknowledge and Human Freedom: The Coherence of Theism: Omniscience*. Leiden and New York: E. J. Brill, 1990.

_____. "The Empty Tomb of Jesus." In *In Defense of Miracles: A Comprehensive Case for God's Action in History*, ed. R. Douglas Geivett and Gary R. Habermas, 247-261. Downers Grove, Ill.: InterVarsity, 1997.

_____. *The Existence of God and the Beginning of the Universe*. San Bernardino, Calif.: Here's Life, 1979.

_____. *The Historical Argument for the Resurrection of Jesus During the Deist Controversy*. Texts and Studies in Religion, vol. 23. Lewiston, N.Y.: Edwin Mellen Press, 1985.

_____. *The* Kalâm *Cosmological Argument*. Library of Philosophy and Religion. New York: Macmillan, 1979.

_____. *Knowing the Truth about the Resurrection*. Ann Arbor: Servant, 1991.

_____. *No Easy Answers*. Chicago: Moody, 1990.

_____. *The Only Wise God: The Compatibility of Divine Foreknowledge and Human Freedom*. Grand Rapids: Baker, 1987.

_____. "Politically Incorrect Salvation." In *Christian Apologetics in the Postmodern World*, ed. Timothy R. Phillips and Dennis L. Ockholm, 75-97. Downers Grove, Ill.: InterVarsity, 1995.

_____. *Reasonable Faith: Christian Truth and Apologetics*. Wheaton, Ill.: Crossway, 1994. Revised version of *Apologetics: An Introduction*. Chicago: Moody, 1984.

_____. "The Teleological Argument and the Anthropic Principle." In *The Logic of Rational Theism: Exploratory Essays*, ed. William Lane Craig and Mark S. McLeod, 127-153. Problems in Contemporary Philosophy, vol. 24. Lewiston, N.Y.: Edwin Mellen Press, 1990.

_____. *Time and Eternity: Exploring God's Relationship to Time*. Westchester, Ill.: Crossway Books, 2001.

Craig, William Lane, and John Dominic Crossan. *Will the Real Jesus Please Stand Up? A Debate Between William Lane Craig and John Dominic Crossan*. Moderated by William F. Buckley, Jr. Edited by Paul Copan. With responses from Robert J. Miller, Craig L. Blomberg, Marcus Borg, and Ben Witherington III. Grand Rapids: Baker, 1998.

Craig, William Lane, and Mark S. McLeod, eds. *The Logic of Rational Theism: Exploratory Essays*. Problems in Contemporary Philosophy, vol. 24. Lewiston, N.Y.: Edwin Mellen Press, 1990.

Craig, William Lane, and Quentin Smith. *Theism, Atheism, and Big Bang Cosmology*. Oxford: Clarendon, 1993.

Craig, William Lane, and Walter Sinnott-Armstrong. *God? A Debate between a Christian and an Atheist*. Point/Counterpoint Series. James P. Sterba, series ed. New York: Oxford University Press, 2004.

Crouzel, Henri. *Origen*, trans. A. S. Worrell. San Francisco: Harper & Row, 1989.

Crumpacker, Mary M. "Clark's Axiom: Something New?" *Journal of the Evangelical Theological Society* 32 (1989): 355-365.

Cuneo, Terrence D. "Combatting the Noetic Effects of Sin: Pascal's Strategy for Natural Theology." *Faith and Philosophy* 11 (1994): 645-662.

Cunliffe, Christopher, ed. *Joseph Butler's Moral and Religious Thought: Tercentenary Essays.* Oxford: Clarendon; New York: Oxford University Press, 1992.

Cunningham, Richard B. *C. S. Lewis: Defender of the Faith.* Philadelphia: Westminster Press, 1967.

Dalgarno, Melvin, and Eric Matthews, eds. *The Philosophy of Thomas Reid*, Philosophical Studies, vol. 42. Dordrecht and Boston: Kluwer Academic Publishers, 1989.

Davidson, Hugh M. *The Origins of Certainty: Means and Meanings in Pascal's "Pensées."* Chicago: University of Chicago Press, 1979.

Davies, Brian. *The Thought of Thomas Aquinas.* Oxford: Clarendon, 1992.

_____, ed. *Thomas Aquinas: Contemporary Philosophical Perspectives.* Oxford and New York: Oxford University Press, 2002.

_____, and Gillian R. Evans, eds. *Anselm of Canterbury: The Major Works.* Oxford World's Classics. Oxford and New York: Oxford University Press, 1998.

_____, and Brian Leftow, eds. *The Cambridge Companion to Anselm.* Cambridge Companions to Philosophy. New York: Cambridge University Press, 2004.

Davis, Caroline Franks. *The Evidential Force of Religious Experience.* New York: Oxford University Press, 1989.

Davis, Stephen T. *Encountering Evil: Live Options in Theodicy.* Atlanta: John Knox, 1981.

_____. *God, Reason and Theistic Proofs.* Reason and Religion series. Grand Rapids: Eerdmans, 1997.

De Greef, Wulfert. *The Writings of John Calvin: An Introductory Guide*, trans. Lyle D. Bierma. Grand Rapids: Baker, 1993.

Demarest, Bruce A. *General Revelation: Historical Views and Contemporary Issues.* Grand Rapids: Zondervan, 1982.

Denning-Bolle, Sara J. "Christian Dialogue as Apologetic: The Case of Justin Martyr Seen in Historical Context." *Bulletin of the John Rylands Library* 69 (1987): 492-510.

Dennis, Lane T., ed. *Francis A. Schaeffer: Portraits of the Man and His Work.* Westchester, Ill.: Crossway, 1986.

Dennison, William D. *Paul's Two-Age Construction and Apologetics.* Lanham, Md.: University Press of America, 1985.

DeWeese, Garrett J., and Joshua Rasmussen. "Hume and the *Kalam* Cosmological Argument." In *In Defense of Natural Theology: A Post-Humean Assessment*, ed. James F. Sennett and Douglas R. Groothuis, 123-49. Downers Grove, Ill.: InterVarsity, 2005.

Depoe, John. "Rejuvenating Christian Apologetics in the Twenty-first Century: Taking Hints from Søren Kierkegaard." Baylor University, 2002. Accessed online at < http://www.johndepoe.com/Kierkegaard_Apologetics.pdf >.

Diehl, David W. "Divine Omniscience in the Thought of Charles Hartshorne and Cornelius Van Til: A Systemic Comparative Study." Ph.D. diss. Hartford Seminary Foundation, 1978.

_____. "Evangelicalism and General Revelation: An Unfinished Agenda." *Journal of the Evangelical Theological Society* 30 (1987): 441-55.

_____. "Historical Apologetics." Class syllabus, The King's College, 1974.

_____. "Van Til's Epistemic Argument: A Case of Inadvertent Natural Theology." Faculty paper. The King's College, n.d.

Dillenberger, John, ed. *Martin Luther: Selections from His Writings.* Garden City, N.Y.: Doubleday, 1961.

Dooyeweerd, Herman. *In the Twilight of Western Thought: Studies in the Pretended Autonomy of Philosophical Thought* (Nutley, N.J.: Craig Press, 1972.

_____. *A New Critique of Theoretical Thought,* trans. David H. Freeman, William S. Young, and H. De Jongste. 4 vols. Nutley, N.J.: Presbyterian & Reformed, 1953-1957; bound as two volumes, 1969.

_____. *Roots of Western Culture: Pagan, Secular, and Christian Options,* trans. John Kraay. Toronto: Wedge, 1979.

Dorrien, Gary. *The Barthian Revolt in Modern Theology: Theology without Weapons.* Louisville, Ky.: Westminster John Knox Press, 2000.

Dorsett, Lyle W. *The Essential C. S. Lewis.* New York: Collier, 1988.

Dowey, Edward A. Jr. *The Knowledge of God in Calvin's Theology.* Expanded edition. Grand Rapids: Eerdmans, 1994. Original edition, New York: Columbia University Press, 1952.

Downing, David C. *The Most Reluctant Convert: C. S. Lewis's Journey to Faith.* Downers Grove, Ill.: InterVarsity, 2002.

_____. *Planets in Peril: A Critical Study of C.S. Lewis's Ransom Trilogy.* Amherst: University of Massachusetts Press, 1995.

Droge, Arthur J. "Justin Martyr and the Restoration of Philosophy." *Church History* 56 (1987): 303-319.

Dulles, Avery. *A History of Apologetics.* 2d ed., Modern Apologetics Library, San Francisco: Ignatius Press, 2005. Orig. publ. New York: Corpus Books, 1971.

Dunn, John. *Locke: A Very Short Introduction.* Updated ed. Oxford and New York: Oxford University Press, 2003.

Duriez, Colin. *The C. S. Lewis Handbook.* Grand Rapids: Baker, 1994.

_____. "Francis Schaeffer." In *Handbook of Evangelical Theologians,* ed. Walter E. Elwell, 245-259. Grand Rapids: Baker, 1993.

Dyrness, William. *Christian Apologetics in a World Community*. Downers Grove, Ill.: InterVarsity, 1983.

Edgar, William. "Two Christian Warriors: Cornelius Van Til and Francis A. Schaeffer Compared." *Westminster Theological Journal* 57 (1995): 57-80.

_____. *Reasons of the Heart: Recovering Christian Persuasion*. Hourglass Books. Grand Rapids: Baker, 1996.

Elders, Leo J. *The Philosophical Theology of St. Thomas Aquinas*. Leiden: E. J. Brill, 1990.

Ellul, Jacques. *Living Faith*, trans. Peter Heinegg. San Francisco: Harper & Row, 1983.

_____. *What I Believe*, trans. Geoffrey W. Bromiley. Grand Rapids: Eerdmans, 1989.

Erickson, Millard J. *Postmodernizing the Faith: Evangelical Responses to the Challenge of Postmodernism*. Grand Rapids: Baker, 1998.

Erlandson, Doug. "The Resurrection of Thomism." *Antithesis* 2, 3 (May/June 1991).

Evans, C. Stephen. "Apologetic Arguments in *Philosophical Fragments*." In *"Philosophical Fragments" and "Johannes Climacus,"* ed. Robert L. Perkins, 63-83. International Kierkegaard Commentary, vol. 7. Macon, Ga.: Mercer University Press, 1994.

_____. "Apologetics in a New Key: Relieving Protestant Anxieties over Natural Theology." In *The Logic of Rational Theism: Exploratory Essays*, ed. William Lane Craig and Mark S. McLeod. Problems in Contemporary Philosophy, vol. 24. Lewiston, N.Y.: Edwin Mellen Press, 1990.

_____. *Despair: A Moment or a Way of Life*. Downers Grove, Ill.: InterVarsity, 1971.

_____. *Existentialism: The Philosophy of Despair and the Quest for Hope*. Grand Rapids: Zondervan, 1984; Dallas: Probe Books, 1989.

_____. *Faith Beyond Reason: A Kierkegaardian Account*. Reason & Religion. Grand Rapids: Eerdmans, 1998.

_____. *The Historical Christ and the Jesus of Faith: The Incarnational Narrative as History*. Oxford: Oxford University Press, 1996.

_____. *Philosophy of Religion: Thinking about Faith*. Contours of Christian Philosophy. Downers Grove, Ill.: InterVarsity, 1985.

_____. "A Privileged Calling." In *Storying Ourselves: A Narrative Perspective on Christians in Psychology*, ed. D. John Lee, 187-209. Christian Explorations in Psychology. Grand Rapids: Baker, 1993.

_____. *The Quest for Faith: Reason and Mystery as Pointers to God* (Downers Grove, Ill.: InterVarsity, 1986.

_____. *Why Believe? Reason and Mystery as Pointers to God*. Grand Rapids: Eerdmans; Leicester: Inter-Varsity Press, 1996.

Evans, Calvin D., comp. *Søren Kierkegaard: Remnants, 1944-1980 and Multi-Media, 1925-1991*. Fontanus Monograph Series. Montreal: McGill University Libraries, 1993.

Evans, Gillian R. *Anselm*. Outstanding Christian Thinkers. Wilton, Conn.: Morehouse, 1989.

_____. *Anselm and Talking about God*. Oxford: Clarendon; New York: Oxford University Press, 1978.

Everdell, William R. *Christian Apologetics in France, 1730-1790: The Roots of Romantic Religion*. Texts and Studies in Religion, vol. 31. Lewiston, N.Y.: Edwin Mellen Press, 1987.

Fee, Gordon D. *The First Epistle to the Corinthians*. New International Commentary on the New Testament. Grand Rapids: Eerdmans, 1987.

Feinberg, John S. *The Many Faces of Evil: Theological Systems and the Problem of Evil*. Grand Rapids: Zondervan, 1994.

Feinberg, Paul D. "Cumulative Case Apologetics." In *Five Views on Apologetics*, edited by Steven B. Cowan, 148-172. Grand Rapids: Zondervan, 2000.

Fischer, Robert H. "Place of Reason in Luther's Theology." *Lutheran Quarterly* 16 (1964): 41-48.

Flew, Antony. "The Presumption of Atheism." In *God, Freedom, and Immortality*. Buffalo: Prometheus Books, 1984. Reprint of *The Presumption of Atheism* (1976).

_____. *God and Philosophy*. New York: Harcourt, Brace & World, 1966. Reprinted with a new Introduction. Buffalo, N.Y.: Prometheus Books, 2005.

_____, and Gary R. Habermas. "My Pilgrimage from Atheism to Theism: A Discussion between Antony Flew and Gary R. Habermas." *Philosophia Christi* 6 (2004): 197-211.

Fodor, Jim, and Frederick Christian Bauerschmidt, eds. *Aquinas in Dialogue: Thomas for the Twenty-first Century*. New York: Blackwell, 2004.

Foreman, Paul. "The Theology of Reinhold Niebuhr." LeadershipU. < http://www.leaderu.com/isot/docs/niehbr3.html >.

Forsyth, P. T. *The Principle of Authority*. 2d ed. London: Independent Press, 1952.

Fortin, John R., ed. *Saint Anselm: His Origins and Influence*. Texts and Studies in Religion 91. Lewiston, N.Y.: Edwin Mellen Press, 2001.

Frame, John M. *Apologetics to the Glory of God: An Introduction*. Phillipsburg, N.J.: Presbyterian & Reformed, 1994.

_____. *Cornelius Van Til: An Analysis of His Thought*. Phillipsburg, N.J.: Presbyterian & Reformed, 1995.

_____. *Doctrine of the Knowledge of God: A Theology of Lordship*. Phillipsburg, N.J.: Presbyterian & Reformed, 1987.

_____. *Evangelical Reunion: Denominations and the Body of Christ*. Grand Rapids: Baker, 1986.

_____. *Medical Ethics: Principles, Persons, and Problems*. Grand Rapids: Baker, 1988.

_____. *Perspectives on the Word of God: An Introduction to Christian Ethics*. Phillipsburg, N.J.: Presbyterian & Reformed, 1990.

_____. "Presuppositional Apologetics." In *Five Views on Apologetics*, ed. Steven B. Cowan, 208-231. Grand Rapids: Zondervan, 2000.

_____. *Van Til: The Theologian*. Phillipsburg, N.J.: Harmony Press, 1976.

Gaffin, Richard B., Jr. "Some Epistemological Reflections on 1 Cor 2:6-16." *Westminster Theological Journal* 57 (1995): 103-124.

Gallie, Roger D. *Thomas Reid and "The Way of Ideas."* Dordrecht and Boston: Kluwer Academic Publishers, 1989.

Gamble, Richard C. ed. Articles on Calvin and Calvinism, 10 vols. New York: Garland, 1992.

Ganssle, Gregory E., and David M. Woodruff, eds. *God and Time: Essays on the Divine Nature*. New York: Oxford University Press, 2002.

Garff, Joakim. *Søren Kierkegaard: A Biography*, trans. Bruce H. Kirmmse. Princeton: Princeton University Press, 2000.

Gärtner, Bertil. *The Areopagus Speech and Natural Revelation*. Acta seminarii neotestamentici upsaliensis, vol. 24. Lund: Gleerup, 1955.

Geehan, E. R., ed. *Jerusalem and Athens: Critical Discussions on the Philosophy and Apologetics of Cornelius Van Til*. Nutley, N.J.: Presbyterian & Reformed, 1971.

Geisler, Norman L. *Baker Encyclopedia of Christian Apologetics*. Grand Rapids: Baker, 1999.

_____. *Christian Apologetics*. Grand Rapids: Baker, 1976.

_____. *Is Man the Measure? An Evaluation of Contemporary Humanism*. Grand Rapids: Baker, 1983.

_____. "Johannine Apologetics." *Bibliotheca Sacra* 136 (1979): 333-343.

_____. *Knowing the Truth about Creation: How It Happened and What It Means for Us*. Ann Arbor, Mich.: Servant, 1989.

_____. *Miracles and Modern Thought*. Grand Rapids: Zondervan, 1982.

_____. *Options in Contemporary Christian Ethics*. Grand Rapids: Baker, 1981.

_____. "Philosophical Presuppositions of Biblical Errancy." In *Inerrancy*, ed. Geisler, 305-324. Grand Rapids: Zondervan, 1979.

_____. *The Roots of Evil*. Grand Rapids: Zondervan, 1978.

_____. *Systematic Theology, Volume One: Introduction, Bible*. Minneapolis: Bethany House, 2002.

_____. *Thomas Aquinas: An Evangelical Appraisal*. Grand Rapids: Baker, 1991; reprint, Eugene, Ore.: Wipf & Stock, 2003.

_____., ed. *What Augustine Says*. Grand Rapids: Baker, 1982.

Geisler, Norman L., and J. Kerby Anderson. *Origin Science: A Proposal for the Creation-Evolution Controversy*. Grand Rapids: Baker, 1987.

Geisler, Norman L., and Paul D. Feinberg. *Introduction to Philosophy: A Christian Perspective.* Grand Rapids: Baker, 1980.

Geisler, Norman L., and Ronald M. Brooks, *When Skeptics Ask: A Handbook of Christian Evidences.* Wheaton, Ill.: Victor, 1990.

Geisler, Norman L., and William D. Watkins. *Worlds Apart: A Handbook on World Views.* 2nd ed. Grand Rapids: Baker, 1989.

Geisler, Norman L., and Winfried Corduan. *Philosophy of Religion.* 2nd ed. Grand Rapids: Baker, 1988.

Geisler, Norman L., with Frank Turek *I Don't Have Enough Faith to Be an Atheist.* Foreword by David Limbaugh. Wheaton, Ill.: Good News Publishers—Crossway Books, 2004.

Geivett, R. Douglas. "The Evidential Value of Miracles." In *In Defense of Miracles: A Comprehensive Case for God's Action in History*, ed. R. Douglas Geivett and Gary R. Habermas, 178-95. Downers Grove, Ill.: InterVarsity, 1997.

_____. *Evil and the Evidence for God: The Challenge of John Hick's Theodicy.* Afterword by John Hick. Philadelphia: Temple University Press, 1993.

_____. ""The *Kalam* Cosmological Argument." In *To Everyone an Answer: A Case for the Christian Worldview: Essays in Honor of Norman L. Geisler*, ed. Francis J. Beckwith, William Lane Craig, and J. P. Moreland, 61-76. Downers Grove, Ill.: InterVarsity Press, 2004.

Geivett, R. Douglas, and Brendan Sweetman, eds. *Contemporary Perspectives on Religious Epistemology.* New York and Oxford: Oxford University Press, 1992.

Geivett, R. Douglas, and Gary R. Habermas, eds. *In Defense of Miracles: A Comprehensive Case for God's Action in History.* Downers Grove, Ill.: InterVarsity, 1997.

George, Timothy. *Theology of the Reformers.* Nashville: Broadman, 1985.

Gerrish, B. A. *Grace and Reason: A Study in the Theology of Luther.* Oxford: Clarendon, 1962.

Gerstner, John H. *The Rational Biblical Theology of Jonathon Edwards*, Vol. 1. Powhatan, Va.: Berea Publications, and Orlando, Fla.: Ligonier Ministries, 1991.

_____. "Warfield's Case for Biblical Inerrancy." In *God's Inerrant Word: An International Symposium on the Trustworthiness of Scripture*, ed. John Warwick Montgomery, 115-142. Minneapolis: Bethany House, 1974.

Gilson, Étienne. *The Christian Philosophy of St. Augustine.* Translated by L. E. M. Lynch. New York: Random House, 1960.

_____. *The Christian Philosophy of St. Thomas Aquinas.* Translated by L. K. Shook. New York: Random House, 1956.

_____. *Reason and Revelation in the Middle Ages.* New York: Scribner, 1938.

Given, Mark D. "Not Either/Or but Both/And in Paul's Areopagus Speech." *Biblical Interpretation* 3 (1995): 356-372.

Gooch, Paul W. *Partial Knowledge: Philosophical Studies in Paul*. Notre Dame, Ind.: University of Notre Dame Press, 1987.

Gootjes, N. H. "The Sense of Divinity: A Critical Examination of the Views of Calvin and Demarest." *Westminster Theological Journal* 48 (1986): 337-350.

Gornall, Thomas. *Philosophy of God: The Elements of Thomist Natural Theology*. Oxford: Blackwell; London: Darton, Longman & Todd, 1962.

Goud, Johan F. "Origen (185-254)." In *Bringing into Captivity Every Thought: Capita Selecta in the History of Christian Evaluations of Non-Christian Philosophy*, ed. Jacob Klapwijk, Sander Griffioen, and Gerben Groenewoud, 29-47. Christian Studies Today. Lanham, Md.: University Press of America, 1991.

Grant, Robert M. *Greek Apologists of the Second Century*. Philadelphia: Westminster, 1988.

Grave, S. A. "Able and Fair Reasoning of Butler's *Analogy*." *Church History* 47 (1978): 298-307.

_____. "Reid, Thomas." In *The Encyclopedia of Philosophy*, ed. Paul Edwards, 7:118-121. New York: Macmillan and Free Press, 1967.

_____. *The Scottish Philosophy of Common Sense*. Oxford: Clarendon, 1960.

Green, Michael, and Alister McGrath. *How Shall We Reach Them? Defending and Communicating the Christian Faith to Nonbelievers*. Nashville: Nelson, Oliver-Nelson, 1995.

Greenleaf, Simon. *The Testimony of the Evangelists*. New York: James Cockcroft, 1874.

Gregory, Thomas M. "Apologetics before and after Butler." In *Pressing Toward the Mark: Essays Commemorating Fifty Years of the Orthodox Presbyterian Church*, ed. Charles G. Dennison and Richard C. Gamble, 351-367. Philadelphia: Committee for the Historian of the Orthodox Presbyterian Church, 1986.

Grier, James M., Jr. "The Apologetic Value of the Self-Witness of Scripture." *Grace Theological Journal* 1 (1980): 71-76.

Grislis, Egil. "Calvin's Use of Cicero in the Institutes I:1-5—A Case Study in Theological Method." In *The Organizational Structure of Calvin's Theology*, ed. Richard C. Gamble, 1-33. Articles on Calvin and Calvinism 7. New York: Garland Publishing, 1992. Reprinted from *Archiv fur Reformationsgeschichte* 62 (1971): 5-37.

Groothuis, Douglas R. "Are All Bets Off? A Defense of Pascal's Wager." *Philosophia Christi* 3 (2001).

_____. "Are Theistic Arguments Religiously Useless? A Pascalian Objection Examined." *Trinity Journal* NS 15 (1994): 147-61.

_____. *On Pascal*. Belmont, Calif.: Wadsworth, 2002.

_____. "Proofs, Pride, and Incarnation: Is Natural Theology Theologically Taboo?" *Journal of the Evangelical Theological Society* 38 (1995): 67-76.

_____. "To Prove or Not to Prove: Pascal on Natural Theology." Ph.D. diss. University of Oregon, 1993.

_____. *Truth Decay: Defending Christianity against the Challenges of Postmodernism.* Downers Grove, Ill.: InterVarsity, 2000.

_____. "An Unwarranted Farewell to Pascal's Wager: A Reply to Alan Carter," *Philosophia Christi* 4 (2002).

Guerra, Anthony J. "Polemical Christianity: Tertullian's Search for Certainty." *Second Century* 8 (1991): 109-123.

Habermas, Gary R. *Dealing with Doubt.* Chicago: Moody, 1990.

_____. "Evidential Apologetics." In *Five Views on Apologetics*, edited by Steven B. Cowan, 92-121. Grand Rapids: Zondervan, 2000.

_____. "Greg Bahnsen, John Warwick Montgomery, and Evidential Apologetics." *Global Journal of Classical Theology* 3, 1 (March 2002). Accessed online at < http://www.trinitysem.edu/journal/toc_v3n1.html >.

_____. *The Historical Jesus: Ancient Evidence for the Life of Christ.* Joplin, Mo.: College Press, 1996.

_____. "Paradigm Shift: A Challenge to Naturalism." *Bibliotheca Sacra* 146 (1989): 437-50.

_____. "The Personal Testimony of the Holy Spirit to the Believer and Christian Apologetics." *Journal of Christian Apologetics* 1 (1997): 49-64.

_____. "The Resurrection Appearances of Jesus." In *In Defense of Miracles: A Comprehensive Case for God's Action in History*, ed. R. Douglas Geivett and Gary R. Habermas, 262-275. Downers Grove, Ill.: InterVarsity, 1997.

_____. "Resurrection Claims in Other Religions." *Religious Studies* 25 (1989): 167-177.

_____. *The Resurrection of Jesus: An Apologetic.* Grand Rapids: Baker, 1980.

Habermas, Gary R., and Antony G. N. Flew. *Did Jesus Rise from the Dead? The Resurrection Debate.* Edited by Terry L. Miethe. San Francisco: Harper & Row, 1987.

Habermas, Gary R., and Michael R. Licona. *The Case for the Resurrection of Jesus.* Grand Rapids: Kregel, 2004.

Habermas, Gary R., and J. P. Moreland. *Immortality: The Other Side of Death.* Chicago: Moody, 1991.

Hackett, Stuart C. *The Reconstruction of the Christian Revelation Claim: A Philosophical and Critical Apologetic.* Grand Rapids: Baker, 1984.

_____. *The Resurrection of Theism: Prolegomena to Christian Apology*, 2nd ed. Grand Rapids: Baker, 1982.

Hagopian, David G., ed. *The Genesis Debate: Three Views on the Days of Creation.* Foreword by Norman L. Geisler. Mission Viejo, Calif.: Crux Press, 2001.

Hakkenberg, Michael A. "The Battle over the Ordination of Gordon H. Clark." In *Pressing Toward the Mark: Essays Commemorating Fifty Years of the Orthodox Presbyterian Church*, ed.

Charles G. Dennison and Richard C. Gamble, 329-350. Philadelphia: Committee for the Historian of the Orthodox Presbyterian Church, 1986.

Halsey, Jim S. *For a Time Such as This: An Introduction to the Reformed Apologetic of Cornelius Van Til.* Phillipsburg, N.J.: Presbyterian & Reformed, 1978.

Halverson, William H. *A Concise Introduction to Philosophy.* 3rd ed. New York: Random House, 1976.

Hammond, Nicholas. *The Cambridge Companion to Pascal.* Cambridge Companions to Religion. New York and Cambridge: Cambridge University Press, 2003.

Hankey, W. J. *God in Himself: Aquinas' Doctrine of God as Expounded in the "Summa Theologiae."* New York: Oxford University Press, 1987.

Hannay, Alastair, and Gordon D. Morino, eds. *The Cambridge Companion to Kierkegaard.* Cambridge Companions to Philosophy. Cambridge and New York: Cambridge University Press, 1998.

Hanna, Mark M. *Crucial Questions in Apologetics.* Grand Rapids: Baker, 1981.

Hare, John E. "The Problem of Evil." In *Evidence for Faith: Deciding the God Question,* ed. John Warwick Montgomery, 231-52. Cornell Symposium on Evidential Apologetics, 1986. Dallas: Probe Books, 1991; distributed by Word Publishing.

Hart, Hendrik, Johan Van der Hoeven, and Nicholas Wolterstorff, eds. *Rationality in the Calvinian Tradition.* Christian Studies Today. Lanham, Md.: University Press of America, 1983.

Hart, Trevor. "A Capacity for Ambiguity? The Barth-Brunner Debate Revisited." *Tyndale Bulletin* 44 (1993): 289-305.

Hartshorne, Charles. *Anselm's Discovery: A Re-examination of the Ontological Proof for God's Existence.* La Salle, Ill.: Open Court, 1965.

Harvey, Van A. *A Handbook of Theological Terms.* New York: Macmillan, 1964.

Hauck, Robert J. "They Saw What They Saw: Sense Knowledge in Early Christian Polemic." *Harvard Theological Review* 81 (1988): 239-249.

Haught, John. *Science and Religion: From Conflict to Conversation.* Mahwah, N.J.: Paulist, 1995.

Hazen, Craig. "'Ever Hearing but Never Understanding': A Response to Mark Hutchins's Critique of John Warwick Montgomery's Historical Apologetics." *Global Journal of Classical Theology* 3, 1 (March 2002). Accessed online at < http://www.trinitysem.edu/journal/toc_v3n1.html >.

Helm, Paul. "John Calvin: The *Sensus Divinitatis,* and the Noetic Effects of Sin." *International Journal for Philosophy of Religion* 43 (1998): 87-108.

_____. "Thomas Reid, Common Sense and Calvinism." In *Rationality in the Calvinian Tradition,* ed. Hendrik Hart, Johan van der Hoeven, and Nicholas Wolterstorff, 71-89. Christian Studies Today. Lanham, Md.: University Press of America, 1983.

Helseth, Paul K. "The Apologetical Tradition of the OPC: A Reconsideration." *Westminster Theological Journal* 60 (1998): 109-29.

_____. "B. B. Warfield's Apologetical Appeal to 'Right Reason': Evidence of a 'Rather Bald Rationalism'?" *Scottish Journal of Theology* 16 (1998): 156-77.

_____. "J. Gresham Machen and 'True Science': Machen's Apologetical Continuity with Old Princeton's Right Use of Reason," *Premise* 5, 1 (1998). Found online 10/27/2005 at < http://homepage.mac.com/shanerosenthal/reformationink/pkhmachen.htm >. Longer version of "Apologetical Tradition of the OPC."

Henderson, R. D. "How Abraham Kuyper Became a Kuyperian." *Christian Scholar's Review* 22 (1992): 22-35.

Henry, Carl F. H. *Confessions of a Theologian*. Waco, Tex.: Word, 1986.

_____. *God, Revelation, and Authority*. 6 vols. Waco, Tex.: Word, 1976-1983.

Hereen, Fred. *Show Me God: What the Message from Space Is Telling Us about God*. Wonders That Witness, vol. 1. Wheeling, Ill.: Searchlight Publications, 1995.

Heslam, Peter S. *Creating a Christian Worldview: Abraham Kuyper's Lectures on Calvinism*. Grand Rapids and Cambridge, U.K.: Eerdmans; Carlisle: Paternoster Press, 1998.

Hick, John, and Arthur C. McGill, eds. *The Many-Faced Argument: Recent Studies on the Ontological Argument for the Existence of God*. London: Macmillan, 1968.

Hicks, Peter. *The Philosophy of Charles Hodge: A Nineteenth Century Evangelical Approach to Reason, Knowledge, and Truth*. Studies in American Religion, vol. 65. Lewiston, N.Y.: Edwin Mellen Press, 1997.

Hillman, Dennis Roy. "The Use of Basic Issues in Apologetics from Selected New Testament Apologies." Th.M. thesis. Dallas Theological Seminary, 1979.

Himmelstrup, Jens. *Søren Kierkegaard: International Bibliography*. Copenhagen: Nyt Nordisk Forlag, 1962.

Hodge, Archibald Alexander, and Benjamin B. Warfield. "Inspiration." *Presbyterian Review* 6 (April 1881): 225-260.

Hodge, Charles. *Systematic Theology*, 3 vols. Reprint, Grand Rapids: Eerdmans, 1981. Originally published 1875.

Hoehner, Harold W. *Chronological Aspects of the Life of Christ*. Grand Rapids: Zondervan, 1978.

Hoeksema, Herman. *The Clark–Van Til Controversy*. Jefferson, Md.: Trinity Foundation, 1995.

Hoffecker, W. Andrew. *Piety and the Princeton Theologians: Archibald Alexander, Charles Hodge, and Benjamin Warfield*. Grand Rapids: Baker, 1981.

Hoitenga, Dewey J., Jr. *Faith and Reason from Plato to Plantinga: An Introduction to Reformed Epistemology*. Albany: State University of New York Press, 1991.

_____. "The Noetic Effects of Sin: A Review Article." *Calvin Theological Journal* 38 (2003): 68-102.

Honderich, Ted. *Butler*. Arguments of the Philosophers. New York: Routledge & Kegan Paul, 1986.

Honer, Stanley M., and Thomas C. Hunt. *Invitation to Philosophy: Issues and Options*. 4th ed. Belmont, Calif.: Wadsworth, 1982.

Hoover, Arlie J. *The Case for Christian Theism*. Grand Rapids: Baker, 1976.

Hopkins, Jasper. *A Companion to the Study of St. Anselm*. Minneapolis: University of Minnesota Press, 1972.

Horton, Michael Scott. "Legal Rather than Evangelical Knowledge: Calvin on the Limits of Natural Theology." *Modern Reformation Journal* 7, no. 1 (1998): 28-31.

House, H. Wayne. "The Value of Reason in Luther's View of Apologetics." *Concordia Journal* 7 (1981): 65-67.

Howard-Snyder, Daniel. "God, Evil, and Suffering." In *Reason for the Hope Within*, ed. Michael J. Murray, 76-115. Grand Rapids, and Cambridge, U.K.: Eerdmans, 1999.

Howe, Frederic R. *Challenge and Response: A Handbook of Christian Apologetics*. Grand Rapids: Zondervan, 1982.

Hughes, Philip Edgecumbe, ed. *Creative Minds in Contemporary Theology*. 2nd ed. Grand Rapids: Eerdmans, 1969.

Hume, David. *An Enquiry Concerning Human Understanding*. 3rd ed. Revised by P. H. Nidditch. Oxford: Clarendon, 1975. Originally published 1777.

Hutchens, Steven Mark. "Knowing and Being in the Context of the Fundamentalist Dilemma: A Comparative Study of the Thought of Karl Barth and Carl F. H. Henry." Th.D. diss. Lutheran School of Theology at Chicago, 1989.

Hutchison, John C. "Darwin's Evolutionary Theory and 19th-Century Natural Theology." *Bibliotheca Sacra* 152 (1995): 334-54.

Jaki, Stanley L. *God and the Cosmologists*. Washington, D.C.: Regnery Gateway, 1989.

Jastrow, Robert. *God and the Astronomers*. New York: Norton, 1978.

Jenkins, John I. *Knowledge and Faith in Thomas Aquinas*. Cambridge and New York: Cambridge University Press, 1997.

Johnson, Phillip E. *Darwin on Trial*. Washington, D.C.: Regnery Gateway, 1991.

Jones, Charles Andrews, III. "Charles Hodge, the Keeper of Orthodoxy: The Method, Purpose and Meaning of His Apologetic." Ph.D. diss., Drew University, 1989.

Jones, Timothy Paul. "John Calvin and the Problem of Philosophical Apologetics." *Perspectives in Religious Studies* 23 (1996): 387–403.

Jorgensen, Aage, and Stephane Hogue. "Søren Kierkegaard Literature 1881-1981: A Bibliography." *Kierkegaardiana* 16 (1993).

Kalbeek, L. *Contours of a Christian Philosophy: An Introduction to Herman Dooyeweerd's Thought*, ed. Bernard Zylstra and Josina Zylstra. Toronto: Wedge, 1975.

Kant, Immanuel. *Critique of Pure Reason.* Translated by J. M. D. Meiklejohn. Great Books of the Western World, vol. 42, 1-250. Chicago: Encyclopaedia Britannica, 1952.

_____. *Critique of Pure Reason.* Translated by Norman Kemp Smith. New York: St. Martin's Press, 1965.

Kegley, Charles W., and Robert W. Bretall, eds. *Reinhold Niebuhr: His Religious, Social, and Political Thought.* New York: Macmillan, 1956; reprint, New York: Pilgrim Press, 1984.

Keith, Alexander. *Evidence of the Truth of the Christian Religion Derived from the Literal Fulfillment of Prophecy,* 6th ed. New York: Harper, 1841.

Keith, Graham A. "Justin Martyr and Religious Exclusivism." *Tyndale Bulletin* 43 (1992): 57-80.

Kenny, Anthony. *The Five Ways: St. Thomas Aquinas' Proofs of God's Existence.* New York: Schocken, 1969. Reprint, Notre Dame, Ind.: University of Notre Dame Press, 1980.

_____, ed. *Aquinas: A Collection of Critical Essays.* Modern Studies in Philosophy. Notre Dame, Ind.: University of Notre Dame Press, 1976.

Kierkegaard, Søren. *Concluding Unscientific Postscript to "Philosophical Fragments,"* vol. 1, *Text,* ed. Howard V. Hong and Edna H. Hong. Princeton, N.J.: Princeton University Press, 1992.

_____. *The Essential Kierkegaard,* ed. Howard V. Hong and Edna H. Hong. Princeton: Princeton University Press, 2000.

_____. *On Authority and Revelation,* trans. Walter Lowrie. Princeton, N.J.: Princeton University Press, 1955.

_____. *A Kierkegaard Anthology,* ed. Robert Bretall. Princeton, N.J.: Princeton University Press, 1946.

_____. *Philosophical Fragments; Johannes Climacus,* ed. and trans. Howard V. Hong and Edna H. Hong. Princeton, N.J.: Princeton University Press, 1985.

_____. *The Point of View for My Work as an Author.* In *A Kierkegaard Anthology,* ed. Robert Bretall. Princeton, N.J.: Princeton University Press, 1946.

_____. *Søren Kierkegaard's Journals and Papers,* ed. Howard V. Hong and Edna H. Hong. 7 vols. Bloomington: Indiana University Press, 1967-1978.

Kilgallen, John J. "Acts 17:22-31: An Example of Interreligious Dialogue." *Studia Missionalia* 43 (1994): 43-60.

Kirmmse, Bruce. *Kierkegaard in Golden Age Denmark.* Bloomington and Indianapolis: Indiana University Press, 1990.

Klapwijk, Jacob. "Antithesis and Common Grace." In *Bringing into Captivity Every Thought:* Capita Selecta *in the History of Christian Evaluations of Non-Christian Philosophy,* ed. Jacob Klapwijk, Sander Griffioen, and Gerben Groenewoud, 169-90. Christian Studies Today. Lanham, Md.: University Press of America, 1991.

_____. "Rationality in the Dutch Neo-Calvinist Tradition." In *Rationality in the Calvinian Tradition*, ed. Hendrik Hart, Johan van der Hoeven, and Nicholas Wolterstorff, 93-111. Christian Studies Today. Lanham, Md.: University Press of America, 1983.

Klemke, E. D. *Studies in the Philosophy of Kierkegaard*. The Hague: Martinus Nijhoff, 1976.

Klooster, Fred H. *The Incomprehensibility of God in the Orthodox Presbyterian Conflict*. Franeker: T. Wever, 1951.

_____. *The Significance of Barth's Theology: An Appraisal with Special Reference to Election and Reconciliation*. Grand Rapids: Baker, 1961.

Knudsen, Robert D. "Apologetics and History." In *Life Is Religion: Essays in Honor of H. Evan Runner*, ed. Henry Vander Goot, 119-33. Saint Catharines, Ont.: Paideia Press, 1981.

_____. "Progressive and Regressive Tendencies in Christian Apologetics." In *Jerusalem and Athens: Critical Discussions on the Philosophy and Apologetics of Cornelius Van Til*, edited by E. R. Geehan, 275-298. Nutley, N.J.: Presbyterian & Reformed, 1971.

Kobes, Wayne A. "Sphere Sovereignty and the University: Theological Foundations of Abraham Kuyper's View of the University and Its Role in Society." Ph.D. diss., Florida State University, 1993.

Koivisto, Rex A. "Clark Pinnock and Inerrancy: A Change in Truth Theory?" *Journal of the Evangelical Theological Society* 24 (1981): 138-151.

Kooi, Cornelis van der. *As in a Mirror: John Calvin and Karl Barth on Knowing God: A Diptych*, trans. Donald Mader. Studies in the History of Christian Traditions 120. Leiden: Brill, 2005.

Koons, Robert C. "Faith, Probability and Infinite Passion: Ramseyian Decision Theory and Kierkegaard's Account of Christian Faith." *Faith and Philosophy* 10 (1993): 145-160. Accessed online at < http://www.utexas.edu/cola/depts/philosophy/faculty/koons/kierk.pdf >.

Krailsheimer, A. J. *Pascal*. Past Masters. New York: Hill & Wang, 1980.

Kreeft, Peter. *Between Heaven and Hell: A Dialog Somewhere Beyond Death with John F. Kennedy, C. S. Lewis and Aldous Huxley*. Downers Grove, Ill.: InterVarsity, 1982.

_____. *C. S. Lewis for the Third Millennium: Six Essays on "The Abolition of Man."* San Francisco: Ignatius, 1994.

_____. *Christianity for Modern Pagans: Pascal's Pensées Edited, Outlined, and Explained*. San Francisco: Ignatius Press, 1993.

_____. *Fundamentals of the Faith*. San Francisco: Ignatius, 1988.

_____. "Introduction: Why Debate the Existence of God?" In *Does God Exist? The Great Debate*, by J. P. Moreland and Kai Nielsen. Nashville: Thomas Nelson, 1993.

_____. *Making Sense Out of Suffering*. Ann Arbor: Servant, 1986.

_____. *Socrates Meets Jesus*. Downers Grove, Ill.: InterVarsity, 1987. Reprinted with new introduction, 2002.

_____. *A Summa of the "Summa": The Essential Philosophical Passages of St. Thomas Aquinas' "Summa Theologica" Edited and Explained for Beginners*. San Francisco: Ignatius, 1990.

_____. *Yes or No?* 2nd ed. San Francisco: Ignatius, 1991.

Kreeft, Peter, and Ronald K. Tacelli. *Handbook of Christian Apologetics: Hundreds of Answers to Crucial Questions*. Downers Grove, Ill.: InterVarsity, 1994.

Kretzmann, Norman. "Faith Seeks, Understanding Finds: Augustine's Charter for Christian Philosophy." In *Christian Philosophy,* ed. Thomas P. Flint, 1-36. Notre Dame, Ind.: University of Notre Dame Press, 1988.

_____, and Eleonore Stump, eds. *The Cambridge Companion to Aquinas*. Cambridge and New York: Cambridge University Press, 1993.

Kuhn, Thomas S. *The Structure of Scientific Revolutions*, 2nd ed. Chicago: University of Chicago Press, 1970.

Kuyper, Abraham. *Abraham Kuyper: A Centennial Reader*, ed. James D. Bratt. Grand Rapids: Eerdmans, 1998.

_____. *De Gemeene Gratie*, 2nd ed., 3 vols. Kampen: J. H. Kok, 1931, 1932.

_____. *Lectures on Calvinism*. Grand Rapids: Eerdmans, 1931.

_____. *Principles of Sacred Theology*. Grand Rapids: Eerdmans, 1968. Reprint of *Encyclopedia of Sacred Theology: Its Principles*, trans. Hendrik De Vries. Introduction by B. B. Warfield. New York: Scribner, 1898.

_____. *The Work of the Holy Spirit*, trans. with notes by Henri De Vries. New York: Funk & Wagnalls, 1900; Chattanooga: AMG Publishers, 1995.

La Croix, Richard R. *Proslogion II and III: A Third Interpretation of Anselm's Argument*. Leiden: E. J. Brill, 1972.

Laoye, John Anjola. "Augustine's Apologetic Use of the Old Testament as Reflected Especially in the 'De Civitate Dei.'" Th.D. diss., Southern Baptist Theological Seminary, 1972.

Lapointe, Francois, comp. *Søren Kierkegaard and His Critics: An International Bibliography of Criticism*. Westport, Conn.: Greenwood, 1980.

Leffel, Jim. "Our New Challenge: Postmodernism." In *The Death of Truth*, ed. Dennis McCallum. Minneapolis: Bethany House, 1996.

Lehrer, Keith. *Thomas Reid*. Arguments of the Philosophers. London and New York: Routledge, 1989.

Leftow, Brian. "The Ontological Argument." In *The Oxford Handbook of Philosophy of Religion*, ed. William J. Wainwright, 80-115. Oxford and New York: Oxford University Press, 2005.

Lewis, C. S. *The Abolition of Man*. New York: Macmillan, 1947.

_____. *Christian Reflections*, ed. Walter Hooper. Grand Rapids: Eerdmans, 1967.

_____. *The Chronicles of Narnia*. 7 vols. New York: Macmillan, 1950-1956.

_____. *God in the Dock: Essays on Theology and Ethics*. Edited by Walter Hooper. Grand Rapids: Eerdmans, 1970.

_____. *Letters of C. S. Lewis*, ed. W. H. Lewis. London: Geoffrey Bles, 1966.

_____. *Mere Christianity*. Rev. and enlarged ed. New York: Macmillan, 1960.

_____. *Miracles: A Preliminary Study*. 2nd ed. New York: Macmillan, 1960.

_____. "On Obstinacy in Belief." In *The World's Last Night and Other Essays*, 13-30. New York: Harcourt, Brace & World, 1960.

_____. *Out of the Silent Planet*. New York: Macmillan, 1943.

_____. *Perelandra*. New York: Macmillan, 1944.

_____. *The Pilgrim's Regress: An Allegorical Apology for Christianity*. Grand Rapids: Eerdmans, 1933; rev. ed., New York: Sheed & Ward, 1944.

_____. *The Problem of Pain*. London: Centenary Press, 1940; New York: Macmillan, 1943; paperback ed., 1962.

_____. *Of Other Worlds: Essays and Stories*, ed. Walter Hooper. New York: Harcourt, Brace & World, 1966.

_____. *Surprised by Joy: The Shape of My Early Life*. London: Geoffrey Bles, 1955; New York: Harcourt, Brace & World, 1956.

_____. *That Hideous Strength*. New York: Macmillan, 1946.

_____. *The Weight of Glory and Other Addresses*. Grand Rapids: Eerdmans, 1949; New York: Collier, 1980.

Lewis, Gordon R. "Faith and Reason in the Thought of St. Augustine." Ph.D. diss. Syracuse University, 1959.

_____. "Schaeffer's Apologetic Method." In *Reflections on Francis Schaeffer*, ed. Ronald W. Ruegsegger, 69-104. Grand Rapids: Zondervan, 1986.

_____. *Testing Christianity's Truth Claims: Approaches to Christian Apologetics*. Chicago: Moody, 1976.

Lincoln, Andrew T. *Truth on Trial: The Lawsuit Motif in the Fourth Gospel*. Peabody, MA: Hendrickson, 2001.

Lindskoog, Kathryn. *Journey into Narnia*. Pasadena, Calif.: Hope Publishing, 1997.

Lindsley, Art. *C. S. Lewis's Case for Christ: Insights from Reason, Imagination and Faith*. Downers Grove, Ill.: InterVarsity, 2005.

Linton, Irwin H. *A Lawyer Examines the Bible*. Grand Rapids: Baker, 1943.

Littell, Franklin Hamlin, ed. *Reformation Studies: Essays in Honor of Roland H. Bainton*. Richmond: John Knox, 1962.

Livingstone, David N. *Darwin's Forgotten Defenders: The Encounter between Evangelical Theology and Evolutionary Thought*. Grand Rapids: Eerdmans; Edinburgh: Scottish Academic Press, 1987.

_____. "Science and Religion: Towards a New Cartography." *Christian Scholar's Review* 26 (1997): 270-92.

Litwak, Kenneth D. "Israel's Prophets Meet Athens' Philosophers: Scriptural Echoes in Acts 17:22-31." *Biblica* 85 (2004): 199-216.

Livingstone, William D. "The Princeton Apologetic as Exemplified by the Work of Benjamin B. Warfield and J. Gresham Machen: A Study in Modern American Theology, 1880-1930." Ph.D. diss., Yale University, 1948.

Locke, John. *An Essay Concerning Human Understanding*. Great Books of the Western World, vol. 35, 83-395. Chicago: Encyclopaedia Britannica, 1952. Originally published 1689.

_____. *The Reasonableness of Christianity: As Delivered in the Scriptures*, edited by John C. Higgins-Biddle. Clarendon Edition of the Works of John Locke. Oxford and New York: Oxford University Press, 1998. Originally published 1695.

Lønning, Per. *The Dilemma of Contemporary Theology: Prefigured in Luther, Pascal, Kierkegaard, Nietzsche*. Oslo: Universitetsforlaget, 1962; New York: Humanities Press, 1964.

Lowrie, Walter. *Kierkegaard*. 2 vols. New York: Harper, 1962.

Luther, Martin. *Luther's Works*. 56 vols. St. Louis: Concordia; Philadelphia: Fortress, 1955-1986.

_____. *Table Talk*. London: H. G. Bonn, 1857.

Macbeth, Norman. *Darwin Retried: An Appeal to Reason*. Boston: Gambit, 1971.

MacDonald, A. J. *Authority and Reason in the Early Middle Ages*. Hulsean Lectures 1931-32. London: Oxford University Press, 1933.

MacDonald, Neil B. *Karl Barth and the Strange New World within the Bible: Barth, Wittgenstein, and the Metadilemmas of the Enlightenment*. Paternoster Biblical and Theological Monographs. Milton Keynes, U.K.: Paternoster, 2002.

Maclachan, Renton. "With Gentleness and Respect: The Implications for Christian Apologetics of Some Passages from 1 Peter." *Stimulus* 4 (Fall 1996): 30-33.

Manweiler, Robert W. "The Destruction of Tyre." In *The Evidence of Prophecy*, ed. Robert C. Newman, 21-30. Hatfield, Pa.: Biblical Research Institute, 1994.

Mare, W. Harold. "Pauline Appeals to Historical Evidence." *Bulletin of the Evangelical Theological Society* 11 (1968): 121-130.

Marsden, George M. *Reforming Fundamentalism: Fuller Seminary and the New Evangelicalism*. Grand Rapids: Eerdmans, 1987.

Martin, C. F. J. *Thomas Aquinas: God and Explanations*. Edinburgh: Edinburgh University Press, 1997.

Martin, Terence. *The Instructed Vision: Scottish Common Sense Philosophy and the Origins of American Fiction*. Indiana University Humanities, vol. 48. Bloomington: Indiana University Press, 1961; reprint, New York: Kraus Reprint, 1969.

Mauck, John W. *Paul on Trial: The Book of Acts as a Defense of Christianity*. Nashville: Thomas Nelson—Nelson Reference, 2001.

Mayers, Ronald B. *Balanced Apologetics: Using Evidences and Presuppositions in Defense of the Faith*. Grand Rapids: Kregel, 1996. Reprint of *Both/And: A Balanced Apologetic*. Chicago: Moody, 1984.

McClanahan, James Samuel, Jr. "Benjamin B. Warfield: Historian of Doctrine in Defense of Orthodoxy, 1881-1921." Ph.D. diss., Union Theological Seminary [Richmond], 1988.

McCloskey, Patrick L., and Ronald L. Schoenberg. *Criminal Law Advocacy*, vol. 5. New York: Matthew Bender, 1984.

McCormack, Bruce L. "The Being of Holy Scripture Is in Becoming: Karl Barth in Conversation with American Evangelical Criticism." In *Evangelicals & Scripture: Tradition, Authority and Hermeneutics*, ed. Vincent Bacote, Laura C. Miguélez, and Dennis L. Ockholm, 55-75. Downers Grove, Ill.: InterVarsity, 2004.

_____. *Karl Barth's Critically Realistic Dialectical Theology: Its Genesis and Development, 1909-1936*. Oxford: Clarendon, 1995.

McDowell, Josh. *Evidence that Demands a Verdict*. San Bernardino, Calif.: Campus Crusade for Christ, 1972.

McGoldrick, James E. *God's Renaissance Man: Abraham Kuyper*. Darlington, U.K., and Webster, N.Y.: Evangelical Press, 2000.

McGrath, Alister E. *The Intellectual Origins of the European Reformation*. Oxford: Blackwell, 1987.

_____. *Intellectuals Don't Need God and Other Modern Myths: Building Bridges to Faith Through Apologetics*. Grand Rapids: Zondervan, 1993.

_____. *A Life of John Calvin: A Study in the Shaping of Western Culture*. Oxford: Blackwell, 1990.

McKim, Donald K., ed. *The Cambridge Companion to John Calvin*. Cambridge Companions to Religion. New York: Cambridge University Press, 2004.

_____, ed. *The Cambridge Companion to Martin Luther*. Cambridge Companions to Religion. New York and Cambridge: Cambridge University Press, 2003.

_____, ed. *How Karl Barth Changed My Mind*. Grand Rapids: Eerdmans, 1986.

_____, ed. *Readings in Calvin's Theology*. Grand Rapids: Baker, 1984.

McLaren, Brian D. *Finding Faith: A Self-Discovery Guide for Your Spiritual Quest*. Grand Rapids: Zondervan, 1999.

Meek, Esther L. "A Polanyian Interpretation of Calvin's *Sensus Divinitatis*." *Presbyterion* 23 (1997): 8-24.

Meeter, John E., and Roger Nicole. *A Bibliography of Benjamin Breckinridge Warfield*. Nutley, N.J.: Presbyterian & Reformed, 1974.

Middleton, J. Richard, and Brian J. Walsh. *Truth Is Stranger Than It Used to Be: Biblical Faith in a Postmodern Age*. Downers Grove, Ill.: InterVarsity, 1995.

Miethe, Terry L. *A Christian's Guide to Faith and Reason*. Minneapolis: Bethany House, 1987.

Miethe, Terry L., comp. *Augustinian Bibliography, 1970-1980: With Essays on the Fundamentals of Augustinian Scholarship*. Westport, Conn.: Greenwood, 1982.

Miethe, Terry L., and Antony Flew. *Does God Exist? A Believer and an Atheist Debate*. San Francisco: Harper San Francisco, 1991.

Miethe, Terry L., and Gary R. Habermas. *Why Believe? God Exists! Rethinking the Case for God and Christianity*. Joplin, Mo.: College Press, 1993.

Miller, Ed. L., ed. *Believing in God: Readings on Faith and Reason*. Upper Saddle River, N.J.: Prentice Hall, 1996.

Miller, Mark C. "The Hipness unto Death: Søren Kierkegaard and David Letterman—Ironic Apologists to Generation X." *Mars Hill Review* 7 (Winter/Spring 1997): 38-52. Accessed online at < http://www.leaderu.com/marshill/mhr07/kierk1.html >.

Minnema, Theodore. "Reinhold Niebuhr." In *Creative Minds in Contemporary Theology*, ed. Philip E. Hughes, 377-406. 2nd rev. ed. Grand Rapids: Eerdmans, 1969.

Mohler, Richard A., Jr. "Evangelical Theology and Karl Barth: Representative Models of Response." Ph.D. diss. Southern Baptist Theological Seminary, 1989.

Montgomery, John Warwick. "Clark's Philosophy of History." In *The Philosophy of Gordon H. Clark*, ed. Ronald H. Nash. Philadelphia: Presbyterian & Reformed, 1968.

_____. "Editor's Introduction." Special Issue: John Warwick Montgomery's Apologetic. *Global Journal of Classical Theology* 3, 1 (March 2002), online at < http://www.trinity-sem.edu/journal/jwm_intro_v3n1.html >.

_____. "Existence of God." In *Sensible Christianity*. Santa Ana, Calif.: One Way Library, 1976.

_____. *Faith Founded on Fact: Essays in Evidential Apologetics*. Nashville: Thomas Nelson, 1978.

_____. *History and Christianity*. Downers Grove, Ill.: InterVarsity, 1971; reprint, Minneapolis: Bethany House, 1986.

_____. *How Do We Know There Is a God?* Minneapolis: Bethany Fellowship, 1973.

_____. "Introduction: The Apologists of Eucatastrophe." In *Myth, Allegory, and Gospel: An Interpretation of J. R. R. Tolkien/C. S. Lewis/G. K. Chesterton/Charles Williams*, ed. John Warwick Montgomery. Minneapolis: Bethany Fellowship, 1974.

_____. "The Jury Returns: A Juridical Defense of Christianity." In *Evidence for Faith: Deciding the God Question*, ed. Montgomery, 319-341. Cornell Symposium on Evidential Apologetics, 1986. Dallas: Probe Books, 1991; distributed by Word Publishing.

_____. *The Shape of the Past: A Christian Response to Secular Philosophies of History.* Minneapolis: Bethany Fellowship, 1962; reprint, 1975.

_____. *The Suicide of Christian Theology.* Minneapolis: Bethany Fellowship, 1970.

_____. *Where Is History Going? Essays in Support of the Historical Truth of the Christian Revelation.* Minneapolis: Bethany Fellowship, 1969.

_____, ed. *Christianity for the Tough-minded: Essays in Support of an Intellectually Defensible Religious Commitment.* Minneapolis: Bethany Fellowship, 1973.

_____, ed. *Evidence for Faith: Deciding the God Question*, Cornell Symposium on Evidential Apologetics, 1986. Dallas: Probe Books, 1991; distributed by Word Publishing.

_____, ed. *Jurisprudence: A Book of Readings.* Strasbourg, France: International Scholarly Publishers, 1974.

_____, ed. Special Issue: John Warwick Montgomery's Apologetic. *Global Journal of Classical Theology* 3, 1 (March 2002), online at < http://www.trinitysem.edu/journal/ jwm_intro_v3n1.html >.

Moreland, J. P. *Christianity and the Nature of Science.* Grand Rapids: Baker, 1989.

_____. "Kuhn's Epistemology: A Paradigm Afloat." *Bulletin of the Evangelical Philosophical Society* 4 (1981): 33-60.

_____. *Scaling the Secular City: A Defense of Christianity.* Grand Rapids: Baker, 1987.

_____. "Science, Miracles, Agency Theory, and the God-of-the-Gaps." In *In Defense of Miracles: A Comprehensive Case for God's Action in History*, ed. R. Douglas Geivett and Gary R. Habermas, 132-148. Downers Grove, Ill.: InterVarsity, 1997.

_____. "The Scientific Realism Debate and the Role of Philosophy in Integration." *Bulletin of the Evangelical Theological Society* 10 (1987): 38-49.

_____. "Theistic Science and Methodological Naturalism." In *The Creation Hypothesis: Scientific Evidence for an Intelligent Designer*, ed. J. P. Moreland, 41-66. Downers Grove, Ill.: InterVarsity, 1994), 41-66.

_____., ed. *The Creation Hypothesis: Scientific Evidence for an Intelligent Designer.* Downers Grove, Ill.: InterVarsity, 1994.

Moreland, J. P., and Kai Nielsen. *Does God Exist? The Great Debate.* Nashville: Thomas Nelson, 1993.

Moreland, J. P., and William Lane Craig. *Philosophical Foundations for a Christian Worldview.* Downers Grove, Ill.: InterVarsity, 2003.

Moroney, Stephen K. *The Noetic Effects of Sin.* Lanham, Md.: Lexington Books, 2000.

Morris, Thomas V. *Francis Schaeffer's Apologetics: A Critique.* 2nd ed. Grand Rapids: Baker, 1987. Original edition, 1976.

_____. *Making Sense of It All: Pascal and the Meaning of Life.* Grand Rapids: Eerdmans, 1992.

Mossner, Ernest Campbell. *Bishop Butler and the Age of Reason: A Study in the History of Thought.* New York: Macmillan, 1936.

Mourant, John A. "The Augustinian Argument for the Existence of God." In *Inquiries into Medieval Philosophy: A Collection in Honor of Francis P. Clarke,* ed. James F. Ross, 165-184. Contributions in Philosophy, vol. 4. Westport, Conn.: Greenwood Publishing, 1971.

Mouw, Richard. "Dutch Calvinist Philosophical Influences in North America." *Calvin Theological Journal* 24 (1989): 93-120.

Muller, Richard A. *The Unaccommodated Calvin: Studies in the Foundation of a Theological Tradition.* Oxford Studies in Historical Theology. Oxford and New York: Oxford University Press, 1999.

Murray, Michael J., ed. *Reason for the Hope Within.* Grand Rapids, and Cambridge, U.K.: Eerdmans, 1999.

Nash, Ronald H. *Faith and Reason: Searching for a Rational Faith.* Grand Rapids: Zondervan, 1988.

_____. "Gordon H. Clark." In *Handbook of Evangelical Theologians,* ed. Walter A. Elwell, 182-186. Grand Rapids: Baker, 1993.

_____. *The Light of the Mind: St. Augustine's Theory of Knowledge.* Lexington: University Press of Kentucky, 1969.

_____. "Use and Abuse of History in Christian Apologetics." *Christian Scholar's Review* 1 (1971): 217-226.

_____. *Worldviews in Conflict: Choosing Christianity in a World of Ideas.* Grand Rapids: Zondervan, 1992.

_____, ed. *The Philosophy of Gordon H. Clark: A Festschrift.* Philadelphia: Presbyterian & Reformed, 1968. 2nd ed., Jefferson, Md.: Trinity Foundation, 1992.

Natoli, Charles M. "The Role of the Wager in Pascal's Apologetics." *New Scholasticism* 57 (1983): 98-106.

Neill, Stephen. *Anglicanism.* New York: Oxford University Press, 1977.

Nelson, Rudolph. *The Making and Unmaking of an Evangelical Mind: The Case of Edward Carnell.* New York: Cambridge University Press, 1988.

New American Standard Bible. La Habra, Calif.: Lockman Foundation, 1977.

Newbigin, Lesslie. *Proper Confidence: Faith, Doubt, and Certainty in Christian Discipleship.* Grand Rapids: Eerdmans, 1995.

Newman, Robert C. "The Evidence of Cosmology." In *Evidence for Faith: Deciding the God Question*, ed. John Warwick Montgomery, 71-91. Cornell Symposium on Evidential Apologetics, 1986. Dallas: Probe Books, 1991; distributed by Word Publishing.

_____. "Fulfilled Prophecy as Miracle." In *In Defense of Miracles: A Comprehensive Case for God's Action in History*, ed. R. Douglas Geivett and Gary R. Habermas, 217-221. Downers Grove, Ill.: InterVarsity, 1997.

_____. "Israel's History Written in Advance: A Neglected Evidence for the God of the Bible." In *Evidence for Faith: Deciding the God Question*, ed. John Warwick Montgomery, 193-201. Cornell Symposium on Evidential Apologetics, 1986. Dallas: Probe Books, 1991; distributed by Word Publishing.

_____. "The Testimony of Messianic Prophecy." In *Evidence for Faith: Deciding the God Question*, ed. John Warwick Montgomery, 203-214. Cornell Symposium on Evidential Apologetics, 1986. Dallas: Probe Books, 1991; distributed by Word Publishing.

_____. "The Time of the Messiah." In *The Evidence of Prophecy*, ed. Newman, 111-18. Hatfield, Pa.: Biblical Research Institute, 1994.

Nicholi, Armand M. *The Question of God: C. S. Lewis and Sigmund Freud Debate God, Love, Sex, and the Meaning of Life*. New York: Free Press, 2002.

Nichols, Aidan. *Discovering Aquinas: An Introduction to His Life, Work, and Influence*. London: Darton, Longman & Todd, 2002; Grand Rapids: Eerdmans, 2003.

Nichols, Stephen J. *Martin Luther: A Guided Tour of His Life and Thought*. Phillipsburg, N.J.: Presbyterian & Reformed, 2002.

Niebuhr, Reinhold. *Faith and History: A Comparison of Christian and Modern Views of History*. New York: Scribner, 1949.

_____. *Moral Man and Immoral Society: A Study in Ethics and Practice*. New York: Scribner, 1932.

_____. *The Nature and Destiny of Man: A Christian Interpretation*. Gifford Lectures. 2 vols. New York: Scribner, 1941, 1943.

Noebel, David A. *Understanding the Times: The Story of the Biblical Christian, Marxist/Leninist, and Secular Humanist Worldviews*. Manitou Springs, Col.: Summit Ministries, 1991.

Noll, Mark A. "B. B. Warfield." In *Handbook of Evangelical Theologians*, ed. Walter A. Elwell, 26-39. Grand Rapids: Baker, 1993.

_____, ed. *The Princeton Theology, 1812-1921: Scripture, Science, and Theological Method from Archibald Alexander to Benjamin Breckinridge Warfield*. Grand Rapids: Baker, 1983.

Noll, Mark A., and Cassandra Niemczyk. "Evangelicals and the Self-Consciously Reformed." In *The Variety of American Evangelicalism*, ed. Donald W. Dayton and Robert K. Johnston, 204-221. Knoxville: University of Tennessee Press, 1991.

North, Gary. *Foundations of Christian Scholarship: Essays in the Van Til Perspective*. Vallecito, Calif.: Ross House, 1976.

Notaro, Thom. *Van Til and the Use of Evidence*. Phillipsburg, N.J.: Presbyterian & Reformed, 1980.

Nuovo, Victor, ed. *John Locke: Writings on Religion*. Oxford and New York: Oxford University Press, 2002.

O'Connell, Marvin R. *Blaise Pascal: Reasons of the Heart*. Library of Religious Biography. Grand Rapids: Eerdmans, 1997.

O'Hara, Shelley. *Kierkegaard within Your Grasp: The First Step to Understanding Kierkegaard*. Hoboken, N.J.: Wiley, 2004.

Oberman, H. A. *Forerunners of the Reformation: The Shape of Late Medieval Thought, Illustrated by Key Documents*. New York: Holt, Rinehart & Winston, 1966.

Oliphint, Scott. "Jonathon Edwards: Reformed Apologist." *Westminster Theological Journal* 57 (1995): 165-86.

Oppy, Graham. *Ontological Arguments and Belief in God*. Cambridge and New York: Cambridge University Press, 1995.

Origen: Contra Celsum. Translated by Henry Chadwick. Corrected reprint. Cambridge: Cambridge University Press, 1980.

Orr, James. *The Christian View of God and the World*. Corrected reprint of 3rd ed. Grand Rapids: Eerdmans, 1948; Grand Rapids: Kregel, 1989. Originally published as *The Christian View of God and the World as Centering in the Incarnation*. New York: Scribner, 1897.

_____. *The Faith of a Modern Christian*. New York: Hodder & Stoughton, 1910.

_____. *The Faith that Persuades*. Reprint, New York: Harper & Row, 1977.

_____. *The Resurrection of Jesus*. London: Hodder & Stoughton, 1909; reprint, Grand Rapids: Zondervan, 1965.

_____. *The Virgin Birth of Christ*. New York: Scribner, 1907.

Osborn, Eric. *Tertullian: First Theologian of the West*. New York and Cambridge: Cambridge University Press, 1997.

Padgett, Alan G., ed. *Reason and the Christian Religion: Essays in Honour of Richard Swinburne*. Oxford: Clarendon, 1994.

Paley, William. *Natural Theology: or, Evidences of the Existence and Attributes of the Deity, Collected from the Appearances of Nature*. 1802; reprint, Houston: St. Thomas Press, 1972.

Parker, T. H. L. *Calvin: An Introduction to His Thought*. Louisville: Westminster John Knox, 1995.

Parkhurst, Louis G. *Francis Schaeffer: The Man and His Message*. Wheaton, Ill.: Tyndale, 1985.

Partee, Charles. *Calvin and Classical Philosophy*. Leiden, Netherlands: Brill, 1977; Louisville, Ky.: Westminster John Knox Press, 2005.

Pascal, Blaise. *The Mind on Fire: A Faith for the Skeptical and Indifferent.* Introduction by Os Guinness. Abridged (from the *Pensées*) and ed. by James Houston. Regent College Publishing, 2003.

_____. *Pensées.* Translated by A. J. Krailsheimer. Harmondsworth, U.K.: Penguin Books, 1966.

_____. *Thoughts.* Translated by W. F. Trotter. Harvard Classics, vol. 48, 9-317. New York: P. F. Collier & Son, 1910. Republished as *Pensées.* Great Books of the Western World, vol. 33, 169-352. Chicago: Encyclopaedia Britannica, 1952. Also republished as *Pensées.* New York: Dutton, 1958.

Patterson, Bob E. *Carl F. H. Henry.* Makers of the Modern Theological Mind. Waco, Tex.: Word, 1983.

Pearcey, Nancy R. *Total Truth: Liberating Christianity from Its Cultural Captivity.* Foreword by Phillip E. Johnson. Wheaton, Ill.: Crossway Books, 2004.

Pehrson, Boyd. "How Not to Critique Legal Apologetics: A Lesson from a Skeptic's Internet Web Page Objections." Accessed online at < http://www.trinitysem.edu/journal/toc_v3n1.html >.

Pelikan, Jaroslav. *From Luther to Kierkegaard: A Study in the History of Theology.* St. Louis: Concordia, 1967.

Peterson, Michael L. "Reid Debates Hume: Christian Versus Skeptic." *Christianity Today*, 22 September 1978.

Peterson, Michael L., William Hasker, Bruce Reichenbach, and David Basinger. *Reason and Religious Belief: An Introduction to the Philosophy of Religion.* 3d ed. New York: Oxford University Press, 2003.

_____, ed. *Philosophy of Religion: Selected Readings.* 2d ed. New York: Oxford University Press, 2001.

Phillips, Elaine A. "The Fall of Nineveh." In *The Evidence of Prophecy*, ed. Robert C. Newman, 41-51. Hatfield, Pa.: Biblical Research Institute, 1994.

Phillips, Timothy R., and Dennis L. Ockholm, eds. *Christian Apologetics in the Postmodern World.* Downers Grove, Ill.: InterVarsity Press, 1995.

_____. *The Nature of Confession: Evangelicals and Postliberals in Conversation.* Downers Grove, Ill.: InterVarsity, 1996.

Pinnock, Clark. "Assessing Barth for Apologetics." In *How Karl Barth Changed My Mind*, ed. Donald K. McKim, 162-165. Grand Rapids: Eerdmans, 1986.

_____. "Between Classical and Process Theism." In *Process Theology*, ed. Ronald H. Nash, 313-327. Grand Rapids: Baker, 1987.

_____. *A Case for Faith.* Minneapolis: Bethany House, 1987. Previously published as *Reason Enough: A Case for the Christian Faith.* Downers Grove, Ill.: InterVarsity, 1980.

_____. *A Defense of Biblical Infallibility.* International Library of Philosophy and Theology. Philadelphia: Presbyterian & Reformed, 1967; Grand Rapids: Baker, 1972.

_____. "God Limits His Knowledge." In *Predestination and Free Will: Four Views*, ed. David Basinger and Randall Basinger, 141-162. Downers Grove, Ill.: InterVarsity, 1986.

_____. "The Inspiration of Scripture and the Authority of Jesus Christ." In *God's Inerrant Word: An International Symposium on the Trustworthiness of Scripture*, ed. John Warwick Montgomery, 201-218. Minneapolis: Bethany House, 1974.

_____. *Live Now, Brother*. Chicago: Moody, 1972. Reprinted as *Are There Any Answers?* Minneapolis: Bethany House, 1976.

_____. "The Need for a Scriptural, and Therefore a Neo-Classical Theism." In *Perspectives on Evangelical Theology*, edited by Kenneth S. Kantzer and Stanley N. Gundry, 37-42. Papers from the Thirtieth Annual Meeting of the Evangelical Theological Society. Grand Rapids: Baker, 1979.

_____. "The Philosophy of Christian Evidences." In *Jerusalem and Athens: Critical Discussions on the Philosophy and Apologetics of Cornelius Van Til*, ed. E. R. Geehan, 420-425. Philadelphia: Presbyterian & Reformed, 1971.

_____. "A Response to Rex Koivisto." *Journal of the Evangelical Theological Society* 24 (1981): 153-155.

_____. "Schaeffer on Modern Theology." In *Reflections on Francis Schaeffer*, ed. Ronald W. Ruegsegger. Grand Rapids: Zondervan, 1986.

_____. *The Scripture Principle*. San Francisco: Harper & Row, 1984.

_____. *Set Forth Your Case*. Nutley, N.J.: Craig Press, 1968; reprint, Chicago: Moody, 1971.

_____. *Tracking the Maze: An Evangelical Perspective on Modern Theology*. San Francisco: Harper & Row, 1990.

Plantinga, Alvin. "Advice to Christian Philosophers," *Faith and Philosophy* 1 (1984): 253-271. Reprinted in *The Analytic Theist*, ed. James F. Sennett, 296-315. Grand Rapids: Eerdmans, 1998.

_____. *The Analytic Theist: An Alvin Plantinga Reader*, ed. James F. Sennett. Grand Rapids: Eerdmans, 1998.

_____. "A Christian Life Partly Lived." In *Philosophers Who Believe: The Spiritual Journeys of 11 Leading Thinkers*, ed. Kelly James Clark, 45-82. Downers Grove, Ill.: InterVarsity, 1993.

_____. "Christian Philosophy at the End of the Twentieth Century." In *The Analytic Theist: An Alvin Plantinga Reader*, ed. James F. Sennett, 328-52. Grand Rapids: Eerdmans, 1998. Reprinted from *Christian Philosophy at the Close of the Twentieth Century*, ed. Sandy Griffioen and Bert Balk, 29-53. Kampen: Kok, 1995.

_____. *God, Freedom, and Evil*. Grand Rapids: Eerdmans, 1974.

_____. *The Nature of Necessity*. Oxford: Clarendon, 1974.

_____. "Pluralism: A Defense of Religious Exclusivism." In *The Rationality of Belief and the Plurality of Faith: Essays in Honor of William P. Alston*, ed. Thomas D. Senor, 191-

215. Ithaca, N.Y.: Cornell University Press, 1995. Reprinted as "A Defense of Religious Exclusivism." In *The Analytic Theist*, ed. James F. Sennett, 187-209. Grand Rapids: Eerdmans, 1998.

_____. "Reason and Belief in God." In *Faith and Rationality: Reason and Belief in God*, ed. Alvin Plantinga and Nicholas Wolterstorff, 16-93. Notre Dame, Ind.: University of Notre Dame Press, 1983.

_____. "The Reformed Objection to Natural Theology." In *Rationality in the Calvinian Tradition*, ed. Hendrik Hart, Johan Van der Hoeven, and Nicholas Wolterstorff, 363-383. Christian Studies Today. Lanham, Md.: University Press of America, 1983.

_____. "Self-Profile." In *Alvin Plantinga*, ed. James E. Tomberlin and Peter Van Inwagen, 3-97. Profiles: An International Series on Contemporary Philosophers and Logicians, vol. 5. Dordrecht and Boston: D. Reidel, 1985.

_____. *Warrant and Proper Function.* New York: Oxford University Press, 1993.

_____. *Warrant: The Current Debate.* New York: Oxford University Press, 1993.

_____. *Warranted Christian Belief.* New York: Oxford University Press, 2000.

_____, et. al. Book Symposium on *Warranted Christian Belief.* In *Philosophia Christi* 3 (2001).

_____, ed. *The Ontological Argument from St. Anselm to Contemporary Philosophers.* London: Macmillan; Garden City, N.Y.: Doubleday, Anchor Books, 1968.

Plantinga, Alvin, and Nicholas Wolterstorff, eds. *Faith and Rationality: Reason and Belief in God.* Notre Dame, Ind.: University of Notre Dame Press, 1983.

Pojman, Louis P., ed. *The Theory of Knowledge: Classical and Contemporary Readings.* Belmont, Calif.: Wadsworth, 1993.

Portalie, Eugene. *A Guide to the Thought of Saint Augustine.* Translated by Ralph J. Bastian. Library of Living Catholic Thought. Chicago: Henry Regnery, 1960.

Postema, Gerald J. "Calvin's Alleged Rejection of Natural Theology." In *The Organizational Structure of Calvin's Theology*, ed. Richard C. Gamble, 135-146. Articles on Calvin and Calvinism 7. New York: Garland Publishing, 1992. Reprinted from *Scottish Journal of Theology* 24 (1971): 423-434.

Poythress, Vern Sheridan. *God-Centered Biblical Interpretation.* Grand Rapids: Zondervan, 1999.

_____. *Science and Hermeneutics: Implications of Scientific Method for Biblical Interpretation.* Foundations of Contemporary Interpretation, vol. 6. Grand Rapids: Zondervan, Academie, 1988. Published as part of a single volume, *Foundations of Contemporary Interpretation*, ed. V. Philips Long. Grand Rapids: Zondervan, 1996.

_____. *Symphonic Theology: The Validity of Multiple Perspectives in Theology.* Grand Rapids: Zondervan, Academie, 1987.

Praamsma, Louis. *Let Christ Be King: Reflections on the Life and Times of Abraham Kuyper.* Jordan Station, Ont.: Paideia Press, 1985.

Price, Robert M. "Clark H. Pinnock: Conservative and Contemporary." *Evangelical Quarterly* 60 (1988): 157-183.

Purdy, Richard A. "Carl F. H. Henry," in *Handbook of Evangelical Theologians*, ed. Walter A. Elwell, 260-275. Grand Rapids: Baker, 1993.

_____. "Carl Henry and Contemporary Apologetics: An Assessment of the Rational Apologetic Methodology of Carl F. H. Henry in the Context of the Current Impasse between Reformed and Evangelical Apologetics." Ph.D. diss. New York University, 1980.

_____. "Norman Geisler's Neo-Thomistic Apologetics." *Journal of the Evangelical Theological Society* 25 (1982): 351-58. See rejoinder and surrejoinder, 26 (1983): 329-336.

Purtill, Richard L. *C. S. Lewis's Case for the Christian Faith.* San Francisco: Harper & Row, 1985.

_____. "Proofs of Miracles and Miracles as Proofs." *Christian Scholar's Review* 6 (1976): 39-51.

_____. *Reason to Believe.* Grand Rapids: Eerdmans, 1974.

Rakestraw, Robert V. "Clark H. Pinnock." In *Baptist Theologians*, ed. Timothy George and David S. Dockery, 660-684. Nashville: Broadman, 1990.

Ramirez, J. Roland E. "Augustine's Proof for God's Existence from the Experience of Beauty: *Confessions*, X,6," *Augustinian Studies* 19 (1988): 121-130.

_____. "The Priority of Reason over Faith in Augustine." *Augustinian Studies* 13 (1982): 123-131.

Ramm, Bernard. *A Christian Appeal to Reason.* Waco, Tex.: Word, 1972.

_____. *After Fundamentalism: The Future of Evangelical Theology.* San Francisco: Harper & Row, 1983.

_____. *The Christian View of Science and Scripture.* Grand Rapids: Eerdmans, 1954.

_____. *Protestant Christian Evidences.* Chicago: Moody, 1953.

_____. *Varieties of Christian Apologetics: An Introduction to the Christian Philosophy of Religion.* Grand Rapids: Baker, 1962. Revised edition of *Types of Apologetic Systems: An Introductory Study to the Christian Philosophy of Religion.* Wheaton, Ill.: Van Kampen Press, 1953.

Rana, Fazale, and Hugh Ross. *Origins of Life: Biblical and Evolutionary Models Face Off.* Colorado Springs: NavPress, 2004.

Rana, Fazale, with Hugh Ross. *Who Was Adam: A Creation Model Approach to the Origin of Man.* Colorado Springs: NavPress, 2005.

Reid, J. K. S. *Christian Apologetics.* London: Hodder & Stoughton; Grand Rapids: Eerdmans, 1969.

Reid, Thomas. *An Inquiry into the Human Mind: On the Principles of Common Sense: A Critical Edition*, ed. Derek R. Brookes. Edinburgh Edition of Thomas Reid. University Park: Pennsylvania State University Press, 1997.

_____. *Lectures on Natural Theology*, ed. Elmer H. Duncan. Washington: University Press of America, 1981.

Reid, W. Stanford. "Subjectivity or Objectivity in Historical Understanding." In *Jerusalem and Athens: Critical Discussions on the Philosophy and Apologetics of Cornelius Van Til*, edited by E. R. Geehan, 404-419. Nutley, N.J.: Presbyterian & Reformed, 1971.

Reiter, David. "Calvin's 'Sense of Divinity' and Externalist Knowledge of God." *Faith and Philosophy* 15 (1998): 253–69.

Renick, Timothy M. *Aquinas for Armchair Theologians*. Louisville: Westminster John Knox Press, 2002.

Reppert, Victor. "The Argument from Reason and Hume's Legacy." In *In Defense of Natural Theology: A Post-Humean Assessment*, ed. James F. Sennett and Douglas Groothuis, 253-70. Downers Grove, Ill.: InterVarsity, 2005.

_____. *C. S. Lewis's Dangerous Idea: In Defense of the Argument from Reason*. Downers Grove, Ill.: InterVarsity, 2003.

_____, et. al. Symposium on the Argument from Reason. *Philosophia Christi* 5 (2003): 9-89.

Rescher, Nicholas. *Pascal's Wager: A Study of Practical Reasoning in Philosophical Theology*. Notre Dame, Ind.: University of Notre Dame Press, 1985.

Reymond, Robert L. *The Justification of Knowledge: An Introductory Study in Christian Apologetic Methodology*. Phillipsburg, N.J.: Presbyterian & Reformed, 1976.

Richardson, Alan, ed. *A Dictionary of Christian Theology*. Philadelphia: Westminster, 1969.

Riddlebarger, Kim. "The Lion of Princeton: Benjamin Breckinridge Warfield on Apologetics, Theological Method and Polemics." Ph.D. diss., Fuller Theological Seminary, 1997.

Robbins, John W. *Cornelius Van Til: The Man and the Myth*. Jefferson, Md.: Trinity Foundation, 1986).

_____, ed. *Gordon H. Clark: Personal Recollections*. Jefferson, Md.: Trinity Foundation, 1989.

Roberts, Alexander, and James Donaldson, eds. *The Ante-Nicene Fathers: Translations of the Writings of the Fathers Down to A.D. 325*, rev. A. Cleveland Cox, 10 vols. Grand Rapids: Eerdmans, 1969 reprint (1885).

Robinson, Daniel Sommer ed. *The Story of Scottish Philosophy: A Compendium of Selections from the Writings of Nine Pre-eminent Scottish Philosophers, with Biobibliographical Essays*. Reprint, Westport, Conn.: Greenwood, 1979. Originally published 1961.

Rodin, R. Scott. *Evil and Theodicy in the Theology of Karl Barth*. Issues in Systematic Theology 3. New York: Peter Lang, 1997.

Rogers, Eugene F. *Thomas Aquinas and Karl Barth: Sacred Doctrine and the Knowledge of God*. Notre Dame, Ind.: University of Notre Dame Press, 1999.

Rogers, Jack B. "Francis Schaeffer: The Promise and the Problem." *Reformed Journal* 27 (1977): 12-13.

_____. "Van Til and Warfield on Scripture in the Westminster Confession." In *Jerusalem and Athens: Critical Discussions on the Philosophy and Apologetics of Cornelius Van Til*, edited by E. R. Geehan, 154-165. Nutley, N.J.: Presbyterian & Reformed, 1971.

Rogers, Katherin A. "A Defense of Anselm's *Cur Deus Homo* Argument." *Proceedings of the American Catholic Philosophical Association* 74 (2000): 187-200.

Rohde, Peter P. *Søren Kierkegaard: An Introduction to His Life and Philosophy*, trans. Alan M. Williams. London: Allen & Unwin, 1963.

Rosas, L. Joseph, III. "Edward John Carnell." In *Baptist Theologians*, ed. Timothy George and David S. Dockery, 606-626. Nashville: Broadman, 1990.

_____. *Scripture in the Thought of Søren Kierkegaard*. Nashville: Broadman & Holman, 1994.

_____. "The Theology of Edward John Carnell." *Criswell Theological Review* 4 (1990): 351-371.

Ross, Hugh. "Astronomical Evidences for a Personal, Transcendent God." In *The Creation Hypothesis: Scientific Evidence for an Intelligent Designer*, ed. J. P. Moreland, 141-172. Downers Grove, Ill.: InterVarsity, 1994.

_____. *A Matter of Days: Resolving a Creation Controversy*. 2d ed. Colorado Springs: NavPress, 2004. First published in 1994 as *Creation and Time: A Biblical and Scientific Perspective on the Creation-Date Controversy*.

_____. *The Creator and the Cosmos: How the Latest Scientific Discoveries Reveal God*. 3d expanded ed. Colorado Springs: NavPress, 2001.

_____. *The Fingerprint of God*. 3d ed. New Kensington, Pa.: Whitaker House, 2000.

_____. *The Genesis Question: Scientific Advances and the Accuracy of Genesis*. 2d expanded ed. Colorado Springs: NavPress, 2001.

Ruegsegger, Ronald W., ed. *Reflections on Francis Schaeffer*. Grand Rapids: Zondervan, 1986.

Runia, Klass. *Karl Barth's Doctrine of Holy Scripture*. Grand Rapids: Eerdmans, 1962.

Rupp, G. *Culture-Protestantism: German Liberal Theology at the Turn of the Twentieth Century*. Missoula, Mont.: Scholars, 1977.

Rurak, James. "Butler's *Analogy*: A Still Interesting Synthesis of Reason and Revelation." *Anglican Theological Review* 62 (1980): 365-381.

Sabath, Robert A. "LSD and Religious Truth." In *Christianity for the Tough-minded: Essays in Support of an Intellectually Defensible Religious Commitment*, ed. John Warwick Montgomery, 193-201. Minneapolis: Bethany Fellowship, 1973.

Samples, Kenneth Richard. "Augustine of Hippo." In 2 parts. *Facts for Faith* 1 (2001): 36-41; 2 (2001): 34-39.

_____. *Without a Doubt: Answering the 20 Toughest Faith Questions*. Grand Rapids: Baker, 2004.

Sanders, C. *Introduction to Research in English Literary History*. New York: Macmillan, 1952.

Sandnes, Karl Olav. "Paul and Socrates: The Aim of Paul's Areopagus Speech." *Journal for the Study of the New Testament* 50 (1993): 13-26.

Schaeffer, Edith. *L'Abri*. Wheaton, Ill.: Tyndale, 1969.

_____. *The Tapestry*. Waco, Tex.: Word, 1984.

Schaeffer, Francis A. *The Complete Works of Francis A. Schaeffer*. 5 vols. Westchester, Ill.: Crossway Books, 1982.

Schaff, Philip, ed. *The Creeds of Christendom: With a History and Critical Notes*, vol. 3, *The Evangelical Protestant Creeds, with Translations*. Revised by David S. Schaff. New York: Harper & Row, 1931. Reprint, Grand Rapids: Baker, 1993.

Schakel, Peter. *Reason and Imagination in C. S. Lewis: A Study in Till We Have Faces*. Grand Rapids: Eerdmans, 1984.

Schlissel, Steven M., ed. *The Standard Bearer: A Festschrift for Greg L. Bahnsen*. Nacogdoches, Texas: Covenant Media Press, 2002.

Schufreider, Gregory. *Confessions of a Rational Mystic: Anselm's Early Writings*. West Lafayette, Ind.: Purdue University Press, 1994.

Scorgie, Glen G. "James Orr." In *Handbook of Evangelical Theologians*, ed. Walter A. Elwell, 12-25. Grand Rapids: Baker, 1993.

_____. *A Call for Continuity: The Theological Contribution of James Orr*. Macon, Ga.: Mercer University Press, 1988.

Scott, E. F. *The Apologetics of the New Testament*. New York: Putman, 1907.

A Select Library of Nicene and Post-Nicene Fathers of the Christian Church, 1st ser. Grand Rapids: Eerdmans.

Selden, Jonathan. "Aquinas, Luther, Melanchthon, and Biblical Apologetics." *Grace Theological Journal* 5 (1984): 181-95.

Sell, Alan P. F. *Defending and Declaring the Faith: Some Scottish Examples, 1860-1920*. Exeter, U.K.: Paternoster Press; Colorado Springs: Helmers & Howard, 1987.

_____. *John Locke and the Eighteenth-Century Divines*. Cardiffe: University of Wales Press, 1997.

Sennett, James F., and Douglas Groothuis, eds. *In Defense of Natural Theology: A Post-Humean Assessment*. Downers Grove, Ill.: InterVarsity, 2005.

Sherlock, Thomas. *The Tryal of the Witnesses of the Resurrection of Jesus*. London: J. Roberts, 1729. Reprinted in *Jurisprudence: A Book of Readings*, ed. John Warwick Montgomery, 339-449. Strasbourg, France: International Scholarly Publishers, 1974.

Sider, Robert D. "*Credo Quia Absurdum?*" *Classical World* 73 (1980): 417-19.

Siemens, David F. Jr. "Misquoting Tertullian to Anathematize Christianity." *Philosophia Christi* 5 (2003): 563-65.

Silvester, Hugh. *Arguing with God*. Downers Grove, Ill.: InterVarsity, 1971.

Sims, John A. *Edward John Carnell: Defender of the Faith*. Washington, D.C.: University Press of America, 1979.

_____. *Missionaries to the Skeptics: Christian Apologists for the Twentieth Century: C. S. Lewis, E. J. Carnell, and Reinhold Niebuhr*. Macon, Ga.: Mercer University Press, 1995.

Sire, James W. *The Universe Next Door: A Basic Worldview Catalog*. 3rd ed. Downers Grove, Ill.: InterVarsity, 1997.

_____. *Why Should Anyone Believe Anything at All?* Downers Grove, Ill.: InterVarsity, 1994.

Smith, Richard L. "The Supremacy of God in Apologetics: Romans 1:19-21 and the Transcendental Method of Cornelius Van Til." Ph.D. diss., Westminster Theological Seminary, 1996.

Spencer, Aída Besançon. "Romans 1: Finding God in Creation." In *Through No Fault of Their Own? The Fate of Those Who Have Never Heard*, ed. William V. Crockett and James G. Sigountos, 125-135. Grand Rapids: Baker, 1993.

Spencer, Stephen R. "Is Natural Theology Biblical?" *Grace Theological Journal* 9 (1988): 59-72.

Spier, J. M. *An Introduction to Christian Philosophy*. Nutley, N.J.: Craig Press, 1970.

Sprague, Duncan. "The Unfundamental C. S. Lewis: Key Components of Lewis's View of Scripture." *Mars Hill Review* 2 (May 1995): 53-63. Accessed online at < http://www.leaderu.com/marshill/mhr02/lewis1.html >.

Sproul, R. C. *Defending Your Faith: An Introduction to Apologetics*. Wheaton, Ill.: Good News Publishers—Crossway Books, 2003.

_____. *The Psychology of Atheism*. Minneapolis: Bethany Fellowship, 1974.

_____, John Gerstner, and Arthur Lindsley. *Classical Apologetics: A Rational Defense of the Christian Faith and a Critique of Presuppositional Apologetics*. Grand Rapids: Zondervan, Academie, 1984.

Stackhouse, John G., Jr. "'Who Follows in His Train': Edward John Carnell as a Model for Evangelical Theology." *Crux* 21, no. 2 (June 1985): 19-27.

Steen, Peter J. Review of *Set Forth Your Case*. *Westminster Theological Journal* 31 (1968-1969): 101-109.

Stein, Gordon, ed. *An Anthology of Atheism and Rationalism*. Buffalo: Prometheus Books, 1980.

Steinmetz, David C. *Calvin in Context*. New York: Oxford University Press, 1995.

_____. *Luther in Context*. 2d ed. Grand Rapids: Baker Academic, 2002.

Stendahl, Brita K. *Søren Kierkegaard*. Boston: Twayne Publishers, 1976.

Stewart, M. A., ed. *Studies in the Philosophy of the Scottish Enlightenment,* Oxford Studies in the History of Philosophy, vol. 1. Oxford: Clarendon; New York: Oxford University Press, 1990.

Stinson, C. H. *Reason and Sin according to Calvin and Aquinas: The Noetic Effects of the Fall of Man.* Washington, D.C.: Catholic University of America Press, 1966.

Stonehouse, Ned B. *Paul Before the Areopagus and Other Studies.* Grand Rapids: Eerdmans, 1959.

Story, Dan. *Christianity on the Offense: Responding to the Beliefs and Assumptions of Spiritual Seekers.* Grand Rapids: Kregel, 1998.

_____. *Defending Your Faith: How to Answer the Tough Questions.* Nashville: Thomas Nelson, 1992.

Stowers, Stanley K. "Paul on the Use and Abuse of Reason." in *Greeks, Romans, and Christians: Essays in Honor of Abraham J. Malherbe,* ed. David L. Balch, Everett Ferguson, and Wayne A. Meeks, 253-286. Minneapolis: Fortress, 1990.

Strimple, Robert B. "St. Anselm's *Cur deus homo* and John Calvin's Doctrine of the Atonement." In *Anselm: Aosta, Bec and Canterbury,* ed. David E. Luscombe and Gillian R. Evans, 384-60. Sheffield, U.K.: Sheffield Academic Press, 1996.

Stump, Eleonore. *Aquinas.* Arguments of the Philosophers. London and New York: Routledge, 2003.

Swinburne, Richard. "Argument from the Fine-Tuning of the Universe." In *Physical Cosmology and Philosophy,* ed. John Leslie, 154-173. New York: Macmillan, 1990.

_____. *The Christian God.* Oxford: Clarendon, 1994.

_____. *The Coherence of Theism.* Clarendon Library of Logic and Philosophy. Oxford: Clarendon, 1977; rev. ed., 1993.

_____. *The Existence of God.* Oxford: Clarendon, 1979; rev. ed., 1991.

_____. *Faith and Reason.* Oxford: Clarendon, 1981.

_____. "God and Time." In *Reasoned Faith,* ed. Eleanore Stump, 204-222. Ithaca, N.Y.: Cornell University Press, 1993.

_____. "Intellectual Autobiography." In *Reason and the Christian Religion: Essays in Honour of Richard Swinburne,* ed. Alan G. Padgett, 1-18. Oxford: Clarendon; New York: Oxford University Press, 1994.

_____. *Is There a God?* New York: Oxford University Press, 1996.

_____. *Providence and the Problem of Evil.* Oxford: Clarendon, 1998.

_____. *Responsibility and Atonement.* Oxford: Clarendon, 1989.

_____. *Revelation: From Metaphor to Analogy.* Oxford: Clarendon, 1992.

_____. *Simplicity as Evidence of Truth.* Aquinas Lectures. Milwaukee: Marquette University Press, 1997.

Thomas, John Newton. "The Place of Natural Theology in the Thought of John Calvin." In *The Organizational Structure of Calvin's Theology*, ed. Richard C. Gamble, 147-176. Articles on Calvin and Calvinism 7. New York: Garland Publishing, 1992.

Thompson, Josiah. *Kierkegaard*. London: Victor Gollancz, 1974.

Thorne, Phillip R. *Evangelicalism and Karl Barth: His Reception and Influence in North American Evangelical Theology*. Princeton Theological Monograph Series, vol. 40. Allison Park, Pa.: Pickwick, 1995.

Torrance, Thomas F. *Karl Barth: An Introduction to His Early Theology, 1910-1931*. London: SCM, 1962.

Trigg, Joseph Wilson. *Origen: The Bible and Philosophy in the Third Century*. Atlanta: John Knox, 1983.

Trites, Allison A. *The New Testament Concept of Witness*. Cambridge: Cambridge University Press, 1977.

Turner, David L. "Cornelius Van Til and Romans 1:18-21: A Study in the Epistemology of Presuppositional Apologetics." *Grace Theological Journal* 2 (1981): 45-58.

Van Fleteren, Frederick and Joseph C. Schnaubelt, eds. *Twenty-five Years (1969-1994) of Anselm Studies: Review and Critique of Recent Scholarly Views*. Texts and Studies in Religion, vol. 70, Anselm Studies, vol. 3. Lewiston, N.Y.: Edwin Mellen Press, 1996.

Van Til, Cornelius. "The Apologetic Methodology of Francis Schaeffer." Mimeographed paper. Philadelphia: Westminster Theological Seminary, n.d. (1974).

_____. *Apologetics*. Nutley, N.J.: Presbyterian & Reformed, 1976.

_____. *A Christian Theory of Knowledge*. Phillipsburg, N.J.: Presbyterian & Reformed, 1969.

_____. *Christianity and Barthianism*. Nutley, N.J.: Presbyterian & Reformed, 1962.

_____. *Christianity in Conflict*. Philadelphia: Westminster Theological Seminary, 1962.

_____. *Christian-Theistic Evidences*. In Defense of the Faith, vol. 6. Nutley, N.J.: Presbyterian & Reformed, 1976.

_____. *Common Grace and the Gospel*. Nutley, N.J.: Presbyterian & Reformed, 1972.

_____. *The Defense of the Faith*. 1st ed. Philadelphia: Presbyterian & Reformed, 1955.

_____. *The Defense of the Faith*. 3rd ed. Nutley, N.J. and Philadelphia: Presbyterian & Reformed, 1967.

_____. "The Doctrine of Creation and Christian Apologetics." *Journal of Christian Reconstruction* 1, no. 1 (summer 1974): 69-80.

_____. *An Introduction to Systematic Theology*. Nutley, N.J.: Presbyterian & Reformed, 1974.

_____. "My Credo." In *Jerusalem and Athens: Critical Discussions on the Philosophy and Apologetics of Cornelius Van Til*, edited by E. R. Geehan, 3-21. Nutley, N.J.: Presbyterian & Reformed, 1971.

_____. *The New Modernism: An Appraisal of the Theology of Barth and Brunner*. Philadelphia: Presbyterian & Reformed; London: James Clarke, 1946.

_____. *Protestant Doctrine of Scripture*. Nutley, N.J.: Presbyterian & Reformed, 1967.

_____. *Reformed Pastor and Modern Thought*. Nutley, N.J.: Presbyterian & Reformed, 1971.

_____. Review of *Introduction to Christian Apologetics*, by Edward John Carnell. *Westminster Theological Journal* 11 (1948): 45-53. Reprinted in chapter 3 of *The Case for Calvinism*. Philadelphia: Presbyterian & Reformed, 1963.

_____. *A Survey of Christian Epistemology*. In Defense of the Faith, Vol. II. Nutley, N.J.: Presbyterian & Reformed, 1969.

_____. *The Works of Cornelius Van Til, 1895-1987*. CD-ROM. New York: Labels Army Company, 1995.

Vanauken, Sheldon. *A Severe Mercy*. San Francisco: Harper & Row, 1977.

Vos, Arvin. *Aquinas, Calvin, and Contemporary Protestant Thought: A Critique of Protestant Views on the Thought of Thomas Aquinas*. Washington, D.C.: Christian University Press/ Christian College Consortium. Grand Rapids: Eerdmans, 1985.

Wade, Rick. "Blaise Pascal: An Apologist for Our Times." Richardson, Tex.: Probe Ministries, 1998. Online at < http://www.leaderu.com/orgs/probe/docs/pascal.html > (checked 10/27/2004).

Wainwright, William J. "The Nature of Reason: Locke, Swinburne, and Edwards." In *Reason and the Christian Religion: Essays in Honour of Richard Swinburne*, edited by Alan G. Padgett, 91-118. Oxford: Clarendon, 1994.

Waldron, Jeremy. *God, Locke, and Equality: Christian Foundations in Locke's Political Thought*. Cambridge and New York: Cambridge University Press, 2002.

Walker, Andrew, and James Patrick, eds. *A Christian for All Christians: Essays in Honor of C. S. Lewis*. London: Hodder & Stoughton, 1990; Washington, D.C.: Regnery Gateway; Lanham, Md.: National Book Network, 1992.

Wallace, Stan W., ed. *Does God Exist? The Craig—Flew Debate*. Aldershot, Hants, England; Burlington, Vt.: Ashgate, 2003.

Warfield, B. B. "Apologetics." In *Studies in Theology*. The Works of Benjamin B. Warfield, vol. 9. New York: Oxford University Press, 1932; Grand Rapids: Baker, 1981.

_____. *Calvin and Augustine*, ed. Samuel G. Craig. Philadelphia: Presbyterian & Reformed, 1956.

_____. *Calvin and Calvinism*. The Works of Benjamin B. Warfield, vol. 5. New York: Oxford University Press, 1931; reprint, Grand Rapids: Baker, 1981.

_____. *Evolution, Science and Scripture: Selected Writings*, ed. Mark A. Noll and David N. Livingstone. Grand Rapids: Baker Books, 2000.

_____. "False Religions and the True." In Warfield, *Biblical and Theological Studies*, ed. Samuel G. Craig, 560-80. Philadelphia: Presbyterian & Reformed, 1968.

_____. "The Question of Miracles." In *Selected Shorter Writings of Benjamin B. Warfield*, edited by John E. Meeter, 2:167-204. Nutley, N.J.: Presbyterian & Reformed, 1970.

_____. "The Resurrection of Christ a Historical Fact" and "The Resurrection of Christ a Fundamental Doctrine." In *Selected Shorter Writings of Benjamin B. Warfield*, ed. John E. Meeter, 1:178-92 and 1:193-202. Nutley, N.J.: Presbyterian & Reformed, 1970.

_____. *Selected Shorter Writings of Benjamin B. Warfield*, ed. John E. Meeter. 2 vols. Nutley, N.J.: Presbyterian & Reformed, 1970, 1973.

_____. *Studies in Tertullian and Augustine*. New York: Oxford University Press, 1930.

Watkin, Julia. *Historical Dictionary of Kierkegaard's Philosophy*. Metuchen, N.J.: Scarecrow Press, 2000.

Watson, Francis. "The Bible." In *The Cambridge Companion to Karl Barth* ed. John Webster, 57-71. Cambridge, U.K., and New York: Cambridge University Press, 2000.

Watson, Philip S. *Let God Be God! An Interpretation of the Theology of Martin Luther*. London: Epworth Press, 1947; reprint, Philadelphia: Fortress Press, 1970.

Weaver, Gilbert B. "The Concept of Truth in the Apologetic Systems of Gordon Haddon Clark and Cornelius Van Til." Th.D. diss., Grace Theological Seminary, 1967.

_____. "Man: Analogue of God," in *Jerusalem and Athens: Critical Discussions on the Philosophy and Apologetics of Cornelius Van Til*, edited by E. R. Geehan, 321-27. Nutley, N. J.: Presbyterian & Reformed, 1971.

Webster, John, ed. *The Cambridge Companion to Karl Barth*. Cambridge, U.K., and New York: Cambridge University Press, 2000.

Weigel, Arnold D. "A Critique of Bertrand Russell's Religious Position." In *Christianity for the Tough-minded: Essays in Support of an Intellectually Defensible Religious Commitment*, ed. John Warwick Montgomery, 35-61. Minneapolis: Bethany Fellowship, 1973.

Wells, David F. *Reformed Theology in America: A History of Its Modern Development*. Grand Rapids: Eerdmans, 1985.

Wendel, François. *Calvin: Origins and Development of His Religious Thought*. Grand Rapids: Baker, 1996.

Westminster Theological Journal 57, no. 1 (fall 1995). Special Van Til Issue.

Whately, Richard. *Historic Doubts Relative to Napoleon Bonaparte*. New York: Robert Caster, 1849.

_____. *Introductory Lessons on Christian Evidences*. Boston: W. M. Crosby and H. P. Nichols, 1850.

Whitcomb, John C., Jr. "Christian Evidences and Apologetics." Class syllabus. Grace Theological Seminary, n.d.

_____. "Contemporary Apologetics and the Christian Faith." *Bibliotheca Sacra* 134 (1977): 99-106, 195-202, 291-298; 135 (1978): 24-33.

Whitcomb, John C., Jr., and Henry M. Morris. *The Genesis Flood*. Grand Rapids: Baker, 1961.

White, James Emery. *What Is Truth? A Comparative Study of the Positions of Cornelius Van Til, Francis Schaeffer, Carl F. H. Henry, Donald Bloesch, Millard Erickson*. Nashville: Broadman & Holman, 1994.

White, R. E. O. *Luke's Case for Christianity*. Harrisburg, Pa.: Morehouse, 1990.

White, William. *Van Til: Defender of the Faith*. Nashville:Thomas Nelson, 1979.

Wilkins, Michael J., and J. P. Moreland, eds. *Jesus Under Fire: Modern Scholarship Reinvents the Historical Jesus*. Grand Rapids: Zondervan, 1995.

Williams, Rheinallt Nantlais. *Faith, Facts, History, Science—and How They Fit Together*. Wheaton, Illinois: Tyndale House, 1973.

Wippel, John F. *The Metaphysical Thought of Thomas Aquinas: From Finite Being to Uncreated Being*. Monographs of the Society for Medieval and Renaissance Philosophy. Washington, D.C.: Catholic University of America Press, 2000.

Wolfe, David L. *Epistemology: The Justification of Belief*. Contours of Christian Philosophy. Downers Grove, Ill.: InterVarsity, 1982.

Wolfe, Samuel T. *A Key to Dooyeweerd*. Nutley, N.J.: Presbyterian & Reformed, 1978.

Wolters, Albert. "Dutch Neo-Calvinism: Worldview, Philosophy and Rationality." In *Rationality in the Calvinian Tradition*, ed. Hendrik Hart, Johan van der Hoeven, and Nicholas Wolterstorff, 113-131. Christian Studies Today. Lanham, Md.: University Press of America, 1983.

Wolterstorff, Nicholas. "Is Reason Enough? A Review Essay." *Reformed Review* (April 1981): 20-24.

_____. *John Locke and the Ethics of Belief*. Cambridge Studies in Religion and Critical Thought, vol. 2. New York: Cambridge University Press, 1996.

_____. *Reason within the Bounds of Religion*. 2nd ed. Grand Rapids: Eerdmans, 1984.

_____. "Thomas Reid on Rationality." In *Rationality in the Calvinian Tradition*, ed. Hendrik Hart, Johan van der Hoeven, and Nicholas Wolterstorff, 43-69. Christian Studies Today. Lanham, Md.: University Press of America, 1983.

Woodward, Kenneth L. "Guru of Fundamentalism." *Newsweek*, 1 November 1982, p. 88.

Wright, David F. "Christian Faith in the Greek World: Justin Martyr's Testimony." *Evangelical Quarterly* 54 (1982): 77-87.

Wright, N. T. *The Resurrection of the Son of God: Christian Origins and the Question of God, Volume 3*. Minneapolis: Fortress Press, 2003.

Wright, R. K. McGregor. "Paul's Purpose at Athens and the Problem of 'Common Ground.'" Aquila and Priscilla Study Center, 1993. Located 1/6/2005 online at http://www.dtl.org/apologet-ics/wright/athens-1.htm.

Young, Richard Alan. "The Knowledge of God in Romans 1:18-23: Exegetical and Theological Reflections." *Journal of the Evangelical Theological Society* 43 (2000) 695-707.

Young, William. *Toward a Reformed Philosophy: The Development of a Protestant Philosophy in Dutch Calvinistic Thought since the Time of Abraham Kuyper*. Grand Rapids: Piet Hein, 1952.

Zuidema, S. U. "Common Grace and Christian Action in Abraham Kuyper." In *Communication and Confrontation: A Philosophical Appraisal and Critique of Modern Society and Contemporary Thought*. Toronto: Wedge, 1972.

Notes

CHAPTER 1

[1]Martin Batts, "A Summary and Critique of the Historical Apologetic of John Warwick Montgomery" (Th.M. thesis, Dallas Theological Seminary, 1977), 1.

[2]Unless otherwise indicated, all biblical quotations are from the "Updated Edition" of the New American Standard Bible, or NASB (La Habra, Calif.: Lockman Foundation, 1995; Grand Rapids: Zondervan, 1999). Other translations cited include the New International Version (NIV) and the New Revised Standard Version (NRSV).

[3]Greg L. Bahnsen, "Socrates or Christ: The Reformation of Christian Apologetics," in *Foundations of Christian Scholarship: Essays in the Van Til Perspective*, ed. Gary North (Vallecito, Calif.: Ross House, 1976), 191.

[4]Benjamin B. Warfield, "Apologetics," in *Studies in Theology*, The Works of Benjamin B. Warfield, vol. 9 (New York: Oxford University Press, 1932; Grand Rapids: Baker, 1981), 3-21.

[5]Bahnsen, "Socrates or Christ," 193.

[6]E.g., A. B. Bruce, *Apologetics; or, Christianity Defensively Stated*, 3rd ed. (Edinburgh: T. & T. Clark, 1892), 33-34; "Glossary of Technical Terms," in *The New International Dictionary of New Testament Theology*, ed. Colin Brown (Grand Rapids: Zondervan, 1975), 1:51.

[7]The first occurrence of the term known to us is in John Warwick Montgomery, *Faith Founded on Fact: Essays in Evidential Apologetics* (Nashville: Thomas Nelson, 1978), xiii (which uses the form "meta-apologetics").

[8]Mark M. Hanna, *Crucial Questions in Apologetics* (Grand Rapids: Baker, 1981), 94.

[9]Francis R. Beattie, *Apologetics; or, The Rational Vindication of Christianity* (Richmond: Presbyterian Committee of Publications, 1903), 1:56.

[10]Bernard Ramm, *A Christian Appeal to Reason* (Waco, Tex.: Word, 1972), 15-19.

[11]John M. Frame, *Apologetics to the Glory of God: An Introduction* (Phillipsburg, N.J.: Presbyterian & Reformed, 1994), 2.

[12]Robert L. Reymond, *The Justification of Knowledge: An Introductory Study in Christian Apologetic Methodology* (Phillipsburg, N.J.: Presbyterian & Reformed, 1976), 5-7.

[13]In the first edition of this book, we had correlated these four functions of proof, defense, refutation, and persuasion with the four basic approaches of classical, evidential, Reformed, and fideistic apologetics. Although some rough correlations can be made (e.g., refutation is primary in the presuppositionalist wing of Reformed apologetics; persuasion clearly is primary in fideism), they do not hold up consistently.

CHAPTER 2

[1]Unfortunately, there is no satisfactory full-length textbook on the history of apologetics written from an evangelical perspective. The standard textbook remains Avery Cardinal Dulles, *A History of Apologetics* (New York: Corpus Books, 1971; reprint, Eugene, Ore.: Wipf & Stock, 1999; 2d ed., Modern Apologetics Library, San Francisco: Ignatius Press, 2005), a Roman Catholic work that gives scant attention to modern conservative Protestant and evangelical apologetics. (All subsequent citations except as noted are from the second edition.) The second edition adds about six pages on twentieth-century evangelical apologetics (353-59). (For our part, we do not discuss modern Roman Catholic apologetics in this book.) For a liberal Protestant overview, see J. K. S. Reid, *Christian Apologetics* (London: Hodder & Stoughton; Grand Rapids: Eerdmans, 1969). Perhaps the best evangelical survey of the history of apologetics is found in Ronald B. Mayers, *Balanced Apologetics: Using Evidences and Presuppositions in Defense of the Faith* (Grand Rapids: Kregel, 1996), 87-195. For an excellent collection of readings, see L. Russ Bush, ed., *Classical Readings in Christian Apologetics, A.D. 100-1800* (Grand Rapids: Zondervan—Academie, 1983). Bush concludes with a chapter reviewing the history of apologetics since 1800. Closely following the history of apologetics are the following works dealing with specific issues: Bruce A. Demarest, *General Revelation: Historical Views and Contemporary Issues* (Grand Rapids: Zondervan, 1982); William Lane Craig, *The Historical Argument for the Resurrection of Jesus During the Deist Controversy*, Texts and Studies in Religion, vol. 23 (Lewiston, N.Y.: Edwin Mellen Press, 1985). Textbooks on the history of philosophy are also relevant, especially up to about 1750. Besides the standard works in this area, we would single out Colin Brown, *Christianity and Western Thought: A History of Philosophers, Ideas, and Movements*, vol. 1, *From the Ancient World to the Age of Enlightenment* (Downers Grove, Ill.: InterVarsity, 1990).

[2]On New Testament apologetics, see especially E. F. Scott, *The Apologetics of the New Testament* (New York: Putman, 1907); F. F. Bruce, *The Defense of the Gospel in the New Testament*, rev. ed. (Grand Rapids: Eerdmans, 1977).

[3]Cf. Robert M. Bowman, Jr., *Orthodoxy and Heresy: A Biblical Guide to Doctrinal Discernment* (Grand Rapids: Baker, 1991), 71-73.

[4]On the apologetic perspective in Luke-Acts, see Dulles, *History of Apologetics*, 11-14, 19-21; Allison A. Trites, *The New Testament Concept of Witness* (Cambridge: Cambridge University Press, 1977), 128-38; Frederic R. Howe, *Challenge and Response: A Handbook of Christian Apologetics* (Grand Rapids: Zondervan, 1982), 34-46; Mayers, *Balanced Apologetics*, 135-71; Craig, *Historical Argument*, 8-16; F. F. Bruce, "Paul's Apologetic and the Purpose of Acts," *Bulletin of the John Rylands Library* 69 (1986-87): 379-93; R. E. O. White, *Luke's Case for Christianity* (Harrisburg, Pa.: Morehouse, 1990); Loveday Alexander, "The Acts of the Apostles as an Apologetic Text," in *Apologetics in the Roman Empire: Pagans, Jews, and Christians*, ed. Mark Edwards, Martin Goodman, and Simon Price, in association with Christopher Rowland (Oxford and New York: Oxford University Press, 1999), 15-44; and especially John W. Mauck, *Paul on Trial: The Book of Acts as a Defense of Christianity* (Nashville: Thomas Nelson—Nelson Reference, 2001).

[5]The literature on Paul's speech in Athens is voluminous. In addition to commentaries, the following works must be mentioned: Benjamin Breckinridge Warfield, "False Religions and the True," in Warfield, *Biblical and Theological Studies*, ed. Samuel G. Craig (Philadelphia: Presbyterian & Reformed, 1968), 560-80; Ned B. Stonehouse, *Paul Before the Areopagus and Other Studies* (Grand Rapids: Eerdmans, 1959); Bertil Gärtner, *The Areopagus Speech and Natural Revelation*, Acta seminarii neotestamentici upsaliensis, vol. 24 (Lund: Gleerup, 1955); Greg L. Bahnsen, "The Encounter of Jerusalem with Athens," *Ashland Theological Bulletin* 13 (1980): 4-40, reprinted in Greg L. Bahnsen, *Always Ready: Directions for Defending the Faith*, ed. Robert R. Booth (Atlanta: American Vision; Texarkana, Ark.: Covenant Media Foundation, 1996), 235-76; David L. Balch, "The Areopagus Speech: An Appeal to the Stoic Historian Posidonius against Later Stoics and the Epicureans," in *Greeks, Romans, and Christians: Essays*

in Honor of Abraham J. Malherbe, ed. David L. Balch, Everett Ferguson, and Wayne A. Meeks (Minneapolis: Fortress, 1990), 52-79; Marilyn McCord Adams, "Philosophy and the Bible: The Areopagus Speech," *Faith and Philosophy* 9 (1992): 135-49; Darrell L. Bock, "Athenians Who Have Never Heard," in *Through No Fault of Their Own? The Fate of Those Who Have Never Heard*, ed. William V. Crockett and James G. Sigountos (Grand Rapids: Baker, 1993), 117-24; R. K. McGregor Wright, "Paul's Purpose at Athens and the Problem of 'Common Ground,'" Aquila and Priscilla Study Center, 1993, located 1/6/2005 online at http://www.dtl.org/apologetics/wright/athens-1.htm; Karl Olav Sandnes, "Paul and Socrates: The Aim of Paul's Areopagus Speech," *Journal for the Study of the New Testament* 50 (1993): 13-26; John J. Kilgallen, "Acts 17:22-31: An Example of Interreligious Dialogue," *Studia Missionalia* 43 (1994): 43-60; Mark D. Given, "Not Either/Or but Both/And in Paul's Areopagus Speech," *Biblical Interpretation* 3 (1995): 356-72; D. A. Carson, "Athens Revisited," in *Telling the Truth: Evangelizing Postmoderns*, ed. D. A. Carson (Grand Rapids: Zondervan, 2000), 384-98; Kenneth D. Litwak, "Israel's Prophets Meet Athens' Philosophers: Scriptural Echoes in Acts 17:22-31," *Biblica* 85 (2004): 199-216; and J. Daryl Charles, "Paul before the Areopagus: Reflections on the Apostle's Encounter with Cultured Paganism," *Philosophia Christi* 7 (2005): 125-40.

[6]Studies of Romans 1 focusing on its relation to issues of apologetic importance include G. C. Berkouwer, *General Revelation*, Studies in Dogmatics (Grand Rapids: Eerdmans, 1955), 138-72; David L. Turner, "Cornelius Van Til and Romans 1:18-21: A Study in the Epistemology of Presuppositional Apologetics," *Grace Theological Journal* 2 (1981): 45-58; Howe, *Challenge and Response*, 80-86; Demarest, *General Revelation*, 230-46; R. C. Sproul, John Gerstner, and Arthur Lindsley, *Classical Apologetics: A Rational Defense of the Christian Faith and a Critique of Presuppositional Apologetics* (Grand Rapids: Zondervan—Academie, 1984), 40-63; Stephen R. Spencer, "Is Natural Theology Biblical?" *Grace Theological Journal* 9 (1988) 59-72; James Barr, *Biblical Faith and Natural Theology*, Gifford Lectures 1991 (Oxford: Clarendon Press, 1992); Aída Besançon Spencer, "Romans 1: Finding God in Creation," in *Through No Fault of Their Own*, ed. Crockett and Sigountos, 125-35; Richard L. Smith, "The Supremacy of God in Apologetics: Romans 1:19-21 and the Transcendental Method of Cornelius Van Til" (Ph.D. diss., Westminster Theological Seminary, 1996); Richard Alan Young, "The Knowledge of God in Romans 1:18-23: Exegetical and Theological Reflections," *Journal of the Evangelical Theological Society* 43 (2000) 695-707.

[7]Frame, *Apologetics to the Glory of God*, 8.

[8]On the implications of 1 Corinthians 1–2 for philosophy and apologetics, see William D. Dennison, *Paul's Two-Age Construction and Apologetics* (Lanham, Md.: University Press of America, 1985); Paul W. Gooch, *Partial Knowledge: Philosophical Studies in Paul* (Notre Dame, Ind.: University of Notre Dame Press, 1987); Stanley K. Stowers, "Paul on the Use and Abuse of Reason," in *Greeks, Romans, and Christians*, ed. Balch, et. al., 253-86; Richard B. Gaffin, Jr., "Some Epistemological Reflections on 1 Cor 2:6-16," *Westminster Theological Journal* 57 (1995): 103-24.

[9]On Paul's argument in 1 Corinthians 15, in addition to commentaries, see W. Harold Mare, "Pauline Appeals to Historical Evidence," *Bulletin of the Evangelical Theological Society* 11 (1968): 121-30 (which also discusses Acts 17); William Lane Craig, *Historical Argument*, 19-26, 551-60; Craig, *Assessing the New Testament Evidence for the Historicity of the Resurrection of Jesus*, Studies in the Bible and Early Christianity, vol. 16 (Lewiston, N.Y.: Edwin Mellen Press, 1989); Robert M. Bowman, Jr., *Jehovah's Witnesses*, Zondervan Guide to Cults and Religious Movements (Grand Rapids: Zondervan, 1995), 46-48; and especially N. T. Wright, *The Resurrection of the Son of God: Christian Origins and the Question of God, Volume 3* (Minneapolis: Fortress Press, 2003).

[10]Lesslie Newbigin, *Proper Confidence: Faith, Doubt, and Certainty in Christian Discipleship* (Grand Rapids: Eerdmans, 1995), 4-5. On apologetics in John's writings, see further Trites, *New Testament Concept of Witness*, 78-90; Norman L. Geisler, "Johannine Apologetics," *Bibliotheca Sacra* 136 (1979): 333-43; Mayers, *Balanced Apologetics*, 137-43; Craig, *Historical Argument*, 16-19; and see also James Montgomery Boice, *Witness and Revelation in the Gospel of John* (Exeter:

Paternoster, 1970); Andrew T. Lincoln, *Truth on Trial: The Lawsuit Motif in the Fourth Gospel* (Peabody, MA: Hendrickson, 2001).

[11]On 1 Peter 3:15, see Howe, *Challenge and Response*, 15-17; Frame, *Apologetics to the Glory of God*, 1-9, 27-30; William Edgar, *Reasons of the Heart: Recovering Christian Persuasion*, Hourglass Books (Grand Rapids: Baker, 1996), 33-41; Renton Maclachan, "With Gentleness and Respect: The Implications for Christian Apologetics of Some Passages from 1 Peter," *Stimulus* 4 (Fall 1996): 30-33.

[12]On apologetics in the second and third centuries, see Dulles, *History of Apologetics*, 27-55; Henry Chadwick, *Early Christian Thought and the Classical Tradition: Studies in Justin, Clement, and Origen* (Oxford: Clarendon, 1966); Mayers, *Balanced Apologetics*, 173-95; Craig, *Historical Argument*, 26-46; Robert M. Grant, *Greek Apologists of the Second Century* (Philadelphia: Westminster, 1988); Ford Lewis Battles, *The Apologists*, Study Outline 1 (Allison Park, Pa.: Pickwick, 1991); *Apologetics in the Roman Empire: Pagans, Jews, and Christians*, ed. Edwards, Goodman, and Price (1999). The works of the church fathers from this period are still most conveniently found in a set of volumes edited by Alexander Roberts and James Donaldson, *The Ante-Nicene Fathers: Translations of the Writings of the Fathers Down to A.D. 325*, rev. A. Cleveland Cox, 10 vols. (1885; reprint, Grand Rapids: Eerdmans, 1969).

[13]On Justin Martyr, see Henry Chadwick, "Justin Martyr's Defence of Christianity," *Bulletin of the John Rylands Library* 47 (1965): 275-97; Leslie W. Barnard, *Justin Martyr: His Life and Thought* (Cambridge: Cambridge University Press, 1967); David F. Wright, "Christian Faith in the Greek World: Justin Martyr's Testimony," *Evangelical Quarterly* 54 (1982): 77-87; Arthur J. Droge, "Justin Martyr and the Restoration of Philosophy," *Church History* 56 (1987): 303-19; Sara J. Denning-Bolle, "Christian Dialogue as Apologetic: The Case of Justin Martyr Seen in Historical Context," *Bulletin of the John Rylands Library* 69 (1987): 492-510; Graham A. Keith, "Justin Martyr and Religious Exclusivism," *Tyndale Bulletin* 43 (1992): 57-80.

[14]Bahnsen, "Socrates or Christ," 223.

[15]On Origen, see Joseph Wilson Trigg, *Origen: The Bible and Philosophy in the Third Century* (Atlanta: John Knox, 1983); Henri Crouzel, *Origen*, trans. A. S. Worrell (San Francisco: Harper & Row, 1989); Robert J. Hauck, "They Saw What They Saw: Sense Knowledge in Early Christian Polemic," *Harvard Theological Review* 81 (1988): 239-49; Johan F. Goud, "Origen (185-254)," in *Bringing into Captivity Every Thought: Capita Selecta in the History of Christian Evaluations of Non-Christian Philosophy*, ed. Jacob Klapwijk, Sander Griffioen, and Gerben Groenewoud, Christian Studies Today (Lanham, Md.: University Press of America, 1991), 29-47.

[16]Craig, *Historical Argument*, 41-46.

[17]The standard English edition is *Origen: Contra Celsum*, trans. Henry Chadwick, corrected reprint (Cambridge: Cambridge University Press, 1980).

[18]Augustine's many works are most accessible in English in *A Select Library of Nicene and Post-Nicene Fathers of the Christian Church*, 1st ser. (Grand Rapids: Eerdmans), hereafter cited as NPNF. Three of his most important works are conveniently available in one volume found in almost every public library: Augustine, *The Confessions; The City of God; On Christian Doctrine*, Great Books of the Western World, vol. 18 (Chicago: Encyclopaedia Britannica, 1952). The literature on Augustine is enormous. Books of special relevance to Augustine's apologetics include B. B. Warfield, *Studies in Tertullian and Augustine* (New York: Oxford University Press, 1930); Roy W. Battenhouse, ed., *A Companion to the Study of St. Augustine* (New York: Oxford University Press, 1955); Gordon R. Lewis, "Faith and Reason in the Thought of St. Augustine" (Ph.D. diss., Syracuse University, 1959); Étienne Gilson, *The Christian Philosophy of St. Augustine*, trans. L. E. M. Lynch (New York: Random House, 1960); Eugene Portalie, *A Guide to the Thought of Saint Augustine*, trans. Ralph J. Bastian, Library of Living Catholic Thought (Chicago: Henry Regnery, 1960); Ronald H. Nash, *The Light of the Mind: St. Augustine's Theory of Knowledge* (Lexington: University Press of

Kentucky, 1969); Terry L. Miethe, comp., *Augustinian Bibliography, 1970-1980: With Essays on the Fundamentals of Augustinian Scholarship* (Westport, Conn.: Greenwood, 1982); Norman L. Geisler, ed., *What Augustine Says* (Grand Rapids: Baker, 1982); Henry Chadwick, *Augustine* (New York: Oxford University Press, 1986); Curtis Chang, *Engaging Unbelief: A Captivating Strategy from Augustine & Aquinas* (Downers Grove, Ill.: InterVarsity Press, 2000), especially 40-52, 66-93. The periodical *Augustinian Studies* has published numerous relevant articles, for example, J. Roland E. Ramirez, "The Priority of Reason over Faith in Augustine," *Augustinian Studies* 13 (1982): 123-131. Other studies worth noting include Demarest, *General Revelation*, 25-31; Mayers, *Balanced Apologetics*, 85-96; Sproul, Gerstner, and Lindsley, *Classical Apologetics*, 189-96; Craig, *Historical Argument*, 53-60; Norman Kretzmann, "Faith Seeks, Understanding Finds: Augustine's Charter for Christian Philosophy," in *Christian Philosophy*, ed. Thomas P. Flint (Notre Dame, Ind.: University of Notre Dame Press, 1988), 1-36; Dewey J. Hoitenga, Jr., *Faith and Reason from Plato to Plantinga: An Introduction to Reformed Epistemology* (Albany: State University of New York Press, 1991), 57-142; Abraham P. Bos, "Augustine (354-430)," in *Bringing into Captivity Every Thought*, ed. Klapwijk, et. al., 49-66; Byron Bitar, "Augustine, Natural Theology, and General Revelation" (paper presented to the Evangelical Theological Seminary annual convention, 1997); Kenneth Richard Samples, "Augustine of Hippo," in 2 parts, *Facts for Faith* 1 (2001): 36-41; 2 (2001): 34-39; Dulles, *History of Apologetics*, 73-85.

[19]On *The City of God*, see John Anjola Laoye, "Augustine's Apologetic Use of the Old Testament as Reflected Especially in the 'De Civitate Dei'" (Th.D. diss., Southern Baptist Theological Seminary, 1972); Ford Lewis Battles, *Augustine: City of God*, Study Outline 9 (Pittsburgh: Ford Lewis Battles, 1973).

[20]Augustine, *Epistles* 120; *On the Predestination of the Saints* 2.5; *On the Spirit and the Letter* 31.54.

[21]*City of God* 11.3-4; *Confessions* 7.9.14; *Epistles* 120; etc.

[22]*Tractatus on the Gospel of John* 29.6 (NPNF, 7:184).

[23]*Sermons* 76.1-2 (NPNF, 6:481).

[24]*On the Predestination of the Saints* 2.5.

[25]*City of God* 8.5-6, 10; cf. *Tractatus on the Gospel of John* 2.4. On Augustine's arguments for the existence of God, besides works already cited, see John A. Mourant, "The Augustinian Argument for the Existence of God," in *Inquiries into Medieval Philosophy: A Collection in Honor of Francis P. Clarke*, ed. James F. Ross, Contributions in Philosophy, vol. 4 (Westport, Conn.: Greenwood Publishing, 1971); J. Roland E. Ramirez, "Augustine's Proof for God's Existence from the Experience of Beauty: *Confessions*, X,6," *Augustinian Studies* 19 (1988): 121-30.

[26]Augustine, *City of God* 8.12.

[27]*On Faith in Things That Are Not Seen* 5 (NPNF, 3:339).

[28]Ibid., 5-10; *City of God* 22.1-5.

[29]Dulles, *History of Apologetics*, 91. On apologetics and Christian philosophy during this period, see the classic study Étienne Gilson, *Reason and Revelation in the Middle Ages* (New York: Scribner, 1938).

[30]The standard English edition of Anselm's works is *Anselm of Canterbury*, trans. and ed. Jasper Hopkins and Herbert Richardson, 4 vols. (New York: Edwin Mellen Press; London: SCM, 1974-1976). A more accessible collection may be found in Brian Davies and Gillian R. Evans, eds., *Anselm of Canterbury: The Major Works*, Oxford World's Classics (Oxford and New York: Oxford University Press, 1998). Studies of Anselm's thought include Jasper Hopkins, *A Companion to the Study of St. Anselm* (Minneapolis: University of Minnesota Press, 1972); Richard R. La Croix, *Proslogion II and III: A Third Interpretation of Anselm's Argument* (Leiden: E. J. Brill, 1972); Gillian R. Evans, *Anselm and Talking about God* (Oxford: Clarendon; New York: Oxford University

Press, 1978); Evans, *Anselm*, Outstanding Christian Thinkers (Wilton, Conn.: Morehouse, 1989); Marilyn McCord Adams, *"Fides Quaerens Intellectum:* St. Anselm's Method in Philosophical Theology," *Faith and Philosophy* 9 (1992): 409-35; Gregory Schufreider, *Confessions of a Rational Mystic: Anselm's Early Writings* (West Lafayette, Ind.: Purdue University Press, 1994); Frederick Van Fleteren and Joseph C. Schnaubelt, eds., *Twenty-five Years (1969-1994) of Anselm Studies: Review and Critique of Recent Scholarly Views*, Texts and Studies in Religion, vol. 70, Anselm Studies, vol. 3 (Lewiston, N.Y.: Edwin Mellen Press, 1996); John R. Fortin, ed., *Saint Anselm: His Origins and Influence*, Texts and Studies in Religion 91 (Lewiston, N.Y.: Edwin Mellen Press, 2001); David Bradshaw, "Faith and Reason in St. Anselm's *Monologion," Philosophia Christi* 4 (2002): 509-17; Brian Davies and Brian Leftow, eds., *The Cambridge Companion to Anselm*, Cambridge Companions to Philosophy (New York: Cambridge University Press, 2004).

[31]Anselm, *Proslogion* 1, in *Anselm of Canterbury*, ed. Hopkins and Richardson, 1:93.

[32]See chapter 6, n. 30, for a list of modern works on the ontological argument.

[33]Recent studies focusing on *Cur Deus Homo* include Robert B. Strimple, "St. Anselm's *Cur deus homo* and John Calvin's Doctrine of the Atonement," in *Anselm: Aosta, Bec and Canterbury*, ed. David E. Luscombe and Gillian R. Evans (Sheffield, U.K.: Sheffield Academic Press, 1996), 348-60; Katherin A. Rogers, "A Defense of Anselm's *Cur Deus Homo* Argument," *Proceedings of the American Catholic Philosophical Association* 74 (2000): 187-200; F. B. Asiedu, "Anselm and the Unbelievers: Pagans, Jews, and Christians in the *Cur Deus Homo," Theological Studies* 62 (2001): 530-48.

[34]Anselm, "Commendation of This Work to Pope Urban II," in *Why God Became a Man (Cur Deus Homo), in Anselm of Canterbury*, 3:41.

[35]Anselm, preface to *Why God Became a Man*, in ibid., 43.

[36]*Why God Became a Man* 1.1, in ibid., 49; note the reference to 1 Peter 3:15.

[37]*Why God Became a Man* 1.3, in ibid., 52.

[38]Works on Thomas Aquinas are almost innumerable. Popular-level introductions include those by Catholic writer G. K. Chesterton, *St. Thomas Aquinas* (Garden City, N.Y.: Image Books, 1956); evangelical apologist Norman L. Geisler, *Thomas Aquinas: An Evangelical Appraisal* (Grand Rapids: Baker, 1991; reprint, Eugene, Ore.: Wipf & Stock, 2003); and on a lighter note, Timothy M. Renick, *Aquinas for Armchair Theologians* (Louisville: Westminster John Knox Press, 2002), reflecting a mainline Protestant perspective. Other major works on Aquinas are Étienne Gilson, *The Christian Philosophy of St. Thomas Aquinas*, trans. L. K. Shook (New York: Random House, 1956); Frederick C. Copleston, *Aquinas* (Harmondsworth, U.K.: Penguin Books, 1957); Thomas Gornall, *Philosophy of God: The Elements of Thomist Natural Theology* (Oxford: Blackwell; London: Darton, Longman & Todd, 1962); M.-D. Chenu, *Toward Understanding Saint Thomas*, trans. A.-M. Landry and D. Hughes (Chicago: Henry Regnery, 1964); Anthony Kenny, ed., *Aquinas: A Collection of Critical Essays*, Modern Studies in Philosophy (Notre Dame, Ind.: University of Notre Dame Press, 1976); Demarest, *General Revelation*, 34-42; Mayers, *Balanced Apologetics*, 96-103; Arvin Vos, *Aquinas, Calvin, and Contemporary Protestant Thought: A Critique of Protestant Views on the Thought of Thomas Aquinas* (Washington, D.C.: Christian University Press/Christian College Consortium; Grand Rapids: Eerdmans, 1985); W. J. Hankey, *God in Himself: Aquinas' Doctrine of God as Expounded in the "Summa Theologiae"* (New York: Oxford University Press, 1987); Leo J. Elders, *The Philosophical Theology of St. Thomas Aquinas* (Leiden: E. J. Brill, 1990); Brian Davies, *The Thought of Thomas Aquinas* (Oxford: Clarendon, 1992); Norman Kretzmann and Eleonore Stump, eds., *The Cambridge Companion to Aquinas* (Cambridge and New York: Cambridge University Press, 1993); John I. Jenkins, *Knowledge and Faith in Thomas Aquinas* (Cambridge and New York: Cambridge University Press, 1997); Eugene F. Rogers, *Thomas Aquinas and Karl Barth: Sacred Doctrine and the Knowledge of God* (Notre Dame, Ind.: University of Notre Dame Press, 1999); Brian Davies, ed., *Thomas Aquinas: Contemporary Philosophical Perspectives* (Oxford and

New York: Oxford University Press, 2002); Aidan Nichols, *Discovering Aquinas: An Introduction to His Life, Work, and Influence* (London: Darton, Longman & Todd, 2002; Grand Rapids: Eerdmans, 2003); Eleonore Stump, *Aquinas*, Arguments of the Philosophers (London and New York: Routledge, 2003); Jim Fodor and Frederick Christian Bauerschmidt, eds., *Aquinas in Dialogue: Thomas for the Twenty-first Century* (New York: Blackwell, 2004). On Aquinas as an apologist, see especially Chang, *Engaging Unbelief*, especially 52-64, 94-136, 174-84.

[39]Thomas Aquinas, *Summa Contra Gentiles*, trans. Anton C. Pegis (Notre Dame, Ind., and London: University of Notre Dame Press, 1975).

[40]Thomas Aquinas, *Summa Theologiae: Latin Text and English Translation, Introduction, Notes, Appendices and Glossaries* (London: Blackfriars, 1974). An accessible edition that includes all of Part I and generous portions of Parts II and III is Saint Thomas Aquinas, *The Summa Theologica*, trans. Fathers of the English Dominican Province, rev. Daniel J. Sullivan, 2 Vols.; Great Books of the Western World, vols. 19-20 (Chicago: Encyclopaedia Britannica, 1952). See also Peter Kreeft, *A Summa of the "Summa": The Essential Philosophical Passages of St. Thomas Aquinas' "Summa Theologica" Edited and Explained for Beginners* (San Francisco: Ignatius, 1990).

[41]The literature on Aquinas's "five ways" is astonishingly vast. In addition to the sources already cited, see especially Anthony Kenny, *The Five Ways: St. Thomas Aquinas' Proofs of God's Existence* (New York: Schocken, 1969; reprint, Notre Dame, Ind.: University of Notre Dame Press, 1980); William Lane Craig, *The Cosmological Argument from Plato to Leibniz* (New York: Macmillan, 1980), 152-205; C. F. J. Martin, *Thomas Aquinas: God and Explanations* (Edinburgh: Edinburgh University Press, 1997); John F. Wippel, *The Metaphysical Thought of Thomas Aquinas: From Finite Being to Uncreated Being*, Monographs of the Society for Medieval and Renaissance Philosophy (Washington, D.C.: Catholic University of America Press, 2000).

[42]See further Craig, *Historical Argument*, 61-70.

[43]On the origins of the Reformation and the teachings of the Reformers, see H. A. Oberman, *Forerunners of the Reformation: The Shape of Late Medieval Thought, Illustrated by Key Documents* (New York: Holt, Rinehart & Winston, 1966); Timothy George, *Theology of the Reformers* (Nashville: Broadman, 1985); Alister E. McGrath, *The Intellectual Origins of the European Reformation* (Oxford: Blackwell, 1987).

[44]See chapter 16 for a detailed discussion of Luther's approach to apologetics.

[45]See chapter 12 on Calvin's approach to apologetics.

[46]On apologetics and related developments during the seventeenth and eighteenth centuries, see Demarest, *General Revelation*, 61-91; Craig, *Historical Argument*, 71-352; William R. Everdell, *Christian Apologetics in France, 1730-1790: The Roots of Romantic Religion*, Texts and Studies in Religion, vol. 31 (Lewiston, N.Y.: Edwin Mellen Press, 1987); Brown, *Christianity and Western Thought*, 159-234.

[47]Only the briefest survey of apologetics since the Enlightenment will be given here, since more extended discussions of the work of post-Enlightenment apologists will be presented in later chapters of the book. General studies relating to the history of apologetics during this period include Demarest, *General Revelation*, 93-225; Alan P. F. Sell, *Defending and Declaring the Faith: Some Scottish Examples, 1860-1920* (Exeter, U.K.: Paternoster Press; Colorado Springs: Helmers & Howard, 1987); Brown, *Christianity and Western Thought*, 235-330.

CHAPTER 3

[1]Dulles, *History of Apologetics* (1st ed.), 246.

[2]Edwin A. Burtt, *Types of Religious Philosophy* (New York: Harper & Row, 1939), 448.

[3]For a comparison of this classification with that in other books on apologetics, see Appendix.

[4]E.g., *Five Views on Apologetics*, ed. Cowan (see Appendix).

[5]The usual name for the most popular form of Reformed apologetics is *presuppositionalism*, a term that has been used for the apologetic systems developed by Cornelius Van Til and Gordon H. Clark. However, the Reformed apologetical tradition is broader than Clark and Van Til. In particular, the apologetic thought of Alvin Plantinga would not properly be termed a form of presuppositionalism. Hence, we have chosen to use the broader term.

[6]For a list of ten questions or issues that overlap somewhat the dozen questions considered here, see Bernard Ramm, *Varieties of Christian Apologetics: An Introduction to the Christian Philosophy of Religion* (Grand Rapids: Baker, 1962), 17-27. Ramm's questions deal with philosophy, proofs of God's existence, truth, sin, revelation, certainty, common ground, faith, evidences, and faith and reason. Seven of these ten questions are also used, apparently independent of Ramm, as focus points in Mayers, *Balanced Apologetics*, 13, 95-96, 102-103, 116-18, 123-25, 132-33, 214-17.

CHAPTER 4

[1]R. C. Sproul, John Gerstner, and Arthur Lindsley, *Classical Apologetics: A Rational Defense of the Christian Faith and a Critique of Presuppositional Apologetics* (Grand Rapids: Zondervan—Academie, 1984), 210.

[2]Introductions to Warfield include Mark A. Noll, "B. B. Warfield," in *Handbook of Evangelical Theologians*, ed. Walter A. Elwell (Grand Rapids: Baker, 1993), 26-39; Stanley W. Barnberg, "Our Image of Warfield Must Go," *Journal of the Evangelical Theological Society* 34 (1991): 229-41. Important works on Warfield, especially relevant to apologetics, include the following: William D. Livingstone, "The Princeton Apologetic as Exemplified by the Work of Benjamin B. Warfield and J. Gresham Machen: A Study in Modern American Theology, 1880-1930" (Ph.D. diss., Yale University, 1948); Woodrow Behannon, "Benjamin B. Warfield's Concept of Religious Authority" (Th.D. diss., Southwestern Baptist Theological Seminary, 1964); John H. Gerstner, "Warfield's Case for Biblical Inerrancy," in *God's Inerrant Word: An International Symposium on the Trustworthiness of Scripture*, ed. John Warwick Montgomery (Minneapolis: Bethany House, 1974), 115-42; John E. Meeter and Roger Nicole, *A Bibliography of Benjamin Breckinridge Warfield* (Nutley, N.J.: Presbyterian & Reformed, 1974); W. Andrew Hoffecker, *Piety and the Princeton Theologians: Archibald Alexander, Charles Hodge, and Benjamin Warfield* (Grand Rapids: Baker, 1981); Mark A. Noll, ed., *The Princeton Theology, 1812-1921: Scripture, Science, and Theological Method from Archibald Alexander to Benjamin Breckinridge Warfield* (Grand Rapids: Baker, 1983); James Samuel McClanahan, Jr., "Benjamin B. Warfield: Historian of Doctrine in Defense of Orthodoxy, 1881-1921" (Ph.D. diss., Union Theological Seminary [Richmond], 1988); Kim Riddlebarger, "The Lion of Princeton: Benjamin Breckinridge Warfield on Apologetics, Theological Method and Polemics" (Ph.D. diss., Fuller Theological Seminary, 1997); Paul K. Helseth, "B. B. Warfield's Apologetical Appeal to 'Right Reason': Evidence of a 'Rather Bald Rationalism'?" *Scottish Journal of Theology* 16 (1998): 156-77; and Owen Anderson, *Benjamin B. Warfield and Right Reason: The Clarity of General Revelation and Function of Apologetics* (Lanham, Md.: University Press of America, 2005).

[3]Warfield's most important writings can be found in two collections: The Works of Benjamin B. Warfield, 10 vols. (reprint, Grand Rapids: Baker, 1981), which are individually titled; and *Selected Shorter Writings of Benjamin B. Warfield*, ed. John E. Meeter, 2 vols. (Nutley, N.J.: Presbyterian & Reformed, 1970, 1973); hereafter cited as *Shorter Writings*.

[4]Westminster Seminary's apologetic changed directions from the Old Princeton approach under the leadership of Westminster's professor of apologetics, Cornelius Van Til (see chapter 12).

[5]Warfield, "Christianity and Our Times," in *Shorter Writings*, 1:48-49.

[6]Warfield, "Apologetics," in *Studies in Theology*, 17-18.

[7]See especially Warfield, *Calvin and Augustine*, ed. Samuel G. Craig (Philadelphia: Presbyterian & Reformed, 1956).

[8]Warfield, "Apologetics," in *Studies in Theology*, 11.

[9]Ibid., 13.

[10]Archibald Alexander Hodge and Benjamin B. Warfield, "Inspiration," *Presbyterian Review* 6 (April 1881): 227.

[11]Riddlebarger, "The Lion of Princeton," 83-132, 268-332.

[12]Ibid., 83, 329-30.

[13]Ibid., 101-105, 329 n. 212.

[14]Ibid., 106-120.

[15]Ibid., 108, quoting Warfield, "The Question of Miracles," in *Shorter Writings*, 2:181.

[16]Warfield, "Apologetics," in *Studies in Theology*, 5.

[17]Works about Lewis of most relevance to his apologetics include Richard B. Cunningham, *C. S. Lewis: Defender of the Faith* (Philadelphia: Westminster Press, 1967); John Beversluis, *C. S. Lewis and the Search for Rational Religion* (Grand Rapids: Eerdmans, 1985), which is highly (and, most agree, unfairly) critical of Lewis; Richard L. Purtill, *C. S. Lewis's Case for the Christian Faith* (San Francisco: Harper & Row, 1985); Andrew Walker and James Patrick, eds., *A Christian for All Christians: Essays in Honor of C. S. Lewis* (London: Hodder & Stoughton, 1990; Washington, D.C.: Regnery Gateway; Lanham, Md.: National Book Network, 1992); Colin Duriez, *The C. S. Lewis Handbook* (Grand Rapids: Baker, 1994); Peter Kreeft, *C. S. Lewis for the Third Millennium: Six Essays on "The Abolition of Man"* (San Francisco: Ignatius, 1994); John A. Sims, *Missionaries to the Skeptics: Christian Apologists for the Twentieth Century: C. S. Lewis, E. J. Carnell, and Reinhold Niebuhr* (Macon, Ga.: Mercer University Press, 1995); Scott R. Burson and Jerry L. Walls, *C. S. Lewis and Francis Schaeffer: Lessons for a New Century from the Most Influential Apologists of Our Time* (Downers Grove, Ill.: InterVarsity, 1998); Victor Reppert, *C. S. Lewis's Dangerous Idea: In Defense of the Argument from Reason* (Downers Grove, Ill.: InterVarsity, 2003); and Art Lindsley, *C. S. Lewis's Case for Christ: Insights from Reason, Imagination and Faith* (Downers Grove, Ill.: InterVarsity, 2005). For a stimulating perspective on Lewis that does not overtly support his position, see Armand M. Nicholi, *The Question of God: C. S. Lewis and Sigmund Freud Debate God, Love, Sex, and the Meaning of Life* (New York: Free Press, 2002).

[18]Lewis wrote voluminously, and many of his writings, while not expressly works of apologetics, had an apologetic function or relevance. His most important and directly apologetical works were *Mere Christianity* (New York: Macmillan, 1952); *Miracles: A Preliminary Study*, 2nd ed. (New York: Macmillan, 1960); *The Problem of Pain* (New York: Macmillan, 1962); *Christian Reflections*, ed. Walter Hooper (Grand Rapids: Eerdmans, 1967); and *God in the Dock: Essays on Theology and Ethics*, ed. Walter Hooper (Grand Rapids: Eerdmans, 1970).

[19]On Lewis's conversion, see especially David C. Downing, *The Most Reluctant Convert: C. S. Lewis's Journey to Faith* (Downers Grove, Ill.: InterVarsity, 2002). Even those well read in Lewis will learn much about the context of his thought from this insightful book.

[20]Lewis, "Answers to Questions on Christianity," in *God in the Dock*, 58.

[21]Michael Maudlin, "1993 Christianity Today Book Awards," *Christianity Today*, 5 April 1993, 28, cited in Burson and Walls, *C. S. Lewis & Francis Schaeffer*, 31.

[22]Lewis, *The Pilgrim's Regress: An Allegorical Apology for Christianity* (Grand Rapids: Eerdmans, 1933; rev. ed., New York: Sheed & Ward, 1944).

[23]Lewis, *Surprised by Joy: The Shape of My Early Life* (London: Geoffrey Bles, 1955; New York:

Harcourt, Brace & World, 1956).

[24]Lewis, *Out of the Silent Planet* (New York: Macmillan, 1943); *Perelandra* (New York: Macmillan, 1944); *That Hideous Strength* (New York: Macmillan, 1946); *The Chronicles of Narnia*, 7 vols. (New York: Macmillan, 1950-1956). Helpful studies of these books include David C. Downing, *Planets in Peril: A Critical Study of C.S. Lewis's Ransom Trilogy* (Amherst: University of Massachusetts Press, 1995); Kathryn Lindskoog, *Journey into Narnia* (Pasadena, Calif.: Hope Publishing, 1997); Peter Schakel, *Reason and Imagination in C. S. Lewis: A Study in Till We Have Faces* (Grand Rapids: Eerdmans, 1984).

[25]*Letters of C. S. Lewis*, ed. W. H. Lewis (London: Geoffrey Bles, 1966), 167, cited in Burson and Walls, *C. S. Lewis & Francis Schaeffer*, 166.

[26]C. S. Lewis, "Sometimes Fairy Stories May Say Best What's to Be Said," in *Of Other Worlds: Essays and Stories*, ed. Walter Hooper (New York: Harcourt, Brace & World, 1966), 37; cf. Burson and Walls, 166.

[27]Burson and Walls, *C. S. Lewis & Francis Schaeffer*, 46.

[28]Lyle W. Dorsett, *The Essential C. S. Lewis* (New York: Collier, 1988), 3, cited in Burson and Walls, *C. S. Lewis & Francis Schaeffer*, 12-13.

[29]*Time*, 7 April 1980, 66, quoted in Purtill, *C. S. Lewis's Case for the Christian Faith*, 1.

[30]Duncan Sprague, "The Unfundamental C. S. Lewis: Key Components of Lewis's View of Scripture." *Mars Hill Review* 2 (May 1995): 53-63, accessed online at < http://www.leaderu.com/marshill/mhr02/lewis1.html >.

[31]Geisler, *Baker Encyclopedia of Christian Apologetics*, 42; David K. Clark, *Dialogical Apologetics: A Person-Centered Approach to Christian Defense* (Grand Rapids: Baker, 1993), 108.

[32]Lewis, "Christian Apologetics," in *God in the Dock*, 92.

[33]The evidentialist John Warwick Montgomery, in some comments he made on the first edition of this book, describes Lewis as his "mentor" and expresses incredulity that "C. S. Lewis is put in the same bed with Norman Geisler" ("Editor's Introduction," Special Issue: John Warwick Montgomery's Apologetic, *Global Journal of Classical Theology* 3, 1 [March 2002], online at < http://www.trinitysem.edu/journal/jwm_intro_v3n1.html >. Of course, there are significant differences between Lewis and Geisler (and no doubt significant similarities between Lewis and Montgomery). Yet the approaches of Lewis and Geisler are sufficiently alike (prove that God exists [if necessary], then present the evidence for Christ) that they may be placed in the same "family" or basic type of apologetics.

[34]The most important books authored by Geisler alone that are of special importance to apologetics include *Christian Apologetics* (Grand Rapids: Baker, 1976); *The Roots of Evil* (Grand Rapids: Zondervan, 1978); *Miracles and Modern Thought* (Grand Rapids: Zondervan, 1982); *Baker Encyclopedia of Christian Apologetics* (Grand Rapids: Baker, 1999); and *Systematic Theology, Volume One: Introduction, Bible* (Minneapolis: Bethany House, 2002). Geisler has also co-authored numerous books, the most important of which for our purposes are *Philosophy of Religion*, 2d ed. with Winfried Corduan (Grand Rapids: Baker, 1988); with William D. Watkins, *Worlds Apart: A Handbook on World Views*, 2d ed. (Grand Rapids: Baker, 1989); with Ronald M. Brooks, *When Skeptics Ask: A Handbook of Christian Evidences* (Wheaton, Ill.: Victor, 1990); and with Frank Turek, *I Don't Have Enough Faith to Be an Atheist*, Foreword by David Limbaugh (Wheaton, Ill.: Good News Publishers—Crossway Books, 2004). See also *To Everyone an Answer: A Case for the Christian Worldview: Essays in Honor of Norman L. Geisler*, ed. Francis J. Beckwith, William Lane Craig, and J. P. Moreland (Downers Grove, Ill.: InterVarsity Press, 2004).

[35]In 2003, Geisler resigned his membership in ETS in protest of the society's retaining Clark Pinnock as a member. According to Geisler, Pinnock's view of Scripture is incompatible with biblical

inerrancy as understood historically in the ETS.

[36]Very little has been written either positively or negatively about Geisler's apologetics or his thought generally. One brief article critiquing Geisler's apologetic method is Richard A. Purdy, "Norman Geisler's Neo-Thomistic Apologetics," *Journal of the Evangelical Theological Society* 25 (1982). A more recent article that critiques the apologetic of Geisler and other classical apologists is Doug Erlandson, "The Resurrection of Thomism," *Antithesis* 2, 3 (May/June 1991).

[37]This 12-point argument is prominently featured in Geisler and Turek, *I Don't Have Enough Faith to Be an Atheist*, and is also developed in a series available in video and audio formats entitled "12 Points that Show Christianity Is True" (http://www.impactapologetics.com/).

[38]All page references in this section are from Geisler and Corduan, *Philosophy of Religion*. Since the book was originally authored by Geisler alone, and since our focus here is on Geisler's apologetic, in the text we refer to the book simply as Geisler's.

[39]All references in this section are to Geisler, *Christian Apologetics*.

[40]Kreeft's most important apologetics-oriented works include *Between Heaven and Hell: A Dialog Somewhere Beyond Death with John F. Kennedy, C. S. Lewis and Aldous Huxley* (Downers Grove, Ill.: InterVarsity, 1982); *Making Sense Out of Suffering* (Ann Arbor: Servant, 1986); *Socrates Meets Jesus* (Downers Grove, Ill.: InterVarsity, 1987; reprinted with new introduction, 2002); *Fundamentals of the Faith* (San Francisco: Ignatius, 1988); *Yes or No?* 2d ed. (San Francisco: Ignatius, 1991); and with Ronald K. Tacelli, *Handbook of Christian Apologetics: Hundreds of Answers to Crucial Questions* (Downers Grove, Ill.: InterVarsity, 1994). Note that Kreeft has books published by the evangelical Protestant firm InterVarsity Press, others by the Catholic firm Ignatius Press, and still others by the ecumenical firm Servant Books.

[41]Peter Kreeft, ed., *A Summa of the "Summa": The Essential Philosophical Passages of St. Thomas Aquinas' "Summa Theologica" Edited and Explained for Beginners* (San Francisco: Ignatius, 1990).

[42]All parenthetical references in this section are to Kreeft and Tacelli, *Handbook of Christian Apologetics*.

[43]Kreeft's interest in and affinity for Lewis is typified by his recent book, *C. S. Lewis for the Third Millennium: Six Essays on "The Abolition of Man"* (San Francisco: Ignatius Press, 1994).

[44]The essay "Man or Rabbit?" (388-392) was taken from Lewis, *God in the Dock*, 108-113.

[45]Peter Kreeft, *Between Heaven and Hell*, 32-33.

[46]See Craig's books *The Existence of God and the Beginning of the Universe* (San Bernardino, Calif.: Here's Life, 1979); *The Kalām Cosmological Argument*, Library of Philosophy and Religion (New York: Macmillan, 1979); *The Cosmological Argument from Plato to Leibniz* (New York: Macmillan, 1980); and Paul Copan and William Lane Craig, *Creation Out of Nothing: A Biblical, Philosophical, and Scientific Exploration* (Grand Rapids: Baker Academic; Leicester, England: Apollos, 2004).

[47]See *The Historical Argument for the Resurrection of Jesus During the Deist Controversy*, Texts and Studies in Religion, vol. 23 (Lewiston, N.Y.: Edwin Mellen Press, 1985); *Assessing the New Testament Evidence for the Historicity of the Resurrection of Jesus*, Studies in the Bible and Early Christianity, vol. 16 (Lewiston, N.Y.: Edwin Mellen Press, 1989); *Knowing the Truth about the Resurrection* (Ann Arbor: Servant, 1991).

[48]Craig argues that God knows all things, including all future events, but in no sense predestines or predetermines the future. This is not a question that will be explored in this book. There are two notable introductions to the most prevalent views within evangelicalism: David Basinger and Randall Basinger, eds., *Predestination and Free Will: Four Views*, by John Feinberg, Norman Geisler, Bruce Reichenbach, and Clark Pinnock (Downers Grove, IL: InterVarsity Press, 1986); and another 'Four Views' book to which Craig contributed: James K. Beilby and Paul R. Eddy, eds.,

Divine Foreknowledge: Four Views, by Gregory A. Boyd, David Hunt, William Lane Craig, and Paul Helm (Downers Grove, Ill.: InterVarsity, 2001).

[49]In addition to his contribution to *Divine Foreknowledge: Four Views* (see previous note), see Craig, *Divine Foreknowledge and Human Freedom: The Coherence of Theism: Omniscience* (Leiden and New York: E. J. Brill, 1990); *The Only Wise God: The Compatibility of Divine Foreknowledge and Human Freedom* (Grand Rapids: Baker, 1987); "Politically Incorrect Salvation," in *Christian Apologetics in the Postmodern World*, ed. Timothy R. Phillips and Dennis L. Ockholm (Downers Grove, Ill.: InterVarsity, 1995), 75-97.

[50]See especially William Lane Craig, *Time and Eternity: Exploring God's Relationship to Time* (Westchester, Ill.: Crossway Books, 2001), and his contribution to *God and Time: Essays on the Divine Nature*, ed. Gregory E. Ganssle and David M. Woodruff (New York: Oxford University Press, 2002).

[51]Craig, *Reasonable Faith: Christian Truth and Apologetics* (Wheaton, Ill.: Crossway, 1994). This book is a revised version of *Apologetics: An Introduction* (Chicago: Moody, 1984).

[52]J. P. Moreland and William Lane Craig, *Philosophical Foundations for a Christian Worldview* (Downers Grove, Ill.: InterVarsity, 2003).

[53]Craig also engaged an atheist philosopher in an extremely technical written debate on the cosmological argument: William Lane Craig and Quentin Smith, *Theism, Atheism, and Big Bang Cosmology* (Oxford: Clarendon, 1993).

[54]This debate was published with responses from four biblical scholars: *Will the Real Jesus Please Stand Up? A Debate between William Lane Craig and John Dominic Crossan*, moderated by William F. Buckley, Jr., ed. Paul Copan, with responses from Robert J. Miller, Craig L. Blomberg, Marcus Borg, and Ben Witherington III (Grand Rapids: Baker, 1998). Crossan is a former co-chair of the ultraliberal "Jesus Seminar." See also *Jesus' Resurrection: Fact or Figment? A Debate on the Resurrection between William Lane Craig and Gerd Lüdemann*, ed. Paul Copan and Ronald Tacelli (Downers Grove, Ill.: InterVarsity, 2000).

[55]*Does God Exist? The Craig—Flew Debate*, ed. Stan W. Wallace (Aldershot, Hants, England; Burlington, Vt.: Ashgate, 2003). See also William Lane Craig and Walter Sinnott-Armstrong, *God? A Debate between a Christian and an Atheist*, Point/Counterpoint Series, James P. Sterba, series ed. (New York: Oxford University Press, 2004).

[56]"My Pilgrimage from Atheism to Theism: A Discussion between Antony Flew and Gary R. Habermas," *Philosophia Christi* 6 (2004): 197-211. See below, chapter 10 n. 36 (p. 608).

[57]Craig, "Classical Apologetics," in *Five Views on Apologetics*, ed. Steven B. Cowan, Counterpoint series (Grand Rapids: Zondervan, 2000), 26-55; see our comments on this book in the Appendix.

[58]All parenthetical references in this section are from Craig's *Reasonable Faith*.

CHAPTER 5

[1]Geisler, *Christian Apologetics*, 29-46.

[2]Geisler, *Baker Encyclopedia of Christian Apologetics*, 428.

[3]Warfield, "Apologetics,"in *Studies in Theology*, 8-9.

[4]Geisler, *Baker Encyclopedia of Christian Apoloogetics*, 427.

[5]Warfield, "Apologetics," in *Studies in Theology*, 15; so also "Introduction to Francis R. Beattie's Apologetics," in *Shorter Writings*, 2:99; "A Review of *De Zekerheid des Geloofs*," in *Shorter Writings*, 2:114 (where the word *not* has been accidentally omitted!).

[6]Warfield, "The Deity of Christ," in *Shorter Writings*, 1:152.

[7]Geisler, *Christian Apologetics*, 133-36, 141-45.

[8]Ibid., 43.

[9]See below, chapter 6, for details on Geisler's cosmological argument.

[10]For examples of this line of reasoning, see Winfried Corduan, *No Doubt about It: The Case for Christianity* (Nashville: Broadman & Holman, 1997), 36-38; Paul Copan, *"True for You, but Not for Me": Deflating the Slogans that Leave Christians Speechless* (Minneapolis: Bethany House, 1998), 23-25. We used this same argument in *An Unchanging Faith in a Changing World: Understanding and Responding to Issues that Christians Face Today* (Nashville: Nelson, Oliver, 1997), 54-57.

[11]C. S. Lewis, "On Obstinacy in Belief," in *The World's Last Night and Other Essays* (New York: Harcourt, Brace & World, 1960), 18.

[12]Ibid., 20, 21.

[13]William Lane Craig, in Craig and Crossan, *Will the Real Jesus Please Stand Up*, 160.

[14]All parenthetical references in this section are from Craig's *Reasonable Faith*. Craig gives a very similar exposition of his approach in his essay, "Classical Apologetics," in *Five Views on Apologetics*, ed. Cowan, 26-55.

[15]As Craig observes in an endnote, the term comes from Edward John Carnell, but Craig applies the concept to apologetics in a way that differs from Carnell's approach (326 n. 24).

[16]Norman Geisler, *Knowing the Truth about Creation: How It Happened and What It Means for Us* (Ann Arbor, Mich.: Servant, 1989), 79.

[17]Mayers, *Balanced Apologetics*, 7-8.

[18]Warfield, "Apologetics," in *Studies in Theology*, 4.

[19]Ibid., 5.

[20]Ibid., 7.

[21]Lewis, *Mere Christianity*, 6; see 6-9.

[22]Lewis, "Christian Apologetics," in *God in the Dock*, ed. Walter Hooper (Grand Rapids: Eerdmans, 1970), 90.

[23]All parenthetical references in this paragraph are to Norman L. Geisler and Paul D. Feinberg, *Introduction to Philosophy: A Christian Perspective* (Grand Rapids: Baker, 1980).

[24]Lewis, *The Weight of Glory and Other Addresses* (Grand Rapids: Eerdmans, 1949; New York: Collier, 1980), 50.

[25]Stuart C. Hackett, *The Resurrection of Theism: Prolegomena to Christian Apology*, 2nd ed. (Grand Rapids: Baker, 1982), 20.

[26]J. P. Moreland and William Lane Craig, *Philosophical Foundations for a Christian Worldview* (Downers Grove, Ill.: InterVarsity, 2003). Parenthetical references in this paragraph are to this book.

[27]B. B. Warfield, "Christianity and Our Times," in *Shorter Writings*, 1:49.

[28]Lewis, "Christian Apologetics," in *God in the Dock*, 100-101.

[29]Lewis, "Dogma and the Universe," in *God in the Dock*, 39.

[30]Lewis, "Religion and Rocketry," in *World's Last Night*, 84.

[31]Geisler, *Knowing the Truth about Creation*, 110.

[32]Ibid., 96, 97.

33See, for example, B. B. Warfield, "Charles Darwin's Religious Life: A Sketch in Spiritual Biography," in *Studies in Theology*, 541-82; "Darwin's Arguments against Christianity and against Religion," in *Shorter Writings*, 2:132-41. For a collection of his writings pertaining to science arranged in chronological order, see B. B. Warfield, *Evolution, Science and Scripture: Selected Writings*, ed. Mark A. Noll and David N. Livingstone (Grand Rapids: Baker Books, 2000). Cf. David N. Livingstone, *Darwin's Forgotten Defenders: The Encounter between Evangelical Theology and Evolutionary Thought* (Grand Rapids: Eerdmans; Edinburgh: Scottish Academic Press, 1987); W. Brian Aucker, "Hodge and Warfield on Evolution," *Presbyterion* 20 (1994): 131-42.

34C.S. Lewis, "The Funeral of a Great Myth," in *Christian Reflections*, ed. Walter Hooper (Grand Rapids: Eerdmans, 1967), 85.

35Geisler, *Knowing the Truth about Creation*, 96-97, cf. 153-54. Craig's treatment of the age of the universe is discussed in chapter 6.

36See especially J. P. Moreland, "Kuhn's Epistemology: A Paradigm Afloat," *Bulletin of the Evangelical Philosophical Society* 4 (1981): 33-60; "The Scientific Realism Debate and the Role of Philosophy in Integration," *Bulletin of the Evangelical Theological Society* 10 (1987): 38-49; *Scaling the Secular City: A Defense of Christianity* (Grand Rapids: Baker, 1987), 185-223; *Christianity and the Nature of Science* (Grand Rapids: Baker, 1989); "Theistic Science and Methodological Naturalism," in *The Creation Hypothesis: Scientific Evidence for an Intelligent Designer*, ed. J. P. Moreland (Downers Grove, Ill.: InterVarsity, 1994), 41-66; "Science, Miracles, Agency Theory, and the God-of-the-Gaps," in *In Defense of Miracles: A Comprehensive Case for God's Action in History*, ed. R. Douglas Geivett and Gary R. Habermas (Downers Grove, Ill.: InterVarsity, 1997), 132-48; and Part IV, "Philosophy of Science," in Moreland and Craig, *Philosophical Foundations for a Christian Worldview*, 305-90. In places in his writings Moreland refers to himself as an evidentialist, but this is always in a broader sense of an apologist who uses "rational argumentation and evidence . . . as epistemic support for Christian theism" (Moreland, *Christianity and the Nature of Science*, 205 n. 42). Moreland's approach borrows from evidentialism in the narrower sense of the term (as we use it in this book), but in general seems fairly classified as a classical approach.

37Moreland, *Christianity and the Nature of Science*, 103-108; *Scaling the Secular City*, 197; Moreland and Craig, *Philosophical Foundations*, 347-48.

38*Christianity and the Nature of Science*, 103-138; *Scaling the Secular City*, 198-200; *Philosophical Foundations*, 348-50.

39*Christianity and the Nature of Science*, 205-206.

40Ibid., 206-211; see also *Philosophical Foundations*, 326-45.

41*Christianity and the Nature of Science*, 13.

42*Scaling the Secular City*, 200-208; *Philosophical Foundations*, 350-52.

43*Christianity and the Nature of Science*, 23-35; *Scaling the Secular City*, 208-213.

44*Christianity and the Nature of Science*, 221-34.

45*Scaling the Secular City*, 214-23.

46Ibid., 33-41, 52-55.

47Warfield, "How to Get Rid of Christianity," in *Shorter Writings*, 1:59.

48Parenthetical references are to Geisler, *Christian Apologetics*.

49This material is repeated—some of it verbatim—and augmented in "Appendix Two: Do Historical Facts Speak for Themselves?" in Geisler, *Systematic Theology, Volume One: Introduction, Bible*, 585-89.

[50]Parenthetical references in this section are to Geisler and Corduan, *Philosophy of Religion*.

[51]William Lane Craig, in *The Craig—Flew Debate*, ed. Wallace, 23, 24.

[52]Ibid., 179.

CHAPTER 6

[1]Craig, "A Classical Apologist's Closing Remarks," in *Five Views on Apologetics*, ed. Cowan, 320-21.

[2]Archibald Alexander Hodge and Benjamin B. Warfield, "Inspiration," *Presbyterian Review* 6 (April 1881): 227.

[3]Other good examples include Stuart C. Hackett, *The Reconstruction of the Christian Revelation Claim: A Philosophical and Critical Apologetic* (Grand Rapids: Baker, 1984); Winfried Corduan, *No Doubt About It: The Case for Christianity* (Nashville: Broadman & Holman, 1997).

[4]Geisler, *Christian Apologetics*, 353.

[5]Richard L. Purtill, *Reason to Believe* (Grand Rapids: Eerdmans, 1974), 119.

[6]Stephen Neill, *Anglicanism* (New York: Oxford University Press, 1977), 123.

[7]Gordon R. Lewis, *Testing Christianity's Truth Claims: Approaches to Christian Apologetics* (Chicago: Moody, 1976), 204; cf. Purtill, *Reason to Believe*, 119-27. We should note that Gordon Lewis is not, strictly speaking, a classical apologist, but rather advocates the approach taken by Edward John Carnell (see chapter 20).

[8]Norman L. Geisler, "Philosophical Presuppositions of Biblical Errancy," in *Inerrancy*, ed. Geisler (Grand Rapids: Zondervan, 1979), 305-24.

[9]Ibid., 306.

[10]James W. Sire, *The Universe Next Door: A Basic Worldview Catalog*, 3d ed. (Downers Grove, Ill.: InterVarsity, 1997), 17.

[11]Ibid., 194.

[12]In the first edition of the book (1976), postmodernism was not discussed.

[13]The chart is based in part on Peter Kreeft, "Introduction: Why Debate the Existence of God?" in *Does God Exist? The Debate Between Theists and Atheists*, by J. P. Moreland and Kai Nielsen (Buffalo: Prometheus Books, 1993), 15, and in part on Norman Geisler and William D. Watkins, *Worlds Apart: A Handbook on World Views*, 2d ed. (Grand Rapids: Baker, 1989), 16. It should be noted that in practice religions sometimes combine elements of more than one of these worldviews. For example, some forms of Hinduism affirm both pantheism and polytheism.

[14]C. S. Lewis, letter to Sheldon Vanauken, in *A Severe Mercy* (San Francisco: Harper & Row, 1977), 89-90.

[15]Lewis, "God in the Dock," in *God in the Dock*, 244.

[16]See Geisler, *Christian Apologetics*, 168-69, 186-87, 207-208, 223-24; Geisler and Watkins, *Worlds Apart*, 60-61, 101, 139, 180-81, 210-11, 249-50.

[17]Warfield, "Christianity and Revelation," in *Shorter Writings*, 1:23.

[18]Geisler, *Christian Apologetics*, 187.

[19]Ibid., 188.

[20]Ibid., 189.

21Hackett, *Resurrection of Theism*, 365.

22Cf. C.S. Lewis, "Christian Apologetics," in *God in the Dock*, 92, quoted earlier in chapter 4 of this book.

23Warfield, "Atheism," in *Shorter Writings*, 1:39.

24Ibid., 1:38.

25Warfield, "God," in *Shorter Writings*, 1:70, 71.

26On this argument, see especially Victor Reppert, *C. S. Lewis's Dangerous Idea: In Defense of the Argument from Reason* (Downers Grove, Ill.: InterVarsity, 2003); Symposium on the Argument from Reason (Reppert, et. al.), *Philosophia Christi* 5, 1 (2003): 9-89; "The Argument from Reason and Hume's Legacy," in *In Defense of Natural Theology: A Post-Humean Assessment*, ed. James F. Sennett and Douglas Groothuis (Downers Grove, Ill.: InterVarsity, 2005), 253-70.

27G. K. Chesterton, *Orthodoxy*, Image Books (Garden City, N.Y.: Doubleday, 1959 [1903]), 106-110; C. S. Lewis, *The Abolition of Man* (New York: Macmillan, 1947); *Mere Christianity* (New York: Macmillan, 1952).

28Parenthetical references in this paragraph are to C. S. Lewis, *Mere Christianity*, rev. and enlarged ed. (New York: Macmillan, 1960).

29Modern works on the ontological argument include Karl Barth, *Anselm:* Fides Quaerens Intellectum: *Anselm's Proof of the Existence of God in the Context of His Theological Scheme*, 2d ed. (London: SCM; Richmond: John Knox, 1960); Charles Hartshorne, *Anselm's Discovery: A Re-examination of the Ontological Proof for God's Existence* (La Salle, Ill.: Open Court, 1965); John Hick and Arthur C. McGill, eds., *The Many-Faced Argument: Recent Studies on the Ontological Argument for the Existence of God* (London: Macmillan, 1968); Alvin Plantinga, ed., *The Ontological Argument from St. Anselm to Contemporary Philosophers* (London: Macmillan; Garden City, N.Y.: Doubleday, Anchor Books, 1968); Alvin Plantinga, *The Nature of Necessity* (Oxford: Clarendon, 1974); Sproul, Gerstner, and Lindsley, *Classical Apologetics*, 93-108; Norman Geisler and Winfried Corduan, *Philosophy of Religion*, 2d ed. (Grand Rapids: Baker, 1988), 123-49; Graham Oppy, *Ontological Arguments and Belief in God* (Cambridge and New York: Cambridge University Press, 1995); Brian Leftow, "The Ontological Argument," in *The Oxford Handbook of Philosophy of Religion*, ed. William J. Wainwright (Oxford and New York: Oxford University Press, 2005), 80-115.

30See Geisler and Corduan, *Philosophy of Religion*, 143.

31Ibid., 148.

32William Lane Craig, *The Existence of God and the Beginning of the Universe* (San Bernardino, Calif.: Here's Life, 1979); *The Kalām Cosmological Argument*, Library of Philosophy and Religion (New York: Macmillan, 1979); *The Cosmological Argument from Plato to Leibniz* (New York: Macmillan, 1980); and Paul Copan and William Lane Craig, *Creation Out of Nothing: A Biblical, Philosophical, and Scientific Exploration* (Grand Rapids: Baker Academic; Leicester, England: Apollos, 2004). Many other apologists and philosophers have written on the subject since Craig, and all of them are heavily indebted to him. Two recent studies worth mentioning are those by evidentialist R. Douglas Geivett, "The *Kalam* Cosmological Argument," in *To Everyone an Answer*, ed. Beckwith et. al., 61-76; and Garrett J. DeWeese and Joshua Rasmussen, "Hume and the *Kalam* Cosmological Argument," in *In Defense of Natural Theology*, ed. Sennett and Groothuis, 123-49.

33Moreland, *Scaling the Secular City*, 18; see 18-42 for Moreland's own excellent presentation of the argument.

34Craig, *Reasonable Faith*, 92-94.

35Ibid., 94-100.

36Ibid., 116.

[37]Ibid., 100-116. The scientific argument for God's existence is discussed in chapter 10.

[38]For a recent defense by another evangelical scholar, see W. David Beck, "A Thomistic Cosmological Argument," in *To Everyone an Answer*, ed. Beckwith et. al., 95-107 (a book of essays in honor of Geisler).

[39]Geisler and Corduan, *Philosophy of Religion*, 207.

[40]Ibid., 175.

[41]Purtill, *Reason to Believe*, 52.

[42]The word *theodicy* comes from the Greek words *theos* (God) and *dikaios* (just), and thus means the project of explaining God's justice in light of the evil in God's world. Although the word might be taken to imply that apologists are "defending God," the point really is not to defend or justify *God*, but to defend or justify *belief in God* in light of the problem of evil.

[43]Geisler and Corduan, *Philosophy of Religion*, 313, emphasis in original.

[44]Ibid., 310.

[45]Ibid., 328.

[46]Hugh Silvester, *Arguing With God* (Downers Grove, Ill.: InterVarsity, 1971), 61.

[47]Geisler and Corduan, *Philosophy of Religion*, 339-40.

[48]Ibid., 353-56.

[49]Arlie J. Hoover, *The Case for Christian Theism* (Grand Rapids: Baker, 1976), 256.

[50]Geisler and Corduan, *Philosophy of Religion*, 363.

[51]Ibid., 379-85.

[52]Warfield, "Christianity and Revelation," in *Shorter Writings*, 1:26-27 (quote on 27).

[53]Craig, *Reasonable Faith*, 155.

[54]Ibid., 51.

[55]Ibid., 174.

[56]C.S. Lewis, "Miracles," in *God in the Dock*, 27.

[57]"Impossible," a song by Richard Rodgers and Oscar Hammerstein II, in their 1957 musical play *Cinderella*.

[58]Lewis, "Miracles," 27.

[59]Hoover, *Case for Christian Theism*, 139.

[60]Geisler, *Christian Apologetics*, 329, where these are numbers (2) and (3), with point (1) being the reliability of the New Testament. But this point may also be treated as part of the argument for (2). Thus at its simplest level the argument involves two steps.

[61]The term *trilemma* apparently originated with Josh McDowell in his extremely popular apologetic book *Evidence that Demands a Verdict* (San Bernardino, Calif.: Campus Crusade for Christ, 1972).

[62]Kreeft and Tacelli, *Handbook of Christian Apologetics*, 165, 171. Kreeft and Tacelli use the terms *Lord, liar, lunatic, guru,* and *myth* to designate the five alternatives. An interesting variation on this argument is found in Kenneth Richard Samples, *Without a Doubt: Answering the 20 Toughest Faith Questions* (Grand Rapids: Baker, 2004), 104-119, who adds and refutes another alternative (that Jesus was an extraterrestrial). See also Kenneth D. Boa and Robert M. Bowman, Jr., *20 Compelling Evidences that God Exists: Discover Why Believing in God Makes So Much Sense* (Colorado Springs: Cook Communications—Victor Academic, 2005), 203-16.

[63]Geisler, *Christian Apologetics*, 314-22, especially 316.

[64]Kreeft and Tacelli, *Handbook of Christian Apologetics*, 165.

[65]Ibid., 166-67.

[66]Ibid., 169.

[67]Lewis, *Mere Christianity*, 56; cf. "What Are We to Make of Jesus Christ?" in *God in the Dock*, 156-60.

CHAPTER 7

[1]Geisler, *Christian Apologetics*, 41.

[2]R. C. Sproul, *The Psychology of Atheism* (Minneapolis: Bethany Fellowship, 1974), 28-29.

[3]Ibid., 29.

[4]Sire, *Universe Next Door*, 18.

[5]Geisler, *Christian Apologetics*, 151.

[6]Montgomery, *Faith Founded on Fact*, xiv.

[7]Geisler, *Christian Apologetics*, 129, emphasis deleted.

[8]Ibid., 131.

[9]Hanna, *Crucial Questions in Apologetics*, 99.

[10]Geisler and Corduan, *Philosophy of Religion*, 171-72.

[11]Geisler, *Baker Encyclopedia of Christian Apologetics*, 401.

[12]John C. Whitcomb, "Christian Evidences and Apologetics" (class syllabus, Grace Theological Seminary, n.d.), 13.

[13]Hoover, *Case for Christian Theism*, 116.

[14]Thomas V. Morris, *Francis Schaeffer's Apologetics: A Critique*, 2d ed. (Grand Rapids: Baker, 1987), 52.

[15]Ibid., 53. Morris applies this criticism to the writings of Francis Schaeffer, who uses classic apologetic arguments within a moderately Reformed apologetic framework (see chapter 20).

[16]Ibid.

CHAPTER 8

[1]Paley's work has been reprinted many times; we refer here to William Paley, *Natural Theology: or, Evidences of the Existence and Attributes of the Deity, Collected from the Appearances of Nature* (1802; reprint, Houston: St. Thomas Press, 1972).

[2]Ibid., 394.

[3]Ibid., 398.

[4]See especially William Lane Craig, *The Historical Argument for the Resurrection of Jesus During the Deist Controversy*, Texts and Studies in Religion 23 (Lewiston, N.Y.: Edwin Mellen Press, 1985).

[5]Locke's epistemology is developed in *An Essay Concerning Human Understanding* (1689); a convenient edition is found in Great Books of the Western World, vol. 35 (Chicago: Encyclopaedia Britannica, 1952), 83-395. His chief apologetic work was *The Reasonableness of Christianity: As Delivered in the Scriptures* (1695); a recent edition is that edited by John C. Higgins-Biddle,

Clarendon Edition of the Works of John Locke (Oxford and New York: Oxford University Press, 1998). A valuable collection of Locke's religious thought is Victor Nuovo, ed., *John Locke: Writings on Religion* (Oxford and New York: Oxford University Press, 2002).

[6]For a brief summary of Locke's apologetics, see Craig, *Reasonable Faith*, 22-23. Important studies and reference works include Richard Ashcraft, "Faith and Knowledge in Locke's Philosophy," in *John Locke: Problems and Perspectives*, ed. John W. Yolton (New York: Cambridge University Press, 1969); Vere Chappell, ed., *The Cambridge Companion to Locke* (New York: Cambridge University Press, 1994); Nicholas Wolterstorff, *John Locke and the Ethics of Belief*, Cambridge Studies in Religion and Critical Thought, vol. 2 (New York: Cambridge University Press, 1996); Alan P. F. Sell, *John Locke and the Eighteenth-Century Divines* (Cardiffe: University of Wales Press, 1997); John Dunn, *Locke: A Very Short Introduction*, updated ed. (Oxford and New York: Oxford University Press, 2003). A recent significant work on Locke's political philosophy with insight into his philosophy of religion is Jeremy Waldron, *God, Locke, and Equality: Christian Foundations in Locke's Political Thought* (Cambridge and New York: Cambridge University Press, 2002).

[7]Thomas Sherlock, *The Tryal of the Witnesses of the Resurrection of Jesus* (London: J. Roberts, 1729), 98. This book is reprinted in its entirety in John Warwick Montgomery, ed., *Jurisprudence: A Book of Readings* (Strasbourg, France: International Scholarly Publishers, 1974), 339-449 (the quote appears on 436).

[8]Quotations in this section are taken from Joseph Butler, *The Analogy of Religion*, Introduction by Ernest C. Mossner; Milestones of Thought (New York: Frederick Ungar, 1961). Butler's *Analogy* has gone through numerous editions. Works on Butler include Ernest Campbell Mossner, *Bishop Butler and the Age of Reason: A Study in the History of Thought* (New York: Macmillan, 1936); S. A. Grave, "Able and Fair Reasoning of Butler's *Analogy*," *Church History* 47 (1978): 298-307; James Rurak, "Butler's *Analogy*: A Still Interesting Synthesis of Reason and Revelation," *Anglican Theological Review* 62 (1980): 365-81; Ted Honderich, *Butler*, Arguments of the Philosophers (New York: Routledge & Kegan Paul, 1986); Thomas M. Gregory, "Apologetics before and after Butler," in *Pressing Toward the Mark: Essays Commemorating Fifty Years of the Orthodox Presbyterian Church*, ed. Charles G. Dennison and Richard C. Gamble (Philadelphia: Committee for the Historian of the Orthodox Presbyterian Church, 1986), 351-367; Christopher Cunliffe, ed., *Joseph Butler's Moral and Religious Thought: Tercentenary Essays* (Oxford: Clarendon; New York: Oxford University Press, 1992).

[9]Works on James Orr include Glen G. Scorgie, "James Orr," in *Handbook of Evangelical Theologians*, ed. Walter A. Elwell (Grand Rapids: Baker, 1993), 12-25; Scorgie, *A Call for Continuity: The Theological Contribution of James Orr* (Macon, Ga.: Mercer University Press, 1988); Robert D. Knudsen, "Apologetics and History," in *Life Is Religion: Essays in Honor of H. Evan Runner*, ed. Henry Vander Goot (Saint Catharines, Ont.: Paideia Press, 1981), 119-33. Knudsen's essay analyzes Orr's thought from a Reformed apologetic perspective.

[10]His best-known book was originally entitled *The Christian View of God and the World as Centering in the Incarnation*. The standard edition is *The Christian View of God and the World*, corrected reprint of 3rd ed. (New York: Scribner, 1897; reprint, Grand Rapids: Eerdmans, 1948; Grand Rapids: Kregel, 1989). His other books include *The Faith of a Modern Christian* (New York: Hodder & Stoughton, 1910); *The Faith that Persuades* (reprint, New York: Harper & Row, 1977); *The Resurrection of Jesus* (London: Hodder & Stoughton, 1909; reprint, Grand Rapids: Zondervan, 1965); and *The Virgin Birth of Christ* (New York: Scribner, 1907).

[11]All parenthetical references in this section are to Orr, *Christian View of God and the World*.

[12]Pinnock's works include *A Defense of Biblical Infallibility*, International Library of Philosophy and Theology (Philadelphia: Presbyterian & Reformed, 1967; Grand Rapids: Baker, 1972); *Set Forth Your Case* (Nutley, N.J.: Craig Press, 1968; reprint, Chicago: Moody, 1971); *Live Now, Brother* (Chicago: Moody, 1972), reprinted as *Are There Any Answers?* (Minneapolis: Bethany House, 1976);

A Case for Faith (Minneapolis: Bethany House, 1987), previously published as *Reason Enough: A Case for the Christian Faith* (Downers Grove, Ill.: InterVarsity, 1980); *The Scripture Principle* (San Francisco: Harper & Row, 1984); and *Tracking the Maze: An Evangelical Perspective on Modern Theology* (San Francisco: Harper & Row, 1990). One of his most important later articles related to apologetics was "Assessing Barth for Apologetics," in *How Karl Barth Changed My Mind*, ed. Donald K. McKim (Grand Rapids: Eerdmans, 1986), 162-165. Works about Pinnock include Peter J. Steen, review of *Set Forth Your Case*, in *Westminster Theological Journal* 31 (1968-1969): 101-109; Nicholas Wolterstorff, "Is Reason Enough? A Review Essay," *Reformed Review* (April 1981): 20-24; Robert M. Price, "Clark H. Pinnock: Conservative and Contemporary," *Evangelical Quarterly* 60 (1988): 157-83; and Robert V. Rakestraw, "Clark H. Pinnock," in *Baptist Theologians*, ed. Timothy George and David S. Dockery (Nashville: Broadman, 1990), 660-84.

[13]Pinnock, *Set Forth Your Case*, 86.

[14]Pinnock, *A Case for Faith*, 18, 120.

[15]Ibid., 120.

[16]Ibid., 88.

[17]Pinnock, "The Philosophy of Christian Evidences," in *Jerusalem and Athens: Critical Discussions on the Philosophy and Apologetics of Cornelius Van Til*, ed. E. R. Geehan (Philadelphia: Presbyterian & Reformed, 1971), 420-25, quote on 425.

[18]Notably *A Defense of Biblical Infallibility;* "The Inspiration of Scripture and the Authority of Jesus Christ," in *God's Inerrant Word: An International Symposium on the Trustworthiness of Scripture*, ed. John Warwick Montgomery (Minneapolis: Bethany House, 1974), 201-218.

[19]Pinnock, *The Scripture Principle*, especially 57-59. On Pinnock's views on inerrancy, see Rex A. Koivisto, "Clark Pinnock and Inerrancy: A Change in Truth Theory?" *Journal of the Evangelical Theological Society* 24 (1981): 138-51; and Pinnock, "A Response to Rex Koivisto," 153-55, in the same volume.

[20]Montgomery's most important apologetics works are *The Shape of the Past: A Christian Response to Secular Philosophies of History* (Minneapolis: Bethany Fellowship, 1962; reprint, 1975); *History and Christianity* (Downers Grove, Ill.: InterVarsity, 1971; reprint, Minneapolis: Bethany House, 1986); *Where Is History Going? Essays in Support of the Historical Truth of the Christian Revelation* (Minneapolis: Bethany Fellowship, 1969); *The Suicide of Christian Theology* (Minneapolis: Bethany Fellowship, 1970); *How Do We Know There Is a God?* (Minneapolis: Bethany Fellowship, 1973); and *Faith Founded on Fact: Essays in Evidential Apologetics* (Nashville: Thomas Nelson, 1978). He is also the editor of *Christianity for the Tough-minded: Essays in Support of an Intellectually Defensible Religious Commitment* (Minneapolis: Bethany Fellowship, 1973) and *Evidence for Faith: Deciding the God Question*, Cornell Symposium on Evidential Apologetics, 1986 (Dallas: Probe Books, 1991; distributed by Word Publishing).

[21]In *Evidence for Faith*, 319-41; parenthetical references in this section are to this essay.

[22]Patrick L. McCloskey and Ronald L. Schoenberg, *Criminal Law Advocacy*, vol. 5 (New York: Matthew Bender, 1984), section 12.01 (b).

[23]Montgomery, "Introduction: The Apologists of Eucatastrophe," in *Myth, Allegory, and Gospel: An Interpretation of J. R. R. Tolkien/C. S. Lewis/G. K. Chesterton/Charles Williams*, ed. Montgomery (Minneapolis: Bethany Fellowship, 1974), 28, 30.

[24]Richard Swinburne, *The Coherence of Theism*, Clarendon Library of Logic and Philosophy (Oxford: Clarendon, 1977; rev. ed., 1993); *The Existence of God* (Oxford: Clarendon, 1979; rev. ed., 1991); and *Faith and Reason* (Oxford: Clarendon, 1981).

[25]Swinburne, *Responsibility and Atonement* (Oxford: Clarendon, 1989); *Revelation: From Metaphor*

to Analogy (Oxford: Clarendon, 1992); *The Christian God* (Oxford: Clarendon, 1994); and *Providence and the Problem of Evil* (Oxford: Clarendon, 1998).

[26]Swinburne, "Intellectual Autobiography," in *Reason and the Christian Religion: Essays in Honour of Richard Swinburne*, ed. Alan G. Padgett (Oxford: Clarendon, 1994), 8.

[27]Swinburne, *Is There a God?* (New York: Oxford University Press, 1996), 2.

[28]In *Is There a God*, chapter 1 (3-19), Swinburne summarizes the argument of his book *The Coherence of Theism*.

[29]Swinburne, *Coherence of Theism*, 295.

[30]Ibid., 176, 220-221; cf. *Existence of God*, 91-92; *Is There a God*, 8-9.

[31]Swinburne, *Is There a God*, 19.

[32]Swinburne, "Intellectual Autobiography," 10.

[33]Swinburne, *Existence of God*, 288-289, 291.

[34]Swinburne, *Is There a God*, 140.

[35]Montgomery, "Introduction: The Apologists of Eucatastrophe," in *Myth, Allegory, and Gospel*, 17.

CHAPTER 9

[1]Bernard Ramm, *Protestant Christian Evidences* (Chicago: Moody, 1953), 16-32.

[2]William Kingdon Clifford, "The Ethics of Belief," in *An Anthology of Atheism and Rationalism*, ed. Gordon Stein (Buffalo: Prometheus Books, 1980), 282. The article was first published in 1877 and soon thereafter in Clifford's *Lectures and Essays*, ed. Leslie Stephen and Frederick Pollock (London: Macmillan, 1879). It has been reprinted several times, for example, in *The Theory of Knowledge: Classical and Contemporary Readings*, ed. Louis P. Pojman (Belmont, Calif.: Wadsworth, 1993).

[3]Dan Story, *Christianity on the Offense: Responding to the Beliefs and Assumptions of Spiritual Seekers* (Grand Rapids: Kregel, 1998), 69.

[4]Montgomery, "The Theologian's Craft: A Discussion of Theory Formation and Theory Testing in Theology," in *Suicide of Christian Theology*, 274.

[5]Montgomery, *Faith Founded on Fact*, xxii-xxiii.

[6]Montgomery, "The Jury Returns: A Juridical Defense of Christianity," in *Evidence for Faith*, 335; see our review of this essay in the preceding chapter.

[7]Montgomery, "The Death of the 'Death of God,'" in *Suicide of Christian Theology*, 125.

[8]Montgomery, *Faith Founded on Fact*, 233.

[9]Montgomery, "Death of the 'Death of God,'" in *Suicide of Christian Theology*, 122.

[10]Montgomery, "Clark's Philosophy of History," in *The Philosophy of Gordon H. Clark*, ed. Ronald H. Nash (Philadelphia: Presbyterian & Reformed, 1968), 387.

[11]Montgomery, *Where Is History Going*, 137.

[12]Montgomery, *Shape of the Past*, 139.

[13]Montgomery, *History and Christianity*, 79.

[14]Montgomery, *Faith Founded on Fact*, 59.

[15]Montgomery, "Clark's Philosophy of History," in *Philosophy of Gordon H. Clark*, edited by Nash, 388.

[16]Montgomery, "How Muslims Do Apologetics," in *Faith Founded on Fact*, 98.

[17]Francis Beckwith, *David Hume's Argument against Miracles: A Critical Analysis* (Lanham, Md.: University Press of America, 1989), 122-23.

[18]See Norman Macbeth, *Darwin Retried: An Appeal to Reason* (Boston: Gambit, 1971); Phillip E. Johnson, *Darwin on Trial* (Washington, D.C.: Regnery Gateway, 1991).

[19]Story, *Christianity on the Offense*, 66, emphasis in original.

[20]Montgomery, *Shape of the Past*, 141.

[21]Ibid., 266.

[22]Jim Leffel, "Our New Challenge: Postmodernism," in *The Death of Truth*, ed. Dennis McCallum (Minneapolis: Bethany House, 1996), 31, quoted in Story, *Christianity on the Offense*, 160.

[23]Story, *Christianity on the Offense*, 170.

[24]Ibid., 385. Mavrodes, it should be noted, is not an evidentialist.

[25]Batts, "Summary and Critique of the Historical Apologetic of John Warwick Montgomery," 46.

[26]Montgomery, "Existence of God," in *Sensible Christianity* (Santa Ana, Calif.: One Way Library, 1976), cassette tapes, vol. 2, tape 1.

[27]Montgomery, *Faith Founded on Fact*, 40.

[28]Ibid., xx.

[29]John A. Bloom, "Why Isn't the Evidence Clearer?" in *Evidence for Faith*, 305-317.

[30]Ibid., 313.

[31]Montgomery, "The Theologian's Craft," in *Suicide of Christian Theology*, 267-313.

[32]Montgomery, "The Suicide of Christian Theology and a Modest Proposal for Its Resurrection," in *Suicide of Christian Theology*, 37.

[33]Ibid., 40.

[34]Richard Swinburne, *The Coherence of Theism*, 220-24; "God and Time," in *Reasoned Faith*, ed. Eleanore Stump (Ithaca, N.Y.: Cornell University Press, 1993), 204-222.

[35]Ibid., 176.

[36]Clark H. Pinnock, "The Need for a Scriptural, and Therefore a Neo-Classical Theism," in *Perspectives on Evangelical Theology*, Papers from the Thirtieth Annual Meeting of the Evangelical Theological Society, edited by Kenneth S. Kantzer and Stanley N. Gundry (Grand Rapids: Baker, 1979), 37-42; "God Limits His Knowledge," in *Predestination and Free Will: Four Views*, ed. David Basinger and Randall Basinger (Downers Grove, Ill.: InterVarsity, 1986), 141-62; "Between Classical and Process Theism," in *Process Theology*, ed. Ronald H. Nash (Grand Rapids: Baker, 1987), 313-27.

[37]See chapter 4, note 36.

[38]Beckwith has written extensively in defense of Christian ethics as well as on other issues of apologetic significance. His earliest apologetic book, *Baha'i* (Minneapolis: Bethany House, 1985), closely follows Montgomery's form of evidentialism. More recent works reflect a more philosophically developed evidentialism. See *David Hume's Argument Against Miracles;* and "History and Miracles," in *In Defense of Miracles: A Comprehensive Case for God's Action in History*, ed. R. Douglas Geivett and Gary R. Habermas (Downers Grove, Ill.: InterVarsity, 1997), 86-98.

[39]See especially R. Douglas Geivett, *Evil and the Evidence for God: The Challenge of John Hick's*

Theodicy, afterword by John Hick (Philadelphia: Temple University Press, 1993); "The Evidential Value of Miracles," in *In Defense of Miracles*, 178-95.

[40]The distinction presented here is a fairly standard one, and seems to have been first articulated by the philosopher C. D. Broad. See, for example, Stanley M. Honer and Thomas C. Hunt, *Invitation to Philosophy: Issues and Options*, 4th ed. (Belmont, Calif.: Wadsworth, 1982), 10-14; William H. Halverson, *A Concise Introduction to Philosophy*, 3rd ed. (New York: Random House, 1976), 10-16; Geisler and Feinberg, *Introduction to Philosophy*, 14-17.

[41]Montgomery, "Clark's Philosophy of History," in *Philosophy of Gordon H. Clark*, edited by Nash, 100.

[42]Montgomery, *Faith Founded on Fact*, 98.

[43]John Warwick Montgomery, ed., *Christianity for the Tough-minded: Essays in Support of an Intellectually Defensible Religious Commitment* (Minneapolis: Bethany Fellowship, 1973).

[44]Swinburne defends this assertion in relation to science in *Simplicity as Evidence of Truth*, Aquinas Lectures (Milwaukee: Marquette University Press, 1997).

[45]See especially Swinburne's reply to Mackie on this point in an appendix to the revised edition of *The Existence of God*, 293-97.

[46]*Is There a God*, 25-26; *Existence of God*, 64-66.

[47]Parenthetical references in this and the next paragraph are taken from Geivett, *Evil and the Evidence for God*.

[48]Beckwith, *David Hume's Argument against Miracles*, 33-34; "History and Miracles," in *In Defense of Miracles*, edited by Geivett and Habermas, 92-93.

[49]J. Oliver Buswell, Jr., *A Systematic Theology of the Christian Religion* (Grand Rapids: Zondervan, 1972), 1:72-101.

[50]Swinburne, *Existence of God*, especially chapters 7–9.

[51]Montgomery, *Christianity for the Tough-Minded*, 26-27; *Suicide of Christian Theology*, 256-58.

[52]Montgomery, *Christianity for the Tough-Minded*, 26.

[53]Robert C. Newman, "The Evidence of Cosmology," in *Evidence for Faith*, 88.

[54]See the web site http://reasons.org.

[55]Hugh Ross, *The Fingerprint of God*, 3d ed. (New Kensington, Pa.: Whitaker House, 2000); *The Creator and the Cosmos: How the Latest Scientific Discoveries Reveal God*, 3d expanded ed. (Colorado Springs: NavPress, 2001); *The Genesis Question: Scientific Advances and the Accuracy of Genesis*, 2d expanded ed. (Colorado Springs: NavPress, 2001); *A Matter of Days: Resolving a Creation Controversy*, 2d ed. (Colorado Springs: NavPress, 2004), first published in 1994 as *Creation and Time*; Fazale Rana and Hugh Ross, *Origins of Life: Biblical and Evolutionary Models Face Off* (Colorado Springs: NavPress, 2004); Fazale Rana with Hugh Ross, *Who Was Adam: A Creation Model Approach to the Origin of Man* (Colorado Springs: NavPress, 2005); see also Hugh Ross and Gleason L. Archer, "The Day-Age View," and their replies to other viewpoints, in *The Genesis Debate: Three Views on the Days of Creation*, ed. David G. Hagopian, Foreword by Norman L. Geisler (Mission Viejo, Calif.: Crux Press, 2001).

[56]Hugh Ross, *A Matter of Days*, 16.

[57]Ibid., 20.

[58]See most recently Gary Habermas, "Evidential Apologetics," in *Five Views on Apologetics*, edited by Cowan, 92-121, which emphasizes historical evidences. The essay by Paul D. Feinberg, "Cumulative Case Apologetics," 148-72, presents a variant form of evidentialism that includes but

de-emphasizes historical evidences.

[59]Swinburne, *Existence of God*, 291.

[60]Montgomery, "The Jury Returns," in *Evidence for Faith*, 319.

[61]Swinburne, *Existence of God*, chapter 10; *Providence and the Problem of Evil* (Oxford: Clarendon, 1998), especially Part II.

[62]Montgomery, *Shape of the Past*, 41.

[63]Ibid.

[64]Montgomery, *Suicide of Christian Theology*, 367.

[65]Dennis Roy Hillman, "The Use of Basic Issues in Apologetics from Selected New Testament Apologies" (Th.M. thesis, Dallas Theological Seminary, 1979), 41.

[66]Ronald H. Nash, "Use and Abuse of History in Christian Apologetics," *Christian Scholar's Review* 1 (1971): 223.

[67]Montgomery, "Clark's Philosophy of History," 375.

[68]Montgomery, *Where Is History Going*, 203.

[69]Robert A. Sabath, "LSD and Religious Truth," in *Christianity for the Tough-minded*, ed. Montgomery, 198-99.

[70]Ibid., 199.

[71]Clark Eugene Barshinger, "Existential Psychology and Christian Faith," in *Christianity for the Tough-minded*, ed. Montgomery, 171-72.

[72]Montgomery, *Shape of the Past*, 140.

CHAPTER 10

[1]Montgomery, "Death of the 'Death of God,'" in *Suicide of Christian Theology*, 106.

[2]All parenthetical citations in this section are from Montgomery, *History and Christianity*. The same material is found in Montgomery, *Where Is History Going*, 37-52.

[3]C. Sanders, *Introduction to Research in English Literary History* (New York: Macmillan, 1952).

[4]See, for example, Montgomery, "The Jury Returns," in *Evidence for Faith*, edited by Montgomery, 322-23; Moreland, *Scaling the Secular City: A Defense of Christianity* (Grand Rapids: Baker, 1987), 134; Beckwith, *Baha'i*, 43-50; Steven Collins, *Championing the Faith: A Layman's Guide to Proving Christianity's Claims* (Tulsa: Virgil W. Hensley, 1991), 78; Dan Story, *Defending Your Faith: How to Answer the Tough Questions* (Nashville:Thomas Nelson, 1992), 38-47. Apologists of a more classical orientation have also used this threefold test, including one of the present authors; see Ken Boa and Larry Moody, *I'm Glad You Asked*, 2d ed. (Wheaton, Ill.: Victor, 1994), 90-99.

[5]On fulfilled prophecy in apologetics, see Geisler, *Baker Encyclopedia of Christian Apologetics*, 609-617.

[6]Alexander Keith, *Evidence of the Truth of the Christian Religion Derived from the Literal Fulfillment of Prophecy*, 6th ed. (New York: Harper, 1841).

[7]Bernard Ramm, *Protestant Christian Evidences* (Chicago: Moody Press, 1953), 85.

[8]John A. Bloom, "Truth Via Prophecy," in *Evidence for Faith*, edited by Montgomery, 175-76.

[9]Ibid., 176-77.

[10]Ibid., 179-86; Robert W. Manweiler, "The Destruction of Tyre," and Elaine A. Phillips, "The Fall

of Nineveh," in *The Evidence of Prophecy*, ed. Robert C. Newman (Hatfield, Pa.: Biblical Research Institute, 1994), 21-30 and 41-51 respectively; Robert C. Newman, "Fulfilled Prophecy as Miracle," in *In Defense of Miracles*, ed. Geivett and Habermas, 217-21.

[11]Robert C. Newman, "Israel's History Written in Advance: A Neglected Evidence for the God of the Bible," in *Evidence for Faith*, ed. Montgomery, 193-201.

[12]Ibid., 193.

[13]See further *The Evidence of Prophecy*, ed. Newman, which contains three essays on Israel's history as fulfilling biblical prophecy.

[14]Newman, "The Testimony of Messianic Prophecy," in *Evidence for Faith*, ed. Montgomery, 204-208.

[15]Ibid., 209-212. On Daniel 9:24-27, see especially Harold W. Hoehner, *Chronological Aspects of the Life of Christ* (Grand Rapids: Zondervan, 1978), which argues for an amazingly precise fulfillment of that prophecy in light of the date of Christ's death. See also Robert C. Newman, "The Time of the Messiah," in *The Evidence of Prophecy*, ed. Newman, 111-18. We discuss this prophecy in more detail in *20 Compelling Evidences that God Exists*, 160-69.

[16]Newman, "Testimony of Messianic Prophecy," 212.

[17]Geisler, *Baker Encyclopedia of Christian Apologetics*, 609.

[18]Montgomery, "Death of the 'Death of God,'" in *Suicide of Christian Theology*, 125.

[19]Ibid., 126.

[20]Beckwith, *Baha'i*, 18.

[21]Montgomery, "Death of the 'Death of God,'" in *Suicide of Christian Theology*, 141.

[22]Gary R. Habermas, "Resurrection Claims in Other Religions," *Religious Studies* 25 (1989): 167-177; see also David K. Clark, "Miracles in the World Religions," in *In Defense of Miracles*, ed. Geivett and Habermas, 199-213.

[23]Beckwith, *Baha'i*, 41.

[24]Arnold D. Weigel, "A Critique of Bertrand Russell's Religious Position," in *Christianity for the Tough-minded*, ed. Montgomery, 43.

[25]Swinburne, *Existence of God*, 227, 235, 242-243.

[26]See chapter 6.

[27]William Lane Craig, *The Existence of God and the Beginning of the Universe* (San Bernardino, Calif.: Here's Life, 1979), 55-80; *Reasonable Faith: Christian Truth and Apologetics* (Wheaton, Ill.: Crossway, 1994), 100-116; and his debate book on the subject with Quentin Smith, *Theism, Atheism, and Big Bang Cosmology* (Oxford: Clarendon, 1993).

[28]Notably Moreland, 33-35; Francis Beckwith, *David Hume's Argument against Miracles: A Critical Analysis* (Lanham, Md.: University Press of America, 1989), 73-84.

[29]See the works by Hugh Ross cited in chapter 9, n. 56; see also Newman, "The Evidence of Cosmology," in *Evidence for Faith*, ed. Montgomery, 71-91; Fred Hereen, *Show Me God: What the Message from Space Is Telling Us about God*, Wonders That Witness, vol. 1 (Wheeling, Ill.: Searchlight Publications, 1995).

[30]In addition to the sources already cited, see Boa and Bowman, *20 Compelling Evidences that God Exists*, 51-60, for an overview of the argument; more detailed treatments can be found in Robert Jastrow, *God and the Astronomers* (New York: Norton, 1978); Stanley L. Jaki, *God and the Cosmologists* (Washington, D.C.: Regnery Gateway, 1989).

[31]Geivett, *Evil and the Evidence for God*, 102-103.

[32]Full-length treatments of this subject include John D. Barrow and Frank J. Tipler, *The Anthropic Cosmological Principle* (Oxford: Oxford University Press, 1986); M. A. Corey, *God and the New Cosmology: The Anthropic Design Argument* (Lanham, Md.: Rowman & Littlefield, 1993). Barrow and Tipler report the major findings but reject the idea of divine design; Corey finds the evidence supportive of a divine Designer and Creator.

[33]Hugh Ross, "Astronomical Evidences for a Personal, Transcendent God," in *The Creation Hypothesis: Scientific Evidence for an Intelligent Designer*, ed. J. P. Moreland (Downers Grove, Ill.: InterVarsity, 1994), 141-72; and in several of his books.

[34]Notable discussions include Moreland, *Scaling the Secular City*, 52-55; Richard Swinburne, "Argument from the Fine-Tuning of the Universe," in *Physical Cosmology and Philosophy*, ed. John Leslie (New York: Macmillan, 1990), 154-73; William Lane Craig, "The Teleological Argument and the Anthropic Principle," in *The Logic of Rational Theism: Exploratory Essays*, ed. William Lane Craig and Mark S. McLeod, Problems in Contemporary Philosophy, vol. 24 (Lewiston, N.Y.: Edwin Mellen Press, 1990), 127-53; Robin Collins, "A Scientific Argument for the Existence of God: The Fine-Tuning Design Argument," in *Reason for the Hope Within*, ed. Michael J. Murray (Grand Rapids and Cambridge, U.K.: Eerdmans, 1999), 47-75. We give a popular presentation of the argument aimed at nonbelievers in *20 Compelling Evidences that God Exists*, 61-81.

[35]The table is loosely based on tables by Hugh Ross, e.g., tables 14.1 and 16.1 in *Creator and the Cosmos*, 154, 188.

[36]In 2004, Antony Flew acknowledged that recent scientific discoveries had convinced him that some kind of God along the lines of Aristotle's "God" (a powerful, intelligent being that is the uncaused cause of the universe) probably exists. However, Flew still denied that God had revealed himself in Christianity or any other religion. See "My Pilgrimage from Atheism to Theism: A Discussion between Antony Flew and Gary Habermas," *Philosophia Christi* 6 (2004): 197-211. Flew's extensive discussions and debates with Habermas and other evangelical apologists directly contributed to his rethinking his longstanding position of atheism. However, subsequent publications, including the short introduction to a new edition of Flew's classic atheist book *God and Philosophy* (Buffalo, N.Y.: Prometheus Books, 2005), suggest that Flew's belief in a God was not yet a settled conviction.

[37]Montgomery, "Death of the 'Death of God,'" in *Suicide of Christian Theology*, 101.

[38]All parenthetical citations here and in the following paragraph are from Geivett, *Evil and the Evidence for God*.

[39]Quotations in this paragraph are taken from John E. Hare, "The Problem of Evil," in *Evidence for Faith*, edited by Montgomery, 231-52.

[40]Collins, "A Scientific Argument for the Existence of God," 66.

[41]Beckwith, *David Hume's Argument against Miracles;* see also his "History and Miracles," in *In Defense of Miracles*, edited by Geivett and Habermas, 86-98. Parenthetical references in this section are to the former work by Beckwith; emphasis is in the original.

[42]The inclusion of levitation is odd, but Beckwith likely had the Ascension in mind.

[43]Citing David Hume, *An Enquiry Concerning Human Understanding*, 3rd ed., rev. P. H. Nidditch (Oxford: Clarendon, 1975; original, 1777), 110. Note the similarity to Clifford's evidentialist maxim, discussed at the beginning of chapter 9.

[44]The expression "convergence of independent probabilities" comes from Montgomery, who in turn attributes it to Cardinal John Henry Newman; see Beckwith, "History and Miracles," in *In Defense of Miracles*, ed. Geivett and Habermas, 98; cf. Montgomery, *Faith Founded on Fact*, 55.

[45]Montgomery, *Faith Founded on Fact*, 57.

⁴⁶Gary R. Habermas, *The Resurrection of Jesus: An Apologetic* (Grand Rapids: Baker, 1980); "The Resurrection Appearances of Jesus," in *In Defense of Miracles*, edited by Geivett and Habermas, 262-275; Habermas and Antony G. N. Flew, *Did Jesus Rise from the Dead? The Resurrection Debate*, ed. Terry L. Miethe (San Francisco: Harper & Row, 1987); and more recently, Gary R. Habermas and Michael R. Licona, *The Case for the Resurrection of Jesus* (Grand Rapids: Kregel, 2004).

⁴⁷Craig, *The Historical Argument for the Resurrection of Jesus During the Deist Controversy* (1985); *Assessing the New Testament Evidence for the Historicity of the Resurrection of Jesus*, Studies in the Bible and Early Christianity, vol. 16 (Lewiston, N.Y.: Edwin Mellen Press, 1989); *Knowing the Truth about the Resurrection* (Ann Arbor: Servant, 1991); *Reasonable Faith* (1994), 255-98; "Did Jesus Rise from the Dead?" in *Jesus Under Fire*, ed. Michael J. Wilkins and J. P. Moreland (Grand Rapids: Zondervan, 1995), 141-176; "The Empty Tomb of Jesus," in *In Defense of Miracles*, edited by Geivett and Habermas (1997), 247-261; and Craig and John Dominic Crossan, *Will the Real Jesus Please Stand Up?* (1998).

⁴⁸For example, Habermas and Flew, *Did Jesus Rise from the Dead*, 19-20; Craig and Crossan, *Will the Real Jesus Please Stand Up*, 26-28; and especially Habermas and Licona, *Case for the Resurrection of Jesus*, 43-77. See also Boa and Moody, *I'm Glad You Asked*, 64-66.

⁴⁹Craig and Crossan, *Will the Real Jesus Please Stand Up*, 161-162.

⁵⁰Ibid., 163.

⁵¹See especially Craig, "The Empty Tomb of Jesus," in *In Defense of Miracles*, edited by Geivett and Habermas, 247-261.

⁵²See especially Habermas, "The Resurrection Appearances of Jesus," in *In Defense of Miracles*, edited by Geivett and Habermas, 262-275.

⁵³Habermas and Flew, *Did Jesus Rise from the Dead*, 22-23.

⁵⁴Craig and Crossan, *Will the Real Jesus Please Stand Up*, 160.

⁵⁵ Habermas and Licona, *Case for the Resurrection of Jesus*, 171. Perhaps we should note that this argument works better if one qualifies it to say that Jesus' resurrection would not be a *total* surprise *in retrospect*. The Gospels themselves report that the disciples were quite surprised, no doubt because no amount of preparation could overcome the shock of Jesus' horrific death and the seeming end it put to all their hopes (cf. Luke 24:21).

⁵⁶Craig, *Will the Real Jesus Please Stand Up*, 159.

CHAPTER 11

¹William Dyrness, *Christian Apologetics in a World Community* (Downers Grove, Ill.: InterVarsity, 1983), 58.

²Antony G. N. Flew, *God and Philosophy* (London, 1966), 63.

³Ibid., 141.

⁴Swinburne, *Existence of God*, 14 n.

⁵Geivett, *Evil and the Evidence for God*, 92.

⁶Irwin H. Linton, *A Lawyer Examines the Bible* (Grand Rapids: Baker, 1943), 195.

⁷J. P. Moreland, "Atheism and Leaky Buckets: The Christian Rope Pulls Tighter," in *Does God Exist? The Debate between Theists and Atheists* (Buffalo: Prometheus Books, 1993), 240. Oddly, Moreland goes on to assert that a series of leaky buckets are "related to one another in a chain" while "strands of rope work independently of each other" (240-241). In fact, strands woven into a rope act

in a mutual *dependence* in which the whole is greater than the sum of the parts.

[8]Hanna, *Crucial Questions in Apologetics*, 97.

[9]Diehl, "Historical Apologetics," 6.

[10]Montgomery, *Faith Founded on Fact*, 33-34.

[11]Ronald H. Nash, "Use and Abuse of History in Christian Apologetics," *Christian Scholar's Review* 1 (1971): 217.

[12]W. Stanford Reid, "Subjectivity or Objectivity in Historical Understanding," in *Jerusalem and Athens*, edited by Geehan, 418-419.

[13]Montgomery, "Is Man His Own God?" in *Suicide of Christian Theology*, 261.

[14]Ibid., 263-264.

[15]Montgomery, *Faith Founded on Fact*, 34.

[16]Rheinallt Nantlais Williams, *Faith, Facts, History, Science—and How They Fit Together* (Wheaton, Ill.: Tyndale House, 1973), 85.

[17]Montgomery, *Faith Founded on Fact*, 34.

[18]Several articles explicating and defending Montgomery's apologetic appeared in the *Global Journal of Classical Theology* 3, 1 (March 2002): Ross Clifford, "Justification of the Legal Apologetic of John Warwick Montgomery: An Apologetic for All Seasons"; Gary Habermas, "Greg Bahnsen, John Warwick Montgomery, and Evidential Apologetics"; Craig Hazen, "'Ever Hearing but Never Understanding': A Response to Mark Hutchins's Critique of John Warwick Montgomery's Historical Apologetics"; and Boyd Pehrson, "How Not to Critique Legal Apologetics: A Lesson from a Skeptic's Internet Web Page Objections." These articles were accessed online at < http://www.trinitysem.edu/journal/toc_v3n1.html >.

[19]Geisler, *Christian Apologetics*, 95.

[20]Ibid., 95, emphasis deleted.

[21]Ibid., 96.

[22]Reid, "Subjectivity or Objectivity," in *Jerusalem and Ath*ens, edited by Geehan, 409; cf. Hanna, *Crucial Questions*, 100; Carl F. H. Henry, *God, Revelation, and Authority*, 6 vols. (Waco, Tex.: Word, 1976-1983), 1:231.

[23]Martin Batts, "A Summary and Critique of the Historical Apologetic of John Warwick Montgomery" (Th.M. thesis, Dallas Theological Seminary, 1977), 87-88.

[24]Hanna, *Crucial Questions*, 100.

[25]Dennis Roy Hillman, "The Use of Basic Issues in Apologetics from Selected New Testament Apologies" (Th.M. thesis, Dallas Theological Seminary, 1979), 54.

[26]Gordon H. Clark, *Three Types of Religious Philosophy* (Nutley, N.J.: Presbyterian & Reformed, 1977), 117.

[27]Henry, *God, Revelation and Authority*, 1:231.

[28]John Warwick Montgomery, *The Shape of the Past: A Christian Response to Secular Philosophies of History* (Minneapolis: Bethany Fellowship, 1962; reprint, 1975), 265, emphasis deleted.

[29]Henry, *God, Revelation and Authority*, 1:231.

[30]Hanna, *Crucial Questions*,100.

[31]Thom Notaro, *Van Til and the Use of Evidence* (Phillipsburg, N.J.: Presbyterian & Reformed,

1980), 102, 105.

[32]Henry, *God, Revelation and Authority*, 1:220.

[33]Montgomery, "The Place of Reason—Part 1," *His*, February 1966, 12.

[34]Hillman, "Use of Basic Issues in Apologetics," 55.

CHAPTER 12

[1]See chapter 2 on Augustine and Anselm. On the importance of Augustine in Reformed apologetics, see Dewey J. Hoitenga, Jr., *Faith and Reason from Plato to Plantinga: An Introduction to Reformed Epistemology* (Albany: State University of New York Press, 1991), 57-142.

[2]Works on Calvin include B. B. Warfield, *Calvin and Calvinism*, The Works of Benjamin B. Warfield, vol. 5 (New York: Oxford University Press, 1931; reprint, Grand Rapids: Baker, 1981); Donald K. McKim, ed., *Readings in Calvin's Theology* (Grand Rapids: Baker, 1984); William J. Bouwsma, *John Calvin: A Sixteenth Century Portrait* (New York: Oxford University Press, 1988); Alister E. McGrath, *A Life of John Calvin: A Study in the Shaping of Western Culture* (Oxford: Blackwell, 1990); Wulfert De Greef, *The Writings of John Calvin: An Introductory Guide*, trans. Lyle D. Bierma (Grand Rapids: Baker, 1993); Edward A. Dowey, Jr., *The Knowledge of God in Calvin's Theology*, expanded ed. (Grand Rapids: Eerdmans, 1994; original, New York: Columbia University Press, 1952); T. H. L. Parker, *Calvin: An Introduction to His Thought* (Louisville: Westminster John Knox, 1995); David C. Steinmetz, *Calvin in Context* (New York: Oxford University Press, 1995); Ford Lewis Battles, *Interpreting John Calvin*, ed. Robert Benedetto (Grand Rapids: Baker, 1996); François Wendel, *Calvin: Origins and Development of His Religious Thought* (Grand Rapids: Baker, 1996); Timothy Paul Jones, "John Calvin and the Problem of Philosophical Apologetics," *Perspectives in Religious Studies* 23 (1996): 387–403; Richard A. Muller, *The Unaccommodated Calvin: Studies in the Foundation of a Theological Tradition*, Oxford Studies in Historical Theology (Oxford and New York: Oxford University Press, 1999); Donald K. McKim, ed., *The Cambridge Companion to John Calvin* (New York: Cambridge University Press, 2004); and the excellent collection in Richard C. Gamble, ed., Articles on Calvin and Calvinism, 10 vols. (New York: Garland, 1992). For an annually updated list of resources, see the Calvin Bibliography of the H. Henry Meeter Center for Calvin Studies at Calvin College (online at http://www.calvin.edu/meeter/bibliography/).

[3]Parenthetical citations are taken from John Calvin, *Institutes of the Christian Religion*, ed. John T. McNeill, trans. Ford Lewis Battles, Library of Christian Classics, vols. 20-21 (Philadelphia: Westminster, 1960). Citations follow the standard reference to book, chapter, and section. An excellent companion is Ford Lewis Battles, *An Analysis of the "Institutes of the Christian Religion" of John Calvin*, assisted by John R. Walchenbach (Phillipsburg, N.J.: P & R, 2001).

[4]On this subject in Calvin, see C. H. Stinson, *Reason and Sin according to Calvin and Aquinas: The Noetic Effects of the Fall of Man* (Washington, D.C.: Catholic University of America Press, 1966); Paul Helm, "John Calvin: The *Sensus Divinitatis*, and the Noetic Effects of Sin," *International Journal for Philosophy of Religion* 43 (1998): 87-108; Stephen K. Moroney, *The Noetic Effects of Sin* (Lanham, Md.: Lexington Books, 2000); Dewey J. Hoitenga, "The Noetic Effects of Sin: A Review Article," *Calvin Theological Journal* 38 (2003): 68-102.

[5]Based on Battles, *Interpreting John Calvin*, 183 (who extends the analysis down to 1.14).

[6]Cf. the famous exchange on this issue between Emil Brunner and Karl Barth in *Natural Theology*, trans. Peter Fraenkel (London: Geoffrey Bles, Centenary Press, 1946; reprint, Eugene, Ore.: Wipf & Stock, 2002). For an analysis of this debate, placing it in its historical context, see Trevor Hart, "A Capacity for Ambiguity? The Barth-Brunner Debate Revisited," *Tyndale Bulletin* 44 (1993): 289-305.

[7]On the *sensus divinitatis* in Calvin, see N. H. Gootjes, "The Sense of Divinity: A Critical Examination of the Views of Calvin and Demarest," *Westminster Theological Journal* 48 (1986): 337-350; Esther L. Meek, "A Polanyian Interpretation of Calvin's *Sensus Divinitatis*," *Presbyterion* 23 (1997): 8-24; Helm, "John Calvin"; David Reiter, "Calvin's 'Sense of Divinity' and Externalist Knowledge of God," *Faith and Philosophy* 15 (1998): 253–69.

[8]Alvin Plantinga, "The Reformed Objection to Natural Theology," in *Rationality in the Calvinian Tradition*, ed. Hendrik Hart, Johan Van der Hoeven, and Nicholas Wolterstorff, Christian Studies Today (Lanham, Md.: University Press of America, 1983), 363-83.

[9]See Egil Grislis, "Calvin's Use of Cicero in the Institutes I:1-5—A Case Study in Theological Method," in *The Organizational Structure of Calvin's Theology*, ed. Richard C. Gamble; Articles on Calvin and Calvinism 7 (New York: Garland Publishing, 1992), 1-33; reprinted from *Archiv fur Reformationsgeschichte* 62 (1971): 5-37. More broadly, see Charles Partee, *Calvin and Classical Philosophy* (Leiden, Netherlands: Brill, 1977; Louisville, Ky.: Westminster John Knox Press, 2005).

[10]Cf. Plantinga, "Reformed Objection to Natural Theology," 367.

[11]See further John Newton Thomas, "The Place of Natural Theology in the Thought of John Calvin," and Gerald J. Postema, "Calvin's Alleged Rejection of Natural Theology," in *The Organizational Structure of Calvin's Theology*, 153-54 and 135-46 respectively; the latter is reprinted from *Scottish Journal of Theology* 24 (1971): 423-34; Michael Scott Horton, "Legal Rather than Evangelical Knowledge: Calvin on the Limits of Natural Theology," *Modern Reformation Journal* 7, no. 1 (1998): 28-31; Edward Adams, "Calvin's View of Natural Knowledge of God," *International Journal of Systematic Theology* 3, 3 (2001): 280-92.

[12]Ramm, *Varieties of Christian Apologetics*, 178.

[13]Calvin, *Concerning Scandals*, trans. John W. Fraser (Grand Rapids: Eerdmans, 1978), 18.

[14]Ibid., 25.

[15]Ibid., 20.

[16]On these and other streams of Reformed thought, see *Reformed Theology in America: A History of Its Modern Development*, ed. David F. Wells (Grand Rapids: Eerdmans, 1985).

[17]On Scottish Common Sense Realism and Scottish philosophy in general, see S. A. Grave, *The Scottish Philosophy of Common Sense* (Oxford: Clarendon, 1960); Daniel Sommer Robinson, ed., *The Story of Scottish Philosophy: A Compendium of Selections from the Writings of Nine Pre-eminent Scottish Philosophers, with Biobibliographical Essays* (1961; reprint, Westport, Conn.: Greenwood, 1979); Alexander Broadie, *The Tradition of Scottish Philosophy: A New Perspective on the Enlightenment* (Edinburgh: Polygon; Savage, Md.: Barnes & Noble, 1990); M. A. Stewart, ed., *Studies in the Philosophy of the Scottish Enlightenment*, Oxford Studies in the History of Philosophy, vol. 1 (Oxford: Clarendon; New York: Oxford University Press, 1990).

[18]The contemporary Reformed apologist who has given the most attention to the thought of Thomas Reid is Nicholas Wolterstorff. Our discussion here follows Wolterstorff's treatment in "Thomas Reid on Rationality," in *Rationality in the Calvinian Tradition*, ed. Hart, et. al., 43-69. Additional studies include S. A. Grave, "Reid, Thomas," in *The Encyclopedia of Philosophy*, ed. Paul Edwards (New York: Macmillan and Free Press, 1967), 7:118-21; Stephen F. Barker and Tom L. Beauchamp, eds., *Thomas Reid: Critical Interpretations* (Philadelphia: University City Science Center, 1976); Michael L. Peterson, "Reid Debates Hume: Christian Versus Skeptic," *Christianity Today*, 22 September 1978; Ronald E. Beanblossom and Keith Lehrer, eds., *Thomas Reid: Inquiry and Essays* (Indianapolis: Hackett, 1983); Paul Helm, "Thomas Reid, Common Sense and Calvinism," in *Rationality in the Calvinian Tradition*, 71-89; Melvin Dalgarno and Eric Matthews, eds., *The Philosophy of Thomas Reid*, Philosophical Studies, vol. 42 (Dordrecht and Boston: Kluwer Academic Publishers, 1989); Roger D. Gallie, *Thomas Reid and "The Way of Ideas"* (Dordrecht

and Boston: Kluwer Academic Publishers, 1989); Keith Lehrer, *Thomas Reid*, Arguments of the Philosophers (London and New York: Routledge, 1989); Kelly James Clark, *Return to Reason: A Critique of Enlightenment Evidentialism and a Defense of Reason and Belief in God* (Grand Rapids: Eerdmans, 1990), 143-51.

[19]Thomas Reid, *An Inquiry into the Human Mind: On the Principles of Common Sense: A Critical Edition*, ed. Derek R. Brookes, Edinburgh Edition of Thomas Reid (University Park: Pennsylvania State University Press, 1997), 4 (Dedication). The statement is also quoted (from another edition) in Wolterstorff, "Thomas Reid on Rationality," 44.

[20] Kelly James Clark, *Return to Reason*, 146-47.

[21]Reid, *Inquiry into the Human Mind*, ed. Brookes, 33 (2.6); cf. Wolterstorff, "Thomas Reid on Rationality," 51.

[22]Reid, *Essays* 1.2, quoted in Wolterstorff, "Thomas Reid on Rationality," 54-55. Wolterstorff characterizes this line of argument as ad hominem (53-55), but that does not seem to be correct. As Wolterstorff himself recognizes, Reid was arguing not merely that certain skeptics *don't* live consistently with their skeptical principles, but that people in general *can't* live that way. Given that this is Reid's point, his argument is not ad hominem.

[23]Reid, *Inquiry into the Human Mind*, ed. Brookes, 68 (5.7); cf. Wolterstorff, "Thomas Reid on Rationality," 55; Clark, *Return to Reason*, 147-48.

[24]Reid, *Essays* 2.20, quoted in Wolterstorff, "Thomas Reid on Rationality," 58.

[25]Helm comments that Reid's philosophy was "compatible with, if it does not actually entail," the *"a posteriori* apologetic stance . . . best exemplified in the work of Paley and Butler." Helm, "Thomas Reid, Common Sense and Calvinism," 80.

[26]Reid, *Essays* 6.6, quoted in Wolterstorff, "Thomas Reid on Rationality," 61-62.

[27]Reid, *Lectures on Natural Theology*, ed. Elmer H. Duncan (Washington: University Press of America, 1981), 2, cited in Wolterstorff, "Thomas Reid on Rationality," 62.

[28]Derek R. Brookes, introduction to Reid, *Inquiry into the Human Mind*, ed. Brookes, xxii.

[29]Reid, *Lectures*, 1-2, cited in Wolterstorff, "Thomas Reid on Rationality," 63.

[30]Helm, "Thomas Reid, Common Sense and Calvinism," 81.

[31]See especially Sydney E. Ahlstrom, "The Scottish Philosophy and American Theology," *Church History* 24 (1955): 257-72. On the broader influence of commonsense realism in American culture, see Terence Martin, *The Instructed Vision: Scottish Common Sense Philosophy and the Origins of American Fiction*, Indiana University Humanities, vol. 48 (Bloomington: Indiana University Press, 1961; reprint, New York: Kraus Reprint, 1969).

[32]On Old Princeton, see especially W. Andrew Hoffecker, *Piety and the Princeton Theologians: Archibald Alexander, Charles Hodge, and Benjamin Warfield* (Grand Rapids: Baker, 1981); Mark A. Noll, ed., *The Princeton Theology, 1812-1921: Scripture, Science, and Theological Method from Archibald Alexander to Benjamin Breckinridge Warfield* (Grand Rapids: Baker, 1983).

[33]Charles Hodge, *Systematic Theology*, 3 vols. (1875; reprint, Grand Rapids: Eerdmans, 1981). Parenthetical references in the following paragraphs are from volume 1 of this work. On Hodge's apologetic, besides the works cited above, see especially Charles Andrews Jones III, "Charles Hodge, the Keeper of Orthodoxy: The Method, Purpose and Meaning of His Apologetic" (Ph.D. diss., Drew University, 1989); Peter Hicks, *The Philosophy of Charles Hodge: A Nineteenth Century Evangelical Approach to Reason, Knowledge, and Truth*, Studies in American Religion, vol. 65 (Lewiston, N.Y.: Edwin Mellen Press, 1997).

[34]On the influence of Dutch Calvinism in America, see James D. Bratt, *Dutch Calvinism in Modern*

America: A History of a Conservative Subculture (Grand Rapids: Eerdmans, 1984); Richard Mouw, "Dutch Calvinist Philosophical Influences in North America," *Calvin Theological Journal* 24 (1989): 93-120. Two articles on Dutch Calvinist philosophy during the past century are Jacob Klapwijk, "Rationality in the Dutch Neo-Calvinist Tradition," and Albert Wolters, "Dutch Neo-Calvinism: Worldview, Philosophy and Rationality," in *Rationality in the Calvinian Tradition*, ed. Hart, et. al., 93-111 and 113-31 respectively.

[35]An accessible introduction to Kuyper's thought is his *Lectures on Calvinism* (Grand Rapids: Eerdmans, 1931), originally the Stone Lectures at Princeton University in 1898. A recent collection of readings from Kuyper is *Abraham Kuyper: A Centennial Reader*, ed. James D. Bratt (Grand Rapids: Eerdmans, 1998). See further Louis Praamsma, *Let Christ Be King: Reflections on the Life and Times of Abraham Kuyper* (Jordan Station, Ont.: Paideia Press, 1985); R. D. Henderson, "How Abraham Kuyper Became a Kuyperian," *Christian Scholar's Review* 22 (1992): 22-35 (an excellent introduction); Wayne A. Kobes, "Sphere Sovereignty and the University: Theological Foundations of Abraham Kuyper's View of the University and Its Role in Society" (Ph.D. diss., Florida State University, 1993); James D. Bratt, "In the Shadow of Mt. Kuyper: A Survey of the Field," *Calvin Theological Journal* 31 (1996): 51-66 (one of several articles on Kuyper in the same issue); Peter S. Heslam, *Creating a Christian Worldview: Abraham Kuyper's Lectures on Calvinism* (Grand Rapids and Cambridge, U.K.: Eerdmans; Carlisle: Paternoster Press, 1998); James E. McGoldrick, *God's Renaissance Man: Abraham Kuyper* (Darlington, U.K., and Webster, N.Y.: Evangelical Press, 2000). For a discussion of Kuyper's views on apologetics, see Ramm, *Varieties of Christian Apologetics*, 179-95.

[36]Abraham Kuyper, *Principles of Sacred Theology* (Grand Rapids: Eerdmans, 1968). (Parenthetical page references in the text are to this work.) This book is a reprint of *Encyclopedia of Sacred Theology: Its Principles*, trans. Hendrik De Vries, introduction by B. B. Warfield (New York: Scribner, 1898).

[37]Kuyper's principle work on common grace, *De Gemeene Gratie*, 2nd ed., 3 vols. (Kampen: J. H. Kok, 1931, 1932), has not yet been translated into English. Helpful overviews of this work and of Kuyper's doctrine of common grace include S. U. Zuidema, "Common Grace and Christian Action in Abraham Kuyper," in *Communication and Confrontation: A Philosophical Appraisal and Critique of Modern Society and Contemporary Thought* (Toronto: Wedge, 1972); Jacob Klapwijk, "Antithesis and Common Grace," in *Bringing into Captivity Every Thought: Capita Selecta in the History of Christian Evaluations of Non-Christian Philosophy*, ed. Jacob Klapwijk, Sander Griffioen, and Gerben Groenewoud, Christian Studies Today (Lanham, Md.: University Press of America, 1991), 169-90; Kobes, "Sphere Sovereignty and the University" (1993), 122-49.

[38]Kuyper, *Lectures on Calvinism*, 132-33.

[39]Ibid., 11.

[40]Kuyper, *The Work of the Holy Spirit*, trans. with notes by Henri De Vries (New York: Funk & Wagnalls, 1900; Chattanooga: AMG Publishers, 1995), 440.

[41]Kuyper, *Lectures on Calvinism*, 199.

[42]Ibid., 11.

[43]Ibid., 12.

[44]See William Young, *Toward a Reformed Philosophy: The Development of a Protestant Philosophy in Dutch Calvinistic Thought since the Time of Abraham Kuyper* (Grand Rapids: Piet Hein, 1952).

[45]Dooyeweerd is notoriously difficult to understand, especially for those not familiar with Dutch thought. Standard introductions to his thought include J. M. Spier, *An Introduction to Christian Philosophy* (Nutley, N.J.: Craig Press, 1970); L. Kalbeek, *Contours of a Christian Philosophy: An Introduction to Herman Dooyeweerd's Thought*, ed. Bernard Zylstra and Josina Zylstra (Toronto:

Wedge, 1975); Samuel T. Wolfe, *A Key to Dooyeweerd* (Nutley, N.J.: Presbyterian & Reformed, 1978). A difficult but important study of Dooyeweerd is Vincent Brümmer, *Transcendental Criticism and Christian Philosophy: A Presentation and Evaluation of Herman Dooyeweerd's "Philosophy of the Cosmonomic Idea"* (Franeker: T. Wever, 1961). Edwin Mellen Press (of Lewiston, N.Y.) is publishing in many volumes *The Collected Works of Herman Dooyeweerd*.

[46]Herman Dooyeweerd, *A New Critique of Theoretical Thought*, trans. David H. Freeman, William S. Young, and H. De Jongste, 4 vols. (Nutley, N.J.: Presbyterian & Reformed, 1953-1957; bound as two volumes, 1969). All parenthetical references in the following paragraphs are to this work, with the volume number preceding the colon and the page reference following it.

[47]Two of the best editions of Immanuel Kant's *Critique of Pure Reason* in English are the translations by J. M. D. Meiklejohn in Great Books of the Western World, vol. 42 (Chicago: Encyclopaedia Britannica, 1952), 1-250, and the translation by Norman Kemp Smith (New York: St. Martin's Press, 1965).

[48]See further Brümmer, *Transcendental Criticism and Christian Philosophy*, 27-28.

[49]Herman Dooyeweerd, *In the Twilight of Western Thought: Studies in the Pretended Autonomy of Philosophical Thought* (Nutley, N.J.: Craig Press, 1972), 32.

[50]Ibid., 39-52; Herman Dooyeweerd, *Roots of Western Culture: Pagan, Secular, and Christian Options*, trans. John Kraay (Toronto: Wedge, 1979), 15-22, 148-56.

[51]The only book-length biography of Van Til is William White, *Van Til: Defender of the Faith* (Nashville:Thomas Nelson, 1979), an entirely uncritical work by a close friend of Van Til. For more recent treatments with some perspective, see John M. Frame, *Cornelius Van Til: An Analysis of His Thought* (Phillipsburg, N.J.: Presbyterian & Reformed, 1995), 19-37; Greg L. Bahnsen, *Van Til's Apologetic: Readings and Analysis* (Phillipsburg, N.J.: Presbyterian & Reformed, 1998), 7-20. These two books are by far the most important works on Van Til. An earlier, helpful work developing Van Til's apologetic is Thom Notaro, *Van Til and the Use of Evidence* (Phillipsburg, N.J.: Presbyterian & Reformed, 1980).

[52]On Machen's relation to Van Til, see Greg L. Bahnsen, "Machen, Van Til, and the Apologetical Tradition of the OPC," in *Pressing Toward the Mark: Essays Commemorating Fifty Years of the Orthodox Presbyterian Church*, ed. Charles G. Dennison and Richard C. Gamble (Philadelphia: Committee for the Historian of the Orthodox Presbyterian Church, 1986), 259-94. Bahnsen makes a good case for understanding Machen to be more in agreement with Van Til's approach than critics of Van Til might suppose. For an equally interesting counterpoint emphasizing Machen's agreement with Old Princeton, see Paul Kjoss Helseth, "J. Gresham Machen and 'True Science': Machen's Apologetical Continuity with Old Princeton's Right Use of Reason," *Premise* 5, 1 (1998), found online 10/27/2005 at < http://homepage.mac.com/shanerosenthal/reformationink/pkhmachen.htm >. That article is a longer version of Paul Kjoss Helseth, "The Apologetical Tradition of the OPC: A Reconsideration," *Westminster Theological Journal* 60 (1998): 109-29.

[53]A complete collection of Van Til's writings is available on CD-ROM, *The Works of Cornelius Van Til, 1895-1987* (New York: Labels Army Company, 1995), along with a printed guide by Eric D. Bristley, *A Guide to the Writings of Cornelius Van Til, 1895-1987* (Chicago: Olive Tree Communications, 1995).

[54]Bahnsen, *Van Til's Apologetic*, already mentioned, and *Always Ready: Directions for Defending the Faith*, ed. Robert R. Booth (Atlanta: American Vision; Texarkana, Ark.: Covenant Media Foundation, 1996). The first is a massive tome presenting extensive readings from Van Til's writings (especially *Defense of the Faith*, *A Christian Theory of Knowledge*, *Introduction to Systematic Theology*, and *Survey of Christian Epistemology*, but more than a dozen others as well) with Bahnsen's detailed and insightful analysis and footnotes. The second is a more popular exposition of presuppositionalism that focuses on biblical and practical support for the method. See also Steven

M. Schlissel, ed., *The Standard Bearer: A Festschrift for Greg L. Bahnsen* (Nacogdoches, Texas: Covenant Media Press, 2002).

[55]John M. Frame, *Doctrine of the Knowledge of God: A Theology of Lordship* (Phillipsburg, N.J.: Presbyterian & Reformed, 1987), is an involved analysis of the foundations of theology from a Van Tilian perspective. *Apologetics to the Glory of God: An Introduction* (Phillipsburg, N.J.: Presbyterian & Reformed, 1994) is a well-written primer on apologetics. *Cornelius Van Til: An Analysis of His Thought*, already mentioned, presents a well-rounded introduction to Van Til's life and thought. See also Frame, "Presuppositional Apologetics," in *Five Views on Apologetics*, ed. Cowan, 208-231.

[56]On Carnell, see Van Til, *The Defense of the Faith*, 3rd ed. (Nutley, N.J. and Philadelphia: Presbyterian & Reformed, 1967), 227-33, 242-48. Citations from *Defense of the Faith* are from this third edition except where otherwise noted. On Schaeffer, see Van Til, "The Apologetic Methodology of Francis Schaeffer" (Philadelphia: Westminster Theological Seminary, n.d. [1974]), mimeographed paper. William Edgar has argued that while Van Til and Schaeffer did have some substantive differences, the two were closer than perhaps Van Til himself realized; see Edgar, "Two Christian Warriors: Cornelius Van Til and Francis A. Schaeffer Compared," *Westminster Theological Journal* 57 (1995): 57-80.

[57]Representative examples of critical assessments of Van Til by classical and evidentialist apologists include the following: Hackett, *Resurrection of Theism*, 154-78, 250-60 (who treats Van Til along with Carnell and Gordon Clark); the articles by Gordon R. Lewis, John Warwick Montgomery, and Clark H. Pinnock in *Jerusalem and Athen*, ed. Geehan, 349-61, 380-92, 420-26; Gordon R. Lewis, *Testing Christianity's Truth Claims* (1976), 125-50; Norman L. Geisler, *Christian Apologetics* (1976), 56-64; and especially R. C. Sproul, John Gerstner, and Arthur Lindsley, *Classical Apologetics: A Rational Defense of the Christian Faith and a Critique of Presuppositional Apologetics* (Grand Rapids: Zondervan, Academie, 1984), especially 183-338. For a critique of the last-named work, see Frame, *Cornelius Van Til: An Analysis of His Thought*, 401-422.

[58]Cf. Bahnsen, *Van Til's Apologetic*, 596-612.

[59]Cornelius Van Til, *Common Grace and the Gospel* (Nutley, N.J.: Presbyterian & Reformed, 1972), 184. Parenthetical references in this and the next paragraph are to this work.

[60]Van Til, *Defense of the Faith*, 99.

[61]Cornelius Van Til, *Christian-Theistic Evidences*, In Defense of the Faith, vol. 6 (Nutley, N.J.: Presbyterian & Reformed, 1976), 58.

[62]Cf. Van Til, "My Credo," in *Jerusalem and Athens*, ed. Geehan, 21.

[63]For biographical information about Clark, see especially Ronald H. Nash, "Gordon H. Clark," in *Handbook of Evangelical Theologians*, ed. Elwell, 182-86; John W. Robbins, ed., *Gordon H. Clark: Personal Recollections* (Jefferson, Md.: Trinity Foundation, 1989).

[64]As noted in Nash, "Gordon H. Clark," 183.

[65]Clark and Van Til discuss their differences in Gordon H. Clark, "The Bible as Truth," *Bibliotheca Sacra* 114 (1957): 157-70, reprinted in *God's Hammer: The Bible and Its Critics*, 2nd ed. (Jefferson, Md.: Trinity Foundation, 1987), 24-38; Gordon H. Clark, *The Trinity* (Jefferson, Md.: Trinity Foundation, 1985), 87-101; Van Til, *Protestant Doctrine of Scripture* (Nutley, N.J.: Presbyterian & Reformed, 1967), 62-72; Van Til, *An Introduction to Systematic Theology* (Nutley, N.J.: Presbyterian & Reformed, 1974), 159-73. In the 1940s Herman Hoeksema wrote a series of editorials defending Clark; these have been edited into a book entitled *The Clark–Van Til Controversy* (Jefferson, Md.: Trinity Foundation, 1995). John W. Robbins defends Clark's view in heavy-handed style in *Cornelius Van Til: The Man and the Myth* (Jefferson, Md.: Trinity Foundation, 1986). Studies supportive of Van Til include Fred H. Klooster, *The Incomprehensibility of God in the Orthodox Presbyterian Conflict* (Franeker: T. Wever, 1951), and Gilbert B. Weaver, "The Concept of Truth

in the Apologetic Systems of Gordon Haddon Clark and Cornelius Van Til" (Th.D. diss., Grace Theological Seminary, 1967); Weaver, "Man: Analogue of God," in *Jerusalem and Athens*, ed. Geehan, 321-27; Michael A. Hakkenberg, "The Battle over the Ordination of Gordon H. Clark," in *Pressing Toward the Mark*, ed. Dennison and Gamble, 329-50. For an evenhanded discussion by a Van Tilian, see Frame, *Cornelius Van Til*, 97-113. A recent study putting the matter in some perspective is Mark A. Noll and Cassandra Niemczyk, "Evangelicals and the Self-Consciously Reformed," in *The Variety of American Evangelicalism*, ed. Donald W. Dayton and Robert K. Johnston (Knoxville: University of Tennessee Press, 1991), chapter 12.

[66]Henry's own autobiography is *Confessions of a Theologian* (Waco, Tex.: Word, 1986). Overviews of Henry's life and thought are found in Bob E. Patterson, *Carl F. H. Henry*, Makers of the Modern Theological Mind (Waco, Tex.: Word, 1983); Richard A. Purdy, "Carl F. H. Henry," in *Handbook of Evangelical Theologians*, ed. Elwell, 260-75. Purdy's dissertation on Henry is an important study: "Carl Henry and Contemporary Apologetics: An Assessment of the Rational Apologetic Methodology of Carl F. H. Henry in the Context of the Current Impasse between Reformed and Evangelical Apologetics" (Ph.D. diss., New York University, 1980). See also Steven Mark Hutchens, "Knowing and Being in the Context of the Fundamentalist Dilemma: A Comparative Study of the Thought of Karl Barth and Carl F. H. Henry" (Th.D. diss., Lutheran School of Theology at Chicago, 1989).

[67]Carl F. H. Henry, *God, Revelation, and Authority*, vol. 1, *God Who Speaks and Shows: Preliminary Considerations* (Waco, Tex.: Word, 1976), 10.

[68]Ronald H. Nash, ed., *The Philosophy of Gordon H. Clark: A Festschrift* (Philadelphia: Presbyterian & Reformed, 1968; 2nd ed., Jefferson, Md.: Trinity Foundation, 1992).

[69]See especially Ronald H. Nash, *Faith and Reason: Searching for a Rational Faith* (Grand Rapids: Zondervan, 1988).

[70]Gordon H. Clark, *Three Types of Religious Philosophy* (Nutley, N.J.: Craig Press, 1973), 116.

[71]There is some question whether Clark's treatment of biblical inspiration as the axiom for all knowledge was a novel development in his thought. See Ronald H. Nash, "Gordon Clark's Theory of Knowledge," in *Philosophy of Gordon H. Clark*, ed. Nash, chapter 5, and Mary M. Crumpacker, "Clark's Axiom: Something New?" *Journal of the Evangelical Theological Society* 32 (1989): 355-65.

[72]Clark, *In Defense of Theology* (Milford, Mich.: Mott Media, 1984), 31.

[73]Ibid., 32.

[74]Ibid., 32-33.

[75]Clark, "The Axiom of Revelation," in *Philosophy of Gordon H. Clark*, ed. Nash, 59, 60.

[76]Clark, *A Christian View of Men and Things: An Introduction to Philosophy* (Grand Rapids: Eerdmans, 1952; reprint, Grand Rapids: Baker, 1981), 324.

[77]Clark, *Thales to Dewey: A History of Philosophy* (Boston: Houghton Mifflin, 1957; reprint, Grand Rapids: Baker, 1980), 534.

[78]Clark, *Three Types of Religious Philosophy*, 123.

[79]Additional studies of Clark's thought, besides those already mentioned, include the following: Lewis, *Testing Christianity's Truth Claims* (1976), 100-124; Bahnsen, *Van Til's Apologetic* (1998), 667-72; Geisler, *Baker Encyclopedia of Christian Apologetics* (1999), 150-53.

[80]Alvin Plantinga, "Self-Profile," in *Alvin Plantinga*, ed. James E. Tomberlin and Peter Van Inwagen, Profiles: An International Series on Contemporary Philosophers and Logicians, vol. 5 (Dordrecht and Boston: D. Reidel, 1985), 3-97; "A Christian Life Partly Lived," in *Philosophers Who Believe: The*

Spiritual Journeys of 11 Leading Thinkers, ed. Kelly James Clark (Downers Grove, Ill.: InterVarsity, 1993), 45-82.

[81]Plantinga, "A Christian Life Partly Lived," 51-52; parenthetical references in the next few paragraphs are to this work.

[82]Alvin Plantinga, "Christian Philosophy at the End of the Twentieth Century," in *The Analytic Theist: An Alvin Plantinga Reader*, ed. James F. Sennett (Grand Rapids: Eerdmans, 1998), 346. Thus, the claim that Plantinga "strongly rejects" the idea of an "antithesis between believers and unbelievers" (Steven B. Cowan, review of *Faith Has Its Reasons* [1st ed.], in *Philosophia Christi* 6 [2004]: 372) is mistaken.

[83]Plantinga, "Self-Profile," in *Alvin Plantinga*, ed. Tomberlin and Van Inwagen, 21; parenthetical references in the next several paragraphs are to this work.

[84]Alvin Plantinga and Nicholas Wolterstorff, eds., *Faith and Rationality: Reason and Belief in God* (Notre Dame, Ind.: University of Notre Dame Press, 1983).

[85]Alvin Plantinga, "Afterword," in *Analytic Theist*, ed. Sennett, 353.

[86]Plantinga, "Christian Philosophy at the End of the Twentieth Century," in *Analytic Theist*, ed. Sennett, 336.

[87]Calvin, *Institutes* 3.2.18.

[88]Plantinga, "Christian Philosophy," 336.

[89]Plantinga, *Warrant: The Current Debate* (New York: Oxford University Press, 1993); *Warrant and Proper Function* (New York: Oxford University Press, 1993); and *Warranted Christian Belief* (New York: Oxford University Press, 2000). Parenthetical references in the remainder of this chapter are from *Warranted Christian Belief*.

[90]For some stimulating discussion, see the "Book Symposium on *Warranted Christian Belief*" in *Philosophia Christi* 3 (2001), with articles by Plantinga, R. Douglas Geivett and Greg Jesson, Richard Fumerton, and Paul K. Moser.

[91]Plantinga cites W. K. Clifford, *Lectures and Essays* (London: Macmillan, 1901), 183. Plantinga is here referring to *epistemological evidentialism*, not to be confused with evidentialism in appologetics (see p.156 of this book).

[92]Steven B. Cowan, in his review of the first edition of *Faith Has Its Reasons*, faulted its authors' placing of presuppositionalists and Reformed epistemologists in "the same camp" as "the most obvious error in their classification system" (*Philosophia Christi* 6 [2004]: 372). Cowan registered this complaint despite agreeing with us on specific points of comparison between the two (e.g., "the view that belief in God is properly basic") and despite the fact that we pointed out some of the very differences between the two varieties that Cowan mentioned (e.g., some Reformed epistemologists are less critical of natural theology than presuppositionalists; Plantinga supports a form of the free-will defense against the problem of evil, unlike presuppositionalists). More generally, Cowan's criticism mistakenly treats the four basic types as if they were uniform systems rather than broad categories of approaches to apologetics.

CHAPTER 13

[1]Cornelius Van Til, *Christianity in Conflict* (Philadelphia: Westminster Theological Seminary, 1962). Excerpts from this syllabus are published in Bahnsen, *Van Til's Apologetic*, 287-292.

[2]Van Til, *The Defense of the Faith*, 1st ed. (Philadelphia: Presbyterian & Reformed, 1955), 52, in Bahnsen, *Van Til's Apologetic*, 97.

[3]Van Til, *Introduction to Systematic Theology*, 18, in Bahnsen, *Van Til's Apologetic*, 62.

[4]Van Til, *Introduction to Systematic Theology*, 15, in Bahnsen, *Van Til's Apologetic*, 94.

[5]Van Til, *Defense of the Faith* (1955), 256, in Bahnsen, *Van Til's Apologetic*, 81.

[6]Bahnsen, *Van Til's Apologetic*, 30.

[7]Ibid., 501-502.

[8]Van Til, *Survey of Christian Epistemology* (Nutley, N.J.: Presbyterian & Reformed, 1969), 11, in Bahnsen, *Van Til's Apologetic*, 516.

[9]Van Til, *Defense of the Faith*, 3rd ed. (1967), 99-100.

[10]Frame, *Apologetics to the Glory of God*, 102.

[11]Frame, *Cornelius Van Til: An Analysis of His Thought*, 236.

[12]Ibid., 237.

[13]Cornelius Van Til, *A Christian Theory of Knowledge* (Phillipsburg, N.J.: Presbyterian & Reformed, 1969), 49, 50.

[14]Frame, *Cornelius Van Til: An Analysis of His Thought*, 237.

[15]Frame, *Apologetics to the Glory of God*, 102.

[16]R. J. Rushdoony, "Clark's Philosophy of Education," in *Philosophy of Gordon H. Clark*, ed. Nash, 276.

[17]Van Til, *Defense of the Faith* (1967), 3-5.

[18]Ibid., 260-66; Jack B. Rogers, "Van Til and Warfield on Scripture in the Westminster Confession," in *Jerusalem and Athens*, ed. Geehan, 154-65.

[19]Van Til, *Defense of the Faith*, 80-89; foreword to Jim S. Halsey, *For a Time Such as This: An Introduction to the Reformed Apologetic of Cornelius Van Til* (Phillipsburg, N.J.: Presbyterian & Reformed, 1978), ix.

[20]Robert D. Knudsen, "Progressive and Regressive Tendencies in Christian Apologetics," in *Jerusalem and Athens*, ed. Geehan, 283.

[21]Van Til, *Defense of the Faith*, 142.

[22]Halsey, *For a Time Such as This*, 15.

[23]Van Til, *Defense of the Faith*, 257-59; "My Credo," in *Jerusalem and Athens*, ed. Geehan, 18-19.

[24]Van Til, *Defense of the Faith*, 259. For Van Til's insistence on a Reformed apologetic, see further Van Til, *Christian Theory of Knowledge*, 11-24; *Toward a Reformed Apologetic* (privately printed, 1972); and cf. Bahnsen, *Van Til's Apologetic*, 530-37.

[25]Alvin Plantinga, "Advice to Christian Philosophers," in *Analytic Theist*, ed. Sennett, 296-315 (quote on 297); reprinted from *Faith and Philosophy* 1 (1984): 253-71. Parenthetical page references in the following paragraphs are from the Eerdmans volume.

[26]Cornelius Van Til, *Common Grace and the Gospel*, 8, in Bahnsen, *Van Til's Apologetic*, 109.

[27]Dooyeweerd, *In the Twilight of Western Thought*, 113.

[28]Ibid., 142, 146.

[29]Van Til, *Survey of Christian Epistemology*, xv, in Bahnsen, *Van Til's Apologetic*, 58.

[30]Cornelius Van Til, *Apologetics* (Nutley, N.J.: Presbyterian & Reformed, 1976), 37, in Bahnsen, *Van Til's Apologetic*, 67.

[31]Abraham Kuyper, *Principles of Sacred Theology* (Grand Rapids: Eerdmans, 1968). Quotations from Kuyper in this section are cited from this work.

[32]Abraham Kuyper, *Lectures on Calvinism* (Grand Rapids: Eerdmans, 1931), 133.

[33]Cornelius Van Til, *Christian-Theistic Evidences*, introduction (unnumbered).

[34]Ibid., 51.

[35]Cf. Bahnsen, *Van Til's Apologetic*, 268 n. 20.

[36]Cf. Frame, *Cornelius Van Til: An Introduction to His Thought*, 180 n. 19.

[37]Van Til, *Christian-Theistic Evidences*, 55-56.

[38]Van Til, *Defense of the Faith*, 103.

[39]Van Til, *Christian-Theistic Evidences*, 56.

[40]Ibid., 57.

[41]John C. Whitcomb, Jr., and Henry M. Morris, *The Genesis Flood* (Grand Rapids: Baker, 1961). For a discussion (by an advocate) of the importance of this book to the movement, see Charles A. Clough, "Biblical Presuppositions and Historical Geology: A Case Study," *Journal of Christian Reconstruction* 1, no. 1 (summer 1974): 35-48. This periodical is the work of Christian Reconstructionists, a Calvinist movement emphasizing the ethical, social, and political applications of Van Til's philosophy.

[42]For his advocacy of Van Til's apologetic system, see John C. Whitcomb, Jr., "Contemporary Apologetics and the Christian Faith," *Bibliotheca Sacra* 134 (1977): 99-106, 195-202, 291-98; 135 (1978): 24-33. Some indication of Whitcomb's adherence to a philosophy of science akin to that of Van Til can be seen in the introduction to *The Genesis Flood* (see especially xxi).

[43]Cf. Cornelius Van Til, "The Doctrine of Creation and Christian Apologetics," *Journal of Christian Reconstruction* 1, no. 1 (summer 1974): 69-80.

[44]Van Til, *Christian Theory of Knowledge*, 73; cf. *Defense of the Faith* (1955), 247-51.

[45]Gordon H. Clark, *The Philosophy of Science and Belief in God*, 3rd ed. (Jefferson, Md.: Trinity Foundation, 1996), 36. Parenthetical page references to Clark in this section are to this work.

[46]We are stating here formally what Clark informally expresses.

[47]Thomas S. Kuhn, *The Structure of Scientific Revolutions*, 2nd ed. (Chicago: University of Chicago Press, 1970).

[48]See Vern Sheridan Poythress, *Symphonic Theology: The Validity of Multiple Perspectives in Theology* (Grand Rapids: Zondervan, Academie, 1987); Poythress, *Science and Hermeneutics: Implications of Scientific Method for Biblical Interpretation*, Foundations of Contemporary Interpretation, vol. 6 (Grand Rapids: Zondervan, Academie, 1988); Frame, *Doctrine of the Knowledge of God* (1987), 28-29, 72, 86, etc.; Frame, *Apologetics to the Glory of God* (1994), 200; Frame, *Cornelius Van Til: An Introduction to His Thought* (1995), 133-34.

[49]Kuyper, *Principles of Sacred Theology*, 386-87.

[50]Gordon H. Clark, "Apologetics," in *Contemporary Evangelical Thought*, ed. Carl F. H. Henry (Great Neck, N.Y.: Channel Press, 1957), 140.

[51]Gordon H. Clark, *Religion, Reason, and Revelation* (Nutley, N.J.: Craig Press, 1961; 2nd ed., Jefferson, Md.: Trinity Foundation, 1986), 53.

[52]Gordon H. Clark, *A Christian Philosophy of Education* (Grand Rapids: Eerdmans, 1946), 35, as quoted in Lewis, *Testing Christianity's Truth Claims*, 107.

[53]Van Til, *Defense of the Faith* (1967), 197-99.

[54]Ibid., 199.

⁵⁵Van Til, *Christian-Theistic Evidences*, preface.

⁵⁶Van Til, *Defense of the Faith*, 99.

⁵⁷Van Til, *Christian-Theistic Evidences*, 56-57, emphasis in original.

⁵⁸Ibid., 52.

⁵⁹Van Til, *Defense of the Faith*, 204.

⁶⁰Bahnsen, *Van Til's Apologetic*, 644 n. 197. We may note here in passing that Acts 2:24 has nothing to do with historical argument or even how the Jews were supposed to know that Christ was risen. Peter is simply saying that because Jesus was the Lord of life, it was impossible for him to stay dead.

⁶¹Gordon H. Clark, *Karl Barth's Theological Method* (Philadelphia: Presbyterian & Reformed, 1963), 100.

⁶²Van Til, *Defense of the Faith*, 98.

⁶³Ibid., 98-99, emphasis in original.

⁶⁴Van Til, *Common Grace and the Gospel*, 196.

⁶⁵Ibid., 54.

⁶⁶Van Til, *Survey of Christian Epistemology*, 10.

⁶⁷Ibid., 208.

CHAPTER 14

¹Van Til, *Defense of the Faith*, 105.

²Gordon H. Clark, *In Defense of Theology* (Milford, Mich.: Mott Media, 1984), 33.

³Clark, *Logic*, 2d ed. (Jefferson, Md.: Trinity Foundation, 1988), 120-21. References to Clark in this section are from this work.

⁴Cornelius Van Til, *Introduction to Systematic Theology*, 191.

⁵Van Til, *Defense of the Faith*, 115, 118.

⁶Cornelius Van Til, *Survey of Christian Epistemology*, 12.

⁷Van Til, *Defense of the Faith*, 108.

⁸Plantinga, *Warranted Christian Belief*, 258-66. Citations in the following paragraphs are taken from this book.

⁹Alvin Plantinga, "Pluralism: A Defense of Religious Exclusivism," in *The Rationality of Belief and the Plurality of Faith: Essays in Honor of William P. Alston*, ed. Thomas D. Senor (Ithaca, N.Y.: Cornell University Press, 1995), 191-215. All references to Plantinga in this section are to this article. The article has already been reprinted at least twice: as "A Defense of Religious Exclusivism," in *Analytic Theist*, ed. Sennett, 187-209, and in *Philosophy of Religion: An Anthology*, ed. Louis Pojman (Belmont, Calif.: Wadsworth, 1996).

¹⁰Cornelius Van Til, *Why I Believe in God*, in Bahnsen, *Van Til's Apologetic*, 126.

¹¹Clark, *Christian View of Men and Things*, 231.

¹²This understanding of Clark seems implicit in Bahnsen, *Van Til's Apologetic*, 669-670.

¹³Clark, *Christian View of Men and Things*, 231.

¹⁴Bahnsen, *Van Til's Apologetic*, 524 n. 126.

¹⁵Frame, *Apologetics to the Glory of God: An Introduction*, 38.

[16]Ibid., 42.

[17]Bahnsen, *Van Til's Apologetic*, 524 n. 126.

[18]Ibid.

[19]Ibid., 525 n. 126. (This very long note begins on p. 523 and continues to p. 525.)

[20]Antony Flew, "The Presumption of Atheism," in *God, Freedom, and Immortality* (Buffalo: Prometheus Books, 1984), reprint of a book originally entitled *The Presumption of Atheism* (1976). Flew continued this theme in his published debate with evangelical philosopher and apologist Terry Miethe, *Does God Exist? A Believer and an Atheist Debate* (San Francisco: Harper San Francisco, 1991).

[21]Bahnsen, *Van Til's Apologetic*, 479 n. 28.

[22]Alvin Plantinga, "Reason and Belief in God," in *Faith and Rationality*, ed. Plantinga and Wolterstorff, 16-93. Parenthetical references to Plantinga in the remainder of this section are from this paper.

[23]Alvin Plantinga, *God, Freedom, and Evil* (Grand Rapids: Eerdmans, 1974), 77-84.

[24]Plantinga, *God, Freedom, and Evil*, 112.

[25]*Five Views on Apologetics*, ed. Cowan; all citations in the next two paragraphs are from Kelly James Clark's contributions to this book.

[26]Dooyeweerd, *A New Critique of Theoretical Thought*, 2:38.

[27]Ibid., 40.

[28]Ibid., 2:40-41.

[29]Clark, *Religion, Reason, and Revelation*, 35.

[30]Ibid., 35-38.

[31]Ibid., 39-41.

[32]Ibid., 41.

[33]Nash, "Gordon Clark's Theory of Knowledge," in *The Philosophy of Gordon H. Clark: A Festschrift*, ed. Ronald H. Nash, 157.

[34]Van Til, *Defense of the Faith*, 197.

[35]Ibid., 108-109.

[36]Ibid., 176.

[37]Van Til, *Common Grace and the Gospel*, 49.

[38]Ibid., 190, 192.

[39]Van Til, *Why I Believe in God*, 139, 143.

[40]Cornelius Van Til, *Protestant Doctrine of Scripture*, 56; Van Til, *Christian Theory of Knowledge*, 301; Van Til, *Reformed Pastor and Modern Thought* (Nutley, N.J.: Presbyterian & Reformed, 1971), 12-13, 24; cf. Bahnsen, *Van Til's Apologetic*, 184-86, 192-94.

[41]Van Til, *Common Grace and the Gospel*, 44.

[42]Cf. Bahnsen, *Van Til's Apologetic*, 613 n. 129, where he rather tentatively makes the same point.

[43]Van Til, *Common Grace and the Gospel*, 44.

[44]Gilbert B. Weaver, "Gordon Clark: Christian Apologist," in *The Philosophy of Gordon H. Clark*, ed. Nash, 301.

[45]David Waring Diehl, "Divine Omniscience in the Thought of Charles Hartshorne and Cornelius Van Til: A Systemic Comparative Study" (Ph.D. diss., Hartford Seminary Foundation, 1978), 224-225. Diehl cites Ramm, *Types of Apologetic Systems*, 202. See also Diehl, "Van Til's Epistemic Argument: A Case of Inadvertent Natural Theology" (faculty paper, The King's College, n.d.).

[46]Diehl, "Divine Omniscience," 264.

[47]Ibid., 266.

[48]William Lane Craig, "A Classical Apologist's Response," in *Five Views on Apologetics*, ed. Cowan, 233.

[49]Bahnsen, *Van Til's Apologetic*, 496-529.

[50]Frame, "A Presuppositional Apologist's Closing Remarks," in *Five Views on Apologetics*, ed. Cowan, 359-60.

[51]Westminster Confession of Faith 3.1; 5.1-4, in *The Creeds of Christendom: With a History and Critical Notes*, vol. 3, *The Evangelical Protestant Creeds, with Translations*, ed. Philip Schaff, rev. David S. Schaff, (New York: Harper & Row, 1931; reprint, Grand Rapids: Baker, 1993), 608, 612-13.

[52]Van Til, *Defense of the Faith*, 182.

[53]Clark, *Religion, Reason, and Revelation*, 238.

[54]Van Til, *Defense of the Faith*, 182.

[55]Frame, *Apologetics to the Glory of God*, 165-66.

[56]Clark, *Religion, Reason, and Revelation*, 207.

[57]Van Til, *Defense of the Faith*, 184-85.

[58]Van Til, "My Credo," 10.

[59]Van Til, *Protestant Doctrine of Scripture*, 5, in Bahnsen, *Van Til's Apologetic*, 380.

[60]Bahnsen, *Van Til's Apologetic*, 642.

[61]Ibid., 646.

[62]Van Til, *Defense of the Faith*, 240.

[63]Ibid., 242.

[64]Ibid., 199.

[65]Van Til, "My Credo," 3-21. All references to Van Til in this section are from this article.

CHAPTER 15

[1]Some elements of this dialogue are inspired by a sample apologetic dialogue included by John Frame in his book *Apologetics to the Glory of God: An Introduction*, 203-217. (In Frame's dialogue, John talks to a non-Christian named Al while both are in flight on an airplane.)

[2]Craig, "A Classical Apologist's Response," in *Five Views on Apologetics*, ed. Cowan, 232, 233.

[3]John M. Frame, *Evangelical Reunion: Denominations and the Body of Christ* (Grand Rapids: Baker, 1986); Vern S. Poythress, *Symphonic Theology: The Validity of Multiple Perspectives in Theology* (Grand Rapids: Zondervan, Academie, 1987).

[4]Frame, *Cornelius Van Til: An Analysis of His Thought* (Phillipsburg, N.J.: Presbyterian & Reformed, 1995).

[5]William Edgar, "Two Christian Warriors: Cornelius Van Til and Francis A. Schaeffer Compared." *Westminster Theological Journal* 57 (1995): 57-80.

CHAPTER 16

[1]Some critics of the first edition of *Faith Has Its Reasons* expressed just this complaint—without, however, addressing the reasons we gave for including fideism in the book.

[2]Greg L. Bahnsen, *Van Til's Apologetic: Readings and Analysis* (Phillipsburg, N.J.: Presbyterian & Reformed, 1998), 73.

[3]Alan Richardson, "Fideism," in *A Dictionary of Christian Theology*, ed. Alan Richardson (Philadelphia: Westminster, 1969), 129.

[4]Van A. Harvey, *A Handbook of Theological Terms* (New York: Macmillan, 1964), 99.

[5]C. Stephen Evans, *Faith Beyond Reason: A Kierkegaardian Account*, Reason & Religion (Grand Rapids: Eerdmans, 1998), especially 52, 55.

[6]Evans classifies Van Til as an *irrational* fideist, although he prefaces his comments with the admission that his classification of certain individuals might be challenged; C. Stephen Evans, *Faith Beyond Reason*, 17-19. As we have seen, Van Til argued that Christianity was supremely rational and the only rational system of thought, and developed an argument with which to prove this to non-Christians. Thus, Van Til does not fit Evans's definition of fideism, responsible or otherwise. Evans does a better job backing up his suggestion to classify Plantinga as a responsible fideist (41-47), which is defensible on Evans's definition of the term. We classify Plantinga as a Reformed apologist, but note that some elements of his thought are closer to classical apologetics and other elements have affinities with fideism (as was the case with Abraham Kuyper, whose thought led in different ways to Van Til and Plantinga).

[7]On Tertullian, see B. B. Warfield, *Studies in Tertullian and Augustine* (New York: Oxford University Press, 1930); Cornelius Van Til, *A Christian Theory of Knowledge* (Phillipsburg, N.J.: Presbyterian & Reformed, 1969), 83-109; Robert H. Ayers, *Language, Logic, and Reason in the Church Fathers: A Study of Tertullian, Augustine, and Aquinas*, Altertumswissenschaftliche Texte und Studien 6 (Hildesheim: Georg Olms, 1979); Robert D. Sider, "*Credo Quia Absurdum?*" *Classical World* 73 (1980): 417-19; Timothy D. Barnes, *Tertullian: A Historical and Literary Study*, rev. ed. (Oxford: Clarendon; New York: Oxford University Press, 1985); Anthony J. Guerra, "Polemical Christianity: Tertullian's Search for Certainty," *Second Century* 8 (1991): 109-123; Eric Osborn, *Tertullian: First Theologian of the West* (New York and Cambridge: Cambridge University Press, 1997); Ian Balfour, "Tertullian on and off the Internet," *Journal of Early Christian Studies* 8 (2000): 579-85. Online resources include The Tertullian Project (http://www.tertullian.org/).

[8]Tertullian, *Against Heresies* 7, in Ante-Nicene Fathers, 10 vols. (1885; reprint, Grand Rapids: Eerdmans, 1969), 3:246.

[9]As pointed out by many scholars and apologists; e.g., Norman L. Geisler and Winfried Corduan, *Philosophy of Religion*, 2d ed. (Grand Rapids: Baker, 1988), 87.

[10]Tertullian, *On the Flesh of Christ* 5 (our translation); cf. *Opera*, ed. E. F. Leopold (Leipzig, 1839-1841), 4:66.

[11]See especially David F. Siemens, Jr., "Misquoting Tertullian to Anathematize Christianity," *Philosophia Christi* 5 (2003): 563-65.

[12] An accessible collection of key writings by Luther is John Dillenberger, ed., *Martin Luther: Selections from His Writings* (Garden City, N.Y.: Doubleday, 1961). Useful introductions to Luther include David C. Steinmetz, *Luther in Context*, 2d ed. (Grand Rapids: Baker Academic, 2002); Stephen J. Nichols, *Martin Luther: A Guided Tour of His Life and Thought* (Phillipsburg, N.J.: Presbyterian & Reformed, 2002); Donald K. McKim, ed., *The Cambridge Companion to Martin Luther*, Cambridge Companions to Religion (New York and Cambridge: Cambridge University Press, 2003). Works dealing with Luther's thought of special relevance to apologetics include Philip S. Watson, *Let God Be God! An Interpretation of the Theology of Martin Luther* (London: Epworth

Press, 1947; reprint, Philadelphia: Fortress Press, 1970); B. A. Gerrish, *Grace and Reason: A Study in the Theology of Luther* (Oxford: Clarendon, 1962); several essays in *Reformation Studies: Essays in Honor of Roland H. Bainton*, ed. Franklin Hamlin Littell (Richmond: John Knox, 1962); Robert H. Fischer, "Place of Reason in Luther's Theology," *Lutheran Quarterly* 16 (1964): 41-48; H. Wayne House, "The Value of Reason in Luther's View of Apologetics," *Concordia Journal* 7 (1981): 65-67; Siegbert W. Becker, *The Foolishness of God: The Place of Reason in the Theology of Martin Luther* (Milwaukee: Northwestern Publishing House, 1982); Demarest, *General Revelation*, 43-50; Brown, *Christianity and Western Thought*, 148-151.

¹³Cited in Gerrish, *Grace and Reason*, 8 n. 2.

¹⁴Luther, "Postil [Epistle] for Epiphany," on Isaiah 40:1-6, in *WA* 10, pt. 1/1, 531; cited in Gerrish, 12. *WA* refers to the 1910 Weimar edition *(Weimarer Ausgabe)* of *D. Martin Luthers Werke*, the standard reference. The epistle cited here is not published in the American edition.

¹⁵*WA* 9:43.

¹⁶"The Gospel for the Festival of the Epiphany, Matthew 2[:1-12]," in *LW* 52:165. *LW* refers to the fifty-six-volume American Edition in English of *Luther's Works*, co-published by Concordia Publishing House and Fortress Press.

¹⁷Luther, *Lectures on Jonah: The German Text* (1526), in *LW* 19:53-55 (cf. *WA* 19:206-208), on Jonah 1:5; *Lectures on Galatians 1535, Chapters 1—4*, in *LW* 26:399 (cf. *WA* 40:606-608), on Galatians 4:8-9.

¹⁸Luther, "The Gospel for New Year's Day, Luke 2[:21]," in *LW* 52:150.

¹⁹Luther, *The Disputation Concerning the Passage: "The Word Was Made Flesh"* (1539), in *LW* 38:239-244.

²⁰Luther, *Sermon on Faith and Good Works*, cited in J. K. S. Reid, *Christian Apologetics* (London: Hodder & Stoughton; Grand Rapids: Eerdmans, 1969), 131.

²¹A good, short introduction to Pascal for beginners is Douglas Groothuis, *On Pascal* (Belmont, Calif.: Wadsworth, 2002). Works on Pascal's thought include Hugh M. Davidson, *The Origins of Certainty: Means and Meanings in Pascal's "Pensées"* (Chicago: University of Chicago Press, 1979); A. J. Krailsheimer, *Pascal*, Past Masters (New York: Hill & Wang, 1980); Mayers, *Both/And: A Balanced Apologetic*, 118-125; Francis X. J. Coleman, *Neither Angel nor Beast: The Life and Work of Blaise Pascal* (New York: Routledge & Kegan Paul, 1986); Thomas V. Morris, *Making Sense of It All: Pascal and the Meaning of Life* (Grand Rapids: Eerdmans, 1992); Peter Kreeft, *Christianity for Modern Pagans: Pascal's Pensées Edited, Outlined, and Explained* (San Francisco: Ignatius Press, 1993); Douglas R. Groothuis, "To Prove or Not to Prove: Pascal on Natural Theology" (Ph.D. diss., University of Oregon, 1993); Terrence D. Cuneo, "Combatting the Noetic Effects of Sin: Pascal's Strategy for Natural Theology," *Faith and Philosophy* 11 (1994): 645-662; Marvin R. O'Connell, *Blaise Pascal: Reasons of the Heart*, Library of Religious Biography (Grand Rapids: Eerdmans, 1997); Rick Wade, "Blaise Pascal: An Apologist for Our Times" (Richardson, Tex.: Probe Ministries, 1998), online at < http://www.leaderu.com/orgs/probe/docs/pascal.html > (checked 10/27/2004); Nicholas Hammond, *The Cambridge Companion to Pascal*, Cambridge Companions to Religion (New York and Cambridge: Cambridge University Press, 2003); Kenneth Richard Samples, "Why Should I Gamble on Faith?" in *Without a Doubt: Answering the 20 Toughest Faith Questions* (Grand Rapids: Baker, 2004), 77-87.

²²According to the traditional arrangement, Pascal's "thoughts" are in blocks of sentences and paragraphs and are numbered. Thus citations from the *Pensées* are given here according to numbers, not pages, and are quoted from the translation by W. F. Trotter. It has been published as *Thoughts*, trans. W. F. Trotter, Harvard Classics 48 (New York: P. F. Collier & Son, 1910), 9-317; *Pensées*, Great Books of the Western World 33 (Chicago: Encyclopaedia Britannica, 1952), 169-352; and *Pensées* (New York: Dutton, 1958). See also Blaise Pascal, *The Mind on Fire: A Faith for the*

Skeptical and Indifferent, intro. Os Guinness, abridged and ed. James Houston (Regent College Publishing, 2003).

[23]In addition to the literature already cited, see Charles M. Natoli, "The Role of the Wager in Pascal's Apologetics," *New Scholasticism* 57 (1983): 98-106; Nicholas Rescher, *Pascal's Wager: A Study of Practical Reasoning in Philosophical Theology* (Notre Dame, Ind.: University of Notre Dame Press, 1985); R. Douglas Geivett and Brendan Sweetman, eds., *Contemporary Perspectives on Religious Epistemology* (New York and Oxford: Oxford University Press, 1992), 257-92, and the literature cited there; and see the following exchange: Alan Carter, "On Pascal's Wager; or Why All Bets Are Off," and Douglas Groothuis, "Are All Bets Off? A Defense of Pascal's Wager," *Philosophia Christi* 3 (2001); Alan Carter, "Is the Wager Back On? A Response to Douglas Groothuis," and Douglas Groothuis, "An Unwarranted Farewell to Pascal's Wager: A Reply to Alan Carter," *Philosophia Christi* 4 (2002).

[24]See C. Stephen Evans, *Faith Beyond Reason*, 49-52.

[25]Emil Brunner, *Truth as Encounter* (Philadelphia: Westminster, 1964), 112.

[26]Emil Brunner, *The Christian Doctrine of God*, trans. Olive Wyon (Philadelphia: Westminster, 1950), 100.

[27]Brunner's notion of 'eristics' was in some ways a compromise between classical apologetics and Kierkegaard's fideistic stance. Brunner's one-time mentor and later theological rival, Karl Barth, was thoroughly fideistic, and he strenuously opposed Brunner's eristics.

[28]A fact attested by the many bibliographies on Kierkegaard that have been published; see especially Calvin D. Evans, comp., *Søren Kierkegaard: Remnants, 1944-1980, and Multi-Media, 1925-1991*, Fontanus Monograph Series (Montreal: McGill University Libraries, 1993); Francois Lapointe, comp., *Søren Kierkegaard and His Critics: An International Bibliography of Criticism* (Westport, Conn.: Greenwood, 1980). Two excellent Kierkegaard readers are *A Kierkegaard Anthology*, ed. Robert Bretall (Princeton, N.J.: Princeton University Press, 1946), and *The Essential Kierkegaard*, ed. Howard V. Hong and Edna H. Hong (Princeton: Princeton University Press, 2000). A helpful introductory work is Shelley O'Hara, *Kierkegaard within Your Grasp: The First Step to Understanding Kierkegaard* (Hoboken, N.J.: Wiley, 2004). Among the best reference works are Alastair Hannay and Gordon D. Morino, eds., *The Cambridge Companion to Kierkegaard*, Cambridge Companions to Philosophy (Cambridge and New York: Cambridge University Press, 1998), and Julia Watkin, *Historical Dictionary of Kierkegaard's Philosophy* (Metuchen, N.J.: Scarecrow Press, 2000).

[29]For an especially negative assessment, see E. D. Klemke, *Studies in the Philosophy of Kierkegaard* (The Hague: Martinus Nijhoff, 1976). A number of apologists whose views we profile in this book have written critical assessments of Kierkegaard. See, for example, Gordon H. Clark, *Thales to Dewey: A History of Philosophy* (Grand Rapids: Baker, 1980 reprint of 1957 ed.), 485-91; Cornelius Van Til, *Christianity and Barthianism* (Phillipsburg, N.J.: Presbyterian & Reformed, 1962), 287-307; Edward John Carnell, *The Burden of Søren Kierkegaard* (Grand Rapids: Eerdmans, 1965); Norman L. Geisler, "Kierkegaard, Søren," in *Baker Encyclopedia of Christian Apologetics* (Grand Rapids: Baker, 1999), 405-11. In our opinion, Geisler's assessment of Kierkegaard is especially judicious.

[30]Works on Kierkegaard's life are numerous; see especially Walter Lowrie, *Kierkegaard*, 2 vols. (New York: Harper, 1962); Peter P. Rohde, *Søren Kierkegaard: An Introduction to His Life and Philosophy*, trans. Alan M. Williams (London: Allen & Unwin, 1963); Josiah Thompson, *Kierkegaard* (London: Victor Gollancz, 1974); Brita K. Stendahl, *Søren Kierkegaard* (Boston: Twayne Publishers, 1976); Bruce Kirmmse, *Kierkegaard in Golden Age Denmark* (Bloomington and Indianapolis: Indiana University Press, 1990); Joakim Garff, *Søren Kierkegaard: A Biography*, trans. Bruce H. Kirmmse (Princeton: Princeton University Press, 2000). For a recent survey by an evangelical writer, see L. Joseph Rosas III, *Scripture in the Thought of Søren Kierkegaard* (Nashville: Broadman & Holman, 1994).

[31]The collection we will rely on is *Søren Kierkegaard's Journals and Papers*, ed. Howard V. Hong and Edna H. Hong, 7 vols. (Bloomington: Indiana University Press, 1967-1978), hereafter referred to as *JP* in parenthetical references in the text. The first locator is the entry number, after which are given the volume and page numbers. Entries and excerpts from Kierkegaard's unpublished writings are arranged alphabetically by topics.

[32]Søren Kierkegaard, *The Point of View for My Work as an Author*, in *A Kierkegaard Anthology*, ed. Robert Bretall (Princeton, N.J.: Princeton University Press, 1946), 325.

[33]Kierkegaard, *Point of View*, 326.

[34]Ibid., 332.

[35]Søren Kierkegaard, *Concluding Unscientific Postscript to "Philosophical Fragments,"* vol. 1, *Text*, ed. Howard V. Hong and Edna H. Hong (Princeton, N.J.: Princeton University Press, 1992), 617.

[36]Søren Kierkegaard, *On Authority and Revelation*, trans. Walter Lowrie (Princeton, N.J.: Princeton University Press, 1955), 59.

[37]Kierkegaard, *Concluding Unscientific Postscript*, 557.

[38]C. Stephen Evans, "Apologetic Arguments in *Philosophical Fragments*," in *"Philosophical Fragments" and "Johannes Climacus,"* ed. Robert L. Perkins, International Kierkegaard Commentary, vol. 7 (Macon, Ga.: Mercer University Press, 1994), 63-83. Parenthetical page references in the rest of this section are to this article.

[39]Cf. Søren Kierkegaard, *Philosophical Fragments; Johannes Climacus*, ed. and trans. Howard V. Hong and Edna H. Hong (Princeton, N.J.: Princeton University Press, 1985), 21.

[40]Citing ibid., 22.

[41]Cf. ibid., 35-36.

[42]Citing ibid., 51.

[43]On the apologetic insights to be found in Kierkegaard, see also Robert C. Koons, "Faith, Probability and Infinite Passion: Ramseyian Decision Theory and Kierkegaard's Account of Christian Faith," *Faith and Philosophy* 10 (1993): 145-160, accessed online at < http://www.utexas. edu/cola/depts/philosophy/faculty/koons/kierk.pdf >; Mark C. Miller, "The Hipness unto Death: Søren Kierkegaard and David Letterman—Ironic Apologists to Generation X," *Mars Hill Review* 7 (Winter/Spring 1997): 38-52, accessed online at < http://www.leaderu.com/marshill/mhr07/kierk1. html >; John Depoe, "Rejuvenating Christian Apologetics in the Twenty-first Century: Taking Hints from Søren Kierkegaard," Baylor University, 2002, accessed online at < http://www.johndepoe.com/ Kierkegaard_Apologetics.pdf >.

[44]Barth offers an illuminating account of his life's work in *How I Changed My Mind* (Richmond: John Knox, 1966; Edinburgh: Saint Andrew Press, 1969). His son, the New Testament theologian Markus Barth, wrote an endearing short biography, "My Father: Karl Barth," published in *How Karl Barth Changed My Mind*, ed. Donald K. McKim (Grand Rapids: Eerdmans, 1986), 1-5. See also Geoffrey W. Bromiley, "Karl Barth," in *Creative Minds in Contemporary Theology*, ed. Philip E. Hughes, 2d rev. ed. (Grand Rapids: Eerdmans, 1969), 27-62, especially 27-31; Eberhard Busch, *Karl Barth: His Life from Letters and Autobiographical Texts*, trans. John Bowden, 2d rev. ed. (Philadelphia: Fortress, 1976); Hendrikus Berkhof, *Two Hundred Years of Theology: Report of a Personal Journey*, trans. John Vriend (Grand Rapids: Eerdmans, 1989), 179-207. Studies of the development of Barth's theology include Thomas F. Torrance, *Karl Barth: An Introduction to His Early Theology, 1910-1931* (London: SCM, 1962); Bruce L. McCormack, *Karl Barth's Critically Realistic Dialectical Theology: Its Genesis and Development, 1909-1936* (Oxford: Clarendon, 1995); Gary Dorrien, *The Barthian Revolt in Modern Theology: Theology without Weapons* (Louisville, Ky.: Westminster John Knox Press, 2000); Sung Wook Chung, *Admiration & Challenge: Karl*

Barth's Theological Relationship with John Calvin (New York: Peter Lang, 2002), 15-122. Some interpreters of Barth (following Barth's own self-reflections) emphasize the differences between his early thought and his later, more conservative theology (e.g., Torrance), while others emphasize the continuities and maintain that Barth's later theology retained significant elements of liberalism (e.g., McCormack, Dorrien).

[45]Johann Wilhelm Herrmann (1846-1922) was one of Barth's professors at Marburg; on his theology and his relation to Barth, see Karl Barth, "The Principles of Dogmatics According to Wilhelm Herrmann," in *Theology and Church*, ed. Louise Pettibone Smith (New York: Harper & Row, 1962), 238-71; Berkhof, *Two Hundred Years of Theology*, 143-62, 179-85; McCormack, *Karl Barth's Critically Realistic Dialectical Theology*, 49-77; Dorrien, *Barthian Revolt in Modern Theology*, 15-21, 27-32.

[46]Cf. George Rupp, *Culture-Protestantism: German Liberal Theology at the Turn of the Twentieth Century* (Missoula, Mont.: Scholars, 1977).

[47]Karl Barth, *The Epistle to the Romans*, trans. Sir Edwyn Hoskyns (London: Oxford University Press, 1933 [2d ed.], 1980 [6th ed.]), 10 (in both editions).

[48]On Barth's theological relationship to Calvin, see especially Chung, *Admiration & Challenge: Karl Barth's Theological Relationship with John Calvin*; Cornelis van der Kooi, *As in a Mirror: John Calvin and Karl Barth on Knowing God: A Diptych*, trans. Donald Mader; Studies in the History of Christian Traditions 120 (Leiden: Brill, 2005).

[49]Karl Barth, *Anselm: Fides Quaerens Intellectum*, trans. Ian W. Robertson, 2d ed. (London: SCM; Richmond: John Knox, 1960), 71.

[50]Ibid., 11.

[51]Karl Barth, *Church Dogmatics*, ed. Geoffrey T. Bromiley and Thomas F. Torrance (Edinburgh: T. & T. Clark, 1936-1977), I/1, xiii. The abbreviation *CD* is used throughout for the English translation of this work. Citations refer to volume and part, each of which was actually a separate book (I/1, I/2, II/1, etc.), followed by the page reference.

[52]Geoffrey W. Bromiley was not only the co-editor overseeing the translation of the *Church Dogmatics* into English, but he was also the master at digesting Barth's work for students needing an overview. His *Introduction to the Theology of Karl Barth* (Grand Rapids: Eerdmans, 1979) offers a careful and insightful condensation of the *Church Dogmatics* in about 250 pages. For an even briefer overview, see Bromiley, "Karl Barth," 31-50.

[53]Surveys of evangelical views of Barth include Gregory Bolich, *Karl Barth and Evangelicalism* (Downers Grove, Ill.: InterVarsity, 1980); Richard A. Mohler, Jr., "Evangelical Theology and Karl Barth: Representative Models of Response" (Ph.D. diss., Southern Baptist Theological Seminary, 1989); and especially helpful, Phillip R. Thorne, *Evangelicalism and Karl Barth: His Reception and Influence in North American Evangelical Theology*, Princeton Theological Monograph Series, vol. 40 (Allison Park, Pa.: Pickwick, 1995).

[54]For example, G. C. Berkouwer, *The Triumph of Grace in the Theology of Karl Barth*, trans. H. R. Boer (Grand Rapids: Eerdmans; London: Paternoster Press, 1956); Colin Brown, *Karl Barth and the Christian Message* (Downers Grove, Ill.: InterVarsity, 1967).

[55]Perhaps most notably Bernard Ramm, *After Fundamentalism: The Future of Evangelical Theology* (San Francisco: Harper & Row, 1983).

[56]Especially Cornelius Van Til and others of his theological perspective; see Van Til, *The New Modernism: An Appraisal of the Theology of Barth and Brunner* (Philadelphia: Presbyterian & Reformed; London: James Clarke, 1946); Van Til, *Christianity and Barthianism* (Nutley, N.J.: Presbyterian & Reformed, 1962); Fred H. Klooster, *The Significance of Barth's Theology: An Appraisal with Special Reference to Election and Reconciliation* (Grand Rapids: Baker, 1961).

Taking a somewhat different approach but reaching similar conclusions is Gordon H. Clark, *Karl Barth's Theological Method* (Philadelphia: Presbyterian & Reformed, 1963).

[57]Ramm's *After Fundamentalism* (see n. 54 above) defends Barth's soundness on these basic doctrines, while Van Til, Klooster, and Gordon Clark (see n. 55 above) were among Barth's sharpest critics on these doctrinal issues. *The Cambridge Companion to Karl Barth*, ed. John Webster (Cambridge, U.K., and New York: Cambridge University Press, 2000), contains recent essays on Barth's views on the Trinity, Christology, grace, and salvation by scholars noted for their work on Barth. On Barth's view of the resurrection (usefully contrasted with Bultmann's), see Dorrien, *Barthian Revolt in Modern Theology*, 182-92.

[58]On Barth's view of Scripture, see Klass Runia, *Karl Barth's Doctrine of Holy Scripture* (Grand Rapids: Eerdmans, 1962); Francis Watson, "The Bible," in *Cambridge Companion to Karl Barth*, ed. Webster, 57-71; Neil B. MacDonald, *Karl Barth and the Strange New World within the Bible: Barth, Wittgenstein, and the Metadilemmas of the Enlightenment*, Paternoster Biblical and Theological Monographs (Milton Keynes, U.K.: Paternoster, 2002); Bruce L. McCormack, "The Being of Holy Scripture Is in Becoming: Karl Barth in Conversation with American Evangelical Criticism," in *Evangelicals & Scripture: Tradition, Authority and Hermeneutics*, ed. Vincent Bacote, Laura C. Miguélez, and Dennis L. Ockholm (Downers Grove, Ill.: InterVarsity, 2004), 55-75.

[59]See Bromiley, "Karl Barth," 51-55, for an overview of these and subsidiary problems in Barth's theology.

[60]Barth, CD I/2, 833, quoted in Chung, *Admiration and Challenge*, 14 n. 31.

[61]See *Evangelical Theology in Transition: Theologians in Dialogue with Donald Bloesch*, ed. Elmer M. Colyer (Downers Grove, Ill.: InterVarsity, 1999), featuring contributions by Avery Dulles, Millard Erickson, Clark Pinnock, Thomas F. Torrance, and others.

[62]In fact, he left the pastorate to begin his academic career in 1928, the same year that Donald Bloesch was born. Reinhold Niebuhr's principal writings include *Moral Man and Immoral Society: A Study in Ethics and Practice* (New York: Scribner, 1932); *The Nature and Destiny of Man: A Christian Interpretation*, Gifford Lectures, 2 vols. (New York: Scribner, 1941, 1943); *Faith and History: A Comparison of Christian and Modern Views of History* (New York: Scribner, 1949). On Niebuhr, see Theodore Minnema, "Reinhold Niebuhr," in *Creative Minds in Contemporary Theology*, 377-406; Charles W. Kegley and Robert W. Bretall, eds., *Reinhold Niebuhr: His Religious, Social, and Political Thought* (New York: Macmillan, 1956; reprint, New York: Pilgrim Press, 1984); Paul Foreman, "The Theology of Reinhold Niebuhr," LeadershipU < http://www.leaderu.com/isot/docs/niehbr3.html >. Reinhold is to be distinguished from his brother, H. Richard Niebuhr, another distinguished liberal theologian.

[63]Donald G. Bloesch, *The Christian Witness in a Secular Age: An Evaluation of Nine Contemporary Theologians* (Minneapolis: Augsburg, 1968; reprint, Eugene, Ore.: Wipf & Stock, 2002). Parenthetical page references in the text are to this work.

[64]Donald G. Bloesch, *The Ground of Certainty: Toward an Evangelical Theology of Revelation* (Grand Rapids: Eerdmans, 1971; reprint, Eugene, Ore.: Wipf & Stock, 2002). Parenthetical page references in the text are to this work.

[65]Donald G. Bloesch, *Jesus Is Victor! Karl Barth's Doctrine of Salvation* (Nashville: Abingdon, 1976).

[66]Donald G. Bloesch, *Essentials of Evangelical Theology*, 2 vols. (San Francisco: Harper & Row, 1978, 1979; 2 vols. in 1, Peabody, Mass.: Hendrickson, 2006).

[67]Donald G. Bloesch, *The Future of Evangelical Christianity: A Call for Unity amid Diversity* (Garden City, N.Y.: Doubleday, 1983), 121.

[68]Ibid., 122.

⁶⁹Ibid., 123-24, citing Norman L. Geisler, *Options in Contemporary Christian Ethics* (Grand Rapids: Baker, 1981), 32.

⁷⁰(1) *A Theology of Word and Spirit: Authority and Method in Theology* (1992), (2) *Holy Scripture: Revelation, Inspiration, and Interpretation* (1994); (3) *God the Almighty: Power, Wisdom, Holiness, Love* (1995); (4) *Jesus Christ: Savior and Lord* (1997); (5) *The Holy Spirit: Works and Gifts* (2000); (6) *The Church: Sacraments, Worship, Ministry, Mission* (2002); and (7) *The Last Things: Resurrection, Judgment, Glory* (2004). Each volume is published in Downers Grove, Illinois, by InterVarsity Press. Page references in the text are to the first volume in this series.

⁷¹Citing Jacques Ellul, *Living Faith*, trans. Peter Heinegg (San Francisco: Harper & Row, 1983), 123, 125; *What I Believe*, trans. Geoffrey W. Bromiley (Grand Rapids: Eerdmans, 1989), 306. Oddly, in an endnote Bloesch states that "Ellul is not an irrationalist" since he allows some role to reason, though not in faith (*Word and Spirit*, 285 n. 80). But if Ellul affirms that faith is *illogical*, that would seem to be sufficient to justify classifying him as an irrational fideist.

CHAPTER 17

¹Donald G. Bloesch, *A Theology of Word and Spirit: Authority and Method in Theology* (Downers Grove, Ill.: InterVarsity, 1992), 60-61.

²Bloesch, *Word and Spirit*, 231.

³Karl Barth, *Church Dogmatics*, trans. G. T. Thompson, Harold Knight, et. al., 4 vols. (Edinburgh: T. & T. Clark, 1936-1958), I/1, 31. References in the text to Barth's *Church Dogmatics* will hereafter be cited with *CD*, followed by the volume and part number, and the page reference.

⁴Citing *Fastenpost.* (1525), Sermon on Matt. 8:1f., *WA* 17, Part II, 85, line 10. *WA* refers to the 1910 Weimar edition *(Weimarer Ausgabe)* of *D. Martin Luthers Werke*, the standard reference.

⁵Citing Sermon on Acts 2:14f. (1534).

⁶Gregory A. Clark, "The Nature of Conversion: How the Rhetoric of Worldview Philosophy Can Betray Evangelicals," in *The Nature of Confession: Evangelicals and Postliberals in Conversation*, ed. Timothy R. Phillips and Dennis L. Ockholm (Downers Grove, Ill.: InterVarsity, 1996), 201-218. Parenthetical page references in the text are to this essay.

⁷Bloesch, *Word and Spirit*, 14.

⁸Donald G. Bloesch, *Future of Evangelical Theology: A Call for Unity amid Diversity* (Colorado Springs: Helmers & Howard, 1988), 122-23.

⁹Geoffrey W. Bromiley, *Introduction to the Theology of Karl Barth* (Grand Rapids: Eerdmans, 1979), 5.

¹⁰Karl Barth, "Karl Barth's Table Talk," in *Scottish Journal of Occasional Papers* (London: Oliver & Boyd, 1963), 44, 62.

¹¹Luther, *The Disputation Concerning the Passage: "The Word Was Made Flesh"* (1539), in *LW* 38:238-44. *LW* refers to the fifty-six-volume American Edition in English of *Luther's Works*, co-published by Concordia Publishing House and Fortress Press.

¹²Cited in Gerrish, *Grace and Reason*, 52.

¹³Luther, *Disputation*, in *LW* 38:239-244.

¹⁴Often cited; for example, in Pascal, *Pensées*, trans. A. J. Krailsheimer (Harmondsworth, U.K.: Penguin Books, 1966), 309.

¹⁵Søren Kierkegaard, *Concluding Unscientific Postscript to "Philosophical Fragments,"* vol. 1, *Text*, ed. Howard V. Hong and Edna H. Hong (Princeton, N.J.: Princeton University Press, 1992), 54.

[16]Peter F. Rhode, quoted by Howard A. Johnson, introduction to Kierkegaard, *JP*, 1:xxv.

[17]Johnson, introduction to Kierkegaard, *JP*, 1:xxvi.

[18]Donald G. Bloesch, *Holy Scripture: Revelation, Inspiration, and Interpretation* (Downers Grove, Ill.: InterVarsity, 1994), 113, 114.

[19]Ibid., 117.

[20]Ibid., 98.

[21]Ibid., 37.

[22]Søren Kierkegaard, *Philosophical Fragments; Johannes Climacus*, ed. and trans. Howard V. Hong and Edna H. Hong (Princeton, N.J.: Princeton University Press, 1985), 179; parenthetical page references in the text are to this work.

[23]C. Stephen Evans, "Apologetic Arguments in *Philosophical Fragments*," in *"Philosophical Fragments" and "Johannes Climacus,"* ed. Robert L. Perkins, International Kierkegaard Commentary, vol. 7 (Macon, Ga.: Mercer University Press, 1994), 63-83; see discussion in previous chapter.

[24]Parenthetical page references in text are to this work.

[25]Bloesch, *Word and Spirit*, 202.

[26]Ibid., 203, citing P. T. Forsyth, *The Principle of Authority*, 2d ed. (London: Independent Press, 1952), 55, 328.

CHAPTER 18

[1]Geoffrey W. Bromiley, *Introduction to the Theology of Karl Barth* (Grand Rapids: Eerdmans, 1979), 29.

[2]Parenthetical references in the text are to paragraph numbers, not pages, in Blaise Pascal, *Pensées*, trans. Totter; see chapter 16 for a more detailed exposition of Pascal's arguments with documentation.

[3]In this and other respects, Hume may be seen not so much as a skeptic but as a fideist, or at least someone whose thought prompted the development of modern fideism. See especially Delbert J. Hansen, *Fideism and Hume's Philosophy: Knowledge, Religion and Metaphysics*, Revisioning Philosophy 12 (New York: Peter Lang, 1993).

[4]Kierkegaard, *Concluding Unscientific Postscript*, 1:31.

[5]Kierkegaard, *Philosophical Fragments*, 49; so also *JP* 1334, 2:93.

[6]Kierkegaard, *Concluding Unscientific Postscript*, 485.

[7]Martin Luther, *Table Talk* (London: H. G. Bonn, 1857), 29-30, as quoted in R. Scott Rodin, *Evil and Theodicy in the Theology of Karl Barth*, Issues in Systematic Theology 3 (New York: Peter Lang, 1997), 26.

[8]For discussions of these and other statements by Barth pertaining to the problem of evil, see Rodin, *Evil and Theodicy in the Theology of Karl Barth*.

[9]*Karl Barth's Table Talk*, ed. John D. Godsey (Richmond: John Knox, 1963), 69.

[10]Kierkegaard, *Philosophical Fragments*, 35-36.

[11]Ibid., 51.

[12]C. Stephen Evans, "Apologetic Arguments in *Philosophical Fragments*," in *"Philosophical Fragments" and "Johannes Climacus,"* ed. Robert L. Perkins, International Kierkegaard Commentary, vol. 7 (Macon, Ga.: Mercer University Press, 1994), 69.

CHAPTER 19

[1]Douglas Groothuis, *Truth Decay: Defending Christianity against the Challenges of Postmodernism* (Downers Grove, Ill.: InterVarsity, 2000), 11.

CHAPTER 20

[1]C. S. Lewis, "On Obstinacy in Belief," in *The World's Last Night*, 17.

[2]B. B. Warfield, *Calvin and Augustine*, ed. Samuel G. Craig (Philadelphia: Presbyterian & Reformed, 1956).

[3]Evans, *Faith Beyond Reason*, 55 (see 55-64).

[4]See B. B. Warfield, *Calvin and Calvinism*, The Works of Benjamin B. Warfield, vol. 5 (New York: Oxford University Press, 1931; reprint, Grand Rapids: Baker, 1981).

[5]Cf. Geisler, *Baker Encyclopedia of Christian Apologetics*, 111-12.

[6]Gordon R. Lewis, *Testing Christianity's Truth Claims*, 176.

[7]Edgar Sheffield Brightman (1884-1953) was a philosopher in the tradition of idealism. He taught that God is a finite being who brought the universe into its created form out of a preexistent chaos and is working to perfect the universe and himself.

[8]Lewis, *Testing Christianity's Truth Claims*, 11. Note that for some reason Lewis changes the order of Carnell's books, discussing *Kingdom of Love* (in chapter 9) before *Christian Commitment* (in 10), and therefore "psychology" (which deals with love) before "ethics" (which deals with justice).

[9]Edward John Carnell, *An Introduction to Christian Apologetics: A Philosophic Defense of the Trinitarian-Theistic Faith* (Grand Rapids: Eerdmans, 1948; 4th ed., 1953); *A Philosophy of the Christian Religion* (Grand Rapids: Eerdmans, 1952); *Christian Commitment: An Apologetic* (New York: Macmillan, 1957; reprint, Grand Rapids: Baker, 1982); *The Kingdom of Love and the Pride of Life* (Grand Rapids: Eerdmans, 1960).

[10]Carnell, *Kingdom of Love*, 6.

[11]Edward John Carnell, *The Burden of Søren Kierkegaard* (Grand Rapids: Eerdmans, 1965).

[12]The only published biography of Carnell is Rudolph Nelson, *The Making and Unmaking of an Evangelical Mind: The Case of Edward Carnell* (New York: Cambridge University Press, 1988). For background on Carnell's life and work at Fuller, see George M. Marsden, *Reforming Fundamentalism: Fuller Seminary and the New Evangelicalism* (Grand Rapids: Eerdmans, 1987). Introductions to Carnell's apologetic and theology include Bernard L. Ramm, "Edward John Carnell," in *Types of Apologetic Systems: An Introductory Study to the Christian Philosophy of Religion* (Wheaton, Ill.: Van Kampen Press, 1953), 210-36; Lewis, *Testing Christianity's Truth Claims* (1976), 176-284; John A. Sims, *Edward John Carnell: Defender of the Faith* (Washington, D.C.: University Press of America, 1979); John G. Stackhouse, Jr., "'Who Follows in His Train': Edward John Carnell as a Model for Evangelical Theology," *Crux* 21, no. 2 (June 1985): 19-27; L. Joseph Rosas III, "Edward John Carnell," in *Baptist Theologians*, ed. Timothy George and David S. Dockery (Nashville: Broadman, 1990), 606-626; Rosas, "The Theology of Edward John Carnell," *Criswell Theological Review* 4 (1990): 351-71; John A. Sims, "Part Two: Edward John Carnell," in *Missionaries to the Skeptics* (1995), 95-148.

[13]Carnell, *Introduction*, 57. Carnell's four major works are cited in the text as *Introduction*, *Philosophy*, *Commitment*, and *Kingdom* respectively. For full titles, see n. 9 above.

[14]Lewis, *Testing Christianity's Truth Claims*, 178.

[15]Geisler, *Baker Encyclopedia of Christian Apologetics*, 114.

[16]Cornelius Van Til, *Defense of the Faith*, 3d ed. (1967), pp. 225-57; see also Van Til, review of *Introduction to Christian Apologetics*, by Carnell, *Westminster Theological Journal* 11 (1948): 45-53; chapter 3 of *The Case for Calvinism* (Philadelphia: Presbyterian & Reformed, 1963); "Reply" to Gordon R. Lewis, in *Jerusalem and Athens*, ed. Geehan, 361-68.

[17]Van Til, *Defense of the Faith*, 227.

[18]Bahnsen, *Van Til's Apologetic*, 549 and n. 64; see 537-50.

[19]Frame, *Cornelius Van Til: An Analysis of His Thought*, pp. 286-287; see the entire chapter, 285-97.

[20]Ibid., 294.

[21]Kenneth L. Woodward, "Guru of Fundamentalism," *Newsweek*, 1 November 1982, 88.

[22]On Schaeffer's life, see Edith Schaeffer, *L'Abri* (Wheaton, Ill.: Tyndale, 1969) and *The Tapestry* (Waco, Tex.: Word, 1984); Christopher Catherwood, *Five Evangelical Leaders* (Wheaton, Ill.: Harold Shaw, 1985), 113-61; Colin Duriez, "Francis Schaeffer," in *Handbook of Evangelical Theologians*, ed. Walter E. Elwell (Grand Rapids: Baker, 1993), 245-59; Burson and Walls, *C. S. Lewis and Francis Schaeffer* (1998), 34-48.

[23]*The Complete Works of Francis A. Schaeffer*, 5 vols. (Westchester, Ill.: Crossway Books, 1982). Quotations from Schaeffer's writings, and page references in the text, will all be taken from this set, with the volume number preceding the colon and the page reference following.

[24]Louis G. Parkhurst, *Francis Schaeffer: The Man and His Message* (Wheaton, Ill.: Tyndale, 1985); Lane T. Dennis, ed., *Francis A. Schaeffer: Portraits of the Man and His Work* (Westchester, Ill.: Crossway, 1986); Ronald W. Ruegsegger, ed., *Reflections on Francis Schaeffer* (Grand Rapids: Zondervan, 1986); Thomas V. Morris, *Francis Schaeffer's Apologetics: A Critique*, 2d ed. (Grand Rapids: Baker, 1987; original, 1976).

[25]Clark H. Pinnock, "Schaeffer on Modern Theology," in *Reflections on Francis Schaeffer*, ed. Ruegsegger, 186.

[26]Reymond, *Justification of Knowledge*, 145.

[27]Ibid., 146 (cf. 136-48).

[28]Gordon R. Lewis, "Schaeffer's Apologetic Method," in *Reflections on Francis Schaeffer*, ed. Ruegsegger, 71 (cf. 69-104).

[29]Ibid., 94.

[30]As quoted in Jack Rogers, "Francis Schaeffer: The Promise and the Problem," *Reformed Journal* 27 (1977): 12-13.

[31]Quoted in Edgar, "Two Christian Warriors," 59.

[32]Forrest Baird, "Schaeffer's Intellectual Roots," in *Reflections on Francis Schaeffer*, ed. Ruegsegger, 46-55.

[33]See our discussion of Dooyeweerd's philosophy in chapter 12.

[34]Baird takes notice of the connection, but his description of Van Til's apologetic is unsatisfactory (ibid., 55-58). For example, he erroneously asserts that according to Van Til, "the careful development and presentation of Christian evidences is really a waste of time" (57).

[35]Edgar, "Two Christian Warriors," 57-80.

[36]Ibid., 60-64.

[37]Ibid., 70-74.

[38]Ibid., 75.

[39]Ibid., 75.

[40]David K. Clark, *The Pantheism of Alan Watts* (Downers Grove, Ill.: InterVarsity, 1978).

[41]David K. Clark, *The Relation of Tradition to Experience in Mysticism* (Ann Arbor: University Microfilms, 1982).

[42]David K. Clark and Norman L. Geisler, *Apologetics in the New Age: A Christian Critique of Pantheism* (Grand Rapids: Baker, 1990). Parenthetical page references in the following paragraphs are to this book.

[43]David L. Wolfe, *Epistemology: The Justification of Belief*, Contours of Christian Philosophy (Downers Grove, Ill.: InterVarsity, 1982), 50-55.

[44]David K. Clark, *Dialogical Apologetics: A Person-Centered Approach to Christian Defense* (Grand Rapids: Baker, 1993). Parenthetical page references in the following paragraphs are to this book.

[45]Evans has recounted his life and career up to 1991 in "A Privileged Calling," in *Storying Ourselves: A Narrative Perspective on Christians in Psychology*, ed. D. John Lee, Christian Explorations in Psychology (Grand Rapids: Baker, 1993), 187-209.

[46]C. Stephen Evans, *Despair: A Moment or a Way of Life* (Downers Grove, Ill.: InterVarsity, 1971).

[47]C. Stephen Evans, *Existentialism: The Philosophy of Despair and the Quest for Hope* (Grand Rapids: Zondervan, 1984; Dallas: Probe Books, 1989).

[48]C. Stephen Evans, *Philosophy of Religion: Thinking about Faith*, Contours of Christian Philosophy (Downers Grove, Ill.: InterVarsity, 1985); *The Quest for Faith: Reason and Mystery as Pointers to God* (Downers Grove, Ill.: InterVarsity, 1986). The Contours of Christian Philosophy series was edited by Evans himself and included a volume on ethics by his former professor Arthur Holmes and other noted evangelical philosophers.

[49]C. Stephen Evans, *The Historical Christ and the Jesus of Faith: The Incarnational Narrative as History* (Oxford: Oxford University Press, 1996), 233. Parenthetical page references in the following paragraphs are to this book.

[50]C. Stephen Evans, "Apologetics in a New Key: Relieving Protestant Anxieties over Natural Theology," in *The Logic of Rational Theism: Exploratory Essays*, ed. William Lane Craig and Mark S. McLeod, Problems in Contemporary Philosophy, vol. 24 (Lewiston, N.Y.: Edwin Mellen Press, 1990), 70, 75.

[51]C. Stephen Evans, *Why Believe? Reason and Mystery as Pointers to God* (Grand Rapids: Eerdmans; Leicester: Inter-Varsity Press, 1996), 19. Parenthetical page references in the following paragraphs are to this book.

[52]Evans, *Historical Christ*, 32. Parenthetical page references in the following paragraphs are to this book.

[53]Evans, *Why Believe*, 73. Parenthetical page references in the following paragraphs are to this book.

[54]Evans, *Historical Christ*, 25. Parenthetical page references in the following paragraphs are to this book.

[55]For most of the biographical information presented here, see Frame, *Cornelius Van Til*, 15-18.

[56]John M. Frame, *The Doctrine of the Knowledge of God: A Theology of Lordship* (Phillipsburg, N.J.: Presbyterian & Reformed, 1987). All parenthetical page references in the text in this section are to this book.

[57]John M. Frame, *Apologetics to the Glory of God: An Introduction* (Phillipsburg, N.J.: Presbyterian & Reformed, 1994).

[58]John M. Frame, *Medical Ethics: Principles, Persons, and Problems* (Grand Rapids: Baker,

1988); *Perspectives on the Word of God: An Introduction to Christian Ethics* (Phillipsburg, N.J.: Presbyterian & Reformed, 1990).

[59]On hermeneutics, see Vern Sheridan Poythress, *Science and Hermeneutics: Implications of Scientific Method for Biblical Interpretation*, Foundations of Contemporary Interpretation, vol. 6 (Grand Rapids: Zondervan, Academie, 1988), later published as part of a single volume, *Foundations of Contemporary Interpretation*, ed. V. Philips Long (Grand Rapids: Zondervan, 1996); and Poythress, *God-Centered Biblical Interpretation* (Grand Rapids: Zondervan, 1999).

[60]Vern Sheridan Poythress, *Symphonic Theology: The Validity of Multiple Perspectives in Theology* (Grand Rapids: Zondervan, Academie, 1987).

[61]Cf. Frame, *Doctrine of the Knowledge of God*, 75.

[62]John M. Frame, *Van Til: The Theologian* (Phillipsburg, N.J.: Harmony Press, 1976), 5 n. 10.

[63]Frame, *Cornelius Van Til*, 16.

[64]Frame, *Apologetics*, 71.

[65]Ibid., 72, 73.

[66]Ibid., 76.

[67]Van Til, *Christian-Theistic Evidences*, 56-57, emphasis in original.

[68]Frame, *Apologetics to the Glory of God*, 81.

[69]Ibid., 27.

[70]Frame, *Apologetics*, 2-3 and n. 5. Parenthetical page references in the remainder of this paragraph are to this book.

CHAPTER 21

[1]Ian G. Barbour, *Religion and Science: Historical and Contemporary Issues* (San Francisco: Harper San Francisco, 1997), 77-105.

[2]John Haught, *Science and Religion: From Conflict to Conversation* (Mahwah, N.J.: Paulist, 1995); cf. Barbour, *Religion and Science*, 338 n. 1.

[3]Michael Peterson, William Hasker, Bruce Reichenbach, and David Basinger, *Reason and Religious Belief: An Introduction to the Philosophy of Religion*, 3d ed. (New York and Oxford: Oxford University Press, 2003), 246-66.

[4]David N. Livingstone, "Science and Religion: Towards a New Cartography," *Christian Scholar's Review* 26 (1997): 270-92 (quote on 271).

CHAPTER 22

[1]Sproul, Gerstner, and Lindsley, *Classical Apologetics*, 93-108.

[2]Terry L. Miethe and Gary R. Habermas, *Why Believe? God Exists! Rethinking the Case for God and Christianity* (Joplin, Mo.: College Press, 1993), 65-71.

[3]See especially Alvin Plantinga, *The Nature of Necessity* (Oxford: Clarendon, 1974).

[4]Karl Barth, *Anselm: Fides Quaerens Intellectum: Anselm's Proof of the Existence of God in the Context of His Theological Scheme*, trans. Ian W. Robertson, 2nd ed. (London: SCM; Richmond: John Knox, 1960).

[5]Cowan, review of *Faith Has Its Reasons* (1st ed.), in *Philosophia Christi* 6 (2004): 371.

[6]For a recent discussion focusing on two of the problems (the deductive and inductive problems of

evil), see Daniel Howard-Snyder, "God, Evil, and Suffering," in *Reason for the Hope Within*, ed. Murray, 76-115.

CHAPTER 23
[1]Kenneth D. Boa, *Conformed to His Image: A Practical Handbook to Spiritual Formation* (Grand Rapids: Zondervan, 2001), Appendix A.

APPENDIX
[1]Bernard L. Ramm, *Types of Apologetic Systems* (Wheaton, Ill.: Van Kampen Press, 1953).

[2]Bernard L. Ramm, *Varieties of Christian Apologetics: An Introduction to the Christian Philosophy of Religion* (Grand Rapids: Baker, 1962).

[3]Gordon R. Lewis, *Testing Christianity's Truth Claims: Approaches to Christian Apologetics* (Chicago: Moody, 1976). Parenthetical references in the text are to this book.

[4]Norman L. Geisler, "Apologetics, Types of," in *Baker Encyclopedia of Christian Apologetics* (Grand Rapids: Baker, 1999), pp. 41-44. Parenthetical references in this section are to this book.

[5]Steven B. Cowan, ed., *Five Views on Apologetics*, Counterpoint series (Grand Rapids: Zondervan, 2000). Parenthetical references in this section are to this book. Parts of this section first appeared as a review (by Bowman) in *Facts for Faith* 1, no. 2 (2000): 61.

List of Tables and Charts

Name Index

The names of the 25 authors whose views receive special attention are printed in boldface type as are the pages in which their views (and those of select other authors) receive sustained attention. Endnotes pages are shown in italics. Most names appearing only in the bibliography and notes are not indexed.

Subject Index

The twelve major subjects are printed in boldface type as are the page numbers of the five sections in which each is discussed most directly.

abduction, 157

absolutes, absolute truth, 39-40, 43, 148, 163-64, 174, 200, 262, 271-72, 281, 286, 315, 395, 447, 449-50, 478, 491-92, 512; God as absolute, 260-61, 288, 294, 302-3, 318, 320, 324, 329, 356-57, 403, 441, 473, 487, 503; absolute knowledge, 85, 144, 221, 492; absolute faith, commitment, 39, 75, 150, 159, 370, 471; moral absolutes, 37, 96-97, 119, 503; absolutizing non-absolutes, 239-40, 473, 480

absurd, absurdity, 65-66, 99, 129, 144, 339, 345, 349-51, 362, 375-76, 381, 383, 402, 406, 437, 441, 489

agnosticism, agnostics, 60, 93, 145, 169, 182, 187, 326, 461, 498

anthropic principle, 187, *608*

anthropological argument, 97

antinomies, 159, 299; *see also* paradox

anti-Semitism, 124

antithesis, antithetical, 94, 352, 374, 397; in Reformed apologetics, xvii, 25-26, 221-23, 233, 242, 248, 266, 276, 290, 294, 296, 521, *618*

apologetic, defined, 4

apologetics, defined, 4

apologia, 1-3, 6-7, 13

apologist, defined, 4

apologists, differences among, 513-15

apology, 1, 3, 4, 10, 11, 77, 340, 373, 377, 500; defined, 3, 54

a posteriori, 172, 289, 613; *a priori*, 72, 83, 98, 100, 106, 108, 151, 171, 172, 254, 278, 289, 301, 426, 432

archē, Archimedean point, 240

Aristotelianism, 19-20, 50, 128, 426, 496

Arminianism, 40, 64, 166-67, 200, 242, 264-65, 286, 493, 495, 520

axiom, 160-62, 234, 245-46, 273, 281-82, 286-89, 314, 317, 345, 366, 375, 384, 407, 432, *617*

Barmen Declaration, 353, 398, 450

Bayes's theorem, 169-70

begging the question. *See* circular reasoning

Bible. *See* Scripture

biblical criticism, xii, 43, 51, 67, 81, 111, 145, 147, 183, 195, 255, 276, 384, 418, 422, 463, 469

big bang, 100, 186, 203

Book of Mormon, 91

Buddhism, Buddha, 93, 153, 169, 185, 210, 291, 453

burden of proof, 81, 156, 189, 295-96, 327, 329

Calvin College, 241, 247-48, 460, 464, *611*

Catholics, Catholicism, 20-22, 27, 30, 32, 36, 51, 61, 124, 166, 242, 248, 286, 310, 342, 358, 361, 363, 375, 493-94, 520, *584, 588, 593*

cause and effect, 24, 97, 102, 163, 193, 228, 230, 299, 402, 429, 507

cause, God as, 37, 60, 81, 97, 100-102, 187, 299-301, 305-7, 318-20, 429, 476, 521, *608*

certainty, xi, 18, 21, 26, 33, 40, 62, 74, 80, 115-16, 139, 144, 147-48, 159-60, 191, 199, 211, 221, 228, 230, 233-37, 242-43, 245, 251, 260, 274, 279-80, 297, 314, 332, 340, 344, 362-63, 376, 383, 385, 387-89, 401, 410, 430, 445-46, 458, 464-65, 469-70, 477-79, 493-94, 505-6, *590*

chance, 265, 271, 302-3, 307, 309, 316, 318-19, 442

Christ. *See* Jesus

circular reasoning, 84, 90, 133, 176, 180, 215, 249, 267, 300, 323-24, 330, 395, 408, 431-32, 454, 462, 470, 478, 487

classical apologetics, xiv, xvi-xvii, 29-40 *passim*, 45, 528-33, *583*; discussed, **48-136**; and evidentialism, 139, 141, 150-57 *passim*, 160, 162-63, 166-68, 172-73, 179, 184-85, 187-88, 191, 194, 199-200, 202-3, 212, 214, 216, 218, *606*; and Reformed apologetics, 221-22, 224, 228, 232, 235, 242, 256, 259-60, 262, 264, 268, 279-80, 290, 304, 307, 313-19, 329-30, *616*; and fideism, 341, 343, 345, 362, 365, 369, 372, 392, 410, *624, 626*; and integrative approaches, 425-27, **428-29**, 434, **440-43**, 446, 453-61

passim, 466, 468, 473, **475-76**, 481, 484, **487-88**, 489-511 *passim*, 517-21

combinationalism, 60, 131-32

common grace, 217, 232-34, 449, 500, *614*

common ground, 25, 33, 40, 83, 130, 134-36, 281-82, 303, 354, 360, 374, 434-35, 454, 457, *590*

common sense, 24, 161, 228-30, 431, 515

Common Sense Realism, 24, 26, 227-31, 242, *612*

complementarianism, of science and theology, 378

cosmological argument, 16, 23, 29-30, 50, 58-67 *passim*, 73, 81, 95-97, 99-102, 113, 117, 119-20, 133-34, 140, 172-73, 186, 194, 202, 224, 298-301, 311, 318, 441-43, 476, 505, 515, 521, *594, 598-99*; *kālam* argument, 66-67, 99-102, 113, 134, 186, 194, 298, *598*; *see also* cause, God as

cosmology, 84, 173, 178, 186, 456; *see also* big bang

cosmonomic philosophy, 238; *see also* Dooyeweerd

creation, 12, 16, 30, 35, 59-60, 68, 81-84, 87, 89, 103-7, 119, 123, 143, 145, 179, 194, 204, 228, 239-40, 242, 265, 272, 301, 303, 316, 328, 350, 356-57, 402, 406, 432, 435, 447, 490, 497, 506, 523

creationism, 82-84, 117, 120, 173, 201, 204, 272, 316, 320, 520; old-earth and young-earth, 82, 84, 117, 120, 173, 201, 204, 272, 316, 320, 520

Creator, 16, 24, 34, 37-38, 54, 89, 103, 107, 112, 122, 126, 140, 184, 224, 226, 230, 240, 294, 300-301, 305, 318, 322, 329, 355-56, 402, 434, 441, 473, 508, *608*

Crusades, 124

cults, 295

cumulative, cumulative-case argument, 10, 45, 62, 66, 68, 143, 153, 170, 179, 182, 186, 196, 212, 218, 313, 456-62 *passim*, 468, 488, 504, 531-33, 605-6

deductive reasoning, 28, 35, 37, 68, 71, 75, 87, 89, 99-100, 115, 119-20, 128, 131-133, 153, 157-58, 160, 167, 170-172, 188-89, 191, 199, 202, 211, 212, 243-245, 256, 260-61, 273-74, 276, 288, 301, 304, 313-14, 318, 345, 365, 426, 428-430, 432, 458-59, 466, 493, 504-506, 519, *635*

defeaters, 255, 297-98, 471

design, 254, 271; arguments from or to, 23-24, 37, 58, 66, 81, 84, 95-97, 119, 133, 140, 172-73, 186-87, 193, 202-203, 224, 228-29, 298, 300-301, 379, 429, 442, 476, 487, 504-505, 521, *608*; *see also* teleological argument

determinism, 108, 299, 304-7, 311, 318-19, 506-7

direct and indirect argument, 37-38, 261, 347-51, 411-12, 435-36, 476, 488-89; direct, 72, 279, 521; indirect, 43, 294, 301, 383, 406, 420, 448, 451, 502, 504

dogmatism, 23, 56, 60, 81, 160, 176, 193, 215, 231, 238-39, 246, 315, 331, 333, 451, 474-75, 494, 498

dualism (good and evil), 55, 59, 102-3, 441-42

dualism, in ground motives, 25-26, 239-40, 447

Eastern religion and philosophy, 74, 76, 92, 94, 103, 109, 111-12, 116, 119, 148, 174, 184-85, 262, 324, 332, 453; *see also* Buddhism; Hinduism; Taoism

empiricism, 22, 141, 147, 152-53, 160, 215, 218, 259-60, 263, 429, 432, 443, 473, 480, 484, 529, 533

Enlightenment, 23, 25, 136, 238, 248, 257, 262, 384, 386, 463, 469-70, 488, 589

Epicureans, xi, 10

epistemic argument, 303, 320, 520; *see also* transcendental argument

epistemological evidentialism, 156, 232, 253, 608

epistemology, 5, 24, 33-34, 39-40, 67, 71, 79, 88, 115, 168, 216, 229, 232, 239, 242, 249, 251, 259-61, 268, 273, 276, 283, 298, 436, 444-45, 450, 458-60, 463-64, 469, 472-74, 479-80, 484, 495-96, 532, 600; defined, 39; *see also* Reformed epistemology

epistemology of suspicion, 156

eschatological verification, 104

evangelism, 6, 7, 76, 88, 148, 329, 360, 367, 439, 446, 453, 499, 515

evidentialism (in apologetics), xiv, xvi-xvii, 29-40 *passim*, 45, 528-33; discussed, **137-218**, 604-6; not epistemological evidentialism, 156; and classical apologetics, 52-54, 56, 60, 62, 65, 68-69, 89-90, 110, 113, 592, 596, 598; and Reformed apologetics, 221, 228, 231-32, 235, 256, 259-60, 262, 268, 277, 279-80, 290, 304, 307-8, 313-19, 329-31, 616; and fideism, 339, 365, 369, 380-87; and integrative approaches, 425-28, **429-31**, 435, 437, **443-46**, 453-73 *passim* (especially **460-64**), **476-79**, 481, 484, 487, **488-89**, 491-510 *passim*, 515, 518-21

evil, problem of, xii, xvii, 36-38, 43, 58, 59, **102-5**, 113, 119-24, **188-90**, 197, 203-4, 229, 249, 251, 266-67, **304-7**, 311, 318,

ontological argument;
teleological argument;
transcendental argument

God, omniscience of, 64, 141, 152, 166,
189, 294

gospel, 2, 9, 11, 12, 20-21, 27, 40, 66,
130, 143, 146-47, 150, 159,
163, 176-77, 180, 204, 226,
283, 285-86, 289-90, 340-41,
356, 360, 362, 367, 372, 375,
387, 392, 428, 436, 441, 446,
481, 490-91, 504, 513

Gospels, 15, 30, 44, 66, 109-111, 119,
125-127, 148, 180, 181, 183,
195, 197, 202, 206-208, 418,
462, 463, 466, 503, 509, 510,
517, 520, *609*

ground motive, 239, 240, 447

Hindus, Hinduism, xii, 36, 37, 93, 124,
126, 210, 291, 322, *597*

historical model, of apologetics, 161

history, xiv-xv, 7, 9-10, 14-16, 32-34,
41, 44, 49, 58-61, 66, **84-86**,
87, 90, 104, 107-108, 113, 115,
117-18, 120, 124, 127, 140-41,
143, 145, 152, 162-64, 167-68,
174-76, 178, 180-83, 187, 191,
196-97, 199, 201-202, 204,
213, 216, 227, 238, 246-248,
259, 263, 273, **275-80**, 283-84,
290, 293-94, 304, 307, 309,
313-14, 316, 319-20, 333,
352-53, 356, 362, 365-66, 372,
377, **380-87**, 391-92, 396, 402,
405-409, 426, 430-31, 438,
440, 443-44, 447-48, 452, 462,
498-99, 502, 506, 520, 521,
523, 525, *584, 589, 607*

Holy Spirit. *See* Spirit

humanism, 20, 63, 130, 166, 168, 246

illusionism, 59, 102-103

image of God, 68, 244, 265, 277, 280-
283, 314, 317, 320, 329, 432,
435, 438, 520

immanentism, 240

Incarnation, 132, 145, 213-14, 251, 350-
51, 355, 371, 375-377, 381,
383, 406, 420, 426, *601*

inductive reasoning, 42, 68, 71, 75, 89,
118, 140-41, 144, 147, 152,
157, 159, 164, 169-73, 186,
189-91, 195-96, 199-200, 204,
211, 230, 243, 245, 260-61,
273, 276, 278-79, 304, 307,
314-16, 318, 331-32, 365, 444,
459, 463-64, 489, 499, 504,
506, 519, *635*

inerrancy. *See* Scripture, inerrancy and
infallibility of

inference, 150, 193, 195-96, 230, 245,
254, 277, 488; to the best
explanation, 170, 196, 212

infinite regress (*regressus in infinitum*),
100, 101, 172, 261, 299, 432

Inquisitions, 124

inspiration. *See* Scripture, inspiration of

integrative approaches, xi, xv, 425, 427,
471-72, 480, 483-91, 513, 519,
522

intelligent design, 37, 84, 500, *596*; *see
also* design, argument from

internalist epistemology, 464

International Council on Biblical
Inerrancy, 91, 244

irrationalism, 26, 243, 263-64, 315, 320,
338, 354, 363, 378, 391, 420,
448, 492, *630*

Islam, Muslims, xii, 17, 30, 37, 60, 66-
67, 89, 93, 99, 118, 124, 143,
174, 184, 210, 246, 291, 293-
295, 324-25, 461, *604*

Israel, 11-14, 94, 119, 124, 126, 183,
197, 279, 291, 325, 386, 404,
467, *584-86, 588, 607, 621*

Jesus, *passim*, especially 12-16, 65-69,
109-13, 175-180, **194-97**,
202-211, **309-311**, **406-408**,
509-10

Jesus Seminar, 67, 594

Jews. *See* Israel; Judaism

Judaism, 14, 17, 30, 37, 60, 89, 93, 112, 118, 180, 183-84, 294, 489

justification by faith. *See* faith alone (*sola fide*)

kalām. See cosmological argument

karma, 205, 322

knowledge, *passim*, especially 28-31, **71-77**, 83-86, **155-64**, 173-76, 221-24, 233-40, **259-64**, 313-18, **365-71**, 380-84, 409-12, 419-22, 470-75, **484-93**

Koran. *See* Qur'an

law, apologetics and. *See* legal evidence model

law of (non)contradiction, 34, 69, 72, 76, 127-28, 131, 158, 287, 428, 430, 432, 443

laws of logic, 28, 128, 300, 303, 440, 473

laws of nature, 108; *see also* scientific laws

leaky bucket analogy, 212, *609*

legal evidence model, 30, 141-42, 148-49, 161, 194, 498-99

liberalism (theological modernism), 25, 27, 28, 241, 264, 352, 353, 377, 396, 447, 451, 494, *628*

line of despair, 447-449, 452

logic, xiv, 6, 11-12, 19, 21, 26, 28, 29, 34, 37, 59, 63, 66, 68, 71-73, 75-76, 87, 89, 92, 99, 103, 115, 119, 122, 127-36 *passim*, 155, 157-160, 164, 168, 186, 188-89, 203, 213-14, 230, 242, 244-45, 256, 260, 264, 266, 270, 273-74, 276, 286-88, 293, 298, 300, 303, 314, 329-30, 340-41, 368, 376-77, 395, 428-29, 432, 441, 445-54 *passim*, 473-74, 478, 484-86, 495, 499, 504, 529; laws of, 28, 128, 300, 303, 440, 473; *see also* abduction; circular reasoning; deductive reasoning; fallacies; inductive reasoning; inference; law of (non)contradiction;

self-defeating or self-refuting arguments or positions

logical positivism, 266, 436

logos, 13, 286-87

love, 38, 42, 68, 104, 123, 210, 307, 343, 347, 351, 357, 366, 398, 399, 401, 406, 411, 414-15, 418, 421, 428, 438-39, 452-53, 467, 480, 489, 491, 510, 521, *632*

metaphysical, 15, 78, 96, 104, 108-109, 142, 147, 150, 158, 176, 215-16, 243, 261, 275, 300, 303, 342, 377, 425, 434, 437, 448

metaphysics, 79, 216, 264, 268, 436, 495

metapologetic, metapologetics, 4, 39, 40, 42, 115, 199, 313, 409, 483

mind, argument from, 186

minds, argument from other, 229

miracles, xii-xiii, xv, 15, 17, 20, 23-24, 27, 37, 43-44, 50-62 *passim*, 66-68, 84, 93, 97, **105-109**, 111, 113, 117, 119, 125, 129, 141-43, 150-51, 161, 164, 171, 174, 179-80, 182, 185, 187, **191-94**, 197, 202-204, 210, 213-14, 226, 234, 276, 279, 283, **307-309**, 317, 319, 331, 345, 384, **404-406**, 408, 411, 461, 462, 486, 498-99, 505-506, **507-509**, 510, 517, 519, 521

models, of apologetics, *see* historical model; legal evidence model; scientific model; *and see* classical apologetics; evidentialism; Reformed apologetics; fideism; of science and theology, 83, 496-97; of theology, 165-66, 230; *see also* paradigms

modernism (theological). *See* liberalism

modernism (philosophical). *See* postmodernism

monism, 92, 94

moral argument, 66, 96, 97, 119, 120, 186, 461, 521

Muslims. *See* Islam

myth, 55, 82, 111, 126, 207-208, 356, 380, 417, *599; see also* history

natural law, 107, 120, 192, 307, 508; *see also* laws of nature

natural revelation. *See* general revelation

natural theology, 23, 27, 36, 45, 133, 140-41, 164, 197, 223, 230, 234, 250-51, 254, 257, 298-99, 302-303, 351, 356, 379, 401-402, 432, 461, 466, 527-28, *618*

naturalism-of-the-gaps, 192-93

neoorthodoxy, 175, 346, 352, 359, 361, 437, 450

neutrality, 25, 66, 133, 136, 160, 260, 277, 285, 293, 354, 386, 396, 454, 456, 463, 475, 498

New Age movement, 74, 76, 92, 94, 116, 122, 205, 332, 453-55, 542, *634*

New Testament, 1-3, 6, 9-10, 13-14, 24, 29, 32, 50-51, 57, 60-61, 64, 66-67, 75, 90, 106, 110-112, 126-27, 145, 148-49, 176, 180-81, 187, 195-197, 206-208, 297, 348, 349, 377, 388, 392, 403, 412, 419, 462, 467, 469, 473, 477

noetic structure, 253; effects of sin, *see* sin, noetic effects of

non-realism, 274-75, 316

objections, 5, 6, 9, 15, 18, 20, 23, 31, 35, 37-39, 41-43, 54, 59, 61-64, 66, 79, 80, 84, 91, 97, 101-108 *passim*, 113, 116, 128, 133, 135-36, 140-51 *passim*, 163, 189, 194-95, 212, 214, 223, 225-27, 237, 245, 248, 251, 253-56, 276, 280, 286, 291-92, 297, 306, 308, 324, 332, 350, 367, 374, 388, 391, 401-402, 419, 421, 455, 463, 465, 470,

471, 479-80, 495, 504, 518, 530

objective, objectivity, 40, 102, 133, 135-36, 230, 263, 369-71, 383, 388-89, 403, 420; objective facts, evidence, or data, 78, 85, 161, 168, 190, 200, 270-71, 280, 316, 430, 436-37, 468-69, 492, 529; objective experience, 177; objective methods, 162-63, 170; objective morality, 24, 96, 262; objectivity in historical knowledge, 42, 66, 85-86, 120, 148, 160, 164, 175-77, 182, 204, 213, 215, 217, 320, 362, 410, 463, 520; objective reality, truth, 76, 86, 106, 162, 178, 262-63, 465, 491-92; objectivity in science, 187

objectivism, 169, 388

Old Testament, 10, 12, 61, 93, 118, 164, 182-184, 197, 276, 392, 399, 403, 407, 510, *587*

omniscience. *See* God omniscience of

ontological argument, 17, 20, 23, 50, 58, 66, 73, 95-96, 98-99, 119, 133, 140, 172, 202, 298, 301, 426, 506, 588, 598

operationalism, in science, 274, 316; see realism and nonrealism in science

pagans, paganism, 12, 14-17, 20, 21, 222, 234, 340, 373, 395, 489

palingenesis, 233, 234, 240, 269

panentheism, 60, 92-93, 98

pantheism, 30, 37, 60, 63, 92-95, 106, 134, 294, 436, 442, 453-455, 597

paradigms, 10, 27, 28, 79, 115, 167, 199, 253, 275, 313, 409, 456, 493, 494, 516, 528; *see also* models

paradox, 25, 36, 132, 159, 183, 338-340, 342, 350, 354, 361, 372, 375-76, 381-82, 385, 393, 401, 417, 467, 496, 504, 508-510, 521

Quintilemma, 110, 120

Qur'an, 91, 246, 295, 324-25; *see also* Islam

rationalism, 31-32, 35, 39, 60, 68, 71-74, 76, 131-32, 146, 161, 182, 218, 227-28, 230-31, 259-60, 263, 315, 330, 361-62, 366, 372, 391, 396, 432, 448, 456, 473-74, 480, 484, 516, 529

reason, *passim*; *see* logic

realism and nonrealism in science, 83, 173, 201, 274-75, 316

reductio ad absurdum, 475; *see also* absurd

Reformation, 9, 20-21, 51, 440, 447, 494

Reformed apologetics, xiv, 4, 26, 31-32, 34-36, 40, 45; discussed, **219-334**; and evidentialism, 153, 160, 218; and fideism, 338-39, 341, 358, 387, 404-405; and integrative approaches, 425, 427-28, **431-35, 446-50**, 453-55, 460, **464-65**, 466, **474-75**, 484, **489**, 494, 496-97, 502, 506, 509, 518, 528

Reformed epistemology, 31, 45, 248-250, 298, 464-65, 487, 488, 506, 531, 532

Reformed theology, xiv, 232, 264, 265, 271, 281, 319, 359, 372, 426, 472, 474, 494, 506, 529

refutation, function of apologetics, 5-7, 79, 91, 108-109, *583*

regeneration, 233, 237, 240, 246, 260, 269, 281, 283, 286, 314, 317

reincarnation, 205, 322

relativism, 31, 66, 74, 76, 84, 116, 163-64, 175, 200, 275, 396, 420, 441, 445-46, 449, 491; *see also* postmodernism

religion, xii, 3, 5-6, 12, 14, 22-23, 37-38, 41, 43, 52-55, 57-58, 72, 74, 76, 78, 83-84, **91-95**, 98, 103, 116, 124-25, 130, 142-43, 156, 167-68, 176, 182, **184-85**, 193, 210, 227, 232, 234-35, 249, 255, 269-70, 276, 280, 283, **290-95**, 313, 321-22, 324-25, 341, 343-345, 348, 360, 373, 380, 386, 394, **395-400**, 411-12, 416-17, 419, 453, 467, 496-97, 500, **503**, 521

religious experience, 58, 62, 86-87, 117, 128, 151, 177, 201, 202, 280-81, 296-97, 316, 337, 425, 456, 462, 527-28, 530

religious language, 58, 59, 252

resurrection (of Jesus), 9-12, 15, 24, 28-30, 35, 44, 53, 57, 61, 64-65, 67-68, 75, 89, 107, 110, 114, 141-42, 146-50, 153, 156, 164, 166, 175-77, 179, 183, 187, **191-97**, 200-204, 207-209, 213-14, 218, 276-79, 291, 308-309, 319, 332, 339-40, 356-58, 366, 386, 430, 456, 461-62, 467-68, 476-77, 487-89, 491, 498-99, 509-10, 521, 531, *609, 629*

revelation, *passim*, especially 19-27, 50-53, 228-237, 355-358, 386-389, 396-399, 404-408

Scholastics, 20, 341, 375-76

science, xiv-xv, 2, 4, 6, 9, 22, 29-30, 33-34, 36-37, 40-41, 53, 55, 64, 74, 77, **80-84**, 85, 87-88, 100, 105-106, 108, 115, 117-18, 139-40, 142, 151-52, 157, 159, 161-63, 165, 168-69, **171-73**, 178, 186-87, 190-94, 199, 201, 203-204, 211, 215, 218, 230, 233-34, 246, 262, **268-75**, 278, 283, 285, 290, 308, 313, 315-16, 328, 365-66, 369, **378-80**, 385, 409-10, 430-31, 438, 442-45, 448, 495, **496-97**, 500, 515, 520, 527

scientific laws, 34, 151, 191, 273; *see also* laws of nature

scientific method, 34, 161-62, 204, 215, 270-71

scientific model, of apologetics, 140, 161-62, 171-72, 430

scientism, 83-84

Scripture, *passim*, especially 24-27, **90-91**, 164-66, **180-84**, 221-26, 229-31, 244-46, 270-72, **286-90**, 301-303, 309-11, 314-17, 356-58, 369-71, 278-80, **391-95**, 405-407, 410-12, 484-86, **501-502**, 503, 519-21, *629-31*; inerrancy and infallibility of, 27, 30, 90-91, 147, 216, 358, 391, 422, 447, 495, 516, *593, 602*; inspiration of, 35, 42, 60, 89-91, 118, 120, 147, 180, 183-84, 202, 204, 265, 286, 317, 344, 346, 371, 519, 521, *617*; *see also* New Testament; Old Testament

secular, secularism, secularization, 58, 86, 111, 130, 213-14, 232, 244, 450, 497

seed of religion, 234

self-attesting, self-authenticating, 65, 75, 178, 289-90, 309-311, 319-20, 324, 387, 395, 404, 406, 410, 412, 501-502, 508, 510, 521, 530

self-defeating or self-refuting arguments or positions, 60, 74, 76, 83-84, 93-95, 116, 120, 163, 252-53, 255, 271, 290, 320, 429, 441, 455, 491

sensus divinitatis (sense of divinity), 223-24, 254, 282, 302, 327, *612*

sin, 18-21, 35, 38, 41, 59, 78, 84, 103-104, 145, 210-211, 217, 222, 227, 230, 232, 234, 237, 254-55, 263, 265, 267, 277, 280-283, 304-308, 314, 318, 320, 328, 340-41, 356-358, 360, 387, 414, 416-17, 429, 433; noetic effects of, 222, 237, 255; the Fall, 78, 272, 576, *611*

skepticism, xii, 21, 23-24, 27, 36, 51, 54, 57, 59, 64, 84, 87, 110, 113, 134, 140, 142, 145, 181, 183, 188, 192-194, 196, 203, 227-

229, 238, 246, 250, 267, 293, 300, 308, 319, 332-33, 344, 373, 462, 508, *613*

Spirit, 21, 116, 118, 160, 177, 222, 231, 233, 246, 254, 264, 268, 281-83, 289-90, 314, 328, 340, 355-68, 389, 400, 407-410, 417, 420, 437, 468-71, 484-86, 491, 514, 516, 520-22; witness of, 65, 69, 75-77, 120, 200, 204, 224-26, 236, 320, 357, 370-71, 394, 409, 412, 464-65, 469, 471, 477-78

Stoics, Stoicism, xi, 10, 12, 14, 339, 340

subjective, subjectivity, 31, 36, 45, 71, 84-86, 102, 148, 162, 164, 166, 174-75, 177, 201, 363, 370-71, 383, 385, 388, 403, 410, 420, 436, 465, 469, 472, 480, 527-28

subjectivism, 40, 76, 163, 337, 388, 420, 436, 473, 480, 484

supernatural, 44, 52, 58, 79, 90, 97, 106-109, 114, 140, 147, 155, 191, 197, 230, 282, 345, 426, 463, 487, 499, 502, 513; supernaturalism, 25, 140

synoptic starting point, 432, 435

systematic consistency, 60, 66, 75, 91, 429, 430, 433-437, 531

Taoism, 122

teleological argument. *See* design

theistic proofs. *See* God, existence of

theology, *passim*, especially 51-55, **77-78**, 79-80, 161-63, **164-67**, 221-23, 229-32, **264-65**, 266, 284-86, 351-63, **371-75**, 472-74, **493-95**, 496-97, 527-29

total depravity, 232, 280

transcendence, in human desire and experience, xii, 55, 58, 86-87, 117, 280, 291, 436, 438, 500; of God, 18, 36-37, 72, 86, 92, 95-96, 106, 126, 132, 185, 245, 263, 294, 300, 319, 368, 487

transcendental argument, 29, 238, 240,
   244-46, 256, 261, 271, 178-
   79, 283, 288, 295, 302-303,
   314-18, 320, 329-30, 332, 365,
   428-29, 433, 449-50, 459, 466,
   475-76, 487-89, 499, 505, 515,
   520

transcendent aspect of knowledge, 484-
   86, 504, 520

trilemma, 27, 599; *see also*
   Quintilemma

truth. *See* knowledge

verification, 6, 34, 58, 104, 142, 146,
   157, 168, 182, 191, 273, 406,
   443-445, 448-49

verificationalism (apologetic approach),
   443-45, 528; cf. 133

verificationism (epistemological theory).
   See logical positivism

vindication, apologetics as, 1, 2, 5, 10,
   140, 210, 226, 279, 329, 332,
   386

Virgin Birth, 52, 106-107

Wager argument, 344, 385, 400-401,
   479-80, 517, *626*

Westminster Confession of Faith, 304,
   306, *619, 623*

Westminster Theological Seminary, 26,
   52, 241, 304, 331, 427, 439,
   446, 448, 472

Wheaton College, 243, 427, 459-60

witness, apologetics as, 6, 237, 360, 373,
   388, 419, 422, 500, 510

witness of the Holy Spirit. *See* Spirit

witnesses, historical testimony of, 111,
   149, 171, 174, 206-207, 276,
   387, 444, 462-63, 502, 510

worldviews, xi-xii, 5-6, 15, 19, 25-26,
   30, 34, 37, 42-43, 51, 55, 57,
   59-60, 62, 68, 71, 75, 79, 83,
   85, 89, 91-95, 98, 106-108,
   113, 116-20, 129-36, 143,
   145-46, 157-58, 160, 162, 168,
   172, 174, 176, 179, 183-84,
   188, 199-200, 204, 213-15,

217, 221, 226, 239-40, 246,
   261, 269, 275, 280, 293-295,
   300-301, 307, 313, 318-320,
   331-32, 357, 369-70, 409, 429,
   431, 433, 440-442, 444, 454-
   459, 478, 485, 487-88, 498,
   500, 503, 508, 517, 519-521,
   597

Scripture Index

Genesis

book—83, 272, 497
1-3—379-80
1:1—441
1:3—12
2:17—263
3:5, 22—263
50:20—307

Exodus

book—44, 485

1 Kings

18—508

Job

book—403

Psalms

14:1—5
22—183
33:6, 9—12
36:9—235
110—183

Isaiah

9:6-7—183
40—399
41:21-23—182
42:6-7—183
44:7-8—182
49:5-6—183
52:13-53:12—183

Ezekiel

26—183

Daniel

7:13-14—183
9:24-27—183, *607*

Micah

5:2—183

Jonah

1:5—625

Haggai

2:3-9—183

Zechariah

9:9—183

Matthew

book—181, 183, 418,
510, 520
5:7—514
11:27—235
28:11-15—195-96

Mark

book—125, 181, 195,
207, 418, 510,
520

Luke

book—9-11, 66, 181,
510, 520
1:1-4—9, 207, 444,
510
12:11—1
21:14—1
24:21—*609*

John

book—12-13
1:1—12-13, 287
1:8—510
1:9—12
1:14—12-13
1:17—178
1:18—12

2:18-22—214
5:30-47—510
7:17—178
11—508
13:34-35—452
14:6—366, 370, 396,
436
17:21—452
19:35—207-208
20:24-29—164, 177
20:30-31—13, 444

Acts

1:3—187
2:22-36—164
2:24—279, *621*
2:36—10, 279
14:15-17—10
17:16-34—xi, **10-11**,
50, *584-85*
17:23—11
17:28—340
19:33—1
20:35—514
22:1—1
24:10—1
25:8, 16—1
26:2, 24—1
26:26—164

Romans

book—352, 354
1-2—11, *585*
1:18-25—11
1:18—11
1:20—16
1:21—**11**
1:28—11
2:15—2
8:28—307
10:9-13—499
10:17—178
12:6-8—514-15